An Anthology of Interracial Literature

An Anthology
of Interracial Literature

Black-White Contacts in the
Old World and the New

EDITED BY

Werner Sollors

New York University Press

NEW YORK AND LONDON

NEW YORK UNIVERSITY PRESS
New York and London
www.nyupress.org

Library of Congress Cataloging-in-Publication Data
An anthology of interracial literature :
Black-white contacts in the Old World and the New /
edited by Werner Sollors.
p. cm.
Includes bibliographical references (p.   ) and index.
ISBN 0–8147–8143–8 (cloth : alk. paper) —
ISBN 0–8147–8144–6 (pbk. : alk. paper)
1. Blacks—Literary collections.
2. Race relations—Literary collections.
I. Sollors, Werner
PN6071.B57A58   2003
808.8'0355—dc21   2003056105

New York University Press books are printed on acid-free paper,
and their binding materials are chosen for strength and durability.

Manufactured in the United States of America

c 10 9 8 7 6 5 4 3 2 1
p 10 9 8 7 6 5 4 3 2 1

Contents

Acknowledgments   ix

Introduction   1

BEFORE COLOR PREJUDICE

1   "Riddle" (5th century B.C.)   7
     Cleobulus

2   From *Parzival* (1197–1210)   8
     Wolfram von Eschenbach

ARABIAN NIGHTS AND ITALIAN RENAISSANCE NOVELLAS

3   From *The Book of the Thousand Nights and One Night*   57

4   From *Il Novellino* (1475)   69
     Masuccio Salernitano

5   From *Hecatommithi* (1565)   85
     Giambattista Giraldi Cinzio

LOVE POETRY IN BLACK AND WHITE

6   "The Beautiful Slave-Girl" (1614)   97
     Giambattista Marino

7   "A Negress Courts Cestus, a Man of a Different Colour" (1633)   99
     George Herbert

8   "A Faire Nimph Scorning a Black Boy Courting Her" (1658)   101
     John Cleveland

9   "The Inversion" (1657), "One Enamour'd on a *Black-moor*" (1657),
     "A Black Nymph Scorning a Fair Boy Courting Her" (1657)   103
     Eldred Revett

10   "To Mrs. Diana Cecyll" (1665), "The Brown Beauty" (1665),
     "Sonnet of Black Beauty" (1665),
     "Another Sonnet to Black It Self" (1665)   107
     Edward Herbert of Cherbury

11   "In Laudem Æthiopissæ" (1778)   110
     James de la Cour

     FROM COLONIAL EXOTICISM AND THE
     NOBLE SAVAGE TO ANTISLAVERY WRITING

12   *The Isle of Pines* (1668)   115
     Henry Neville

13   From *Oroonoko: A Tragedy in Five Acts* (1696)   132
     Thomas Southerne

14   "On a Young Lady's Weeping at *Oroonooko*" (1732),
     "To a Gentleman in Love with a Negro Woman" (1732)   143
     John Whaley

15   Two Versions of the Story of Inkle and Yarico   145

16   *The Dying Negro* (1773)   152
     Thomas Day and John Bicknell

17   Letter to James Tobin (1788)   161
     Olaudah Equiano

     BLACK AND WHITE IN EUROPE
     AND THE AMERICAS, 1800–1870

18   *The Engagement in Santo Domingo* (1811)   167
     Heinrich von Kleist

19   *Ourika* (1823)   189
     Claire de Duras

20   *The Blackamoor of Peter the Great* (1827–1828)   208
     Alexander Pushkin

21   "The Quadroons" (1842)   232
     Lydia Maria Child

22   From *Georges* (1843)   240
     Alexandre Dumas

23   From *Beyond the Seas* (1863–1864)   253
     Theodor Storm

24   "The Quadroon Girl" (1842)   278
      Henry Wadsworth Longfellow

25   "The Runaway Slave at Pilgrim's Point" (1848)   280
      Elizabeth Barrett Browning

26   "The Pilot's Story" (1860)   288
      William Dean Howells

27   From *Mulatto: An Original Romantic Drama in Five Acts* (1840)   292
      Hans Christian Andersen

28   *The Octoroon; or, Life in Louisiana: A Play in Five Acts* (1859)   300
      Dion Boucicault

29   From *Black and White: A Drama in Three Acts* (1869)   337
      Wilkie Collins and Charles Fechter

30   From *Miscegenation: The Theory of the Blending of the Races,*
      Applied to the American White Man and Negro (1863)   350
      David Goodman Croly and George Wakeman

Realism and Local Color

31   *Madame Delphine* (1881)   383
      George Washington Cable

32   From "The Pariah" (1895)   421
      James Edwin Campbell

33   "Boitelle" (1889)   424
      Guy de Maupassant

34   "The Father of Désirée's Baby" (1893)   431
      Kate Chopin

35   "Uncle Wellington's Wives" (1899)   436
      Charles W. Chesnutt

Harlem Renaissance and Modernism

36   "The Mulatto to His Critics" (1918)   461
      Joseph Seamon Cotter, Jr.

37   "The Octoroon" (1922), "Cosmopolite" (1922), "The Riddle" (1925)   462
      Georgia Douglas Johnson

38   From *The Vengeance of the Gods* (1922)   464
      William Pickens

39   "Hope" (1922)   473
         Waldo Frank

40   "Withered Skin of Berries" (1923)   476
         Jean Toomer

41   "Confession" (1929)   498
         Margery Latimer

42   *All God's Chillun Got Wings* (1924)   504
         Eugene O'Neill

43   "Near White" (1925), "Two Who Crossed a Line" (1925)   530
         Countée Cullen

44   "Cross" (1925), "Mulatto" (1927),
     Mulatto: A Tragedy of the Deep South (1935)   532
         Langston Hughes

45   "The Mulatto" (1925), "Near-White" (1932)   559
         Claude McKay

46   "The Pink Hat" (1926)   573
         Caroline Bond Day

47   "Ballad of Pearl May Lee" (1945)   577
         Gwendolyn Brooks

FROM THE 1960S TO THE PRESENT

48   *The Owl Answers* (1963)   583
         Adrienne Kennedy

49   From *Oxherding Tale* (1982)   594
         Charles Johnson

50   From *The Darker Face of the Earth* (1994)   606
         Rita Dove

51   From *Buck* (2001)   634
         Francesca J. Petrosino

52   From *The Secret Life of Fred Astaire* (2001)   653
         Itabari Njeri

     Sources   667

     Index   673

     About the Editor   675

Acknowledgments

This anthology is the result of the long years of work that went into the making of my book *Neither Black Nor White Yet Both: Thematic Explorations of Interracial Literature* (1997); and I am indebted to all colleagues, scholars, and friends who helped me research and who commented on earlier versions of that study. Students enrolled in a course on interracial literature urged me to turn the required readings into a book. I wish to thank Niko Pfund, who was enthusiastic about such a project at an early stage, and Eric Zinner, Emily Park, Despina Papazoglou Gimbel, Nicholas Taylor, Nicholas Mirra, and all the people at New York University Press for their encouragement and help in producing this volume. I am grateful to Lawrence Buell and the Hyder E. Rollins Publication Fund at Harvard University for defraying a part of the permission fees; to Erica Michelstein for her excellent research and editorial assistance as well as for her help with the permissions requests; to Rosalie Morales Kearns for expertly copyediting the manuscript; and to Peter Becker for his assistance in reading proof. Finally, I would like to thank Francesca Petrosino for drafting the biographical notes for this volume, for helping at various crisis moments to keep this anthology afloat, and for permitting me to publish scenes from her play *Buck*. I am grateful to Itabari Njeri for allowing me to include a chapter from her forthcoming novel *The Secret Life of Fred Astaire*, to Judith Ryan for the right to publish her new translation of Theodor Storm's *Von jenseit des Meeres*, to Norman Shapiro for permission to publish his new translation of Marino's "The Beautiful Slave-Girl," to Jesper Sørensen for a draft translation of Hans Christian Andersen's *Mulatten*, and to Christoph Lohmann for help with the English versification of Andersen's play.

I also wish to thank the various copyright holders for permission to reprint previously published copyright materials. They are listed in the "Sources" section at the end of the book.

Introduction

An idealized hero of racially mixed origin becomes the love interest of a young woman and a middle-aged woman. A white knight meets his half-black half-brother in battle. A white woman marries a black hero. Black and white exchange amorous verses emphasizing racial difference. Love stories are perverted by the slave trade. Revolutionary events pit rebellious black heroes against the status quo and turn mixed-race heroes into rebels against their own white fathers. Infidelity and jealousy mix with racial hatred and the wish for revenge. Black-white triangles are examined in their comic and tragic potential. A beautiful black woman turns melancholy in a white world. A planter sells his own daughter to a slave trader. A slave mother kills her child by a rapist-master. A white-looking person of partly African ancestry passes for white. A mixed-blood woman from the West Indies falls in love with and happily marries her European cousin. A mixed-blood mother engineers a "white" marriage to ensure her daughter's upward mobility even if it means denying that she is her daughter. A master and a slave change places for a single night. A European man listens to his parents' advice and does not marry the African woman he loves. A person convinced of his or her whiteness finds out the truth about his or her ancestry. An interracial marriage turns sour. The birth of a child brings a crisis. A single character is divided into black and white aspects. Such are the story lines found on the following pages.

This is the first anthology of the literary theme of black-white encounters, of love and family stories that cross—or are crossed by—what came to be considered racial boundaries. It is a theme that makes for unusual intersections of the plots of love and family relations with issues of society and politics. Unlike such themes as "autumn" or "war" (but to some extent like such themes as "lesbian love"), this literature includes representations that were themselves affected by the taboo that has at times surrounded interracial life stories. How does the representation of a human activity fare when the activity in question is, in some cases, under very serious debate and censure? Interracial love and marriage were, for example, criminalized in the English colonies and for four-fifths of the span of United States history. Yet the theme was also represented in periods and areas of the world in which no such censure existed. It could thus be expected to be represented neutrally as well as threateningly, in a paranoid as well as in a romanticized fashion, and such representations could further be expected to change as interracialism became decriminalized, more commonplace, and so widespread as to become an accepted part of the commercial culture, and, indeed, so much a part of ordinary and socially sanctioned human life that the emotions some of the earlier writers brought to this theme seem almost beyond comprehension today.

Except for a few very recent works, the anthology ends shortly after such "normalization" has set in, marked in the United States by the 1967 Supreme Court decision of *Loving v. Virginia*, which declared interracial marriage bans unconstitutional, and at the time of a great outpouring of interracial writing, for which this book provides a historical background and literary counterpoint. Generally, the process of selection was not guided by any prior definition of the term "interracial" or by a wish to present only works that will not give offense to anybody. Instead, it was inspired by the hope that the reader will see how the major and minor literature that is sampled on these pages has helped to define "black," "white," and their interactions in the world of writing. This anthology does not so much say what interracialism "is" but how writers have imagined it, both from the "inside" of such experiences and from the "outside."

From Cleobulus's ancient Greek riddle to the tormented encounters in the modern United States seems a very long trajectory, indeed; and this anthology includes samplings of a German medieval chivalric romance, *The Arabian Nights*, Italian Renaissance novellas, and Renaissance love lyric from Italy and England. There are also dramatic scenes and plays from Denmark, England, and the United States; modern novellas and short stories from France, Russia, Germany, England, and America; as well as essays, a pamphlet, autobiographical sketches, and numerous poems, among them many rarely anthologized ones by African American writers. The authors of the selections include some of the great names of world literature—Wolfram von Eschenbach, Marino, George Herbert, Kleist, Pushkin, Hans Christian Andersen, Longfellow, Dumas, Maupassant, Eugene O'Neill, and Langston Hughes. Also represented are less well-known writers who have focused on interracial relations from a variety of angles, be they erotic exploit, tragedy, comedy, melodrama, antislavery agitation, gothic, sentimental romance, satire, or local color fiction. In what may well be the fullest selection of interracially themed writings by African American and biracial authors, they are here represented by Olaudah Equiano, James Edwin Campbell, Charles Waddell Chesnutt, Joseph Seamon Cotter, Jr., Georgia Douglas Johnson, William Pickens, Jean Toomer, Countée Cullen, Langston Hughes, Claude McKay, Caroline Bond Day, Gwendolyn Brooks, Adrienne Kennedy, Charles Johnson, Rita Dove, Francesca J. Petrosino, and Itabari Njeri.

The collection contains some rare and hard-to-find sources. The selections from Wolfram's medieval epic *Parzival*, concerning his father Gamuret's love for the African queen Belakané and their biracial son, Feirefis, are presented in Jessie Weston's verse translation. The widely influential, sentimental Inkle and Yarico tale is included in its full version from the *Spectator*, as is an excerpt from its first verse adaptation from the *London Magazine*—which transforms Yarico from an American Indian into an African woman. Claire de Duras's once immensely popular tearjerker *Ourika* is included in a lively period translation. The complete extant text of Pushkin's historical novel fragment *The Blackamoor of Peter the Great* is also here. A chapter from *Georges*, the only novel by the prolific Alexandre Dumas in which he focused on a biracial hero, is included, as are the sadly resolved American version and the British happy ending of Dion Boucicault's play *The Octoroon*. Readers will be glad to find here the often-cited pamphlet *Miscegenation*, which coined that ominous word, as a Civil War–era political hoax intended to help prevent Lincoln's reelection. Further rarities are Wilkie Collins and Charles Fechter's little-known play *Black and White*, William Dean Howells's poem "The Pilot's Story," and Georgia Douglas Johnson's poem "The Octoroon." Jean Toomer's "Withered Skin of Berries" is printed together with two tales by his closest associates, his friend Waldo Frank's odd story "Hope" and his first wife Margery Latimer's "Confession."

Included are also several works that have never before been translated into English, among them Marino's foundational sonnet "The Beautiful Slave-Girl," scenes from Hans Christian Andersen's high-toned verse play *Mulatto*, in which the biracial hero Horatio charms not only one but two white women, the younger of whom marries him at the end, and the remarkable novella by Theodor Storm, *From Beyond the Seas*.

Some may find it surprising to reread familiar works in this interracial context ("Was that really how *The Arabian Nights* began?" the reader might ask of the story of King Shehriyar and his brother) or to read unfamiliar scenes by well-known authors ("Why have I never heard of Andersen's play *Mulatto*?" a fan of his fairy tales might say). The interracial advocacy letter by Olaudah Equiano/Gustavus Vassa may be as new to some readers as the extent to which interracial themes appeared in modern African American writing from the Civil War to the present. But it is also worthwhile to read the less well-known works, from Giraldi's story "A Moorish Captain Takes to Wife a Venetian Dame" (which served as the source for Shakespeare's *Othello*) to Henry Neville's odd *Isle of Pines*, or to read the poems by Eldred Revett, John Cleveland, Edward Herbert of Cherbury, John Whaley, Thomas Day and John Bicknell, and James de la Cour. In many minor works the generic sense of the conventions that govern the representation of interracial themes may become more apparent than in the more outstanding ones.

This *Anthology of Interracial Literature* covers a broad range of texts, spanning a very long period, and stemming from many national and linguistic origins (though with a strong focus on Europe and the United States). It includes high literary genres, from epic to poetry to novella. Its broad array of texts invites the reader to undertake comparative explorations, be they of different works whose titles include terms like "Mulatto" or "Quadroon," or of various works of literature set in revolutionary contexts. This book could be read by genre, from Renaissance lyrics that play with "black" and "white" to the modern poems by Gwendolyn Brooks and Langston Hughes, from the amazingly biased and misogynous, adultery-and-revenge-driven tales from *The Arabian Nights* or Masuccio's *Novellino* to the many modern answers to that tradition given in stories by Kate Chopin and Charles Chesnutt or in the hilarious excerpt from the novel *Oxherding Tale* by Charles Johnson. Particularly rich is the possibility to read dramatic scenes and complete plays in a historical arrangement, from Thomas Southerne's interracialized adaptation of Aphra Behn's *Oroonoko* through the nineteenth-century plays by Andersen, Boucicault, and Collins to the modern dramatic versions in O'Neill's *All God's Chillun Got Wings*, Langston Hughes's *Mulatto: A Tragedy of the Deep South*, the wonderfully complex play by Adrienne Kennedy, *The Owl Answers*, the modern interracial version of Oedipus in

Rita Dove's play *The Darker Face of the Earth*, and Francesca J. Petrosino's *Buck* (2001), which explores the tragicomic potential of conventions and forms a contemporary conclusion to this book.

Most selections are prefaced by brief biographical sketches, drafted especially for this volume by Francesca Petrosino.

Before Color Prejudice

Before Color Prejudice is the apt title of a study by the classicist Frank M. Snowden, Jr., who documents how Egyptian, Greek, Roman, and early Christian sources "point to a highly favorable image of blacks and white-black relations differing markedly from those that have developed in more color-conscious societies." Color contrasts were viewed as part of a natural order, and notions of descent were flexible: of course, day could give birth to night, and night to day, as Cleobulus's riddle also suggests. For example, in Heliodorus's novel *Aethiopica* (not included here), the black queen Persinne gives birth to a white daughter. Color was an accidental, not an essential quality in antiquity and in the Christian Middle Ages. According to Snowden, most of the early commentators on the Bible read the famous passage from the *Song of Songs* "I am black and beautiful" (Nigra sum et formosa)—not, as in the King James version, "black *but* comely." Christian symbolism did develop a color contrast between "hell's darkness and the light of heaven." This is the phrasing from Wolfram von Eschenbach's medieval epic *Parzival*. Yet the metaphoric contrast does not apply to racially different people. Thus Wolfram says about his African queen Belakané that "unlike to the dew-dipped roses was her colour, yea, black as night," and sees her also as representing "purity untarnished."

1

"Riddle"

Cleobulus

The philosopher Cleobulus was born on the island of Rhodes around the fifth century B.C. Diogenes of Laertius credits him with the authorship of nearly three thousand lines of proverb-like songs and riddles, few of which have survived. The answer to the enigma included here is that the *year* is the father of twelve *months*, each of which has thirty *days* and thirty *nights*.

ΚΛΕΟΒΟΥΛΟΥ ΑΙΝΙΓΜΑ

Εἶς ὁ πατήρ, παῖδες δυοκαίδεκα· τῶν δὲ ἑκύστῳ
παῖδες <δὶς> τριήκοντα διάνδιχα εἶδος ἔχουσαι·
αἱ μὲν λευκαὶ ἔασιν ἰδεῖν, αἱ δ᾽ αὖτε μέλαιναι·
ἀθάνατοι δέ τ᾽ ἐοῦσαι, ἀποφθινύθουσιν ἅπασαι.

An Enigma of Cleobulus

There is one father and twelve children. Each of these has twice thirty children of different aspect; some of them we see to be white and the others black, and though immortal, they all perish.

TRANSLATED BY W. R. PATON

From *Parzival*

Wolfram von Eschenbach

Much of what we know of the life of a medieval German knight named Wolfram von Eschenbach (ca. 1170–1220) can be deduced from his own literary creations: *Willehalm*, a poem of battle, and *Parzival*, a knightly romance and Grail quest. Wolfram claims to have first heard the story of Parzival from heathen legends told to his master, Kiot, and his emphasis on the envy of Western Christian leaders for the prosperity of their Eastern heathen counterparts locates the poem's action in the ninth century. But Wolfram's vibrant storytelling and position in the epic as narrator rather than simple writer indicate that much of the action was germane to the thirteenth century and to Wolfram himself. To stock characters of knights and kings Wolfram adds dignified older men, dewy-eyed children, and active women. He lashes out at the contemporary poets who assumed his ignorance. Wolfram's subtlety, sarcasm, and skill make *Parzival* an epic not only of Parzival's life but also of Wolfram's own.

Wolfram's own additions to the traditional romances of the Grail are remarkable and include the interracial love story of Parzival's father, Gamuret, king of Anjou, who, on a quest for knightly adventures, goes to Baghdad and the African kingdom Zassamank, where he comes to queen Belakané's rescue and marries her. Their son, Feirefis, whom Parzival later encounters, is described as "piebald," resembling "written parchment, both black and white." Books 1 and 15, which are reprinted here in Jessie Weston's English verse translation from the Middle High German original, suggest the uniqueness of Wolfram von Eschenbach's accomplishment.

Book I: Gamuret

Argument

In the Introduction the poet tells of the evil of doubt and unsteadfastness—against which he would warn both men and women; he will tell them a tale which shall speak of truth and steadfastness, and in which many strange marvels shall befall.

Book 1 tells how Gamuret of Anjou at the death of his father, King Gandein, refused to become his brother's vassal, and went forth to seek fame and love-guerdon for himself. How he fought under the Baruch before Alexandria, and came to Patelamunt. How Queen Belakané was accused of having caused the death of her lover Eisenhart, and was besieged by two armies, which Friedebrand, King of Scotland, Eisenhart's uncle, had brought against her. How Gamuret defeated her foemen, and married the Queen, and became King of Assagog and Zassamank. How he grew weary

for lack of knightly deeds, and sailed away in secret from Queen Belakané, and left her
a letter telling of his name and race. How Feirifis was born, and how Gamuret came to
Seville.

If unfaith in the heart find dwelling, then the soul it shall reap but woe;
And shaming alike and honour are his who such doubt shall show,
For it standeth in evil contrast with a true man's dauntless might,
As one seeth the magpie's plumage, which at one while is black and white.
And yet he may win to blessing; since I wot well that in his heart,
Hell's darkness, and light of Heaven, alike have their lot and part.
But he who is false and unsteadfast, he is black as the darkest night,
And the soul that hath never wavered stainless *its* hue and white!

This my parable so fleeting too swift for the dull shall be,
Ere yet they may seize its meaning from before their face 'twill flee,
As a hare that a sound hath startled: yea, metal behind the glass,
And a blind man's dream yield visions that as swift from the eye do pass,
For naught shall they have that endureth! And at one while 'tis bright and sad,
And know of a truth that its glory but for short space shall make ye glad.
And what man shall think to grip me, where no hair for his grasp shall grow,
In the palm of mine hand? The mystery of a close clasp he sure doth know!

If I cry aloud in such peril, it 'seemeth my wisdom well.
Shall I look for truth where it fleeteth? In the fire that the stream doth quell,
Or the dew that the sun doth banish? Ne'er knew I a man so wise,
But was fain to learn the wisdom my fable doth ill disguise,
And the teaching that springeth from it: for so shall he ne'er delay
To fly and to chase as shall fit him, to shun and to seek alway,
And to give fitting blame and honour. He who knoweth the twain to tell,
In their changing ways, then wisdom has tutored that man right well.
And he sits not o'er-long at leisure, nor his goal doth he overreach,
But in wisdom his ways discerning, he dealeth with all and each.
But his comrade, of heart unfaithful, in hell-fire shall his portion be,
Yea, a hailstorm that dims the glory of a knightly fame is he.
As a short tail it is, his honour, that but for two bites holds good,
When the steer by the gad-fly driven doth roam thro' the lonely wood.

And tho' manifold be my counsel not to *men* alone I'ld speak,
For fain would I show to women the goal that their heart should seek.
And they who shall mark my counsel, they shall learn where they may bestow
Their praise and their maiden honour; and the manner of man shall know
Whom they freely may love and honour, and never may fear to rue
Their maidenhood, and the true love they gave him of heart so true.
In God's sight I pray all good women to keep them in wisdom's way,

For true shame on all sides doth guard them: such bliss I for them would pray.
But the false heart shall win false honour—How long doth the thin ice last,
If the sun shineth hot as in August? So their praise shall be soon o'erpast.

Many women are praised for beauty; if at heart they shall be untrue,
Then I praise them as I would praise it, the glass of a sapphire hue
That in gold shall be set as a jewel! Tho' I hold it an evil thing,
If a man take a costly ruby, with the virtue the stone doth bring,
And set it in worthless setting: I would liken such costly stone
To the heart of a faithful woman, who true womanhood doth own.
I would look not upon her colour, nor the heart's roof all men can see,
If the heart beateth true beneath it, true praise shall she win from me!

Should I speak of both man and woman as I know, nor my skill should fail,
O'er-long would it be my story. List ye now to my wonder-tale:
And this venture it telleth tidings of love, and anon of woe,
Joy and sorrow it bringeth with it. 'Stead of *one* man if *three* ye know,
And each one of the three hath wisdom and skill that outweigh my skill,
Yet o'erstrange shall they find the labour, tho' they toil with a right goodwill
To tell ye this tale, which I think me to tell ye myself, alone,
And worn with their task and weary would they be ere the work was done.

A tale I anew will tell ye, that speaks of a mighty love;
Of the womanhood of true women; how a man did his manhood prove;
Of one that endured all hardness, whose heart never failed in fight,
Steel he in the face of conflict: with victorious hand of might
Did he win him fair meed of honour; a brave man yet slowly wise
Is he whom I hail my hero! The delight he of woman's eyes,
Yet of woman's heart the sorrow! 'Gainst all evil his face he set;
Yet he whom I thus have chosen my song knoweth not as yet,
For not yet is he born of whom men this wondrous tale shall tell,
And many and great the marvels that unto this knight befell.

Now they do to-day as of old time, where a foreign law holds sway
(Yea, in part of our German kingdom, as ye oft shall have heard men say),
Whoever might rule that country, 'twas the law, and none thought it shame
('Tis the truth and no lie I tell ye) that the elder son might claim
The whole of his father's heirdom—And the younger sons must grieve,
What was theirs in their father's lifetime, they perforce at his death must leave.
Before, all was theirs in common, now it fell unto one alone.
So a wise man planned in his wisdom, that the eldest the lands should own,
For youth it hath many a fair gift, but old age knoweth grief and pain,
And he who is poor in his old age an ill harvest alone doth gain.
Kings, Counts, Dukes (and no lie I tell ye) the law holdeth all as one,
And no man of them all may inherit, save only the eldest son,

And methinks 'tis an evil custom—So the knight in his youthful pride,
Gamuret, the gallant hero, lost his Burg, and his fair lands wide,
Where his father had ruled with sceptre and crown as a mighty king,
Till knighthood, and lust of battle, to his death did the monarch bring.

And all men were sore for his sorrow, who truth and unbroken faith
Bare ever throughout his lifetime, yea even unto his death.
Then the elder son he summoned the princes from out his land,
And knightly they came, who rightly might claim from their monarch's hand,
To hold, as of yore, their fiefdoms. So came they unto his hall,
And the claim of each man he hearkened, and gave fiefs unto each and all.

Now hear how they dealt—As their true heart it bade them, both great and small,
They made to their king petition, with one voice from the people all,
That to Gamuret grace and favour he would show with true brother's hand,
And honour himself in the doing. That he drive him not from the land
But give him, within his kingdom, a fair Burg that all men might see,
That he take from that Burg his title, and be held of all tribute free!—
Nor the king was ill-pleased at their pleading, and he quoth, "A small grace, I trow,
Have ye asked, I would e'en be better than your prayer, as ye straight shall know,
Why name ye not this my brother as Gamuret Angevin?
Since Anjou is my land, I think me the title we *both* may win!"

Then further he spake, the monarch, "My brother in sooth may seek
Yet more from my hand of favour than my mouth may as swiftly speak,
With me shall he have his dwelling—I would that ye all should see
How one mother alike hath borne us; his riches but small shall be,
While I have enough; of free hand would I give him both lands and gold,
That my bliss may be ne'er held forfeit by Him, Who can aye withhold,
Or give, as He deemeth rightful!" Then the princes they heard alway,
How the king would deal well with his brother, and they deemed it a joyful day!

And each one bowed him low before him. Nor Gamuret long delayed,
But he spake as his heart would bid him, and friendly the words he said:
"Now hearken, my lord and brother, if vassal I think to be
To thee, or to any other, then a fair lot awaiteth me.
But think thou upon mine honour, for faithful art thou and wise,
And give counsel as shall beseem thee, and help as thou shalt devise.
For naught have I now save mine armour, if within it I more had done,
Then far lands should speak my praises, and remembrance from men were won!"

Then further he spake, the hero: "Full sixteen my squires shall be,
And six of them shall bear harness; four pages give thou to me
Of noble birth and breeding, and nothing to them I'll spare
Of all that my hand may win them. Afar in the world I'ld fare,

(Somewhat I ere now have journeyed,) if Good Fortune on me shall smile,
I may win from fair women favour. If a woman I serve awhile,
And to serve her she hold me worthy, and my heart speaketh not amiss,
True knight shall I be and faithful! God show me the way of bliss!
As comrades we rode together (but then o'er thy land did reign
The King Gandein, our father), and sorrow and bitter pain
We bare for Love's sake! At one while I knew thee as *thief* and *knight*,
Thou couldst serve, and thou couldst dissemble, for the sake of thy lady bright.
Ah! could I steal love as thou couldst, if my skill were but like to thine,
That women should show me favour, then a blissful lot were mine!"

"Alas! that I ever saw thee," spake, sighing, the king so true,
"Who lightly, with words of mocking, my heart would in pieces hew
And would fain that we part asunder! One father hath left us both
A mighty store of riches, I would share with thee, nothing loth.
Right dear from my heart I hold thee; red gold and jewels bright,
Folk, weapons, horse, and raiment, take thou as shall seem thee right,
That thou at thy will mayst journey, and thy free hand to all be known.
Elect do we deem thy manhood, didst thou Gylstram as birthplace own,
Or thou camest here from Rankulat, yet still would that place be thine,
Which thou holdest to-day in my favour; true brother art thou of mine!"

"Sir King, thou of need must praise me, so great is thy courtesy!
So, courteous, thine aid be given, if thou and my mother free
Will share with me now your riches, I mount upward, nor fear to fall,
And my heart ever beateth higher—Yet I know not how I should call
This life, which my left breast swelleth! Ah! whither wouldst go mine heart?
I would fain know where thou shalt guide me—'Tis time that we twain should part."

And all did the monarch give him, yea, more than the knight might crave,
Five chargers, picked and chosen, the best in his land he gave
High-couraged, swift to battle; and many a cup of gold,
And many a golden nugget, for naught would his hand withhold.
Four chests for the road he gave him, with many a jewel rare
Were they filled. Then the squires he took him who should for the treasure care,
And well were they clad and mounted; and none might his grief withhold
When the knight gat him unto his mother, who her son in her arms did fold.

Spake the woman, as woman grieving: "Wilt thou tarry with me no more,
King Gandein's son? Woe is me! yet my womb this burden bore
And the son of my husband art thou. Is the eye of God waxed blind,
Or His ear grown deaf in the hearing, that my prayer doth no credence find?
Is fresh sorrow to be my portion? I have buried my heart's desire,
And the light of mine eyes; will He rob me, who have suffered a grief so dire,

Who judgeth with righteous judgment? Then the tale it hath told a lie,
That spake of His help so mighty, Who doth help unto me deny!"

"God comfort thee," quoth the hero, "for the death of my father dear,
For truly we both must mourn him—But I think from no lips to hear
Such wailing for my departing! As valour shall show the way,
I seek knighthood in distant countries—So it standeth with me to-day."

Quoth the queen, "Since to high love's service thou turnest both hand and heart,
Sweet son, let it not displease thee to take of my wealth a part
That may serve thee upon thy journey; let thy chamberlain take from me
Four chests, each a pack-horse burden, and heavy their weight shall be.
And within, uncut, there lieth rich silk of Orient rare,
No man as yet hath cut it, and many a samite fair.
Sweet son, I prithee tell me what time thou wilt come again,
That my joy may wax the greater, and I look for thee not in vain!"

"Nay, that I know not, Lady, nor the land that shall see my face,
But wherever I take my journey, thou hast shown unto me such grace
As befitteth knightly honour: and the king he hath dealt with me
In such wise that grateful service his rewarding shall ever be.
And this trust have I, O Lady, that for this thou wilt love him more
Henceforward, whate'er the future yet keepeth for me in store."

And as the venture telleth, to the hand of this dauntless knight,
Thro' the favour he won from a woman, and the working of true love's might,
Came a token fair, and its value was full thousand marks, I trow,
E'en to-day an a Jew were craving a pledge, he would deem enow
Such jewel, and ne'er disdain it—'Twas sent by his lady true,
And fame did he win in her service, and her love and her greeting knew,
Yet seldom his pain found easing—Then the hero he took his leave
Of mother, brother, and brother's kingdom, and many I ween must grieve
Since his eyes never more beheld them. And all who his friends had been,
Ere he passed from the land of his fathers, tho' the grace were but small, I ween,
He gave them of thanks full measure; he deemed they too much had done,
And, courteous, little thought him, that of right he their love had won!
Straighter his heart than straightness; did one of his praises speak
In a full and fitting measure, then doubt were not far to seek,
But ask ye of those his neighbours, or of men who in distant lands
Had seen his deeds, then the marvel ye were swifter to understand.

And Gamuret he trode ever where Temperance aye should guide,
And naught else might rule his doings, nor he boasted him in his pride
But bare great honour meekly; from loose ways he e'er had flown;

And he thought him, the gallant hero, that none bare on earth a crown,
Were they King, or Queen, or Kaiser, whom he deemed of his service worth
Were they not the mightiest reckoned of all monarchs that be on earth.
This will in his heart he cherished—Then men spake, at Bagdad did reign
A monarch so strong and powerful, that homage he well might claim
From two-thirds or more of earth's kingdoms. The heathen his name held great,
And they spake of him as the Baruch, and kings did on his bidding wait,
And crownéd heads were his servants; and his office it lasts to-day—
See how Christian men baptizèd to Rome wend their pilgrim way,
So there was the heathen custom. At Bagdad was their papal right,
And the Baruch as 'seemed his office purged their sins with his word of might.

From Pompey and Ipomidon, two brothers of Babylon,
Nineveh, the town of their fathers, the Baruch with force had won,
And bravely 'gainst him they battled. Then came the young Angevin,
And the Baruch he showed him favour, yea, he did to his service win
Gamuret the gallant hero—And he deemed it were well he bore
Other arms than Gandein his father had given to him of yore.
Then the hero he well bethought him; on his charger's cloth they laid
An anchor of ermine fashioned, and the same at his will they made
For shield alike and vesture—And green as the emerald rare
Was his riding-gear, and 'twas fashioned and wrought of Achmardi fair,
('Tis a silken stuff,) and he bade them to make of it at his will
Both blazoned coat and surcoat, (than velvet 'tis richer still;)
And he bade them to sew upon it the anchor of ermine white,
And with golden threads inwoven was the badge of this gallant knight.

And his anchors they never tested or mainland or haven fair
And found in that place abiding—But the hero must further bear
Thro' many a land, a brave guest, the load of this heraldry,
And behind the sign of this anchor but short space might his resting be,
And nowhere he found abiding—The tale of the lands he saw,
And the vessels in which he sailed him? If the truth unto ye I swore,
On mine own oath must I swear it, and my knightly honour true
In such wise as the venture told me; other witness I never knew!

And men say that his manly courage held the prize in far heathendom,
In Morocco's land, and in Persia, and elsewhere he high honour won,
At Damascus and at Aleppo, and where knightly deeds should be:
In Arabia and lands around it was he held of all conflict free,
For no man might dare withstand him, he won him such crown of fame;
And his heart for honour lusted, and all deeds were brought to shame,
And became as naught before him, as all men bare witness true
Who a joust with him had ridden, and Bagdad of his glory knew.

And his heart never failed or faltered, but onward his course he bare
To Zassamank's land and kingdom; there all men wept that hero fair,
Eisenhart, who in knightly service gave his life for a woman's smile;
Belakané thereto constrained him, sweet maid she, and free from guile.
(Since her love she never gave him, for love's sake did the hero die,)
And his kinsmen would fain avenge him, and with force and with subtlety
Their armies beset the maiden, but in sooth she could guard her well
Ere Gamuret came to her kingdom, and her wrath on her foemen fell.
For the Prince Friedebrand of Scotland; and his host that against her came
By ship, ere he left her kingdom had she wasted with fire and flame.

Now hear what befell our hero; storm-driven he was that day,
And scarce might he win to safety, and his boat in the haven lay
Beneath the royal palace; and the folk they beheld him there,
And he looked around on the meadow, and he saw many tents stand fair
Around the town, save the sea-coast, and two armies he thought to see.
Then he bade them to tell the story, and whose that fair Burg should be?
Since he knew it not, nor his shipmen—And an answer they straightway gave,
'Twas Patelamunt; then the townsfolk a boon from the knight would crave,
And their speech it was soft and friendly—In the name of their gods they'ld pray
He should help them, so great their peril that in danger of death they lay.

When the young Angevin had hearkened to the tale of their bitter pain,
He proffered to them his service for such payment as knight may gain,
(As it oft shall befit a hero)—They should say for what goodly prize
He should dare the hate of their foemen? And they answered him in this wise
With one mouth the hale and the wounded—Naught would they from
    him withhold,
But lord should he be of their treasure, of their jewels alike and gold,
A fair life should he lead among them!—But such payment he little sought,
For many a golden nugget from Araby had he brought.
And dark as night were the people who in Zassamank dwelt alway—
And the time it seemed long unto him that he need in their midst must stay—
But he bade them prepare a lodging, and methinks it became them well
The best of their land to give him, since awhile he with them would dwell.
And the women they looked from the windows, and they gazed on the noble knight,
And they looked on his squires, and his harness, how 'twas fashioned for deeds
    of might.
Then they saw how the knight, free-handed, on his shield of ermine bare
Full many a pelt of sable; the Queen's Marshal he read it fair,
The badge, for a mighty anchor, and little he rued the sight,
If his eye spake the truth unto him ere this had he seen the knight,
Or one who bare his semblance—At Alexandria it needs must be,
When the Baruch besieged the city—and unequalled in strife was he!

So rode the gallant hero, in stately guise and meet;
Ten pack-horses heavy-laden they led first adown the street,
And twenty squires behind them; and his people they went before,
And lackeys, cooks, and cook-boys, at the head of the train they saw.
And stately I ween his household, twelve pages of lineage high
Rode next to the squires, well-mannered, and trained in all courtesy,
And Saracens were among them; and behind them in order fair
Came chargers eight, and a covering of sendal did each one bear.
But the ninth it bore a saddle, and the shield ye have known ere now
Was borne by a squire beside it, and joyful his mien, I trow.
And trumpeters rode behind it, for in sooth they must needs be there,
And a drummer he smote his tambour, and swung it aloft in air.
And as naught had the hero deemed it, this pomp, if there failed to ride
Men who on the flute were skilful, and three fiddlers were at their side,
And they hasted not nor hurried; and behind them the hero came,
And his shipman he rode beside him, a wise man of goodly fame.

And much folk was within the city, and Moors were both man and maid.
Then the hero he looked around him, and, lo! many a shield displayed,
Battle-hewn and with spear-thrust piercèd they hung on each wall and door.
And wailing and woe was their portion; for the knight at each window saw
Many men lie sorely wounded, who to breathe the air were fain,
And e'en tho' a leech might tend them no help might they think to gain
Who were hurt too sore for healing—In the field had they faced the foe,
And such shall be their rewarding who in conflict no flight will know—
Many horses were led towards him, sword-hewn and with lance thrust through;
And on each side stood dusky maidens, and black as the night their hue.

Then his host gave him kindly greeting—and of joy did he reap his meed—
A rich man was he and mighty, and many a knightly deed
With thrust and blow had his hand wrought when his post at the gate he found;
And many a knight was with him, and bandaged their heads and bound,
And their hands in slings were holden; yet tho' sorely wounded still
They did many deeds of knighthood, nor were lacking in strength and skill.

Then the Burg-grave of the city, with fair words did he pray his guest
To deal with him and his household in such wise as should seem him best.
And the host, he led the hero to his wife, and courteously
Did Gamuret kiss the lady, small joy in the kiss had he!
Then they sat them down to the table, and e'en as the feast was o'er,
The Marshal he gat him swiftly to the queen, and the tidings bore,
And craved from her goodly payment, as to messenger shall be due.
And he spake, "It shall end in gladness, the grief that erewhile we knew,
We have welcomed here, O Lady, a knight of such gallant mien,
We must thank the gods who have sent him, for our need they have surely seen."

"Now tell me upon thine honour who this gallant knight may be?"
"Lady, a dauntless hero, and the Baruch's man is he,
An Angevin he, of high lineage; Ah me! little did he spare
Himself, when his foemen seeking he forth to the field would fare.
How wisely, with skill and cunning, he avoided the threatening blow,
And turned him again to the onslaught! Much sorrow he wrought his foe—
Ere this have I seen him battle, when the princes of Babylon
Their city of Alexandria had fain from the Baruch won,
And with force from its walls would drive him, and many a man lay dead
In the overthrow of their army, for their venture was but ill-sped.
And such deeds did he do, this hero, that no counsel was theirs but flight:
And there did I hear his praises, for all spake of this gallant knight
As one who, without denial, had won him, in many a land,
The crown of true knightly honour, by the strength of his own right hand."

"Now fain would I speak with the hero, see thou to the time and way;
E'en now might he ride to the castle, for peace shall be kept to-day.
Were it better that I should seek him? He is other than we in face,
Pray Heaven it not displease him, but our need with the knight find grace!
I would that I first might know this, ere the rede from my folk I hear
That I show to this stranger honour—If it pleaseth him to draw near,
Say, how shall I best receive him? Shall the knight be so nobly born
That my kiss be not lost, if I kiss him?" "Nay, hold me of life forsworn
If he be not of kings the kinsman! Lady, this word I'll bear
To thy princes, that they shall clothe them in raiment both fit and fair,
And stand before thee, in due order, ere yet to thy court we ride,
And the same shalt thou say to thy ladies—In the city he doth abide;
I will ride below, and will bring him to thy palace, a worthy guest,
For no fair or knightly virtue shall be lacking that noble breast."

But little space they delayed them, for the Marshal, with ready skill,
Strove that all in such wise be ordered as should pleasure his lady's will.
But soon did they bear to the hero rich garments, he did them on,
And this hath the venture told me that their cost should be hardly won;
And thereon lay the anchors, heavy, and wrought of Arabian gold,
For so had he willed. Then the hero, who fair payment for love had told
A charger bestrode that 'fore Babylon a knight rode, for jousting fain,
From the saddle did Gamuret smite him, and I wot it hath wrought him pain.

If his host thought to ride beside him? He and his gallant knights?
Yea, in sooth they would do so, gladly—So wended they up the height,
And dismounted before the palace; and many a knight stood there,
And each, as was fit, had clothed him in raiment both rich and fair.
And his pages they ran before him, and each twain they went hand in hand,
And in marvellous fair arraying he saw many ladies stand.

And the queen, her eyes brought her sorrow as she looked on the Angevin,
So lovely was he to look on that he needs must an entrance win
Thro' the gates of her heart, if 'twere anguish or joy that within he bore,
Tho' her womanhood 'gainst all comers had held them fast closed before.

Then a space did she step towards him, and a kiss from her guest she prayed;
And, herself, by the hand she took him and they sat them, both man and maid
In a window wide, that looked forth from the palace upon the foe,
And a covering of wadded samite was spread o'er the couch below.
Is there aught that than day is lighter? Then it likeneth not the queen!
Yet else was she fair to look on, as a woman should be, I ween,
But unlike to the dew-dipped roses was her colour, yea, black as night.
And her crown was a costly ruby, and thro' it ye saw aright
Her raven head. Then as hostess she spake to her guest this word,
That greatly she joyed at his coming, "Sir Knight, I such tale have heard
Of thy knightly strength and prowess—Of thy courtesy, hear me fair,
For fain would I tell of my sorrow, and the woe that my heart doth bear!"

"My help shall not fail thee, Lady! What hath grieved, or doth grieve thee now,
I think me aside to turn it, to thy service my hand I vow!
I am naught but one man only—Who hath wronged or now wrongeth thee
My shield will I hold against him—Little wroth shall thy foeman be!"

Then a prince he spake out courteous, "The foe would we little spare,
Did our host not lack a captain, since Friedebrand hence must fare.
He defendeth afar his kingdom—A king, one Hernant by name
(Whom he slew for the sake of Herlindè) his kinsmen against him came,
And evil enow have they wrought him, nor yet from their strife forbear—
Yet he left here full many a hero, and among them, Duke Heuteger
With his gallant deeds of knighthood, and his army, hath pressed us sore,
They have skill and strength for the conflict. And many a soldier more
With Gaschier of Normandy came here, and a hero wise is he.
Many knights hath he brought to this country (and wrathful guests they be):
Kailet of Hoscurast. All these hath he brought upon our fair land
With his comrades four, and his soldiers, the Scottish king Friedebrand!
And there, to the West, by the sea-coast doth Eisenhart's army lie,
And their eyes shall be fain for weeping; nor in secret, nor openly
Hath one seen them, and failed to marvel at their grief and their sorrow sore,
Since their lord hath been slain in battle with the heart's rain their eyes run o'er."

Then the guest courteous spake to his hostess, "I would, an it seem thee right,
Thou shouldst say why thy foeman threaten, why they seek thee with warlike might!
Thou hast here many gallant heroes, it grieveth me sore to see
Thy land thus with hate o'erladen, for woe must it bring to thee."

"Wouldst thou know? Then, Sir Knight, I will tell thee—A knight did me
    service true,
And the fruit of all manly virtue his life as its decking knew,
And gallant and wise was the hero, and his faith as a goodly tree
Was fast-rooted, and none so courteous but were shamed by his courtesy.
And modest was he as a woman, tho' dauntless and strong, I trow,
And a knight e'en as he free-handed ere his day never land might know.
(But they that shall come hereafter, other folk shall their doings see.)
A fool was he in false dealing, and a Moor, as myself shall be;
And his father's name was Tánkaneis, a king of a kingly heart,
And his son, he who was my lover, men knew him as Eisenhart.
That for love's sake I took his service, as a woman I did not well,
It hath brought me but lasting sorrow since no joy to his portion fell,
They deem I to death betrayed him! Yet such treason were far from me,
Tho' his folk bring such charge against me; and dear to my heart was he,
Far dearer than *they* e'er held him. Nor witnesses here shall fail
To speak to the truth of my saying, if it please them to tell the tale.
His gods and mine, they know it, the truth—I must sorrow deep
Since my womanly shame hath brought him a guerdon I needs must weep!

"Thus he won in my maiden service much honour by knighthood fair,
I thought thus to prove my lover; his deeds did his worth declare.
For my sake he put off his harness (that which like to a hall doth stand
Is a lofty tent, the Scotch folk they brought it into this land),
Then e'en tho' he bare no armour his body he little spared,
For he held his life as worthless, many ventures unarmed he dared.
As the matter so stood between us, a prince who my man should be,
Prothizilas did men call him, a bold knight, from all cowardice free,
Rode forth in search of venture, and evil for him that day
For there, in Assagog's forest, his death in waiting lay.
In a knightly joust he met it, and there too he found his end
The gallant knight who faced him—'Twas Prince Eisenhart, my friend.
For both of the twain were piercèd with a spear thro' heart and shield,
And I, alas! poor woman, must weep for that fatal field.
And ever their death doth grieve me, and sorrow from love shall grow,
And never henceforth as my husband a man do I think to know."

Then e'en tho' she was a heathen Gamuret he bethought him well,
That a heart more true and tender ne'er in woman's breast might dwell.
Her purity was her baptism, and as water that washed her o'er
Was the rain that streamed from her eyelids o'er her breast, and the robe
    she wore;
All her joy did she find in sorrow, and grief o'er her life did reign—
Then the queen she looked on the hero, and in this wise she spake again:

"With his army the king of Scotland hath sought me across the sea,
For the knight was son to his uncle; yet no ill can he do to me,
If here the truth be spoken, that is worse than the grief I knew
For Eisenhart's death!" and sorely she sighed that lady true;
And many a glance thro' her tear-drops on Gamuret shyly fell,
And her eyes to her heart gave counsel, and his beauty it pleased her well,
(And she knew how to judge a fair face, since fair heathen she oft had seen,)
And the root of true love and longing it sprang up the twain between.
She looked upon him, and his glances, they answering sought her own—
Then she bade them to fill the wine-cup, had she dared, it were left undone,
And she grieved she might not delay it, since to many a hero brave
Who spake with the maids this wine-cup the signal of parting gave.
Yet her body was e'en as his body, and his look did such courage give
To the maid, that she thought henceforward in the life of the knight to live.

Then he stood upright, and he spake thus, "Lady, I weary thee,
Too long methinks do I sit here, I were lacking in courtesy!
As befitting true knight and servant I mourn for thy woe so great,
Lady, do thou command me, I will on thy bidding wait.
Wherever thou wilt, there I wend me. I will serve thee in all I may!"
And the lady she quoth in answer, "I believe thee, Sir Knight, alway!"

Then his kindly host the Burg-grave, of his labour would nothing spare
Lest the hours of his stay be heavy; and he asked if he forth would fare,
And ride round the walls of the city? "The battle-field shalt thou see,
And how we would guard our portals!" then Gamuret courteously
Made answer, he fain would see it, the field where they late had fought,
And the place where brave deeds of knighthood had by gallant hands been wrought.

And noble knights rode with him adown from the palace hall,
Some were wise, some were young and foolish,—So rode they around the wall
To sixteen gates, and they told him not one of them might they close
Since Eisenhart's death called for vengeance—"So wrathful shall be our foes
Our conflict it resteth never, but we fight both by night and day,
Nor our portals since then we fasten, but open they stand alway.
At eight of our gates they beset us, true Eisenhart's gallant knights,
And evil shall they have wrought us; spurred by anger each man doth fight,
The princes of lofty lineage, the king of Assagog's ban!"
And there floated before each portal a banner, so pale and wan,
With a piercèd knight upon it. When Eisenhart lost his life
His folk chose to them this symbol, as badge in the coming strife.
"But against these arms have we others, wherewith we their grief would still,
And thus shalt thou know our banner; 'twas wrought at our lady's will,
Two fingers in oath she stretcheth, that never such grief she knew
As Eisenhart's death hath brought her (true sorrow for heart so true),

And so doth it stand the semblance of our queen, on a samite white
Belakané in sable fashioned,—Since against us they came in might,
(To avenge him for whom she sorrows) so she looks from our portals high.
And proud Friedebrand's mighty army doth to eight of our gates stand nigh,
Baptized men, from o'er the waters. A prince doth each portal hold,
And forth from the gate he sallies, with his banners and warriors bold."

"From the host of Gaschier the Norman, a count have we captive ta'en,
And heavy methinks the ransom we may hope from that knight to gain;
He is sister's son to Kailet, and the harm *he* to us hath done
His nephew I ween shall pay for! Yet such prize have we seldom won.
Here have we no grassy meadow, but sand, thirty gallops wide
Betwixt the tents and the trenches; here many a joust we ride."

And further his host would tell him, "One knight, he doth never fail
To ride forth, a fair joust seeking. (If his service shall nought avail
With her who hath sent him hither, what boots it how well he fight?)
Proud Heuteger is the hero, of him may I speak with right
For since our besiegers threaten there dawneth never a day
But before the gates 'neath the castle, that knight doth his charger stay.
And oft from that dauntless hero many tokens we needs must bear,
That he smote through our shields at his spear-point, and costly their worth and rare
When the squire from the shield doth break them. Many knights 'fore his joust
    must fall;
He would that all men may behold him, and our women they praise him all.
And he who is praised of women, one knoweth that he doth hold
The prize in his hand, and his heart's joy in full measure shall aye be told!"

But now would the sun, grown weary, its wandering rays recall;
'Twas time that the ride was ended—Then he sought with his host the hall,
And the evening meal was ready; and I needs of that feast must tell,
'Twas laid in a fitting order, and knightly 'twas served, and well.
And the queen with mien so stately she unto his table came,
(Here stood the fish, there the heron) and she counted it not for shame
To ride adown from her palace, that herself she might be aware
If they cared for the guest as 'twas fitting, and with her rode her maidens fair.
Low she knelt (and but ill it pleased him) and cut as it seemed her best
For the knight a fitting portion; she was glad in her goodly guest.
And she filled for him the wine-cup, and care for his needs would take,
And well did he mark, the hero, her mien, and the words she spake.
And his fiddlers sat at the table, and over against the knight
Was his chaplain: with shy looks shamefast, he spake to the lady bright:

"I looked not to find such welcome as, Lady, thou gavest me,
Too much must I deem the honour! If rede I might give to thee,

Then to-day I had claimed naught from thee save was due to my worth alone,
Nor adown the hill hadst thou ridden, nor such service to me hadst shown.
And, Lady, if I may venture to make unto thee request,
Let me live but as best befits me, thou dost honour o'ermuch thy guest!"

Yet her kindly care she stayed not; for she stept to his page's seat
And with gentle words and friendly she prayed them to freely eat,
This she did her guest to honour: and the noble lads, I trow,
Bare goodwill to the royal lady. Nor the queen methinks was slow
To pass where the host was seated and his lady, the Burg-gravine,
And she raised the golden goblet, and she spake as should fit a queen:
"Now unto your care I give him, our guest, and I rede ye both
Since the honour is yours, to hearken, and do my will nothing loth!"
And she bade them farewell, and she turned her, and passed to her guest once more,
Whose heart for her sake was heavy; and such sorrow for him she bore,
And her heart and her eyes they answered, and they spake to her sorrow yea!
And courteous she spake, the lady, "Sir Knight, thou the word shalt say,
And whate'er be thy will, I will do it, for I hold thee a worthy guest.
Now give me, I pray, dismissal; if here thou in peace shalt rest,
Of that shall we all be joyful." Her torch-holders were of gold,
And four tapers they bare before her, so she rode to her fortress-hold.

Nor long at the board they lingered—The hero was sad, and gay,
He was glad for the honour done him, yet a sorrow upon him lay,
And that was strong Love's compelling, that a proud heart and courage high
Can bend to her will, and gladness shall oft at her bidding fly.

Then the hostess she passed to her chamber, yea, e'en as the meal was o'er;
And a couch did they spread for the hero, and love to the labour bore.
And the host to his guest spake kindly, "Now here shall thy sleep be sweet,
Thou shalt rest thro' the night that cometh, to thy need shall such rest be meet."
Then he spake to his men, and he bade them they should hence from the hall away,
And the noble youths his pages, their couches around his lay
Each one with the head toward his master, for so was the custom good;
And tapers so tall and flaming alight round the chamber stood.
Yet ill did it please the hero that so long were the hours of night,
For the Moorish queen so dusky, had vanquished his heart of might.
And he turned as a willow wand bendeth, till his joints they were heard to crack,
The strife and the love that he craved for he deemed he o'er-long did lack.
And his heart-beats they echoed loudly, as it swelled high for knighthood fain,
And he stretched himself as an archer who bendeth a bow amain.
And so eager his lust for battle that sleepless the hero lay
Till he saw the grey light of morning, though as yet it should scarce be day.
And his chaplain for Mass was ready, and to God and the knight they sing,
For so did he give commandment. Then he bade them his harness bring,

And he rode where a joust should wait him, and that self-same hour would ride
A horse that could charge the foeman, and turn swiftly to either side,
And answer to bit and bridle if its rider would backward draw.
And the watchers, both man and woman, his helm in the gateway saw,
And the anchor shone fair upon it; and no man ere this might see
So wondrous fair a hero, for like to a god was he!

And strong spears they bare for his using—How then was he decked, the knight?
With iron was his charger covered, as should serve for a shield in fight,
And above lay another covering, nor heavy methinks it weighed,
'Twas a samite green; and his surcoat and blazoned coat were made
Of Achmardi, green to look on, and in Araby fashioned fair,
And no lie I tell, but the shield-thongs that the weight of the shield should bear
Were of silk and gold untarnished, and jewel-bedecked their pride,
And the boss of the shield was covered with red gold, in the furnace tried.
He served but for love's rewarding; sharp conflict he held it light;
And the queen she looked from her window, with many a lady bright.
And see, there Heuteger held him, who the prize ne'er had failed to gain;
When he saw the knight draw nearer, in swift gallop across the plain,
He thought, "Now whence came this Frenchman? Who hither this knight hath sent?
If a *Moor* I had thought this hero, my wit were to madness bent!"

No whit they delayed the onslaught, from gallop to swifter flight
Each man spurred amain his charger; and as fitting a valiant knight
Nor one would evade the other, but would meet him in jousting fair,
From brave Heuteger's spear the splinters flew high thro' the summer air,
But his foeman so well withstood him that he thrust him from off his steed
Adown on the grass; but seldom might he win for his joust such meed!
And his foe in his course rode o'er him, and trode him unto the ground,
Yet he sprang up again, and valiant, fresh lust for the strife he found,
But Gamuret's lance had pierced him thro' the arm, and he bade him yield,
And he knew he had found his master, and he spake from the foughten field,
"Now who shall have o'erthrown me?" and the victor he swiftly spake,
"Gamuret Angevin do men call me!" then he quoth, "Thou my pledge canst take!"

Then his pledge the knight took, and straightway he sent him within the wall,
And much praise did he win from the women who looked from the castle hall.
And swiftly there came towards him, Gaschier of Normandy,
A proud and wealthy hero and mighty in strife was he.
And Gamuret made him ready, for a second joust he'ld ride,
And strong and new was his spear-shaft, and the iron was both sharp and wide,
And the strangers they faced each other—But unequal their lot, I trow,
For Gaschier and his gallant charger full swiftly were they laid low,
And the knight with his arms and harness he fell in the shock of strife;
If he thought it for good or for evil, by his pledge must he win his life.

Then Gamuret quoth, the hero, "Thou hast pledged unto me thine hand,
Yet the weapon it well hath wielded! Ride thou to the Scottish band,
And bid them to cease from troubling; if they to thy will are fain,
Thou canst follow me to the city." Then the knight hied him o'er the plain.
If he prayed them, or gave commandment, they did at the last his will,
And the Scottish host they rested, and from conflict they held them still.

Then Kailet spurred swift towards him, but Gamuret turned his rein,
His cousin he was, and near kinsman, why then bring him grief and pain?
And the Spaniard cried loudly on him; on his helm he an ostrich bare,
And so far as I know to tell ye the knight he was decked so fair
With silken raiment goodly, and long were his robes and wide,
And the plain rang clear with the chiming of sweet bells as he o'er it hied.
The flower he of manly beauty, and his fairness it held the field,
Save for two who should come hereafter, and his fame unto theirs must yield;
But Parzival and brave Beau-corps, King Lot's son, they are not here,
Not yet were they born, but hereafter for their beauty men held them dear!

Then Gaschier he grasped his bridle. "Now checked will it be thy race,
So I tell thee upon mine honour, if the Angevin thou shalt face
Who there my pledge hath taken. Sir Knight, thou shalt list my prayer
And hearken unto my counsel; in Gamuret's hand I sware
From strife aside to turn thee: stay thy steed then for my sake,
For mighty is he in conflict!" Then aloud King Kailet spake,
"Is he Gamuret my cousin, and son unto King Gandein?
Then I care not with him to battle, no foe shall he be of mine!
Take thine hand from off my bridle"—"Nay, further thou shalt not fare
Till mine eyes have first beheld thee, with thine head of the helmet bare,
For *mine* with blows is deafened!" Then his helmet the prince unbound.
And yet, tho' with him he fought not, Gamuret other foemen found.

And the day had grown to high morning—And the folk who the joust might see
Were glad at heart, and they gat them to their bulwarks right speedily,
For he was as a net before them, and none might escape his hold.
And he chose him another charger, so the tale unto me was told,
And it flew, and the earth it spurnèd, and its work could aright fulfil,
Bold when the knight would battle, yet its speed could he check at will.
And what would he do the rider? His valour I praise alway,
For he rode where the Moorish army to the west by the sea-coast lay.

Thence a prince, Rassalig men called him, forgat not each coming morn
(He was Assagog's richest hero, to riches and honour born
Since he came of a royal lineage) to take from the camp his way
He would fain joust before the city—But his strength it was quelled that day
By Anjou's dauntless hero; and a dusky maid made moan

(Since 'twas she who sent him hither) that her knight should be thus o'erthrown.
For a squire brought, without his bidding, to his master, brave Gamuret,
A spear, with light reed-shaft fashioned, and its point 'gainst the Moor he set,
And with it he smote the paynim from his steed down upon the sand,
Nor longer he bade him lie there than as surety he pledged his hand.
So the strife it had found its ending, and the hero had won him fame;
Then Gamuret saw eight banners toward the city that onward came,
And he bade the conquered hero the force with his word to stay,
And follow him to the city. And that word must he needs obey.

Nor Gaschier delayed his coming; and unto the Burg-grave told
How his guest sought for further conflict nor his wrath might the host withhold.
If he swallowed not iron as an ostrich, nor his wrath did on stones assuage
'Twas but that he might not find them! Then he gnashed his teeth for rage,
And he growled as a mighty lion, and the hair of his head he tare,
And he quoth, "So the years of my lifetime a harvest of folly bear,
The gods they had sent to my keeping a valiant and worthy friend,
If with strife he shall be o'erladen, then mine honour hath found an end;
Sword and shield they shall little profit—Yea, shame he would on me cast
Who should bring this to my remembrance!" Then swift from his place he passed,
And he gat him into the portal, and a squire towards him drew,
And he bare a shield that was painted with a knight by a spear pierced thro',
In Eisenhart's land was it fashioned; and a helmet his hand must hold,
And a sword that Rassalig carried in battle, that heathen bold,
But now was he parted from it whose fame was in every place;
Were he slain unbaptized I think me, God had shown to this hero grace!

And e'en as the Burg-grave saw it, ne'er of yore was his joy so great,
For the coat-of-arms he knew it—So he rode thro' the city gate,
And without, his guest had halted, young hero he, not yet old,
As one of a joust desirous, and his bridle the Burg-grave bold,
Lahfilirost was his name, he grasped it, and he led him within the wall;
And I wot well no other foeman that day 'neath his spear must fall.

Quoth Lahfilirost the Burg-grave, "Sir Knight, thou shalt tell to me
If thine hand Rassalig hath vanquished?" "Then our land from all strife is free;
For he of the Moors is chieftain, the men of true Eisenhart
Who have brought unto us such sorrow—But now shall our woe depart,
'Twas a wrathful god who bade him thus seek us with all his host,
But his weapons to naught are smitten, and to folly is turned his boast!"

Then he led him in (ill it pleased him) and there met then the royal maid,
And she loosened the bands of his vizor, and her hand on his bridle laid,
To her care must the Burg-grave yield it: nor his squires to their task were slack,
For they turned them about, and swiftly they rode on their master's track.

So men saw the queen so gracious lead her guest thro' the city street
Who here should be hailed the victor—Then she lighted her on her feet,
"Ah me! but thy squires are faithful! Fear ye lest your lord be lost?
Without ye shall he be cared for; take his steed, here am I his host!"

And above found he many a maiden: then her hands of dusky hue
The queen set unto his harness, and disarmed the knight so true.
And the bed-covering was of sable, and the couch it was spread so fair,
And in secret a hidden honour they did for the knight prepare,
For no one was there to witness—The maidens they might not stay,
And the door was fast closed behind them, and Frau Minne might have her way.
So the queen in the arms of her true love found guerdon of sweet delight,
Tho' unlike were the twain in their colour, Moorish princess and Christian knight!

Then the townsfolk brought many an offering to the gods who had seen their woe.
That which Rassalig needs must promise ere he from the field might go
That he did, in all truth and honour, yet heavy was he at heart,
And afresh sprang the fount of his sorrow for his prince gallant Eisenhart.
And the Burg-grave he heard of his coming; then loud rang the trumpet call,
And no man of Zassamank's princes but came to the palace hall.
They gave Gamuret thanks for the honour he had won in the field that day,
Four-and-twenty had fallen before him, and their chargers he bore away,
And three chieftains had he made captive. And there rode in the princes' train
Many gallant knights, in the courtyard of the palace did they draw rein.
And the hero had slept and eaten, and clad him in raiment fair,
Chief host was he, for his body fit garments would they prepare.
And she who afore was a maiden but now was a wife would take
Her lord by the hand, forth she led him, and unto her princes spake:
"My body and this my kingdom are vassals unto this knight,
If so be that his foemen fearing, resist not his hand of might!"

Then Gamuret spake, and his bidding was courteous, for hero meet,
"Sir Rassalig, go thou nearer, with a kiss thou my wife shalt greet;
And Sir Gaschier, thou shalt do likewise." Then the Scotch knight proud Heuteger
He bade on the lips to kiss her (and the wounds won in joust he bare).

Then he bade them all be seated, and standing, he wisely spake:
"I were fain to behold my kinsman, if he who did captive take
The knight shall have naught against it—As kinsman it seemeth me
That I find here no other counsel save straightway to set him free!"
Then the queen she smiled, and bade them go swiftly and seek the knight,
And then thro' the throng he pressed him, that count so fair and bright,
Yet bare he the wounds of knighthood, and bravely and well had fought;
With the host of Gaschier the Norman the land of the Moors he sought.

He was courteous; his sire a Frenchman   he was Kailet's sister's son,
Killirjacac his name; in the service   of fair women fair meed he won,

And the fairest of men they deemed him.   When Gamuret saw his face
(For like were they each to the other,   as men of a kindred race)
He bade his queen to kiss him   and embrace him as kinsman true,
And he spake, "Now come thou and greet me!"   and the knight to his arms he drew,
And he kissed him, and each was joyful   that the other he here might meet:
And Gamuret quoth unto him,   "Alas! cousin fair and sweet,
What doth thy young strength in this conflict?   Say, if woman hath sent thee here?"
"Nay, never a woman sent me,   with my cousin I came, Gaschier,
He knoweth why he hath brought me—   A thousand men have I,
And I do to him loyal service—   To Rouen in Normandy
I came, where his force was gathered,   and many a youthful knight
I brought from Champagne in mine army;   'neath his banner we fain would fight.
Now evil hath turned against him   what of cunning is hers and skill,
Thou wilt honour thyself if thou free him   for my sake, and cure his ill!"

"Thyself shalt fulfil thy counsel!   Go thou, take with thee Gaschier,
I would fain see my kinsman Kailet,   do thou bring him unto me here!"
So they wrought out the host's desiring,   and brought him at his behest,
And in loving wise and kindly   did Gamuret greet his guest;
And ofttimes the queen embraced him,   and kissed him with kisses sweet:
And nothing it wronged her honour   in such wise the prince to greet,
He was cousin unto her husband,   by birth was himself a king.
Then smiling his host spake to him,   "God knows, 'twere an evil thing,
Had I taken from thee Toledo,   and thy goodly land of Spain
For Gascogny's king, who wrathful   doth plague thee with strife amain;
'Twere faithless of me, Sir Kailet,   since mine aunt's son thou sure shalt be;
The bravest of knights shall be with thee;   say, who forced this strife on thee?"

Then out spake the proud young hero,   "My cousin Schiltung bade
(Since his daughter Friedebrand wedded)   that I lend to the king mine aid.
For the sake of his wife hath he won him,   yea even from me alone
Six thousand chosen heroes,   who valour and skill have shown.
And other men did I bring him,   but a part they shall hence have sailed,
For the Scottish folk came they hither,   brave bands who in strife ne'er failed.
And there came to his aid from Greenland,   strong heroes who bravely fought,
Two mighty kings, and a torrent   of knighthood with them they brought,
And many a goodly vessel: and they pleased me, those men of might—
And here for his sake came Morhold,   who hath cunning and skill in fight."

"But now have they turned them homewards,   and that which the queen shall say
Even that will I do with mine army,   her servant am I alway!

Thou shalt thank me not for this service, from kinsman 'twas due, I ween.
Now *thine* are these gallant heroes, if like mine they baptized had been
And were even as they in colour, then never a monarch crowned
But if they should fight against him, of conflict his fill had found!
But I marvel what here hath brought thee? Say, how didst thou reach this strand?"
"Yestreen I came, and this morning I am lord o'er this goodly land!
The queen by the hand she took me, and with love I myself would shield,
For so did my wit give counsel—" "Yea, so hast thou won the field,
Those sweet weapons two hosts have vanquished!" "Thou wouldst say, since I fled
    from *thee*,
So loudly on me thou calledst, say, what wouldst thou force from me?
Let us speak of the thing in friendship!" "Thine anchor I failed to know,
But seldom mine aunt's brave husband Gandein, did such token show!"
"But I, I knew well thine ostrich with the snake's head upon thy breast,
Aloft stood thy bird so stately, nor hid it within a nest!"

"And I saw in thy mien and bearing that that pledge would have 'seemed thee ill
Which two heroes afore had given, tho' first had they fought their fill."
"E'en such fate as theirs were my portion—But this thing I needs must say,
Tho' little I like a devil, were he victor as thou this day
For love of his gallant doings the women had deemed him sweet,
Yea, as sugar were fain to eat him!" "Now thou praisest me more than meet!"
"Nay, of flattery know I little, thou shalt see that I hold thee dear
In other wise!" Then the hero bade Rassalig draw anear.

And courteous he spake, King Kailet, "My kinsman with valiant hand
Hath made of thee here his captive?" "Yea, Sire, so the thing doth stand,
And I hold him for such a hero that Assagog's kingdom fair
Should fail not to yield him homage, since the crown he may never wear,
Our prince Eisenhart! In her service was he slain who shall now be wife
To thy kinsman, as knight so faithful he gave for her love his life.
With my kiss have I sealed forgiveness, yet my lord and my friend I lost!
If thy cousin by knightly dealing will repay of his death the cost
I will fold my hands as his vassal: and wealth shall be his and fame,
All that Eisenhart from Tankaneis as his heritage thought to claim.
Embalmed here the hero lieth, and I gaze on his wounds each day
Since this spear thro' his true heart piercing, my lord and my king did slay!"

Then he drew it forth from his bosom by a silken cord so fine,
And the heroes saw the spear-blade 'neath his robe on his bare chest shine.
And he quoth, "It is now high morning, if my lord Sir Killirjacac
My token will bear to my princes, with him will the knights ride back."
And a finger-ring he sent them: dark as hell were those heroes all
And they rode who were there of princes, thro' the town to the castle hall.

As his vassals he gave with their banners to Assagog's lords their land,
And each one rejoiced in the fiefdom he won from his ruler's hand,
But the better part was his portion, Gamuret's, as their lord and king.
And these were the first—as they passed hence their homage they fain would bring
The princes of Zassamank's kingdom, and they came in their order due,
And each as their queen had bade them, they took from his hand anew
Their land, and the fruit it should bear them, as to each man was fit and right,
And poverty fled from his presence. Now he who was slain in fight
And in life was a prince by lineage, Prothizilas, he had left
A Dukedom fair, and this country which was thus of its lord bereft
He gave unto him who much honour had won by his strong right hand,
The Burg-grave, in combat dauntless—With its banners he took the land.

Then Assagog's noble princes took the Scotch Duke, proud Heuteger,
And Gaschier, the Norman hero, to their lord did they lead them there,
And he spake them free for their asking, and they thanked brave Gamuret.
Then Heuteger of Scotland with prayers did these knights beset,
"Now give to our lord the armour, as prize for his deeds so brave,
That Eisenhart's life took from us, when to Friedebrand he gave
That which was of our land the glory—Forfeit of joy the knight,
And dead on his bier he lieth, since no love might his love requite—"
And earth knoweth naught so goodly, the helm it was strong and hard,
Yea even of diamond fashioned, in battle a goodly guard.
Then Heuteger sware unto them, if the land of his lord he saw
He would pray of his hand the armour, and send it to them once more.

And this did he swear them freely—Then leave would the princes pray
Who stood in the royal presence, and they wend from the hall their way.
And tho' sorely the land was wasted, yet Gamuret scattered free
Such royal gifts and goodly as if laden with gold each tree.
And costly I ween the presents that vassal and friend must share
From the open hand of the hero; and the queen deemed it right and fair.

Full many a bitter conflict had been fought ere the bridal feast,
But peace had the foeman sealèd, and the land was from strife released;
(Nor this song I myself have woven, but so was it told to me)
And Eisenhart did they bury with honours right royally.
To his grave did his kinsmen bear him, and the gold that his lands might bring
In a whole year long, did they spend there, of their free will they did this thing.
And Gamuret bade his kinsfolk his riches and lands to hold
And use as they would; tho' they craved not such boon from the hero bold.

At dawn from before the fortress the foe would their camp withdraw,
And those who were there departed; many litters with them they bore.

And the field was left unsheltered, save for one tent so great and fair,
And the king he bade his servants that tent to his vessel bear.
And he said to his folk that to Assagog would he take it, and yet I wot
He did with that speech deceive them, for Assagog saw him not.

Now that proud and gallant hero, his heart gave him little rest
Since he found there no deeds of knighthood, and gladness forsook his breast;
Yet his dusky wife was dearer than e'en his own life might be,
Ne'er knew he a truer lady whose heart was from falsehood free,
She forgat not what 'seemed a woman, and with her as comrades good
Went purity untarnished, and the ways of true womanhood.

He was born in Seville's fair city whom the knight would hereafter pray,
When he grew of his sojourn weary, to sail with him far away;
For many a mile had he led him, and he brought him unto this place,
And a Christian was he, the steersman, nor like to a Moor in face.
And wisely he spake, "Thou shalt hide it from them who a dark skin bear,
Too swift is my barque for pursuing, from hence shall we quickly fare!"

Then his gold it was borne to the vessel. Now of parting I needs must tell,
By night did he go, the hero, and his purpose he hid it well;
But when from his wife he sailèd, in her womb did she bear his child:
And fair blew the wind, and the breezes bare him hence o'er the waters wild.

And the lady she found a letter, and 'twas writ by her husband's hand;
And in French (for she well could read it) did the words of the writing stand:
"Here one love to another speaketh—As a thief have I stolen away
That mine eyes might not see thy sorrow—But this thing I needs must say,
Wert thou, e'en as I, a Christian I ever should weep for thee,
For e'en now I must sorely mourn thee. If it chance that our child shall be
In face like unto one other, then his is a dowry fair,
Of Anjou was *he* born, and Frau Minne for his lady he did declare.
Yet was he in strife a hailstorm, ill neighbour unto his foe;
That his grandsire hath been King Gandein, this I will that my son shall know.
Dead he lay thro' his deeds of knighthood; and his father the same death won,
Addanz was his name, and unsplintered his shield hath been seen of none;
And by birth he hath been a Breton, and two brothers' sons were they,
He and the brave Pendragon, and their sires' names I here will say;
For Lassalies he hath been the elder, and Brickus was his brother's name,
And Mazadan was their father whom a fay for her love did claim.
Terre-de-la-schoie did they call her, to Fay-Morgan she led the king,
For he was her true heart's fetters; and my race from those twain did spring.
And fair shall they be, and valiant, and as crownèd kings they reign—
If lady, thou'lt be baptizèd thou mayst win me to thee again!"

Yet had she no thought of anger, but she spake, "Ah! too soon 'tis o'er,
Of a sooth would I do his bidding, would it bring him to me once more.
In whose charge hath my courteous hero left the fruit of his love so true?
Alas! for the sweet communion that we twain for a short space knew!
Shall the strength of my bitter sorrow rule body and soul alway?"
And she quoth, "Now his God to honour, his will would I fain obey,
And gladly I'ld be baptizèd, and live as should please my love!"
And sorrow with her heart struggled, and e'en as the turtle dove
Her joy sought the withered branches, for the same mind was hers, I ween,
When the mate of the turtle dieth, she forsaketh the branches green.

Then the queen at the time appointed bare a son, who was dark and light,
For in him had God wrought a wonder, at one while was he black and white.
And a thousand times she kissed him where white as his sire's his skin.
And she named the babe of her sorrows Feirefis Angevin.
And he was a woodland-waster, many spears did he shatter fair,
And shields did he pierce—as a magpie the hue of his face and hair.

Now a year and more was ended since Gamuret won such fame
At Zassamank, and his right hand the victor's prize might claim,
And yet o'er the seas he drifted, for the winds vexed the hero bold.
Then a silken sail red gleaming he saw, and the barque did hold
The men whom the King of Scotland, Friedebrand, sent upon their way
At the bidding of Queen Belakané: from her would they pardon pray
That ever he came against her, tho' in sooth he had lost the more.
And with them the diamond helmet, the corslet and sword they bore,
And hosen e'en such as the harness, and a marvel it needs must be
That the barque was thus borne towards him, as the venture hath told to me!
And they gave him the goodly armour, and an oath unto them he swore
That his mouth it should speak their message, an he came to the queen
    once more.
And they parted; and one hath told me that the sea bare him onward bound
Till he came to a goodly haven, and in Seville his goal he found.
And with gold did he pay his steersman right well for his guidance true,
And they parted, those twain, and sorrow the heart of that steersman knew!…

Book XV: Feirefis

Argument

Book xv tells how Parzival met with a mighty heathen, with whom he fought fiercely,
and how he was well-nigh vanquished. How he found the heathen to be his brother,
Feirefis Angevin, and how the twain rode together to the court of King Arthur.

Of the welcome given to Feirefis by King Arthur and his knights; of his riches; and of the kings conquered by the two brothers.

How a feast of the Round Table was holden, and how Kondrie bare tidings of Parzival's election to the Grail Kingdom, and summoned him, his wife, and his son Lohengrin, to Monsalväsch; and how Parzival and Feirefis rode thither with Kondrie as their guide.

Now many were sorely angered that I told not this tale afore
Since it wearied them naught in the hearing—Now my words I withhold no more,
But I give ye to wit full truly, as my mouth may the story tell,
The end of this wondrous venture for methinks it shall please ye well.
Ye shall know how the king, Anfortas, of his wound was made whole again—
Of the queen doth the venture tell us, who in far Pelrapär did reign;
How she kept a pure heart and loyal till the day of her great reward,
And earth's fairest crown was her guerdon at the hand of her faithful lord.
Ye shall hear the tale of its winning, if my skill fail me not alway;
Yet first must ye list the labour that Parzival wrought that day.

Now, tho' dauntless his hand had striven, but as children his foemen all,
And ne'er would I risk my hero might I rule that which shall befall.
I must sorrow sore for his peril, and fain would I speak him free,
But now must I trust that Good Fortune the shield of his heart may be.
For purity, and high courage, side by side in his heart they lay,
And ne'er had he cherished cowardice, nor shrunk from the knightly fray;
And I deem this shall surely give him such strength he his life may hold,
Since fierce strife draweth nigh unto him, and his foe is a hero bold.
For he meeteth a prince of battles who dauntless to strife doth ride,
And unbaptized was the foeman who rode here in his heathen pride.

Full soon had he come, our hero, to a mighty woodland shade,
And without, in the light of the dawning, his armour a knight displayed.
'Twere a marvel could I, a poor man, of the riches now speak to ye
That the heathen he bare as his decking, so costly their worth should be.
If more than enough I told ye, yet more would be left to tell;
Yet I would not his wealth were hidden—What of riches, I ween, shall dwell
In Bretagne alike and England, and be tribute to Arthur's might,
They had paid not the stones that, shining, glowed fair on his armour bright.
His blazoned coat was costly, and naught but the truth I say,
Ruby and Chalcedony, ye had held them not fair that day.
And bright as the sun was his vesture, on the mount of Agremontein,
In the glowing fires, Salamanders had welded that garment's shine.
There jewels rare and precious, with never a fault or flaw,
Glowed dark and light; of their nature, I ween, I can tell no more!

His desire was for love's rewarding, and the winning of high renown,
He had won from the hands of fair women the jewels that his pride did crown.
For the favour Frau Minne showed him with joy did his proud heart beat,
And it swelled high with manly courage, as is for a lover meet.
As reward for his deeds of knighthood on his helmet a beast he bare,
Ecidemon, all poisonous serpents they must of its power beware,
For of life and of strength doth it rob them, if they smell it but from afar—
Thopedissimonté, Assigarzionté, Thasmé, and Arabia,
They scarce of such silk might boast them as was covering for his steed—
He sought, that mighty heathen, in a woman's love his meed,
And therefore he bravely decked him, and fain would his courage prove,
And his manhood, it urged him onward to battle for sake of love.

Now the knight, so young and gallant, in a haven beside the wood,
But little known, on the water had anchored his ships so good.
And his armies were five-and-twenty, and they knew not each other's speech—
'Twas a token fair of his riches, and the lands that his power might reach,
As the armies, so were the kingdoms that did service unto his hand—
And Moors and Saracens were they, and unlike was each warlike band,
And the hue of their skins was diverse—Thus gathered from lands afar
Ye might see in his mighty army strange weapons of heathen war.

So thus, in search of adventure, from his army this man would ride,
In the woodland green he wandered, and waited what should betide.
And since thus it well doth please them, so let them ride, these kings,
Alone, in search of ventures, and the fair fame that combat brings.
Yet Parzival rode not lonely, methinks he had comrades twain,
Himself, and the lofty courage that lord o'er his soul did reign.
And that he so bravely fought here might win from a woman praise,
If falsehood should not mislead her, that injustice should rule her ways.

So spurred they against each other, who were lambs in their purity,
Yet as lions were they bold and dauntless, 'twas a sight for a man to see!
Ah! woe is me for their meeting, for the world and its ways are wide,
And they well might have spared each other, nor, guiltless, to battle ride.
I should sorrow for him whom I brought here, save my heart did this comfort hold,
That the Grail shall with strength endue him, and Love shelter the hero bold,
Since he was of the twain the servant, nor his heart ever wavering knew,
And ever his hand was ready to serve them with service true.

My skill little wit doth give me this combat that here befell,
In fitting words and knightly, from beginning to end to tell.
But the eye of each flashed triumph as the coming foe he saw,
And the heart of each knight waxed joyful, as they nearer to battle draw.

Yet sorrow, I ween, was nigh them, true hearts, from all falsehood free,
And each bare the heart of the other, and should comrade and stranger be!

Nor may I asunder part them, the paynim and Christian knight,
Hatred they show to each other, tho' no cause have they here for fight.
And methinks this of joy shall rob them, who, as true women, share their pain
Who risk their lives for a woman! May they part, ere one here be slain!

As the lion-cub, that its mother beareth dead, doth to life awake
At the aweful voice of its father, so these twain, as the spear-shafts break
Arouse to fresh life, and to honour, I ween, are they newly born,
For many a joust have they ridden and many a spear outworn.
Then they tighten the hanging bridle, and they take to their aim good care,
That each on the shield of the other, as he willeth, shall smite him fair.
And no point do they leave unguarded, and they give to their seat good heed,
As men who are skilled in jousting, and sharply each spurs his steed.

And bravely the joust was ridden, and each gorget asunder broke,
And the spears bent not, but in splinters they flew from each mighty stroke;
And sore was he wroth, the heathen, that this man might his joust abide,
For never a knight but had fallen who a course 'gainst his spear would ride.
Think ye that their swords they wielded as their chargers together drew?
Yea, the combat was sharp and bitter, and each must give proof anew
Alike of his skill and his manhood—The strange beast, Ecidemon,
Had many a wound, and beneath it the helmet sore blows had won;
And the horses were hot and wearied, and many new turns they tried—
Then down they sprung from their chargers, and their sword-blades afresh
    they plied.

And the heathen wrought woe to the Christian, "Thasmé!" was his battle-cry,
And when "Tabronit!" he shouted he drew ever a step anigh.
And the Christian, he showed his valour in many an onslaught bold;
So pressed they upon each other—Nor would I the tale withhold
Of how the fight was foughten, yet must I the strife bemoan,
How, one flesh and one blood thus sharing, each wrought evil unto his own;
For both were the sons of one father, and brothers, I ween, were they,
And methinks upon such foundation faith and friendship their stone should lay!

And love ne'er had failed the heathen, and his heart was for combat fain,
For the love of Queen Sekundillé fresh honour he thought to gain;
Tribalibot's land she gave him, and she was his shield in strife—
So bravely he fought, how think ye that the Christian might guard his life?
On love let his thoughts be steadfast, else sure is he here undone,
And he hath from the hand of the heathen in this combat his death-blow won.
O thou Grail, by thy lofty virtue such fate from thy knight withhold!

Kondwiramur, thine husband in such deadly stress behold!
Here he standeth, of both the servant, in such danger and peril sore
That as naught ye may count the ventures he hath dared for your sake of yore!
Then on high flashed the sword of the heathen, and many such blow had slain,
To his knee Parzival was beaten—Now see how they fought, the twain,
If twain ye will still account them, yet in sooth shall they be but one,
For my brother and I are one body, e'en as husband and wife are one!

The heathen wrought woe to the Christian—Of Asbestos, I ween, his shield,
That wondrous wood that never to flame or decay shall yield;
I'sooth, right well she loved him who gave him a gift so fair,
Turquoise, Chrysoprase, Emerald, Ruby, rich jewels beyond compare
Decked with shining lines its surface, on the boss shone a precious stone,
Antrax, afar they call it, as Carbuncle it here is known.
And as token of love, for his guarding, Sekundillé the queen would give
That wondrous beast, Ecidemon—in her favour he fain would live,
And e'en as she willed he bare it, as his badge, did that gallant knight—
Here with purity faith joined issue, and truth with high truth would fight.

For love's sake upon the issue of this combat each risked his life,
Each had pledged his hand to the winning of honour and fame in strife;
And the Christian, in God he trusted since the day that he rode away
From the hermit, whose faithful counsel had bidden him trust alway
In Him who could turn his sorrow into bliss without thought of bale—
To Him should he pray for succour, whose succour should never fail.

And fierce and strong was the heathen, when "Tabronit," he cried,
For there, 'neath the mount Kaukasus did the queen, Sekundill', abide;
Thus gained he afresh high courage 'gainst him who ne'er knew of yore
The weight of such deadly combat, for in sooth was he pressed full sore—
To defeat was he aye a stranger, and ne'er had he seen its face,
Tho' his foemen right well must know it, as they yielded them to his grace!

With skill do they wield their weapons, and sparks spring from the helmets fair,
And a whistling wind ariseth as the blades cleave the summer air;
God have Gamuret's son in His keeping! and the prayer it shall stand for both,
For the twain shall be one nor, I think me, to own it were either loth.
For had they but known each other their stake ne'er had been so great,
For blessing, and joy, and honour, were risked on that combat's fate,
For he who shall here be victor, if true brother and knight he be,
Of all this world's joy is he forfeit, nor from grief may his heart be free!

Sir Parzival, why delay thee to think on thy queen and wife,
Her purity and her beauty, if here thou wouldst save thy life?
For the heathen, he bare two comrades who kindled his strength anew,

The one, in his strong heart, steadfast, lay ever a love so true;
And the other, the precious jewels that burnt with a mystic glow,
Thro' whose virtue his strength waxed greater, and his heart must fresh
      courage know.
And it grieveth me sore that the Christian was weary and faint with fight,
Nor swiftly might he avoid him, and his blows they were robbed of might;
And if the twain fail to aid thee, O thou gallant Parzival,
Thy queen and the Grail, then I think me this thought it shall help thee well,
Shall thy fair babes thus young be orphaned? Kardeiss and Lohengrin,
Whom thy wife, e'en as thou didst leave her, for her joy and her hope must win—
For children thus born in wedlock, the pledge of a love so pure,
I ween are a man's best blessing, and a joy that shall aye endure!

New strength did he win, the Christian, and he thought, none too soon, I ween,
On his love so true and faithful, on Kondwiramur, his queen,
How he won his wife at the sword's point, when sparks from the helm did spring
'Neath the mighty blows he dealt him, Klamidé, the warrior king.
"Tabronit! and Thasmé!" and above them rung clear his battle-cry,
"Pelrapär!" as aloud he cried it to his aid did his true love fly,
O'er kingdoms four she sought him, and her love gave him strength anew,
And lo! from the shield of the heathen the costly splinters flew,
Each one a hundred marks' worth—and the sword so strong and keen
That Ither of Gaheviess bare first brake sheer on the helmet's sheen,
And the stranger, so rich and valiant, he stumbled, and sought his knee—
For God, He no longer willed it that Parzival lord should be
Of this weapon of which in his folly he had robbed a gallant knight—
Then up sprang afresh the heathen who ne'er before fell in fight,
Not yet is the combat ended, and the issue for both shall stand
In the power of the God of battles, and their life lieth in His hand!

And a gallant knight was the heathen, and he spake out, right courteously,
(Tho' the tongue was the tongue of a heathen yet in fair French his speech
      should be,)
"Now I see well, thou gallant hero, thou hast no sword wherewith to fight,
And the fame shall be small I win me if I fight with an unarmed knight,
But rest thee awhile from conflict, and tell me who thou shalt be,
For the fame that so long I cherished it surely had fallen to thee
Had the blow not thy sword-blade shattered—Now, let peace be betwixt us twain,
And our wearied limbs will we rest here ere we get us to strife again."
Then down on the grass they sat them, and courteous and brave were they,
Nor too young nor too old for battle—fit foemen they were that day!

Then the heathen, he spake to the Christian, "Believe me, Sir Knight, that ne'er
Did I meet with a man so worthy the crown of such fame to bear
As a knight in strife may win him—Now, I prithee, tell thou to me

Thy name, and thy race, that my journey may here not unfruitful be!"
Quoth the son of fair Herzeleide, "Thro' *fear* shall I tell my name?
For thou askest of me such favour as a victor alone may claim!"
Spake the heathen prince from Thasmé, "Then that shame shall be mine, I ween,
For first will I speak my title, and the name that mine own hath been;
'Feirefis Angevin' all men call me, and such riches are mine, I trow,
That the folk of full many a kingdom 'neath my sceptre as vassals bow!"

Then, e'en as the words were spoken, to the heathen quoth Parzival,
"How shall '*Angevin*' be thy title, since as heirdom to *me* it fell,
Anjou, with its folk and its castles, its lands and its cities fair?
Nay, choose thee some other title, if thou, courteous, wouldst hear my prayer!
If thro' thee I have lost my kingdom, and the fair town Beàlzenan,
Then wrong hadst thou wrought upon me ere ever our strife began!
If one of us twain is an Angevin then by birthright that one am I!—
And yet, of a truth, was it told me, that afar 'neath an Eastern sky,
There dwelleth a dauntless hero, who, with courage and knightly skill,
Such love and such fame hath won him that he ruleth them at his will.
And men say, he shall be my brother—and that all they who know his name
Account him a knight most valiant, and he weareth the crown of fame!"

In a little space he spake further, "If, Sir Knight, I thy face might see,
I should know if the truth were told me, if in sooth thou art kin to me.
Sir Knight, wilt thou trust mine honour, then loosen thine helmet's band,
I will swear till once more thou arm thee to stay from all strife mine hand!"

Then out he spake, the heathen, "Of such strife have I little fear,
For e'en were my body naked, my sword, I still hold it here!
Of a sooth must thou be the vanquished, for since broken shall be thy sword
What availeth thy skill in combat keen death from thine heart to ward,
Unless, of free will, I spare thee? For, ere thou couldst clasp me round,
My steel, thro' the iron of thy harness, thy flesh and thy bone had found!"
Then the heathen, so strong and gallant, he dealt as a knight so true,
"Nor mine nor thine shall this sword be!" and straight from his hand it flew,
Afar in the wood he cast it, and he quoth, "Now, methinks, Sir Knight,
The chance for us both shall be equal, if further we think to fight!"

Quoth Feirefis, "Now, thou hero, by thy courteous breeding fair,
Since in sooth thou shalt have a brother, say, what face doth that brother bear?
And tell me here of his colour, e'en as men shall have told it thee."
Quoth the Waleis, "As written parchment, both black and white is he,
For so hath Ekuba told me." "Then that brother am I alway,"
Quoth the heathen—Those knights so gallant, but little they made delay,
But they loosed from their heads the helmet, and they made them of iron bare,
And Parzival deemed that he found there a gift o'er all others fair,

For straightway he knew the other, (as a magpie, I ween, his face,)
And hatred and wrath were slain here in a brotherly embrace.
Yea, friendship far better 'seemed them, who owed to one sire their life,
Than anger, methinks, and envy—Truth and Love made an end of strife.
Then joyful he spake, the heathen, "Now well shall it be with me,
And I thank the gods of my people that Gamuret's son I see.
Blest be Juno, the queen of heaven, since, methinks, she hath ruled it so,
And Jupiter, by whose virtue and strength I such bliss may know,
Gods and goddesses, I will love ye, and worship your strength for aye—
And blest be those shining planets, 'neath the power of whose guiding ray
Thither have made my journey—For ventures I here would seek,
And found *thee*, brother, sweet and aweful, whose strong hand hath made me weak.
And blest be the dew, and the breezes, that this morning my brow have fanned.
Ah! thou courteous knight who holdest love's key in thy valiant hand!
Ah! happy shall be the woman whose eyes on thy face shall light,
Already is bliss her portion who seeth so fair a sight!"

"Ye speak well, I would fain speak better of a full heart, had I the skill;
Yet alas! for I lack the wisdom, tho' God knoweth, of right goodwill
The fame of your worth and valour by my words would I higher raise,
And as eye, and as heart should serve me, the twain, they should speak your praise;
As your fame and your glory lead them, so behind in your track they fare—
And ne'er from the hand of a foeman such peril hath been my share
As the peril your hand hath wrought me! and sooth are these words I say."
In this wise quoth the knight of Kanvoleis; yet Feirefis spake alway;

"With wisdom and skill, I wot well, hath Jupiter fashioned thee,
Thou true and gallant hero! Nor thy speech shall thus distant be,
For '*ye*' thou shalt no more call me, of one sire did we spring we twain."
And with brotherly love he prayed him he would from such speech refrain
And henceforward "*thou*" to call him, yet Parzival deemed it ill,
And he spake, "Now, your riches, brother, shall be e'en as the Baruch's still,
And ye of us twain are the elder, my poverty and my youth
They forbid me '*thou*' to call ye, or discourteous were I in truth."

Then the Prince of Tribalibot, joyful, with many a word would praise
His god, Jupiter, and to Juno thanksgiving he fain would raise,
Since so well had she ruled the weather, that the port to which he bound
He had safely reached, and had landed, and there had a brother found.

Side by side did they sit together, and neither forgot the grace
Of courtesy, to the other, each knight fain had yielded place.
Then the heathen spake, "My brother, wilt thou sail with me to my land
Then two kingdoms, rich and powerful, will I give thee into thine hand.
Thy father and mine, he won them when King Eisenhart's life was run,

Zassamank and Assagog are they—to no man he wrong hath done,
Save in that he left me orphaned—of the ill that he did that day
As yet have I not avenged me, for an ill deed it was alway.
For his wife, the queen who bare me, thro' her love must she early die,
When she knew herself love-bereavèd, and her lord from her land did fly
Yet gladly that knight would I look on, for his fame hath been told to me
As the best of knights, and I journey my father's face to see!"

Then Parzival made him answer, "Yea I, too, I saw him ne'er;
Yet all men they speak well of him, and his praises all lands declare,
And ever in strife and conflict to better his fame he knew,
And his valour was high exalted, and afar from him falsehood flew.
And women he served so truly that all true folk they praised his name,
And all that should deck a Christian lent honour unto his fame,
For his faith it for aye stood steadfast, and all false deeds did he abhor,
But followed his true heart's counsel—Thus ever I heard of yore
From the mouth of all men who knew him, that man ye were fain to see,
And I ween ye would do him honour if he yet on this earth might be,
And sought for fame as aforetime—The delight of all women's eyes
Was he, till king Ipomidon with him strove for knighthood's prize,
At Bagdad the joust was ridden, and there did his valiant life
For love's sake become death's portion, and there was he slain in strife;
In a knightly joust we lost him from whose life do we spring, we twain;
If here ye would seek our father, then the seas have ye sailed in vain!"

"Alas, for the endless sorrow!" quoth the knight. "Is my father dead?
Here joy have I lost, tho' it well be that joy cometh in its stead.
In this self-same hour have I lost me great joy, and yet joy have found,
For myself, and thou, and my father, we three in one bond are bound;
For tho' men as *three* may hold us, yet I wot well we are but *one*,
And no wise man he counts that kinship 'twixt father, methinks, and son,
For in truth for more must he hold it—With *thyself* hast thou fought to-day,
To strife with *myself* have I ridden, and I went near myself to slay;
Thy valour in good stead stood us, from myself hast thou saved my life—
Now Jupiter see this marvel, since thy power so hath ruled the strife
That from death hast thou here withheld us!" Then tears streamed from his
     heathen eyes,
As he laughed and wept together—Yea, a Christian such truth might prize,
For our baptism truth should teach us, since there are we named anew
In the Name of Christ, and all men they hold the Lord Christ for true!

Quoth the heathen, e'en as I tell ye, "No longer will we abide
In this place, but if thou, my brother, for a short space with me wilt ride,
From the sea to the land will I summon, that their power be made known to thee,
The richest force that Juno e'er guided across the sea.

And in truth, without thought of falsehood, full many a gallant knight
Will I show thee, who do me service, and beneath my banners fight,
With me shalt thou ride towards them." Then Parzival spake alway,
"Have ye then such power o'er these people that your bidding they wait to-day
And all the days ye are absent?" Quoth the heathen, "Yea, even so,
If for half a year long I should leave them, not a man from the place would go,
Be he rich or poor, till I bade him. Well victualled their ships shall be,
And neither the horse nor his rider setteth foot on the grassy lea,
Save only to fetch them water from the fountain that springeth fair,
Or to lead their steeds to the meadow to breathe the fresh summer air."

Then Parzival quoth to his brother, "If it be so, then follow me
To where many a gracious maiden, and fair pleasures, ye well may see,
And many a courteous hero who shall be to us both akin—
Near by with a goodly army lieth Arthur, the Breton king,
'Twas only at dawn I left them, a great host and fair are they,
And many a lovely lady shall gladden our eyes to-day."

When he heard that he spake of women, since he fain for their love would live,
He quoth, "Thou shalt lead me thither, but first thou shalt answer give
To the question I here would ask thee—Of a truth shall we kinsmen see
When we come to the court of King Arthur? For ever 'twas told to me
That his name it is rich in honour, and he liveth as valiant knight"—
Quoth Parzival, "We shall see there full many a lady bright,
Nor fruitless shall be our journey, our own folk shall we find there,
The men of whose race we have sprung, men whose head shall a king's
        crown bear."

Nor longer the twain would sit there, and straightway did Parzival
Seek again the sword of his brother that afar in the woodland fell,
And again the hero sheathed it, and all hatred they put away,
And e'en as true friends and brothers together they rode that day.

Yet ere they might come to King Arthur men had heard of the twain a tale—
On the self-same day it befell so that the host, they must sore bewail
The loss of a gallant hero, since Parzival rode away—
Then Arthur, he took good counsel, and he spake, "Unto the eighth day
Would they wait for Parzival's coming, nor forth from the field would fare"—
And hither came Gramoflanz' army, and they many a ring prepare,
And with costly tents do they deck them, and the proud knights are lodged
        full well,
Nor might brides e'er win greater honour than here to these four befell.
Then from Château Merveil rode thither a squire in the self-same hour,
And he said, in their column mirrored, had they seen in their fair watchtower
A mighty fight, and a fearful—"And where'er men with swords have fought,

I wot well, beside this combat their strife shall be held as naught."
And the tale did they tell to Gawain, as he sat by King Arthur's side,
And this knight, and that, spake wondering to whom might such strife betide?
Quoth Arthur the king, "Now I wager that I know of the twain *one* knight,
'Twas my nephew of Kanvoleis fought there, who left us ere morning light!"

And now, lo the twain rode hither—They had foughten a combat fair,
As helmet and shield sore dinted with sword-stroke might witness bear.
And well skilled were the hands that had painted these badges of strife, I trow,
(For 'tis meet in the lust of combat that a knight's hand such skill should show,)
Then they rode by the camp of King Arthur—As the heathen knight rode past
Full many a glance of wonder at his costly gear was cast.
And with tents the plain was covered—Then rode they to Gawain's ring,
And before his tent they halted—Did men a fair welcome bring,
And lead them within, and gladly behold them? Yea, even so,
And Gawain, he rode swiftly after when he did of their coming know;
For e'en as he sat by King Arthur he saw that his tent they sought,
And, as fitted a courteous hero, joyful greeting to them he brought.

And as yet they bare their armour—Then Gawain, the courteous knight,
He bade his squires disarm them—In the stress of the deadly fight
Ecidemon, the beast, was cloven; the robe that the heathen ware
In many a place bare token of the blows that had been its share,
'Twas a silk of Saranthasmé, decked with many a precious stone,
And beneath, rich, snow-white, blazoned with his bearings his vesture shone.
And one over against the other stood the gems in a double row;
By the wondrous Salamanders was it woven in fierce flame's glow!
All this glory a woman gave him, who would stake on his skill in strife
Her crown alike and her kingdom, as she gave him her love and life.
'Twas the fair Queen Sekundillé (and gladly he did her will,
And were it for joy or for sorrow he hearkened her bidding still)
And, e'en as her true heart willed it, of her riches was he the lord,
For her love, as his rightful guerdon, had he won him with shield and sword.

Then Gawain, he bade his people of the harness to have good care,
That naught should be moved from its station, shield, or helmet, or vesture fair.
And in sooth a gift too costly e'en the blazoned coat had been
If poor were the maid who a love-gift would give to her knight, I ween,
So rich were the stones that decked it, the harness of pieces four—
And where wisdom with goodwill worketh, and of riches there be full store,
There love well can deck the loved one! And proud Feirefis, he strove
With such zeal for the honour of women, he well was repaid by Love!

And soon as he doffed his harness they gazed on the wondrous sight,
And they who might speak of marvels said, in sooth, that this heathen knight,

Feirefis, was strange to look on! and wondrous marks he bore—
Quoth Gawain to Parzival, "Cousin, I ne'er saw his like before,
Now who may he be, thy comrade? For in sooth he is strange to see!"
Quoth Parzival, "Are we kinsmen, then thy kinsman this knight shall be,
As Gamuret's name may assure thee—Of Zassamank is he king,
There my father he won Belakané who this prince to the world did bring."
Then Gawain, he kissed the heathen—Now the noble Feirefis
Was black and white all over, save his mouth was half red, I wis!

Then they brought to the twain fair raiment, and I wot well their cost was dear.
(They were brought forth from Gawain's chamber.) Then the ladies, they drew anear,
And the Duchess she bade Sangivé and Kondrie first kiss the knight
Ere she and Arnivé proffered in greeting their lips so bright.
And Feirefis gazed upon them, and, methinks, he was glad at heart
At the sight of their lovely faces, and in joy had he lot and part.

Then Gawain spake to Parzival, "Cousin, thou hast found a new battle-field,
If aright I may read the token of thy helmet and splintered shield,
Sore strife shall have been your comrade, both thine and thy brother's too!
Say, with whom did ye fight so fiercely?" Then Parzival spake anew,
"No fiercer fight have I foughten, my brother's hand pressed me sore
To defend me, no charm more potent than defence 'gainst death's stroke I bore.
As this stranger, whom yet I knew well, I smote, my sword brake in twain,
Yet no fear did he show, and 'vantage he scorned of mischance to gain,
For afar did he cast his sword-blade, since he feared lest 'gainst me he sin,
Yet naught did he know when he spared me that we twain were so near akin.
But now have I won his friendship, and his love, and with right goodwill
Would I do to him faithful service as befitteth a brother still!"

Then Gawain spake, "They brought me tidings of a dauntless strife and bold,
In Château Merveil the country for six miles may ye well behold,
The pillar within the watch-tower showeth all that within that space
Doth chance,—and he spake, King Arthur, that *one* who there strife did face,
Should be *thou* cousin mine of Kingrivals, now hast thou the tidings brought,
And we know of a sooth the combat was even as we had thought.
Now believe me, the truth I tell thee, for eight days here our feast we'ld hold
In great pomp, and await thy coming, shouldst thou seek us, thou hero bold.
Now rest here, ye twain, from your combat—but methinks, since ye thus did fight,
Ye shall each know the other better, and hatred shall own love's might."

That eve would Gawain sup early, since his cousin of far Thasmé,
Feirefis Angevin, and his brother, had tasted no food that day.
And high and long were the cushions that they laid in a ring so wide,
And many a costly covering of silk did their softness hide.
And long, and wide, and silken, were the clothes that above them went,

And the store of Klingsor's riches they spread forth within the tent.
Then four costly carpets silken, and woven so fair to see,
Did they hang one against the other, so the tale it was told to me;
And beneath them, of down were the pillows, and each one was covered fair,
And in such wise the costly couches for the guests would the squires prepare.

And so wide was the ring that within it six pavilions right well might stand
Nor the tent ropes should touch each other—(Now wisdom doth fail mine hand,
I will speak no more of these marvels). Then straightway Gawain he sent
To King Arthur, he fain would tell him who abode here within his tent,
He had come, the mighty heathen, of whom Ekuba erst did tell
On Plimizöl's plain! And the tidings they rejoiced King Arthur well.

And he who should bear the tidings, he was Iofreit, and Idol's son;
And he bade the king sup early, and so soon as the meal was done,
With his knights and his host of ladies, to ride forth a train so fair,
And a fit and worthy welcome for Gamuret's son prepare.
Quoth the king, "All who here are worthy, of a sooth, will I bring with me."
Quoth Iofreit, "Ye fain will see him, so courteous a knight is he,
And a marvel is he to look on—From great riches he forth must fare,
For the price of his coat emblazoned is such as no man might bear,
And no hand might count its equal, not in Löver or Brittany,
Or in England, or e'en from Paris to Wizsant beside the sea—
Nay, all the rich lands between them, were their wealth in the balance weighed,
Then the cost of his goodly raiment, I think me, were yet unpaid!"

Then again came the knight Iofreit, when he to the king had told
The guise that should best befit him when he greeted the heathen bold.
And within the tent of Gawain the seats were ordered fair,
In courteous rank and seemly, and the guests to the feast repair.
And the vassals of Orgelusé, and the heroes within her train
Who gladly for love had served her, they sate there beside Gawain.
Their seats they were on his right hand, on his left were Klingsor's knights,
And over against the heroes sat many a lady bright,
All they who were Klingsor's captives, in sooth were they fair of face,
And Parzival and his brother, by the maidens they took their place.

Then the Turkowit, Sir Florant, and Sangivé, that noble queen,
Sat over against each other, and in like wise, the board between,
Sat Gowerzein's Duke, brave Lischois, and his wife, the fair Kondrie.
Iofreit and Gawain forgat not each other's mate to be,
As of old would they sit together, and together, as comrades, eat.
The Duchess, with bright eyes shining, by Arnivé must find her seat,
Nor forgat they to serve each other with courteous and kindly grace—
At the side sat fair Orgelusé, while Arnivé by Gawain found place.

And all shame and discourteous bearing from the circle must take their flight,
And courteous they bare the viands to each maid and each gallant knight.
Then Feirefis looked on his brother, and he spake unto Parzival;
"Now Jupiter ruled my journey so that bliss to my lot would fall
Since his aid shall have brought me hither, and here mine own folk I see,
And I praise the sire that I knew not, of a gallant race was he!"

Quoth the Waleis, "Ye yet shall see them, a folk ye right well may love,
With Arthur their king and captain, brave knights who their manhood prove.
So soon as this feast is ended, as methinks it will be ere long,
Ye shall see them come in their glory, many valiant men and strong.
Of the knights of the good Round Table there shall sit at this board but three,
Our host, and the knight Iofreit, and such honour once fell to me,
In the days that I showed me worthy, that they prayed me I would be one
Of their band, nor was I unwilling, but e'en as they spake 'twas done."

Now 'twas time, since all well had eaten, the covers to bear away
From before both man and maiden, and this did the squires straightway.
The host would no longer sit there; then the Duchess and Arnivé spake,
And they prayed that the twain, Sangivé and Kondrie, they with them might take
And go to the strange-faced heathen, and entreat him in courteous wise—
When Feirefis saw them near him, from his seat did the prince arise,
And with Parzival, his brother, stepped forward the queens to meet,
By his hand did the Duchess take him, and with fair words the knight
        would greet;
And the ladies and knights who stood there she bade them be seated all—
Then the king and his host came riding, with many a trumpet call;
And they heard the sound of music, of tambour, and flute, and horn,
With many a blast drew nearer the king of Arnivé born;
And the heathen this pomp and rejoicing must hold for a worthy thing—
And Guinevere rode with King Arthur, so came they to Gawain's ring;
And goodly the train that followed of ladies and gallant knights,
And Feirefis saw among them fair faces with youth's tints bright;
And King Gramoflanz rode among them, for Arthur's guest was he,
And Itonjé, his love so loyal, true lady, from falsehood free!

Then the gallant host dismounted, with many a lady sweet,
And Guinevere bade Itonjé her nephew, the heathen, greet.
Then the queen herself drew anear him, and she kissed the knight Feirefis,
And Gramoflanz and King Arthur received him with friendly kiss;
And in honour they proffered service unto him, those monarchs twain,
And many a man of his kinsfolk to welcome the prince was fain.
And many a faithful comrade Feirefis Angevin had found,
Nor in sooth was he loth to own here that he stood upon friendly ground.

Down they sat them, both wife and husband, and many a gracious maid,
And many a knight might find there (if in sooth he such treasure prayed,)
From sweet lips sweet words of comfort—If for wooing such knight were fain,
Then from many a maid who sat there no hatred his prayer would gain,
No true woman shall e'er be wrathful if a true man for help shall pray,
For ever the right she holdeth to yield, or to say him "Nay,"
And if labour win joy for payment then such guerdon shall true love give—
And I speak but as in my lifetime I have seen many true folk live—
And service sat there by rewarding, for in sooth 'tis a gracious thing
When a knight may his lady hearken, for joy shall such hearing bring.

And Feirefis sat by King Arthur, nor would either prince delay
To the question each asked the other courteous answer to make straightway—
Quoth King Arthur, "May God be praised, for He honoureth us I ween,
Since this day within our circle so gallant a guest is seen,
No knight hath Christendom welcomed to her shores from a heathen land
Whom, an he desired my service, I had served with such willing hand!"

Quoth Feirefis to King Arthur, "Misfortune hath left my side,
Since the day that my goddess Juno, with fair winds and a favouring tide,
Led my sail to this Western kingdom! Methinks that thou bearest thee
In such wise as he should of whose valour many tales have been told to me;
If indeed thou art called King Arthur, then know that in many a land
Thy name is both known and honoured, and thy fame o'er all knights doth stand."

Quoth Arthur, "Himself doth he honour who thus spake in my praise to thee
And to other folk, since such counsel he won of his courtesy
Far more than of my deserving—for he spake of his kindly will.
Yea, in sooth shall my name be Arthur, and the tale would I hearken still
Of how to this land thou camest, if for *love's* sake thou bearest shield,
Then thy love must be fair, since to please her thou ridest so far afield!
If her guerdon be not withholden then love's service shall wax more fair,
Else must many a maid win hatred from the knight who her badge doth bear!"

"Nay, 'twas otherwise," quoth the heathen; "Now learn how I came to thee,
I led such a mighty army, they who guardians of Troy would be,
And they who its walls besiegèd, the road to my hosts must yield—
If both armies yet lived, and lusted to face me on open field,
Then ne'er might they win the victory, but shame and defeat must know
From me and my host, of a surety their force would I overthrow!—
And many a fight had I foughten, and knightly deeds had done,
Till as guerdon at length the favour of Queen Sekundillé I won.
And e'en as her wish so my will is, and her love to my life is guide,
She bade me to give with a free hand, and brave knights to keep at my side,

And this must I do to please her; and I did even as she would,
'Neath my shield have I won as vassals full many a warrior good,
And her love it hath been my guerdon—An Ecidemon I bear
On my shield, even as she bade me, at her will I this token wear.
Since then, came I e'er in peril, if but on my love I thought
She hath helped me, yea, Jupiter never such succour in need hath brought!"

Quoth Arthur, "Thy gallant father, Gamuret, he hath left thee heir
To the heart that on woman's service thus loveth afar to fare.
Of such service I too can tell thee, for but seldom hath greater deeds
Been done for a woman's honour, or to win of her love the meed,
Than were done for the sake of the Duchess who sitteth beside us here.
For her love many gallant heroes have splintered full many a spear,
Yea, the spear-shafts were e'en as a forest! And many have paid the cost
Of her service in bitter sorrow, and in joy and high courage lost!"

And then the tale he told him of the fame that Gawain had found,
And the knights of the host of Klingsor, and the heroes who sat around,
And of Parzival, his brother, how he fought fierce combats twain,
For the sake of Gramoflanz' garland, on Ioflanz' grassy plain;
"And what other have been his ventures, who never himself doth spare
As thro' the wide world he rideth, that shall he himself declare;
For he seeketh a lofty guerdon, and he rideth to find the Grail.
And here shall it be my pleasure that ye twain, without lack or fail,
Shall tell me the lands and the peoples against whom ye shall both
        have fought."
Quoth the heathen, "I'll name the princes whom I here as my
        captives brought":

"King Papirus of Trogodjenté, Count Behantins of Kalomident,
Duke Farjelastis of Africk, and King Tridanz of Tinodent;
King Liddamus of Agrippé, of Schipelpjonte King Amaspartins,
King Milon of Nomadjentesin, of Agremontin, Duke Lippidins;
Gabarins of Assigarzionté, King Translapins of Rivigatas,
From Hiberborticon Count Filones, from Sotofeititon, Amincas,
From Centrium, King Killicrates, Duke Tiridé of Elixodjon,
And beside him Count Lysander, from Ipopotiticon.
King Thoaris of Orastegentesein, from Satarthjonté Duke Alamis,
And the Duke of Duscontemedon, and Count Astor of Panfatis.
From Arabia King Zaroaster, and Count Possizonjus of Thiler,
The Duke Sennes of Narjoclin, and Nourjenté's Duke, Acheinor,
Count Edisson of Lanzesardin, Count Fristines of Janfusé,
Meiones of Atropfagenté, King Jetakranc of Ganpfassasché,
From Assagog and Zassamank princes, Count Jurans of Blemunzîn.
And the last, I ween, shall a Duke be, Affinamus of Amantasîn!"

"Yet one thing for a shame I deemed it—In my kingdom 'twas told to me
Gamuret Angevin, my father, the best of all knights should be
That ever bestrode a charger—Then so was my will and mind,
That, afar from my kingdom faring, my father I thought to find;
And since then strife hath been my portion, for forth from my kingdoms twain
A mighty host and powerful 'neath my guidance hath crossed the main,
And I lusted for deeds of knighthood; if I came to a goodly land,
Then I rested not till its glory paid tribute into mine hand.
And thus ever I journeyed further—I won love from two noble queens,
Olympia and Klauditté; Sekundillé the third hath been.
And well have I served fair women!—Now first must I learn to-day
That my father is dead! My brother, the tale of thy ventures say."

And Parzival quoth, "Since I seek it, The Grail, in full many a fight,
Both far and near, have I striven, in such wise as beseems a knight,
And my hand of their fame hath robbed them who never before might fall—
If it please ye the tale to hearken, lo! here will I name them all!"

"King Schirniel of Lirivoin, and his brother of Avendroin, King Mirabel,
King Piblesun of Lorneparz, of Rozokarz, King Serabel,
Of Sirnegunz, King Senilgorz, and Strangedorz of Villegarunz,
Rogedal the Count of Mirnetalle and Laudunal of Pleyedunz.
From Semblidag King Zyrolan, from Itolac Onipreiz,
From Zambron the Count Plenischanz, and Duke Jerneganz of Jeropleis,
Count Longefiez of Teuteleunz, Duke Marangliess of Privegarz,
From Lampregun Count Parfoyas, from Pictacon Duke Strennolas;
Postefar of Laudundrehte, Ascalon's fair king, Vergulacht,
Duke Leidebron of Redunzehte, and from Pranzile Count Bogudaht,
Collevâl of Leterbé, Jovedast of Arl, a Provençal,
Count Karfodyas of Tripparûn, all these 'neath my spear must fall.
In knightly joust I o'erthrew them the while I The Grail must seek!
Would I say those I felled in *battle*, methinks I o'er-long must speak,
It were best that I here keep silence—Of those who were known to me,
Methinks that the greater number I here shall have named to ye!"

From his heart was he glad, the heathen, of his brother's mighty fame,
That so many a gallant hero 'neath his hand had been put to shame,
And he deemed in his brother's honour he himself should have honour won,
And with many a word he thanked him for the deeds that he there had done.

Then Gawain bade his squires bear hither (yet e'en as he knew it not)
The costly gear of the heathen, and they held it was fair I wot.
And knights alike and ladies, they looked on its decking rare,
Corslet, and shield, and helmet, and the coat that was blazoned fair.
Nor narrow nor wide the helmet—And a marvel great they thought

The shine of the many jewels in the costly robe inwrought,
And no man I ween shall ask me the power that in each did dwell,
The light alike and the heavy, for I skill not the tale to tell;
Far better might they have told it, Heraclius or Hercules
And the Grecian Alexander; and better methinks than these
Pythagoras, the wise man, for skilled in the stars was he,
And so wise that no son of Adam I wot well might wiser be.

Then the women they spake, "What woman so e'er thus hath decked this knight
If he be to her love unfaithful he hath done to his fame despite."
Yet some in such favour held him, they had been of his service fain—
Methinks the unwonted colour of his face did their fancy gain!
Then aside went the four, Gawain, Arthur, Gramoflanz, and Parzival,
(And the women should care for the heathen, methinks it would please
      them well.)

And Arthur willed ere the morrow a banquet, rich and fair,
On the grassy plain before him they should without fail prepare,
That Feirefis they might welcome as befitting so brave a guest.
"Now be ye in this task not slothful, but strive, as shall seem ye best,
That henceforth he be one of our circle, of the Table Round, a knight."
And they spake, they would win that favour, if so be it should seem him right.
Then Feirefis, the rich hero, he brotherhood with them sware;
And they quaffed the cup of parting, and forth to their tents would fare.
And joy it came with the morning, if here I the truth may say,
And many were glad at the dawning of a sweet and a welcome day.

Then the son of Uther Pendragon, King Arthur, in this wise spake:
For Round Table a silk so costly, Drianthasmé, he bade them take—
Ye have heard how it once was ordered, afar on Plimizöl's plain,
How they spread them there a Round Table, in such wise was it spread again—
'Twas cut in a round, and costly it was, and right fair to see,
And on the green turf around it the seats of the knights should be.
It was even a goodly gallop from the seats to the Table Round,
For the Table's self it was not, yet the likeness they there had found.
And a cowardly man might shame him to sit there with such gallant knights,
And with sin would his food be tainted since he ate it not there of right.

Thro' the summer night 'twas measured, the ring, both with thought and care,
And from one end unto the other with pomp they the seats prepare.
And the cost were too great for a poor king, as they saw it in noontide light,
When the trappings, so gay and costly, shone fair in the sun-rays bright.
Gramoflanz and Gawain would pay it, the cost, since within their land
He was but a guest, King Arthur, tho' he dealt with a generous hand.

And the night, it seldom cometh but, as it is wont, the sun
Bringeth back the day and the daylight when the hours of the night are run;
And e'en so it befell, and the dawning was clear and calm and bright,
And many a flowery chaplet crowned the locks of many a knight;
And with cheeks and lips unpainted saw ye many a lovely maid,
And, if Kiot the truth hath spoken, knight and lady they were arrayed
In diverse garb and fashion, with head-gear both high and low,
As each in their native country their faces were wont to show—
'Twas a folk from far kingdoms gathered and diverse their ways were found—
If to lady a knight were lacking she sat not at the Table Round,
But if she for knightly service had promised a guerdon fair,
She might ride with her knight, but the others, they must to their tents repair.

When Arthur the Mass had hearkened, then Gramoflanz did they see
With Gowerzein's Duke and Florant; to the king came the comrades three,
And each one a boon would crave here, for each of the three was fain
To be one of the good Round Table, nor this grace did they fail to gain.
And if lady or knight would ask me who was richest of all that band,
Who sat as guests in the circle, and were gathered from every land,
Then here will I speak the answer, 'twas Feirefis Angevin,
But think not from my lips of his riches a further tale to win.

Thus in festive guise, and gaily, they rode to the circle wide,
And often to maid had it chancèd (so closely the guests must ride).
Were her steed not well girthed she had fallen—with banners waving high
From every side of the meadow to each other the groups drew nigh;
And a Buhurd fair was ridden without the Table Round,
And in courtly guise and skilful no man rode *within* its bound;
There was space without for the chargers, and they handled their steeds with skill,
And rode each one against the other till the ladies had looked their fill.

Then in order fair they seat them when 'twas time for the guests to eat,
And cup-bearer, steward, and butler, they bethink them as shall be meet,
How, courteous, to do their office—No lack of food had they,
And many a maid was honoured as she sat by her knight that day.
And many thro' fond heart's counsel had been served by knightly deed—
And Feirefis, and the Waleis, to the maidens they gave good heed,
And they looked on the one and the other, and a fair choice was theirs, I ween,
For never on field or meadow may the eye of man have seen
So many sweet lips and fair faces as shone there at the Table Round,
And the heathen was glad for their beauty, and the joy that his heart had found.

Now hail to the hour that cometh, and the tidings they soon shall hear
From the welcome lips of a maiden who draweth the host anear;

For a maiden came towards them, and her raiment was fair to see,
And e'en as in France the custom so 'twas fashioned right cunningly.
Her mantle was costly velvet, and blacker, I ween, its hue
Than the coat of a sable jennet; and with gold was it woven thro'
With turtle-doves, all shining, the badge of the Grail were they.
And they looked and they marvelled at her as toward them she made her way,
For swiftly she came, and her head-gear was high and white, her face
With many a veil was shrouded, and her features no man might trace.

Then with even pace and seemly she rode o'er the turf so green,
And saddle and reins and trappings were costly enow I ween;
And they let her within the circle—Now she who would tidings bring
No fool was she, but wise maiden—So rode she around the ring,
And they showed her where sat King Arthur, nor her greeting should fail that day,
In French was her speech, and in this wise the monarch she fain would pray;
They should wreak not on her their vengeance for the words that she spake of yore,
But hearken unto her message since welcome the news she bore.
And the king and the queen she pleaded to give unto her their aid,
That she failed not to win from the hero the grace that she fain had prayed.

Then to Parzival she turned her, since his place by the king's was found,
And she stayed not, but down from her charger she sprang swiftly unto the ground,
And with courteous mien, as beseemed her, fell low at the hero's feet,
And, weeping, she prayed that in friendship her coming he now would greet,
And forget his wrath against her, and forgive her without a kiss.
And they joined to her prayer their pleadings, King Arthur and Feirefis.
Of a sooth Parzival must hate her, yet he hearkened to friendship's prayer,
And of true heart and free forgave her—Tho' I say not the maid was fair,
Yet methinks she was honour-worthy—Then swiftly she sprang upright,
And thanked those who had won her pardon for the wrong she had done the knight.

Then she raised her hand to her head-gear, were it wimple or veil, no less
Was it cast on the ground, and all men knew Kondrie, the sorceress.
And they knew of the Grail the token and the badge that the maiden bare,
And all men I ween must marvel—Her face it was e'en as fair
As man and maiden saw it when to Plimizöl's banks she came,
Of her countenance have I told ye, and to-day was it still the same,
And yellow her eyes as the topaz, long her teeth, and her lips in hue
Were even as is a violet, that man seeth not *red* but *blue*!

Yet methinks had her will been evil she had borne not the head-gear rare
That aforetime, on Plimizöl's meadow, it had pleasured the maid to wear.
The sun it had worked no evil, if its rays thro' her hair might win
Yet scarce had they shone so fiercely as to darken one whit her skin.

Then courteous she stood, and she spake thus, and good were her words to hear,
In the self-same hour her tidings came thus to the listening ear;
"Oh! well is thee, thou hero, thou Gamuret's son so fair,
Since God showeth favour to thee whom Herzeleide of old did bear.
And welcome is he, thy brother, Feirefis, the strange of hue,
For the sake of my Queen Sekundillé, and the tidings that erst I knew
Of the gallant deeds of knighthood that his valiant hand hath done,
For e'en from the days of his childhood great fame for himself he won!"

And to Parzival she spake thus, "Now rejoice with a humble heart,
Since the crown of all earthly blessings henceforward shall be thy part,
For read is the mystic writing—The Grail, It doth hail thee king,
And Kondwiramur, thy true wife, thou shalt to thy kingdom bring,
For the Grail, It hath called her thither—Yea, and Lohengrin, thy son,
For e'en as thou left her kingdom twin babes thou by her hadst won.
And Kardeiss, he shall have in that kingdom a heritage rich I trow!
And were no other bliss thy portion than that which I tell thee now—
That with true lips and pure, thou shalt greet him, Anfortas the king, again,
And thy mouth thro' the mystic question shall rid him of all his pain,
For sorrow hath been his portion—If joy's light thro' thy deed shall shine
On his life, then of all earth's children whose bliss shall be like to thine?"

Seven stars did she name unto him in Arabic, and their might,
Right well Feirefis should know it, who sat there, both black and white.
And she spake, "Sir Parzival, mark well the names that I tell to thee,
There is Zevâl the highest planet, and the swift star Almustri;
Almaret and the shining Samsi, great bliss unto thee they bring,
Alligafir is fifth, and Alketer stands sixth in the starry ring;
And the nearest to us is Alkamer; and no dream shall it be, my rede,
For the bridle of heaven are they, to guide and to check its speed,
'Gainst its swiftness their power, it warreth—Now thy sorrow is passed away,
For far as shall be their journey, and far as shall shine their ray,
So wide is the goal of thy riches and the glory thine hand shall win,
And thy sorrow shall wane and vanish—Yet this thing It holds for sin,
The Grail and Its power, It forbids thee unlawful desire to know,
And the company of sinners henceforth must thou shun, I trow;
And riches are thine, and honour, but from these shall thy life be free—
Now thy youth was by sorrow cherished, and her lesson she taught to thee,
But by joy she afar is driven, for thou hast thy soul's rest won,
And in grief thou o'er-long hast waited for the joy that is now begun."

Nor seemed ill to the knight her tidings—Thro' joy must his eyelids know
A rain of crystal tear-drops from a true heart's overflow.
And he quoth, "If thou speakest, Lady, the thing that indeed shall be,

If God as his knight doth claim me, and they are elect with me,
My wife and my child, then I wot well, tho' a sinful man am I,
God looketh with favour on me, and hath dealt with me wondrously!
Of a sooth hast thou here repaid me for the grief thou on me hast brought,
Yet I deem well thy wrath had spared me save that evil myself had wrought,
Nor to bliss was I then predestined—but thou bringest such tidings fair
That my sorrow hath found an ending—And these arms do thy truth declare,
For when by the sad Anfortas I sat in Monsalväsch' hall,
Full many a shield I looked on that hung fair on the castle wall,
And with turtle-doves all were blazoned, such as shine on thy robe to-day.
But say, to the joy that awaits me, when and how may I take my way,
For I would not there were delaying?" Then she quoth, "Lord and master dear,
But *one* knight alone shall ride with thee; choose thou from these warriors here
And trust thou to my skill and knowledge to guide thee upon thy way,
For thy succour Anfortas waiteth, wouldst thou help him, make no delay!"

Then they heard, all they who sat there, how Kondrie had come again
And the tidings she bare; and teardrops fell soft like a summer's rain
From the bright eyes of Orgelusé, since Parzival should speak
The words that should heal Anfortas, nor that healing be long to seek.
Then Arthur, the fame-desirous, spake to Kondrie in courtesy,
"Now, Lady, wilt ride to thy lodging? Say, how may we care for thee?"
And she quoth, "Is she here, Arnivé, what lodging she shall prepare,
That lodging shall well content me till hence with my lord I fare;
If a captive she be no longer, then fain would I see them all,
The queen, and the other ladies, whom Klingsor, in magic thrall,
For many a year hath fettered"—Then they lifted her on her steed,
Two knights, and unto Arnivé did the faithful maiden speed.

Now the feast drew nigh to its ending—By his brother sat Parzival,
And he prayed him to be his comrade, nor his words did unheeded fall,
For Feirefis spake him ready to Monsalväsch' Burg to ride—
In the self-same hour upstood they, the guests, o'er the ring so wide,
And Feirefis prayed this favour from Gramoflanz, the king,
If in sooth he should love his cousin of that love he would token bring;
"Both thou and Gawain, ye must help me, whether princes or kings they be,
Or barons, or knights, none betake them from this field till my gifts they see.
Myself had I shamed if I rode hence and never a gift should leave,
And the minstrel-folk they shall wait here till they gifts from my hand receive.
And Arthur, this thing would I pray thee, seek that none of these knights disdain,
Tho' lofty their birth, a token of friendship from me to gain;
For the shame, on thyself shalt thou take it—one so rich shall they ne'er
    have known—
Give me messengers unto the haven that the presents to all be shown!"

Then they sware them unto the heathen that no man of them should depart
From the field till four days were ended, and the heathen was glad at heart,
And wise messengers Arthur gave him, who should forth to the haven fare—
Feirefis took him ink and parchment, and a letter he bade them bear,
Nor the writing, I ween, lacked tokens of his hand from whom it came,
And seldom methinks a letter such goodly return might claim!

Then soon must the messengers ride hence—Parzival stood the host before,
And in French did he tell the story from Trevrezent learnt of yore,
How The Grail, throughout all ages, may never by man be known,
Save by him whom God calleth to It, whose name God doth know alone.
And the tale shall be told in all lands; no conflict may win that prize,
And 'tis vain on that Quest to spend them, since 'tis hidden from mortal eyes!

And for Parzival and his brother the maidens must mourn that day,
Farewell they were loth to bid them—Ere the heroes rode on their way
Thro' the armies four they gat them, and they prayed leave from each and all,
And joyful, they took their journey, well armed 'gainst what might befall.
And the third day hence to Ioflanz from the heathen's host they brought
Great gifts, so rich and costly, men ne'er on such wealth had thought.
Did a king take of them, his kingdom was rich for evermore—
And to each as beseemed his station the precious gifts they bore,
And the ladies, they had rich presents, from Triant and Nouriente—
How the others rode I know not, but the twain, they with Kondrie went!

TRANSLATED BY JESSIE L. WESTON

Arabian Nights and Italian Renaissance Novellas

Story cycles had probably existed for a long time in varying oral versions when the use of a frame narrative and a loose method of organizing tales were introduced. One very popular example was the collection that ultimately became known as *Alf Laylah wa Laylah* (Thousand Nights and One Night). The ruse that holds the tales together is that a dramatically cuckolded and hence misogynous king is kept from following his habit of slaughtering a woman every morning by the brave daughter of a vizier, who keeps the king's attention by telling a new story each day. Storytelling thus serves as a method of staving off violence, of which the stories themselves are full. In the Italian Renaissance novellas by Masuccio and Giraldi Cinzio there are echoes of this thematic focus on cuckoldry and misogynous revenge, often associated with the inclusion of slaves, Muslims, or Africans in the adultery plot.

From *The Book of the Thousand Nights and One Night*

The stories that are familiar to us as part of *The Book of the Thousand Nights and One Night*, also called *The Arabian Nights*, have actually been subject to centuries of editing by their various tellers. Tenth-century Arabic historians noted that the stories had been translated to Arabic from a Persian collection called *The Thousand Tales*. While there are no extant editions of *The Thousand Tales*, it can be inferred that this Persian collection was the source of the stories themselves as well as the narrative framework of *The Thousand Nights*, in which a king will murder one wife every morning unless a woman named Shehrzad can retain his interest in her tales. In the oral transmission the number of tales and the details of each story would vary from teller to teller, as the diversity of subsequent written accounts indicates. Storytellers also added their own anecdotes to *The Thousand Tales* and gradually increased the core of tenth-century Persian stories to the present collection. The *Arabian Nights* tales circulated widely and were apparently known to some Italian Renaissance novella writers, who drew on them. The French Orientalist Jean Antoine Galland was the first Westerner to translate them, into French; he published them between 1704 and 1707. The first major Arabic-to-English translation was undertaken by Dr. Edward William Lane between 1838 and 1840, yet he omitted certain tales he found boring, repetitive, or lewd. Among the tales of interracial interest are the "Story of the Eunuch Bekhit" and "The Man from Yemen and His Six Slave Girls." The tales presented here in the translation by John Payne are "Story of King Shehriyar and His Brother" (which is among the oldest parts of the story cycle and constitutes the opening of the collection's frame narrative, providing a rationale for its storytelling); and "Story of the Enchanted Youth" (which reveals the violent emotions unleashed by adulterous love relations between high-standing women and slaves).

Story of King Shehriyar and His Brother

In the name of God, the Compassionate, the Merciful! Praise be to God, the Lord of the two worlds, and blessing and peace upon the Prince of the Prophets, our lord and master Mohammed, whom God bless and preserve with abiding and continuing peace and blessing until the Day of the Faith! Of a verity, the doings of the ancients become a lesson to those that follow after, so that men look upon the admonitory events that have happened to others and take warning, and come to the knowledge of what befell bygone peoples and are restrained thereby. So glory be to Him who hath appointed the things that have been done aforetime for an example to those that come after! And of these admonitory instances are the histories called the Thousand Nights and One Night, with all their store of illustrious fables and relations.

It is recorded in the chronicles of the things that have been done of time past that there lived once, in the olden days and in bygone ages and times, a king of the kings of the sons of Sasan, who reigned over the Islands of India and China and was lord of armies and guards and servants and retainers. He had two sons, an elder and a younger, who were both valiant cavaliers, but the elder was a stouter horseman than the younger. When their father died, he left his empire to his elder son, whose name was Shehriyar, and he took the government and ruled his subjects justly, so that the people of the country and of the empire loved him well; whilst his brother Shahzeman became King of Samarcand of Tartary. The two kings abode each in his own dominions, ruling justly over their subjects and enjoying the utmost prosperity and happiness, for the space of twenty years, at the end of which time the elder king yearned after his brother and commanded his Vizier to repair to the latter's court and bring him to his own capital. The Vizier replied, "I hear and obey," and set out at once and journeyed till he reached King Shahzeman's court in safety, when he saluted him for his brother and informed him that the latter yearned after him and desired that he would pay him a visit; to which King Shahzeman consented gladly and made ready for the journey and appointed his Vizier to rule the country in his stead during his absence. Then he caused his tents and camels and mules to be brought forth and encamped, with his guards and attendants, without the city, in readiness to set out next morning for his brother's kingdom. In the middle of the night, it chanced that he bethought him of somewhat he had forgotten in his palace: so he returned thither privily and entered his apartments, where he found his wife asleep in his own bed, in the arms of one of his black slaves. When he saw this, the world grew black in his sight, and he said to himself, "If this is what happens whilst I am yet under the city walls, what will be the condition of this accursed woman during my absence at my brother's court?" Then he drew his sword and smote the twain and slew them and left them in the bed and returned presently to his camp, without telling any one what had happened. Then he gave orders for immediate departure and set out at once and travelled till he drew near his brother's capital, when he despatched vaunt-couriers to announce his approach. His brother came forth to meet him and saluted him and rejoiced exceedingly and caused the city to be decorated in his honour. Then he sat down with him to converse and make merry; but King Shahzeman could not forget the perfidy of his wife and grief grew on him more and more and his colour changed and his body became weak. Shehriyar saw his condition, but attributed it to his separation from his country and his kingdom, so let him alone and asked no questions of him, till one day he said to him, "O my brother, I see that thou art grown weak of body and hast lost thy colour." And Shahzeman answered, "O my brother, I have an internal wound;" but did not tell him about his wife. Said Shehriyar, "I wish thou wouldst ride forth with me a-hunting; maybe it would lighten thy heart." But Shahzeman refused; so his brother went out to hunt without him. Now there were in King Shahzeman's apartments lattice-windows overlooking his brother's garden, and as the former was sitting looking on the garden, behold a gate of the palace opened, and out came twenty damsels and twenty black slaves, and among them his brother's wife, who was wonderfully fair and beautiful. They all came up to a fountain, where the girls and slaves took off their clothes and sat down together. Then the queen called out, "O Mesoud!" And there came to her a black slave, who embraced her and she him. Then he lay with her, and on like wise did the other slaves with the girls. And they ceased not from kissing and clipping and clicketing and carousing until the day began to wane. When the King of Tartary saw this, he said to himself, "By Allah, my mischance was lighter than this!" And his grief and chagrin relaxed from him and he said, "This is more grievous than what happened to me!" So he put away his melancholy and ate and drank. Presently, his brother came back from hunting and they saluted each other: and Shehriyar looked at Shahzeman and saw that his colour had returned and his face was rosy and he ate heartily, whereas before he ate but little. So he said to him, "O my brother, when I last saw thee, thou wast pale and wan; and now I see that the colour has returned to thy face. Tell me how it is with thee." Quoth Shahzeman, "I will tell thee what caused my loss of colour, but excuse me from acquainting thee with the cause of its return to me." Said Shehriyar, "Let me hear first what was the cause of thy pallor and weakness." "Know then, O my brother," rejoined Shahzeman, "that when thou sentest thy vizier to bid me to thee, I made ready for the journey and had actually quitted my capital city, when I remembered that I had left behind me a certain jewel, that which I gave thee. So I returned to my palace, where I found my wife asleep in my bed, in the arms of a black slave. I slew them both and came to thee: and it was for brooding over this affair, that I lost my colour and became weak. But forgive me if I tell thee not the cause of my restoration to health." When his brother heard this, he said to him, "I conjure thee by Allah, tell me the reason of thy recovery!" So he told him all that he had seen, and Shehriyar said, "I must see this with my own eyes." "Then," replied Shahzeman, "feign to go forth to hunt and hide thyself in my lodging and thou shalt see all this and have ocular proof of the truth." So Shehriyar ordered his attendants to prepare to set out at once; whereupon the troops encamped without the city and he himself went forth with them and sat in his pavilion, bidding his servants admit no one. Then he disguised himself and returned secretly to King Shahzeman's palace and sat with him at the lattice overlooking the garden, until the damsels and their mistress came out with the slaves and did as his brother had reported, till the call to afternoon prayer. When King Shehriyar saw this, he was as one distraught and said to his brother, "Arise, let us depart hence, for we have no concern with kingship, and wander till we find one to whom the like has happened as to us: else our death were better than our life." Then they went out by a postern of the palace and journeyed days and nights till they came to a tree standing in the midst of a meadow, by a spring of water, on the shore of the salt sea: and they drank of the stream and sat down by it to rest. When the day was somewhat spent, behold, the sea became troubled and there rose from it a black column, that ascended to the sky and made towards the meadow. When the princes saw this, they were afraid and climbed up to the top of the tree, which was a high one, that they might see what was the matter; and behold, it was a genie of lofty stature, broad-browed and wide-chested, bearing on his head a coffer of glass with seven locks of steel. He landed and sat down under the tree, where he set down the coffer, and opening it, took out a smaller one. This also he opened, and there came forth a damsel slender of form and dazzlingly beautiful, as she were a shining sun, as says the poet Uteyeh:

> She shines out in the dusk, and lo! the day is here, And all the trees flower
>   forth with blossoms bright and clear,
> The sun from out her brows arises, and the moon, When she unveils her
>   face, doth hide for shame and fear.
> All living things prostrate themselves before her feet, When she un-
>   shrouds and all her hidden charms appear;
> And when she flashes forth the lightnings of her glance, She maketh eyes
>   to rain, like showers, with many a tear.

When the genie saw her, he said to her, "O queen of noble ladies, thou whom indeed I stole away on thy wedding night, I have a mind to sleep awhile." And he laid his head on her knees and fell asleep. Presently the lady raised her eyes to the tree and saw the two kings among the branches: so she lifted the genie's head from her lap and laid it on the ground, then rose and stood beneath the tree and signed to them to descend, without heeding the Afrit. They answered her, in the same manner, "God on thee! excuse us from this." But she rejoined by signs, as who should say, "If you do not come down, I will wake the Afrit on you, and he will kill you without mercy." So they were afraid and came down to her, whereupon she came up to them and offered them her favours, saying, "To it, both of you, and lustily; or I will set the Afrit on you." So for fear of him, King Shehriyar said to his brother Shahzeman, "O brother, do as she bids thee." But he replied, "Not I; do thou have at her first." And they made signs to each other to pass first, till she said, "Why do I see you make signs to each other? An you come not forward and fall to, I will rouse the Afrit on you." So, for fear of the genie, they lay with her one after the other; and when they had done, she bade them arise, and took out of her bosom a purse containing a necklace made of five hundred and seventy rings, and said to them, "Know ye what these are?" They answered, "No." And she said, "Every one of the owners of these rings has had to do with me in despite of this Afrit. And now give me your rings, both of you." So each of them took off a ring and gave it to her. And she said to them, "Know that this genie carried me off on my wedding night and laid me in a box and shut the box up in a glass chest, on which he clapped seven strong locks and sank it to the bottom of the roaring stormy sea, knowing not that nothing can hinder a woman, when she desires aught, even as says one of the poets:

> I rede thee put no faith in womankind, Nor trust the oaths they lavish all
>   in vain:
> For on the satisfaction of their lusts Depend alike their love and their dis-
>   dain.
> They proffer lying love, but perfidy Is all indeed their garments do con-
>   tain.
> Take warning, then, by Joseph's history, And how a woman sought to do
>   him bane;
> And eke thy father Adam, by their fault, To leave the groves of Paradise
>   was fain.

Or as another says:

Out on you! blame confirms the blamed one in his way. My fault is not so
　　great indeed as you would say.
If I'm in love, forsooth, my case is but the same As that of other men be-
　　fore me, many a day.
For great the wonder were if any man alive From women and their wiles
　　escape unharmed away!

When the two kings heard this, they marvelled and said, "Allah! Allah! There is no
power and no virtue save in God the Most High, the Supreme! We seek aid of God
against the malice of women, for indeed their craft is great!" Then she said to them,
"Go your ways." So they returned to the road, and Shehriyar said to Shahzeman, "By
Allah, O my brother, this Afrit's case is more grievous than ours. For this is a genie
and stole away his mistress on her wedding night and clapped her in a chest, which he
locked with seven locks and sank in the midst of the sea, thinking to guard her from
that which was decreed by fate; yet have we seen that she has lain with five hundred
and seventy men in his despite, and now with thee and me to boot. Verily, this is a
thing that never yet happened to any, and it should surely console us. Let us therefore
return to our kingdoms and resolve never again to take a woman to wife; and as for
me, I will show thee what I will do." So they set out at once and presently came to the
camp outside Shehriyar's capital and, entering the royal pavilion, sat down on their
bed of estate. Then the chamberlains and amirs and grandees came in to them and
Shehriyar commanded them to return to the city. So they returned to the city and
Shehriyar went up to his palace, where he summoned his Vizier and bade him forthwith put his wife to death. The Vizier accordingly took the queen and killed her,
whilst Shehriyar, going into the slave girls and concubines, drew his sword and slew
them all. Then he let bring others in their stead and took an oath that every night he
would go in to a maid and in the morning put her to death, for that there was not one
chaste woman on the face of the earth. As for Shahzeman, he sought to return to his
kingdom at once; so his brother equipped him for the journey and he set out and
fared on till he came to his own dominions. Meanwhile, King Shehriyar commanded
his Vizier to bring him the bride of the night, that he might go in to her: so he
brought him one of the daughters of the amirs and he went in to her, and on the morrow he bade the Vizier cut off her head. The Vizier dared not disobey the King's commandment, so he put her to death and brought him another girl, of the daughters of
the notables of the land. The King went in to her also, and on the morrow he bade the
Vizier kill her; and he ceased not to do thus for three years, till the land was stripped
of marriageable girls, and all the women and mothers and fathers wept and cried out
against the King, cursing him and complaining to the Creator of heaven and earth
and calling for succour upon Him who heareth prayer and answereth those that cry to
Him; and those that had daughters left fled with them, till at last there remained not a
single girl in the city apt for marriage. One day the King ordered the Vizier to bring
him a maid as of wont: so the Vizier went out and made search for a girl, but found
not one and returned home troubled and careful for fear of the King's anger. Now this
Vizier had two daughters, the elder called Shehrzad and the younger Dunyazad, and
the former had read many books and histories and chronicles of ancient kings and

stories of people of old time: it is said indeed that she had collected a thousand books of chronicles of past peoples and bygone kings and poets. Moreover, she had read books of science and medicine; her memory was stored with verses and stories and folk-lore and the sayings of kings and sages, and she was wise, witty, prudent and well-bred. She said to her father, "How comes it that I see thee troubled and oppressed with care and anxiety? Quoth one of the poets:

> 'Tell him that is of care oppressed, That grief shall not endure alway,
> But even as gladness fleeteth by, So sorrow too shall pass away.'"

When the Vizier heard his daughter's words, he told her his case, and she said, "By Allah, O my father, marry me to this king, for either I will be the means of the deliverance of the daughters of the Muslims from slaughter or I will die and perish as others have perished." "For God's sake," answered the Vizier, "do not thus adventure thy life!" But she said, "It must be so." . . .

Story of the Enchanted Youth

"My father was King of the city that stood in this place, and his name was Mohammed, Lord of the Black Islands, which are no other than the four hills of which thou wottest. He reigned seventy years, at the end of which time God took him to Himself, and I succeeded to his throne and took to wife the daughter of my father's brother, who loved me with an exceeding love, so that, whenever I was absent from her, she would neither eat nor drink till she saw me again. With her I lived for five years, till one day she went out to go to the bath, and I bade the cook hasten supper for us against her return. Then I entered the palace and lay down on the bed where we were wont to lie and ordered two slave-girls to sit, one at my head and the other at my feet, and fan me. Now I was disturbed at my wife's absence and could not sleep, but remained awake, although my eyes were closed. Presently I heard the damsel at my head say to the other one, 'O Mesoudeh, how unhappy is our lord and how wretched is his youth, and oh, the pity of him with our accursed harlot of a mistress!' 'Yes, indeed,' replied Mesoudeh; 'may God curse all unfaithful women and adulteresses! Indeed, it befits not that the like of our lord should waste his youth with this harlot, who lies abroad every night.' Quoth the other, 'Is our lord then a fool, that, when he wakes in the night and finds her not by his side, he makes no enquiry after her?' 'Out on thee,' rejoined Mesoudeh; 'has our lord any knowledge of this or does she leave him any choice? Does she not drug him every night in the cup of drink she gives him before he sleeps, in which she puts henbane? So he sleeps like a dead man and knows nothing of what happens. Then she dresses and scents herself and goes forth and is absent till daybreak, when she returns and burns a perfume under his nose and he awakes.' When I heard the girls' talk, the light in my eyes became darkness, and I thought the night would never come. Presently, my wife returned from the bath, and they served up supper and we ate and sat awhile drinking and talking as usual. Then she called for my sleeping-draught and gave me the cup: and I feigned to drink it, but made shift to pour it into my bosom and lay down at once and began to snore as if I slept. Then said she, 'Sleep out thy night and never rise again! By Allah, I hate thee and I hate thy person; I am sick of thy company and I know not when God will take away thy life!' Then she rose and donned her richest clothes and perfumed herself and girt on my sword and opened the palace gate and went out. I rose and followed her, and she passed through the streets of the city, till she came to the gate, when she muttered words I understood not: and straightway the locks fell off and the gate opened. She went forth and fared on among the rubbish heaps, I still following her without her knowledge, till she came to a reed fence, within which was a hut of brick. She entered the hut and I climbed up on the roof and looking down, saw my wife standing by a scurvy black slave, with blubber lips, one of which overlapped the other, like a coverlet, and swept up the sand from the gravel floor, lying upon a bed of sugarcane refuse and wrapped in an old cloak and a few rags. She kissed the earth before him, and he raised his head to her and said, 'Out on thee! why hast thou tarried till now? There have been some of my kinsmen the blacks here, drinking; and they have gone away, each with his wench; but I refused to drink on account of thine absence.' 'O my lord and my love and solace of my eyes,' answered she, 'dost thou not know that I am married to my cousin, and that I hate to look upon him and abhor myself in his company. Did I not fear for thy sake, I would not let the sun rise again till his city was a heap of ruins wherein the owl and the raven should hoot and wolves and foxes harbour; and I would transport its stones behind the mountain Caf.' 'Thou liest, O accursed one!' said the black, 'and I swear by the valour of the blacks (else may our manhood be as that of the whites!) that if thou tarry again till this hour, I will no longer keep thee company nor join my body to thine! O accursed one, wilt thou play fast and loose with us at thy pleasure, O stinkard, O bitch, O vilest of whites?' When I heard and saw what passed between them, the world grew dark in my eyes and I knew not where I was; whilst my wife stood weeping and humbling herself to him and saying, 'O my love and fruit of my heart, if thou be angry with me, who is left me, and if thou reject me, who shall shelter me, O my beloved and light of mine eyes?' And she ceased not to weep and implore him till he forgave her. Then she was glad and rose and putting off her clothes, said to the slave, 'O my lord, hast thou aught here for thy handmaid to eat?' 'Take the cover off yonder basin,' answered he; 'thou wilt find under it cooked rats' bones, and there is a little millet beer left in this pot. Eat and drink.' So she ate and drank and washed her hands and mouth; then lay down, naked, upon the rushes, beside the slave, and covered herself with the rags. When I saw this, I became as one distraught and coming down from the roof, went in by the door. Then I took the sword she had brought and drew it, thinking to kill them both. I struck first at the slave's neck and thought I had made an end of him; but the blow only severed the flesh and the gullet, without dividing the jugulars. He gave a loud gurgling groan and roused my wife, whereupon I drew back, after I had restored the sword to its place, and returning to the palace, lay down on my bed till morning, when my wife came and awoke me, and I saw that she had cut off her hair and put on mourning garments. 'O my cousin,' said she, 'do not blame me for this I have done; for I have news that my mother is dead, that my father has fallen in battle and that both my brothers are dead also, one of a snake-bite and the other of a fall from a precipice, so that I have good reason to weep and lament.' When I heard this, I did not reproach her, but said to her, 'Do what thou wilt: I will not baulk thee.' She ceased not to mourn and lament for a whole year, at the end of which time she said to me, 'I wish to build me in thy palace a tomb with a cupola and set it apart for mourning and call it House of Lamentations.' Quoth I, 'Do what seemeth good to thee.' So she built herself a house of mourning, roofed with a dome, and a monument in the midst like the tomb of a saint. Thither she transported the slave and lodged him in the tomb. He was exceeding weak and from the day I wounded him he had remained unable to do her any service or to speak or do aught but drink; but he was still alive, because his hour was not yet come. She used to visit him morning and evening in the mausoleum and carry him wine and broths to drink and weep and make moan over him; and thus she did for another year, whilst I ceased not to have patience with her and pay no heed to her doings, till one day I came upon her unawares and found her weeping and saying, 'Why art thou absent from my sight, O delight of my heart? Speak to me, O my life! speak to me, O my love!' And she recited the following verses:

> My patience fails me for desire: if thou forgettest me, My heart and all my
> soul can love none other after thee.
> Carry me with thee, body and soul, wherever thou dost fare; And where
> thou lightest down to rest, there let me buried be.
> Speak but my name above my tomb; the groaning of my bones, Turning
> towards thy voice's sound, shall answer drearily.

And she wept and recited the following:

> My day of bliss is that whereon thou drawest near to me; And that,
> whereon thou turn'st away, my day of death and fear.
> What though I tremble all the night and be in dread of death, Yet thine
> embraces are to me than safety far more dear.

And again the following:

> Though unto me were given all that can make life sweet, Though the
> Chosroës' empire, yea, and the world were mine,
> All were to me in value less than a midge's wing, If that mine eyes must
> never look on that face of thine!

When she had finished, I said to her, 'O my cousin, let thy mourning suffice thee: for weeping profiteth nothing.' She replied, 'Thwart me not, or I will kill myself.' So I held my peace and let her go her way: and she ceased not to mourn and weep for the space of another year. At the end of the third year, I came into the mausoleum one day, vexed at something that had crossed me and weary of this excessive affliction, and found her by the tomb under the dome, saying, 'O my lord, I never hear thee speak to me, no, not one word. Why dost thou not answer me, O my lord?' And she recited the following verses:

O tomb, O tomb, have his beauties ceased, or does thy light indeed, The
  sheen of the radiant countenance, no more in thee abound?
O tomb, O tomb, thou art neither earth nor heaven unto me: How comes
  it then that sun and moon at once in thee are found?

When I heard this, it added wrath to my wrath, and I said, 'Alas! how much more
of this mourning?' and I repeated the following [parody of her] verses:

O tomb, O tomb, has his blackness ceased, or does thy light indeed, The
  sheen of the filthy countenance, no more in thee abound?
O tomb, thou art neither kitchen-stove nor sewer-pool for me! How
  comes it then that mire and coal at once in thee are found?

When she heard this, she sprang to her feet and said, 'Out on thee, thou dog! it
was thou that didst thus with me and woundedst the beloved of my heart and hast
afflicted me and wasted his youth, so that these three years he hath lain, neither dead
nor alive!' 'O foulest of harlots and filthiest of whorish doxies of hired slaves,' answered I, 'it was indeed I who did this!' And I drew my sword and made at her to kill
her; but she laughed and said, 'Avaunt, thou dog! Thinkst thou that what is past can
recur or the dead come back to life? Verily, God has given into my hand him who did
this to me and against whom there was in my heart fire that might not be quenched
and insatiable rage.' Then she stood up and pronouncing some words I did not understand, said to me, 'Let one half of thee by my enchantments become stone and the
other half remain man.' And immediately I became as thou seest me and have remained ever since neither sitting nor standing and neither dead nor alive. Then she
enchanted the city with all its streets and gardens and turned it into the lake thou
wottest of, and the inhabitants, who were of four religions, Muslims, Christians, Magians and Jews, she changed to fish of various colours, the Muslims white, the Christians blue, the Magians red and the Jews yellow; and the four islands she turned into
four mountains encompassing the lake. Moreover, the condition to which she has reduced me does not suffice her: but every day she strips me and gives me a hundred
lashes with a whip, so that the blood runs down me and my shoulders are torn. Then
she clothes my upper half in a shirt of hair-cloth and over that she throws these rich
robes." And he wept and repeated the following verses:

Lord, I submit myself to Thee and eke to Fate, Content, if so Thou please,
  to suffer and to wait.
My enemies oppress and torture me full sore: But Paradise at last, belike,
  shall compensate.
Though Fate press hard on me, I trust in the Elect, The Accepted One of
  God, to be my advocate.

With this the King turned to him and said, "O youth, after having rid me of one
trouble, thou addest another to me: but tell me, where is thy wife and where is the
wounded slave?" "The slave lies in the tomb under the dome," answered the youth,

"and she is in the chamber over against the gate. Every day at sunrise, she comes out and repairs first to me and strips off my clothes and gives me a hundred strokes with the whip; and I weep and cry out, but cannot stir to keep her off. When she has done torturing me, she goes down to the slave with the wine and broth on which she feeds him; and to-morrow at sunrise she will come." "O youth," rejoined the King, "by Allah, I will assuredly do thee a service by which I shall be remembered and which men shall chronicle to the end of time!" Then he sat down by the youth and talked with him till nightfall, when they went to sleep. At peep of day, the King rose and put off his clothes and drawing his sword, repaired to the mausoleum, where, after noting the paintings of the place and the candles and lamps and perfumes burning there, he sought for the slave till he came upon him and slew him with one blow of the sword; after which he took the body on his back and threw it into a well that was in the palace. Then he returned to the dome and wrapping himself in the black's clothes, lay down in his place, with his drawn sword by his side. After awhile, the accursed enchantress came out and, going first to her husband, stripped him and beat him with the whip, whilst he cried out, "Alas! the state I am in suffices me. Have mercy on me, O my cousin!" But she replied, "Didst thou show me any mercy or spare my beloved?" And beat him till she was tired and the blood ran from his sides. Then she put the hair shirt on him and the royal robes over it, and went down to the dome with a goblet of wine and a bowl of broth in her hands. When she came to the tomb, she fell a-weeping and wailing and said, "O my lord, speak to me!" And repeated the following verse:

> How long ere this rigour pass away and thou relent? Is it not yet enough
> of the tears that I have spent?

And she wept and said again, "O my lord, speak to me!" The King lowered his voice and knotting his tongue, spoke after the fashion of the blacks and said, "Alack! alack! there is no power and no virtue but in God the Most High, the Supreme!" When she heard this, she screamed out for joy and swooned away; and when she revived, she said, "O my lord, can it be true and didst thou indeed speak to me?" The King made his voice small and said, "O accursed woman, thou deservest not that I should speak to thee!" "Why so?" asked she; and he replied, "Because all day thou tormentest thy husband and his cries disturb me, and all night long he calls upon God for help and invokes curses on thee and me and keeps me awake from nightfall to daybreak and disquiets me; and but for this, I had been well long ago. This is what has hindered me from answering thee." Quoth she, "With thy leave, I will release him from his present condition." "Do so," said the King, "and rid us of his noise." "I hear and obey," answered she, and going out into the palace, took a cup full of water and spoke over it certain words, whereupon the water began to boil and bubble as the cauldron bubbles over the fire. Then she went up to the young King and sprinkled him with it, saying, "By the virtue of the words I have spoken, if thou art thus by my spells, quit this shape for thy former one." And immediately he shook and rose to his feet, rejoicing in his deliverance, and said, "I testify that there is no god but God and that Mohammed is His apostle, may God bless and preserve him!" Then she said to him, "Depart hence and do not return, or I will kill thee." And she screamed out in his face. So he went out from before her, and she returned to the dome and going down into the tomb, said, "O my lord, come forth to me, that I may see thy goodly form!" The King replied in a weak voice, "What hast thou done? Thou hast rid me of the branch, but not of the root." "O my beloved, O my little black," said she, "what is the root?" "Out on thee, O accursed one!" answered he. "Every night, at the middle hour, the people of the city, whom thou by thine enchantments didst change into fish, lift up their heads from the water and cry to God for help and curse thee and me; and this is what hinders my recovery: so do thou go quickly and set them free, and after return and take me by the hand and raise me up; for indeed health returns to me." When she heard this speech of the King, whom she supposed to be the slave, she rejoiced and said, "O my lord, on my head and eyes be it, in the name of God!" Then she went out, full of joy, and ran to the lake and taking a little of the water in her hand, spoke over it words that might not be understood, whereupon there was a great stir among the fish; and they raised their heads to the surface and stood upright and became men as before. Thus was the spell dissolved from the people of the city and the lake became again a populous city, with its streets and bazaars, in which the merchants bought and sold, and every one returned to his employment; whilst the four hills were restored to their original form of islands. Then the enchantress returned to the King and said to him, "O my lord, give me thy noble hand and arise." "Come nearer to me," answered he, in a faint voice. So she came close to him, and he took his sword and smote her in the breast, that the steel came forth, gleaming, from her back. He smote her again and cut her in twain, and she fell to the ground in two halves. Then he went out and found the young King standing awaiting him and gave him joy of his deliverance, whereupon the youth rejoiced and thanked him and kissed his hand. Quoth the Sultan, "Wilt thou abide in this thy city or come with me to mine?" "O King of the age," rejoined he, "dost thou know how far it is from here to thy capital?" And the Sultan replied, "Two and a half days' journey." "O King," said the other, "if thou sleepest, awake! Between thee and thy capital is a full year's journey to a diligent traveller; and thou hadst not come hither in two days and a half, save that the city was enchanted. But, O King, I will never leave thee, no, not for the twinkling of an eye!" The Sultan rejoiced at his words and said, "Praised be God, who hath bestowed thee upon me! Thou shalt be my son, for in all my life I have never been blessed with a son." And they embraced each other and rejoiced with exceeding great joy. Then they returned to the palace, and the young King bade his officers make ready for a journey and prepare his baggage and all that he required. The preparations occupied ten days, at the end of which time the young King set out in company of the Sultan, whose heart burned within him at the thought of his long absence from his capital, attended by fifty white slaves and provided with magnificent presents. They journeyed day and night for a whole year, and God ordained them safety, till they drew near the Sultan's capital and sent messengers in advance to acquaint the Vizier with his safe arrival. Then came out the Vizier and the troops, who had given up all hope of the Sultan's return, and kissed the ground before him and gave him joy of his safety. So he entered his palace and sat down on his throne and the Vizier came in to him, to whom he related all that had befallen him with the young King: and the Vizier gave the latter joy of his deliverance. Then all things being set in order, the Sultan gave largesse to many of his people and sending for the fisherman who had brought him the enchanted fish and had thus been the first cause of the delivery of the people of the Black Islands, bestowed on him a dress of honour and enquired of his condition and whether he had any children, to which he replied that he had three children, two daughters and one son. So the King sent for them and taking one daughter to wife, married the other to the young King and made the son his treasurer. Moreover, he invested his Vizier with the sovereignty of the Black Islands and despatched him thither with the fifty officers, who had accompanied the young King thence, giving him robes of honour for all the amirs. So the Vizier kissed hands and set out for the Black Islands. The fisherman became the richest man of his time, and he and his daughters and the two Kings their husbands abode in peace till death came to them.

Translated by John Payne

From *Il Novellino*

Masuccio Salernitano

Tommaso Guardati (1410–1475), secretary to the prince of Salerno, used the nom de plume Masuccio Salernitano for his sole literary endeavor, a collection of novellas called *Il Novellino*. Masuccio continued a tradition dating to Boccaccio by dividing his stories into five themes of ten novellas each: the transgressions of church figures, the consequences of jealousy, the faults of women, the generosity of princes, and tragedies. He diverges from Boccaccio in his use of storytellers: Masuccio himself is the narrator. Among Masuccio's novellas is the first general construction of the story of Romeo and Juliet. The novellas included here, "A Lady of Trapani Becomes Enamoured of a Moor," "A Young Man Loves a Certain Lady Who Does Not Love Him in Return," and "A Young Girl Is Beloved by Many Suitors," come from the third section of the book, which is devoted to the faults of women, who are, as in *The Arabian Nights*, represented in adulterous relations across boundaries that bring out the most exaggeratedly violent reactions in their husbands, toward whose flaws the narrator is far more lenient.

Novel the Twenty-second

Argument

A lady of Trapani becomes enamoured of a Moor, and lets him have knowledge of her. She robs her husband, and then takes flight to Barbary in company with the aforesaid Moor and a Turkish girl. Whereupon the husband, in order to avenge himself, follows them, having put on a certain disguise, and slays the Moor and his wife. Then he returns with the Turkish girl to Trapani, and, having made her his wife, he lives with her a long time in great happiness.

TO THE MAGNIFICENT SIGNOR GALEAZZO SANSEVERINO

Exordium

Forasmuch as my weary but still unsatiated pen is not equal to the heavy task of setting forth to you by description the deeds, more natural to monstrous beasts than to human beings, which are commonly wrought by members of that most base and wicked female sex, I mean to let all those things concerning which I myself gathered experience in the early years of my youth stand apart from what I have learned about women and their deeds in my present season of old age. Nevertheless, in order to win my way to the end of the journey I have begun, I will not hold back from writing in this place concerning certain wicked deeds wrought by this evil-natured brood and since become a scandal in the mouths of the vulgar, and from giving full intelligence of the same to all such as are well endowed with virtue and good manners. And, certes, while dealing with these I will not be niggard of my speech you-ward, knowing that it is meet to reckon you amongst the most virtuous, but will tell you a story anent the unnatural and libidinous desire which overcame a certain woman of Trapani. From the hearing of this I doubt not at all—supposing there should still abide within you any faith as to women at large—that you will hereafter abandon all trust in the female sex on account of the hatred you will feel for this woman's crime. Now let me wish that you, free and untrammeled as you are, may find much joy in the course of your flourishing youth. Farewell!

The Narrative

Trapani, a noble city of Sicily, is situated, as many know, in the furthermost regions of the island, and is, in sooth, almost a nearer neighbour to Africa than any other Christian country, for which reason the Trapanese are often wont, at such times as they may be cruising about in their ships of war, to sail up and down along the shores and the inlets of the country of the Moors, wherefrom they continually gather the most valuable booty. At certain times, however, they suffer defeat and are plundered in their turn, and on this account it often happens that, in order to negotiate as to the ransoms to be paid for the release of prisoners on one side or the other, they arrange a truce between themselves, and transport their merchandize and buy and sell, carrying on their dealings together without hindrance. For the reasons above given it is the case that there are to be found very few Trapanese who are not as well acquainted with the country of the Moors as with their own.

Not a great time ago it chanced that a gentleman of Trapani, called by name Nicolao d'Aguito, in his day renowned as a most famous corsair, after he had many times harried and despoiled the coasts of Barbary, returned to his home and took to himself as wife a young woman of great beauty; and having had born to him several children by her, he settled down to lead his life in honourable wise. Amongst the other servants and slaves whom he kept in his house was a certain Moor of Tripoli in Barbary, who was called by name Elia, a young fellow strong and robust of body, but ugly beyond all measure. The wife of Nicolao, assailed by hot and unbridled wantonness, having no regard to the breaking of her marriage vow (of which sacrament, indeed, they rarely take much account except they be compelled thereto by circumstance), considering naught either that this fellow was a slave and she a free woman, or that she was fair and he beyond measure hideous, or that she was a Christian, he a Moor, or that by reason of this last-named consideration she would give offence to God, to the law, and to her honour, remembered only that he was young and lusty, and would on this account satisfy her carnal desires better than could her husband. Wherefore she at once set to work with all her will to make trial whether the Moor would know how to bear himself as a valiant man-at-arms in as capable a manner as he used in carrying burdens of inordinate weight upon his shoulders. Having made trial of his powers once and again, and having fully satisfied herself that the judgment she had formed of him had not deceived her, she determined to follow her bent as long as her course of life and her husband's wealth should suffice therefor.

Now, although it seemed that the world must be going very well with the Moor, and that he might for many reasons be quite contented with the game he was called upon to play, nevertheless—seeing that he was by nature akin to the birds of prey, which, being left at liberty, always seek to return to their own abandoned nests, although as long as they are in the keeping of the falconer they are daily fed with excellent and delicate meats, while when they shift for themselves they rarely secure their prey—this Moor, in spite of all the flattering words and the rich gifts and the love lavished upon him without ceasing by his beautiful mistress, would constantly dream of a flight to his own home. And, as he was both cunning and wicked by nature, he began to put on sad and melancholy humours in the presence of his mistress, and was wont at such times as she showed herself wishful to take her pleasure with him to deny her the same. On account of these moods, she being mightily ill content therewith, urged him continually to let her know the cause of his melancholy, for she was disposed to leave nothing undone which might work for his cure. In answer the Moor let her know in plain terms that he would never be satisfied until he should have returned to his own home, and the lady, when she listened to these words, was smitten with a sorrow the like of which she had never felt before, and she strove with all her powers, using many and most convincing arguments the while, to persuade him to abide contented in his present condition. Nay, further, she promised, if she might thereby win the Moor's approval, to poison her husband in order that they might seize upon his estate. The Moor, however, would not assent to this proposition, but with great cunning stood firm to the resolution he had taken; wherefore she fixed upon the desperate course of eloping with him into Barbary, and when she told him her resolution he listened to her words with exceeding great pleasure.

In order that there might be no delay in carrying out their enterprise, they awaited the season when a fresh and steady Tramontano wind should be blowing, and when Messer Nicolao should be gone to Mazzara to despatch certain business of his. Then one night the Moor and certain other slaves took a ship which had been furnished with all equipment necessary for a voyage, and having carried on board the lady—who had with her a young and very beautiful Turkish girl—with as many light and delicate articles for her use as their hurried flight allowed, they issued forth from the city and took to the ship. They were so well sped by good fortune on their way that on the following day they found themselves close upon the Moorish coast. After they had landed, and all their companions had gone their divers ways into their own lands, Elia, in the company of the lady and the Turkish girl, journeyed to Tripoli, and there they were received by all his friends with the most sumptuous feasts and rejoicings.

When he had tarried a few days in his house, enjoying the booty he had taken, the Moor, either urged on thereto by the justice of God, which never suffers any wrongdoing to go long unpunished, or convinced by some thoughts which may have sprung from his own brain, determined that it was neither in his power nor in his duty to give either faith or love or hope to this wicked and abandoned woman, who, driven along by her own insatiate lechery, had deceived the husband who had loved her better than he had loved his own life; had abandoned her children, a deed which must of a surety cause no small wonderment, and had forsaken alike her country and the laws of her God. For the reasons aforesaid he began, after the lapse of a few days, to hold her in such savage hatred and disgust that not only was he unable to bestow upon her such caresses as he was wont to give her, but even found it a hard business to speak a word to her. Neither could he trust himself to look towards her; and, beyond this, whensoever she might commit the slightest fault, he would cudgel her as lustily as if he were the captain of a galley and she the slave. Wherefore the foolish woman, finding herself reduced to a state of extreme wretchedness, began to repent when it was too late, and bewept the misery of her life, together with all the ill-doing of which she had been guilty. In sooth, she would much sooner have died outright than have lived on, and would have welcomed death with the greatest joy as the one cure for all her troubles.

When the wretched Nicolao returned to his home, and heard the most odious and most shameful tidings which awaited him there, everyone who reads will be able to judge for himself how great must have been the grief and the tears and the sorrowing which possessed the poor wight. Indeed, he fell into so desperate a mood that over and over again he came within an ace of plunging a sharp knife into his heart's core, knowing well enough that to continue to live, weighed down by such a burden of disgrace, would be much worse than death itself. Nevertheless, after having given way to his grief for a certain time, he began to take thought that he would be greatly lacking in all that was due to the maintenance of his fair fame were he, out of cowardice, to make an end of his life. Wherefore he determined to go like a man, and to lose his life in that same place where he had already lost both his honour and his riches. Now he was at all times a man of great courage, and his nature was farther strengthened by the justice of the undertaking which he had in hand; so, without waiting to take counsel either with his friends or his relations, he bade come together secretly ten or a dozen bold and sprightly young men, and, after they had during the night armed and got in readiness a small bark fit for sea-roving, they set sail together, and directed their course towards the Barbary coast.

After a few days' voyaging, Nicolao arrived at the spot he had been seeking, and when the crew had drawn the ship up on the beach about ten miles distant from Tripoli, he covered her up with the sea-weed, which is very abundant in those parts, and bade his companions conceal themselves withinside the galley, letting no one be aware of their presence, until such time as they would have the opportunity of seizing for themselves a vast booty. Furthermore, he bade them await his return for the space of eight days and no longer; for, supposing that he should not come back within that time, they might hold it for certain that he had either met his death or had been taken prisoner by his adversaries. After he had allowed his beard to grow to some length, and had disguised himself in Moorish clothing, he, being well acquainted with the language spoken by the people of Tripoli, recommended himself to God and departed from his companions, having everything about him in order, and being very eager to carry out the vengeance he had planned against his wife and the Moor.

Now one day, when Nicolao, who indeed knew that country and all the neighbouring parts thereto belonging, but too well, was walking along beside a little river very near to the city, a spot which many women of the place were wont to frequent for the purpose of blanching their linen, it suddenly came into his mind that perchance the Turkish girl—whom he believed to be much attached to him—might have come there from the house where his wife was abiding, either to fetch water or for some other household task. And then, by the will of chance, who had likewise made ready the vengeance he was to work, and the penalty he was to exact for the losses he had suffered, it was ordained that, at the very moment when he came to the place, he espied the girl making her way back to the house bearing a vessel of water. Wherefore he, hurrying on with rapid steps, overtook her and spake thus, weeping the while: "Lucia, can it be that the great love which I have borne towards you for these many years past—a love which has led me to bring you up in my house as if you had been my own daughter—has found so little place in your heart that you, too, are ready to deceive me?" Lucia, turning round and recognizing her master both by his speech and by his countenance, was overcome by the most heartfelt compassion for him, and ran weeping to embrace him, because in sooth she loved him more than anyone else in the world, and with good reason. Then she implored his pardon, saying that her mistress had induced her to accompany herself and the Moor to that place by using the greatest deceit. Wherefore it seemed to Nicolao, when the girl went on to talk of trifling matters, that this was not the place for such discourse, he being anxious not to lose any more time before he should put into execution the cruel scheme he had devised. So, like an astute man, he determined that he would use as messenger this one who had herself been deceived in the first instance.

After he had let her tell him in a few words of the wretched life which his wife was now leading, he besought her that she would commend him lovingly to his wife, and beg her that she would be pleased to remember him who had loved her and still loved her so very dearly, and likewise to bear in mind the love of her children and her own honour. Also to say how he, having received intelligence even in Trapani of the wretchedness and misery she was suffering, had come after her to place his life in peril so as to deliver her from all her trouble, thinking not so much of forgiving her the fault she had committed against him as to take her back once more as the mistress of his life and of all his goods. And he spake to the girl many other similar words, all of them seductive and full of flattery—words which might well have moved even a heart of marble to pity. The kind-hearted slave, urged on by the prayers of her beloved master, and overcome by pity, found that for the present she could say or do nothing more than beg him come back to this place at the same hour the next day, and that, with regard to whatsoever yet remained to be done, he should leave the ordering thereof to her.

Having bidden farewell to him and gone back to the house, she told her mistress, with many bitter tears, by what means and on what errand her husband had come thither, letting her know exactly everything he had said and adding that, if in this matter she would deign to follow the advice of her poor servant, she would do well. The girl went on to say that it appeared to her, even if Messer Nicolao should play them false, it would still be better to die quickly and at once by the hand of a Christian, her husband and her lord, than to suffer daily a hundred deaths from a Moor who had formerly been her servant and slave. And thus, urging her by many kind and loving words, she heartened her mistress so much that the unhappy lady, without taking any time to consider her answer, and acting as hastily as when she had lightly, and without any good reason, let herself be carried away by her lust to commit so enormous an offence, made answer to the slave that she was prepared to carry out all the wishes of her husband, without considering at all how richly she deserved punishment at his hands. And after they had discussed together, as women are wont to do, many and various schemes, they settled that on the following night they would, in secret and cautious wise, let Nicolao gain entrance to the house, and afterwards do whatever he might command.

On the following day Lucia went at the usual time for water, and found her master already at the place she had assigned, and rejoicing amain she said to him, "Your wife is quite ready to carry out whatsoever commands you may lay upon her, and to go hence with you at any time and in whatever fashion you may please to order. Nevertheless, it has seemed good to her, and to me likewise, that you, so as not to let your presence here be known to anyone, should return with me to the house, where we will bestow you in hiding. Meantime we will keep a good watch, and when it shall appear to us that the time is ripe, we will set to work to bring our wishes and your own to the end we desire." Nicolao, lending the most perfect faith to Lucia's words, and knowing at the same time that there was no other way whereby he might bring his scheme to a successful issue, went after Lucia, following her afar off; and, having made good his entrance to the house of the Moor without being seen or heard by anyone, Lucia straightway took him and put him in hiding in a certain dark corner where the firewood was kept—a spot to which no one was wont to go save herself. Here they kept him close for six days on account of an accident which did not allow them to do otherwise, because at this particular time the Moors were celebrating a certain feast, and every evening Elia would entertain a great number of his friends at a sumptuous banquet in his own house, but in spite of this Nicolao was every day visited and fed in his darksome hole, sometimes by his wife and sometimes by Lucia.

After the feasting was over, Elia was left in the house without any other male companion, and he fell into a slumber so sound and heavy that the loudest peal of thunder would scarce have awakened him; whereupon the wife, ignorant of what Messer Nicolao was minded to do, beyond taking her and the Turkish girl away with him, let him be brought into the room where the Moor was sleeping like a log. The husband, when he saw that everything had been got in order as he desired, and that he must needs despatch quickly the affair, gave command to his wife, bidding her lay hands on all the money and jewels that she could carry away, for that he was about to depart forthwith; whereupon she lost her head somewhat and went about the house, opening now this casket and now that. In the meantime Nicolao, having chosen his time, softly approached the bed where the Moor lay asleep, and, taking in hand a knife meet for the deed, he dexterously severed the veins of the Moor's throat without making any noise, and left him lying there dead. Then he went towards his wife, who was on the floor stooping down beside an open cassone, searching for some jewels which she had seen in the Moor's possession, and having taken with both his hands the lid of the cassone, he let it descend on the neck of his wife, crushing and forcing it down upon her in such wise that he killed her then and there without even letting her cry out "Alas!"

As soon as he had brought this deed to pass he caught up certain bags filled with pistoles, and divers rich jewels and dainty little gems, and, having carefully made of the same a package, threw it into Lucia's lap, who was overwhelmed with fear at the sight of the corpses of the murdered folk, and was standing in dire terror of her own life. Then he spake thus to her: "My daughter, I have now done all the work which my heart willed me to carry out; so nothing now remains except to return to my companions, forasmuch as, with the passing of this night, will come to an end the season during which they were bound to await my return. And I will likewise take you with me, not only because it pleases me so to do, but also as a reward for the great services you have wrought on my behalf. And moreover, from the boon which I mean to confer upon you, you shall judge whether or not I ought to be charged with the vice of ingratitude." Lucia, when she listened to these words, which were in sooth vastly different from what she in her doubt and uncertainty had expected, rejoiced greatly in her heart, and forthwith declared that she was ready to do whatsoever he might command. Thereupon they went silently out of the house, and, having come to the gate of the curtilage, they opened the same by means of certain small instruments of iron which they had brought with them for the purpose. Then they took to their heels and went along at a pace which was rather quick than slow, and in due time they arrived at the place where Messer Nicolao had left his friends, who at that very same moment were launching their boat in the sea, and getting ready for their departure, for the reason that they had lost all hope of ever seeing him again.

And when they had brought to an end the manifestations of joy they made at the sight of him, they all went on board without any further delay, and, the winds and seas being propitious and calm, they made a short and prosperous voyage to Trapani. When the people heard of their arrival, and knew in what fashion Nicolao had worked his vengeance on the Moor, and how he had punished his wife for her offence, they all praised him highly thereanent, over and beyond the universal delight there was manifested on account of his return. Also Nicolao, so as not to show himself ungrateful for the many benefits he had received from Lucia, took her for his wife, and hereafter found her very dear to him, holding her in great honour as long as he lived.

Masuccio

It may well be said that the wickedness of this woman of Trapani was very great and horrible in its nature—not so much perhaps for the reason that she let herself be mastered by a base slave, as for taking flight with him into Barbary. But, be this as it may, we must assuredly set down the husband as a man of singular virtue, seeing that, without the least reserve, he placed his honour before his life; and, although Fortune was prodigal of her favours in helping him on, it may not be denied that in boldness of heart he showed himself superior to any other man. And what shall we say of the generosity and gratitude which he exhibited towards Lucia, by which he not only changed her from a slave into a free woman, but also joined himself with her in matrimonial union? And certes, seeing that by her aid she restored to him his life, his honour, and his wealth, and let him issue victorious from the undertaking upon which his heart was set, no reward, however great, would have been sufficient for her, except the gift of himself to her, which in sooth he duly made. Therefore it seems to me that, in what respect soever we may give praise and give it worthily, it should be given especially in the case last named, for in the same measure as ingratitude surpasses every other vice, thankfulness for benefits received outdoes all other virtues....

Novel the Twenty-fourth

Argument

A young man loves a certain lady who does not love him in return. Whereupon, having concealed himself in her house, he sees from the place where he is hidden a black Moor taking his pleasure with her. The young man comes forward, and with many insulting words reproves the wicked nature of the woman, and finds his former love for her turned to hatred.

TO THE EXCELLENT COUNT OF ALTAVILLA

Exordium

Because it is my wish, most excellent Signor, to dedicate to you the novel which I have now in hand, I have determined, so as not to turn my pen against those who have never given me any occasion for offence, to keep silent in this story, not only concerning the present condition of the lady and of the lover, but also to conceal the name of the city in which the events of this story came to pass. In it I will let you hear of a strange and very painful adventure which befell a certain ill-starred lover, who found himself brought to such a pass that he was forced to take a part which could not have been, otherwise than most irksome to a man of his high and gentle nature, even after canvassing fully the same. On this account I beg you—if at any time after reading what is aforesaid written you may find yourself hot-blooded and warmed with the fire of love—that you will give me at your pleasure a well-balanced opinion of the adventure, and tell me what course the unhappy lover should have followed, and whether or not he deserves praise with regard to the issue.

The Narrative

In a famous city of Italy there lived not long ago a certain youth of no mean station and influence, very comely to look upon both in face and figure, of most courteous manners, and abounding in every virtue, to whom a thing happened which in sooth happens not seldom to young men of his sort, that is to say, he became very deeply enamoured of a gracious and beautiful lady, the wife of one of the foremost gentlemen of the city aforesaid. And the lady becoming aware of this passion of his, and marking how every day he went about scheming and contriving some method by which he might win his way into her good graces, determined, as is the inborn habit of women, to entangle the poor wight by the working of her art and ingenuity, in her craftily-laid nets on the very first occasion when they might accidentally foregather. To accomplish this task did not cost her much travail; and as soon as she was assured that she had him in hold in such a fashion that it would be no easy matter for him to withdraw himself from the toils, she soon began to let him see little by little that she had scant liking for him, so that he might not for any length of time taste any pleasure or contentment by reason of his love. Thus she went on without ceasing to show him that she set very little store upon himself or upon anything that he did.

On account of this treatment the luckless lover had to endure a life of discontent and intolerable vexation, and, taking account that all his jousting and lavish spending of money, and all the other notable services which he performed on her behalf without intermission, worked no advantage to his cause, but rather seemed to furnish occasion for some fresh show of disdain from her, he essayed over and over again to withdraw himself from the enterprise which he had in hand, and to let his thoughts wander in some other direction. But whenever it became apparent to the lady that he was turning his mind towards this purpose, and that his amorous fervour showed signs of cooling, she would straightway in some fresh fashion of beguilement favour him anew, and thus induce him to set about playing the same game as heretofore. Then, when she knew that she had lured him back according to her plan, she would once more trim her sails for the contrary course, and bring him again into a state of wretchedness. And this deed she would execute with all the skill of an artist, not merely for the sake of vaunting herself as one of the company of honest and beautiful women, for the reason that she had kept so proper a lover in suspense so long, but also that the lover himself might serve as testimony of her simulated virtue, whereby everyone would be constrained to regard as false any evil doings of hers which might hereafter become publicly known.

It thus happened that the ill-fated youth, spending his life for several years in such evil and blameworthy case, without winning for himself so much as a single word to give him hope, determined that, even though he should meet his death thereby, he would stealthily break into the house of the lady, and there work out his purpose as fortune might allow. Wherefore, having got advice as to the season when the gentleman, the husband of the lady in question, would go forth from the city on certain business of his own, and be absent therefor several days, he carefully made entrance to the premises late one evening, and hid himself in an outhouse adjoining the courtyard which was used for storing fodder. He then took his stand behind some empty casks which had been bestowed there, and in this station he remained all the night through, buoyed up with the hope that when the lady should quit the house next morning and betake herself to church, he might be able to find an opportunity of gaining entrance to her chamber, and, once there, to hide himself under her bed, so that the following night he might make trial of his final venture. But, as was the will of his fate, which in sooth ever followed upon his traces, giving him a worse to-morrow for a bad to-day, the lady did not stir out of the house that morning on account of some unlooked-for accident; therefore the young man, having kept his station until the time of nones, with all the pain and patience he was wont to feel and exercise, without any result, made up his mind still to abide there until the following morning. He took a scanty meal off some sweetmeats which he had brought with him for that purpose, and with much weariness of spirit, and with mighty little hope he kept himself without making a sound in the hiding place aforesaid.

Now when a good part of the day had rolled by, he heard a noise and saw come into the courtyard a muleteer, a black Moor who belonged to the household, bringing with him two loads of firewood, which he began to unload forthwith in the courtyard. On account of the noise which he made the lady went to her chamber-window, and at once took to rating the Moor that he had spent so long a time over his errand, and had brought back with him such a mean and miserable lot of wood. The Moor gave her little or nothing in the way of answer, but simply went on easing his mules in their harness and adjusting their packsaddles; and, this done, he entered the storehouse wherein the young man lay concealed in order to fetch some oats for his beasts. As soon as he had finished his task, lo and behold! the lady appeared and went likewise into the storehouse, and after plying the Moor with words of the kind she had lately thrown at him by way of banter, she began to sport with him in tender wise with her hand; and as she went on from one endearment to another, the wretched lover, who stood wonder-stricken, and for his own sake wishful that he could have been worse even than a Moor, if only he could have won the favour which was now being granted to the black without any labour on his part, beheld the lady go and make fast the door, and then, without further ado or demur, throw herself down upon the mules' saddles which lay there, and draw the horrible black fellow towards her. He, without waiting for any farther invitation, at once set himself to his task, and gave the vile wanton what she desired. Alas for you, you goodly youths! Alas, for you, you loyal and blameless lovers! who are wont without ceasing to place your honour and your riches and your life as well in jeopardy for the sake of women faithless and corrupt as this one. Come forward every one of you at this point of my story, and let each one, bearing in mind the while his own case, give me, according to the best judgment he can use, a righteous opinion as to what would have been the meetest course for the wretched youth to follow at this supreme juncture. Certes, according to my own humble understanding, any design of vengeance which he might have framed in his mind with respect to the deed which he had now seen done before his very eyes, would have failed to do full justice.

But to complete my story I will narrate to you truly, what the poor young man felt stirred up to do, after hastily taking counsel with himself. When he had looked upon this deed as aforesaid, and had felt that it went beyond his power to endure the same (his fervent love being changed meantime to hate), he came forth from his lurking-place with his naked sword in his hand, harbouring in his mind the fell purpose of putting an end to the lives of both of them at one thrust; but in that moment of time he felt himself withheld by a certain whisper of reason, which bade him consider well the shameful use he would be making of his sword in staining it with the death of such a base hound, and of such a vile and abandoned woman, as he now deemed her whom he had heretofore rated as the very flower of virtue. Wherefore, having rushed upon them with a terrible cry, he said: "Ah me! how woebegone and wretched is my life, how horrible, how monstrous are the deeds which my cruel fortune has brought before my eyes!" Then, turning towards the Moor, he said: "You, insolent dog that you are, I know not if there be aught for me to say to you, after giving you a word of praise anent your forecast in this matter, except to tell you that I shall remain for ever your debtor because you have delivered me out of the clutches of this savage bitch, who has, in sooth, bereft me of all my welfare and peace of mind." The lady, as soon as she beheld her lover, grew pale as one half dead, and everyone may judge for himself what manner of thoughts possessed her. She, who would sooner have been brought face to face with death—and with reason—had in the meantime cast herself down at the feet of her lover, not to cry him mercy, but to beseech him that he would without farther tarrying give her the death-stroke which was her just meed. Thereupon he, who had by this time made ready the reply he was minded to give her, said: "Oh, wicked and most wanton she-wolf, shame and eternal infamy of all the residue of womankind! through what frenzy, through what passion, through what lustful desire have you suffered yourself to be overcome and subjected to a black hound, a brute beast, or, as it is more meet to say, a monstrous spawn of the earth, like this snarling cur to whom you have given, as a repast, your own corrupt and infected flesh? And though it might appear to you a fine thing to let me be torn and harassed all these years for the sake of this fellow, ought you not at least to have had some care for your own good repute, for the honour of mankind, and for the love which is borne to you by your husband, as well as that which you are in duty bound to bear towards him? He, certes, appears to me to be the most gallant, courteous, and accomplished gentleman now living in this land of ours. Of a surety I know not what else to say than to affirm that you women in the main, unbridled crew as you are, cannot be induced—when you are concerned with those matters which make for your lustful indulgence—by shame, or by fear, or by conscience, to draw any distinction between master and servant, noble and peasant, comely and frightful, so long as, according to your faulty judgment, the fellow upon whom your choice may fall is able and willing to play a lusty part between the sheets. As to that same death which you beg me with such persistence to give to you, it does not seem that you need ask it at my hands so pressingly, forasmuch as, with your name so blackened and disgraced and clouded with shame, you may well and truly reckon yourself as being even worse than dead in the future. Nay, rather I am fain you should still live on in the world, in order that you may be to your own self a testimony of your own unutterable crimes; and that, as often as you may get sight of me, you may suffer anew the pangs of death in calling back to memory your former life, and all the squalor thereof. Wherefore, abide still here on earth, and may bad luck cling to you; indeed, the savour which arises from your tainted person is so great and so foul that I cannot endure to remain any longer in your neighbourhood."

And then, because it was late, he went his way and returned to his own house, without being perceived of anyone, and the lady, who had not given him a single word in reply to what he had said, withdrew sadly to her own room, letting fall many piteous tears. The young man after this adventure gave up the use of the banner which he had heretofore borne in his jousting and tilting matches, and caused to be made another one which carried as a device a fierce black greyhound holding in its paws and its teeth the naked figure of a very beautiful woman, which it was rending and devouring. Every time that the lady saw this ensign it was to her as if an icy blade were being plunged into the very core of her heart, and in such wise this wicked woman, being thus vexed every day, was pierced and torn in spirit without respite.

Masuccio

On account of the monstrous nature of the incident which I have just set before you, I am doubtful whether we should give the lover our highest praise in that he did the one thing which became a man of noble spirit to do, or heap our censure upon the wicked woman, seeing that she, in a way exactly similar, put into practice those same methods which all the others, who are even worse than she, use when nothing happens to interrupt the easy working of their designs. We may therefore hold it as an undoubted fact that those women are indeed rare who, when the opportunity may be given, do not go pirating the goods of whomsoever they may meet—a fact of which every day gives us clear testimony, and our belief in it may be yet further confirmed by the novel which follows. In this the young woman whom I intend to make the subject of my story, the one and singular daughter of her father, desired to be also one and singular in making choice of the very worst of all the many lovers who came to woo her.

Novel the Twenty-fifth

Argument

A young girl is beloved by many suitors, and whilst feeding them with hope, cozens them one and all. One of these pursues her more closely than the others. She, however, has criminal converse with a slave of the house, who lets this thing be known to the lover. Whereupon she dies of grief, and the young man, having purchased the slave, lets him go free.

TO THE ILLUSTRIOUS LORD, MESSER GIULIO D'ACQUAVIVA, DUKE OF ATRI

Exordium

For the reason that I am advised, my illustrious and worthy sir, that you have many a time gathered no small diversion from the reading of my rude unpolished novels, and spoken fair of the same in many words of praise, I am in no way minded to withhold from you your portion of these fruits of mine which seem to please your taste. And because I have, in this part of my book, let fly my shafts at womankind as a target, I am fain to inscribe one of the missiles aforesaid to you, as one who has a good knowledge of this perverse brood, in order that, in the company of any other of their misdeeds which may have come under your notice, this one may cause you to take up, in a worthy spirit and when occasion may arise, the just quarrel which I have with the whole sex. In this wise you will every day lay me under a still greater obligation to you.

The Narrative

According to a report which I once heard from the mouth of a merchant of Ancona, there lived in that city not a great while ago a very rich merchant, well known all through Italy, who had an only daughter named Geronima, very young and beautiful, but vain beyond measure. Now this damsel, who thus gloried herself overmuch on account of her beauties of person, was firmly set in the belief that the greater the number of lovers she might each day bind to her service the greater would be the price at which her beauty would be appraised. For this reason she not only kept fast bound to her all those whom she had already ensnared, but she turned her thoughts to no other aim than to devise plans for the capture of still more victims by new arts of beguilement. So, without letting any one of them ever have a taste of the supreme fruit she held in store, she fed them with wind and leaves and flowers, but she never suffered one of them to go out of her presence altogether void of hope.

And while she went on priding herself over this game of trifling, it chanced that a certain youth of a very noble house, of a comely person and well endowed with all the virtues, applied himself with keener ardour than any others of the suitors had put forth to the task of winning this finished artist in coquetry. In sooth, he let himself be borne away so far into the depths of the sea of love that, notwithstanding the difference and disparity of their several estates, he would assuredly have taken her to wife if it had not been that he, being a poor man, deemed that others would have held him worthy of censure for that he, out of meanness of soul or greed of wealth, had thus made a market of his ancient nobility. Nevertheless, the father of the young damsel aforesaid plied him with importunity without ceasing, setting before him how great would be the profit and advantage which must accrue to him through an alliance of this sort. But the young man, albeit he did not look upon any of these proposals with favour, contrived nevertheless with great ingenuity to keep the business in suspense, so that he might determine whether he might not by a cunning trick bring this scheme to a successful issue. Thus, having planned to enter into relations with some one or other of the household of the young girl, he found that the only one of the servants he could use for this purpose was a certain black Moor belonging to her father, a youth named Alfonso, and for a Moor not ill-looking. He was wont to go about with a stout strap, and let himself out at a price, to carry burdens on his back for whomsoever might have need of his services.

Now the young man, under the pretence of employing this fellow for some errand, would often let him come to his house, treating him with much kindness and caressing, giving him plenty of good things to eat and money to spend on his pleasures, alluring him in such wise that in the end Alfonso became more devoted to him than to his rightful master. Then, as soon as the young man was fully assured that he might trust the Moor, he began to ask him to speak fair of him in the damsel's hearing; and, continuing to discourse in the same strain, he said one day, "My good Alfonso, if in sooth there be any man in the world of whom I am envious, it is of you; forasmuch as fortune gives you free leave to behold and to address your mistress whensoever you wish." And with these and with other very passionate words he went on without ceasing, tempting the slave to listen to him and to do him the service he desired. Wherefore the Moor, who was indeed in no wise lacking in wit and caution, and who was likewise in a measure cognizant of his master's intention to make a match between this young man and his daughter, determined that it would be a grievous waste if such a worthy and well-mannered gentleman as this should, under the name and guise of matrimony, be entangled in toils so fraudulent. So one day in his ill-wrought speech he bade the young man to lay aside entirely this love of his, for the reason that Geronima was a most evil-minded girl, and that he himself had many a time had intercourse with her, having done this thing rather by compulsion than of his own free will. When the poor young lover heard spoken such monstrous words as these, it seemed to him as if his soul was taking its flight from his body; however, collecting his wits somewhat, he put to the Moor many narrow and searching questions, only to find himself more clearly convinced, especially as Alfonso in the end offered to let him see the fact for himself, and as it were to touch it with his own hand—a proposition which he most readily accepted.

In order to carry out this scheme without letting waste any long time over the same, he caused to be made for himself forthwith a strap or band exactly similar to that worn by the Moor, with a certain device thereto by means of which he could put it on or take it off at will in such wise as is the habit of porters. On that same night, when he had determined to betake himself to witness the monstrous spectacle which was to be shown to him, he went to a painter who was his friend and had himself painted black from head to foot, and then, when he had put on certain rags which belonged to the Moor, together with the porter's band, and had changed himself in his carriage and in every other necessary respect, no one would have taken him for aught else than a real porter. As soon as it was nightfall he was led by Alfonso into the merchant's house, and was furthermore made to lie down on a mean, dirty bed. Then the Moor, after he had given full information as to the wonted doings of the abandoned girl, went his way to sleep in the stable.

The young man had not waited a great time before he heard a sound which told him that the door of the place where he lay was being stealthily unfastened, and when it was fully opened he saw and recognized Geronima, the damsel whom he had loved beyond all others, enter the place, bearing a little candle in her hand and glancing on every side to see whether peradventure some other one might not have come into the room. But when she saw that, according to her belief, there was no one else therein except her Alfonso, she went close beside the bed, and, remarking that he was black and suspecting nothing, she quenched the light and lay down by his side, and began straightway according to her wont to awake the sleeping beast.

The wretched lover, when he saw things had so fallen out that, in order to accomplish what he had hitherto desired beyond aught else, he must needs have his heart wrung with grief—when he discovered that his lover's anguish had shaken his manhood in such wise that he would vainly attempt the end he had looked to attain—was several times on the point of letting it be known who he was, and assailing the unpar-

alleled wickedness of the young girl with unbounded and scathing rebukes. But after
carefully considering the affair, he reckoned that he would not himself get full satisfaction from the adventure, except it should be duly brought to its appointed issue,
and except the damsel should in the end be left by him covered with shame and grief
and sorrow. Whereupon he determined once for all to put compulsion on his hu-
mour, chilled as it was by grief and indignation, and then, by a punishment of the sort
aforesaid, to work vengeance upon the girl, not only on his own account, but likewise
on account of all the many others who had been befooled and flouted by her. So with
no slight difficulty he brought to completion the course he had resolved to pursue.
And when he had done this, he began to address her, his indignation raging strong
and fierce as ever, in the following words: "Ah foolish, insensate, profligate wretch,
headstrong and insolent beast that you are! Where are now all the charms with which
you were wont to trick yourself out? Where is now your pride, you who deemed yourself fair beyond all others, and imagined in your haughtiness that, with the aid of this
and of your wealth, you could touch the very heavens with your head? Where are
those broods of ill-starred lovers of yours, wretches whom you fed with false hopes,
while every day you mocked and derided them? Where is now that foolhardy insolence which led you to seek to get me for your husband? What manner of flesh was it
you were minded to give me for my enjoyment? Was it the same which you had already given as a meet repast to a black carrion crow, to a filthy porter, to a savage
hound, clad in vile rags and loaded with chains? As you must of a certainty be aware,
I have ever been careful how I might with all manner of artifices deck out my person
with divers fine garments, and use pleasant odours, solely with the desire of exhibiting
myself in your sight in fashion which would please you; but, finding that naught I
could do proved of any avail, I bethought me of putting on this dress, the habit of the
basest menial, in which you saw me when you first came in. Of this you assured yourself by examining me closely with a lighted candle, and were no doubt mightily
pleased with what you thought you had found. And afterwards I, as you yourself must
know well, found it no light task to labour in the field which by right belongs to this
Moor. Before this you will, I doubt not, have discovered by the sound of my voice that
I am the man whom you have befooled and fed with wind for these many years past
by means of your wheedling looks. Moreover, it grieves me to think that you, beguiled
by holding me so completely under your yoke, may have been able to boast in the past
that you had bettered your former condition a hundred thousandfold; though, indeed, you may now set this down as your last bit of good fortune, for be assured that I
would rather let myself be cut in quarters than ever again admit that you are worthy
of being mated with myself. Nor need you flatter yourself that you will be able, as
heretofore, to let quench your hot lust in the arms of your beloved Moor; for it is by
his hand that I now find myself unshackled from the bonds which your lures have cast
around me, and as some reward for the great service he has wrought me I have determined to make a free man of him and release him from the servitude he owes to your
father. And if you should ever henceforth take it upon yourself to dupe or to feed with
false hopes any goodly youths in such fashion as you have befooled them in the past,
or to put your flouts upon them anew, be well assured that this scheming of yours will
be baulked, forasmuch as I myself will set to work to let this abominable wickedness

of yours become the public talk in every part of this our city, and I will make your name the byword in the mouths of the common folk, and thereby let eternal disgrace fall upon you. In sooth, I shall never deem that I have vituperated you enough for the vile and wicked profligacy you have practised. But these rags which I now wear, and the clothes upon this bed—which have been to you heretofore so gracious and sweet-smelling and pleasant—stink in my nostrils so horribly that I am constrained to go my way forthwith; therefore get you gone quickly hence, and on your way call for me your worthy lover, who is waiting in the stable, in order that he may convey me privately out of this dark prison in which I am not inclined to tarry any longer."

The woebegone and most wretched Geronima, who indeed knew full well who was the man she had with her the very first word he spoke, would assuredly have made an end straightway to her miserable life had a knife meet for such a deed been in her hand. All the time he was speaking, she, without giving him back a single word in reply, went on with her bitter weeping, and at last, according to his command, she got up from the bed and called the Moor in a soft voice. Then, as the young man wished, she let them both out of the house, and after she had locked the door she returned to her own chamber, and there, under the colour of some excuse, she thenceforth remained grief-stricken to death, and shedding as many tears as a well full of water would have supplied. In a few days' time she died, whether by grief or by poison I know not. The noble youth, having let the whole affair get noised abroad, and having likewise enjoyed no small pleasure from the punishment and death of the young girl, purchased the Moor and set him at liberty. He himself, now that he was delivered and unfettered from his passion, lived happily for a long time, taking much pleasure in his lusty youth.

Masuccio

What man having listened to this novel will hereafter nurse any doubts concerning the crowning profligacy of womankind? If he should turn over in his mind the stories I have told, will it not appear to him as though he had seen the same with his own eyes? I, who from very shame of myself am kept back from telling you (for I, like the rest of men, was born of a woman) how, when they are assailed by overpowering lust and unbridled rage, they employ certain means for saving their credit, in order that, as they believe, their offence may be less. If you who read this understand my meaning, there is no need for me to say anything more to you; but if you should still be in doubt, then find someone else who may declare the purport of these obscure terms of mine. I am still bound to write of divers others who, being blinded by their fiery lust, and fearing that their secret should be known, or that they should abase themselves to the conversation of men of mean estate, have not shrunk from submitting themselves to brute beasts—things of which I have heard tell as the very truth, and have myself had experience, even as a matter which I could touch with my own hands. Such nefarious working as this is in sooth for the most part practised by the very women who hold themselves to be wise beyond all others.

TRANSLATED BY W. G. WATERS

5

From *Hecatommithi*

Giambattista Giraldi Cinzio

The Italian playwright, literary critic, and prose writer Giambattista Giraldi (1504–1573) was known widely as Il Cinzio or Cynthio. He began writing novellas in 1528. His play *Orbecche* (1541) was the first original Italian tragedy in classical style. *Gli Hecatommithi*, or *The Hundred Stories*, one of which follows here, was published in 1565 and contained source material for eight of Giraldi's own plays as well as Shakespeare's *Measure for Measure*. The story included, "A Moorish Captain Takes to Wife a Venetian Dame," was the source for *Othello*.

A Moorish Captain Takes to Wife a Venetian Dame

There once lived in Venice a Moor, who was very valiant and of a handsome person; and having given proofs in war of great skill and prudence, he was highly esteemed by the Signoria of the Republic, who in rewarding deeds of valour advanced the interests of the State.

It happened that a virtuous lady of marvellous beauty, named Disdemona, fell in love with the Moor, moved thereto by his valour; and he, vanquished by the beauty and the noble character of Disdemona, returned her love; and their affection was so mutual that, although the parents of the lady strove all they could to induce her to take another husband, she consented to marry the Moor; and they lived in such harmony and peace in Venice that no word ever passed between them that was not affectionate and kind.

Now it happened at this time that the Signoria of Venice made a change in the troops whom they used to maintain in Cyprus, and they appointed the Moor commander of the soldiers whom they dispatched thither. Joyful as was the Moor at the honour proffered him, such dignity being only conferred on men of noble rank and well-tried faith, and who had displayed bravery in arms,—yet his pleasure was lessened when he reflected on the length and dangers of the voyage, fearing that Disdemona would be pained at his absence. But Disdemona, who had no other happiness in the world than the Moor, and who rejoiced to witness the testimony of his valour her husband had received from so powerful and noble a Republic, was all impatient that he should embark with his troops, and longed to accompany him to so honourable a post. And all the more it vexed her to see the Moor so troubled; and not knowing what could be the reason, one day, when they were at dinner, she said to him, "How is it, O Moor, that when so honourable a post has been conferred on you by the Signoria, you are thus melancholy?"

The Moor answered Disdemona, "My pleasure at the honour I have received is disturbed by the love I bear you; for I see that of necessity one of two things must happen,—either that I take you with me to encounter the perils of the sea, or, to save you from this danger, I must leave you here in Venice. The first could not be otherwise than serious to me, for all the toil you would have to bear and every danger that might befall you would cause me extreme anxiety and pain, yet, were I to leave you behind me, I should be hateful to myself, since in parting from you I should part from my own life."

Disdemona, on hearing this, replied: "My husband, what thoughts are these that wander through your mind? Why let such things disturb you? I will accompany you whithersoe'er you go, were it to pass through fire, as now to cross the water in a safe and well-provided ship; if indeed there are toils and perils to encounter, I will share them with you. And in truth I should think you loved me little were you to leave me here in Venice, denying me to bear you company, or could believe that I would liefer bide in safety here than share the dangers that await you. Prepare then for the voyage with all the readiness which the dignity of the post you hold deserves."

The Moor, in the fulness of his joy, threw his arms around his wife's neck, and with an affectionate and tender kiss exclaimed, "God keep you long in such love, dear wife!" Then speedily donning his armour, and having prepared everything for his expedition, he embarked on board the galley with his wife and all his troops, and, setting sail, they pursued their voyage, and with a perfectly tranquil sea arrived safely at Cyprus.

Now amongst the soldiery there was an Ensign, a man of handsome figure, but of the most depraved nature in the world. This man was in great favour with the Moor, who had not the slightest idea of his wickedness; for, despite the malice lurking in his heart, he cloaked with proud and valorous speech and with a specious presence the villainy of his soul with such art that he was to all outward show another Hector or Achilles. This man had likewise taken with him his wife to Cyprus, a young, and fair, and virtuous lady; and being of Italian birth she was much loved by Disdemona, who spent the greater part of every day with her.

In the same Company there was a certain Captain of a troop, to whom the Moor was much affectioned. And Disdemona, for this cause, knowing how much her husband valued him, showed him proofs of the greatest kindness, which was all very grateful to the Moor. Now the wicked Ensign, regardless of the faith that he had pledged his wife, no less than of the friendship, fidelity, and obligation which he owed the Moor, fell passionately in love with Disdemona, and bent all his thoughts to achieve his conquest; yet he dared not to declare his passion openly, fearing that, should the Moor perceive it, he would at once kill him. He therefore sought in various ways, and with secret guile, to betray his passion to the lady; but she, whose every wish was centred in the Moor, had no thought for this Ensign more than for any other man; and all the means he tried to gain her love had no more effect than if he had not tried them. But the Ensign imagined that the cause of his ill success was that Disdemona loved the Captain of the troop; and he pondered how to remove him from her sight. The love which he had borne the lady now changed into the bitterest hate, and, having failed in his purposes, he devoted all his thoughts to plot the death of the Captain of the troop and to divert the affection of the Moor from Disdemona. After revolving in his mind various schemes, all alike wicked, he at length resolved to accuse her of unfaithfulness to her husband, and to represent the Captain as her paramour. But knowing the singular love the Moor bore to Disdemona, and the friendship which he had for the Captain, he was well aware that, unless he practised an artful fraud upon the Moor, it were impossible to make him give ear to either accusation; wherefore he resolved to wait until time and circumstance should open a path for him to engage in his foul project.

Not long afterwards it happened that the Captain, having drawn his sword upon a soldier of the guard, and struck him, the Moor deprived him of his rank; whereat Disdemona was deeply grieved, and endeavoured again and again to reconcile her husband to the man. This the Moor told to the wicked Ensign, and how his wife importuned him so much about the Captain that he feared he should be forced at last to receive him back to service. Upon this hint the Ensign resolved to act, and began to work his web of intrigue. "Perchance," said he, "the lady Disdemona may have good reason to look kindly on him."

"And wherefore?" said the Moor.

"Nay, I would not step 'twixt man and wife," replied the Ensign, "but let your eyes be witness to themselves."

In vain the Moor went on to question the officer,—he would proceed no further; nevertheless, his words left a sharp, stinging thorn in the Moor's heart, who could think of nothing else, trying to guess their meaning and lost in melancholy. And one day, when his wife had been endeavouring to pacify his anger toward the Captain, and praying him not to be unmindful of ancient services and friendship for one small fault, especially since peace had been made between the Captain and the soldier he had struck, the Moor was angered, and exclaimed, "Great cause have you, Disdemona, to care so anxiously about this man! Is he a brother, or your kinsman, that he should be so near your heart?"

The lady, with all gentleness and humility, replied, "Be not angered, my dear lord; I have no other cause to bid me speak than sorrow that I see you lose so dear a friend as, by your own words, this Captain has been to you; nor has he done so grave a fault that you should bear him so much enmity. Nay, but you Moors are of so hot a nature that every little trifle moves you to anger and revenge."

Still more enraged at these words, the Moor replied, "I could bring proofs—by heaven it mocks belief! but for the wrongs I have endured revenge must satisfy my wrath."

Disdemona, in astonishment and fright, seeing her husband's anger kindled against her, so contrary to his wont, said humbly and with timidity, "None save a good intent has led me thus to speak with you, my lord; but to give cause no longer for offence, I'll never speak a word more on the subject."

The Moor, observing the earnestness with which his wife again pleaded for the Captain, began to guess the meaning of the Ensign's words; and in deep melancholy he went to seek that villain and induce him to speak more openly of what he knew.

Then the Ensign, who was bent upon injuring the unhappy lady, after feigning at first great reluctance to say aught that might displease the Moor, at length pretended to yield to his entreaties, and said, "I can't deny it pains me to the soul to be thus forced to say what needs must be more hard to hear than any other grief; but since you will it so, and that the regard I owe your honour compels me to confess the truth, I will no longer refuse to satisfy your questions and my duty. Know, then, that for no other reason is your lady vexed to see the Captain in disfavour than the pleasure that she has in his company whenever he comes to your house, and all the more since she has taken an aversion to your blackness."

These words went straight to the Moor's heart; but in order to hear more (now that he believed true all that the Ensign had told him) he replied, with a fierce glance, "By heavens, I scarce can hold this hand from plucking out that tongue of thine, so bold, which dares to speak such slander of my wife!"

"Captain," replied the Ensign, "I looked for such reward for these my faithful offices,—none else; but since my duty, and the jealous care I bear your honour, have carried me thus far, I do repeat, so stands the truth, as you have heard it from these lips; and if the lady Disdemona hath, with a false show of love for you, blinded your eyes to what you should have seen, this is no argument but that I speak the truth. Nay, this same Captain told it me himself, like one whose happiness is incomplete until he can declare it to another; and, but that I feared your anger, I should have given him, when he told it me, his merited reward, and slain him. But since informing you of what concerns you more than any other man brings me so undeserved a recompense, would I had held my peace, since silence might have spared me your displeasure."

Then the Moor, burning with indignation and anguish, said, "Make thou these eyes self-witnesses of what thou tell'st, or on thy life I'll make thee wish thou hadst been born without a tongue."

"An easy task it would have been," replied the villain, "when he was used to visit at your house; but now that you have banished him, not for just cause, but for mere frivolous pretext, it will be hard to prove the truth. Still, I do not forego the hope to make you witness of that which you will not credit from my lips."

Thus they parted. The wretched Moor, struck to the heart as by a barbed dart, returned to his home, and awaited the day when the Ensign should disclose to him the truth which was to make him miserable to the end of his days. But the evil-minded Ensign was, on his part, not less troubled by the chastity which he knew the lady Disdemona observed inviolate; and it seemed to him impossible to discover a means of making the Moor believe what he had falsely told him; and, turning the matter over in his thoughts in various ways, the villain resolved on a new deed of guilt.

Disdemona often used to go, as I have already said, to visit the Ensign's wife, and remained with her a good part of the day. Now, the Ensign observed that she carried about with her a handkerchief, which he knew the Moor had given her, finely embroidered in the Moorish fashion, and which was precious to Disdemona, nor less so to the Moor. Then he conceived the plan of taking this kerchief from her secretly, and thus laying the snare for her final ruin. The Ensign had a little daughter, a child three years of age, who was much loved by Disdemona, and one day, when the unhappy lady had gone to pay a visit at the house of this vile man, he took the little child up in his arms and carried her to Disdemona, who took her and pressed her to her bosom; whilst at the same instant this traitor, who had extreme dexterity of hand, drew the kerchief from her sash so cunningly that she did not notice him, and overjoyed he took his leave of her.

Disdemona, ignorant of what had happened, returned home, and, busy with other thoughts, forgot the handkerchief. But a few days afterwards, looking for it and not finding it, she was in alarm, lest the Moor should ask her for it, as he oft was wont to do. Meanwhile, the wicked Ensign, seizing a fit opportunity, went to the Captain of the troop, and with crafty malice left the handkerchief at the head of his bed without his discovering the trick, until the following morning, when, on his getting out of bed, the handkerchief fell upon the floor, and he set his foot upon it. And not being able to imagine how it had come into his house, knowing that it belonged to Disdemona, he resolved to give it to her; and waiting until the Moor had gone from home, he went to the back door and knocked. It seemed as if fate conspired with the Ensign to work the death of the unhappy Disdemona. Just at that time the Moor returned home, and hearing a knocking at the back door, he went to the window, and in a rage exclaimed, "Who knocks there?" The Captain, hearing the Moor's voice, and fearing lest he should come down stairs and attack him, took to flight without answering a word. The Moor went down, and opening the door hastened into the street and looked about, but in vain. Then, returning into the house in great anger, he demanded of his wife who it was that had knocked at the door. Disdemona replied, as was true, that she did not know; but the Moor said, "It seemed to me the Captain."

"I know not," answered Disdemona, "whether it was he or another person."

The Moor restrained his fury, great as it was, wishing to do nothing before consulting the Ensign, to whom he hastened instantly, and told him all that had passed, praying him to gather from the Captain all he could respecting the affair. The Ensign, overjoyed at the occurrence, promised the Moor to do as he requested, and one day he took occasion to speak with the Captain when the Moor was so placed that he could see and hear them as they conversed. And whilst talking to him of every other subject than of Disdemona, he kept laughing all the time aloud, and, feigning astonishment, he made various movements with his head and hands, as if listening to some tale of marvel. As soon as the Moor saw the Captain depart, he went up to the Ensign to hear what he had said to him. And the Ensign, after long entreaty, at length said, "He has hidden from me nothing, and has told me that he has been used to visit your wife whenever you went from home, and that on the last occasion she gave him this handkerchief which you presented to her when you married her."

The Moor thanked the Ensign, and it seemed now clear to him that, should he find Disdemona not to have the handkerchief, it was all true that the Ensign had told to him. One day, therefore, after dinner, in conversation with his wife on various subjects, he asked her for the kerchief. The unhappy lady, who had been in great fear of this, grew red as fire at this demand; and to hide the scarlet of her cheeks, which was closely noted by the Moor, she ran to a chest and pretended to seek the handkerchief, and after hunting for it a long time, she said, "I know not how it is—I cannot find it; can you, perchance, have taken it?"

"If I had taken it," said the Moor, "why should I ask it of you? but you will look better another time."

On leaving the room, the Moor fell to meditating how he should put his wife to death, and likewise the Captain of the troop, so that their death should not be laid to his charge. And as he ruminated over this day and night, he could not prevent his wife's observing that he was not the same towards her as he had been wont; and she said to him again and again, "What is the matter? What troubles you? How comes it that you, who were the most light-hearted man in the world, are now so melancholy?"

The Moor feigned various reasons in reply to his wife's questioning, but she was not satisfied, and, although conscious that she had given the Moor no cause, by act or deed, to be so troubled, yet she feared that he might have grown wearied of her; and she would say to the Ensign's wife, "I know not what to say of the Moor; he used to be all love towards me; but within these few days he has become another man; and much I fear that I shall prove a warning to young girls not to marry against the wishes of their parents, and that the Italian ladies may learn from me not to wed a man whom nature and habitude of life estrange from us. But as I know the Moor is on such terms of friendship with your husband, and communicates to him all his affairs, I pray you, if you have heard from him aught that you may tell me of, fail not to befriend me." And as she said this, she wept bitterly.

The Ensign's wife, who knew the whole truth (her husband wishing to make use of her to compass the death of Disdemona), but could never consent to such a project, dared not, from fear of her husband, disclose a single circumstance: all she said was, "Beware lest you give any cause of suspicion to your husband, and show to him by every means your fidelity and love."—"Indeed I do so," replied Disdemona, "but it is all of no avail."

Meanwhile the Moor sought in every way to convince himself of what he fain would have found untrue, and he prayed the Ensign to contrive that he might see the handkerchief in the possession of the Captain. This was a difficult matter to the wicked Ensign; nevertheless, he promised to use every means to satisfy the Moor of the truth of what he said.

Now, the Captain had a wife at home who worked the most marvellous embroidery upon lawn, and seeing the handkerchief, which belonged to the Moor's wife, she resolved, before it was returned to her, to work one like it. As she was engaged in this task, the Ensign observed her standing at a window, where she could be seen by all the passers-by in the street, and he pointed her out to the Moor, who was now perfectly convinced of his wife's guilt. Then he arranged with the Ensign to slay Disdemona and the Captain of the troop, treating them as it seemed they both deserved. And the Moor prayed the Ensign that he would kill the Captain, promising eternal gratitude to him. But the Ensign at first refused to undertake so dangerous a task, the Captain being a man of equal skill and courage; until at length, after much entreating and being richly paid, the Moor prevailed on him to promise to attempt the deed.

Having formed this resolution, the Ensign, going out one dark night, sword in hand, met the Captain on his way to visit a courtesan, and struck him a blow on his right thigh, which cut off his leg and felled him to the earth. Then the Ensign was on the point of putting an end to his life, when the Captain, who was a courageous man and used to the sight of blood and death, drew his sword, and, wounded as he was, kept on his defence, exclaiming with a loud voice, "I'm murdered!" Thereupon the Ensign, hearing the people come running up, with some of the soldiers who were lodged thereabouts, took to his heels to escape being caught; then turning about again, he joined the crowd, pretending to have been attracted by the noise. And when he saw the Captain's leg cut off, he judged that, if not already dead, the blow must, at all events, end his life; and whilst in his heart he was rejoiced at this, he yet feigned to compassionate the Captain as he had been his brother.

The next morning the tidings of this affair spread through the whole city, and reached the ears of Disdemona; whereat she, who was kind-hearted and little dreamed that any ill would betide her, evinced the greatest grief at the calamity. This served but to confirm the Moor's suspicions, and he went to seek for the Ensign, and said to him, "Do you know that my wife is in such grief at the Captain's accident that she is well nigh gone mad."

"And what could you expect, seeing he is her very soul?" replied the Ensign.

"Ay, soul forsooth!" exclaimed the Moor; "I'll draw the soul from out her body; call me no man if that I fail to shut the world upon this wretch."

Then they consulted of one means and another—poison and daggers—to kill poor Disdemona, but could resolve on nothing. At length the Ensign said, "A plan comes to my mind, which will give you satisfaction and raise cause for no suspicion. It is this: the house in which you live is very old, and the ceiling of your chamber has many cracks; I propose we take a stocking, filled with sand, and beat Disdemona with it till she dies; thus will her body bear no signs of violence. When she is dead we can pull down a portion of the ceiling, and thus make it seem as if a rafter falling on her head had killed the lady. Suspicion cannot rest on you, since all men will impute her death to accident."

This cruel counsel pleased the Moor, and he only waited for a fitting time to execute the plot. One night, when he and Disdemona had retired to bed, the Ensign, whom the Moor had concealed in a closet which opened into the chamber, raised a noise in the closet, according to a concerted plan; whereat the Moor said to his wife, "Did you not hear that noise?"

"Indeed I heard it," she replied.

"Rise," said the Moor, "and see what 'tis."

The unhappy Disdemona rose from bed, and the instant she approached the closet, out rushed the Ensign, and being strong and of stout nerve, he beat her cruelly with the bag of sand across her back; upon which Disdemona fell to the ground, scarce able to draw her breath; but with the little voice she had left, she called upon the Moor for aid. But the Moor, leaping from bed, exclaimed, "Thou wickedest of women, thus has thy falseness found its just reward, the recompense to wives who, counterfeiting love, place horns upon their husbands' brows."

The wretched lady, hearing these words, and feeling that she was near her end, (for the Ensign had given her another blow,) appealed to the justice of Heaven, since justice here had failed her, in proof of her fidelity and truth; and as she was thus calling Heaven to witness, the wicked Ensign inflicted a third blow, under which she sank lifeless on the floor.

Then the Ensign and the Moor, laying Disdemona on the bed and wounding her head, pulled down part of the ceiling of the chamber, as they had arranged; whereupon the Moor began to call aloud for help, exclaiming that the house was falling. Hearing this uproar, the neighbours all came running up, and there found Disdemona lying dead beneath a rafter,—a sight which, from the good life of that poor lady, did fill all hearts with sorrow.

On the following day Disdemona was buried, followed to the grave by the universal grief of the people. But Heaven, the just regarder of all hearts, willed not that so wicked a deed should go unpunished. Ere long the Moor, whom Disdemona had loved more than her own life, began to feel such sorrow at her loss that he went wandering about as one bereft of reason, searching in every part of the house. And reflecting in his thoughts that the Ensign had been the cause that he had lost, with Disdemona, all joy in life, he conceived so deep a hatred to that wicked man he could not bear to set eyes on him, and had it not been for his fear of the inviolable justice of the Signoria of Venice, he would have slain him openly. But being unable to do this with safety, he deprived him of his rank, and would not allow him to remain in his Company; whereat such an enmity arose between the two that no greater or more deadly can be imagined.

The Ensign, that wickedest of all bad men, now turned his thoughts to injuring the Moor; and seeking out the Captain, whose wound was by this time healed, and who went about with a wooden leg in place of the one that had been cut off, he said to him, "'Tis time you should be avenged for your lost limb; and if you will come with me to Venice, I'll tell you who the malefactor is, whom I dare not mention to you here for many reasons; and I will bring you proofs."

The Captain of the troop, whose anger returned fiercely, but without knowing why, thanked the Ensign, and went with him to Venice. On arriving there the Ensign told him that it was the Moor who had cut off his leg, on account of the suspicion he had formed of Disdemona's conduct with him; and for that reason he had slain her, and then spread the report that the ceiling had fallen and killed her. Upon hearing which, the Captain accused the Moor to the Signoria, both of having cut off his leg and killed his wife, and called the Ensign to witness the truth of what he said. The Ensign declared both charges to be true, for that the Moor had disclosed to him the whole plot, and had tried to persuade him to perpetrate both crimes; and that, having afterwards killed his wife out of jealousy he had conceived, he had narrated to him the manner in which he had perpetrated her death.

The Signoria of Venice, when they heard of the cruelty inflicted by a barbarian upon a lady of their city, commanded that the Moor's arms should be pinioned in Cyprus, and he be brought to Venice, where, with many tortures, they sought to draw from him the truth. But the Moor, bearing with unyielding courage all the torment, denied the whole charge so resolutely that no confession could be drawn from him. But, although by his constancy and firmness he escaped death, he was, after being confined for several days in prison, condemned to perpetual banishment, in which he was eventually slain by the kinsfolk of Disdemona, as he merited. The Ensign returned to his own country, and, following up his wonted villainy, he accused one of his companions of having sought to persuade him to kill an enemy of his, who was a man of noble rank; whereupon this person was arrested and put to the torture; but when he denied the truth of what his accuser had declared, the Ensign himself was likewise tortured to make him prove the truth of his accusations; and he was tortured so that his body ruptured, upon which he was removed from prison and taken home, where he died a miserable death. Thus did Heaven avenge the innocence of Disdemona; and all these events were narrated by the Ensign's wife, who was privy to the whole, after his death, as I have told them here.

TRANSLATED BY JOHN EDWARD TAYLOR

Love Poetry in Black and White

A new genre of love poetry emerged in the Renaissance as the result of the success of Francesco Petrarca, whose love poems for Laura became the occasion for an explosion of imagery that was later conventionalized as Petrarchism. In numerous sonnets the poet Giambattista Marino pushed the new sensibilities and techniques into "baroque" directions, sometimes called Marinism. The imagery became more far-fetched; there were frosty antitheses and a prevailing love for puns, "concetti"—which found their equivalents in what is known in English writing as metaphysical conceits. Marino wrote a sonnet on an interracial love situation in this manner, employing the traditional rhetoric of racial contrasts for aesthetic purposes. It was this fit between the color difference of lovers and the rhetorical needs of Marinism for contrasts and for clever ways of bridging them that made this genre of poems work. There are also echoes in it to the biblical *Song of Songs*. In the English tradition, it was a Latin poem by George Herbert that may have inspired many English seventeenth- and eighteenth-century poems that followed it, among them those by John Cleveland, Eldrett Revett, Edward Herbert of Cherbury, and James de la Cour.

"The Beautiful Slave-Girl"

Giambattista Marino

By 1623 Giambattista Marino (1569–1625) had reached the peak of his popularity as a poet, satirist, and prose writer who could unite both ancient and modern. His chief work, *L'Adone*, a narrative poem of the Renaissance epic with its foundation in classical mythology, displays the trademark harmony, lush imagery, varied metaphorical patterns, and elaborate technique and baroque language that would come to be called Marinism. He is surpassed among Italian writers only by Petrarch in appeal and emulation (though Marino's popularity faded by the end of the seventeenth century). Marino's sonnet "Bella schiava" (1614), here presented in the Italian original together with a new verse translation by Norman R. Shapiro, is a love poem that playfully develops a set of paradoxically resolved contrasts between black and white, ebony and ivory, slave status and enslavement of the heart.

Bella schiava

Negra sì, ma se' bella, o di Natura
fra le belle d'Amor leggiadro mostro;
Fosca è l'alba appo te, perde e s'oscura
presso l'ebano tuo l'avorio e l'ostro.

Or quando, or dove il mondo antico o il nostro
vide sì viva mai, sentì sì pura
o luce uscir di tenebroso inchiostro,
o di spento carbon nascere arsura?

Servo di chi m'è serva, ecco ch'avolto
porto di bruno laccio il core intorno,
che per candida man non fia mai sciolto.

La 've più ardi, o Sol, sol per tuo scorno
un Sole è nato; un Sol, che nel bel volto
porta la Notte, ed ha negli occhi il Giorno.

The Beautiful Slave-Girl

Black you are, one of Nature's monsters, yes;
yet fairest of Love's beauties must you be:
powder seems dark; fine ivory, dark no less;
and dawn turns dusk, beside your ebony.

Has our world ever, or Antiquity,
seen light so pure, so sprightly, effervesce
and, lustrous, spring from ink's dark mystery,
or fire flare, new, from spent coals' lifelessness?

A slave to her, my slave, come I, heart twined
about with tawny cords: her tribute, quite;
nor white be hands that would this heart unbind.

Where most you burn, O Sun, for your despite
a Sun is born; borne in its eyes I find
the light of Day, and on its fair face, Night.

TRANSLATED BY NORMAN R. SHAPIRO

"A Negress Courts Cestus, a Man of a Different Colour"

George Herbert

George Herbert (1593–1633) is lauded as a metaphysical devotional poet of the stature of John Donne, his lifelong friend. Born in Wales and educated at Cambridge University, Herbert was ordained an Anglican deacon in 1624 and became a priest in 1630. Though he wrote mostly sacred poetry, he did compose verses on secular love, most notably in an influential Latin poem, "Aethiopissa ambit Cestum diversi coloris Virum," translated into English as "A Negress Courts Cestus, a Man of a Different Colour." Readers have seen in this poem an early principled refutation of color prejudice and an articulation of the maxim that black is beautiful. Herbert's poem contains many of the rhetorical contrasts that later poets would employ.

Aethiopissa ambit Cestum diversi coloris Virum

Quid mihi si facies nigra est? hoc, Ceste, colore
    Sunt etiam tenebrae, quas tamen optat amor.
Cernis ut exusta semper sit fronte viator;
    Ah longum, quae te deperit, errat iter.
Si nigro sit terra solo, quis despicit arvum?
    Claude oculos, et erunt omnia nigra tibi:
Aut aperi, et cernes corpus quas projicit umbras;
    Hoc saltem officio fungar amore tui.
Cum mihi sit facies fumus, quas pectore flammas
    Jamdudum tacite delituisse putes?
Dure, negas? O fata mihi praesaga doloris,
    Quae mihi lugubres contribuere genas!

A Negress Courts Cestus, a Man of a Different Colour

What if my face be black? O Cestus, hear!
    Such colour Night brings, which yet Love holds dear.
You see a Trav'ller has a sunburnt face;
    And I, who pine for thee, a long road trace.
If earth be black, who shall despise the ground?
    Shut now your eyes, and, lo, all black is found;

Or ope, a shadow-casting form you see;
    This be my loving post to fill for thee.
Seeing my face is smoke, what fire has burn'd
    Within my silent bosom, by thee spurn'd!
Hard-hearted man, dost still my love refuse?
    Lo, Grief's prophetic hue my cheek imbues!

TRANSLATED BY ALEXANDER B. GROSART

"A Faire Nimph Scorning a Black Boy Courting Her"

John Cleveland

John Cleveland (1613–1658) distinguished himself as a scholar at Cambridge before being drawn in to the English Civil Wars on the side of the royalists. Literary scholars attribute to him the origination of the use of extreme, almost discordant, metaphysical conceits, a technique known as Clevelandism. His 1658 poem "A Faire Nimph Scorning a Black Boy Courting Her" is not only inspired by Herbert's "A Negress Courts Cestus, a Man of a Different Colour" but is virtually identical with a poem of the same title published by Eldred Revett, making the determination of authorship difficult in this case.

NYMPH. Stand off, and let me take the aire,
   Why should the smoak pursue the faire?
BOY. My face is smoak, thence may be guest
   What flames within have scorch'd my brest.
NYMPH. The flame of love I cannot view,
   For the dark Lanthorne of thy hue.
BOY. And yet this Lanthorne keeps loves Taper
   Surer then yours, that's of white paper.
   Whatever Midnight hath been here,
   The Moon-shine of your face can cleare.
NYMPH. My Moon of an Ecclipse is 'fraid,
   If thou should'st interpose thy shade.
BOY. Yet one thing (sweet-heart) I will ask,
   Take me for a new fashion'd Mask.
NYMPH. Done: but my bargaine shall be this,
   I'le throw my Maske off when I kiss.
BOY. Our curl'd embraces shall delight
   To checquer limbs with black and white.
NYMPH. Thy inke, my paper, make me guesse,
   Our Nuptiall bed will prove a Presse;
   And in our sports, if any come,
   They'l read a wanton Epigram.
BOY. Why should my Black thy love impaire?
   Let the darke shop commend the ware:

Or if thy love from black forbeares,
I'le strive to wash it of with teares.

NYMPH. Spare fruitless teares, since thou must needs
Still weare about thee mourning weeds:
Teares can no more affection win,
Then wash thy Æthiopian skin.

"The Inversion"
"One Enamour'd on a Black-moor"
"A Black Nymph Scorning a Fair Boy Courting Her"

Eldred Revett

Little is known about the English poet Eldred Revett; even the dates of his birth and death are uncertain. In 1657 he published a verse collection, *Selected Poems: Humane and Divine*, which included a poem by Revett's contemporary and occasional poetic addressee Richard Lovelace. Revett's work appeared in several other poetry volumes in the 1650s. In his poems "The Inversion," "One Enamour'd on a *Black-moor*," and "A Black Nymph Scorning a Fair Boy Courting Her," he continues the Marino-Herbert tradition but in going back also to classical conventions of nymphs and satyrs, draws out more of the comic implications of the genre of white-black love poetry.

The Inversion

NYMPH. Stand off fair Boy, thou wilt affright
My solitude with sudden light.
BOY. My face is light, thence may be guest
The truth of my transparent brest.
NYMPH. The truth of Love I cannot view.
For the full lustre of thy hew.
BOY. The lustre's sooner pervious made
Then your impenitrable shade.
What-ever Noon, my day doth trim,
Your thick how-ever Mist may dim.
NYMPH. My mist would fear to break away
If you should intermix your ray.
BOY. Our curled embraces shall delight
With Limbs to shuffle day and night:
NYMPH. Thy light my darkness make me fear
Our bed a *Chaos* would appear;
And in our sports did any pass,
They'd see the indigested Mass.

BOY. Yet one thing sweet-heart let me crave,
       Me for a new-false mirror have;
NYMPH. Yes, but my bargain must request,
       I throw my glass by, when undrest:
BOY. Why should my hue thee less delight,
       Let the Star-foyles set of the night:
       Or if thy love from light forbeares,
       I'le strive to put it out with teares.
NYMPH. Spare fruitless teares, since thou must needs
       Still have on thy transfigur'd weeds,
       Teares can no more affection win,
       Then over-cast thy Angell Skin.

One Enamour'd on a Black-moor

What a strange love doth me invade,
Whose fires must *cool* in that *dark shade*!
Round her such *solitudes* are seen
As she were all *Retir'd within*,
And did in hush't up silence lye
(*Though single*) a *Conspiracy*.
How did my passion find her out,
That is with *Curtains drawn about?*
(And though her eye do *cent'nell keep*)
She is all over else asleep;
And I expect when she my sight,
Should strike with universal light.
A scarce seen thing she glides, were gon
If touch'd, *an Apparition*,
To immortality that dip't
Hath *newly* from her *Lethe slipt*.
No feature here we can define
By this, or that illustrious line,
Such curiosity is not
Found in an *un-distinguisht blot*:
This beauty puts us from the part
We all have tamely *got by hart*,
Of Roses here there Lillies grow,
Of Saphyre, Corall, Hills of snow:
These *Rivulets* are *all ingrost*.
And all in one *Black Ocean lost*
The treasures *lock't up* we would get
Within the *Ebon Cabinet*;
And he that *Ravishes must pick*

Open the quaint *Italian Trick.*
She is her *own close mourning in,*
(At Natures charge) a *Cypress skin.*
Our common Parent else to blot,
A moal on the white mold, a spot.
Dropt it with her own *Statute Ink,*
And the *new temper'd Clay* did *sink*:
So the fair figure doth remain,
Her ever since *Record in grain.*
Ixion's sometime armfull might
Swell with, perhaps, a *fleece more bright*;
But she as *soft* might be allow'd,
The *goddesse's deputed cloud*;
Though sure from our distinct embrace,
Centaurs had been a *dapple Race.*
Thou pretious *Night-piece* that art made,
More valuable in thy *shade.*
From which when the weak tribe depart,
The skilfull *Master* hugs his art.
Thou dost not to our dear surprise
Thine own *white marble* statue rise;
And yet no more a price dost lack,
Clean built up of the *polisht' black.*
Thou *like* no *Pelops* hast supply
Of *an one joynt* by *Ivory.*
But art miraculously set,
Together *totally* with *Jet.*
Nor can I count that bosome cheap,
That lyes not a cold winter heap:
Where pillow yet I warmly can,
In *down* of the *contrary swan*;
Let who will wilde enjoyments dream;
And tipple from another stream;
Since he with equall pleasure dwells,
That lyes at these dark fontinells;
These fair, Round, *sphears* contemplate on
So just in the proportion.
And in the *lines* of either breast,
Find the rich *countries of the East.*
They not as in the *milkie* hue,
Are *broke* into *Raw streaks* of *blew.*
But have in the *more-lived* stains,
The *very Violets* of *Veins,*
They rise the *Double-headed* Hill,
Whose tops *shade one another still*;

Between them lyes that *spicy Nest*,
That the *last Phoenix scorch'd*, and *blest*.
What fall's from her is rather made
Her own (just) picture, than her shade:
And where she walks the Sun doth hold
Her pourtrai'd in a frame of gold.

A Black Nymph Scorning a Fair Boy Courting Her

NYMPH. Fond Boy, thy vain pursuit give o're,
   Since I thy shadow go before.
BOY. Ah fly not Nymph! We may pursue,
   And shadows overtake like you.
NYMPH. I pass howe're in course away
   The night to thy succeeding day.
BOY. If night thou art, oh! be not gone,
   Till thou have stood a triple one:
   Though Jove I fear, would then invade.
   Not his Alcmena, but the shade.
NYMPH. So should the thunderer embrace,
   A cloud in his own goddess place.
BOY. So let us but commixt a while,
   Distinguish one anothers foyl;
   That to advantage we may tell,
   How either beauty doth excell.
NYMPH. I need not thy betraying light,
   To shew how far I am from white;
   And to the piece that nature made,
   I dare be no improving shade.
BOY. Then my dark Angell, I can charm
   Thee (circled) in mine either arm.
NYMPH. See! From thy flight embraces broke
   Secure I vanish in my smoke.

"To Mrs. Diana Cecyll"
"The Brown Beauty"
"Sonnet of Black Beauty"
"Another Sonnet to Black It Self"

Edward Herbert of Cherbury

Edward Herbert of Cherbury (1583–1648), the older brother of the metaphysical poet George Herbert, was a well-traveled diplomat who authored several works of philosophy and history as well as an autobiography. The four poems included here are from his posthumously published collection *Occasional Verses* (1665). "To Mrs. Diana Cecyll" addresses a woman, real or fictional, whose beauty differs from "pale and whitely" standards. "The Brown Beauty" praises Phaie (Greek for "dusky") for uniting in herself the white beauty of northern nations with the aspect of "the Moor and Indian." In "Sonnet of Black Beauty" and "Another Sonnet to Black It Self," the reader witnesses a new scientific approach to colors that makes for a particularly philosophical poetry.

To Mrs. Diana Cecyll

Diana Cecyll, that rare beauty thou dost show
      Is not of Milk, or Snow,
   Or such as pale and whitely things do ow.
But an illustrious Oriental Bright,
Like to the Diamonds refracted light,
Or early Morning breaking from the Night.

Nor is thy hair and eyes made of that ruddy beam,
      Or golden-sanded stream,
   Which we find still the vulgar Poets theme,
But reverend black, and such as you would say,
Light did but serve it, and did shew the way,
By which at first night did precede the day.

Nor is that symmetry of parts and form divine
      Made of one vulgar line,
   Or such as any know how to define,

But of proportions new, so well exprest,
That the perfections in each part confest,
Are beauties to themselves, and to the rest.

Wonder of all thy Sex! let none henceforth inquire
        Why they so much admire,
    Since they that know thee best ascend no higher;
Only be not with common praises woo'd
Since admiration were no longer good,
When men might hope more th[a]n they understood.

The Brown Beauty

1.
While the two contraries of Black and White,
In the Brown *Phaie* are so well unite,
That they no longer now seem opposite,
    Who doubts but love, hath this his colour chose,
    Since he therein doth both th' extremes compose,
    And as within their proper Centre close?

2.
Therefore as it presents not to the view
That whitely raw and unconcocted hiew,
Which Beauty Northern Nations think the true;
    So neither hath it that adust aspect,
    The *Moor* and *Indian* so much affect,
    That for it they all other do reject.

3.
Thus while the White well shadow'd doth appear,
And black doth through his lustre grow so clear,
That each in other equal part doth bear;
    All in so rare proportion is combin'd,
    That the fair temper, which adorns her mind,
    Is even to her outward form confin'd.

4.
Phaie, your Sexes honour, then so live,
That when the World shall with contention strive
To whom they would a chief perfection give,
    They might the controversie so decide,
    As quitting all extreams on either side,
    You more th[a]n any may be dignify'd.

Sonnet of Black Beauty

Black beauty, which above that common light,
    Whose Power can no colours here renew
    But those which darkness can again subdue,
Do'st still remain unvary'd to the sight,

And like an object equal to the view,
    Art neither chang'd with day, nor hid with night;
    When all these colours which the world call bright,
And which old Poetry doth so persue,

Are with the night so perished and gone,
    That of their being there remains no mark,
Thou still abidest so intirely one,
    That we may know thy blackness is a spark
Of light inaccessible, and alone
    Our darkness which can make us think it dark.

Another Sonnet to Black It Self

Thou Black, wherein all colours are compos'd,
    And unto which they all at last return,
    Thou colour of the Sun where it doth burn,
And shadow, where it cools, in thee is clos'd
Whatever nature can, or hath dispos'd
    In any other Hue: from thee do rise
Those tempers and complexions, which disclos'd,
    As parts of thee, do work as mysteries,
Of that thy hidden power; when thou dost reign
    The characters of fate shine in the Skies,
And tell us what the Heavens do ordain,
    But when Earth's common light shines to our eys,
Thou so retir'st thy self, that thy disdain
    All revelation unto Man denys.

"In Laudem Æthiopissæ"

James de la Cour

James de la Cour—or Delacour—(1709–1781) was a clergyman. No further biographical information is available about the author of the 1778 poem "In Laudem Æthiopissæ," a later Latin contribution to the white-black love poetry tradition.

In Laudem Æthiopissæ

Est mihi (siqua mihi est) sine fuco, fraude, vel arte,
Nescia mutari forma, suique tenax:
Unguentis utor nullis, medicamine nullo,
Quid juvet, ignoro, regia mellis aqua;
Nec maculis stellata, hic interspergor, et illic,
Non equidem nigra nigrior esse velim;
Lotio sola mihi est de pura et simplice lympha,
Et vereor quam sit vanus et iste labor.
At nivei mihi sunt, pœti sine pulvere dentes,
Quale nec Indorum purius albet ebur;
Sideribus similes fulgere videtis ocellos,
Angliacam possint qui decorare nurum.
Mollitiem talpæ superant mea labra, quis, ecquis
Libabit——quam sunt oscula mollicula?
Sin minus oblectem tot flammas inter et ignes,
(Usque adeo est nostræ lux inimica cuti)
Si placet extingui tantum mandate lucernas,
Protenus in tenebris altera Thais, ero.

In Praise of a Negress

What shape I have, that form is all my own,
To art a stranger, and to modes unknown;
To paint or patches, perfum'd fraud, no friend,
Nor know what stays or honey-water mend:
No spotted moons deform my jetty face,

I would be blacker than that speckled race!
My simple lotion is the purer rain,
And e'en that wash is labour took in vain.
But my pearl teeth, without tobacco's aid,
On snow or Indian iv'ry cast a shade!
My eyes eclipse the stars in all their flame,
Such as may not e'en Albions daughters shame!
My softer skin with the mole's velvet vies,
Ah! who will on those altars sacrifice?
But if I please less in the sultry day,
My colour with the candles dies away;
Since to our hue the light is deem'd a foe,
Night will a THAIS in my charms bestow.

From Colonial Exoticism and the Noble Savage
to Antislavery Writing

Colonial expansion and the introduction of the African slave trade changed the European view of the world. Racialization became more forceful, permeating even such apparently utopian island fantasies as Henry Neville's *Isle of Pines*, in which racial difference matters for the account of Philippa and her descendants, the Phills. Along with, and attempting to counter, these newly debasing images came a Noble Savage literature that idealized heroic natives, both Indian and African. Wylie Sypher delineated the features of what he termed the "Noble Negro" tradition: "the invidious contrast between the exemplary savage and the sordid white man; the more invidious contrast between the princely and the ordinary Negro; the pseudo-African setting; great bursts of natural rhetoric; the blurring of Indian with Negro . . . ; and the tone of sentiment and primitivism." He specifies that the two legends sustaining that tradition were that of Oroonoko, who dies stoically at the hands of his white captors and tormentors, and that of the Englishman Inkle, who sells his beloved native woman Yarico into slavery. Both legends were immensely popular and retold in a great variety of versions. The growing intensity of the issues of the slave trade and slavery in the course of the eighteenth century transformed what readers took to be the moral of these stories, just as it transformed and politicized interracial love poetry. The employment of interracial themes in the struggle against the slave trade is brought to an almost manifesto-like political point in a public letter by Olaudah Equiano.

The Isle of Pines

Henry Neville

As a member of Parliament, Henry Neville (1620–1694) was embroiled in the political conflicts of his day. The government of Oliver Cromwell had him expelled from London in 1654, but he returned to Parliament in 1658. His political opponents lodged charges of atheism and blasphemy against him, and he was briefly imprisoned for treason but was released for lack of evidence. In 1668 Neville published *The Isle of Pines*, presented here in its entirety. An odd utopian island fantasy in which the boundaries of class and race are crossed, this short, popular book was followed by an anonymously published sequel and by imitations, and became part of the modern island literature of which *Robinson Crusoe* is now the most famous example. Among Neville's works are several other pieces of fiction as well as a 1675 translation of the works of Machiavelli.

Two Letters concerning the Island of Pines to a Credible person in Covent Garden

Amsterdam, *June* the 29th 1668.
It is written by the last Post from Rochel, *to a Merchant in this City, that there was a* French *ship arrived, the Master and Company of which reports, that about 2 or 300 Leagues Northwest from* Cape Finis Terre, *they fell in with an Island, where they went on shore, and found about* 2000 English *people without cloathes only some small coverings about their middle, and that they related to them, that at their first coming to this Island (which was in Queen* Elizabeths *time) they were but five in number men and women, being cast on shore by distress or otherwise, and had there remained ever since, without having any correspondence with any other people, or any ship coming to them. This story seems very fabulous, yet the Letter is come to a known Merchant, and from a good hand in* France, *so that I thought fit to mention it, it may be that there may be some mistake in the number of the Leagues, as also of the exact point of the Compass, from* Cape Finis Terre; *I shall enquire more particularly about it. Some* English *here suppose it may be the Island of* Brasile *which have been so oft sought for, Southwest from* Ireland, *if true, we shall hear further about it; Your friend and Brother,*   Abraham Keek.

Amsterdam, *July* the 6th, 1668.
It is said that the ship that discovered the Island, of which I hinted to you in my last, is departed from Rochel, *on her way to* Zealand, *several persons here have writ thither to enquire for the said Vessel, to know the truth of this business. I was promised a Copy of*

the Letter that came from France, *advising the discovery of the Island above said, but it's not yet come to my hand; when it cometh, or any further news about this Island, I shall acquaint you with it,*

Your Friend and Brother,
A. Keek.

The Isle of PINES, Discovered Near to the Coast of Terra Australis Incognita, by Henry Cornelius Van Sloetten, in a Letter to a friend in London, declaring the truth of his Voyage to the East Indies

Sir,

I Received your Letter of this second instant, wherein you desire me to give you a further account concerning the Land of *Pines*, on which we were driven by distress of Weather the last Summer, I also perused the Printed Book thereof you sent me, the Copy of which was surreptiously taken out of my hands, else should I have given you a more fuller account upon what [o]ccasion we came thither, how we were entertained, with some other circumstances of note wherein that relation is defective. To satisfie therefore your desires, I shall briefly yet fully give you a particular account thereof, with a true Copy of the Relation itself; desiring you to bear with my blunt Phrases, as being more a Seaman then a Scholler.

April the *26th 1667*. We set sail from *Amsterdam*, intending for the *East-Indies*; our ship had to name the place from whence we came, the *Amsterdam* burthen 350. Tun, and having a fair gale of Wind, on the 27 of *May* following we had a sight of the high Peak of *Tenriffe* belonging to the *Canaries*, we have touched at the Island *Palma*, but having endeavoured it twice, and finding the winds contrary, we steered on our couse by the Isles of *Cape Verd*, or *Insulæ Capitis Viridis*, where at St. *James's* we took in fresh water, with some few Goats, and Hens, wherewith that Island doth plentifully abound.

June the 14. We had a sight of *Madagascar*, or the Island of St. *Laurence*, an Island of 4000 miles in compass, and scituate under the Southern Tropick; thither we steered our course, and trafficked with the inhabitants for Knives, Beads, Glasses and the like, having in exchange thereof Cloves and Silver. Departing from thence, we were incountred with a violent storm, and the winds holding contrary, for the space of a fortnight, brought us back almost as far as the Isle *Del Principe*; during which time many of our men fell sick, and some dyed, but at the end of that time it pleased God the wind favoured us again, and we steered on our course merrily, for the space of ten days: when on a sudden we were encountered with such a violent storm, as if all the four winds together had conspired for our destruction, so that the stoutest spirit of us all quailed, expecting every hour to be devoured by that merciless element of water, sixteen dayes together did this storm continue, though not with such violence as at the first, the Weather being so dark all the while, and the Sea so rough, that we knew not in what place we were, at length all on a sudden the Wind ceased, and the Air cleared, the Clouds were all dispersed, and a very serene Sky followed, for which we gave hearty thanks to the Almighty, it being beyond our expectation that we should have escaped the violence of that storm.

At length one of our men mounting the Main-mast espyed fire, an evident sign of some Countrey near adjoyning, which presently after we apparently discovered, and steering our course . . . nigher, we saw several persons promiscuously running about the shore, as it were wondering and admiring at what they saw: Being now near to the Land, we manned out our long Boat with ten persons, who approaching the shore, asked them in our *Dutch* Tongue 𝔚𝔞𝔱 𝔈𝔭𝔩𝔞𝔫𝔱 𝔦𝔰 𝔇𝔦𝔱? to which they returned this Answer in English, *That they knew not what we said.* One of our Company named *Jeremiah Hanzen* who understood *English* very well, hearing their words discourst to them in their own Language; so that in fine we were very kindly invited on shore, great numbers of them flocking about us, admiring at our Cloaths which we did wear, as we on the other side did to find in such a strange place, so many that could speak *English*, and yet to go naked.

Four of our men returning back in the long Boat to our Ships company, could hardly make them believe the truth of what they had seen and heard, but when we had brought our ship into harbour, you would have blest your self to see how the naked Islanders flocked unto us, so wondering at our ship, as if it had been the greatest miracle of Nature in whole World.

We were very courteously entertained by them, presenting us with such food as that Countrey afforded, which indeed was not to be despised; we eat of the Flesh both of Beasts, and Fowls, which they had cleanly drest, though with no great curiosity, as wanting materials, wherewithal to do it; and for bread we had the inside or Kernel of a great Nut as big as an Apple, which was very wholsome, and sound for the body, and tasted to the Pallat very delicious.

Having refreshed our selves, they invited us to the Pallace of their Prince or chief Ruler, some two miles distant off from the place where we landed; which we found to be about the bigness of one of our ordinary village houses, it was supported with rough unhewn pieces of Timber, and covered very artificially with boughs, so that it would keep out the greatest showers of Rain, the sides thereof were adorned with several sorts of Flowers, which the fragrant fields there do yield in great variety. The Prince himself (whose name was *William Pine* the Grandchild of *George Pine* that was first on shore in this Island) came to his Pallace door and saluted us very courteously, for though he had nothing of Majesty in him, yet had he a courteous noble and deboneyre spirit, wherewith your English Nation (especially those of the Gentry) are very much indued.

Scarce had he done saluting us when his Lady or Wife, came likewise forth of their House or Pallace, attended on by two Maid-servants, she was a woman of an exquisite beauty, and had on her head as it were a Chaplet of Flowers, which being intermixt with several variety of colours became her admirably. Her privities were hid with some pieces of old Garments, the Relicts of those Cloaths (I suppose) of them which first came hither, and yet being adorned with Flowers those very rags seemeth beautiful; and indeed modesty so far prevaileth over all the Female Sex of that Island, that with grass and flowers interwoven and made strong by the peelings of young Elms (which grow there in great plenty) they do plant together so many of them as serve to cover those parts which nature would have hidden.

We carried him as a present some few Knives, of which we thought they had great need, an Ax or Hatchet to fell Wood, which was very acceptable unto him, the Old one which was cast on shore at the first, and the only one that they ever had, being now so quite blunt and dulled, that it would not cut at all, some few other things we also gave him, which he very thankfully accepted, inviting us into his House or Pallace, and causing us to sit down with him, where we refreshed our selves again, with some more Countrey viands which were no other then such we tasted of before; Prince and peasant here faring alike, nor is there any difference betwixt their drink, being only fresh sweet water, which the rivers yield them in great abundance.

After some little pause, our Companion (who could speak *English*) by our request desired to know of him something concerning their Original and how that people speaking the Language of such a remote Countrey should come to inhabit there, having not, as we could see, any ships or Boats amongst them the means to bring them thither, and which was more, altogether ignorant and meer strangers to ships, or shipping, the main thing conducible to that means, to which request of ours, the courteous Prince thus replyed.

Friends (for so your actions declare you to be, and shall by ours find no less) know that we are inhabitants of this Island of no great standing, my Grandfather being the first that ever set foot on this shore, whose native Countrey was a place called *England*, far distant from this our Land, as he let us to understand; He came from that place upon the Waters, in a thing called a Ship, of which no question but you may have heard; several other persons were in his company, not intending to have come hither (as he said) but to a place called *India*, when tempestuous weather brought him and his company upon this Coast, where falling among the Rocks his ship split all in pieces; the whole company perishing in the Waters, saving only him and four women, which by means of a broken piece of that Ship, by Divine assistance got on Land.

What after passed (said he) during my Grandfathers life, I shall show you in a Relation thereof written by his own hand, which he delivered to my Father being his eldest Son, charging him to have a special care thereof, and assuring him that time would bring some people or other thither to whom he would have him to impart it, that the truth of our first planting here might not be quite lost, which his commands my Father dutifully obeyed; but no one coming, he at his death delivered the same with the like charge to me, and you being the first people, which (besides our selves) ever set footing in this Island, I shall therefore in obedience to my Grandfathers and Fathers commands, willingly impart the same unto you.

Then stepping into a kind of inner room, which as we conceived was his lodging Chamber, he brought forth two sheets of paper fairly written in *English*, (being the same Relation which you had Printed with you at *London*) and very distinctly read the same over unto us, which we hearkened unto with great delight and admiration, freely proffering us a Copy of the same, which we afterward took and brought away along with us; which Copy hereafter followeth.

A Way to the East *India's* being lately discovered by Sea, to the South of *Affrick* by certain *Portugals*, far more safe and profitable then had been heretofore; certain *English* Merchants encouraged by the great advantages arising from the Eastern Commodities, to settle a Factory there for the advantage of Trade. And having to that purpose obtained the Queens Royal Licence *Anno Dom.* 1569. 11. or 12. *Eliz.* furnisht out for those parts four ships, my Master being sent as Factor to deal and Negotiate for them, and to settle there, took with him his whole Family, (that is to say) his Wife, and one Son of about twelve years of age, and one Daughter of about fourteen years, two Maidservants, one *Negro* female slave, and my Self, who went under him as his Book-keeper, with this company on Monday the third of *April* next following, (having all necessaries for Housekeeping when we should come there, we Embarqued our selves in the good ship called the *India Merchant*, of about four hundred and fifty Tuns bur-then, and having a good wind, we on the fourteenth day of *May* had sight of the *Ca-naries*, and not long after of the Isles of *Cape Vert*, or *Verd*, where taking in such things as were necessary for our Voyage, and some fresh Provisions, we stearing our course South, and a point East, about the first of *August* came within sight of the Island of St. *Hellen*, where we took in some fresh water, we then set our faces for the Cape of Good hope, where by Gods blessing after some sickness, whereof some of our company died, though none of our family; and hitherto we had met with none but calm weather, yet so it pleased God, when we were almost in sight of St. *Laurence*, an Island so called, one of the greatest in the world, as Marriners say, we were overtaken and dispersed by a great storm of Wind, which continued with such violence many days, that losing all hope of safety, being out of our own knowledge, and whether we should fall on Flats or Rocks, uncertain in the nights, not having the least benefit of the light, we feared most, always wishing for day, and then for Land, but it came too soon for our good; for about the first of *October*; our fears having made us forget how the time passed to a certainty; we about the break of day discerned Land (but what we knew not) the Land seemed high and Rockey, and the Sea continued still very stormy and tempestuous, insomuch as there seemed no hope of safety, but looked suddenly to perish. As we grew near Land, perceiving no safety in the ship, which we looked would suddenly be beat in pieces: The Captain, my Master, and some others got into the long Boat, thinking by that means to save their lives, and presently after all the Seamen cast themselves overboard, thinking to save their lives by swimming, onely my self, my Masters Daughters, the two Maids, and the *Negro* were left on board, for we could not swim, but those that left us, might as well have tarried with us, for we saw them, or most of them perish, our selves now ready after to follow their fortune, but God was pleased to spare our lives, as it were by miracle, though to further sor-row; for when we came against the Rocks, our ship having endured two or three blows against the Rocks, (being now broken and quite foundred in the Waters, we having with much ado gotten our selves on the Bowsprit, which being broken off, was driven by the Waves into a small Creek, wherein fell a little River, which being en-compassed by the Rocks, was sheltered from the Wind, so that we had opportunity to land our selves, (though almost drowned) in all four persons, besides the *Negro*: when we were got upon the Rock, we could perceive the miserable Wrack to our great ter-rour, I had in my pocket a little Tinder-box and Steel, and Flint to strike fire at any time upon occasion, which served now to good Purpose, for its being so close, pre-served the Tinder dry, with this, and the help of some old rotten Wood which we got together, we kindled a fire and dryed our selves, which done, I left my female company, and went to see, if I could find any of our Ships company, that were escaped, but could hear of none, though I hooted and made all the noise I could; neither could I perceive the footsteps of any living Creature (save a few Birds, and other Fowls). At length it drawing towards the Evening, I went back to my company, who were very much troubled for want of me. I being now all their stay in this lost condition, we were at first affraid that the wild people of the Countrey might find us out, although we saw no footsteps of any not so much as a Path; the Woods round about being full of Briers and Brambles, we also stood in fear of wild Beasts, of such also we saw none, nor sign of any: But above all, and that we had greatest reason to fear, was to be starved to death for want of Food, but God had otherwise provided for us as you shall know hereafter; this done, we spent our time in getting some broken pieces of Boards, and Planks, and some of the Sails and Rigging on shore for shelter; I set up two or three Poles, and drew two or three of the Cords and Lines from Tree to Tree, over which throwing some Sail-cloathes and having gotten Wood by us, and three or four Sea-gowns, which we had dryed, we took up our Lodging for that night altogether (the *blackmoor* being less sensible then the rest we made our Centry) we slept soundly that night, as having not slept in three or four nights before (our fears of what happened preventing us) neither could our hard lodging, fear, and danger hinder us we were so over watcht.

On the morrow, being well refresht with sleep, the winde ceased, and the weather was very warm; we went down the Rocks on the sands at low water, where we found great part of our lading, either on shore or floating near it. I by the help of my company, dragged most of it on shore; what was too heavy for us broke, and we unbound the Casks and Chests, and, taking out the goods, secured all; so that we wanted no clothes, nor any other provision necessary for Housekeeping, to furnish a better house than any we were like to have; but no victuals (the last water having spoiled all) only one Cask of bisket, being lighter than the rest was dry; this served for bread a while, and we found on Land a sort of fowl about the bigness of a Swan, very heavie and fat, that by reason of their weight could not fly, of these we found little difficulty to kill, so that was our present food; we carried out of *England* certain Hens and Cocks to eat by the way, some of these when the ship was broken, by some means got to land, & bred exceedingly, so that in the future they were a great help unto us; we found also, by a little River, in the flags, store of eggs, of a sort of foul much like our Ducks, which were very good meat, so that we wanted nothing to keep us alive.

On the morrow, which was the third day, as soon as it was morning, seeing nothing to disturb us, I lookt out a convenient place to dwell in, that we might build us a Hut to shelter us from the weather, and from any other danger of annoyance, from wild beasts (if any should finde us out: So closse by a large spring which rose out of a high hill over-looking the Sea, on the side of a wood, having a prospect towards the Sea) by the help of an Ax and some other implements (for we had all necessaries, the working of the Sea, having cast up most of our goods) I cut down all the straightest poles I could find, and which were enough for my purpose, by the help of my company (necessity being our Master) I digged holes in the earth setting my poles at an equal distance, and nailing the broken boards of the Caskes, Chests, and Cabins, and such like to them, making my door to the Seaward, and having covered the top, with sail-clothes strain'd, and nail'd, I in the space of a week had made a large Cabbin big enough to hold all our goods and our selves in it, I also placed our Hamocks for lodging, purposing (if it pleased God to send any Ship that way) we might be transported home, but it never came to pass, the place, wherein we were (as I conceived) being much out of the way.

We having now lived in this manner full four months, and not so much as seeing or hearing of any wild people, or of any of our own company, more th[a]n our selves (they being found now by experience to be all drowned) and the place as we after found, being a large Island, and disjoyned, and out of sight of any other Land, was wholly uninhabited by any people, neither was there any hurtful beast to annoy us: But on the contrary the countrey so very pleasant, being always clothed with green, and full of pleasant fruits, and variety of birds, ever warm, and never colder th[a]n in *England* in *September*: So that this place (had it the culture, that skilful people might bestow on it) would prove a *Paradise*.

The Woods afforded us a sort of Nuts, as big as a large Apple, whose kernel being pleasant and dry, we made use of instead of bread, that fowl before mentioned, and a sort of water-fowl like Ducks, and their eggs, and a beast about the size of a Goat, and almost such a like creature, which brought two young ones at a time, and that twice a year, of which the Low Lands and Woods, were very full, being a very harmless creature and tame, so that we could easily take and kill them: Fish, also, especially Shell-fish (which we could best come by) we had great store of, so that in effect as to Food we wanted nothing; and thus, and by such like helps, we continued six moneths, without any disturbance or want.

Idleness and Fulness of every thing begot in me a desire of enjoying the women, beginning now to grow more familiar, I had perswaded the two Maids to let me lie with them, which I did at first in private, but after, custome taking away shame (there being none but us) we did it more openly, as our Lusts gave us liberty; afterwards my Masters Daughter was content also to do as we did; the truth is, they were all handsome Women when they had Cloathes, and well shaped, feeding well. For we wanted no Food, and living idlely, and seeing us at Liberty to do our wills, without hope of ever returning home made us thus bold: One of the first of my Consorts with whom I first accompanied (the tallest and handsomest) proved presently with child, the second was my Masters Daughter, and the other also not long after fell into the same condition: none now remaining but my *Negro*, who seeing what we did, longed also for her share; one Night, I being asleep, my *Negro*, (with the consent of the others) got closse to me, thinking it being dark, to beguile me, but I awaking and feeling her, and perceiving who it was, yet willing to try the difference, satisfied my self with her, as well as with one of the rest: that night, although the first time, she proved also with child, so that in the year of our being here, all my women were with child by me, and they all coming at different seasons, were a great help to one another.

The first brought me a brave Boy, my Masters Daughter was the youngest, she brought me a Girl, so did the other Maid, who being something fat sped worse at her labour: the *Negro* had no pain at all, brought me a fine white Girl, so I had one Boy and three Girls, the Women were soon well again, and the two first with child again before the two last were brought to bed, my custome being not to lie with any of them after they were with child, till others were so likewise, and not with the black at all after she was with child, which commonly was at the first time I lay with her, which was in the night and not else, my stomach would not serve me, although she was one of the handsomest Blacks I had seen, and her children as comly as any of the rest; we had no clothes for them, and therefore when they had suckt, we laid them in Mosse to sleep, and took no further care of them, for we knew, when they were gone more would come, the Women never failing once a year at least, and none of the Children (for all the hardship we put them to) were ever sick; so that wanting now nothing but Cloathes, nor them much neither, other then for decency, the warmth of the Countrey and Custome supplying that Defect, we were now well satisfied with our condition, our Family beginning to grow large, there being nothing to hurt us, we many times lay abroad on Mossey Banks, under the shelter of some Trees, or such like (for having nothing else to do) I had made me several Arbors to sleep in with my Women in the heat of the day, in these I and my women passed the time away, they being never willing to be out of my company.

And having now no thought of ever returning home, as having resolved and sworn each to other, never to part or leave one another, or the place; having by my several wives, forty seven Children, Boys and Girls, but most Girls, and growing up apace, we were all of us very fleshly, the Country so well agreeing with us, that we never ailed any thing; my *Negro* having had twelve, was the first that left bearing, so I never medled with her more: My Masters Daughter (by whom I had most children, being the youngest and handsomest) was most fond of me, and I of her. Thus we lived for sixteen years, till perceiving my eldest Boy to mind the ordinary work of Nature, by seeing what we did, I gave him a Mate, and so I did to all the rest, as fast as they grew up, and were capable: My Wives having left bearing, my children began to breed apace, so we were like to be a multitude; My first Wife brought me thirteen children, my second seven, my Masters Daughter fifteen, and the *Negro* twelve, in all forty seven.

After we had lived there twenty two years, my *Negro* died suddenly, but I could not perceive any thing that ailed her; most of my children being grown, as fast as we married them, I sent them and placed them over the River by themselves severally, because we would not pester one another; and now they being all grown up, and gone, and married after our manner (except some two or three of the youngest) for (growing my self into years) I liked not the wanton annoyance of young company.

Thus having lived to the sixtieth year of my age, and the fortieth of my coming thither, at which time I sent for all of them to bring their children, and there were in number descended from me by these four Women, of my Children, Grand-children, and great Grand-children, five hundred sixty five of both sorts, I took off the Males of one Family, and married them to the Females of another, not letting any to marry their sisters, as we did formerly out of necessity. so blessing God for his Providence and goodness, I dismist them, I having taught some of my children to read formerly, for I had left still the Bible, I charged it should be read once a moneth at a general meeting: At last one of my Wives died being sixty eight years of age, which I buried in a place, set out on purpose, and within a year after another, so I had none now left but my Masters Daughter, and we lived together twelve years longer, at length she died also, so I buried her also next the place where I purposed to be buried my self, and the tall Maid my first Wife next me on the other side, the *Negro* next without her, and the other Maid next my Masters Daughter. I had now nothing to mind, but the place whether I was to go, being very old, almost eighty years, I gave my Cabin and Furniture that was left to my eldest son after my decease, who had married my eldest Daughter by my beloved Wife, whom I made King and Governour of all the rest: I informed them of the Manners of *Europe*, and charged them to remember the Christian Religion, after the manner of them that spake the same Language, and to admit no other, if hereafter any should come and find them out.

And now once for all, I summoned them to come to me, that I might number them, which I did, and found the estimate to contain in or about the eightieth year of my age, and the fifty ninth of my coming there; in all, of all sorts, one thousand seven hundred eighty and nine. Thus praying God to multiply them, and send them the true light of the Gospel, I last of all dismist them: For, being now very old, and my sight decayed, I could not expect to live long. I gave this Narration (written with my own hand) to my eldest Son, who now lived with me, commanding him to keep it, and if any strangers should come hither by chance: to let them see it, and take a Copy of it if they would, that our name be not lost from off the earth. I gave this people (descended from me) the name of the ENGLISH PINES, *George Pine* being my name, and my Masters Daughters name *Sarah English*, my two other Wives were *Mary Sparkes*, and *Elizabeth Trevor*, so their severall Descendants are called the ENGLISH, the SPARKS, and the TREVORS, and the PHILLS, from the Christian Name of the Negro, which was *Philippa*, she having no surname: And the general name of the whole the ENGLISH PINES; whom God bless with the dew of Heaven, and the fat of the Earth, AMEN.

After the reading and delivering unto us a Coppy of this Relation, then proceeded he on in his discourse.

My Grandfather when he wrote this, was as you hear eighty yeares of age, there proceeding from his Loyns one thousand seven hundred eighty nine children, which he had by them four women aforesaid: My Father was his eldest son, and was named *Henry*, begotten of his wife *Mary Sparkes*, whom he apointed chief Governour and Ruler over the rest; and having given him a charge not to exercise tyranny over them, seeing they were his fellow brethren by Fathers side (of which there could be no doubt made of double dealing therein) exhorting him to use justice and sincerity amongst them and not to let Religion die with him, but to observe and keep those Precepts which he had taught them he quietly surrendred up his soul, and was buried with great lamentation of all his children.

My father coming to rule, and the people growing more populous, made them to range further in the discovery of the Countrey, which they found answerable to their desires, full both of Fowls and Beasts, and those too not hurtful to mankinde; as if this Country (on which we were by providence cast without arms or other weapons to defend our selves, or offend others,) should by the same providence be so inhabited as not to have any need of such like weapons of destruction wherewith to preserve our lives.

But as it is impossible, but that in multitudes disorders will grow, the stronger seeking to oppress the weaker; no tye of Religion being strong enough to chain up the depraved nature of mankinde, even so amongst them mischiefs began to rise, and they soon fell from those good orders prescribed them by my Grandfather. The source from whence those mischiefs spring, was at first, I conceive, the neglect of hearing the Bible read, which (according to my Grandfathers proscription) was once a moneth at a general meeting, but now many of them wandring far up into the Country, they quite neglected the coming to it, with all other means of Christian instruction, whereby the sence of sin being quite lost in them, they fell to whoredoms, incests, and adulteries; so that what my Grand-father was forced to do for necessity, they did for wantonness; nay not confining themselves within the bound of any modesty, but brother and sister lay openly together; those who would not yeild to their lewd embraces, were by force ravished, yea many times endangered of their lives. To redress those enormities, my father assembled all the Company near unto him, to whom he declared the wickedness of those their brethren; who all with one consent agreed that they should be severely punished; and so arming themselves with boughs, stones, and such like weapons, they marched against them, who having notice of their coming, and fearing their deserved punishment, some of them fled into woods, others passed over a great River, which runneth through the heart of our Countrey, hazarding drowning to escape punishment; But the grandest offender of them all was taken, whose name was *John Phill*, the second son of the *Negro-woman* that came with my Grandfather into this Island. He being proved guilty of divers ravishings & tyrannies committed by him, was adjudged guilty of death, and accordingly was thrown down from a high Rock into the Sea, where he perished in the waters. Execution being done upon him, the rest were pardoned for what was past, which being notified abroad, they returned from those Desart and Obscure places, wherein they were hidden.

Now as Seed being cast into stinking Dung produceth good and wholesome Corn for the sustentation of mans life, so bad manners produceth good and wholesome Laws for the preservation of Humane Society. Soon after my Father with the advice of some few others of his Counsel, ordained and set forth these Laws to be observed by them.

1. That whosoever should blaspheme or talk irreverently of the name of God should be put to death.
2. That who should be absent from the monethly assembly to hear the Bible read, without sufficient cause shown to the contrary, should for the first default be kept without any victuals or drink, for the space of four days, and if he offend therein again, then to suffer death.
3. That who should force or ravish any Maid or Woman should be burnt to death, the party so ravished putting fire to the wood that should burn him.
4. Whosoever shall commit adultery, for the first crime the Male shall lose his Privities, and the Woman have her right eye bored out, if after that she was again taken in the act, she should die without mercy.
5. That who so injured his Neighbour, by laming of his Limbs, or taking any thing away which he possesseth, shall suffer in the same kind himself by loss of Limb;

and for defrauding his Neighbour, to become servant to him, whil'st he had made him double satisfaction.

6. That who should defame or speak evil of the Governour, or refuse to come before him upon Summons, should receive a punishment by whipping with Rods, and afterwards be exploded from the society of all the rest of the inhabitants.

Having set forth these Laws, he chose four several persons under him to see them put in Execution, whereof one was of the *Englishes*, the Off-spring of *Sarah English*; another of his own Tribe, the *Sparks*; a third of the *Trevors*, and the fourth of the *Phills*; appointing them every year at a certain time to appear before him, and give an account of what they had done in the prosecution of those Laws.

The Countrey being thus settled, my Father lived quiet and peaceable till he attained to the age of ninety and four years, when dying, I succeeded in his place, in which I have continued peaceably and quietly till this very present time.

He having ended his Speech, we gave him very heartily thanks for our information, assuring him we should not be wanting to him in anything which lay in our powers, wherewith we could pleasure him in what he should desire; and thereupon proferred to depart, but before our going away, he would needs engage us to see him, the next day, when was to be their great assembly or monethly meeting for the celebration of their Religious Exercises.

Accordingly the next day we came thither again, and were courteously entertained as before, In a short space there was gathered such a multitude of people together as made us to admire; and first there was several Weddings celebrated, the manner whereof was thus. The Bridegroom and Bride appeared before him who was their Priest or Reader of the Bible, together with the Parents of each party, or if any of their Parents were dead, then the next relation unto them, without whose consent as well as the parties to be married, the Priest will not joyn them together: but being satisfied in those particulars, after some short Oraizons, and joyning of hands together, he pronounces them to be man and wife: and with exhortations to them to live lovingly towards each other, and quietly towards their neighbors, he concludes with some prayers, and so dismisses them.

The Weddings being finished, all the people took their places to hear the Word read, the new married persons having the honour to be next unto the Priest that day, after he had read three or four chapters he fell to expounding the most difficult places therein, the people being very attentive all that while, this exercise continued for two or three hours, which being done, with some few prayers he concluded, but all the rest of that day was by the people kept very strictly, abstaining from all manner of playing or pastimes, with which on other dayes they use to pass their time away, as having need of nothing but victuals, and that they have in such plenty as almost provided to their hands.

Their exercises of Religion being over, we returned again to our Ship, and the next day, taking with us two or three Fowling-pieces, leaving half our Company to guard the Ship, the rest of us resolved to go up higher into the Country for a further discovery: All the way as we passed the first morning, we saw abundance of little Cabbins or Huts of these inhabitants, made under Trees, and fashioned up with boughs, grass, and such like stuffe to defend them from the Sun and Rain; and as we went along, they came out of them much wondering at our Attire, and standing aloof off from us as if they were afraid, but our companion that spake English, calling to them in their own Tongue, and giving them good words, they drew nigher, some of them freely proffering to go along with us, which we willingly accepted; but having passed some few miles, one of our company espying a Beast like unto a Goat come gazing on him, he discharged his Peece, sending a brace of Bullets into his belly, which brought him dead upon the ground; these poor naked unarmed people hearing the noise of the Peece, and seeing the Beast lie tumbling in his gore, without speaking any words betook them to their heels, running back again as fast as they could drive, nor could the perswasions of our Company, assuring them they should have no hurt, prevail any thing at all with them, so that we were forced to pass along without their company: all the way that we went we heard the delightful harmony of singing Birds, the ground very fertile in Trees, Grass, and such flowers, as grow by the production of Nature, without the help of Art; many and several sorts of Beasts we saw, who were not so much wild as in other Countries; whether it were as having enough to satiate themselves without ravening upon others, or that they never before saw the sight of man, nor heard the report of murdering Guns, I leave it to others to determine. Some Trees bearing wild Fruits we also saw, and of those some whereof we tasted, which were neither unwholsome nor distastful to the Pallate, and no question had but Nature here the benefit of Art added unto it, it would equal, if not exceed many of our *Europian* Countries; the Vallyes were every where intermixt with running streams, and no question but the earth hath in it rich veins of Minerals, enough to satisfie the desires of the most covetous.

It was very strange to us, to see that in such a fertile Countrey which was as yet never inhabited, there should be notwithstanding such a free and clear passage to us, without the hinderance of Bushes, Thorns, and such like stuff, wherewith most Islands of the like nature are pestered: the length of the Grass (which yet was very much intermixt with flowers) being the only impediment that we found.

Six dayes together did we thus travel, setting several marks in our way as we went for our better return, not knowing whether we should have the benefit of the Stars for our guidance in our going back, which we made use of in our passage: at last we came to the vast Ocean on the other side of the Island, and by our coasting it, conceive it to be of an oval form, only here and there shooting forth with some Promontories. I conceive it hath but few good Harbours belonging to it, the Rocks in most places making it inaccessible. The length of it may be about two hundred, and breadth one hundred miles, the whole in circumference about five hundred miles.

It lyeth about seventy six degrees of Longitude, and twenty of Latitude, being scituate under the third Climate, the longest day being about thirteen hours and fourty five minutes. The weather as in all Southern Countries, is far more hot than with us in *Europe*; but what is by the Sun parched in the day, the night again refreshes with cool pearly dews. The Air is found to be very healthful by the long lives of the present inhabitants, few dying there till such time as they come to good years of maturity, many of them arriving to the extremity of old age.

And now speaking concerning the length of their Lives, I think it will not be amisse in this place to speak something of their Burials, which they used to do thus.

When the party was dead, they stuck his Carkass all over with flowers, and after carried him to the place appointed for Burial, where setting him down, (the Priest having given some godly Exhortations concerning the frailty of life) then do they take stones (a heap being provided there for that purpose) and the nearest of the kin begins to lay the first stone upon him, afterwards the rest follows, they never leaving till they have covered the body deep in stones, so that no Beast can possibly come to him, and this shift were they forced to make, having no Spades or Shovels wherewith to dig them Graves; which want of theirs we espying, bestowed a Pick-ax and two Shovels upon them.

Here might I add their way of Christening Children, but that being little different from yours in *ENGLAND*, and taught them by *GEORGE PINES* at first which they have since continued, I shall therefore forbear to speak thereof.

After our return back from the discovery of the Countrey, the Wind not being fit for our purpose, and our men also willing thereto, we got all our cutting Instruments on Land, and fell to hewing down of Trees, with which, in a little time, (many hands making light work) we built up a Pallace for this *William Pines* the Lord of that Countrey; which, though much inferiour to the houses of your Gentry in *England*. Yet to them which never had seen better, it appeared a very Lordly Place. This deed of ours was beyond expression acceptable unto him, loading us with thanks for so great a benefit, of which he said he should never be able to make a requital.

And now acquainting him, that upon the first opportunity we were resolved to leave the Island, as also how that we were near Neighbours to the Countrey of *England*, from whence his Ancestors came; he seemed upon the news to be much discontented that we would leave him, desiring, if it might stand with our commodity to continue still with him, but seeing he could not prevail, he invited us to dine with him the next day, which we promised to do, against which time he provided, very sumptuously (according to his estate) for us, and now was he attended after a more Royal manner then ever we saw him before, both for number of Servants, and multiplicity of Meat, on which we fed very heartily; but he having no other Beverage for us to drink, then water, we fetched from our Ship a Case of Brandy, presenting some of it to him to drink, but when he had tasted of it, he would by no means be perswaded to touch thereof again, preferring (as he said) his own Countrey Water before all such Liquors whatsoever.

After we had Dined, we were invited out into the Fields to behold their Country Dauncing, which they did with great agility of body; and though they had no other then only Vocal Musick (several of them singing all that while) yet did they trip it very neatly, giving sufficient satisfaction to all that beheld them.

The next day we invited the Prince *William Pines* aboard our Ship, where was nothing wanting in what we could to entertain him, he had about a dozen of Servants to attend on him he much admired at the Tacklings of our Ship, but when we came to discharge a piece or two of Ordnance, it struck him into a wonder and amazement to behold the strange effects of Powder; he was very sparing in his Diet, neither could he, or any of his followers be induced to drink any thing but Water: We there presented him with several things, as much as we could spare, which we thought would any wayes conduce to their benefit, all which he very gratefully received, assuring us of his real love and good will, whensoever we should come thither again.

And now we intended the next day to take our leaves, the Wind standing fair, blowing with a gentle Gale *South* and by *East*, but as we were hoising of our Sails, and weighing Anchor, we were suddenly Allarm'd with a noise from the shore, the Prince, *W. Pines* imploring our assistance in an Insurrection which had happened amongst them, of which this was the cause.

Henry Phil, the chief Ruler of the Tribe or Family of the *Phils*, being the Off-spring of *George Pines* which he had by the *Negro*-woman; this man had ravished the Wife of one of the principal of the Family of the *Trevors*, which act being made known, the *Trevors* assembled themselves alltogether to bring the offender unto Justice: But he knowing his crime to be so great, as extended to the loss of life: sought to defend that by force, which he had as unlawfully committed, whereupon the whole Island was in a great hurly burly, they being two great Potent Factions, the bandying of which against each other, threatned a general ruin to the whole State.

The Governour *William Pines* had interposed in the matter, but found his Authority too weak to repress such Disorders; for where the Hedge of Government is once broken down, the most vile bear the greatest rule, whereupon he desir'd our assistance, to which we readily condescended, and arming out twelve of us went on Shore, rather as to a surprize then fight, for what could nakedn[e]ss do to encounter with Arms. Being conducted by him to the force of our Enemy, we first entered into parley, seeking to gain them rather by fair means then force, but that not prevailing, we were necessitated to use violence, for this *Henry Phill* being of an undaunted resolution, and having armed his fellows with Clubs and Stones, they sent such a Peal amongst us, as made us at the first to give back, which encouraged them to follow us on with great violence, but we discharging off three or four Guns, when they saw some of themselves wounded, and heard the terrible reports which they gave, they ran away with greater speed then they came. The Band of the *Trevors* who were joyned with us, hotly pursued them, and having taken their Captain, returned with great triumph to their Governour, who sitting in Judgment upon him, he was adjudged to death, and thrown off a steep Rock into the Sea, the only way they have of punishing any by death, except burning.

And now at last we took our solemn leaves of the Governour, and departed from thence, having been there in all, the space of three weeks and two dayes, we took with us good store of the flesh of a Beast which they call there *Reval*, being in tast different either from Beef or Swines-flesh, yet very delightful to the Pallate, and exceeding nutrimental. We took also with us alive, divers Fowls which they call *Marde*, about the bigness of a Pullet, and not different in taste, they are very swift of flight, and yet so fearless of danger, that they will stand still till such time as you catch them: We had also sent us in by the Governour about two bushels of eggs, which as I conjecture were the *Mards* eggs, very lussious in taste, and stren[g]thening to the body.

June 8. We had a sight of *Cambaia*, a part of the *East Indies*, but under the Government of the great *Cham* of *Tartary*; here our Vessel springing a leak, we were forced to put to shore, receiving much dammage in some of our Commodities; we were forced to pay the Pump for eighteen hours together, which, had that miscarried, we had inevitably have perished; here we stai'd five dayes mending our Ship, and drying some of our Goods, and then hoising Sail, in four days time more we came to *Calecute*.

This *Calecute* is the chief Mart Town and Staple of all the *Indian* Traffique, it is very populous, and frequented by Merchants of all Nations. Here we unladed a great part of our Goods, and taking in others, which caused us to stay there a full Moneth, during which space, at leisure times I went abroad to take a survey of the City, which I found to be large and populous, lying for three miles together upon the Sea-shore. Here is a great many of those persons whom they call *Brachmans*, being their Priests or Teachers whom they much reverence. It is a custome here for the King to give to some of those *Brachmain*, the hanselling of his Nuptial Bed; for which cause, not the Kings, but the Kings sisters sons succeed in the Kingdom, as being more certainly known to be of the true Royal blood: And these sisters of his choose what Gentleman they please, on whom to bestow their Virginities; and if they prove not in a certain time to be with child, they betake themselves to these *Brachman Stalions*, who never fail of doing their work.

The people are indifferently civil and ingenious, both men and women imitate a Majesty in their Train and Apparel, which they sweeten with Oyles and Perfumes: adorning themselves with Jewels and other Ornaments befitting each Rank and Quality of them.

They have many odd Customs amongst them which they observe very strictly; as first, not knowing their Wives after they have born them two children: Secondly, not accompanying them, if after five years cohabi[ta]tion they can raise no issue by them, but taking others in their rooms: Thirdly, never being rewarded for any Military exploit, unless they bring with them an enemies Head in their Hand, but that which is strangest, and indeed most barbarous, is that when any of their friends falls sick, they will rather chuse to kill him, then that he should be withered by sickness.

Thus you see there is little employment there for Doctors, when to be sick, is the next warrant for to be slain, or perhaps the people may be of the mind rather to kill themselves, then to let the Doctors do it.

Having dispatched our business, and fraighted again our Ship, we left *Calecute*, and put forth to Sea, and coasted along several of the Islands belonging to *India*, at *Camboia* I met with our old friend Mr. *David Prire*, who was overjoyed to see me, to whom I related our Discovery of the Island of *Pines*, in the same manner as I have related it to you; he was then but newly recovered of a Feaver, the Air of that place not being agreeable to him; here we took in good store of Aloes, and some other Commodities, and victualled our Ship for our return home.

After four dayes sailing, we met with two *Portugal* Ships which came from *Lisbon*, one whereof had in a storm lost its Top-mast, and was forced in part to be towed by the other. We had no bad weather in eleven dayes space, but then a sudden storm of Wind did us much harm in our Tacklings, and swept away one of our Sailors off from the Fore Castle. *November* the sixth had like to have been a fatal day unto us, our Ship striking twice upon a Rock, and at night was in danger of being fired by the negligence of a Boy, leaving a Candle carelesly in the Gun-room; the next day we were chased by a Pyrate of *Argiere*, but by the swiftness of our Sails we out ran him.

December the first we came again to *Madagascar*, where we put in for a fresh recruit of Victuals and Water.

During our abode here, there hapned a very great Earthquake, which tumbled down many Houses; The people of themselves are very Unhospitable and Treacherous, hardly to be drawn to Traffique with any people; and now, this calamitie happening upon them, so enraged them against the Christians, imputing all such calamities to the cause of them, that they fell upon some *Portugals* and wounded them, and we seeing their mischievous Actions, with all the speed we could put forth to Sea again, and sailed to the Island of St. *Hellens.*

Here we stayed all the *Christmas Holy-dayes*, which was ver[y] much celebrated by the Governour there under the King of *Spain*: Here we furnished our selves with all necessaries which we wanted; but upon our departure, our old acquaintance Mr. *Petrus Ramazina*, coming in a Skiff out of the Isle *del Principe*, or the Princes Island, retarded our going for the space of two dayes, for both my self and our Purser had Emergent business with him, he being concerned in those Affairs of which I wrote to you in *April* last: Indeed we cannot but acknowledge his Courtesies unto us, of which you know he is never sparing. *January* the first, we again hois[t]ed Sail, having a fair and prosperous gail of Wind, we touched at the *Canaries*, but made no tarriance, desirous now to see our Native Countrey; but the Winds was very cross unto us for the space of a week, at last we were favoured with a gentle Gale, which brought us on merrily; though we were on a sudden stricken again into a dump; a Sailor from the main Mast discovering five Ships, which put us all in a great fear, we being Richly Laden, and not very well provided for Defence; but they bearing up to us, we found them to be *Zealanders* and our Friends; after many other passages concerning us! not so much worthy of Note, we at last safel[y] arrived at home, *May 26, 1668.*

Thus Sir, have I given you a brief, but true Relation of our Voyage, Which I was the more willing to do, to prevent false Copies which might be spread of this nature: As for the Island of *Pines* itself, which caused me to Write this Relation, I suppose it is a thing so strange as will hardly be credited by some, although perhaps knowing persons, especially considering our last age being so full of Discoveries, that this Place should lie Dormant for so long a space of time; Others I know, such Nullifidians as will believe nothing but what they see, applying that Proverb unto us, *That Travelors may lye by authority.* But Sir, in writing to you, I question not but to give Credence, you knowing my disposition so hateful to divulge Falsities; I shall request you to impart this my Relation to Mr. *W.W.* and Mr. *P.L.* remembring me very kindly unto them, not forgetting my old acquaintance Mr. *J.P.* and Mr. *J.B.* no more at present, but only my best respects to you and your second self, I rest

Yours in the best of friendship,
Henry Cornelius Van Sloetten.
July 22, 1668.

Post-Script

One thing concerning the Isle of *Pines*, I had almost quite forgot, we had with us an *Irish* man named *Dermot Conelly* who had formerly been in *England*, and had learned there to play on the Bag-pipes, which he carried to Sea with him; yet so un Englished he was, that he had quite forgotten your Language, but still retained his Art of Bag-pipe-playing, in which he took extraordinary delight; being one day on Land in the Isle of *Pines*, he played on them, but to see the admiration of those naked people concerning them, would have striken you into admiration; long time it was before we could perswade them that it was not a living creature, although they were permitted to touch and feel it, and yet are the people very intelligible, retaining a great part of the Ingenuity and Gallantry of the *English* Nation, though they have not that happy means to express themselves; in this respect we may account them fortunate, in that possessing little, they enjoy all things, as being contented with what they have, wanting those alurements to mischief, which our *European* Countries are enriched with. I shall not dilate any further, no question but time will make this Island known better to the world; all that I shall ever say of it is, that it is a place enriched with Natures abundance, deficient in nothing conducible to the sustentation of mans life, which were it Manured by Agri-culture and Gardening, as other of our *European* Countries are, no question but it would equal, if not exceed many which now pass for praise worthy.

From *Oroonoko: A Tragedy in Five Acts*

Thomas Southerne

The Loyal Brother, the first production by the Dublin-born playwright Thomas Southerne (1660–1746), was performed at Drury Lane in London in 1682. Southerne spent several years in military service, but by 1690 he had returned to the theater with *Sir Anthony Love*. Five more of his plays were produced in rapid succession, but after *The Fate of Capua* in 1700, no more plays were staged for almost thirty years. His 1726 return, *Money the Mistress*, was booed off stage and marked the end of Southerne's dramatic ambitions. A writer who responded to the tastes of his audience, Southerne is a link between Restoration and eighteenth-century drama. His *Oroonoko: A Tragedy in Five Acts* (1696), of which act 2 is reprinted here, transposed Aphra Behn's novella into an interracial tragedy by representing the African king Oroonoko's wife as white.

DRAMATIS PERSONAE.

OROONOKO	*Master Betty.*
ABOAN	*Mr. C. Kemble.*
GOVERNOR	*Mr. Murray.*
BLANDFORD	*Mr. Brunton.*
STANMORE	*Mr. Claremont.*
CAPTAIN DRIVER	*Mr. Emery.*
HOTMAN	*Mr. Creswell.*

PLANTERS.

Messrs. Atkins—Beverly—Davenport—Field—
Harley—King—Klanert—Lee—Menage.

IMOINDA	*Miss Smith.*
WIDOW	*Mrs. Emery.*

SLAVES.

Messrs. Abbot—T. Blanchard—Bologna—Goodwin—Jefferies—
Lewiss—Powers—Sarjant—Treby—Truman—Wilde.

Mesdames—Bologna—Cox—Dibdin—Follet, and Ratchford.

SCENE—*Surinam.*

Act the Second

SCENE I.

Enter OROONOKO *and* BLANDFORD.

ORO. You know my story, and you say you are
  A friend to my misfortunes: that's a name
  Will teach you what you owe yourself and me.

BLAN. I'll study to deserve to be your friend.
  When once our noble Governor arrives,
  With him you will not need my interest:
  He is too generous not to feel your wrongs.
  But be assur'd I will employ my pow'r,
  And find the means to send you home again.

ORO. I thank you, sir.——My honest wretched friends!
  (*Sighing.*)
  Their chains are heavy: they have hardly found
  So kind a master. May I ask you, sir,
  What is become of them: perhaps I should not.
  You will forgive a stranger.

BLAND. I'll inquire,
  And use my best endeavours, where they are,
  To have them gently us'd.

ORO. Once more I thank you.
  You offer every cordial that can keep
  My hopes alive, to wait a better day.
  What friendly care can do, you have apply'd.
  But, oh! I have a grief admits no cure.

BLAN. You do not know, sir——

ORO. Can you raise the dead?
  Pursue and overtake the wings of time?
  And bring about again the hours, the days,
  The years that made me happy?

BLAN. That is not to be done.

ORO. No, there is nothing to be done for me.
  (*Kneeling and kissing the earth.*)
  Thou god adored! thou ever glorious sun!
  If she be yet on earth, send me a beam
  Of thy all-seeing pow'r to light me to her!
  Or if thy sister goddess has preferr'd
  Her beauty to the skies, to be a star;
  O tell me where she shines, that I may stand
  Whole nights, and gaze upon her.

BLAN. I am rude, and interrupt you.

ORO. I am troublesome:

But pray give me your pardon. My swoll'n heart
Bursts out its passage, and I must complain.
O! can you think of nothing dearer to me?
Dearer than liberty, my country, friends,
Much dearer than my life? That I have lost—
The tend'rest, best belov'd, and loving wife.

BLAND. Alas! I pity you.

ORO. Do pity me:
Pity's a-kin to love; and every thought
Of that soft kind is welcome to my soul.
I would be pity'd here.

BLAN. I dare not ask
More than you please to tell me: but, if you
Think it convenient to let me know
Your story, I dare promise you to bear
A part in your distress, if not assist you.

ORO. Thou honest-hearted man! I wanted such,
Just such a friend as thou art, that would sit
Still as the night, and let me talk whole days
Of my Imoinda. O! I'll tell thee all
From first to last; and pray observe me well.

BLAND. I will most heedfully.

ORO. There was a stranger in my father's court,
Valu'd and honour'd much: he was a white,
The first I ever saw of your complexion:
Of many virtues, and so fam'd in arms,
He still commanded all my father's wars.
I was bred under him. One fatal day,
The armies joining, he before me stepp'd,
Receiving in his breast a poison'd dart
Levell'd at me; he dy'd within my arms.
I've tir'd you already.

BLAN. Pray go on.

ORO. He left an only daughter, whom he brought
An infant to Angola. When I came
Back to the court, a happy conqueror,
Humanity oblig'd me to condole
With this sad virgin for her father's loss,
Lost for my safety. I presented her
With all the slaves of battle, to atone
Her father's ghost. But when I saw her face,
And heard her speak, I offer'd up myself
To be the sacrifice. She bow'd and blush'd;
I wonder'd and ador'd. The sacred pow'r,
That had subdu'd me, then inspir'd my tongue,

Inclin'd her heart, and all our talk was love.

BLAN. Then you were happy.

ORO. O! I was too happy.
I marry'd her: and tho' my country's custom
Indulg'd the privilege of many wives,
I swore myself never to know but her.
She grew with child, and I grew happier still.
O my Imoinda! But it could not last.
Her fatal beauty reach'd my father's ears:
He sent for her to court; where, cursed court,
No woman comes, but for his am'rous use.
He raging to possess her, she was forc'd
To own herself my wife. The furious king
Started at incest: but grown desperate,
Not daring to enjoy what he desir'd,
In mad revenge, which I could never learn,
He poison'd her, or sent her far, far off,
Far from my hopes ever to see her more.

BLAN. Most barbarous of fathers! the sad tale
Has struck me dumb with wonder.

ORO. I have done.
I'll trouble you no farther: now and then
A sigh will have its way: that shall be all.

(*Enter* STANMORE.)

STAN. Blandford, the Lieutenant Governor is gone to your plantation. He desires
you will bring the Royal Slave with you. The sight of his fair mistress,
he says, is an entertainment for a prince; he would have his opinion
of her.

ORO. Is he a lover?

BLAN. So he says himself: he flatters a beautiful slave that I have, and calls her
mistress.

ORO. Must he then flatter her to call her mistress?
I pity the proud man, who thinks himself
Above being in love; what, tho' she be a slave,
She may deserve him.

BLAN. You shall judge of that, when you see her, sir.

ORO. I go with you.

(*Exeunt.*)

SCENE II.
A Plantation.

LIEUTENANT GOVERNOR *following* IMOINDA.

GOV. I have disturb'd you, I confess my fault,
My fair Clemene; but begin again,
And I will listen to your mournful song,

Sweet as the soft complaining nightingale's.
While every note calls out my trembling soul,
And leaves me silent, as the midnight groves,
Only to shelter you;—sing, sing again,
And let me wonder at the many ways
You have to ravish me.

IMO. O, I can weep
Enough for you and me, if that will please you.

GOV. You must not weep: I come to dry your tears,
And raise you from your sorrow.

IMO. Can that be,
When all your actions, and your looks, convince me
That you wou'd keep me here, still far from those,
For whom the tears I shed must flow for ever?—

GOV. They must not sure—be all the past forgotten;—
Look forwards now, where better prospects rise,
New pleasures court you, and new friends invite.

IMO. Alas! can I—I know not what to say—
Nature has form'd you of a diff'rent kind,
Or thus you cou'd not talk; and shou'd I reason
From what I feel, you wou'd not understand me.

GOV. O, yes; my heart has all the soft sensations,
Has all, that friendship, and that love inspires—

IMO. Let your heart answer for me, then:—cou'd you,
Forc'd to some distant land, unknown, forlorn,
A slave, dependent on another's will,
Cut off from all that habit has endear'd,
Cut off from friendship, from domestic joy—
Could you forget all these?—Alas! they're past—
(*Bursts into tears.*)

GOV. O, fair Clemene! there is yet a passion
Which can obliterate all the joys and pains
That others have impress'd; make room for that,
And all I wish is done—look upon me:
Look with the eyes of kind indulging love,
That I may have full cause for what I say:
I come to offer you your liberty,
And be myself the slave. You turn away.
(*Following her.*)
But every thing becomes you. I may take
This pretty hand: I know your modesty
Would draw it back: but you will take it ill,
If I should let it go, I know you would.
You shall be gently forc'd to please yourself;
That you will thank me for.

(*She struggles and gets her hand from him, then he offers to kiss her.*)
Nay, if you struggle with me, I must take——

IMO. You may my life, that I can part with freely.

(*Exit.*)

(*Enter* BLANDFORD, STANMORE, *and* OROONOKO.)

BLAN. So, Governor, we don't disturb you, I hope.
    Your mistress has left you: you were making love; she is thankful for the
        honour, I suppose.

GOV. Quite insensible to all I say and do:
    When I speak to her, she sighs, or weeps,
    But never answers me as I would have her.

STAN. There's something nearer than her slavery, that touches her.

BLAN. What do her fellow-slaves say of her; can't they find the cause?

GOV. Some of them, who pretend to be wiser than the rest, and hate her, I sup-
        pose for being used better than they are, will needs have it that she is
        with child.

BLAN. Poor wretch! if it be so, I pity her:
    She has lost a husband, who perhaps was dear
    To her, and then you cannot blame her.

ORO. If it be so, indeed you cannot blame her.
    (*Sighing.*)

GOV. No, no; it is not so: if it be so,
    I must still love her; and, desiring still,
    I must enjoy her.

BLAN. Try what you can do with fair means, and welcome.

GOV. I'll give you ten slaves for her.

BLAN. You know she is our Lord Governor's: but if I could dispose of her, I
        would not now, especially to you.

GOV. Why not to me?

BLAN. I mean against her will. You are in love with her;
    And we all know what your desires would have:
    Love stops at nothing but possession.
    Were she within your pow'r you do not know
    How soon you would be tempted to forget
    The nature of the deed, and, may be, act
    A violence, you after would repent.

ORO. 'Tis godlike in you to protect the weak.

GOV. Fie, fie, I would not force her. Though she be a slave, her mind is free, and
        should consent.

ORO. Such honour will engage her to consent.
    Shall we not see the wonder?

GOV. Have a care;
    You have a heart, and she has conqu'ring eyes.

ORO. I have a heart: but if it could be false
    To my first vows, ever to love again,

These honest hands should tear it from my breast,
And throw the traitor from me. O! Imoinda!
Living or dead, I can be only thine.

BLAN. Imoinda was his wife: she's either dead,
Or living, dead to him; forc'd from his arms
By an inhuman father. Another time
I'll tell you all.

(*To the* GOVERNOR.)

STAN. The slaves have done their work;
And now begins their evening merriment.

BLAN. The men are all in love with fair Clemene
As much as you, and try their little tricks
To entertain her, and divert her sadness.
May be she is among them: shall we see?

(*Exeunt.*)

SCENE III.

SLAVES, MEN, WOMEN, *and* CHILDREN, *upon the Ground; some rise and dance.*

Enter the LIEUTENANT GOVERNOR, STANMORE, *and* OROONOKO, *as Spectators;*
CAPTAIN DRIVER *and several* PLANTERS, *with their Swords drawn.*

A Bell rings.

CAPT. Where are you, Governor? Make what haste you can
To save yourself and the whole colony.
I bade 'em ring the bell.

Gov. What is the matter?

1 PLAN. The Indians are come down upon us; they have plunder'd some of the
plantations already, and are marching this way as fast as they can.

Gov. What can we do against them?

BLAN. We shall be able to make a stand, till more planters come in to us.

2 PLAN. There are a great many more without, if you would show yourself, and
put us in order.

Gov. There's no danger of the white slaves; they'll not stir. Blandford, come you
along with me: some of you stay here to look after the black slaves.

(*All go out but the* CAPTAIN *and six* PLANTERS, *who all at once seize* OROONOKO.)

1 PLAN. Ay, ay, let us alone.

CAPT. In the first place, we secure you, sir,
As an enemy to the government.

ORO. Are you there, sir? You are my constant friend.

1 PLAN. You will be able to do a great deal of mischief.

CAPT. But we shall prevent you: bring the irons hither. He has the malice of a
slave in him, and would be glad to be cutting his masters' throats. I
know him. Chain his hands and feet, that he may not run over to
them. If they have him, they shall carry him on their backs, that I can
tell them.

(*As they are chaining him,* BLANDFORD *enters, and runs to them.*)

    BLAN. What are you doing there?

    CAPT. Securing the main chance: this is a bosom enemy.

    BLAN. Away, you brutes: I'll answer with my life for his behaviour; so tell the
            Governor.

CAPT. AND PLAN. Well, sir, so we will.

(*Exeunt* CAPTAIN *and* PLANTERS.)

    ORO. Give me a sword, and I'll deserve your trust.

(*Enter the* LIEUTENANT GOVERNOR *and* PLANTERS.)

    BLAN. Hell and the devil! they drive away our slaves before our faces. Governor,
            can you stand tamely by, and suffer this? Clemene, sir, your mistress,
            is among them.

    GOV. We throw ourselves away, in the attempt to rescue them.

    ORO. A lover cannot fall more glorious,
            Than in the cause of love. He, that deserves
            His mistress' favour, will not stay behind:
            I'll lead you on, be bold, and follow me.

(*Exeunt.*)

(*Enter* IMOINDA.)

    IMO. I'm tost about by my tempestuous fate,
            And no where must have rest; Indians, or English!
            Whoever has me, I am still a slave
            No matter whose I am, since I'm no more
            My royal master's; since I'm his no more.
            O, I was happy! nay, I will be happy,
            In the dear thought that I am still his wife,
            Though far divided from him.

(*Draws off to a corner of the stage.*)

(*After a shout, enter the* LIEUTENANT GOVERNOR, OROONOKO, BLANDFORD, STANMORE, *and the* PLANTERS.)

    GOV. Thou glorious man! thou something greater sure
            Than Cæsar ever was! that single arm
            Has sav'd us all: accept our general thanks.

(*All bow to* OROONOKO.)

            And what we can do more to recompense
            Such noble services, you shall command.
            Clemene too shall thank you——she is safe——
            Look up, and bless your brave deliverer.

(*Brings* CLEMENE *forward, looking down on the ground.*)

    ORO. Bless me indeed!

    BLAN. You start!

    ORO. O, all you gods!
            Who govern this great world, and bring about
            Things strange, and unexpected, can it be?

    GOV. What is't you stare at so?

Oro. Answer me, some of you; you who have pow'r,
And have your senses free: or are you all
Struck thro' with wonder too?
(*Looking still fixed on her.*)
Plan. What would you know?
Oro. My soul steals from my body thro' my eyes;
All that is left of life I'll gaze away,
And die upon the pleasure.
Gov. This is strange!
Oro. If you but mock me with her image here:
If she be not Imoinda——
(*She looks upon him, and faints; he runs to her.*)
Ha! she faints!
Nay, then it must be she; it is Imoinda:
My heart confesses her, and leaps for joy,
To welcome her to her own empire here.
I feel her all, in ev'ry part of me.
O! let me press her in my eager arms,
Wake her to life, and with this kindling kiss
Give back that soul, she only lent to me. (*Kisses her.*)
Imoinda! Oh! thy Oroonoko calls.
(Imoinda *coming to life.*)
Imo. My Oroonoko! Oh! I can't believe
What any man can say. But, if I am
To be deceiv'd, there's something in that name,
That voice, that face——(*Staring at him.*)
O! if I know myself, I cannot be mistaken.
(*Runs and embraces* Oroonoko.)
Oro. Never here:
You cannot be mistaken: I am yours,
Your Oroonoko, all that you would have,
Your tender loving husband.
Imo. All indeed
That I would have: my husband! then I am
Alive, and waking to the joys I feel:
They were so great, I could not think them true;
But I believe all that you say to me:
For truth itself and everlasting love
Grows in this breast, and pleasure in these arms.
Oro. Take, take me all: inquire into my heart,
(You know the way to ev'ry secret there)
My heart the sacred treasury of love:
And if, in absence, I have misemploy'd
A mite from the rich store: if I have spent
A wish, a sigh, but what I sent to you;

        May I be curs'd to wish, and sigh in vain,
        And you not pity me.

IMO. O! I believe,
        And know you by myself. If these sad eyes,
        Since last we parted, have beheld the face,
        Of any comfort; or once wish'd to see
        The light of any other heav'n but you,
        May I be struck this moment blind, and lose
        Your blessed sight, never to find you more.

ORO. Imoinda! O, this separation
        Has made you dearer, if it can be so,
        Than you were ever to me. You appear
        Like a kind star to my benighted steps,
        To guide me on my way to happiness:
        I cannot miss it now. Governor, friend,
        You think me mad: but let me bless you all,
        Who any way have been the instruments
        Of finding her again. Imoinda's found!
        And every thing that I would have in her.

(*Embracing her.*)

STAN. Where's your mistress now, Governor?

GOV. Why, where most men's mistresses are forced to be sometimes,
        With her husband, it seems! But I won't lose her so!

(*Aside.*)

STAN. He has fought lustily for her, and deserves her.
        I'll say that for him.

BLAN. Sir, we congratulate your happiness: I do most heartily.

(*To* OROONOKO.)

GOV. And all of us; but how comes it to pass——

ORO. That will require
        More precious time than I can spare you now.
        I have a thousand things to ask of her,
        And she as many more to know of me.
        But you have made me happier, I confess,
        Acknowledge it, much happier, than I
        Have words, or pow'r, to tell you. Captain, you,
        Ev'n you, who most have wrong'd me, I forgive.
        I will not say you have betray'd me now:
        I'll think you but the minister of fate,
        To bring me to my lov'd Imoinda here.

IMO. How, how shall I receive you; how be worthy
        Of such endearments, all this tenderness?
        These are the transports of prosperity,
        When fortune smiles upon us.

ORO. Let the fools,

Who follow fortune, live upon her smiles.
All our prosperity is plac'd in love,
We have enough of that to make us happy.
This little spot of earth, you stand upon,
Is more to me than the extended plains
Of my great father's kingdom. Here I reign
In full delights, in joys to pow'r unknown;
Your love my empire, and your heart my throne.

(*Exeunt.*)

"On a Young Lady's Weeping at Oroonooko"
"To a Gentleman in Love with a Negro Woman"

John Whaley

No biographical information is available about the writer whose two 1732 poems continue the *Oroonooko* theme and the genre of white-black love poetry.

On a Young Lady's Weeping at Oroonooko

At Fate's approach whilst Oroonooko Groans,
Imoinda's Fate, undaunted at his own;
Dropping a gen'rous Tear Lucretia Sighs,
And views the Heroe with Imoinda's Eyes.
When the Prince strikes who envy's not the Deed?
To be so Wept, who wou'd not wish to Bleed?

To a Gentleman in Love with a Negro Woman

Don't Blush, dear Sir, your Flame to own,
    Your sable Mistress to Approve;
Thy Passion other Breasts have known,
    And Heroes justify your Love.

By Æthiopian Beauty mov'd,
    Perseus was clad in Martial Arms;
And the World's Lord too feeble prov'd
For Cleopatra's jetty Charms.

What tho' no sickly White and Red,
    With short liv'd Pride adorn the Maid?
The deeper Yew, its Leaves ne'er Shed,
    While Roses and while Lillies Fade.

What tho' no conscious blush Appear;
    The Tincture of a guilty Skin?
Her's is a Colour that will wear,
    And honest Black ne'er harbours Sin.

Think'st thou such Blood, in Slaves can roll,
    Think'st thou such Lightnings can arise,
Such Pow'r was lodg'd to pierce the Soul,
    In vulgar and Plebeian Eyes?

No, Sir, by Air, and Form, and Dress,
    Thy Fusca, of uncommon Race,
No doubt an Indian Princess is;
    And swarthy King's her Lineage Grace.

Such decent Modesty and Ease!—
    But, least my Rapture be Suspected,
Cease, prying jealous Lover, cease,
    Nor judge the Muse too much Affected.

Me paler Northern Beauties move,
    My Bosom other Darts receives,
Think not I'll Toast an Indian Love,
While Fielding or a Shirley Lives.

Two Versions of the Story of Inkle and Yarico

The periodical essay was pioneered by the longtime friends and collaborators Richard Steele (1672–1729) and Joseph Addison (1672–1719), who founded the *Spectator* in 1711. The *Spectator* occupied a half folio and was built around a fictional club of characters, led by Mr. Spectator, who by turns reported on the doings of daily life, lampooned popular plays and actors, and puzzled over the "fair sex."

The *Spectator* firmly avoided partisanship and emphasized instead the moral traits that would develop in its readers religious devoutness and general goodwill. Publication ended in 1712, but Addison resurrected the *Spectator* in 1714 for a one-volume run, and its influence was felt long after it ceased production. Dozens of periodicals of the later eighteenth century modeled their content and style on the *Spectator*'s straightforwardness and grace.

The *London Magazine*, which was founded in 1732 and continued production until 1785, combined snippets of newspaper essays and birth, death, and marriage records with entire sections of poetry and original essays.

Two versions of the immensely popular story of Inkle and Yarico are presented here. The first appeared in the *Spectator* in 1711. The second, published in the *London Magazine* in 1734, was one of many poetic versions of the story, and it is the first to cast Yarico as an African rather than American Indian woman.

From the *Spectator* (1711)

Arietta is visited by all Persons of both Sexes, who have any Pretence to Wit and Gallantry. She is in that time of Life which is neither affected with the Follies of Youth, or Infirmities of Age; and her Conversation is so mixed with Gaiety and Prudence, that she is agreeable both to the Young and the Old. Her Behaviour is very frank, without being in the least blameable; and as she is out of the Tract of any amorous or ambitious Pursuits of her own, her Visitants entertain her with Accounts of themselves very freely, whether they concern their Passions or their Interests. I made her a Visit this Afternoon, having been formerly introduced to the Honour of her Acquaintance, by my Friend *Will. Honeycomb*, who has prevailed upon her to admit me sometimes into her Assembly, as a civil, inoffensive Man. I found her accompanied with one Person only, a Common-Place Talker, who, upon my Entrance, rose, and after a very slight Civility sat down again; then turning to *Arietta*, pursued his Discourse, which I found was upon the old Topick, of Constancy in Love. He went on with great Facility in repeating what he talks every Day of his Life; and, with the Ornaments of insignificant Laughs and Gestures, enforced his Arguments by Quotations out of Plays and Songs, which allude to the Perjuries of the Fair, and the general Levity of Women. Methought he strove to shine more than ordinarily in his Talkative Way, that he might insult my Silence, and distinguish himself before a Woman of *Arietta*'s Taste and Understanding. She had often an Inclination to interrupt him, but could find no Opportunity, 'till the Larum ceased of its self; which it did not 'till he had repeated and murdered the celebrated Story of the *Ephesian* Matron.

Arietta seemed to regard this Piece of Raillery as an Outrage done to her Sex, as indeed I have always observed that Women, whether out of a nicer Regard to their Honour, or what other Reason I cannot tell, are more sensibly touched with those general Aspersions, which are cast upon their Sex, than Men are by what is said of theirs.

When she had a little recovered her self from the serious Anger she was in, she replied in the following manner.

Sir, When I consider, how perfectly new all you have said on this Subject is, and that the Story you have given us is not quite two thousand Years Old, I cannot but think it a Piece of Presumption to dispute with you: But your Quotations put me in Mind of the Fable of the Lion and the Man. The Man walking with that noble Animal, showed him, in the Ostentation of Human Superiority, a Sign of a Man killing a Lion. Upon which the Lion said very justly, *We Lions are none of us Painters, else we could show a hundred Men killed by Lions, for one Lion killed by a Man.* You Men are Writers, and can represent us Women as Unbecoming as you please in your Works, while we are unable to return the Injury. You have twice or thrice observed in your Discourse, that Hipocrisy is the very Foundation of our Education; and that an Ability to dissemble our Affections, is a professed Part of our Breeding. These, and such other Reflections, are sprinkled up and down the Writings of all Ages, by Authors, who leave behind them Memorials of their Resentment against the Scorn of particular Women, in Invectives against the whole Sex. Such a Writer, I doubt not, was the celebrated *Petronius*, who invented the pleasant Aggravations of the Frailty of the *Ephesian* Lady; but when we consider this Question between the Sexes, which has been either a Point of Dispute or Raillery ever since there were Men and Women, let us take Facts from plain People, and from such as have not either Ambition or Capacity to embellish their Narrations with any Beauties of Imagination. I was the other Day amusing my self with *Ligon*'s Account of *Barbadoes*; and, in Answer to your well-wrought Tale, I will give you (as it dwells upon my Memory) out of that honest Traveller, in his fifty fifth Page, the History of *Inkle* and *Yarico*.

Mr. *Thomas Inkle* of *London*, aged 20 Years, embarked in the *Downs* on the good Ship called the *Achilles*, bound for the *West-Indies*, on the 16th of *June* 1647, in order to improve his Fortune by Trade and Merchandize. Our Adventurer was the third Son of an eminent Citizen, who had taken particular Care to instill into his Mind an early Love of Gain, by making him a perfect Master of Numbers, and consequently giving him a quick View of Loss and Advantage, and preventing the natural Impulses of his Passions, by Prepossession towards his Interests. With a Mind thus turned, young *Inkle* had a Person every way agreeable, a ruddy Vigour in his Countenance, Strength in his Limbs, with Ringlets of fair Hair loosely flowing on his Shoulders. It happened, in the Course of the Voyage, that the *Achilles*, in some Distress, put into a Creek on the Main of *America*, in Search of Provisions: The Youth, who is the Hero of my Story, among others, went ashore on this Occasion. From their first Landing they were observed by a Party of *Indians*, who hid themselves in the Woods for that Purpose. The *English* unadvisedly marched a great distance from the Shore into the Country, and were intercepted by the Natives, who slew the greatest Number of them. Our Adventurer escaped among others, by flying into a Forest. Upon his coming into a remote and pathless Part of the Wood, he threw himself, tired and breathless, on a little Hillock, when an *Indian* Maid rushed from a Thicket behind him: After the first Surprize, they appeared mutually agreeable to each other. If the *European* was highly Charmed with the Limbs, Features, and wild Graces of the Naked *American*; the *American* was no less taken with the Dress, Complexion and Shape of an *European*, covered from Head to Foot. The *Indian* grew immediately enamoured of him, and consequently sollicitous for his Preservation: She therefore conveyed him to a Cave, where she gave him a Delicious Repast of Fruits, and led him to a Stream to slake his Thirst. In the midst of these good Offices, she would sometimes play with his Hair, and delight in the Opposition of its Colour, to that of her Fingers: Then open his Bosome, then laugh at him for covering it. She was, it seems, a Person of Distinction, for she every day came to him in a different Dress, of the most beautiful Shells, Bugles and Bredes. She likewise brought him a great many Spoils, which her other Lovers had presented to her; so that his Cave was richly adorned with all the spotted Skins of Beasts, and most Party-coloured Feathers of Fowls which that World afforded. To make his Confinement more tolerable, she would carry him in the Dusk of the Evening, or by the favour of Moon-light, to unfrequented Groves and Solitudes, and show him where to lye down in Safety, and sleep amidst the Falls of Waters, and Melody of Nightingales. Her Part was to watch and hold him in her Arms, for fear of her Country-men, and wake him on Occasions to consult his Safety. In this manner did the Lovers pass away their Time, till they had learn'd a Language of their own, in which the Voyager communicated to his Mistress, how happy he should be to have her in his Country, where she should be Cloathed in such Silks as his Wastecoat was made of, and be carried in Houses drawn by Horses, without being exposed to Wind or Weather. All this he promised her the Enjoyment of, without such Fears and Alarms as they were there Tormented with. In this tender Correspondence these Lovers lived for several Months, when *Yarico*, instructed by her Lover, discovered a Vessel on the Coast, to which she made Signals, and in the Night, with the utmost Joy and Satisfaction accompanied him to a Ships-Crew of his Country-Men, bound for *Barbadoes*. When a Vessel from the Main arrives in that Island, it seems the Planters come down to the Shoar, where there is an immediate Market of the *Indians* and other Slaves, as with us of Horses and Oxen.

To be short, Mr. *Thomas Inkle*, now coming into *English* Territories, began seriously to reflect upon his loss of Time, and to weigh with himself how many Days Interest of his Mony he had lost during his stay with *Yarico*. This Thought made the Young Man very pensive, and careful what Account he should be able to give his Friends of his Voyage. Upon which Considerations, the prudent and frugal young Man sold *Yarico* to a *Barbadian* Merchant; notwithstanding that the poor Girl, to incline him to commiserate her Condition, told him that she was with Child by him: But he only made use of that Information, to rise in his Demands upon the Purchaser.

I was so touch'd with this Story, (which I think should be always a Counterpart to the *Ephesian* Matron) that I left the Room with Tears in my Eyes; which a Woman of *Arietta*'s good Sense, did, I am sure, take for greater Applause, than any Compliments I could make her.

From the *London Magazine* (1734)

Ye virgin train, an artless *dame* inspire,
Unlearnt in schools, unblest with natal fire,
To save this story from devouring fate,
And the dire arts of faithless man relate.
A youth I sing, in face and shape divine,
In whom both art and nature did combine
With heavenly skill to mingle ev'ry charm,
As gods of old did fair *Pandora* form.
Stranger to virtue, this deceiver held
The box of mischiefs in his breast conceal'd;
His outward form each female heart enflam'd;
His inward beauty lurking avarice stain'd.
    Insatiate love of gold, and hope of gain,
Encourag'd him to cut the yielding main;
By winds, or waves, or the decrees of heaven,
His bark upon a barbarous coast was driven;
Possest by men who thirst for human blood,
Who live in caves, or thickets of the wood:
Untaught to plant (yet corn and fruits abound,
And fragrant flowers enamel all the ground.)
Distrest, he landed on this fatal shore,
With some companions, which were soon no more;
The savage race their trembling flesh devour,
Off'ring oblations to th'infernal power.
Dreadfully suppliant, human limbs they tore,
(accursed rites!) and quaft their streaming gore.
Immortal *Jove* stoop'd from his azure sky,
Grieving a form so like his own shou'd dye;
On the fair youth *mercurial* speed bestow'd;
Swifter than thought he reach'd the shady wood.
    Beneath a nightly shade he panting lies,
Screen'd by all-pitying *Jove* from hostile eyes;
Yet gloomy sorrows and unmanly fears
Swell'd his sad breast which he bedew'd with tears:
When lo! a negro virgin chanc'd to rove

Thro' the thick mazes of the madding grove,
Whose glitt'ring shells and elegant undress,
With various plumes, a noble birth confess.
With reverential fear, the well-shap'd maid
Thought him a god, and low obeisance paid.
His face like polish'd marble did appear;
His silken robe, and long-curl'd flaxen hair
Amaz'd the nymph; nor less her sparkling eyes,
And naked beauty, did the youth surprize.
Low at her feet, in suppliant posture laid,
With speaking eyes, he thus addrest the maid.
    O let soft pity touch that lovely breast!
Succour a man, by various ills opprest:
Such finish'd grace does thro' your person shine,
Sure 'tis enliven'd by a soul divine.
    The tender negro look'd a kind reply
Thro' pearls of pity, dropping from her eye;
With hands uplifted, did the gods implore,
That her relentless countrymen no more
Might stain their native land with human gore.
He seiz'd her hand, with tender passion prest,
While copious tears both love and fear confest.
The pitying maid view'd him with yielding eyes,
And from each bosom mutual sighs arise.
    His safety, now, became her only care,
A secret cave she knew, and bid him there;
Adorn'd it with the spoils of leopards slain,
Which other lovers ventur'd life to gain.
Through mazy thickets, and a pathless wood
She prest, advent'rous, with delicious food.
Daily her hand a rich repast did bring
Of ripen'd fruits, and waters from the spring:
But when declining, toward the close of day,
The crimson sun sets weary on the sea,
Strait to a shady grove, where fountains rise,
From woods defended, and inclement skies;
Where the wing'd warblers of the air conspire
From several boughs, to form a heavenly quire,
Adorn'd with fragrant flowers, and ever-green,
She leads the youth (delightful silvan scene!)
Where he, in peaceful slumbers, takes his rest,
Forgets his fears, and calms his tim'rous breast.
    In soft repose the beauteous lover lies,
While *Yarico* with care unseals her eyes;
With anxious fear the matchless maid attends,

Careful to save him from her barb'rous friends.
    The flowing curls which o'er his shoulders play'd
With artless beauty, pleas'd the negro maid;
She thought her fingers, when entangled there,
Like clouds uncircling *Berenice's* hair:
The graceful youth confessing equal fire,
Did her just symmetry of shape admire.
    Oft would he say; my *Yarico*, with thee
(My only bliss!) cou'd I my country see,
If ever I forget my vows of love,
Unblest, abandon'd, may I friendless rove.
To thee, alone, I owe the vital air;
My love and gratitude for ever share.
I'll gems provide, and silks of curious art,
With gifts expressive of my grateful heart:
Thou in a house by horses drawn shalt ride,
With me, thy faithful lover, by thy side:
The female train shall round with envy gaze,
Wonder, and silent sigh unwilling praise.
    Pleas'd with his words, desiring more to please,
She from a craggy cliff survey'd the seas;
A bark she spy'd, and did by signs implore,
That they would touch upon the sandy shore.
With joy she ran—My love, make haste away,
A Vessel waits us, on the foaming sea.
Soon he the vessel's lofty side ascends,
And finds them to be countrymen, and friends.
With lovely *Yarico*, puts off to sea;
With equal joy they plough the watry way.
    When the fair youth, despairing, calls to mind
All hopes eluded of his wealth design'd;
Riches the seat of his affection seize,
And faithful *Yarico* no more can please.
Unhappy maid! To wasting sorrows born,
And fated evils undeserv'd to mourn.
    This youth was born too near the northern pole,
Which chill'd each virtue in his frozen soul:
But near the sun, the nymph her birth confest,
Where ev'ry virtue glow'd within her breast,
Thus oar lies in the earth, unfinish'd, cold;
But purg'd by fire, it brightens into gold.
    Propitious *Zephyrs*, fill their swelling sails;
They make *Barbadoes*, blest with prosp'rous gales.
The planters thick'ning on the key appear,
To purchase negroe slaves, if any there;

When the false youth, by cursed avarice sway'd,
Horrid to mention! sells his faithful maid.

    Amaz'd and trembling, silently she mourn'd,
While speaking tears her radiant eyes adorn'd.
Low at his feet, the lovely mourner lay;
Nor would to words her swelling heart give way.
She grasps his knees, in vain attempts to speak,
At length her words in moving accent, break:
O much lov'd youth, in tender pity spare
A helpless maid, my long-try'd faith revere.
From you this worst of human ills to prove,
Must break a heart that overflows with love.
Break not my heart, nor drive me to despair,
Lest you deface your lovely image there.
Ah! do not with consummate woe undo
A soul, that father, mother, country, left for you.
What sorrows must my tender parents mourn,
By me forsaken, never to return?
Transfer'd from them, to you my love I gave;
Unjust return! to sell me for a slave.
Oh call to mind the sacred oaths you've given.
Remember there are thunderbolts in heaven.
But if the swelling sorrows in my breast
Your heart of adamant can still resist,
Yet let the infant in my womb I bear,
The blessing taste of your paternal care.

    He thrust her from him with remorseless hand,
For her condition rais'd his first demand.
Pleas'd with success he cheerfully returns,
While the hapless *Yarico* in bondage mourns.
The merchants all the prudent youth admire,
That could, so young, a trading soul acquire.

16

The Dying Negro

Thomas Day and John Bicknell

The famous 1773 poem *The Dying Negro* was a collaborative effort by the English writers Thomas Day (1748–1789) and John Bicknell (1746–1787). Bicknell had come across a story in the *London Courant* about a black slave who had escaped his ship to become baptized and marry a white servant. Captured by his master upon his return, the slave killed himself in despair. Bicknell enlisted Day's aid in creating a poetic account of the story to publicize the evils of African slavery. *The Dying Negro* (which is reprinted here) was a success, inspiring antislavery sentiment in England and propelling Day into a politically responsive literary career. Among the opponents to the slave trade who admired the poem was Olaudah Equiano, who quoted it in his 1789 *Interesting Narrative*.

Advertisement

The following POEM was occasioned by an article of news which appeared last week in the London papers, intimating that "a Black, who a few days before, ran away from his master, and got himself christened, with intent to marry his fellow-servant, a white woman, being taken, and sent on board the Captain's ship, in the Thames; took an opportunity of shooting himself through the head."

The Author trusts, that in an age and country, in which we boast of philanthropy, and generous sentiments, few persons, (except *West-Indians*) can read the above paragraph, without emotions similar to those, which inspired the following lines. They who are not more inclined to sympathize with the *master*, than the *servant*, upon the occasion,—will perhaps not be displeased at an attempt to delineate the feelings of the latter, in the situation above described.—

> "Such artless plaints as nature might inspire,
> But smooth'd and fitted to the sounding lyre."

Whatever reception this little piece may meet with from others, the Author can never regret that portion of time as lost, which he has employed in paying this small tribute of humanity to the misery of a fellow-creature.

A Poetical Epistle, &c.

Blest with thy last sad gift—the power to dye,
At length, thy shafts, stern fortune, I defy;
Welcome, kind pass-port to an unknown shore!—
The world and I are enemies no more.
This weapon ev'n in chains the brave can wield,
And vanquish'd, quit triumphantly the field.

   Yet ere this execrated being close,
Ere one determin'd stroke end all my woes.
O thou whom late I call'd too fondly mine,
Dearer than life, whom I with life resign!
How shall I soothe thy grief, my destin'd bride!
One sad farewell, one last embrace denied?
For oh! thy tender breast my pangs will share,
Bleed for my wounds, and feel my deep despair.
Thy tears alone will grace a wretch's grave,
A wretch, whom only thou would'st wish to save.
Take these last sighs—to thee my soul I breathe—
Fond love in dying groans, is all I can bequeathe.

   Why did I, slave, beyond my lot aspire?
Why didst thou fan, fair maid, the growing fire?
Full dear, for each deluding smile of thine
I pay, nor at thy fatal charms repine.
For thee I bade my drooping soul revive;
For thee alone I could have borne to live;
And love, I said, shall make me large amends,
For persecuting foes, and faithless friends;
Fool that I was! enur'd so long to pain,
To trust to hope, or dream of joy again.
Joy, stranger guest, too soon my faith betray'd,
And love but points to death's eternal shade,
There while I rest from mis'ry's galling load,
Be thou the care of every pitying God!
Nor may that Dæmon's unpropitious power,
Who shed his influence on my natal hour,
Pursue thee too with unrelenting hate,
And blend with mine the colour of thy fate.
For thee may those soft hours return again,
When pleasure led thee o'er the smiling plain,
Ere, like some hell-born spectre of dismay,
I cross'd thy path, and darken'd all the way.

Ye waving groves, that from this cell I view!
Ye meads, now glitt'ring with the morning dew!
Ye flowers that blush on yonder purple shore,
That at my baneful step shall fade no more,
A long farewell!—I ask no vernal bloom—
No pageant wreaths to deck an outcast's tomb.
—Let serpents hiss and night-shade blacken there,
To mark the friendless victim of despair!

    And better in th' untimely grave to rot,
The world and all it's cruelties forgot,
Than dragg'd once more beyond the Western main,
To groan beneath some dastard planter's chain,
Where my poor countrymen in bondage wait,
The long enfranchisement of ling'ring fate.
Oh! my heart sinks, my dying eyes o'erflow,
When mem'ry paints the picture of their woe!
For I have seen them, ere the dawn of day,
Rouz'd by the lash, go forth their chearless way,
And while their souls with shame and anguish burn,
Salute with groans unwelcome morn's return,
And, chiding every hour the slow-pac'd sun
Pursue their toils, till all his race was run,
Without one hope—to mitigate their pain—
One distant hope, their freedom to regain;
Then like the dull unpitied brutes repair
To stalls more wretched, and to coarser fare,
Thank Heav'n, one day of misery was o'er,
And sink to sleep, and wish to wake no more.
Sleep on! dear, lost companions in despair,
Whose suff'rings still my latest tears shall share!
Sleep, and enjoy the only boon of Heav'n
To you in common with your tyrants giv'n.
O while soft slumber from their couches flies,
Still may its balmy blessings seal your eyes;
Awhile in sweet oblivion lull your woes,
And brightest visions gladden your repose!
Let fancy now, unconscious of the change,
Thro' your own climes, and native forests range,
Still waft ye to each well-known stream and grove,
And visit every long-lost scene ye love!
—I sleep no more—nor in the midnight shade,
Invoke ideal phantoms to my aid,
Nor wake again, abandon'd and forlorn,
To find each dear delusion fled at morn;

A slow-consuming death I will not wait,
But snatch at least one sullen boon from fate;
Yon ruddy streaks the rising sun proclaim,
That never more shall beam upon my shame;
Bright orb! for others let thy glory shine—
The gloomy privilege to die, be mine.
Beneath such wrongs let pallid Christians live,
Such they can perpetrate, and may forgive.

    And thou, whose impious avarice and pride
Thy God's blest symbol to my brows denied,
Forbade me or the rights of man to claim,
Or share with thee a Christian's hallow'd name,
Thou too farewell!—for not beyond the grave,
Thy power extends, nor is my dust thy slave.
Go bribe thy kindred ruffians with thy gold,
But dream not nature's rights are bought and sold.
In vain Heav'n spread so wide the swelling sea;
Vast watry barrier, 'twixt thy world and me;
Swift round the globe, by earth nor heav'n controul'd,
Fly proud oppression and dire lust of gold.
Wheree'er the thirsty hell-hounds take their way,
Still nature bleeds, and man becomes their prey.
In the wild wastes of Afric's sandy plain,
Where roars the lion through his drear domain,
To curb the savage monarch in the chace,
There too Heav'n planted man's majestic race;
Bade reason's sons with nobler titles rise,
Lift high their brow sublime, and scan the skies.
What tho' the sun in his meridian blaze
On their scorch'd bodies dart his fiercest rays?
What tho' no rosy tints adorn their face,
No silken ringlets shine with flowing grace?
Yet of etherial temper are their souls,
And in their veins the tide of honour rolls;
And valour kindles there the hero's flame,
Contempt of death, and thirst of martial fame.
And pity melts the sympathizing breast,
Ah! fatal virtue!—for the brave distrest.

    My tortur'd breast, O sad remembrance spare!
Why dost thou plant thy keenest daggers there,
And shew me what I was, and aggravate despair?
Ye streams of Gambia, and thou sacred shade!
Where, in my youth's first dawn I joyful stray'd,

Oft have I rouz'd amid your caverns dim,
The howling tiger, and the lion grim,
In vain they gloried in their headlong force,
My javelin pierc'd them in their raging course.
But little did my boding mind bewray,
The victor and his hopes were doom'd a prey
To human beasts more fell, more cruel far than they.
Ah! what avails it that in every plain,
I purchas'd glory with my blood in vain?
Ah! what avails the conqu'ror's laurel meed,
The generous purpose or the dauntless deed?
Fall'n are my trophies, blasted is my fame,
Myself become a thing without a name,
The sport of haughty Lords and ev'n of slaves the shame.

 Curst be the winds, and curst the tides that bore
These European robbers to our shore!
O be that hour involv'd in endless night,
When first their streamers met my wond'ring sight,
I call'd the warriors from the mountain's steep,
To meet these unknown terrors of the deep;
Rouz'd by my voice, their generous bosoms glow,
They rush indignant, and demand the foe,
And poize the darts of death and twang the bended bow.
When lo! advancing o'er the sea-beat plain,
I mark'd the leader of a warlike train.
Unlike his features to our swarthy race.
And golden hair play'd round his ruddy face.
While with insidious smile and lifted hand,
He thus accosts our unsuspecting band.
"Ye valiant chiefs, whom love of glory leads
"To martial combats, and heroic deeds;
"No fierce invader your retreat explores,
"No hostile banner waves along your shores.
"From the dread tempests of the deep we fly,
"Then lay, ye chiefs, these pointed terrors by.
"And O, your hospitable cares extend,
"So may ye never need the aid ye lend!
"So may ye still repeat to every grove
"The songs of freedom, and the strains of love!"
Soft as the accents of the traitor flow,
We melt with pity, and unbend the bow;
With lib'ral hand our choicest gifts we bring,
And point the wand'rers to the freshest spring.
Nine days we feasted on the Gambian strand,

And songs of friendship echo'd o'er the land.
When the tenth morn her rising lustre gave,
The chief approach'd me by the sounding wave.
"O, youth," he said, "what gifts can we bestow,
"Or how requite the mighty debt we owe?
"For lo! propitious to our vows, the gale
"With milder omens fills the swelling sail.
"To-morrow's sun shall see our ships explore
"These deeps, and quit your hospitable shore.
"Yet while we linger, let us still employ
"The number'd hours in friendship and in joy;
"Ascend our ships, their treasures are your own,
"And taste the produce of a world unknown."

 He spoke; with fatal eagerness we burn,
Ah! wretches, destin'd never to return!
The smiling traitors with insidious care,
The goblet proffer, and the feast prepare,
'Till dark oblivion shades our closing eyes,
And all disarm'd each fainting warrior lies,
O wretches! to your future evils blind!
O morn for ever present to my mind!
When bursting from the treach'rous bands of sleep,
Rouz'd by the murmers of the dashing deep,
I woke to bondage, and ignoble pains,
And all the horrors of a life in chains.
Where were your thunders in that dreadful hour,
Ye Gods of Afric! where your heavenly power?
Did not my prayers, my groans, my tears invoke
Your slumb'ring justice to direct the stroke?
No power descended to assist the brave,
No lightnings flash'd, and I became a slave.
From Lord to Lord my wretched carcase sold,
In Christian traffic, for their sordid gold:
Fate's blackest clouds still gather'd o'er my head;
And now they burst, and mix me with the dead.

 Yet when my fortune cast my lot with thine,
And bade beneath one roof our labours join,
Surpriz'd I felt the tumults of my breast
Lull'd by thy beauties, and subside to rest.
Delusive hopes my changing soul enflame,
And gentler transports agitate my frame.
What tho' obscure thy birth, superior grace
Beam'd in the glowing features of thy face;

Ne'er had my youth such winning softness seen,
Where Afric's sable beauties danc'd the green,
When some bright maid receiv'd her lover's vow,
And bound the offer'd chaplet to her brow;
While on thy languid eyes I fondly gaze,
And tremble while I meet their azure rays,
O mildest virgin, thou did'st not despise
The humble homage of a captive's sighs.
By heav'n abandon'd and by man betray'd,
Each hope resign'd of comfort or of aid,
Thy gen'rous love could every sorrow end,
In thee I found a mistress and a friend;
Still as I told the story of my woes,
With heaving sighs thy lovely bosom rose;
The trick'ling drops of liquid chrystal stole
Down thy fair cheek, and mark'd thy pitying soul;
Dear drops! upon my bleeding heart, like balm
They fell, and soon my wounded soul grew calm,
Then my lov'd country, parents, friends forgot;
Heaven I absolv'd, nor murmur'd at my lot,
Thy sacred smiles could every pang remove,
And liberty became less dear than love.
    —Ah! where is now that voice which lull'd my woes?
That Angel-face, which sooth'd me to repose?
By Nature tempted, and with passion blind,
Are these the joys Hope whisper'd to my mind?
Is this the end of constancy like thine?
Are these the transports of a flame like mine?
My hopes, my joys, are vanish'd into air,
And now of all that once engag'd my care,
These chains alone remain, this weapon and despair!

    —So may thy life's gay prospects all be curst,
And all thy flatt'ring hopes like bubbles burst,
Thus end thy golden visions, son of pride!
Whose ruthless ruffians tore me from my bride;
That beauteous prize Heav'n had reserv'd at last,
Sweet recompence for all my sorrows past.
O may thy harden'd bosom never prove
The tender joys of friendship or of love!
Yet may'st thou, doom'd to hopeless flames a prey,
In disappointed passion pine away!
And see thy fair-one, to a rival's arms,
Obdurate to thy vows, resign her charms.

Why does my ling'ring soul her flight delay?
Come, lovely maid, and gild the dreary way!
Come, wildly rushing with disorder'd charms,
And clasp thy bleeding lover to thy arms,
Close his sad eyes, receive his parting breath,
And sooth him sinking in the shades of death!
O come—thy presence can my pangs beguile,
And bid th' inexorable tyrant smile;
Transported will I languish on thy breast,
And sink in raptures to eternal rest:
The hate of men, the wrongs of fate forgive,
Forget my woes, and almost wish to live.
—Ah! rather fly, lest ought of doubt controul
The dreadful purpose lab'ring in my soul,
Tears must not bend me, nor thy beauties move,
This hour I triumph over fate and love.

    —Again with tenfold rage my bosom burns,
And all the tempest of my soul returns,
Now fiery transports rend my madding brain,
And death extends his shelt'ring arms in vain;
For unreveng'd I fall, unpitied die;
And with my blood glut Pride's insatiate eye!

    Thou Christian God, to whom so late I bow'd,
To whom my soul its fond allegiance vow'd,
When crimes like these thy injur'd pow'r prophane,
O God of Nature! art thou call'd in vain?
Did'st thou for this sustain a mortal wound,
While Heav'n, and Earth, and Hell, hung trembling round?
That these vile fetters might my body bind,
And agony like this distract my mind?
On thee I call'd with reverential awe,
Ador'd thy wisdom, and embrac'd thy law;
Yet mark thy destin'd convert as he lies,
His groans of anguish, and his livid eyes,
These galling chains, polluted with his blood,
Then bid his tongue proclaim thee just and good!
But if too weak thy boasted power to spare,
Or suff'rings move thee not, O hear despair!
Thy hopes, and blessings I alike resign,
But let revenge, let swift revenge be mine!
Be this proud bark, which now triumphant rides,
Toss'd by the winds, and shatter'd by the tides!
And may these fiends, who now exulting view

The horrors of my fortune, feel them too!
Be their's the torment of a ling'ring fate,
Slow as thy justice, dreadful as my hate,
Condemn'd to grasp the riven plank in vain,
And [chased] by all the monsters of the main,
And while they spread their sinking arms to thee,
Then let their fainting souls remember me!

17

Letter to James Tobin

Olaudah Equiano

The writer Olaudah Equiano (ca. 1745–1797), also known as Gustavus Vassa, was born in what is now Nigeria and was enslaved as a child. He underwent the Middle Passage on a slave vessel, was sold in Barbados, and became captain's servant and "able seaman" on various British ships. He purchased his freedom from a Montserrat merchant in 1766 and later moved to England, where he became an active force in the struggle to end the profitable slave trade, by then a predominantly British enterprise. Equiano married the Englishwoman Susanna Cullen in 1792, and they had two daughters. His autobiography, *The Interesting Narrative of the Life of Olaudah Equiano*, was published in 1789 and was popular enough to go through nine editions and to be translated into other languages. It inspired English, American, and European opponents to the slave trade, though the Anglo-American treaty to end the trade was signed only in 1807. In the following letter, published in the *Public Advertiser* in 1788 in response to a pro-slave trade writer, Equiano advocates interracial marriage. In the same year he petitioned Queen Charlotte to end the slave trade.

To J. T. [James Tobin] Esq;
Author of the BOOKS called CURSORY REMARKS & REJOINDER.

Sir,

That to love mercy and judge rightly of things is an honour to man, no body I think will deny; but "if he understandeth not, nor sheweth compassion to the sufferings of his fellow-creatures, he is like the beasts that perish." Psalm lix verse 20.

Excuse me, Sir, if I think you in no better predicament than that exhibited in the latter part of the above clause; for can any man less ferocious than a tiger or a wolf attempt to justify the cruelties inflicted on the negroes in the West Indies? You certainly cannot be susceptible of human pity to be so callous to their complicated woes! Who could but the Author of the Cursory Remarks so debase his nature, as not to feel his keenest pangs of heart on reading their deplorable story? I confess my cheek changes colour with resentment against your unrelenting barbarity, and wish you from my soul to run the gauntlet of Lex Talionis at this time; for as you are so fond of flogging others, it is no bad proof of your deserving a flagellation yourself. Is it not written in the 15th chapter of Numbers, the 15th and 16th verses, that there is the same law for the stranger as for you?

Then, Sir, why do you rob him of the common privilege given to all by the Universal and Almighty Legislator? Why exclude him from the enjoyment of benefits which he has equal right to with yourself? Why treat him as if he was not of like feeling? Does civilization warrant these incursions upon natural justice? No.—Does religion? No.—Benevolence to all is its essence, and do unto others as we would others should do unto us, its grand precept—to Blacks as well as Whites, all being the children of the same parent. Those, therefore, who transgress those sacred obligations, and here, Mr. Remarker, I think you are caught, are not superior to brutes which understandeth not, nor to beasts which perish.

From your having been in the West Indies, you must know that the facts stated by the Rev. Mr. Ramsay are true; and yet regardless of the truth, you controvert them. This surely is supporting a bad cause at all events, and brandishing falsehood to strengthen the hand of the oppressor. Recollect, Sir, that you are told in the 17th verse of the 19th chapter of Leviticus, "You shall not suffer sin upon your neighbour"; and you will not I am sure, escape the upbraidings of your conscience, unless you are fortunate enough to have none; and remember also, that the oppressor and the oppressed are in the hands of the just and awful God, who says, Vengeance is mine and I will repay—repay the oppressor and the justifier of the oppression. How dreadful then will your fate be? The studied and torturing punishments, inhuman, as they are, of a barbarous planter, or a more barbarous overseer, will be tenderness compared to the provoked wrath of an angry but righteous God! who will raise, I have the fullest confidence, many of the sable race to the joys of Heaven, and cast the oppressive white to that doleful place, where he will cry, but will cry in vain, for a drop of water!

Your delight seems to be in misrepresentation, else how could you in page 11 of your Remarks, and in your Rejoinder, page 35, communicate to the public such a glaring untruth as that the oath of a free African is equally admissible in several courts with that of a white person? The contrary of this I know is the fact at every one of the islands I have been, and I have been at no less than fifteen. But who will dispute with such an invective fibber? Why nobody to be sure; for you'll tell, I wish I could say truths, but you oblige me to use ill manners, you lie faster than Old Nick can hear them. A few shall stare you in the face:

What is your speaking of the laws in favour of the Negroes?

Your description of the iron muzzle?

That you never saw the infliction of a severe punishment, implying thereby that there is none?

That a Negro has every inducement to wish for a numerous family?

That in England there are no black labourers?

That those who are not servants, are in rags or thieves?

In a word, the public can bear testimony with me that you are a malicious slanderer of an honest, industrious, injured people!

From the same source of malevolence the freedom of their inclinations is to be shackled—it is not sufficient for their bodies to be oppressed, but their minds must also? Iniquity in the extreme! If the mind of a black man conceives the passion of love for a fair female, he is to pine, languish, and even die, sooner than an intermarriage be allowed, merely because the complexion of the offspring should be tawney—A more foolish prejudice than this never warped a cultivated mind—for as no contamination of the virtues of the heart would result from the union, the mixture of colour could be of no consequence. God looks with equal good-will on all his creatures, whether black or white—let neither, therefore, arrogantly condemn the other.

The mutual commerce of the sexes of both Blacks and Whites, under the restrictions of moderation and law, would yield more benefit than a prohibition—the mind free—would not have such a strong propensity toward the black females as when under restraint: Nature abhors restraint, and for ease either evades or breaks it. Hence arise secret amours, adultery, fornication and all other evils of lasciviousness! hence that most abandoned boasting of the French Planter, who, under the dominion of lust, had the shameless impudence to exult at the violations he had committed against Virtue, Religion, and the Almighty—hence also spring actual murders on infants, the procuring of abortions, enfeebled constitution, disgrace, shame, and a thousand other horrid enormities.

Now, Sir, would it not be more honour to us to have a few darker visages than perhaps yours among us, than inundation of such evils? and to provide effectual remedies, by a liberal policy against evils which may be traced to some of our most wealthy Planters as their fountain, and which may have smeared the purity of even your own chastity?

As the ground-work, why not establish intermarriages at home, and in our Colonies? and encourage open, free, and generous love upon Nature's own wide and extensive plan, subservient only to moral rectitude, without distinction of the colour of a skin?

That ancient, most wise, and inspired politician, Moses, encouraged strangers to unite with the Israelites, upon this maxim, that every addition to their number was an addition to their strength, and as an inducement, admitted them to most of the immunities of his own people. He established marriage with strangers by his own example—The Lord confirmed them—and punished Aaron and Miriam for vexing their brother for marrying the Ethiopian—Away then with your narrow impolitic notion of preventing by law what will be a national honour, national strength, and productive of national virtue—Intermarriages!

Wherefore, to conclude in the words of one of your selected texts, "If I come, I will remember the deeds which he doeth, prating against us with malicious words."

I am Sir,
Your fervent Servant,
GUSTAVUS VASSA, the Ethiopian and the King's late Commissary
for the African Settlement.
Baldwin's Garden, Jan. 1788

Black and White in Europe and the Americas, 1800–1870

In the nineteenth century, the themes of black-white love and marriage and the children of interracial unions became popular with a good number of major writers. Some of the terms for racial mixing created in the Spanish colonies, where they were illustrated by the popular genre of Casta painting, now appeared with greater frequency in the literature, especially "Mulatto," "Quadroon," and "Octoroon." The literary approaches varied, as writers tested their themes in prose fiction, poetry, and drama. These themes are intertwined with motifs of the Haitian and French revolutions in Heinrich von Kleist's radical representation of a tragic failure of trust and in Claire de Duras's turning of the sentimental tradition toward psychology and interiority. Alexander Pushkin's historical novel fragment is marked by extraordinarily sharp ironic detachment. Lydia Maria Child's short story continues the political-sentimental tradition. Alexandre Dumas fictionalizes racist discrimination and racial passing. Theodor Storm's Jenny comes to life in a novella that tells a classic love story. In Henry Wadsworth Longfellow's and Elizabeth Barrett Browning's antislavery poems, the violation of the closest family relations is central; William Dean Howells sounds a classical tone in poeticizing a Mississippi tragedy. Hans Christian Andersen's idealizing Danish verse drama represents a mixed-race hero; the plays by Dion Boucicault and Wilkie Collins reveal the new presence of low comedy, broad dialect, and minstrelsy in the figures of ordinary, nonheroic slaves whose language contrasts sharply with the mixed-race protagonists' standard English. On the stage all parts in such dramas would be played by white actors with different degrees of makeup. In several plays, a slave sale or auction would be held in the last act. The fact that interracial unions constituted a taboo in American public life of the period becomes apparent in the *Miscegenation* pamphlet that closes this section.

18

The Engagement in Santo Domingo

Heinrich von Kleist

The brilliant plays and novellas of the German writer Heinrich von Kleist (1777–1811) received their due recognition only after his death, and were an important influence on later writers, including Kafka and Rilke. His 1811 novella *The Engagement in Santo Domingo*, which is reprinted here in the 1954 translation by Martin Greenberg, sets the tragic love story of the Swiss Gustav von der Ried and the mixed-race woman Toni in the Haitian revolution. The story inspired a contemporary dramatic version by Gustav Körner, which ends with a happy intermarriage, and twentieth-century prose retellings by Anna Seghers and Hans Christoph Buch.

At Port-au-Prince, in the French part of the island of Santo Domingo, on the plantation of M. Guillaume de Villeneuve, there lived at the beginning of this century, in the days when the blacks were killing the whites, a terrible old Negro by the name of Kongo Hoango. This native of the African Gold Coast, who in his youth seemed to possess a loyal and honest disposition, had had countless benefits heaped upon him by his master for having once saved the latter's life during a crossing to Cuba. Not only did M. Guillaume give him his freedom on the spot, and on their return to Santo Domingo set him up in a house and home of his own, but a few years later he also made him, against the custom of the country, overseer of his broad estate and, as Kongo Hoango did not wish to remarry, he gave him instead an old mulatto woman from his plantation named Babekan, to whom the Negro was distantly related by his deceased first wife. Why, when the Negro reached his sixtieth year, M. Guillaume retired him with a large pension and, to cap his kindnesses, he even provided for him in his will; and yet all these proofs of gratitude could not protect M. Villeneuve from the wrath of this ferocious man. In the general frenzy of revenge that flared up in the plantations following the National Convention's ill-considered steps, Kongo Hoango was one of the first to reach for a rifle and, remembering the tyranny that had torn him from his native land, blow his master's brains out. He set fire to the house into which the latter's wife and three children had fled with the other whites of the settlement, laid waste the entire plantation which the heirs who lived in Port-au-Prince might have tried to claim and, after razing every building on the plantation to the ground, he roamed about the region at the head of a band of Negroes he had collected and armed, to help his brothers in the struggle against the whites. Sometimes he would ambush armed companies of travelers crossing the country; at other times, in broad daylight, he would attack the planters barricaded in their settlements and put everyone he found inside to the sword. Indeed, in his inhuman thirst for revenge, he even ordered old Babekan and her daughter, a fifteen-year-old mestizo named Toni, to play a part in this ferocious war which had rejuvenated him completely: seeing that the main building of the plantation, which he now occupied, stood all by itself on the highroad and was often knocked at in his absences by white or Creole refugees seeking food or shelter, he instructed the women to detain these white dogs, as he called them, with help and courtesies until his return. Babekan, who suffered from consumption as the result of a horrible punishment she had received in her youth, used on these occasions to dress up young Toni, whose high-yellow complexion especially suited her for this gruesome deception, in her finest clothes; she encouraged her to refuse none of the strangers' caresses except the ultimate one, which was forbidden her on pain of death; and when Kongo Hoango returned with his Negro band from his forays in the neighborhood, instant death was the fate of the poor fellows who had let themselves be fooled by these tricks.

Now in the year 1803, as everybody knows, General Dessalines advanced on Port-au-Prince with 30,000 Negroes, and all whose skins were white rushed into the place to defend it. For it was the last stronghold of French power in Santo Domingo, and if it fell, every white on the island was lost. It happened that just when old Hoango, who had started out with his following of blacks to carry a load of powder and lead through the French outposts to General Dessalines, was away, somebody knocked at the back door of his house in the darkness and rain of a stormy night. Old Babekan, who was already in bed, got up, opened the window, with just a skirt thrown around her hips, and asked who was there. "In the name of Mary and all the saints," the stranger said in a low voice, as he went over and stood under the window, "before I tell you that, answer just one question!" And, reaching out through the darkness of the night for the old woman's hand, he asked, "Are you a Negress?"

Babekan said, "My goodness, you must certainly be a white man if you would rather face this pitch-black night than a Negress! Come in," she added, "and don't be afraid; it's a mulatto who lives here, and the only other person in the house besides myself is my daughter, a mestizo!" And she shut the window as if she meant to come down to open the door for him; but, pretending that she had trouble finding the key just then, she hastily snatched some clothes from the wardrobe and slipped upstairs into the bedroom to wake her daughter. "Toni!" she said. "Toni!"

"What's the matter, Mother?"

"Quick!" she said. "Get up and get dressed! Here are some clothes, clean linen and stockings. There's a fugitive white man at the door who wants to come in!"

"A white man?" Toni asked, sitting up in bed. She took the clothes the old woman held out to her and said, "Are you sure he is alone, Mother? And is it safe to let him in?"

"There's nothing to worry about," replied the old woman, and lit a candle. "He's unarmed and all alone—he is shaking in every limb, he's so afraid we might attack him!" And while Toni got up and was putting her skirt and stockings on, she lit the large lantern standing in the corner of the room, quickly tied the girl's hair up in a knot on top of her head after the fashion of the country, put a hat on her, and, after lacing up her pinafore, handed her the lantern and told her go down into the yard and bring the stranger in.

Meanwhile the barking of the watchdogs had awakened a boy called Nanky, an illegitimate son of Hoango's by a Negress, who slept with his brother Seppy in one of the outbuildings; and when he saw, by the light of the moon, a solitary figure standing on the back stairs of the house, he ran out at once, as he had been told to do in such cases, to lock the yard gate the man had entered by. The stranger did not understand what these preparations meant and asked the boy, who, he saw with a shudder, was a Negro when he stood near him, who lived in the plantation; and hearing him reply that the estate had passed into Hoango the Negro's hands following the death of M. Villeneuve, the stranger was about to knock him down, snatch the gate key from his hands, and make for the open fields when Toni came out of the house with the lantern in her hand. "Quick," she said, seizing his hand and drawing him toward the door, "in here!" She took care, while saying this, to hold the lantern so that the beam fell full on her face.

"Who are you?" cried the stranger, drawing back as, bewildered for more reasons than one, he stared at her young and charming form. "Who lives in this house where you say I shall find safety?"

"Nobody, by the light of the sun, but my mother and I," said the girl, struggling and straining to draw him along with her.

"What, nobody!" cried the stranger, retreating a step and snatching back his hand. "Didn't the boy just tell me that a Negro called Hoango lives here?"

"No, I say!" said the girl, and stamped her foot in annoyance. "And even if this house did belong to a madman by that name, he is away right now and ten miles off from here!" And then she drew the stranger into the house with both hands, ordered the boy not to tell a soul who was there, and, taking him by the hand, led him upstairs to her mother's room.

"Now," said the old woman, who had overheard the entire conversation from the window and noticed by the lantern light that he was an officer, "what's the meaning of that sword hanging so ready to hand under your arm? We have offered you a refuge in our home," she continued, putting on her glasses, "and thereby endangered our own lives; did you come in here to repay this kindness with treachery, in the customary fashion of your countrymen?"

"Heaven forbid!" replied the stranger, walking up in front of her chair. He caught hold of the old woman's hand, pressed it to his heart, and said, after a hesitant glance or two around the room as he unbuckled the sword from his hip, "You see the most miserable of men before you, but not an ungrateful or a wicked one."

"Who are you?" asked the old woman, pushing a chair toward him with her foot and ordering the girl to go into the kitchen and prepare him as good a supper as could be got ready on short notice.

"I am an officer with the French forces," the stranger replied, "though not, as you may have already guessed, a Frenchman myself; my native land is Switzerland, and my name is Gustav von der Ried. Oh, if only I had never left it for this unhappy island! I come from Fort Dauphin where, as you know, all the whites were murdered, and I hope to reach Port-au-Prince before General Dessalines is able to surround and besiege the town with his troops."

"From Fort Dauphin!" exclaimed the woman. "With a face the color of yours, you managed to come all this way right through the middle of a nigger country in revolt?"

"God and the saints," replied the stranger, "have protected me! And I'm not alone, Granny; a worthy old gentleman, my uncle, is with me, and his wife and five children, not to speak of several men and women servants belong to the family—twelve people in all, whom I had to lead on unspeakably hard night marches, as we cannot show ourselves on the highroad by day, with only the help of two sorry mules."

"Ei, good heavens!" exclaimed the old woman, shaking her head sympathetically and taking a pinch of tobacco. "Where are your people right now?"

"I am sure," replied the stranger after a moment's hesitation, "I can trust you; the color of your face reflects a gleam of my own. The family is about a mile from here, over near the seagull pond, in the wilderness of the mountain woods bordering it, where hunger and thirst forced us to seek shelter the day before yesterday. Last night we sent our servants out to forage for a little bread and wine among the inhabitants of the country, but with no success; they were too afraid, when it came right down to it, of being caught and killed to dare to speak to anybody, with the result that I had to go out myself today, at the risk of my life, and try my luck. But unless I am completely mistaken," he continued, pressing the old woman's hand, "heaven has led me to merciful people who don't share the terrible and unheard-of madness that has seized all the natives of this island. Be good enough to fill a few baskets with food and refreshment and I will pay you well for it; it is only a five days' journey from here to Port-au-Prince, and if you make it possible for us to reach that city we will be eternally grateful to you for having saved our lives."

"Yes," feigned the old woman, "this raging madness. Isn't it just as though the hands of a body or the teeth in a mouth were furious at each other merely because one wasn't made like the other? What can I, whose father came from Santiago on the island of Cuba, do about the glimmer of light that shines upon my face when day breaks? And what can my daughter, who was conceived and born in Europe, do about the fact that the bright day of that continent is reflected in hers?"

"What?" exclaimed the stranger. "You who, according to your whole physiognomy, are a mulatto and therefore of African origin, and the lovely young mestizo who opened the door to me—you face the same doom as we Europeans?"

"Good heavens!" replied the old woman, taking her glasses off her nose. "Do you think the little property we have worked with our hands to acquire through years of weary labor and sorrow doesn't provoke that ferocious gang of hell-begotten brigands? If we had not known how to protect ourselves against their persecution by every trick and skill that self-preservation teaches the weak, you can be sure the shadow of kinship that lies broad across our faces would not have done it!"

"Impossible!" exclaimed the stranger. "Who is persecuting you on this island?"

"The owner of this house," the old woman replied, "the Negro Kongo Hoango! Since the death of M. Guillaume, the former owner of this place, whom his fierce hand struck down at the very start of the uprising, we who, being his relatives, keep house for him have been at the mercy of all his tyranny and violence. For every piece of bread, every bit of drink that we give out of humanity to one or another of the white fugitives that from time to time pass by here on the highroad, we are repaid with his curses and abuse; and he would like nothing better than whipping the blacks up to revenge themselves on us white and creole half-dogs, as he calls us, partly because he wants in general to get rid of us for disapproving of his ferocity against the whites, and partly because he would like to get hold of the little property we would leave behind."

"You unhappy people!" said the stranger. "You pitiable people! And where is this madman right now?"

"With General Dessalines' army," replied the old woman, "to which he and the other blacks belonging to this plantation are bringing a load of powder and lead that the General needed. Unless he goes off on another expedition, we expect him back within ten or twelve days; and if he should then learn, which God forbid, that we gave shelter and protection to a white man on his way to Port-au-Prince while he himself was putting all his strength and energy into the business of ridding the island of the entire race, you can be sure we will all be death's children."

"Heaven, which loves pity and humaneness," answered the stranger, "will protect you in whatever you do for some one unfortunate! And if he did find out," he added, moving closer to the old woman, "seeing that that would draw the Negro's wrath down on you anyhow, and it would do you no good to go back to obeying him even if you wanted to, couldn't you make up your mind now to shelter my uncle and his family in your house for a day or two, at whatever price you care to ask, so that they could recover a bit from the exhaustion of the journey?"

"Young man!" the old woman said in astonishment, "what are you asking? How could I possibly put a party of travelers as large as yours in a house standing on the main road without its becoming known to the people hereabouts?"

"Why not?" insisted the stranger. "If I myself went out to the seagull pond right now and led the party back here before daybreak, and if we put everybody, masters and servants together, in one room, and perhaps even took the precaution, in case of the worst, of carefully locking all the doors and windows?"

The old woman, after considering his proposal for a while, answered that if he tried to lead his party from their mountain glen into the settlement that night, he would be sure to run into a troop of armed Negroes who were reported by several outposts to be on the main road.

"Very well," answered the stranger, "then let us do nothing more for the moment than send a basket of food to my unfortunate people, and put off the business of bringing them into the settlement to the following night. Would you do that, Granny?"

"All right," said the old woman, while the stranger's lips showered kisses on her bony hand. "For the sake of the European who was my daughter's father, I'll do this favor for you, a countryman of his in distress. Sit down at daybreak tomorrow and write a letter to your people, inviting them to come here to me in the settlement; the boy you saw in the yard can carry the letter to them with some provisions, he can pass the night in the mountains with them for safety's sake, and guide the party here, if the invitation is accepted, at the break of the following day."

Meanwhile Toni had returned with the meal she had prepared in the kitchen, and while setting the table jokingly asked the old woman, with a glance at the stranger, "Mother, tell me, has the gentleman got over the fright that took hold of him at the door? Has he convinced himself that neither poison nor a dagger is awaiting him, and that Hoango the Negro is not home?" The mother said with a sigh, "My dear girl, the burnt child, according to the proverb, shuns the flame. The gentleman would have been foolish to have dared to enter the house without first making sure of its inhabitants' race." The girl, standing in front of her mother, described how she had held the lantern up so that its rays fell full on her face. "But his imagination," she said, "was so full of Moors and Negroes that even if a lady from Paris or Marseilles had opened the door, he would have taken her for a Negress." The stranger, slipping his arm gently around her waist, said with embarrassment that the hat she was wearing had prevented him from seeing her face. "If I had been able," he went on, giving her a hug, "to look into your eyes the way I am doing now, I would have been quite willing, even though everything else about you were black, to drink out of a poisoned cup with you." The mother invited him, as he blushed at his own words, to sit down, and Toni took a seat next to him, her elbows propped on the table, and stared into his face as he ate. The stranger asked her how old she was and where she was born, upon which the mother answered to say that she had conceived and given birth to Toni in Paris fifteen years ago, during a trip to Europe she had taken with M. Villeneuve's wife, her former mistress. She added that the Negro Komar, whom she married later, had adopted Toni as his own child, but that her real father was a rich Marseilles merchant named Bertrand, and so her name was Toni Bertrand.

Toni asked him if he knew of such a gentleman in France. The stranger said no, France was a big country, and during the short time he had spent there before embarking for the West Indies he hadn't met anybody by that name. The old woman remarked that anyway M. Bertrand, according to pretty reliable information she had received, was no longer in France. "His ambitious and aspiring nature," she said, "could find no satisfaction within the limits of a middle-class occupation; at the outbreak of the revolution he went into public affairs, and in 1795 accompanied a French Legation to the Turkish court, from where, as far as I know, he has not returned to this day." The stranger took Toni's hand with a smile and said that in that case she was a girl of rich and distinguished birth. He urged her to take advantage of her connection, and ventured to think she had hopes of one day being introduced on her father's arm to a much more brilliant situation than her present one.

"Hardly," remarked the old woman with suppressed feeling. "M. Bertrand, during my pregnancy in Paris, denied in court that he was the father of this child, because he was ashamed in front of a rich young girl he wanted to marry. I shall never forget the brazenness with which he swore the oath right to my face; the consequence for me was a bilious fever, and right after that sixty lashes at M. Villeneuve's order, the result of which was the consumption I suffer from to this very day."

Toni, who was leaning her head pensively on her hand, asked the stranger who he was, where he came from, and where he was going, to which he replied, after a moment of embarrassment caused by the bitterness of the old woman's speech, that he and Herr Strömli's—his uncle's—family, whom he had left behind in the mountain woods near the seagull pond under the protection of two young cousins, came from Fort Dauphin. At the girl's request, he told some of the details of the uprising that had broken out in that city: how at midnight, when everybody was in bed, the blacks, at a treacherously given signal, had started to massacre the whites; how the leader of the Negroes, a sergeant in the French engineers, had immediately set fire to all the ships in the harbor so as to cut off the whites' escape to Europe; how the family had hardly enough time to snatch up a few belongings and flee through the city gates; and how the simultaneous outbreak of uprisings all along the coast had left them no choice but to strike out, with the help of two mules they had got hold of, straight across the island for Port-au-Prince, which was defended by a strong French army and remained the only place still able to offer resistance to the ever growing power of the Negroes.

Toni asked what the whites in the place had done to make themselves so hated. Taken aback, the stranger replied, "It was their whole conduct, as masters of the island, toward the Negroes, which quite frankly I shouldn't attempt to defend—even though things have gone on here in this way for centuries. The craze for freedom that swept all the plantations led the Negroes and Creoles to strike off the chains that burdened them and revenge themselves on the entire white population for all the terrible ill-usage they had suffered at the hands of a few vicious men among the whites. What in particular," he continued after a brief silence, "struck me as frightful and extraordinary was something a young girl did. When the revolt started, this girl, who was of the Negro race, lay sick with the yellow fever which, to make matters even worse, had broken out in the city. Three years before, she had been the slave of a white planter who, out of chagrin at her refusal to gratify his wishes, had treated her very harshly and afterwards sold her to a Creole planter. On the day of the uprising, when the girl learned that the planter, her old master, had run away from the fury of the Negroes to a nearby woodshed, she remembered how he had mistreated her and sent her brother to him at dusk with an invitation to spend the night with her. The miserable fellow, who did not know what disease she had caught or even that she was sick, came and, full of gratitude—for he thought he was saved—clasped her in his arms; but he had spent barely half an hour in her bed, fondling and caressing her, when she suddenly sat up and said, with an expression of cold and ferocious hatred, 'You have been kissing someone with the plague, someone with death in her breast—that's what you have been kissing! Now go and give the fever to all those who are like you!'"

The officer, while the old woman loudly expressed her abhorrence of all this, asked Toni whether she would be capable of such a deed. "Oh no!" Toni said, looking down confused. The stranger put his napkin down on the table and said that the feeling of his own soul was that no amount of tyranny ever practiced by the whites could justify a treachery so base and dreadful. Heaven's vengeance, he said, rising from the table with a passionate expression, would be disarmed by such a deed: the angels themselves in their outrage would side with the unrighteous and, to uphold the human and the divine order, plead their cause. As he said this, he walked over to the window for a moment and looked out into the night, where storm clouds were driving across the face of the moon and the stars; and because it seemed to him that mother and daughter were exchanging looks, although he could not catch a single sign passing between them, a peevish and annoyed feeling came over him; turning around, he asked if they would show him to the room where he was to sleep.

The mother looked at the clock on the wall and remarked that it was already close to midnight, picked up a candle, and asked the stranger to follow her. She led him down a long corridor to his room; Toni carried his coat and the other things he had taken off; the old woman showed him a bed comfortably heaped with pillows, where he was to sleep, and, after telling Toni to prepare a footbath for the gentleman, she wished him good night and left. The stranger stood his sword in a corner of the room and laid the brace of pistols he wore in his belt on the table. While Toni pulled the bed out and covered it with a white sheet, he surveyed the chamber; and as he quickly concluded from the luxury and good taste of its furnishings that it must have been the old owner's bedroom, a feeling of uneasiness fastened itself in his heart like a vulture and he wished himself back in the woods, hungry and thirsty though he had been, with his own people. Meanwhile the girl had carried in, from the kitchen close by, a basin of hot water smelling of aromatic herbs and invited the officer, who had been leaning against the window, to refresh himself with it. The officer took off his neckerchief and vest in silence and sat down on a chair; he started to pull his shoes and stockings off, and, while the girl crouched down on her knees before him and busied herself with the little arrangements for the bath, he studied her attractive form. Her hair, rippling in dark curls, had tumbled over her young breasts as she knelt down; an expression of extraordinary charm played around her lips and over the long lashes that jutted out from her downcast eyes; if not for her color, which repelled him, he would have sworn that he had never seen anything prettier. At the same time he noticed a faint resemblance to somebody, though exactly to whom he himself could not say, which had struck him on first entering the house and which had won his heart completely. He caught hold of her hand as she stood up at one point in her work, and having decided, quite correctly, that there was only one way to find out whether or not the girl had a heart, he drew her down on his lap and asked her if she was already engaged to a young man. "No!" she murmured, dropping her big black eyes in charming confusion. And then she added, without stirring in his lap, that three months ago a young Negro in the neighborhood by the name of Konelly had asked for her hand; but since she was still too young, she had refused him. The stranger, who held her around her slender waist with his two hands, said that where he came from there was an old saying that when a girl reached the age of fourteen years and seven weeks she was old enough to get married. He asked her, while she examined the little gold cross he wore around his neck, how old she was.

"Fifteen years," Toni replied.

"Well then!" said the stranger. "Doesn't he have enough money to set up housekeeping in the way you want?"

Toni, without lifting her eyes to him, replied, "Oh, it isn't that. On the contrary," she went on, letting go of the cross in her hand, "since the recent changes, Konelly has become a rich man; his father has come into all the property that used to belong to his master the planter."

"Then why did you refuse his offer?" the stranger asked. He pushed her hair gently away from her forehead. "Perhaps you didn't like him?" The girl nodded her head quickly and laughed; and when the stranger jokingly whispered in her ear to ask whether it took a white man to win her favor, she hesitated dreamily for a moment and then, as a charming blush flamed in her sunburned face, suddenly pressed herself against his breast. Touched by her grace and sweetness, the stranger called her his own dear girl and took her in his arms, set free, as if by a divine hand, from all his fears. It was impossible for him to think that all the feelings he sensed in her could merely be the wretched expression of a cold and monstrous treachery. The thoughts that had oppressed him scattered like a flock of obscene birds; he reproached himself for having misjudged her heart even for an instant, and, as he rocked her on his knees and drank in her sweet breath, he pressed a kiss upon her forehead in token, as it were, of reconciliation and forgiveness. But meanwhile the girl had suddenly sat up in his arms, thinking she heard someone coming along the corridor to the door; dreamily she straightened her scarf, which had become disarranged, on her breast; but when she realized she was mistaken she turned back to the stranger with a cheerful look and reminded him that the water would get cold if he did not use it right away. "Well?" she said in perplexity, as the stranger said nothing but kept looking at her thoughtfully. "Why do you stare at me so?" She tried to hide her embarrassment by toying with her pinafore, and then exclaimed with a laugh, "You're a strange man, what strikes you so in my appearance?" The stranger passed his hand across his brow while he suppressed a sigh and, lifting her off his lap, said, "An amazing resemblance between you and a friend of mine!"

Toni, who saw that his good spirits were fled, took his hand sympathetically in hers and asked, "Who is she?" To which he replied, after a brief pause, "Her name was Marianne Congreve and she came from Strasbourg. I had met her in that city, where her father was a merchant, just before the outbreak of the Revolution, and was lucky enough to win her consent to marriage and also the approval of her mother. Oh, she was the most faithful soul under the sun; and when I look at you, the terrible and touching circumstances under which I lost her come back to me so vividly that I can hardly restrain my tears."

"What?" asked Toni, pressing against him tenderly and closely. "She is no longer alive?"

"She died," the stranger replied, "and her death taught me for the first time the meaning of everything good and fine. God knows," he continued, resting his head sadly on her shoulder, "how I could have been so rash as to make remarks one evening in a public place about the terrible revolutionary tribunal that had just been set up. I was informed against, then hunted up and down; cheated of their prey when I was lucky enough to escape into the outskirts, the wild mob of my pursuers, who thirsted for a victim, ran to my fiancée's house and, infuriated by her honest avowal that she didn't know where I was, accused her of being in league with me, and with unspeakable wantonness dragged her off to the scaffold instead of me. No sooner was this terrible news brought to me than I dashed out of my hiding place and raced through the crowd to the place of execution, crying out at the top of my voice, "Here, you monsters, here I am!" But she was already standing on the platform of the guillotine, and in reply to a question by the judges, who unfortunately must not have known who I was, she said, turning away from me with a look that remains indelibly stamped on my soul, "I don't know this man!"—upon which, a few seconds later, to the rolling of the drums and the roar of the rabble, the blade, speeded in its release by the impatience of the bloodhounds, dropped down and severed her head from her torso.— How I was saved I do not know; a quarter of an hour later I found myself in the house of a friend, where I fell out of one fainting fit into another, and in the evening, half insane, I was loaded into a cart and carried across the Rhine." At these words the stranger set the girl down and walked to the window; and when she saw him, deeply agitated, press his face into a handkerchief, a feeling of compassion, awakened by many things, came over her; with an abrupt movement she followed him to the window, threw her arms around his neck, and mingled her tears with his.

There is no need to report what happened next, as any reader who has reached this point in our narrative can supply his own words. When the stranger recovered his self-possession, he had no idea where the act he had just committed would lead; but meanwhile he knew that he had been saved, and that here in this house he had nothing to fear now from the girl. Seeing her crying on the bed with folded arms, he tried to do everything possible to calm her. Taking the little gold cross given him by faithful Marianne, his departed bride, from around his neck, and stooping down over Toni with many caresses, he hung his wedding present, as he called it, around her neck. As she went on crying and paid no heed to what he said, he sat down on the edge of the bed and told her, while alternately stroking and kissing her hand, that in the morning he would ask her mother for her hand. He described the little piece of property he owned, free and clear, on the banks of the Aar: a house that was comfortable and roomy enough to accommodate her and her mother, if the latter's age would allow her to make the voyage there; the fields, gardens, meadows, and vineyards; and his worthy old father who would welcome her with grateful affection for having saved his son. Taking her in his arms when her tears continued to course down her cheeks onto the pillow in an unending stream, and quite overcome himself, he begged her to say what harm he had done her and if she could not forgive him. He swore he would never stop loving her, and that it was only in the delirium of his strangely disordered senses that the mixture of desire and fear she inspired in him could have seduced him into doing such a thing. And, last of all, he reminded her that the morning stars were already shining in the sky and that if she stayed in his bed any longer her mother would surely be along and surprise her there; he implored her, for the sake of her health, to get up and rest for several hours in her own bed; extremely alarmed by the state she was in, he asked permission to lift her up in his arms and carry her to her room. But she said nothing in reply to all his urgings, only huddling motionless amid the tumbled pillows of the bed, her head hidden in her arms and quietly sobbing, and at last he had no choice, with the daylight already glimmering through both windows, but to lift her up without further ado; she hung lifelessly over his shoulder as he bore her upstairs to her room, and after putting her down on the bed and repeating, amid a thousand caresses, everything he had already said to her, he again called her his darling bride, pressed a kiss on her cheeks, and hurried back to his own room.

When day had fully dawned, old Babekan went upstairs to her daughter, sat down on her bed, and disclosed her scheme for dealing with the stranger as well as with his traveling companions. Since the Negro Hoango would not be returning for another two days, everything depended on keeping the stranger in the house until that time, without, however, taking in his family, for the presence of so many people might prove dangerous. Her plan was to pretend to the stranger that they had just heard that General Dessalines and his army were headed in their direction, and, as this would make it too risky to bring his family to the house as he desired, they would have to put it off for three days until the General had passed on. The party itself, she concluded, would meanwhile have to be provided with food to keep them from moving on; at the same time, so that Hoango might lay hold of them later, they must be encouraged to imagine they would find refuge in the house. She observed that the project was an important one, since the family was probably carrying a great many possessions with them, and asked her daughter to do everything in her power to help carry out their plans. Toni, sitting up in bed with an angry flush reddening her face, retorted that it was a shameful and atrocious thing to lure people into one's house and then violate the laws of hospitality in such a way. She thought a fugitive who confided himself to their protection should be doubly safe in their house, and she promised her mother that if she did not give up the bloody plan she had just revealed, she, Toni, would go straight to the stranger and tell him what a den of assassins the house was in which he had thought to find his salvation.

"Toni!" exclaimed her mother, putting her hands on her hips and staring at her, wide-eyed.

"Yes," Toni answered, lowering her voice. "What has this young man, who is not even a Frenchman by birth but, as he told us, a Swiss, done to us that we should want to fall on him like robbers and kill and strip him of everything he owns? Do the grievances we have against the planters here apply to the part of the island he comes from? Doesn't everything indicate, rather, what an honorable, upright person he is, a man who shares none of the blame for the injustices the black people may reproach his race with?"

The old woman, noting the girl's extraordinary vehemence, merely observed with trembling lips how astonished she was. She asked what the young Portuguese whom they had clubbed to the ground a short time ago in the gateway, had done to them? She asked what the two Dutchmen were guilty of, who had been slain three weeks before in the courtyard by the bullets of the Negroes. She wanted to know what they had against the three Frenchmen and all the other fugitives of the white race whom they had put out of the way, since the beginning of the rebellion, in their house with rifles, spears and daggers.

"By the light of the sun," retorted her daughter, starting wildly to her feet, "you are very wrong to remind me of those atrocities! For a long time now I have felt only the deepest loathing for the abominations you force me to take part in; I swear to you that I would rather die ten times over to satisfy the vengeance of the Lord for everything I have done, than suffer even one hair of that young man's head to be touched as long as he is in our house."

"Very well," the old woman said, yielding suddenly, "let the stranger leave then! But when Kongo Hoango returns," she said, getting up to leave the room, "and learns that a white man spent a night in our house, you may answer to him for all those tender feelings which move you to defy his express orders and let the stranger go."

This parting remark, which for all its apparent mildness betrayed the old woman's real anger, left the girl more than a little dismayed. She knew her mother's hatred for the whites too well to believe she would let such an opportunity to satisfy it go by. Fearing that she would send immediately to the neighboring plantations for the Negroes to come and overpower the stranger, the girl threw on her clothes and followed her into the downstairs sitting room. As Toni came in, the old woman started away in confusion from the cupboard, where she seemed to be busy with something, and sat down at a spinning wheel. The girl stopped in front of the door and read the proclamation nailed up there that forbade all black people, on pain of death, to give aid and comfort to a white man; and as if panic-stricken at realizing the crime she had been about to commit, she spun around and fell at her mother's feet who, as she well knew, had been watching her from the back. Hugging her knees, she begged her mother's forgiveness for the mad things she had said in the stranger's defense; pleaded in excuse the fact that she had still been in bed in a half-dreaming, half-waking state when her mother had surprised her with the scheme for tricking the stranger; and announced her perfect readiness to hand him over to the vengeance of the law of the land, which had already decided his destruction. The old woman, after a pause in which she looked steadily at the girl, said, "By heaven, your just saying that has saved him his life for today! His food was already poisoned, since you had threatened to take him under your protection, and Kongo Hoango, in keeping with his orders, would at least have had his dead body." And, getting up, she took a pitcher of milk from the table and emptied it out of the window. Toni, not crediting her own senses, stared in horror at her mother. The old woman sat down again and, lifting the girl, who was still on her knees, up from the floor, asked her what it was that could so have changed her way of thinking in the space of one night. Yesterday, after getting his bath ready, had she stayed with the stranger for any length of time? And had she talked with him a great deal? But Toni, whose breast was heaving violently, said nothing in reply to these questions, or nothing definite; she stood there with her eyes cast down and her head in her hands and blamed a dream she had had; but one look at her unhappy mother's breast, she said, stooping quickly to kiss her hand, had reminded her again of all the inhumanity of the race to which this stranger belonged; and she swore, as she turned away and pressed her face into her apron, that as soon as Hoango the Negro returned her mother would see what kind of a daughter she had.

Babekan was still sitting lost in thought, wondering where the girl's strange passion could have sprung from, when the stranger entered the room with a note he had written in his bedroom summoning his people to spend a few days on the Negro Hoango's plantation. He greeted mother and daughter with great cheerfulness and affability, and, handing the paper to the old woman, he asked her to send someone off to the woods right away, just as she had promised, to provide for his people. Babekan got up and put the note away in the cupboard, and said with an alarmed air, "Sir, we must ask you to return to your room immediately. The road is full of passing Negro soldiers who say that General Dessalines and his army are headed in this direction. This house is open to the whole world, and you won't be safe here unless you hide in your bedroom, which faces the yard, and lock the doors as well as shutters as carefully as possible."

"What!" the stranger exclaimed in surprise, "General Dessalines——"

"Don't ask questions!" interrupted the old woman, and she knocked on the floor with a stick three times. "I'll come after you to your bedroom and explain everything there."

The stranger retreated from the room before the old woman's frightened gesticulations, only turning in the doorway to say, "But my people are waiting for me; shouldn't you at least send a messenger to them to——"

"Everything will be taken care of," the old woman broke in, while in response to her knocking the bastard boy whom we have already met entered the room; whereupon she ordered Toni, who had turned her back to the stranger and walked over to the mirror, to pick up a basket of food standing in the corner; and mother, daughter, the stranger, and the boy went upstairs to the bedroom.

There the old woman settled herself comfortably in a chair and told him how all through the night the glow of General Dessalines' camp fires had been seen upon the mountains on the horizon—which in fact was the case, although not one Negro of his army, which was advancing to the southwest against Port-au-Prince, had appeared in the vicinity so far. With this story she was able to throw the stranger into a fever of anxiety, which she then cleverly assuaged by promising him she would do everything in her power to rescue him, even if worst came to worst and troops were quartered in the house. On the stranger's repeated earnest reminders that under these circumstances his family should at least be provided with some food, she took the basket from her daughter's hand and, giving it to the boy, told him he was to go to the seagull pond in the nearby mountains and deliver it to the foreign officer's family whom he would find there. The officer himself, he was to say, was in good hands; friends of the whites, who had suffered much themselves at the hands of the blacks for their sympathies, had pitied him and taken him into their house. She concluded by saying that, just as soon as the highroad was clear of the armed Negro bands which were expected along at any moment, they would arrange to shelter the family, too, in the house.

"Do you understand?" she asked when she had finished. The boy set the basket on his head and answered that he was well acquainted with the seagull pond she had described to him, for he and his friends used to fish there every once in a while, and that he would deliver the message, just as he was given it, to the foreign gentleman's family spending the night there. The stranger, on the woman's asking if he had anything to add, took a ring from his finger and gave it to the boy to deliver to the head of the family, Herr Strömli, as evidence of the truth of his message. After this the mother busied herself with a number of things whose purpose, she said, was to safeguard the stranger; ordered Toni to close the shutters; and, to dispel the darkness that this made in the room, she herself struck a light, though not without some difficulty, as the tinder would not catch, with the tinder box on the mantelpiece. The stranger took advantage of this moment to slip his arm around Toni's waist, put his lips to her ear, and ask her in a whisper whether she had slept well and if he shouldn't perhaps tell her mother what had happened. Toni, however, said nothing to his first question, and her reply to the other, as she twisted out of his grasp, was, "No, not a word, if you love me!" She suppressed the pangs of fear that all her mother's deceitful preparations awakened in her; and on the pretext of getting breakfast for the stranger, she hurried downstairs to the living room.

Trusting to luck that her mother would not miss it, she took from the cupboard the letter in which the stranger in his innocence had asked his family to follow the boy to the settlement and, resolved, if worst came to worst, to die together with him, she raced down the road after the boy. For in her heart and before God she no longer saw the young man as merely a guest to whom she had given shelter and protection, but as her fiancé and husband, and her mind was made up to tell all this quite openly to her mother as soon as his party was numerous enough in the house, counting on the confusion into which the situation would throw the old woman.

"Nanky," she called when she had overtaken the boy in breathless haste on the highroad, "Mother has changed her plans about Herr Strömli's family. Here, take this letter! It is addressed to Herr Strömli, the old man who is the head of the family, and in it is an invitation to spend a few days with all his people at our plantation. Be smart and do everything you can to get them to agree to this; Kongo Hoango the Negro will reward you for it when he returns!"

"All right, Cousin Toni," replied the boy. He put the carefully folded note into his pocket and asked, "Shall I be guide for the party on the way here?"

"Of course," Toni answered, "that goes without saying, since they don't know the country. But as troops may be marching along the road, be sure you don't start out before midnight; once on your way, however, hurry as fast as you can to get here before daybreak.—Can you be depended on?" she asked.

"Just depend on Nanky!" answered the boy. "I know why you're luring these white fugitives to the plantation, and the Negro Hoango will be satisfied with me!"

Returning to the house, Toni carried breakfast up to the stranger, after which mother and daughter cleared the dishes away and returned to the front living room to do their household chores. It was inevitable that the mother should go to the cupboard a little while later where, quite naturally, she missed the letter. Putting her hand to her head for a moment, for she distrusted her memory, she asked Toni where she might have put the letter the stranger had given her. Toni, after a short pause in which she looked at the floor, answered that the stranger had put the letter back in his pocket, as she must surely know, and torn it up in his room in the presence of both of them. The mother stared in astonishment at the girl; she said she distinctly remembered taking the letter from his hand and putting it in the cupboard; but when she had searched it over and over again and could find no trace of the letter, and as several such incidents in the past had made her distrust her own memory, there was nothing for her in the end but to accept her daughter's explanation. However, she could not suppress the keen regret its loss gave her and remarked that it would have been very useful to the Negro Hoango in getting the family to come to the plantation. At midday and in the evening, when Toni was serving the stranger his meals, she sat at the corner of the table talking to him and seized on several occasions to ask him about the letter; but Toni was skillful enough, whenever the conversation approached this dangerous subject, to change or confuse it, so that her mother was never quite able to understand the stranger's explanation of what had actually happened to it. And so the day went by; after supper her mother took the precaution, as she described it, of locking the stranger's room; and after discussing with Toni the tricks she might use to get another such letter from him the next day, she went to bed and told the girl to do the same.

As soon as Toni, who had been longing for this moment, reached her room and felt sure her mother was asleep, she took down the portrait of the Holy Virgin that hung near her bed, propped it on a chair, and knelt before it with clasped hands. She implored the Savior, her divine Son, in a prayer full of infinite devotion, to give her the courage and the resolution to confess the crimes weighing on her young soul to the young man she had given herself to. She vowed to conceal nothing from him, whatever it cost her heart, not even the pitiless and terrible purpose with which she had lured him into the house the day before; yet she prayed that, for the sake of all the steps she had already taken to save him, he would forgive her and take her back to Europe with him as his faithful wife. Wonderfully strengthened by this prayer, she stood up, took the master key that unlocked all the rooms in the house, and without a light crept silently along the narrow passage that traversed the building to the stranger's bedroom. Softly she opened the door and went up to the bed where he lay deep in sleep. The moon shone down on his fresh young face, and the night wind, through the open windows, ruffled the hair on his forehead. Gently she bent over him and, inhaling his sweet breath, spoke his name; but he was lost in a dream that seemed to be about herself, at least she heard his ardent, trembling lips whisper the word "Toni!" several times. An indescribable sadness came over her; she could not gather the resolution to pull him down from the blissful heavens of his imagination into the middle of a common and wretched reality; and, feeling sure that sooner or later he would waken by himself, she knelt beside his bed and covered his dear hand with kisses.

But who can describe the terror that gripped her bosom a few moments later when, from inside the courtyard, she suddenly heard a clatter of men, horses, and weapons and distinctly recognized in it the voice of the Negro Kongo Hoango, who had unexpectedly come back from General Dessalines' camp with his crew. Carefully avoiding the moonlight that threatened to betray her, she ran to the window and hid behind the curtain, where she heard her mother already telling the Negro everything that had happened in his absence, and also that there was a European fugitive in the house. In an undertone the Negro commanded his men to be quiet. When he asked the old woman where the stranger was at that moment, she pointed out the room to him and took this opportunity to tell the Negro about the strange conversation she had had with her daughter about the fugitive. She swore the girl was a traitor, and that the entire plot to capture the stranger was in jeopardy. At all events, the little thief had stolen into his bed at nightfall, as she had seen with her own eyes, where she undoubtedly was taking her ease this very moment; and if the stranger hadn't escaped already, very likely he was being warned this very instant and the means for his escape were

being decided on. The Negro, who had already tested the girl's loyalty in similar circumstances in the past, answered that this was hardly possible. "Kelly!" he called out
in anger, "Omra! Bring your rifles!" And without saying another word, followed by all
his men, he climbed the stairs to the stranger's room.

Toni, under whose eyes this whole scene had been enacted within the space of minutes, stood paralyzed in every limb, as though struck by a lightning bolt. Her first
thought was to wake the stranger; but, for one thing, the soldiers in the yard made escape impossible, and for another, she foresaw his snatching up his arms and running
headlong to his immediate destruction, since the Negroes far outnumbered him. Indeed, the most dreadful possibility she had to consider was that the unfortunate man,
when he found her at his bedside at this time, would take her for a traitor and in the
madness of this terrible delusion charge senselessly right into the arms of the Negro
Hoango instead of heeding her advice. In this moment of unspeakable fear, her eyes
lighted on a rope hanging from a nail in the wall, God knows by what chance. The
Lord himself, she thought, as she snatched down the rope, had put it there to save her
friend and herself. She lashed the young man's hands and feet with the rope and knot-
ted it securely; and after pulling the ends tight without paying any attention to his
tossing and turning, she tied them to the bed frame, pressed a kiss upon his lips in joy
at having mastered the situation for the moment, and rushed out to meet the Negro
Hoango clattering up the stairs.

The Negro, who still did not believe what the old woman had told him about Toni,
stood stock-still in the corridor with his following of torchbearers and armed men,
dumbfounded at seeing her come out of the room. He shouted, "Traitor! Turncoat!"
and, turning to Babekan, who had gone a few steps forward toward the stranger's
door, he asked, "Did the stranger escape?" Babekan, seeing the door open, turned
around without looking in and came back like a madwoman, crying, "The sneak!
She's let him escape! Run and block the exits before he gets out into the open!"

"What's going on?" asked Toni, looking astonished at the old man and the Negroes
around him.

"What's going on?" retorted Hoango, and he grabbed her by the front of her dress
and dragged her toward the room.

"Are you mad?" cried Toni, pushing the old man away as he stiffened at the sight
that met his eyes. "There's the stranger, tied up fast in his bed by me; and, by God, this
isn't the worst thing I've managed in my life!" And, turning her back on him, she sat
down at a table as if in tears. The old man turned to the mother standing flabber-
gasted at his side and said, "Oh, Babekan, what kind of stories have you been deceiv-
ing me with!"

"Thank heavens!" answered the mother, and in embarrassment examined the ropes
with which the stranger was tied. "Here the stranger is, but I can't understand it." The
Negro, thrusting his sword back into its sheath, went over to the bed and asked the
stranger who he was, where he came from, and where he was going. But as the only
thing the latter said amid his violent struggles to free himself was, "Oh, Toni! Oh,
Toni!" in a tone of heart-rending anguish, the mother broke in to say that he was a
Swiss named Gustav von der Ried, and that he had come from the coastal town of
Fort Dauphin with a whole family of European dogs, who were at this moment hiding

in the mountain caves near the seagull pond. Hoango, seeing the girl sitting with her head propped dejectedly in her hands, went over to her and called her his darling girl, patted her cheeks, and asked her forgiveness for the hasty suspicion he had voiced. The old woman, who had also gone to the girl, asked her, with hands on hips and much shaking of her head, why she had tied the stranger to his bed when he had had no suspicion of the danger he was in. Toni, actually crying with grief and rage, turned suddenly on her mother and said, "Because you have no eyes and ears! Because he did so realize the danger he was in! Because he was trying to escape; because he had asked me to help him get away; because he had plotted against your own life and would undoubtedly have carried out his plan at daybreak if I hadn't tied him up in his sleep." The old man patted and soothed the girl and ordered Babekan to say no more about the matter. Then he called over a couple of soldiers armed with rifles to carry out on the spot the law by which the stranger stood condemned; but Babekan whispered to him privately, "No, for heaven's sake, Hoango!" She took him aside and explained that the stranger, before being shot, should be got to write the invitation with the help of which his family could be enticed to the plantation, as it was too risky a business to attack them in the woods. Hoango thought it unlikely that the family was unarmed and gave his approval to this suggestion; but, as it was too late to write the letter, he posted two guards over the white fugitive and, after taking the precaution of examining the prisoner's bonds, which he found too slack and summoned a couple of his men to tighten, he and all his crew left the room and silence gradually descended on the household.

But Toni, who had only pretended to say goodnight to the old man and go to bed when he shook her hand again, got up as soon as she saw that everything was quiet in the house, slipped out of a back gate into the open and, the wildest despair in her heart, raced madly down a path that crossed the highroad in the direction from which Herr Strömli's family would have to come. For the look of contempt that the stranger had flung at her from his bed had gone straight to her heart like a knife thrust; a feeling of burning bitterness began to mingle with her love for him, and she exulted at the thought of dying in this attempt to rescue him. She posted herself, for fear of missing the family, near the trunk of a stone pine which they would have to pass if they had accepted the invitation; and hardly had the first rays of dawn shot across the horizon when, just as it had been arranged, the voice of the boy, Nanky, acting as the party's guide, could be heard in the distance among the trees.

The procession consisted of Herr Strömli and his wife, the latter riding one of the mules; their five children, two of whom, Adelbert and Gottfried, young men of eighteen and nineteen, walked alongside the mule; and three menservants and two maids, one of whom, with an infant at her breast, was riding the other mule: twelve people all told. They moved along slowly, over the path laced with tree roots, toward the pine trunk where Toni, as quietly as possible so as not to scare them, emerged from the shadow of the tree and called out, "Stop!" The boy recognized her immediately; and when she asked him which was Herr Strömli, while men, women, and children crowded around her, he was glad to introduce her to the elderly head of the family, Herr Strömli. "Sir!" Toni said, cutting short his greeting with a resolute voice, "Hoango the Negro with all his crew has unexpectedly returned to the settlement. You can't put up there now except at the peril of your lives; indeed, your nephew, who was unlucky enough to find a welcome there, is lost forever unless you take your arms and follow me to the plantation to free him from the captivity in which he is held by Hoango the Negro!"

"My God!" all the members of the family exclaimed in horror; and the ailing mother, exhausted by the journey, fell to the ground from her mule in a dead faint. While the servant girls rushed up at Herr Strömli's call to help their mistress, Toni, bombarded with questions by the youths, led Herr Strömli and the other men aside for fear of being overheard by the boy, Nanky. She told them everything that had happened, without restraining her tears of shame and remorse: how matters stood in the house at the moment when the young man came along; how their conversation in private had miraculously changed everything; what she had done, in her half-demented panic, when the Negro unexpectedly returned, and how she was now determined to stake her own life on the attempt to rescue him from the captivity in which she herself had put him. "My weapons!" shouted Herr Strömli, running over to his wife's mule to get his rifle. While his strapping sons, Adelbert and Gottfried, and the three brave servants were also arming themselves, he said, "Cousin Gustav has saved the life of more than one of us; now it is our turn to perform the same service for him"; then he lifted his wife, who had regained consciousness, back onto the mule; took the precaution of tying up the hands of Nanky, who was a kind of hostage; sent all the women and children back to the seagull pond under the sole protection of his thirteen-year-old son Ferdinand, who was also armed; and, after questioning Toni, who had taken up a helmet and a pike herself, about the numbers and disposition of the Negroes in the courtyard, and promising, if possible, to spare her mother and Hoango too, he bravely placed himself at the head of his little company and, putting his trust in God, set out, with Toni as his guide, for the plantation.

Toni, as soon as the party had slipped through the back gate, pointed out to Herr Strömli the room in which Hoango and Babekan lay asleep; and while Herr Strömli and his men entered the unlocked house without a sound and seized the Negroes' stacked rifles, she slipped away to the shed where Seppy, Nanky's five-year-old brother, slept. For Nanky and Seppy, old Hoango's bastard children, were very dear to him—especially the latter, whose mother had died only a short time ago; and since the retreat to the seagull pond and the flight from there to Port-au-Prince, which she intended to join, would still be exposed to many dangers even if the Negroes did set the young man free, she concluded, not unwisely, that their holding the boys as a sort of pledge might prove very useful in case they were pursued. She was able to pick the boy up out of his bed and carry him, half asleep in her arms, across to the main building without being seen. Meanwhile Herr Strömli and his men had entered the door of Hoango's room as stealthily as they could; but instead of finding him and Babekan in bed as he expected, both of them, awakened by the noise, were standing, half naked and helpless, in the middle of the room. Herr Strömli raised his rifle and commanded them to surrender or be killed on the spot! But Hoango's only answer was to snatch a pistol from the wall and fire it point-blank into the group, grazing Herr Strömli's head. At this signal, Herr Strömli's band fell upon him fiercely; Hoango, after firing a second shot that pierced a servant through the shoulder, was wounded in the hand by a saber stroke and the two of them, Babekan and the Negro, were thrown to the ground and tied with ropes to the pedestal of a large table.

Meanwhile, awakened by the shots, Hoango's Negroes, twenty or more in number, came rushing from their huts and, hearing old Babekan screaming inside the house, they charged forward furiously to try to recapture their weapons. Herr Strömli, whose wound was trifling, posted his men at the windows of the house and commanded them to empty their rifles at the Negroes to drive them back, but in vain; paying no heed to two of their men already sprawled out dead in the yard, the Negroes were about to fetch axes and crowbars and break down the house door, which Herr Strömli had barred, when Toni, trembling and shaking, entered Hoango's room with the boy Seppy in her arms. Herr Strömli was only too pleased to see her; snatching the boy from her arms, he turned to Hoango, drew his cutlass, and swore he would kill the child on the spot if Hoango did not order his Negroes to fall back. Hoango, whose strength was broken from the blow across the three fingers of his hand, and knowing his own life was in jeopardy if he refused, after a moment's reflection, during which he was lifted from the floor, said that he would do it; escorted to the window by Herr Strömli, he took a handkerchief in his left hand and, signaling to the Negroes in the yard, he shouted for them to leave the door alone and go back to their huts, as he didn't need their help to save his life! At this, the struggle quieted down a little; when his men lingered in the courtyard to discuss things, Hoango, on Herr Strömli's demand, sent out a Negro who had been taken prisoner inside the house to repeat his order. The blacks, as little as they understood what was happening, had no choice but to obey the words of so unmistakable a message; and, abandoning their assault, for which everything stood ready, they went back one by one, grumbling and cursing, to their huts. Herr Strömli had Seppy's hands tied up under Hoango's eyes, told the Negro that his only purpose was to free the officer, his nephew, from his imprisonment on the plantation, and that, if no obstacles were put in the way of their flight to Port-au-Prince, he would have nothing to fear for his own, Hoango's, life, or for that of his children, who would be returned to him. Babekan, when Toni came up to her and, in an irrepressible burst of feeling, put her hand out to say goodbye, knocked it violently aside. She called her a villain and a traitor, and, twisting about against the pedestal of the table to which she was tied, said the vengeance of the Lord would overtake her before she had a chance to enjoy her infamy. Toni replied, "I did not betray you; I am white and engaged to the young man you are holding prisoner; I belong to the race of those you are waging open war against, and shall know how to account to the Lord for my having sided with them!" Thereupon Herr Strömli had a guard posted over the Negro Hoango, whom he had taken care to tie up again and bind to a doorpost; had the servant who lay unconscious on the floor with a smashed shoulderblade lifted up and carried away; and, after telling Hoango that he could come and fetch his two children, Nanky as well as Seppy, a few days later in Sainte Luce, where the first French outposts stood, took Toni, who was a prey to all sorts of feelings and could not keep back her tears, by the hand and led her from the bedroom, amid the curses of Babekan and old Hoango.

Meanwhile Herr Strömli's sons, Adelbert and Gottfried, right after the first main skirmish at the windows had ended, ran at their father's command to their cousin

Gustav's room where, after meeting a stubborn resistance from the two Negroes guarding him, they were lucky enough to overpower them. One lay dead on the floor; the other, with a bad bullet wound, had crawled out into the corridor. The two brothers, the eldest of whom had also been hit, in the thigh, but lightly, untied their beloved cousin; they hugged and kissed him and, handing him a rifle and sidearms, jubilantly told him to follow them to the front room where Herr Strömli, as the victory had already been decided, was probably getting everything ready for their withdrawal. Cousin Gustav, however, sitting halfway up in bed, only gave their hands a friendly squeeze; otherwise he was silent and distracted, and, instead of taking the pistols they held out to him, he raised his right hand and passed it across his forehead with an indescribable expression of woe. The young men, sitting down beside him, asked what was wrong; and when he put his arm around them and leaned his head silently against the younger brother's shoulder, Adelbert thought he was going to faint and was about to get up and bring him a glass of water when Toni, with the boy Seppy on her arm, entered the room, holding Herr Strömli's hand. Gustav instantly changed color; he clung to his two friends for support as he got up, as though he were about to collapse; and before the young men realized what he meant to do with the pistol that he now snatched from their hands, he had already discharged it, gnashing his teeth in rage, full at Toni. The shot went right through her breast; when, with a stifled cry of pain, she took several steps in his direction and, handing the boy to Herr Strömli, collapsed in front of him, he flung the pistol across her body, kicked her away with his foot and, calling her a whore, threw himself back onto the bed. "Monster!" shouted Herr Strömli and his sons. The two young men flung themselves down beside the girl and, lifting her up, they called for one of the old servants who had served them as doctor in several similarly desperate situations in the past; but the girl, with her hand clutched convulsively to her wound, pushed her friends away and gasped out: "Tell him——!" while pointing to the man who had shot her, and again: "Tell him——!"

"What shall we tell him?" cried Herr Strömli—but the approach of death robbed her of the power of speech. Adelbert and Gottfried stood up and shouted at the murderer if he knew that the girl was the one who had saved him; that she loved him and had sacrificed everything, parents and possessions, in order to flee with him to Port-au-Prince? When he lay insensible on the bed, oblivious to their presence, they thundered "Gustav!" in his ears and asked if he could hear them, and shook him and pulled him by the hair. Gustav sat up. He looked at the girl lying bathed in her own blood, and the rage that had given rise to his deed gave way, by a natural succession, to a feeling of ordinary compassion. Herr Strömli, shedding burning tears into his handkerchief, asked, "Why, wretch, did you do it?" Cousin Gustav, rising from the bed and looking at the girl while he wiped the sweat from his brow, replied that she had treacherously tied him up during the night and handed him over to the Negro Hoango. "Oh!" cried Toni, and with an indescribable look stretched her hand out to him. "I tied you up, dearest friend, because——!" But she was incapable of speech, nor could her hand reach him, she fell back again, with a sudden flagging of her strength, into Herr Strömli's lap.

"Why did you tie me up?" asked Gustav, white-faced, kneeling beside her. Herr Strömli, after a long pause punctuated only by the rattling in Toni's throat, during which they waited in vain for her to answer, spoke. "Because, after Hoango's return, there was no other way to save you, you unhappy man; because she wanted to avoid the fight you would certainly have started, because she wanted to gain time until we who, thanks to her, were already hurrying here, could free you with our arms."

Gustav covered his face with his hands. "Oh!" he cried, without looking up, and imagined the earth was sinking under his feet. "Are you telling me the truth?" He put his arms around her and looked into her face, his heart pitiably torn.

"Oh!" cried Toni, and these were her last words: "You shouldn't have distrusted me!" And her noble spirit fled.

Gustav tore his hair. "True, true!" he cried, as his cousins dragged him away from the corpse, "I shouldn't have distrusted you; you were engaged to me by an oath, even though we never said a word about it to one another!" Herr Strömli sorrowfully smoothed down the pinafore over the girl's breast. He urged the servant standing beside him with his few inadequate instruments to extract the bullet he was sure he would find lodged in the breastbone; but all his efforts, as we have said, were in vain, the lead had gone clean through her and her soul had already fled to a better star.

Meanwhile Gustav had gone over to the window; and while Herr Strömli and his sons, weeping silently, considered what to do with the body and whether they should call the mother in, Gustav sent the bullet with which the other pistol was loaded through his brain. This last act of horror robbed the kinsmen of their senses. All their efforts were now turned to him; but the poor unfortunate's skull was completely shattered, with fragments of it clinging to the wall, as he had stuck the pistol right into his mouth. Herr Strömli was the first to get command of himself. For with daylight already shining brightly through the windows, and word being brought in that the Negroes were again to be seen in the courtyard, nothing remained but to think immediately of retreat. The two corpses, which they did not wish to leave behind to the unpredictable mercies of the Negroes, were placed upon a plank, and, reloading their rifles, the grieving column of men set out for the seagull pond. Herr Strömli, with the boy Seppy on his arm, took the lead; the two strongest servants, heaving up the bodies on their shoulders, followed next; the wounded man hobbled behind them on a stick, and Adelbert and Gottfried, with their rifles cocked, marched on either side of the slow-moving funeral cortege. When the Negroes saw how weak the little group was, they rushed out of their huts with spears and pitchforks in their hands and seemed on the point of attacking; but Hoango, whom the party had had the foresight to untie, stepped out onto the stairs of the house and signaled the Negroes to keep back.

"At Sainte Luce," he called to Herr Strömli, who was already passing through the gate with the corpses.

"At Sainte Luce," the latter replied, and the column, unpursued, passed into the open and reached the forest. At the seagull pond, where they found the family, a grave was dug, amid tears and weeping, for the bodies; and after the rings Gustav and Toni wore on their fingers were exchanged, the two were lowered, amid hushed prayers, into the abode of eternal peace. Five days later Herr Strömli, with his wife and children, was fortunate enough to reach Sainte Luce, where he left the two Negro boys behind as he had promised. Arriving at Port-au-Prince shortly before the siege began, he fought on its walls in the cause of the whites; and when the city, after a stubborn defense, fell to General Dessalines, he escaped with the French army aboard the British fleet, after which the family took ship for Europe, reaching their native country, Switzerland, without further incident. There Herr Strömli, with the remainder of his small fortune, brought a piece of property near the Rigi; and even in the year 1807 one could still see, amid the shrubbery of his garden, the monument he had erected to the memory of his nephew, Gustav, and the latter's bride, the faithful Toni.

TRANSLATED BY MARTIN GREENBERG

19

Ourika

Claire de Duras

The first fully dimensioned portrayal of a black person in European literature was created by an aristocratic Frenchwoman, Claire de Duras (1777–1828). Her novella *Ourika*, published in 1823, was based on a true account of a Senegalese child who had been brought to France for her upbringing. The book went through four editions in 1824 alone, was rapidly translated into Italian, German, Spanish, and English, and became such a popular international cult book that it elicited royal comment by Louis XVIII and inspired not only poems, plays, prose sequels, and a famous engraving, but also Ourika clothing styles and hairdos. More significantly, Duras's black female heroine, who considers herself equal to the whites who raised her until she discovers the social consequences of racial difference, offers a counterpoint to the dehumanized African of France's Code Noir. The novella is reprinted here in its entirety in the 1829 Boston translation by George Wallis Haven.

Introduction

A few months after I had left Montpelier and fixed my residence in Paris, where I followed the profession of medicine, I was one morning called to a convent in the suburbs of St. Jacques, to visit a young nun who was sick. The Emperor Napoleon had, a short time before, permitted the rebuilding of some of these convents: the one I now visited was devoted to the education of youth, and belonged to the order of the Ursulines. A part of the edifice had been destroyed during the Revolution. A few arches were all that was now left of the antique church which had protected one side of the cloister. A nun led the way into this cloister, which we traversed, treading on the long flat stones that formed the pavement of these galleries. I at once perceived that there were tombs beneath them: for they all bore inscriptions, nearly effaced by the hand of time. Some of these stones had been broken during the Revolution; and the sister remarked, as she called my attention to them, that they had not yet had time to repair them. I had never before seen the interior of a convent, and the sight was to me entirely novel. From the cloister we passed into the garden, "where," said the nun, "they have carried our sick sister." Just then I perceived her at the extremity of a long alley of lime-trees. She was sitting, and almost entirely hidden beneath her large black veil. "Here is your physician," said the sister, and immediately withdrew.

It was with dread that I approached her; the sight of the tombs had deeply affected my feelings, and I supposed I was about to behold a new victim of the cloisters. All the prejudices of my youth were revived; and my interest in her whom I came to visit was the more increased, as I thought on the malady with which I supposed she was afflicted. She turned herself toward me, and how great was my surprise at beholding a *negress!* My astonishment was still increased by the politeness with which she received me, and the excellence of the language with which she accosted me. "You have come to visit one who is very ill," said she to me; "at present I desire to recover, but I have not always thus wished, and this perhaps is what has fixed my disease so deeply." I questioned her upon the nature of her complaints. "I suffer," said she, "a constant oppression, my fever never leaves me, and I cannot sleep." Her appearance but too well confirmed what she had told me. She was extremely emaciated, her eyes were very bright and large, and her teeth, of a dazzling whiteness, of themselves lit up her countenance. The soul still lived, though the body was destroyed; and she bore all the marks of a long and violent sorrow. Touched beyond expression, I resolved to use all my exertions to restore her. I spoke to her of the necessity of calming her imagination, of diverting her mind, and drawing it away from its painful recollections. "I am happy," said she; "never have I felt so calm and happy." The tones of her voice spoke sincerity. That sweet voice could not deceive; but every moment added to my surprise. "You have not always thought thus," said I; "the traces of very long suffering are impressed upon you." "It is true," answered she; "it was very late ere I found the repose of my heart, but now I am happy." "Then," said I, "'tis the past we must cure; let us trust we may be able: but this past—I must know what it is, before I can hope to cure it." "It is," answered she, "a scene of follies." As she said these words, a tear fell upon her cheek. "And you say," cried I, "you say you are happy!" "Yes," answered she, with firmness, "I am happy, and I would not exchange this happiness for the fortune I once so much envied. I have no secret; my misfortune,—'tis the history of my whole life. My sufferings were so great till the day this convent received me, that my health gradually sunk beneath them. I felt myself sinking, and it gave me joy; for in the future I had no hope. This was a most guilty thought! You see, I am punished for it—and now when I could wish to live, perhaps it will be denied me." I tried to encourage her, and excite hopes of a speedy recovery; but in pronouncing these consoling words, in giving her hopes of life, I know not what sad presentiment it was, that told me it was too late, that death had sealed his victim.

I often repeated my visits to this young nun; the interest I took in her situation appeared to touch her. One day she reverted, of her own accord, to the subject to which I wished to lead her. "The sorrows which I have suffered," said she, "must appear so strange, that I have always felt a great repugnance to disclose them. We cannot judge of the sufferings of others, and confidants are almost always accusers." "Fear it not from me," said I; "I see too plainly the ravages which sorrow has made upon you to doubt your sincerity." "You will find my story true," answered she; "but it will appear most unreasonable." "And even if it does," said I, "will this forbid my sympathy?" "Almost always it does," answered she; "yet if to cure me, you have need to know the sorrows which have destroyed my health, I will confide them to you, when we are a little more acquainted with each other."

I made my visits to the convent more and more frequent; the treatment I prescribed seemed to produce some effect. At length, on one of the last days of summer, finding her alone—beneath the same trees and seated on the same bench as when I first saw her, we resumed the conversation of that day, and she related to me what follows.

Ourika

I was carried away from Senegal at the age of two years, by the Chevalier de B., who was Governor of that place. He pitied my miseries, when he one day saw some slaves carried on board a negro vessel, which was soon to leave the port: my mother was dead, and they forced me on board, notwithstanding my cries. M. de B. purchased me, and upon his arrival in France, gave me to Madame de B., his aunt, one of the most lovely women of her time, one who knew how to unite the most elevated qualities of mind, with the most touching gentleness of heart.

To save me from slavery, to give me Madame de B. for a benefactress,—this was to bestow a double existence upon me. Ungrateful, indeed, must I have been to Providence if I were not happy. And yet, happiness! does it always flow from the gifts of intellect? Much the contrary, I believe. We must pay for the blessing of knowledge by the desire of ignorance; and the fable does not tell us whether Galatea found happiness after she had received life.

It was not till long after this period that I became acquainted with the history of my early days. My own recollections carried me no farther back than the saloon of Madame de B.; there I passed my days, beloved of her, caressed, spoiled by her friends, loaded with presents, flattered and extolled as a most animated and amiable child.

The tone of this society was that of great eagerness to be pleased; but an eagerness which excluded every thing like exaggeration. Praise was bestowed wherever praise was deserved, and censure itself was often withheld where censure was merited; indeed, by a still more benevolent artifice, faults were often construed to be but natural qualities. Here success inspired confidence. One was estimated in Madame de B.'s presence, to the extent of his deserts—indeed, often beyond them, for she unconsciously imparted, as it were, something of herself to her friends; in seeing her, in listening to her, one seemed to be like her.

Clad in an oriental dress and seated at the feet of Madame de B., I listened, although I did not yet understand it, to the conversation of the most distinguished men of the time. I had none of the turbulence of childhood; I was pensive even before I had the power of reflection. I was happy when at the side of Madame de B.; to be there, to listen to her, to obey her, to look up to her in all things; this made my very existence, *love*—and I could ask no more. To exist in the very lap of luxury, to commune with none but the most gifted and amiable minds, did not excite my wonder. I knew no other existence: and yet I felt a great contempt for all that accorded not with the world where my own days were past. Good taste is to the mind what a delicate ear is to sound. While yet a child, the least want of it affected me; I perceived it, even before I could define it; and habit had rendered it essential to my happiness. This disposition it had been dangerous to cultivate, had I known the future; but I knew it not, and it gave me no alarm.

I had arrived at the age of twelve years without the least suspicion that there were any requisites for happiness which I had not. My being a negress gave me no anxiety; they told me I was beautiful, and there was nothing to speak to me of my misfortune; I saw but few other children; one only was my friend, and my color did not prevent his love.

My benefactress had two grandsons, the children of her daughter who died very young. Charles, the younger of the two, was about my own age. Brought up with me, he was my protector, my guide, and my defender, whenever I fell into any trifling errors. When seven years old, he was sent to college. I wept at parting with him; it was my first sorrow. Often did I think of him, though I saw him but seldom. He pursued his studies, and I, to gratify Madame de B. learned all that is essential to a finished education. She fondly believed that I was possessed of every talent. I had a voice, and the most excellent masters were employed to cultivate it; a taste for drawing, and a celebrated painter, a friend of Madame de B., took the charge of directing my attempts; I learned the English and Italian languages, and Madame de B. employed herself in teaching me to read them. She guided my mind, she formed my judgment; in discoursing with her, in discovering all the riches of her mind, I felt my own elevated. It was admiration that opened the ways of knowledge before me. Alas! little did I then think that these delightful studies were to be followed by days of so much bitterness. To please Madame de B. was all I thought of; a smile of approbation on her lips was all my future.

In the meanwhile my studies occupied more and more of my time: a love of the poets now filled my young imagination; without a definite object or design, I suffered my thoughts to roam at will among their beauties, and with all the confidence of youth, I said that Madame de B. knew how to guard my happiness; her tenderness, the manner of my life, every thing served to confirm my error and authorize my blindness. I am about to give you an instance of the attention and preference of which I was the object.

Perhaps you will hardly believe, in seeing me to-day, that I was once celebrated for the elegance and beauty of my form. Madame de B. often praised my gracefulness, and wished that I should perfectly accomplish myself in the art of dancing. In order to exhibit this talent, my benefactress gave a ball, professedly to please her grandsons, but in reality that I might display myself to the greater advantage in a quadrille of the four quarters of the world, in which I was to represent Africa.

Travellers were consulted, books of costumes were read, and works treating of African music were examined; at length they made choice of the *Comba*, the national dance of my country. My partner covered his face with crape: alas! I had no need of putting it upon my own; yet then I made not this reflection. Entirely absorbed in the pleasure of the ball, I danced the *Comba*, with all the flattering success which could follow from the novelty of the sight, and the choice of spectators, the greater part of whom, being friends of Madame de B., were very enthusiastic in their praise, and fancied that they added to her happiness by expressing this sentiment with unrestrained vivacity. The dance on all sides was conducted with great animation; it was a mixture of all measures and attitudes, in which the various passions of love, grief, triumph, and despair were represented. To all these violent workings of the soul, I was then a stranger, and know not what instinct taught me to divine them; yet I succeeded. All joined in applauding me; they surrounded me, they loaded me with praises. This pleasure was without a mixture of sadness; nothing then disturbed my serenity. It was a few days after the ball, that a conversation, which I accidentally heard, opened my eyes and ended my youth.

There was in Madame de B.'s saloon a large silk screen, which concealed a door and extended itself very near one of the windows; between this screen and the window was a table, where I sometimes sat to draw. One day I was finishing with great diligence a miniature; entirely absorbed by my labor, I had remained a long time without moving, and Madame de B. had not a suspicion but that I had gone out, when one of her friends was announced, the Marchioness de ———. She was a woman of a cool judgment and penetrating mind, positive, even to roughness; and this character she carried into her friendship. Sacrifices for what was good and of advantage to her friends, she did not for a moment hesitate to make; yet she expected great returns for this strong attachment. Inquisitive and difficult, her demands equalled her sacrifices, and she was the least beloved of all Madame de B.'s friends. I feared her, although she was kind to me. It was her manner that terrified; to examine even with sternness was in her a proof of interest. Alas! I was so accustomed to gentleness, that justice appeared to me fearful. "Since I find myself alone with you," said Madame de ——— to Madame de B., "I wish to speak with you about Ourika; she becomes daily more fascinating, her mind is fully developed; in conversation she rivals you, full of talent, animated, and easy; but what will become of her? What, in a word, can you do with her?" "Alas," answered Madame de B., "this thought has often occupied my mind, and I confess it fills me with sadness; I love her as if she were my own daughter; I would do every thing to make her happy, and yet when I reflect upon her situation, I see no remedy. Poor Ourika! I see you solitary, for ever solitary in life."

It would be impossible for me to paint to you the effect these words produced upon me. The lightning darts not more swiftly. I saw all: I saw myself a negress, dependent, despised, without fortune, without support, without a single being of my own rank with whom to join my destiny; till this time the plaything, the amusement of my benefactress,—soon to be cast forth from a world to which my rank gave me no title. My blood rushed violently, a cloud came over my eyes, and the rapidity with which my heart beat deprived me for a moment of the power of hearing; but I soon recovered sufficiently to listen to the remainder of the conversation.

"I fear," said Madame de ———, "that you have ruined her happiness. Who, think you, can satisfy her, now that she has lived in the intimacy of your society?" "But she shall still continue there," said Madame de B. "Yes," replied Madame de ———, "as long as she is a child; but she is now fifteen years old; to whom will you marry her, with the sentiments you have inspired her, with the education you have given her? Who would wish to marry a negress? And if, by the gift of wealth, you can find one who will bear the relation of father to her children, he must be one of a condition inferior to her own, one with whom she cannot be happy. Her affections will never be given but to those who cannot reciprocate them." "All this is too true," answered Madame de B.; "but happily she has not the least suspicion of it, and her attachment for me is so strong, that I hope it will long prevent her from reflecting upon her situation. To render her happy she must be reduced to the level of her nation; this I sincerely believe to be impossible. But yet, may not the force of her mind support her above the rank nature has assigned her, she being unable to rest beneath?"

"You indulge a vain, vain hope," said Madame de ———. "Philosophy can support against the evils of fortune, but can avail nothing when we break the relations of nature. Ourika has broken from her destiny: she has intruded herself upon society, without the consent of society, and it will be avenged." "Surely," said Madame de B., "she is wholly innocent of the crime; you are cruel to this unfortunate child." "I am more desirous of her happiness than you yourself are," replied Madame de ———. "I wish her good, you would ruin her." Madame de B. made an impatient reply, and I was just becoming the subject of disagreement between the two friends when company was announced. I passed along behind the screen, escaped from the saloon, and running to my own chamber, a flood of tears calmed for a moment my sorrowful heart.

How great a change was thus wrought in my existence, by the breaking away of the illusion which had till this time encircled me. It was one of those illusions which are like the light of day—fading not alone, but burying all objects with itself in darkness. In the confusion of new thoughts which assailed me, I saw nothing of all that had till that time filled my mind; it was an abyss with all its terrors. The contempt with which I saw myself followed, the society from which I was cast forth, the man, who for the price of gold, might perhaps consent to call my children his own!—all these thoughts sprang up like phantoms before me, and seized upon me like furies: loneliness, above all, the conviction that I must be solitary, for ever solitary in life, as Madame de B. had said; and every moment I repeated, "Alone! forever alone!" Yesterday, what mattered it that I was alone? I knew nothing of it; I perceived it not; I felt how necessary what I loved was to my happiness, but I never thought that the objects of my love had no need of me. Now my eyes were opened, and already had my sorrow let suspicion into my soul.

When I again returned to the saloon, all present were struck with the change in my appearance; they questioned me, and I replied that I was sick: they believed it was so. Madame de B. sent to call Barthez; he examined me with care, felt my pulse, and bluntly said that nothing ailed me. Madame de B. cheered up, and endeavoured to divert and amuse me. I dare not say how ungrateful I was for these attentions of my benefactress; my mind was, as it were, bound up in itself. The benefits which it is delightful to receive, are those which the heart repays; mine was too much filled with bitter reflections to expand itself in gratitude. The same thoughts infinitely combined, filled every moment. They presented themselves under a thousand forms; my imagination gave them the most sombre hues; often my entire nights were passed in tears. I exhausted my pity upon myself; I shuddered at my own appearance—I dared no longer look upon myself in the mirror; when my eyes chanced to rest on my hands, I fancied I saw those of an ape; I exaggerated my own deformity; and my color—it appeared to me the mark of reprobation. "It is this, that separates me from all the beings of my nature, this, that condemns me to solitude! solitude for ever! for ever a stranger to love! For the reward of gold one may perhaps consent that my children should call him father!" My blood rose with indignation at the thought. At one moment I determined to request Madame de B. to return me to my native country; but even there I should have been alone; who could have understood, who comprehended me? Alas! I belonged no more to any one; I was a stranger to the whole human race!

It was not till long after this, that I thought of the possibility of being resigned under my sorrows. Madame de B. was by no means devout, and for the few religious sentiments I possessed, I was indebted to a venerable priest who had prepared me for my first communion. They were sincere feelings, for my character was all sincere; but I did not know that, to support us, they should be mingled with all the actions of life; mine occupied a few moments of my days, and then were strangers to me. My confessor was a holy old man, but little mistrustful; I saw him two or three times each year, and, as I never imagined that sorrows could be faults, I was silent with regard to my sufferings. They sensibly preyed upon my health, but, astonishing their power! they purified my spirit. An eastern sage has said, "He who has never suffered, what does he know?" I saw, that before I was afflicted I knew nothing; my impressions were but sentiments, I formed no judgment; I loved—discourses, actions, persons pleased or displeased my *heart*. Now my mind was separated from these involuntary emotions. Sorrow is like distance, it gives us the proportions of things. Since I had felt myself a stranger to all around me, I had become more difficult to please, and I critically examined all which before that period had given me delight.

This disposition could not escape the notice of Madame de B.; I know not whether she divined the cause. She feared perhaps to increase my sorrows, by leading me to confide them to her. But she showed me still greater kindness than she was wont; she conversed with me without the least reserve, and, to draw me away from my own sorrows, she fixed my attention upon those which touched herself. She judged rightly of my heart: never more could I be bound to life but by the thought that I was necessary, or at least useful, to my benefactress. Still one thought was ever present; I was alone upon the earth, I should die and not one bosom regret my departure. I was unjust to Madame de B.; she loved me, and she had proved her love; yet she was bound by interests far stronger than mine. I never envied the tenderness she showed her grandchildren, especially Charles; but I could have wished that I might say with them: "My Mother!"

As I thought on the ties of domestic life, my sorrows returned with new force upon me; I,—I was never to be a sister, a wife, a mother! Perhaps I fancied more delight in these relations than they really possess; and I forgot the pleasures which were around me, in thinking of those which were forbidden my possession. I had no friend, none on whom to bestow my confidence; that which I felt for Madame de B. flowed rather from habit than affection; yet I believed I felt for Charles all the affection one bears a brother.

All his time had hitherto been past at college; he was now about to leave it and commence his travels. He left home with his elder brother and his tutor; they were to visit England, Germany, and Italy, and to be two years absent. Charles was delighted with the thought, and I was not sorrowful till the moment of separation drew near; for I was always happy in what gave him pleasure. I had never spoken to him of the many thoughts which occupied my mind. I never saw him alone, and it would have taken much time to acquaint him with all my sorrows: then, I am sure, he would have understood me. But there was in Charles, notwithstanding his gentleness and gravity, a love of jest which rendered me timid: it is true he seldom employed it, but upon the folly of affectation; sincerity at once disarmed him. In short, I said nothing to him. His departure served to dissipate my mind, and I thought it well that any sorrow should prey upon me but that which had its home in my bosom.

It was a short time after the departure of Charles that the Revolution assumed a more serious form; I heard nothing spoken of in Madame de B.'s saloon but the great moral and political interests this revolution affected even to their source; they discoursed of what had filled the most elevated minds of all ages. Nothing could be more fitted to form and expand my mind than the sight of this arena, where the most distinguished men called in question points, which the world had not even thought to differ upon till that moment. They examined all subjects to their very foundation, went back to the origin of all institutions, but, too often, only that they might shake and destroy them.

Young as I was, a stranger to all the interests of society, nourishing my secret grief in silence, will you believe that the Revolution wrought a change in my thoughts, gave birth to hope in my heart, and made me for a moment forget my misfortunes? How eagerly the heart grasps at consolation! It for a moment flashed across my mind that my place might be found amid this wild confusion. All fortunes mingled, all ranks confounded, all prejudices dissipated, such a state of society might succeed, that I should be no longer a stranger; and that if I possessed any superiority of intellect, any talent hitherto concealed, it would then be appreciated when my color no longer made me alone in the midst of the world, as it had done till this time. But these very qualities, which I had hoped would be the basis for me to rise upon, soon dispelled my illusion: I could not desire the misery of many, that I alone might be happy. On the other hand, I perceived the folly of those who wished to bow the events of the world to their own will; I saw their selfish, secret views, and condemned the littleness of their characters; their false philanthropy ceased to enchant me, and I renounced my hopes, when I saw that adversity itself did not protect me from contempt. Yet it delighted me to listen to their spirited discussions, though their greatest charm was rapidly fading. The period was past when the desire of pleasing was the only thought,—when success was purchased by the entire sacrifice of self: when the Revolution ceased to be a beautiful theory, when it came home to the intimate interests of every one, conversation was dispute; sharpness, bitterness, and personality took the place of reason. Sometimes, notwithstanding my sadness, I amused myself with these violent opinions, which in truth were seldom more than pretension, affectation, or fear: but the gaiety which flows from sarcasm is not pure; there is too much malignity mingled with it to enliven a heart which rejoices only in innocence. This sarcastic joy may exist and the heart still be sad; perhaps, even, unhappiness makes us more susceptible of it, for the bitterness which the soul cherishes in silence affords a constant nourishment to this gloomy pleasure.

The hope which the Revolution had excited was gone, and the feelings of my mind were unaltered; dissatisfied with my fortune, my sorrows were soothed only by the confidence and kindness of Madame de B. Sometimes, in the midst of discussions whose bitterness she could not restrain, she would fix her eyes sadly upon me;

such a look was consolation to my heart; it seemed to say, "Ourika you alone accord with me!"

The freedom of negroes now became a question of interest: it could not be otherwise than that this question should engage me deeply; it was an illusion in which I even now delight to indulge, that elsewhere at least, there were those who resembled me: they were unhappy, and therefore I believed them good, and interested myself in their fate. Alas! how soon was I undeceived! The massacres of St. Domingo caused a new and rending sorrow: hitherto, I was sad because I belonged to a proscribed race; now, I suffered the shame of belonging to a race of barbarians and assassins.

In the meanwhile the Revolution advanced with rapid steps; terror was seated on all countenances, when men of the most violent measures usurped all the important posts. It was soon evident that they determined to hold nothing sacred: the terrific days of the twentieth of June and the tenth of August served too well to point out their bloody course. Those who had remained of Madame de B.'s society were scattered at this epoch: some sheltered themselves from persecution in distant countries; others concealed themselves, or retired into the provinces. Madame de B. did neither the one nor the other. The feelings of her heart bound her to her home; it dwelt upon the past, and near the tomb of those she loved.

We had lived thus in solitude for some months, when, in the latter part of the year 1792, the decree confiscating the property of emigrants, was issued. In the midst of these disasters, Madame de B. would have thought nothing of the loss of her property, had it not belonged to her grandsons; but by the disposition of it she enjoyed the use of it only. She determined therefore to recall Charles, the younger of the two brothers, and to send the other, who was about twenty years of age, to join the army of Condé. They were now in Italy, continuing the travels they had commenced two years before under circumstances so different. Charles reached Paris the beginning of February 1793, a short time after the execution of the King.

This guilty act filled Madame de B. with excessive sorrow; she yielded herself up to it entirely; her mind was strong and the horror she experienced was commensurate with the enormity of the crime. There is something striking in the deep grief of age; it is never trifling, it is founded on reason. All the energy of Madame de B.'s character was carried into her sufferings; her health was sinking beneath them, yet I did not think that she could be consoled, or even diverted from her sorrows. I wept, I sympathized with her, I tried to elevate my own mind to the rank of hers, that its sufferings might at least equal hers, that they might be borne with hers.

I hardly thought of my own sorrows, while this reign of terror continued; indeed, it would have filled me with shame, to have spoken of my own misery in the midst of so great afflictions; besides I did not now feel my loneliness, while all around me were unhappy too. One's opinions, like one's native country, to bring happiness must be enjoyed with others; he who supports, who defends them, is a brother. I said sometimes to myself, that I, a poor negress, was bound to the most exalted minds by the unjust sufferings we equally endured: the day when virtue and truth should triumph would be a day of triumph to me as well as to them; but, alas! that day was far distant.

As soon as Charles had arrived, Madame de B. left Paris for the country. All her friends were concealed or had fled; her society consisted of scarcely more than an old

Abbot whose daily ridicule of religion had been familiar to me for ten years, and who was now afflicted because the property of the clergy had been sold, and he had lost by it an income of twenty thousand livres. This Abbot accompanied us to St. Germain. His manner in society was mild, or rather it was tranquil: for his calmness had nothing of mildness in it; it resulted from the constitution of his mind, not from the peace of his heart.

The situation of Madame de B. had always enabled her to perform many kind offices. Connected with M. de Choiseul, she had been able, during his long ministry, to exercise her benevolence toward many. Two of the most influential men during this scene of terror had been laid under obligations to Madame de B.; they were not unmindful of it, and gave her proofs of their gratitude. They watched over her continually, and would not suffer her to be accused; many times did they expose their own lives, to save hers from the furious spirits of the Revolution; for it must be remarked that, in those fatal days, the very leaders of the most violent parties, could not do good without danger: it seemed as if, on this desolate earth, the power was given to wickedness alone, so much did all authority proceed from and return to it. Madame de B. was not cast into prison; she was guarded in her own house, under pretence that she was too feeble to endure imprisonment. Charles, the Abbot, and myself remained with her, and we devoted all our attention to her.

Nothing can paint the anxiety and terror in which we passed these days, reading in the journals the condemnation and death of Madame de B.'s friends, and trembling every moment lest her defenders should no longer be able to protect her from the same fate. We knew she was on the point of being condemned, when the death of Robespierre put an end to our horror. Men breathed again; the guards quitted the house of Madame de B., and we four remained in that solitude which is felt, I imagine, after some great calamity by those who have escaped it together. One would believe that the ties of life were drawn closer by affliction: I felt that there at least, I was not a stranger.

If I knew for a moment what it was to be happy, after the illusion of my childhood had vanished, it was in the days which followed these disastrous times. Madame de B. possessed in the highest degree all that constitutes the charm of domestic life: indulgent and easy, one could open the whole heart before her; she could see the wishes of the soul before the lips expressed them. Confidence was never frozen by a severe or unjust interpretation; thoughts were valued according to their true merit; and one was called in judgment for nothing. This quality would have made her friends happy, had she possessed but this alone. But how many charms besides were united in her person! No barrenness, no ennui ever marked her conversation; it flowed from all that was around her; an interest in trifles, so futile in common minds, is the source of a thousand pleasures in the gifted mind; for it is the peculiarity of such to call up forms out of nothing. The most common thought became fruitful as it past from the lips of Madame de B.; her genius, her reason could clothe it in a thousand novel colors.

Charles had Madame de B.'s traits of character; his mind also resembled hers, that is to say, as hers would have been, just, firm, enlarged, if not modified by other qualities; youth knows no modifications; to youth all is good, or all is evil; while age is distinguished by discovering that nothing is perfectly good, nothing entirely evil. Charles possessed the two engaging charms of his age, justice and truth. I have said that he hated even the shadow of affectation; it was his fault, sometimes to see it where it did not exist. Habitually reserved, his confidence was flattering; when it was bestowed, one felt that it was the fruit of esteem, not a bare propensity of character: whatever he gave was valuable, for it did not flow from him involuntarily, and yet all about him was natural. He reposed such confidence in me, that he had not a thought which was not imparted to me. In the evening, seated around the table, we found inexhaustible stores for conversation: our old Abbot took his place with us; he had linked together so many warring ideas, and maintained them with such simple confidence, that he was a boundless source of amusement to Madame de B., whose just and enlightened mind admirably exposed the absurdities of the poor man, who notwithstanding was never thrown out of good humor; she hurled the shafts of good sense so skilfully against his *order of ideas*, that we compared them to the mighty swordthrusts of Roland or Charlemagne.

Madame de B. was fond of walking and every morning roamed in the forest of St. Germain, resting on the arm of the Abbot. Charles and myself followed them at a distance. It was then he spoke to me of all that occupied his thoughts; of his plans, his hopes, especially his views of things, of men, and of events. He concealed nothing from me; he did not fear to impart all to me. So long had he relied upon me that my friendship was as his life to him, he enjoyed it when unconscious of it; he asked of me no interest, no attention; he well knew that in speaking of himself, he spoke to me of myself, and that I was *himself* even more than he was. O the delight of a confidence like this! it makes amends for all, even the loss of happiness itself!

I never thought of imparting to Charles what had caused me so much sadness. I listened to him, and his conversation had I know not what magical effect upon me, that made me forget my sorrows. Had he questioned me, he would have brought them to my mind; then I should have told him all; but he did not even suspect that any thing was hidden. They were accustomed to see me suffer, and Madame de B. did so much to make me happy that she could not but believe I was so. So I ought to have been. I often told myself I ought; I accused myself of ingratitude, of folly. I know not whether I should have dared to confess how far the irremediable evil of my color was the source of my misery. There is something humiliating in this inability to yield to necessity: yes, sorrows like these, when they once gain the mastery of the soul, carry the whole impress of despair. That which intimidated me when with Charles, was the slight turn of severity which pervaded his thoughts. One evening the conversation happened to turn upon pity, and the question was whether the cause or the result of sorrow inspired the deepest interest. Charles maintained the former. He thought all sorrows must be founded in reason. But reason! who shall define it? Is it the same through all the world? And all hearts, have they the same wants? And sorrow, what is it but the unsatisfied longings of the heart?

It was seldom, however, that the conversation of the evening came home to me so touchingly. I tried to divert my thoughts from the subject as much as possible; I had removed all the mirrors from my chamber; I wore gloves constantly; my dress concealed my neck and my arms, and whenever I went out, I covered myself with a large hat and veil, which indeed I often kept on, while I remained at home. Alas! thus did I deceive myself; like children, I shut my eyes, and fancied that no one saw me.

Towards the close of the year 1795, the reign of terror ceased, and men began to resume their stations. The wrecks of Madame de B.'s society were again united around her, and with sadness I saw the circle of her friends increase. My situation in society was so questionable, that as men resumed their natural order, I became more and more an alien. Every time Madame de B.'s saloon was entered by those who had never before frequented it, I felt a new torture. The expression of astonishment mingled with disdain, which I marked upon their countenances, filled me with misery. I was sure of soon being the subject of some group collected around the window, or of some low-voiced conversation: for it must be they would be curious to know how a negress was admitted to the intimate society of Madame de B. I suffered martyrdom while this mystery was unfolding. I wished I could be transported to my own barbarous country, into the midst of the savages who inhabited it; it had fewer terrors for me than this cruel society, which made me answerable for the evil it had done me. The remembrance of these contemptuous looks followed me for days together; they haunted my dreams, they left me not for a moment; they rose up like my own image before me. Alas! it was the image of phantoms, which I suffered to besiege me! Thou hadst not taught me, O my God! to dissipate these shadows; I knew not that in thee alone there is rest.

At present, it was in the heart of Charles that I sought protection; I was proud of his friendship, still more so of his virtues. I regarded him as the perfection of the whole earth. Once, I thought I loved Charles as a brother; but since suffering had become my constant companion, it seemed as if my youth had become age, and I regarded him with the tenderness of a mother. A mother alone could feel that passionate desire for his happiness, for his success; willingly would I have laid down my life to save him the suffering of a moment. I saw, before he himself did, the impression he made on those around him; he was too happy to think of it himself: And this was natural: he had nothing to dread, for nothing had filled him with that constant alarm I felt for the opinions of others; all was harmony in his fortune, in mine all was discord.

One morning, an old friend of Madame de B. came to her house; he brought proposals of marriage for Charles; Mademoiselle de Thémines had become, through a most cruel fate, a rich heiress; she had lost in one day, every relative upon the scaffold; none of them all remained to her, save a great aunt, formerly a nun; she was now her guardian, and considered it her duty to make immediate provision for her settlement, because, being herself more than eighty years old, she feared lest death should remove her, and thus her niece be left alone in the world, and without a protector. Mademoiselle de Thémines possessed every advantage of birth, of fortune, and of education; she was sixteen years of age, beautiful as the day; how could one hesitate? Madame de B. spoke of it to Charles; at first he felt alarmed at marrying so young; soon however he desired to see Mademoiselle de Thémines; they met, and then he hesitated no longer. Anaïs de Thémines was possessed of every quality which would ensure happiness to Charles; beautiful without being conscious of it, and of so unaffected a modesty that all saw she owed to nature this attractive virtue. Madame de Thémines permitted Charles to visit at her house, and he soon became ardently attached. He told me all the progress of his affection, and I was impatient to see this beautiful Anaïs, who was to make the happiness of Charles. At length she came to St. Germain; Charles had spoken to her of me; from her I had not to support that haughty and scrutinizing look which caused me so much horror; she appeared like a spirit of goodness. I assured her of happiness with Charles, I removed all her fears from his youth; I told her that the solid reason of more advanced age had been his at twenty-one; I answered all her questions; she asked me many, for she knew I had been familiar with him from infancy; and to speak his praises was so delightful to me, that I knew not when to cease.

The arrangement of affairs delayed the marriage several weeks. Charles continued his visits to Madame de Thémines, and often remained two or three days together in Paris; these separations afflicted me, and then I was dissatisfied with myself at finding I preferred my own happiness to that of Charles; it was not thus that I was wont to love. The days when he returned were days of festivity; he told me all that had occupied him; and if he had won upon the affection of Anaïs, I shared his joy with him. One day he was describing to me the manner in which he would wish to live with her. "I wish to win her entire confidence," said he to me, "and to bestow all mine upon her; I will conceal nothing from her, she shall know all my thoughts, she shall know every secret movement of my heart; I wish there should be between us a confidence like our own, Ourika." Like our own! The word filled me with sadness; it reminded me that Charles knew not the only secret of my life, and it took from me the power of confiding it to him. By degrees his absence became more and more lengthened; he was seldom at St. Germain except for a few moments; he came on horseback that he might waste less time upon the road, and returned after dinner again to Paris; so that all our evenings were past without him. Madame de B. often jested with him upon his long absences; would that I could have joined her in them!

One day we were strolling in the forest. Charles had been absent almost all the week, when I suddenly perceived him at the extremity of the alley where we were walking; he came on horseback and rode very swiftly. When he was very near the place where we were, he sprung from his horse and joined us in our walk. After talking a few minutes on general topics, we fell back from the rest, and began to converse on the subjects we had so often spoken of before; I made some remark about the past. "The past!" cried he "ah, how great is the change! Had I then any thing to speak of in those times which are past? It seems to me as if life itself was given me within these two months. Ourika, I can never tell you what my feelings toward her are! Sometimes I believe my soul has gone from me and is hers. When she looks upon me, I breathe not; when she blushes, I would prostrate myself at her feet and adore her. When I think that I am to be the protector of this angel, that to me she confides her life, her destiny; ah! then I glory in my being! O that in me she may find her happiness! I will be to her the father, the mother she has lost: but I shall also be her husband, and her affections will be mine! To me will her first love be given; her whole heart will open itself to mine, we shall live the same life, and oh! when the long course of our years is past, may she say that not one hour has flown and she unhappy. How full of joy, Ourika, is the thought that she will be the mother of my children, that from the bosom of Anaïs they will draw their existence! Oh that they may be as gentle, as beautiful as she! O my God! what have I done to deserve happiness like this?"

Alas! at this moment, how different the question I addressed to Heaven! For some instants I listened with indescribable emotion, to this passionate language. "Great God! thou dost bear witness that I rejoiced in the happiness of Charles: but why, why hast thou laden poor Ourika with life? Why was I not suffered to perish on board the negro bark, or upon my mother's bosom? Why did not the sands of my own Africa receive me, and release poor Ourika from the burden of existence? The world—what need has it of Ourika? Why is she condemned to live? That she may live alone, for ever alone, for ever a stranger to love! Oh my God, suffer it not to be! Take away poor Ourika from the earth! There are none to feel her loss. Her life—is it not solitude?" This horrid thought returned upon me with more than wonted power. My limbs bent beneath me, I fell upon my knees, my eyes were closed, and death seemed just ready to receive me.

(In finishing these words the poor nun seemed borne down to the earth by her feelings; the tones of her voice were changed, and the tears flowed over her withered cheeks. I tried to persuade her to suspend her recital; but she refused. "It is nothing:" said she, "for sorrow lives not in my heart; it is cut to the root. God has had compassion on me; he has raised me to himself from the abyss, where I had fallen because I knew him not, neither loved him. Forget not, then that I am happy; though, alas!" added she, "happiness was a stranger to me then.")

To the period of which I now speak, I had borne up under my sorrows. They had destroyed my health, but I had preserved my reason and the empire over myself; my sorrow, like the fruit-destroying worm, had assailed my heart; in my very bosom I carried the seeds of dissolution, while all without bore the traces of life and health. Conversation still pleased, and discussion still animated me; I even preserved a gaiety of spirit, but joy had forsaken my heart. In a word, to this period I was superior to my sorrows; now they crushed me to the earth.

Charles raised me in his arms, and hasted with me to the house. There every aid was rendered me, and I revived. On opening my eyes, I saw Madame de B. standing beside my bed; Charles held my hand in his; they themselves had watched over me, and I saw upon their countenances a mixture of anxiety and sorrow which touched me to the heart; I felt the return of life, and wept. Madame de B. gently wiped away my tears; she spoke not a word to me, she asked me no questions: Charles overwhelmed me with them. I know not what I answered him; I attributed my accident to the heat, the length of the walk: he believed me, and the bitterness returned to my soul when I found that he believed; I dried my tears; I said to myself, "How easily do we deceive those whose interest is far from us;" I withdrew my hand which he was still holding and tried to appear tranquil before him. He left us at five, as was his custom; it wounded me to the heart. I could have wished him anxious and alarmed for me; while I was thus suffering, he would still have left me! I should have forced him to do it—but then I should have been consoled by the thought that he owed the enjoyment of the evening to me. I was very cautious in concealing from Charles this emotion of my heart; the delicate feelings are ever accompanied with bashfulness; if known, unless divined, they are imperfect; they can be shared by two only.

Scarcely had Charles departed, when I was seized with a most violent fever; it still increased upon me the two following days. Madame de B. watched beside me with her usual kindness. She was much afflicted at my situation, and the impossibility of conveying me to Paris, where the marriage of Charles called her on the morrow. The physicians told her that they would answer for my life, if she would leave me at St. Germain; she at length concluded to do so, and manifested so tender an affection for me at parting, that for a moment, it calmed my heart. But after she had left me, the loneliness, complete, unmingled loneliness, the first I had ever felt, threw me into profound despair. Now, now did I realize, what my imagination had so often painted; I languished afar from those I loved; the words of my sad sorrow could not reach their ears: alas! they would have thrown a cloud over their joys. I saw them yielding themselves to all the wildness of delight, afar from the dying Ourika. Ourika had none beside them in the wide world; yet they needed not Ourika; no one had need of her! This horrid thought, that I was a being useless in the world, rent my heart more deeply than all: it gave me such a disgust of life that I sincerely hoped the disease with which I was attacked, would end my being. I did not utter a syllable, I took no notice of any thing around me: this one thought was written distinctly on my mind; *Would that I might die.* At other moments I was more agitated; I recalled every word of that last conversation I had with Charles in the forest; I saw him floating on the sea of pleasure he had pictured to me, while I died forsaken, solitary in death as in life. This caused me more anguish than any other of my afflictions. I summoned up a thousand imaginations to calm it. I fancied to myself Charles, returning to St. Germain; they tell him, "She is dead," and, oh! can you believe it? I rejoiced at his affliction: it avenged me: and for what? merciful God! that he had been the guardian angel of my life? The frightful thought filled me with horror; I felt that if grief was not a fault, yet to be borne on by it as I had been, was guilt. My ideas then took an opposite course; I tried to conquer myself, to find strength within me to struggle with these distracting thoughts; but I sought not this strength in the fountain from which it flows. Shame for my ingratitude overwhelmed me. "Let me die," I repeated to myself, "it is my wish to die; but let not these hated passions assail my heart. Ourika is a disinherited child; but innocence still remains to her: I will not let ingratitude blight and wither it. I shall pass as a shadow from the earth; but in the tomb I shall find peace. O my God! already are they blest; give them also Ourika's share of happiness, and let her die as the leaf of autumn falls. Have my sufferings not yet sufficed?"

When I recovered from this disease, which threatened my life, I fell into a state of languor, proceeding in no small degree from melancholy. Madame de B. established herself at St. Germain after Charles's marriage; here he often came, accompanied by Anaïs, never did he come without her. My sufferings were always more acute when they were present. I know not whether the image of happiness rendered me more sensible to my own misfortune, or whether the presence of Charles awoke the remembrance of our old friendship. I sought sometimes to discover it again, but it could not be recognised. He told me every thing as he had done before; but his present friendship resembled the past, as the artificial flower resembles that of nature; it is the same thing in all but life and fragrance.

Charles attributed the change of my character to the decay of my health; I believe Madame de B. judged more justly of the sadness of my soul, that she divined my silent sorrow, and that she felt most deeply for me: but the time was no longer, when I could administer consolation to others; my own sufferings bade me expend all my pity upon them.

The situation of Anaïs now required that we should return to Paris. Every day added fresh sadness to my heart. This calm happiness of domestic life, these so gentle ties! this innocent love, so tender and yet so passionate! what a spectacle for an unhappy being, destined to pass the sad days of life in solitude! To die and never have been beloved! to die and know no ties but those of dependence and pity! Days and months thus rolled on. I joined in no conversation, I had foregone all my talents; if I endured books, they were those only in which I hoped to find the imperfect picture of the sorrows that devoured me. They were a new poison to my soul, I fed my grief with tears; alone in my chamber, would I for hours together abandon myself to my affliction.

The birth of a son now filled the measure of Charles's happiness: he came hastily to tell me of it, and in the transports of his joy, I discovered the accents of former friendship. How deeply did they rend my bosom! alas! it was the voice of a friend, who was such to me no longer! and all the remembrance of the past came with this voice, to tear open my wounds afresh.

The infant of Charles was beautiful as Anaïs; the picture of this young mother with her son touched all who saw it: I alone, by a sad fortune, was condemned to behold it with bitterness; my heart devoured this image of a happiness, for ever to be a stranger to me, and envy, like a vulture, preyed upon my bosom. "What had I done to those, who thought to bless me by bringing me to this land of exile? Why, why withhold me from the path of my destiny? Then had I been the dark slave of the rich planter; scorched beneath the burning sun, I had tilled the land of another; but I should have had my humble cabin to retire to at night, I should have had a companion of my being, and children of my own color would have called me, Mother! without loathing would they have pressed their little lips to my forehead, they would have reposed upon my bosom and slumbered in my arms! What have I done to be for ever, for ever cut off from affections for which alone my heart was formed! O my God! take me from the world; I feel that I can endure existence no longer."

Upon my knees, in my chamber, did I address to the Creator this impious prayer, when I heard my door open; it was the friend of Madame de B., the Marchioness of ———, who had returned a short time before from England, where she had spent the few last years. It was with terror I saw her approach me; her countenance always reminded me that she had been the first to reveal to me reality; that she had opened that mine of sorrows from which I had drawn so deeply. Since her return to Paris, her presence had always called up the most painful emotions.

"I have come to see you, and converse with you, my dear Ourika," said she to me. "You know how much I have loved you from infancy, and I cannot see you plunging yourself thus in melancholy without the deepest sorrow. Can it be, with the mind you possess, you cannot draw forth brighter images from your condition?" "Intellect, Madam," answered I, "serves only to increase our sorrows: it presents them to us under a thousand varied forms!" "But," replied she, "when our misfortunes are beyond relief, is it not the part of folly to refuse submission, and to struggle thus against necessity? for we do not gain strength by the conflict." "That is true," answered I, "yet in that case, necessity becomes a heavier evil still." "Yet you will grant, Ourika, that reason counsels us to resign ourselves and to divert our thoughts." "Yes, Madam, but to divert the thoughts we must see hope elsewhere." "You can at least create tastes and occupations to employ your hours." "Ah! Madam," said I, "the tastes which one creates are an effort, not a pleasure." "But," continued she, "your talents." "To give pleasure, Madam," answered I, "our talents must have an object; mine are like the flower of the poet, which spreads its fragrance over the desert." "But you forget your friends, whom you may bless with them." "I have no friends, Madam, I have protectors, how different the names!" "Ourika," continued she, "you are rendering yourself most unhappy and useless." "All, all is useless in my life, Madam, even my sorrows." "How can you utter that word of bitterness, you, Ourika, you who showed such devotion, when you remained alone with Madame de B. during the reign of terror?" "Alas! Madam, I am one of those unfortunate spirits, who are strong in the times of calamity, but who flee at the voice of happiness."—"Confide to me your secret, my dear Ourika, open to me your heart: no one feels for you a more sincere interest than I, and perhaps I can soothe your sorrows."—"I have no secret, Madam," answered I; "my situation and my color are all my evil, you know it is so." "How then," said she, "can you deny that deep grief is hidden in your soul? One needs see you but a moment to be satisfied it so." I still continued to tell her that I had unfolded all; she became impatient, she elevated her voice, and I saw the storm was ready to burst upon me. "This then is the boasted candor, the sincerity of which I have heard so much! Ourika, beware; reserve sometimes conducts to falsehood."—"Alas! Madam," said I, "what can I intrust to you, to you who have so long known the wretchedness of my condition? To you, less than to any one can I tell any thing new of my sorrow."—"In vain would you strive to persuade me of that," answered she; "but since you refuse me your confidence, since you affirm that you have no secret I will take upon myself to point one out to you. Yes, Ourika, all your sorrows, all your griefs flow but from an unhallowed, a foolish passion; and were you not mad for love with Charles, you could easily bear up with being a negress. Farewell, Ourika, I leave you, and, I frankly say, with far less interest for you than when I came hither." She departed, as she pronounced these words. I was as if annihilated. What a revelation had she made to me! What frightful light had been darted into the abyss of my sorrows! "Great God! such light didst thou once cast into the depths of hell, and the darkness mourned for its miserable inhabitants. What! I, a criminal passion! This, is it this which has devoured my heart! This desire to hold my place in the chain of beings, this longing for the affections of nature, this dread of solitude, were they but the regrets of a guilty love! And when I thought I envied only the *image* of happiness, was it the happiness itself that was the object of my impious wishes? But what have I done, that one should believe me attainted with this hopeless passion? Is it then impossible to love aught but life with innocence? That mother, who is casting herself into the jaws of the lion to save her child, what feeling animates her? Those brothers, those sisters who are willing to die together on the scaffold and offer to God their prayers, before they ascend, is it guilty love that binds them together?

Humanity even, does it not offer each day examples of supreme devotion? Why then
may I not love Charles thus, the companion of my childhood, the protector of my
youth? And yet, I know not what voice it was within me that cried, that they were
right, that I was guilty. Great God! and must I receive remorse too into my desolate
heart? Ourika must know the bitterness of every sorrow, she must drink of the cup of
every affliction! Yet now my very tears are guilty! to think of him—it is forbidden me!
What! suffering itself forbidden me!"

These frightful thoughts crushed me to the earth like the hand of death. The same
night I was seized with a fever and in less than three days my life was despaired of: the
physician said, if they wished me to receive the sacraments, not a moment was to be
lost. They sent for my confessor; he had died a few days before. Madame de B. then
sent for the parish-priest; he came, and administered to me the extreme unction for I
was too far gone to receive the *viaticum*: I was conscious of nothing, and they expected every moment would terminate my being. Then it was that God had mercy
upon me; he began by restoring me to life: contrary to the fears of all, my strength
sustained me. I struggled thus about five days; at length my consciousness returned.
Madame de B. did not leave me for a moment, and Charles seemed to have recovered
his former affection. The priest visited me every day; he wished to take advantage of
the first moment of returning strength, for me to confess. I also earnestly desired it; I
know not what movement carried me to God, and made me feel the need of casting
myself into his arms and seeking my rest there. The priest heard the confession of my
sins; he was not terrified at the condition of my soul; like an old mariner he was familiar with every tempest. He consoled my sufferings for the passion of which I was
accused: "Your heart is pure," said he, "it is against yourself alone that you have done
evil; yet for that you are no less guilty. God will demand an account of the personal
happiness he has intrusted to you; and yours, how have you disposed of it? This happiness is in our hands, for it dwells in the fulfilment of our duties; have you regarded
them alone? God is the home of man; Where have you sought your own? Yet be not
disheartened. Pray to God, Ourika; he is ready, he is stretching forth his arms to receive you; with him is no respect of persons: all hearts are equal before his eyes, and
your's deserves to become worthy of him." It was thus this venerable man encouraged
the poor Ourika. These simple words carried to my soul a peace it had never known
before; I meditated upon them continually; and constantly drew as from a rich mine,
some new reflection from them. I saw, that, in truth, I had never known my duties:
God has given them to the solitary as well as to those immersed in the society of life;
and if he has cut them off from the ties of blood, has he not given them the family of
the human race? "The sister of charity," said I, "is not alone in life, although she has
renounced all: she has created a family of her choice, she is the mother of orphans, the
daughter of the aged poor, the sister of all the unfortunate. The men of the world,
have they not often sought a voluntary solitude? They have wished to be alone with
God; they have renounced all pleasures, that they might in silence adore the pure
source of all excellence and happiness; they have striven in the secrecy of their
thoughts to render their souls worthy to be presented before the Lord. It is for thee, O
my God! that it is sweet to adorn the heart, to embellish it, as for a day of festivity,
with all the virtues with which thou art well pleased. Alas! what have I done? The mad

plaything of the involuntary emotions of my soul, I have chased after the pleasures of life, and lost happiness in the search. But it is not yet too late; God, in casting me upon this land of strangers, wished perhaps to predestinate me to himself; he has rescued me from barbarism and ignorance; by a miracle of his goodness he has saved me from the vices of slavery and made me to know his law: this law points out my duties, it marks out my way before me: I will follow it, O my God! No longer will I employ thy bounties to offend thee, no longer will I charge my own crimes to thee."

The same day that laid open to me the reality of my situation, brought calmness to my heart. I was astonished at the peace which followed such "tempests of the soul:" a way had been opened for the torrent which was fast wasting its banks, and then it bore its waters to the tranquil sea.

I determined to enter a convent. I spoke of it to Madame de B.; she was sorrowful at the thought, but said to me, "Ourika, I have done you so much evil in attempting to make you happy, that I feel I have no right to oppose your resolution." Charles was more earnest in his resistance; he entreated, he besought me to remain; I said to him; "Suffer me to go, Charles, to the only place where I may be permitted to think, without ceasing, of you."

Here the young nun suddenly ended her story. I continued my care, but alas! it availed nothing; she died at the end of October; she fell with the last leaves of autumn.

TRANSLATED BY GEORGE WALLIS HAVEN

20

The Blackamoor of Peter the Great

Alexander Pushkin

Alexander Pushkin (1799–1837) is widely considered to be Russia's greatest poet and a major influence on modern Russian literature and Russian identity. In the West he is best known for his masterpiece, *Eugene Onegin*, a novel in verse. A member of an aristocratic family, Pushkin held a nominal government appointment in St. Petersburg, where he wrote prolifically and enjoyed wide acclaim among high society. The liberal politics he expressed in his poems made him a frequent object of government suspicion and scrutiny. In 1820 he was exiled from the capital for his subversive poetry; in 1824 he was dismissed from government service for alleged atheism and was placed under house arrest at his mother's country estate. Tsar Nicholas I pardoned him in 1826, and Pushkin returned to court life. In 1837 he died of injuries sustained in a duel.

"The Blackamoor of Peter the Great" (1827–28) was Pushkin's first experiment with historical prose fiction; he paid careful attention to psychological details and employed impersonal narrative voice of ironic detachment from all characters. The subject was an imaginative version of the story of Pushkin's own African great-grandfather, Ibrahim Gannibal. The extant story fragment is reproduced fully here in Paul Debreczeny's translation. According to a diary of one of Pushkin's friends, the plot was to continue with the infidelity of Ibrahim's wife, who was to give birth to a white baby and to be banished to a convent.

1

I am in Paris;
I have begun to live, not just to breathe.
DMITRIEV, "DIARY OF A TRAVELER"

Among the young people whom Peter the Great sent to foreign lands to acquire knowledge needed in the transformed Russian state, there was a blackamoor called Ibrahim, a godson of the Emperor. He received his training at the Military Academy of Paris, graduated with the rank of captain of artillery, distinguished himself in the Spanish War, and returned to Paris severely wounded. The Emperor, engrossed though he was in his vast undertakings, never neglected to inquire after his favorite, and always received laudatory reports about his progress and conduct. Highly satisfied with him, Peter urged him several times to return to Russia, but Ibrahim was in no hurry to do so. He kept excusing himself under various pretexts, such as his wound, his desire to complete his education, and his lack of money. Peter, for his part, acceded to the young man's wishes with indulgence, told him to take care of his health, and expressed his appreciation for his industry, and—though always extremely careful about his own expenses—he liberally provided for his godson from the Treasury, adding fatherly advice and cautionary exhortation to the gold coins.

All historical records show that the frivolity, folly, and luxury of the French of that time was unprecedented. No trace was left by then of the last years of Louis XIV's reign, which had been characterized by fastidious piety at Court and by a grave tone and decorum. The Duke of Orleans, whose brilliant qualities were combined with faults of all kinds, did not possess, unfortunately, one modicum of hypocrisy. The orgies at the Palais Royal were no secret in Paris, and the example was contagious. Just then Law made his appearance on the scene; greed for money was united with thirst for amusement and dissipation; fortunes went to ruin; morality perished; and the French laughed and calculated, while the state was falling apart to the playful tunes of satirical vaudevilles.

Society provided an entertaining spectacle. Education and the demand for amusement drew the different estates together. Wealth, good manners, fame, talent, even eccentricity—all attributes that excited curiosity or promised enjoyment—were accepted with equal indulgence. Literature, scholarship, and philosophy emerged from quiet study rooms to appear in the midst of high society, both bowing to fashion and governing it. Women ruled, but no longer demanded adoration. Superficial courtesy took the place of profound respect. The pranks of the duc de Richelieu—of this Alcibiades of a latter-day Athens—are a matter of historical record, providing an insight into the mores of the period.

> Temps fortuné, marqué par la licence,
> Où la folie, agitant son grelot,
> D'un pied léger parcourt toute la France,
> Où nul mortel ne daigne être dévot,
> Où l'on fait tout excepté pénitence.

As soon as Ibrahim arrived in Paris, his outward appearance, his education and native intelligence, caught everyone's attention. All the ladies, wishing to see *le Nègre du czar* in their drawing rooms, vied with each other in trying to captivate him; the Regent invited him to his merry soirées more than once; he was present at dinner parties enlivened by the youth of Arouet, by the old age of Chaulieu, and by the conversation of Montesquieu and Fontenelle; he did not miss one ball, one festivity, one premiere; in general, he threw himself into the whirl of social life with all the ardor of his youth and race. What daunted Ibrahim, however, was not just the thought of exchanging this libertinage, all these splendid amusements, for the austere simplicity of the Petersburg Court. Other, more powerful bonds tied him to Paris. The young African was in love.

The Countess D., though not in the first bloom of youth, was still renowned for her beauty. At the age of seventeen, right after leaving the convent school, she was married to a man to whom she had not had time to grow attached, a fact that had not particularly worried him, then or later. Rumor ascribed lovers to her, but thanks to the lenient code of high society, she enjoyed a good name simply because she could never be accused of any ridiculous or scandalous escapades. Her house was among the most fashionable, attracting the best Parisian society. Ibrahim was introduced to her by the youthful Merville, generally regarded as her latest lover—a rumor that the young man made every effort to make people believe.

The Countess greeted Ibrahim politely but without fanfare, which flattered him. As a rule, people looked at the young black man as if he were some strange phenomenon—they surrounded him and showered him with salutations and questions. Their curiosity, though disguised as courtesy, offended his pride. The sweet attention of women, almost the sole aim of our efforts, not only did not gladden his heart, but filled it with downright bitterness and indignation. He felt that in their eyes he was a kind of rare animal, a peculiar and alien creature who had been accidentally brought into a world that had nothing in common with it. He even envied people who attracted no one's attention, regarding their insignificance as a happy state.

The thought that, by nature, he was destined not to have his affections reciprocated saved him from presumptuousness and vanity, and this lent a rare charm to his conduct with women. His conversation was simple and demure, and it attracted the Countess D., who had grown tired of the endless jests and subtle insinuations of French wit. He became a frequent guest at her house. Little by little she grew accustomed to the young Black's appearance and even began finding something attractive in that curly head, standing out with its blackness among the powdered wigs in her drawing room. (Ibrahim had been wounded in the head and was wearing a bandage instead of a wig.) He was twenty-seven years old, tall and well built; and quite a few beautiful young women glanced at him with feelings more flattering than mere curiosity, though he in his prejudice either did not notice anything or fancied only flirtation. When, however, his eyes met those of the Countess, his distrustfulness vanished. Her glance conveyed such good nature, her conduct with him was so simple and unaffected, that it was impossible to suspect in her even a shade of coquetry or mockery.

The idea of love had not crossed his mind, but to see the Countess daily was becoming a necessity for him. He sought her out everywhere, and meeting her seemed to him an unexpected favor from heaven each time. The Countess recognized his feelings before he himself did. Whatever you say, love without aspirations and demands touches the feminine heart more surely than all the wiles of seduction. When she was with Ibrahim, the Countess followed every movement he made and listened carefully to every word he said; in his absence she grew thoughtful and sank into her habitual distractedness. Merville was the first to notice this mutual inclination, and he congratulated Ibrahim. Nothing inflames love so much as the encouraging remark of an outsider. Love is blind, and distrustful of itself, eagerly grasps any support. Merville's words awakened Ibrahim. Until then the idea that he might possess the woman he loved had not even occurred to him; now hope suddenly lit up his soul; he fell madly in love. The Countess, frightened of the violence of his passion, tried to counter with friendly exhortations and prudent admonitions, but all in vain; she herself was weakening. Incautiously granted favors followed one another in quick succession. And at last, carried away by the force of the passion she had herself inspired, overpowered by its moment, she gave herself to the ecstatic Ibrahim …

Nothing can be hidden from society's watchful eyes. The Countess's new liaison soon became common knowledge. Some ladies were surprised by her choice, but many found it perfectly natural. Some laughed; others thought she had committed an unforgivable indiscretion. In the first transports of passion, Ibrahim and the Countess did not notice anything, but the double entendres of the men and the caustic remarks of the women soon began to catch their attention. Ibrahim's demure, cold manner had previously protected him from all offensive behavior; now he suffered the attacks with impatience and did not know how to ward them off. The Countess, accustomed to the respect of society, could not resign herself to being the butt of gossip and jests. She would now complain to Ibrahim in tears, now reproach him bitterly, now beg him not to take up her defense lest some useless row bring about her complete ruin.

A new circumstance confounded her situation even further. The consequence of her imprudent love had become apparent. All consolations, counsel, suggestions, were considered, and all rejected. The Countess saw that her ruin was inevitable, and waited for it in despair.

As soon as the Countess's condition became known, common talk started up with renewed vigor. Ladies of sensibility moaned with horror; men took bets on whether the Countess would give birth to a white or black baby. Epigrams proliferated at the expense of her husband—the only person in Paris who knew nothing and suspected nothing.

The fateful moment was approaching. The Countess's situation was terrible. Ibrahim came to see her every day. He watched her spiritual and physical strength gradually wane. Her tears and horror burst forth every minute. At last she felt the first pains. Measures were taken quickly. A pretext was found for sending the Count away. The physician arrived. A couple of days before, a destitute woman had been persuaded to give up her newborn son; now a trusted agent was sent to fetch him. Ibrahim waited in a study right next door to the bedroom where the unfortunate Countess lay. Hardly daring to breathe, he heard her muted groans, the whisperings of the maid, and the doctor's commands. She was in labor for a long time. Every groan rent his heart, every silent interval submerged him in horror … Suddenly he heard the feeble cry of a child; unable to contain his joy, he rushed into the Countess's room. A black baby lay on the bed at her feet. Ibrahim went up to it. His heart throbbed violently. He blessed his son with a shaking hand. The Countess gave a faint smile and stretched her weary hand toward him, but the doctor, anxious to protect the invalid from too much excitement, drew Ibrahim away from her bed. The newborn was placed in a covered basket and taken out of the house by a secret staircase. The other child was brought in, and its cradle placed in the young mother's bedroom. Ibrahim left somewhat reassured. The Count was expected. He returned late, learned about his wife's successful delivery, and was satisfied. Thus the public, which had anticipated an uproarious scandal, was frustrated in its expectations and had to content itself with mere vilifications.

Everything returned to normal, but Ibrahim felt that the course of his life would have to change, since his love affair might sooner or later come to the Count D.'s knowledge. In such a case, whatever the circumstances might be, the ruin of the

Countess would be inevitable. Ibrahim was passionately in love, and was loved with an equal passion, but the Countess was capricious and careless. It was not the first time she had been in love. Revulsion and hatred might replace the most tender feelings in her heart. Ibrahim imagined the moment she would grow cold toward him. He had not experienced the feeling of jealousy before, but now he had a terrifying presentiment of it, and he fancied that the torments of separation would probably be less painful. He contemplated breaking up his ill-fated liaison, leaving Paris, and returning to Russia, where he was being summoned both by Peter and by his own vague sense of duty.

2

> No more does beauty lull me so,
> No more does joy's enchantment linger,
> Nor is my fancy quite so free,
> My spirit so serenely pleased…
> By honor's fever I am seized:
> The sound of glory calls on me!
>
> DERZHAVIN

Days, months went by, but the enamored Ibrahim could not bring himself to leave the woman he had seduced. The Countess became each day more and more attached to him. Their son was being brought up in a remote province. The gossip began to abate, and the lovers enjoyed greater peace, silently remembering the storm that had passed and trying not to think of the future.

One day Ibrahim attended the levee of the Duke of Orleans. Passing by him, the Duke stopped and gave Ibrahim a letter, telling him to read it at leisure. It was a letter from Peter I. The Emperor, guessing the real reason for Ibrahim's extended stay abroad, wrote to the Duke that he did not wish to coerce his foster son in any way, leaving it to him to decide whether he wanted to return to Russia or not, but that he, the Emperor, would in no case leave him without support. This letter touched the very heartstrings of Ibrahim. From that moment his fate was sealed. The next day he informed the Regent of his intention to leave for Russia immediately.

"Think what you're doing," the Duke said to him. "Russia is not your native land; I doubt whether you'll ever have an opportunity to see your own sultry fatherland again, but your long sojourn in France has made you unfit for both the climate and the way of life of semibarbarous Russia. You were not born a subject of Peter's. Listen to me: take advantage of his generous permission. Stay in France, for which you have already shed your blood, and you can rest assured that here, too, your services and talents will earn their just rewards."

Ibrahim sincerely thanked the Duke but remained firm in his decision.

"I'm sorry to see you go," said the Duke, "but, actually, you are right." He promised to release Ibrahim from the service, and reported the whole matter to the Russian Tsar.

Ibrahim was soon ready to leave. He spent the eve of his departure, as he would most evenings, at the house of the Countess D. She was not aware of anything: Ibrahim had not had the heart to reveal his plans to her. She was calm and cheerful. She called him to her side several times and teased him about his pensive mood. After supper all the guests left. Only the Countess, her husband, and Ibrahim remained in the drawing room. The unfortunate Ibrahim would have given anything in the world to be left alone with her, but the Count D. seemed to be so serenely settled by the fireplace that there was no hope of getting rid of him. All three were silent.

"*Bonne nuit,*" said the Countess at last.

Ibrahim's heart sank as he suddenly apprehended the full horror of parting. He stood motionless.

"*Bonne nuit, messieurs,*" repeated the Countess.

He still did not move … At last his vision became blurred, his head began swimming, and he could just barely walk out of the room. Having reached home, he wrote the following letter in an almost unconscious state:

> I am leaving, my dear Léonore, abandoning you forever. I am writing to you because I have not the strength to explain myself to you otherwise.
>
> My happiness could not last. I have enjoyed it in defiance of fate and nature. You were bound to cease loving me: the enchantment was bound to vanish. This thought always haunted me, even at those moments when it seemed I was oblivious to everything, when I lay at your feet intoxicated with your fervent self-sacrifice, with your boundless tenderness … Society, with its fickle ways, ruthlessly persecutes in practice what it permits in theory: its cold mockery would have sooner or later overpowered you, it would have humbled your soaring spirit, and you would in the end have grown ashamed of your passion … What would then have become of me? No! I'd sooner die, I'd sooner leave you, than wait for that terrible moment …
>
> Your tranquility is dearest of all to me, and you could not enjoy it while the gaze of society was fixed on us. Remember everything you have suffered through, all the humiliations, all the torments of fear; remember the terrifying birth of our son. Just think: should I subject you to the same worries and dangers even longer? Why struggle to unite the fate of such a tender and graceful creature with the unlucky lot of a Negro, a pitiful being, scarcely granted the title of man?
>
> Farewell, Léonore, farewell my cherished, my only friend. Abandoning you, I abandon the first and last happy moments of my life. I have neither fatherland nor family. I am leaving for gloomy Russia, where my only comfort will be my complete solitude. Hard work, to which I am going to devote myself from now on, will, if not stifle, at least divert agonizing recollections of those days of rapture and bliss … Farewell, Léonore—I am tearing myself away from this letter as if from your arms; farewell, be happy—and think sometimes of the poor Negro, of your faithful Ibrahim.

The same night he left for Russia.

The journey did not turn out to be quite as grim as he had expected. His imagination prevailed over reality. The farther behind he left Paris, the more vividly, the more immediately, he could recall the forms he had abandoned forever.

He was on the Russian border before he knew it. Autumn was setting in, but the drivers, despite the bad roads, drove him along with the speed of the wind, and on the morning of the seventeenth day of his journey he arrived in Krasnoe Selo, through which the main highway led in those days.

Only twenty-eight versts were left from here to Petersburg. While the horses were being harnessed Ibrahim went into the post station. In the corner a tall man, in a green caftan and with a clay pipe in his mouth, was leaning with his elbows on the table, reading the Hamburg newspapers. Hearing somebody enter, he raised his head.

"Ha! Ibrahim?" he exclaimed, getting up from the bench. "Welcome, godson."

Ibrahim, recognizing Peter, was about to rush up to him with joy, but stopped respectfully. The Emperor came up to him, embraced him, and kissed him on the head.

"I was informed you'd soon be arriving," said Peter, "and I came out to meet you. I've been here waiting for you since yesterday." Ibrahim could not find words to express his gratitude. "Let your carriage follow behind us," continued the Emperor, "while you sit with me. Let's set out for home."

The Emperor's carriage was driven up; he and Ibrahim got in, and they galloped off. They arrived in Petersburg in an hour and a half. Ibrahim looked with curiosity at the newborn capital that had risen from the swamp at the bidding of autocracy. Open dikes, canals without embankments, and wooden bridges testified everywhere to the recent victory of human will over the resistance of the elements. The houses, it seemed, had been erected hastily. There was nothing impressive in the whole city except for the Neva, not yet adorned by a granite frame but already strewn with warships and merchantmen. The Emperor's carriage stopped by the palace in the so-called Tsaritsyn Garden. A woman, aged about thirty-five, attractive and dressed according to the latest Parisian fashion, met Peter on the portico. He kissed her on the lips and, taking Ibrahim by the hand, said:

"Have you recognized my godson, Katenka? Please welcome him and be kind to him as in the old days."

Ekaterina turned her dark, penetrating eyes on Ibrahim and amiably gave him her hand. Two beautiful young girls, tall, graceful, and fresh as roses, stood behind her and respectfully approached Peter.

"Liza," he said to one of them, "do you remember the little black boy who used to steal apples for you from my garden in Oranienbaum? Here he is: I present him to you."

The Grand Duchess laughed and blushed. They entered the dining room. The table had been laid in anticipation of the Emperor's arrival. Peter sat down to dinner with his family, inviting Ibrahim to join them. Over dinner he talked with Ibrahim about various topics, questioning him about the Spanish War, the internal affairs of France, and the Regent, whom he loved though in many ways disapproved of. Ibrahim had a remarkably precise and perceptive mind; Peter was highly satisfied with his answers; on his part he remembered some details of Ibrahim's childhood and related them with such warmth and gaiety that nobody would have suspected this cordial, gracious host of having been the hero of Poltava, the mighty, dreaded reformer of Russia.

After dinner the Emperor, in keeping with Russian custom, retired to rest. Ibrahim was left with the Empress and the duchesses. He did his best to satisfy their curiosity, describing the Parisian way of life, the festivities held in the French capital and its capricious fashions. In the meanwhile some persons of the Emperor's immediate circle were gathering at the palace. Ibrahim recognized the illustrious Prince Menshikov, who, seeing the black man conversing with Ekaterina, cast a haughty glance at him; Prince Iakov Dolgorukii, Peter's stern counselor; the learned Bruce, who had the reputation of a Russian Faust among the people; the young Raguzinskii, Ibrahim's one-time friend; and others who were either bringing reports to the Emperor or awaiting his instructions.

The Emperor reappeared in about two hours.

"Let's see whether you still remember how to carry out your former duty," he said to Ibrahim. "Take a slate and follow me." Peter locked the door of the turnery on the two of them and busied himself with state affairs. One by one he called in Bruce, Prince Dolgorukii, and the chief of police, de Vière; and he dictated several decrees and resolutions to Ibrahim. The latter was astounded by his quick and firm grasp of problems, the power and versatility of his concentration, and the diversity of his activities. When the work was done, Peter pulled out a pocket notebook to check if everything planned for the day had been accomplished. Then, as he was leaving the turnery, he said to Ibrahim:

"It's getting late; you're tired I suppose. Spend the night here as you used to. I'll wake you up in the morning."

Ibrahim, left by himself, could scarcely collect his thoughts. He was in Petersburg; he had once again met the great man in whose company, not yet comprehending his worth, he had spent his childhood. He had to confess to himself, almost with a sense of guilt, that for the first time since their separation the Countess D. had not been the sole preoccupation of his day. He could see that the new way of life that was awaiting him—the work and constant activity—would be able to revive his soul, fatigued by passions, idleness, and an unacknowledged despondency. The thought of being closely associated with a great man and of shaping, together with him, the destiny of a great nation awoke in his heart, for the first time in his life, a noble sentiment of ambition. It was in this state of mind that he lay down on the camp bed prepared for him. His wonted dreams soon carried him to faraway Paris, into the arms of the dear Countess.

3

> Like clouds in summer skies,
> Thus thoughts within us change their fleeting shapes,
> And what we love today, tomorrow we detest.
>
> V. KIUKHELBEKER

The next day Peter woke up Ibrahim as he had promised, and congratulated him on his appointment as first lieutenant in the Preobrazhenskii Regiment's artillery platoon, of which he himself was the captain. The courtiers surrounded Ibrahim, each trying in his own way to show esteem for the new favorite. The haughty Prince

Menshikov shook his hand cordially. Sheremetev inquired after his Parisian acquaintances, and Golovin invited Ibrahim to dinner. Others followed Golovin's example, so much so that Ibrahim received enough invitations to last him at least a month.

Ibrahim's days were unvaried but busy; consequently, he felt no boredom. With every day he became more and more attached to the Emperor, more able to comprehend his lofty mind. To follow the thoughts of a great man is a most engrossing intellectual occupation. Ibrahim saw Peter in the Senate, where Buturlin and Dolgorukii were disputing with him and where he grappled with important legislative matters; watched him in the Admiralty, where he was building Russia's naval might; observed him in the company of Feofan, Gavriil Buzhinskii, and Kopievich, and in his hours of leisure as he examined translations of foreign political writers or visited merchants' warehouses, craftsmen's workshops, scholars' studies. Russia seemed to Ibrahim like an enormous manufacturing plant, where only machines were in motion and where each worker, subject to an established order, was busy with his assignment. He, too, felt obliged to work at his bench, trying to think of the amusements of Parisian life with as little regret as he possibly could. It was more difficult to dismiss from his mind another, dear recollection: he often thought of the Countess D., imagined her just indignation, tears, and despair … At times a dreadful thought took his breath away: the distractions of high society, a new liaison, another lucky man—he shuddered. Jealousy began to seethe in his African blood, and burning tears were ready to course down his black face.

One morning he was sitting surrounded by official papers in his study when he heard a loud greeting in French; turning around in excitement, he found himself in the embrace, accompanied by joyous exclamations, of the young Korsakov, whom he had left behind in Paris, in the whirl of society life.

"I've only just arrived," said Korsakov, "and come directly to see you. All our Parisian acquaintances are missing you and send their regards; the Countess D. enjoined me to summon you to return without fail. Here is a letter from her."

Ibrahim grabbed the letter with a trembling hand and looked at the familiar handwriting on the envelope, not daring to believe his own eyes.

"I'm glad to see that you have not yet died of boredom in this barbarous Petersburg," Korsakov continued. "What do people do here, how do they pass their time? Who is your tailor? Has at least an opera house been established?"

Ibrahim, lost in thought, answered that the Emperor was probably at work in the shipyard. Korsakov burst out laughing.

"I can see that your mind is elsewhere at the moment," he said. "We'll have a good talk later; right now I'll go and present myself to the Emperor." Having said this, he spun around on one heel and ran out of the room.

Left by himself, Ibrahim hastened to open the letter. The Countess tenderly complained, reproaching him for his dissemblance and distrust. "You say," she wrote, "that my tranquility is dearest of all to you. Ibrahim! If that were true, could you have subjected me to the predicament to which the unexpected news of your departure reduced me? You were afraid that I would hold you back, but I assure you that though I love you, I could have sacrificed my love for your well-being and for what you consider your obligation." She concluded the letter with passionate assurances of love and implored him at least to write to her occasionally, even if there was no hope for them ever to meet again.

Ibrahim reread this letter twenty times, kissing the precious lines in ecstasy. He burned with impatience to hear more about the Countess, and was just about ready to go to the Admiralty in the hope of finding Korsakov still there, when the door opened and Korsakov himself reappeared: he had already presented himself to the Emperor and, as usual, seemed to be very satisfied with himself.

"Entre nous," he said to Ibrahim, "the Emperor is a peculiar man: just imagine, when I found him he was wearing some sort of sack-cloth vest and was perched on the mast of a new ship, where I had to clamber after him with my dispatches. Standing on a rope ladder, I did not have enough room even to bow properly and became all confused, which had never happened to me before. But the Emperor, having read the papers I had brought, looked me over from head to foot and was, to all appearances, pleasantly surprised by the taste and refinement of my attire: at least he smiled and invited me to tonight's assembly. But I am a total stranger in Petersburg: during my six-year absence I have completely forgotten the local customs, and I'd like to ask you to please be my mentor, come with me and introduce me."

Ibrahim agreed and hastened to steer the conversation to a topic more interesting to him. "Well, how is the Countess D.?"

"The Countess? As you might expect, she was at first very much upset by your departure; but then, as you might expect, she gradually regained her equanimity and took a new lover. Do you know whom? That lanky Marquis of R. But what are you staring at me for with those Negro eyeballs of yours? Or does all this seem strange to you? Don't you know that lasting grief is not in the nature of the human being, especially of a woman? Think this over thoroughly while I go to take a rest after my journey, and don't forget to come and fetch me."

What sensations filled Ibrahim's heart? Jealousy? Rage? Despair? No; rather a deep, benumbed feeling of depression. He kept repeating to himself: I foresaw this; this had to happen. Then he opened the Countess's letter, read it once more, hung his head, and burst into bitter tears. He wept for a long time. The tears eased his sorrow. Then, looking at his watch, he realized it was time to go. He would have been glad to excuse himself, but the assembly was an official function, and the Emperor rigidly insisted on the attendance of the members of his close circle. Ibrahim got dressed and set out to fetch Korsakov.

Korsakov was sitting in his dressing gown, reading a French book.

"So early?" he asked seeing Ibrahim.

"Mercy," the latter responded; "it's already half past five. We'll be late; get dressed quickly and let's go."

This threw Korsakov into a flurry, and he started ringing with all his might; his servants rushed in; he began dressing hastily. His French valet brought in his red-heeled shoes, his blue velvet breeches, and his pink caftan embroidered with spangles; his wig, quickly powdered in the anteroom, was brought in, and he thrust his close-cropped small head into it; he asked for his sword and gloves, turned around before the mirror about ten times, and declared himself ready. The footman helped him and Ibrahim into their bearskin coats, and the two young men set out for the Winter Palace.

Korsakov showered Ibrahim with questions. Who was the most beautiful woman in Petersburg? Who had the reputation of being the best dancer? What dance was currently in vogue? Ibrahim satisfied his friend's curiosity grudgingly. In the meanwhile they had arrived at the palace. A large number of long sleds, old coaches, and gilded barouches stood in the field already. By the portico there was a large crowd of liveried and mustachioed coachmen, of mace-bearing footmen resplendent in tawdry finery and plumes, of hussars, pages, and awkward-looking haiduks, loaded down with their masters' fur coats and muffs—an indispensable retinue in the opinion of the boyars of that time. Ibrahim's arrival provoked a general murmur among them: "The blackamoor, the blackamoor, the Tsar's blackamoor!" He led Korsakov through this motley crowd of servants as fast as he could. A palace servant opened the doors wide for them, and they entered the hall. Korsakov was dumbfounded … In the large room, lit by tallow candles that burned dimly in the clouds of tobacco smoke, droves of dignitaries with blue sashes across their shoulders, ambassadors, foreign merchants, officers of the Guards in green coats, and shipmasters wearing short jackets with striped trousers were moving up and down to the incessant sound of a brass band. The ladies sat along the walls, the young ones glittering with all the finery of fashion. Gold and silver glistened on their robes; their slim waists rose from their luxuriant hooped skirts like flower stems; diamonds twinkled in their ears, in their long tresses, and around their necks. They cheerfully glanced left and right, waiting for cavaliers and for the dance to begin. The elderly ladies' outfits represented shrewd attempts to combine the new mode of dress with the old styles frowned upon: their head-dresses were very like the Tsaritsa Natalia Kirilovna's sable hat, and their gowns and mantles resembled sarafans and wadded jackets. They attended these newfangled spectacles with more bewilderment, it seemed, than pleasure, and looked askance at the wives and daughters of Dutch skippers who sat in their calico skirts and red blouses, knitting socks, laughing, and chatting among themselves, as if they were at home. Korsakov could not regain his presence of mind. Noticing the newly arrived guests, a servant came up with beer and glasses on a tray.

"Que diable est-ce que tout cela?" said Korsakov to Ibrahim under his breath. Ibrahim could not suppress a smile. The Empress and the grand duchesses, glittering with beauty and elegance, walked through the rows of guests, amicably conversing with them. The Emperor was in another room. Korsakov, wishing to show himself to him, had a hard time pushing his way there through the constantly moving crowd. In that room sat mostly foreigners, solemnly smoking their clay pipes and emptying their earthenware mugs. Bottles of beer and wine, leather pouches with tobacco, glasses of rum punch, and chess-boards were placed on the tables. Peter sat at one of them, playing checkers with a broad-shouldered English skipper. The two of them kept zealously saluting each other with salvos of tobacco smoke, and the Emperor was so preoccupied with an unexpected move of his partner's that he did not notice Korsakov, much as he twisted and turned around them. At this moment a massive gentleman with a massive nosegay on his chest came bustling into the room, to announce in a thunderous voice that the dancing had commenced; then he was gone again, and many of the guests, among them Korsakov, followed after him.

Korsakov was struck by an unexpected sight. Along the whole length of the ballroom, resounding with peals of the most pitiful music, ladies and cavaliers were ranged in two rows, facing one another; the cavaliers bowed low and the ladies curtsied, bending even lower, first straight ahead, then to the right, then to the left, then straight ahead again, to the right again, and so forth. Korsakov stared at this intriguing sport wide-eyed and bit his lips. The bowing and curtsying continued for about half an hour; when it stopped at last, the massive gentleman with the nosegay announced that the ceremonial dance was over, and ordered the musicians to play a minuet. Korsakov rejoiced and prepared to shine. One of the young ladies present attracted him particularly. She was about sixteen, dressed expensively but tastefully; she sat by an elderly man of dignified and stern appearance. Korsakov scampered up to her and asked her to do him the honor of dancing with him. The young beauty looked at him with embarrassment, not knowing, it seemed, what to say to him. The man sitting next to her knitted his brows, looking even more stern. Korsakov stood waiting for her answer, but the gentleman with the nosegay came up to him, led him into the center of the ballroom, and said gravely: "My dear sir, you have committed a breach of etiquette: first, you went up to this young person without the required triple obeisance; secondly, you took it on yourself to select her, though in the minuet the right of choice belongs to the lady, not to the cavalier; for which reasons you are to be severely punished, namely you must drain the *goblet of the Great Eagle*."

Korsakov grew more and more astonished. The guests instantly surrounded him, loudly demanding the immediate execution of the sentence. Peter, hearing the laughter and shouts, and very fond of personally participating in such punishments, came out of the adjacent room. The crowd made way for him, and he entered the circle where the marshal of the assembly stood facing the culprit with an enormous goblet filled with malmsey. He was vainly trying to persuade the condemned to submit to the law voluntarily.

"Aha!" said the Emperor, seeing Korsakov, "you've been caught, brother! Please be so good as to quaff it down, *monsieur*, and don't let me see you wince."

There was no way to escape. The poor fop drained the whole goblet in one gulp and handed it back to the marshal.

"Listen, Korsakov," Peter said to him, "the breeches you're wearing are made of velvet, of a kind even I don't wear, though I am much richer than you. This is extravagance; watch out that I don't fall out with you."

Having listened to this censure, Korsakov wanted to leave the circle, but he lost his balance and almost fell down, to the indescribable joy of the Emperor and the whole merry company. This episode not only did not spoil the unity and interest of the main action, but enlivened it even further. The cavaliers began scraping and bowing, and the ladies curtsying and tapping their heels, with even greater zeal, no longer paying any attention to the rhythm of the music. Korsakov was unable to participate in the general merriment. The lady he had chosen went up to Ibrahim under orders from her father, Gavrila Afanasevich, and casting her blue eyes down, timidly gave him her hand. He danced a minuet with her and led her back to her seat; then he went to look for Korsakov, led him out of the ballroom, put him in a carriage, and took him home. On the way home Korsakov began muttering inaudibly, "Accursed assembly! Accursed goblet of the Great Eagle!," but he soon fell into a deep slumber, unaware of how he arrived home, how he was undressed and put to bed; the next morning he woke up with a headache and could only vaguely remember the scraping and curtsying, the tobacco smoke, the gentleman with the nosegay, and the goblet of the Great Eagle.

4

Our forebears were no hasty eaters,
Not speedily, you would have found,
Did jars and silver pledging-beakers
Of wine and ale go foaming round.

RUSLAN AND LIUDMILA

I must now acquaint my gracious reader with Gavrila Afanasevich Rzhevskii. A descendant of an ancient lineage of boyars, he possessed an enormous estate, was a generous host, loved falconry, and had numerous servants. In other words, he was a true gentleman of the Russian soil; as he himself was fond of saying, he could not endure the German spirit, and in his household he made every effort to preserve the cherished customs of olden times.

His daughter, Natalia Gavrilovna, was seventeen years old. She had been brought up in the old way, that is, surrounded by nurses and nannies, companions and maidservants; she knew how to do gold embroidery, but she was illiterate. On the other hand her father, despite his aversion to everything foreign, gave in to her desire to learn German dances from a captive Swedish officer who lived in their house. This worthy dance teacher was about fifty years old; his right leg had been shot through at Narva and was therefore not quite up to minuets and courants, but with his left one he could execute even the most difficult *pas* with amazing skill and lightness. His pupil did honor to his efforts. She was renowned as the best dancer at the assemblies, which had indeed been one of the things that led Korsakov to his *faux pas*. The latter came to Gavrila Afanasevich to offer his apologies the next day, but the easy manner and dandyish appearance of this young fop did not please the haughty boyar, who subsequently gave him the witty nickname of French monkey.

One festive day Gavrila Afanasevich was expecting several relatives and friends. A long table was being laid in the ancient hall. The guests arrived, accompanied by their wives and daughters, who had at last been freed from their domestic seclusion by the Emperor's decrees and personal example. Natalia Gavrilovna went up to each guest with a silver tray laden with gold cups, and the men emptied their cups, regretting that the kiss that used to accompany such occasions was no longer a custom. They sat down to table. In the place of honor, next to the master of the house, sat his father-in-law, Prince Boris Alekseevich Lykov, a seventy-year-old boyar; the other guests sat according to the rank of their families, thereby evoking the happy old days of the order of precedence. The men were seated on one side, the women on the other. At the end of the table were placed, as usual, the housekeeper in her old-fashioned headgear and bodice, a midget—a prim and wrinkled little darling of thirty—and the captive Swede in his timeworn blue uniform. The table, laden with a great number of dishes, was attended by numerous bustling domestics, among whom the butler was clearly distinguishable by his stern expression, large stomach, and majestic immobility. During the first minutes of the dinner, attention was devoted exclusively to the products of our old-fashioned cuisine; only the clatter of the plates and assiduously laboring spoons disturbed the prevailing silence. At last the host, judging that it was time to divert his guests with pleasant conversation, turned around and asked, "And where is Ekimovna? Call her here."

Several servants were ready to dash off in different directions, but just at that moment an old woman with a powdered and rouged face, bedizened with flowers and trinkets and wearing a damask robe with deep décolletage, danced into the room humming a tune. Her appearance evoked general delight.

"Good day, Ekimovna," said Prince Lykov. "How are you doing?"

"Never felt better, my good friend: singing and dancing, bridegrooms enticing."

"What have you been up to, old goose?" asked the host.

"I've decked myself out, friend, for your dear guests, for the holy day, by the Tsar's command, by the boyars' demand, to give the world a laughing fit with my German outfit."

These words were greeted with loud laughter, and the jester took up her position behind the master's chair.

"A fool may sometimes speak to purpose," said Tatiana Afanasevna, the master's elder sister, whom he sincerely respected. "Today's fashions really make the whole world laugh. Now that even you men have shaved off your beards and put on cut-off caftans, there is little to be said about women's rags; yet, I'll vow, one can't help missing the sarafan, the maiden's ribbon, and the married woman's headdress. Look at today's beauties—you have to laugh and weep at once. The poor things' hair is all fluffed up like tow, greased and bespattered with French flour; their tummies are laced in so tight it's a wonder they don't break into two; and with their petticoats hitched on hoops, they have to get into carriages sideways, and tilt over going through a door. No way to stand, sit, or breathe. Veritable martyrs, the poor darlings."

"My dear Tatiana Afanasevna," said Kirila Petrovich T., a former administrative official of Riazan, who had in that capacity acquired, by hook or crook, three thousand serfs and a young wife, "in my opinion, let the wife dress as she will; I don't mind if she looks like a scarecrow or a Chinese Emperor as long as she doesn't order new dresses every month, throwing away old ones that are still perfectly good. It used to be that the granddaughter was given her grandmother's sarafan in her trousseau, but look at the latest robes: you see them on the lady today, on her serving girl tomorrow. What can you do? It's simply ruining the Russian gentry. A disaster, no two ways about it." As he spoke these words, he looked with a sigh at his Maria Ilinichna, who did not seem to be pleased either by his praise of the olden days or by his railing against the latest customs. The other beauties present shared her discontent but kept silent, because in those days modesty was considered an indispensable attribute of a young woman.

"And who is to blame?" asked Gavrila Afanasevich, filling up his mug with frothy sour kvass. "Aren't we to blame ourselves? The young wenches are playing the fool, and we let them have their way."

"But what can we do if it's not our choice?" rejoined Kirila Petrovich. "There's many a husband would be glad to lock his wife in the tower chamber, but she's summoned to the assembly by drums and clarion. The husband grabs after the whip, the wife grabs after her frippery. Oh, these assemblies! The Lord has inflicted them on us as a punishment for our sins."

Maria Ilinichna was on tenterhooks: she was itching to speak. Finally she could not bear it any longer, and turning to her husband, she asked him with an acid smile just what it was that he found wrong with the assemblies.

"I'll tell you what's wrong with them," answered her husband, flushed. "Since they've begun, husbands have been unable to cope with their wives. Wives have forgotten the Apostle's words, 'Wives, submit yourselves unto your own husbands'; their minds are on new dresses, not on the household; what they care about is catching the eyes of featherbrained officers, not pleasing their husbands. And is it becoming, my dear lady, for a Russian noblewoman to consort with German snuffers and their maidservants? Whoever heard of dancing into the night and parleying with young men? Not with relatives, mind you, but with strangers who haven't even been introduced."

"I'd add a word or two of my own, but even the walls have ears," said Gavrila Afanasevich, frowning. "I must confess the assembly is not to my taste either: it doesn't take long before you run into a drunkard or find yourself forced to drink till you become a public laughingstock. If you don't watch out, some scamp will start playing pranks at the expense of your daughter. Today's young generation's been so utterly spoilt it's beyond belief. Look at the son of the late Evgraf Sergeevich Korsakov, for instance: he created such a scandal with Natasha at the last assembly that it made me blush. The next day, I suddenly notice, somebody's driving straight into my courtyard. Who in the name of heaven could this be, I say to myself; it isn't Prince Aleksandr Danilovich, is it? And who do you think it was? Ivan Evgrafovich! Do you think he could have stopped at the gate and troubled himself to come up to the porch on foot? No, not he! And then? You should have seen how he flew into the house, bowed and scraped, and gibble-gabbled. The fool Ekimovna can imitate him capitally; which reminds me: come, old goose, show us how the overseas monkey carries himself."

Ekimovna the jester seized the lid of a dish, put it under her arm as if holding a hat, and began making grimaces, bowing and scraping to all sides, and muttering words that resembled *monsieur, mamselle, assemblée, pardon.* Once more, general and prolonged laughter testified to the guests' delight.

"The spitting image of Korsakov, as like as two peas," said old Prince Lykov, wiping away the tears of laughter, as calm was gradually restored. "There's no concealing the fact: he's not the first, nor will he be the last, to come back a clown from those German lands to holy Russia. What do our children learn out there? To scrape with their feet and prattle in God knows what tongue, to treat their elders with disrespect, and to dangle after other men's wives. Of all the young people educated abroad (God forgive me), the Tsar's blackamoor's the one that most resembles a man."

"Indeed so," remarked Gavrila Afanasevich; "he is a solid, respectable man; you can't compare him with that good-for-nothing … But who is this now driving through the gate into the courtyard? It isn't that overseas monkey again, is it? What are you gawking here for, idiots?" he continued, addressing his servants. "Run and turn him away, and tell him that in the future, too …"

"Are you raving, graybeard?" the jester Ekimovna interrupted him. "Are you blind? It's the Imperial sled, the Tsar has come."

Gavrila Afanasevich hastily rose from the table; everyone dashed to the windows and indeed beheld the Emperor, who was ascending the steps, leaning on his orderly's shoulder. There was a great commotion. The master of the house rushed to meet the Emperor; the servants ran in all directions as if bereft of reason; the guests were terrified, some of them even wondering how to slip away at the earliest opportunity. Then suddenly Peter's thunderous voice could be heard from the entrance hall; all fell silent; and the Tsar came in, accompanied by the master of the house, who was struck dumb with joy.

"Good day, ladies and gentlemen," said Peter with a cheerful expression on his face. They all bowed low. The Tsar glanced over the crowd quickly, seeking out the host's young daughter; he called her to him. She approached him quite boldly, though she blushed, not only to the ears but down to the shoulders.

"You're becoming prettier by the day," the Emperor said to her, kissing her, as was his habit, on the head. Then he turned to the guests: "Have I disturbed you, ladies and gentlemen? You were eating your dinner; please sit down again, and as for me, Gavrila Afanasevich, would you offer me some aniseed vodka?"

The host dashed to the majestic-looking butler, snatched the tray from his hands, filled a gold goblet himself, and proffered it to the Emperor with a bow. Peter, having downed his liquor, ate a pretzel and asked the guests once more to continue their dinner. All resumed their former places, except for the midget and the housekeeper, who did not dare remain at a table honored by the Tsar's presence. Peter sat down by the master of the house and asked for some cabbage soup. His orderly handed him a wooden spoon inlaid with ivory and a small knife and fork with green bone handles, for he never used anybody's cutlery except his own. The dinner party, which had been noisy and lively with good cheer and conversation only a minute before, now continued in silence and constraint. The host, overawed and overjoyed, ate nothing, and the guests were all stiff, reverentially listening as the Emperor spoke in German with the captive Swede about the campaign of 1701. The jester Ekimovna, to whom the Emperor put several questions, answered with a kind of timid coldness, which (I might say in passing) did not at all testify to innate stupidity. At last the dinner was over. The Emperor, and after him all the guests, rose to their feet.

"Gavrila Afanasevich," he said, "I would like to have a private word with you." And, taking his host by the arm, Peter led him into the drawing room, locking the door behind them. The guests remained in the dining room, discussing the unexpected visit in a whisper; then, not wishing to appear immodest, they soon began to leave one by one, without thanking their host for his hospitality. His father-in-law, daughter, and sister saw the guests off quietly, and finally remained by themselves in the dining room, waiting for the Emperor to emerge.

5

I shall find a wife for thee,
Or a miller I won't be.
FROM ABLESIMOV'S OPERA
The Miller

In half an hour the door opened and Peter came out. He acknowledged the three-fold bow of Prince Lykov, Tatiana Afanasevna, and Natasha with a solemn inclination of the head and went straight through to the entrance hall. The host helped him on with his red fur coat, accompanied him to his sled, and on the porch thanked him once more for the honor. Peter left.

As he returned to the dining room, Gavrila Afanasevich looked very worried. He curtly ordered the servants to clear the table fast, sent Natasha to her room, and informing his sister and father-in-law that he needed to talk to them, led them to the bedroom where he usually rested after dinner. The old Prince lay down on the oak bed; and Tatiana Afanasevna sat in an ancient damask-upholstered armchair, putting a little footstool under her feet. Gavrila Afanasevich locked all the doors, sat on the bed at Prince Lykov's feet, and in a low tone began the conversation with the following words:

"It was not for nothing that the Emperor came to see me: guess what it was his pleasure to speak to me about?"

"How could we know, dear brother?" said Tatiana Afanasevna.

"Did the Tsar command you to govern a province?" asked the father-in-law. "It was high time. Or did he offer you an ambassadorship? Why not? After all, men of nobility, not only scribes, can sometimes be sent to foreign monarchs."

"No," answered the son-in-law, knitting his brow. "I am a man of the old school; our services are not needed these days, though it is quite reasonable to think that an Orthodox Russian nobleman is worth today's upstarts, pancake peddlers, and infidels—but that's another story."

"Then what did he please to talk to you about for such a long time, brother?" asked Tatiana Afanasevna. "You haven't come upon some adversity, have you? The Lord preserve us and have mercy on us!"

"Adversity or no adversity, I must confess it gave me a start."

"But what is it, brother? What is the matter?"

"It concerns Natasha: the Tsar came to arrange a marriage for her."

"Thank God," said Tatiana Afanasevna, making the sign of the cross. "The girl is marriageable, and if the matchmaker is anything to judge by, the bridegroom cannot be unworthy either. God grant them love and good counsel; the honor is great. And for whom does the Tsar seek her hand?"

"Hum," grunted Gavrila Afanasevich, "for whom? That's just it, for whom."

"Who is it then?" repeated Prince Lykov, who had been on the point of nodding off.

"Try to guess," said Gavrila Afanasevich.

"My dear brother," responded the old lady, "how could we guess? There are many eligible men at court; any of them would be glad to take your Natasha. It's not Dolgorukii, is it?"

"No, not Dolgorukii."

"It's just as well; he's so terribly arrogant. Is it Shein then, or Troekurov?"

"No, neither the one nor the other."

"I'm not keen on them either: frivolous young men, too much imbued with the German spirit. Well, is it Miloslavskii?"

"No, not he, either."

"Let him be: rich but stupid. Who then? Eletskii? Lvov? Neither? It's not Raguzinskii, is it? For heaven's sake, I'm at my wit's end. Who is it that the Tsar is asking Natasha's hand for?"

"The blackamoor Ibrahim."

The old lady gasped and clasped her hands. Prince Lykov lifted his head from the pillows and repeated with amazement, "The blackamoor Ibrahim!"

"Brother, my dearest," said the old lady in a tearful voice, "don't destroy the issue of your own flesh and blood, don't throw Natashenka into the clutches of that black devil."

"But how can I refuse the Emperor," objected Gavrila Afanasevich, "when he is promising to reward me with his favor, both me and my whole family?"

"How now," exclaimed the old Prince, whose drowsiness had entirely disappeared, "to give Natasha, my granddaughter, in marriage to a bought Negro!"

"He is not of common birth," said Gavrila Afanasevich. "He is the son of a black sultan. The Moslems captured him and sold him in Constantinople; our ambassador paid a ransom for him and gave him to the Tsar. His elder brother has been to Russia with a sizable ransom and …"

"Gavrila Afanasevich, dear brother," the old lady interrupted him, "we have heard the tales of Bova Korolevich and Eruslan Lazarevich. Tell us rather what you answered to the Emperor's proposal."

"I said that he ruled over us, and it was our duty as his vassals to obey in all things."

At this moment a noise could be heard behind the door. Gavrila Afanasevich went to open it but felt something obstructing it; he gave it a strong push, and when the door opened, they saw Natasha lying prostrate in a swoon on the blood-spattered floor.

When the Emperor had locked himself in with her father, her heart sank. Some premonition whispered to her that the matter concerned her. When Gavrila Afanasevich sent her off, declaring that he had to speak with her aunt and grandfather, she could not resist the promptings of feminine curiosity and quietly stole through the inner apartments to the door of the bedroom. She did not miss one word of the whole horrifying conversation; when she heard her father's last words, the poor thing lost consciousness, and as she fell, she hit her head against the iron-plated chest in which her trousseau was kept.

The servants came running; they lifted Natasha up, carried her to her room, and put her on the bed. After a while she came to and opened her eyes, but she could not recognize either her father or her aunt. A high fever developed. In her delirious state she kept talking about the Tsar's blackamoor and a wedding, and suddenly let out a piercing wail: "Valerian, dear Valerian, my treasure! Save me, here they come, here they come!" Tatiana Afanasevna anxiously glanced at her brother, who blanched, bit his lip, and left the room without a word. He returned to the old Prince, who, unable to climb the stairs, had remained below.

"How is Natasha?" he asked.

"Unwell," answered the distressed father. "Worse than I thought: in her unconscious state she is raving about Valerian."

"Who is this Valerian?" asked the grandfather, alarmed. "Could it be that orphan, the son of a Strelets, whom you took into your house?"

"The very same one," answered Gavrila Afanasevich. "To my misfortune, his father saved my life at the time of the rebellion, and the devil made me take the accursed wolf cub into my house. Two years ago, when he voluntarily enlisted in a regiment, Natasha, saying good-bye to him, burst into tears, and he stood as if petrified. This seemed suspicious to me, and I discussed it with my sister. But since that time Natasha has not mentioned him, and nothing whatever has been heard of him. I thought she had forgotten him, but evidently she hasn't. This decides the matter: she's to marry the blackamoor."

Prince Lykov did not contradict him: it would have been in vain. The Prince returned home; Tatiana Afanasevna remained at Natasha's bedside; Gavrila Afanasevich, having sent for the physician, locked himself in his room, and the house grew silent and gloomy.

The unexpected marriage proposal surprised Ibrahim at least as much as it had Gavrila Afanasevich. This is how it had happened. One time, as Peter was working with Ibrahim, he said to him, "I notice, brother, that you've grown a little listless. Tell me frankly, is there anything you want?"

Ibrahim assured the Emperor that he was happy with his situation and wished for nothing better.

"All right," said the Emperor, "if you feel spiritless for no reason, then I know how to cheer you up."

When they finished their work, he asked Ibrahim, "Did you like the girl with whom you danced the minuet at the last assembly?"

"She is a charming girl, Your Majesty; and she struck me as a modest and good-natured one, too."

"In that case I'll see to it that you get to know her better. Would you like to marry her?"

"I, Your Majesty?"

"Listen, Ibrahim, you are a solitary man, without kith or kin, a stranger to everyone except me. If I should die today, what would become of you tomorrow, my poor blackamoor? You must get settled down while there is still time; you must find support in new connections, entering into alliance with the Russian gentry."

"Your Majesty, I am blessed with Your Highest protection and favor. God grant me that I may not survive my Tsar and benefactor: I ask for no more. But even if I were inclined to marry, would the young lady and her relatives consent? My appearance …"

"Your appearance! What nonsense! You're a fine young man in every way. A young girl must obey the wishes of her parents, and we'll see what old Gavrila Rzhevskii says when I come as your matchmaker." With these words, the Emperor sent for his sleigh and left Ibrahim plunged in profound thought.

"To marry!" mused the African. "And why not? Or am I destined to spend my life in solitude, never experiencing the greatest joys and most sacred obligations of a man, just because I was born below the fifteenth parallel? I cannot hope to be loved, but that is a childish objection. Can one trust love in any case? Does it exist at all in the fickle heart of woman? Having given up sweet libertinage forever, I have succumbed to other allurements, more significant ones. The Emperor is right: I must ensure my future. Marriage with the young Rzhevskaia will affiliate me with the proud Russian gentry, and I will no longer be a newcomer in my adopted fatherland. I will not demand love from my wife: I shall be content with her fidelity. As for her friendship, I will win it by unfailing tenderness, trust, and indulgence."

Ibrahim wanted to get down to work as usual, but his mind wandered. He abandoned his papers and went for a stroll along the embankment of the Neva. Suddenly he heard Peter's voice; turning around he saw the Emperor, who had dismissed his sleigh and was coming after Ibrahim with a cheerful expression on his face.

"It's all accomplished, brother," he said taking Ibrahim by the arm. "I've asked for her hand on your behalf. Tomorrow pay a visit to your father-in-law, but make sure to honor his boyar pride: leave your sleigh at his gate, go across his courtyard on foot, speak about the services he has rendered his country and about the prominence of his family, and he'll become devoted to you. And now," he continued, shaking his cudgel, "walk with me to that scoundrel Danilych's house; I must talk to him about his latest pranks."

Ibrahim, having sincerely thanked Peter for his fatherly solicitude, saw him to the gate of Prince Menshikov's magnificent palace, and returned home.

6

A sanctuary lamp burned quietly before the glass case holding the family's ancient icons in their glittering gold and silver frames. The lamp's flickering flame cast a faint light on the curtained bed and on the little table covered with labeled medicine bottles. A maidservant sat at a spinning wheel close to the stove; the light whir of her spindle was the only sound that disturbed the silence of the bedroom.

"Who is here?" said a weak voice. The maid rose immediately, went to the bed, and gently raised the curtain. "Will it soon be daylight?" asked Natalia.

"It's already noon," answered the maid.

"My God, why is it so dark then?"

"The windows are shuttered, miss."

"Bring me my clothes quickly."

"I can't, miss; it's against the doctor's orders."

"Am I sick then? Since when?"

"It's been two weeks already."

"Has it? To me it seems as if I'd gone to bed only yesterday."

Natasha grew silent, trying to collect her scattered thoughts. Something had happened to her, but exactly what it was she could not remember. The maid still stood in front of her, waiting for her orders. At that moment an indistinct rumble could be heard from downstairs.

"What's that?" asked the sick girl.

"Their Honors have finished dinner," answered the maid. "They're getting up from the table. Tatiana Afanasevna will come up here now."

Natasha, it seemed, was pleased; she feebly moved her hand. The maid pulled the curtain to and sat down at her spinning wheel again.

In a few minutes a head wearing a broad white cap with dark ribbons appeared in the doorway and a subdued voice asked, "How's Natasha?"

"Hello, auntie," said the invalid softly, and Tatiana Afanasevna hastened to her.

"The young mistress has revived," said the maid, cautiously drawing an armchair up to the bed.

The old lady, with tears in her eyes, kissed her niece's pale, languid face and sat down by her. Soon after, the German physician in his black coat and scholar's wig entered the room, felt Natasha's pulse, and announced, first in Latin and then in Russian, that the danger had passed. He asked for paper and ink, wrote out a new prescription, and left. The old lady got up, kissed Natalia once more, and went downstairs to tell Gavrila Afanasevich about the good news.

In the drawing room sat the Tsar's blackamoor, in uniform, with sword by his side and hat in hand, respectfully conversing with Gavrila Afanasevich. Korsakov, stretched out on a soft divan, was listening to them absentmindedly while teasing a good old gray hound; when he had grown tired of that occupation, he went up to a mirror—his usual refuge from boredom—and in the mirror caught sight of Tatiana Afanasevna, who was vainly trying to signal to her brother from the doorway.

"You're wanted, Gavrila Afanasevich," said Korsakov, turning to his host and interrupting Ibrahim. Gavrila Afanasevich promptly went to his sister and closed the door behind him.

"I marvel at your patience," said Korsakov to Ibrahim. "Not only do you listen a whole blessed hour to these ravings about the Rzevskiis' and Lykovs' ancient lineage, but you even add your own virtuous commentary! If I were you, *j'aurais planté là* the old prattler and his whole tribe, including Natalia Gavrilovna, who is putting on airs, pretending to be sick, *une petite santé* ... Tell me honestly, can you be in love with this little *mijaurée*? Listen, Ibrahim, take my advice just this once: honestly, I am wiser than I seem. Give up this freakish idea. Don't marry. It seems to me that your fiancée has no particular liking for you. Anything can happen in this world. For instance, it goes without saying that I cannot complain about my looks; but I have had occasion to deceive husbands who were, I swear, no worse than I. And you yourself … Don't you remember our Parisian friend, Count D.? One cannot rely on woman's fidelity; lucky the man who can contemplate the matter with indifference. But you? Should you, with your passionate, brooding, and suspicious nature, with your flat nose and thick lips, and with that kinky wool on your head, throw yourself into all the dangers of matrimony?"

"I thank you for the friendly advice," Ibrahim interrupted him coldly, "but you know the saying: it's not your duty to rock other people's babies."

"Take care, Ibrahim," answered Korsakov, laughing, "take care not to let it happen that you should illustrate this proverb in a literal sense."

Meanwhile, the conversation going on in the adjacent room was becoming heated.

"You're going to kill her," the old lady was saying. "She will not survive the sight of him."

"But think of it yourself," argued the obstinate brother. "He's been coming here as her bridegroom for two weeks, yet hasn't seen his bride once. He may think at last that her illness is a mere fabrication, that we're only stalling for time in order to find some way to get rid of him. And what will the Tsar say? He has already sent inquiries about Natalia's health three times. Say what you like, I've no intention of quarreling with him."

"The Lord be merciful," said Tatiana Afanasevna, "what will the poor thing come to? Let me at least prepare her for the visit." To this Gavrila Afanasevich agreed, and he returned to the drawing room.

"Thank God," he said to Ibrahim, "the danger has passed. Natalia is much better; if I weren't embarrassed to leave my dear guest, Ivan Evgrafovich, all by himself, I would take you upstairs for a glimpse of your bride."

Korsakov rejoiced over the news and, assuring Gavrila Afanasevich that he had to leave, asked him not to worry about him. He ran out into the entrance hall, giving his host no chance to see him off.

In the meanwhile Tatiana Afanasevna hastened to prepare the invalid for the frightening guest's arrival. Entering the bedroom, she sat down, out of breath, by the bed and took Natasha's hand; but before she was able to utter a word, the door opened. Natasha asked who it was. The old lady, horror-stricken, lost her faculty of speech. Gavrila Afanasevich drew the curtain aside, looked at the patient coldly, and asked how she was. She tried to smile at him, but she could not. Struck by her father's stern glance, she felt apprehensive. Presently it seemed to her that somebody was standing at the head of her bed. She raised her head with an effort and suddenly recognized the Tsar's blackamoor. This brought everything back to her mind, and all the horror of the future presented itself to her imagination. But her exhausted body did not register a visible shock. She let her head fall back on the pillow and closed her eyes … Her heart beat feebly. Tatiana Afanasevna signaled to her brother that the patient wished to go to sleep, and everybody left the room quietly, except for the maidservant, who set to work again at her spinning wheel.

The unlucky beauty opened her eyes and, no longer seeing anyone by her bed, called the maid to her and sent her to fetch the midget. At that same moment, however, the rotund little old elf was already rolling toward her bed like a ball. Lastochka (as the midget was called) had run up the stairs behind Gavrila Afanasevich and Ibrahim as fast as her short legs could carry her, and she hid behind the door, in keeping with the inquisitive nature of her sex. As soon as Natasha saw her, she sent the maid away, and the midget sat down on a little stool by the bed.

Never has such a small body contained such a lively spirit. She meddled in everything, knew everything, fussed about everything. Her shrewd mind and ingratiating manner earned her the love of her masters and the hatred of the rest of the household, over which she ruled despotically. Gavrila Afanasevich listened to her denunciations, complaints, and petty requests; Tatiana Afanasevna perpetually asked for her opinion and took her advice; and Natasha had a boundless attachment to her, entrusting her with all her thoughts and all the stirrings of her sixteen-year-old heart.

"You know, Lastochka," said Natalia, "father is going to marry me to the blackamoor."

The midget sighed deeply and wrinkled up all the more her already wrinkled face.

"Is there no hope?" continued Natasha. "Is father not going to take pity on me?"

The midget shook her little cap.

"Isn't grandpapa or auntie going to intercede for me?"

"No, miss. While you've been sick the blackamoor has succeeded in charming them all. The master is devoted to him, the Prince raves about him, and Tatiana Afanasevna says, 'What a pity he's black; otherwise we couldn't wish for a better bridegroom.'"

"Oh my God, oh my God," groaned poor Natasha.

"Don't grieve, my beauty," said the midget, kissing Natalia's weak hand. "Even if you have to marry the blackamoor, you will have your freedom. Today it's not as it used to be: husbands don't lock up their wives. The blackamoor, they say, is rich; your house will be like a cup brimming over; you'll live in clover …"

"Poor Valerian," said Natasha so softly that the midget could guess more than hear her words.

"That's just it, miss," she said, confidentially lowering her voice. "If the Strelets's orphan weren't quite so much on your mind, you wouldn't rave about him in a fever, and your father wouldn't be angry."

"What?" said the frightened Natasha. "I raved about Valerian, father heard me, father is angry?"

"That's exactly the trouble," answered the midget. "After this, if you start asking him not to marry you to the blackamoor, he will think that the reason is Valerian. There is nothing to be done: you must submit to his paternal will and accept what fate brings you."

Natasha did not utter a single word in protest. The thought that her secret love was known to her father produced a powerful effect on her mind. Only one hope remained for her: to die before the hateful marriage came to pass. This idea comforted her. She submitted to her fate with a faint, sorrowful heart.

7

At the entrance to Gavrila Afanasevich's house, to the right of the passageway, there was a tiny cubicle with one small window. In it stood a simple bed covered with a flannel blanket, and in front of the bed a little deal table, on which a tallow candle burned and some sheets of music lay open. A soldier's old blue coat and a three-cornered hat of the same age hung on the wall; above the hat, a print showing a mounted Charles XII was fastened to the wall with three nails. Notes from a flute resounded through the humble dwelling. Its solitary inhabitant, the captive dance teacher in his nightcap and nankeen dressing gown, was enlivening the monotony of the winter evening by playing old Swedish marches, which reminded him of the gay time of his youth. Having devoted two hours to this exercise, he took his flute apart, put it away in a box, and started undressing.

Just then the latch on his door was lifted, and a tall handsome young man in a uniform entered the room.

The Swede rose to his feet, surprised, before the unexpected visitor.

"You don't recognize me, Gustav Adamych," said the young visitor with feeling. "You don't remember the boy whom you drilled in Swedish musketry and with whom you almost started a fire in this same little room, shooting off a toy cannon."

Gustav Adamych looked at his visitor intently.

"Ah!" he cried at last, embracing him, "god dag to you, so are du here now? Sitt down, your old scamp, so shall ve speak."

TRANSLATED BY PAUL DEBRECZENY

21

"The Quadroons"

Lydia Maria Child

Before she was ostracized from "polite" New England society for her radical antislavery views, Lydia Maria Child (1802–1880) had established a girls' school, founded the first children's periodical in the United States, and published romances and handbooks for housewives. Her 1833 book *An Appeal in Favor of That Class of Americans Called Africans* and other writings in support of African American equality were influential contributions to the abolitionist cause. Child devoted her life to writing and speaking in favor of abolition, helping fugitive slaves to freedom by offering her home as refuge, and editing slave narratives like Harriet Jacobs's 1861 *Incidents in the Life of a Slave Girl*. Child also wrote in support of feminism and equality for Native Americans.

In her 1842 short story "The Quadroons," reprinted here, Child explores the intersection of slavery and family relations. The story inspired African American writers like William Wells Brown, and Child returned to some of its themes in her 1867 novel *The Romance of the Republic*.

> "I promised thee a sister tale,
> Of man's perfidious cruelty:
> Come then and hear what cruel wrong
> Befell the dark Ladie."
>
> Coleridge

Not far from Augusta, Georgia, there is a pleasant place called Sand-Hills, appropriated almost exclusively to summer residences for the wealthy inhabitants of the neighbouring city. Among the beautiful cottages that adorn it was one far retired from the public roads, and almost hidden among the trees. It was a perfect model of rural beauty. The piazzas that surrounded it were wreathed with Clematis and Passion Flower. Magnificent Magnolias, and the superb Pride of India, threw shadows around it, and filled the air with fragrance. Flowers peeped out from every nook, and nodded to you in bye-places, with a most unexpected welcome. The tasteful hand of Art had not learned to *imitate* the lavish beauty and harmonious disorder of Nature, but they lived together in loving unity, and spoke in according tones. The gateway rose in a

Gothic arch, with graceful tracery in iron-work, surmounted by a Cross, around which fluttered and played the Mountain Fringe, that lightest and most fragile of vines.

The inhabitants of this cottage remained in it all the year round, and peculiarly enjoyed the season that left them without neighbours. To one of the parties, indeed, the fashionable summer residents, that came and went with the butterflies, were merely neighbours-in-law. The edicts of society had built up a wall of separation between her and them; for she was a quadroon. Conventional laws could not be reversed in her favour, though she was the daughter of a wealthy merchant, was highly cultivated in mind and manners, graceful as an antelope, and beautiful as the evening star. She had early attracted the attention of a handsome and wealthy young Georgian; and as their acquaintance increased, the purity and bright intelligence of her mind, inspired him with far deeper interest than is ever excited by mere passion. It was genuine love; that mysterious union of soul and sense, in which the lowliest dew-drop reflects the image of the highest star.

The tenderness of Rosalie's conscience required an outward form of marriage; though she well knew that a union with her proscribed race was unrecognised by law, and therefore the ceremony gave her no legal hold on Edward's constancy. But her high poetic nature regarded the reality, rather than the semblance of things; and when he playfully asked how she could keep him if he wished to run away, she replied, "Let the church that my mother loved sanction our union, and my own soul will be satisfied, without the protection of the state. If your affections fall from me, I would not, if I could, hold you by a legal fetter."

It was a marriage sanctioned by Heaven, though unrecognised on earth. The picturesque cottage at Sand-Hills was built for the young bride under her own direction; and there they passed ten as happy years as ever blessed the heart of mortals. It was Edward's fancy to name their eldest child Xarifa; in commemoration of a quaint old Spanish ballad, which had first conveyed to his ears the sweet tones of her mother's voice. Her flexile form and nimble motions were in harmony with the breezy sound of the name; and its Moorish origin was most appropriate to one so emphatically "a child of the sun." Her complexion, of a still lighter brown than Rosalie's, was rich and glowing as an autumnal leaf. The iris of her large, dark eye had the melting, mezzotinto outline, which remains the last vestige of African ancestry, and gives that plaintive expression, so often observed, and so appropriate to that docile and injured race.

Xarifa learned no lessons of humility or shame, within her own happy home; for she grew up in the warm atmosphere of father's and mother's love, like a flower open to the sunshine, and sheltered from the winds. But in summer walks with her beautiful mother, her young cheek often mantled at the rude gaze of the young men, and her dark eye flashed fire, when some contemptuous epithet met her ear, as white ladies passed them by, in scornful pride and ill-concealed envy.

Happy as Rosalie was in Edward's love, and surrounded by an outward environment of beauty, so well adapted to her poetic spirit, she felt these incidents with inexpressible pain. For herself, she cared but little; for she had found a sheltered home in Edward's heart, which the world might ridicule, but had no power to profane. But when she looked at her beloved Xarifa, and reflected upon the unavoidable and dangerous position which the tyranny of society had awarded her, her soul was filled with anguish. The rare loveliness of the child increased daily, and was evidently ripening into most marvellous beauty. The father rejoiced in it with unmingled pride; but in the deep tenderness of the mother's eye there was an indwelling sadness, that spoke of anxious thoughts and fearful forebodings.

When Xarifa entered her ninth year, these uneasy feelings found utterance in earnest solicitations that Edward would remove to France, or England. This request excited but little opposition, and was so attractive to his imagination, that he might have overcome all intervening obstacles, had not "a change come o'er the spirit of his dream." He still loved Rosalie, but he was now twenty-eight years old, and, unconsciously to himself, ambition had for some time been slowly gaining an ascendency over his other feelings. The contagion of example had led him into the arena where so much American strength is wasted; he had thrown himself into political excitement, with all the honest fervour of youthful feeling. His motives had been unmixed with selfishness, nor could he ever define to himself when or how sincere patriotism took the form of personal ambition. But so it was, that at twenty-eight years old, he found himself an ambitious man, involved in movements which his frank nature would have once abhorred, and watching the doubtful game of mutual cunning with all the fierce excitement of a gambler.

Among those on whom his political success most depended, was a very popular and wealthy man, who had an only daughter. His visits to the house were at first of a purely political nature; but the young lady was pleasing, and he fancied he discovered in her a sort of timid preference for himself. This excited his vanity, and awakened thoughts of the great worldly advantages connected with a union. Reminiscences of his first love kept these vague ideas in check for several months; but Rosalie's image at last became an unwelcome intruder; for with it was associated the idea of restraint. Moreover Charlotte, though inferior in beauty, was yet a pretty contrast to her rival. Her light hair fell in silken profusion, her blue eyes were gentle, though inexpressive, and her delicate cheeks were like blush-rose-buds.

He had already become accustomed to the dangerous experiment of resisting his own inward convictions; and this new impulse to ambition, combined with the strong temptation of variety in love, met the ardent young man weakened in moral principle, and unfettered by laws of the land. The change wrought upon him was soon noticed by Rosalie.

> "In many ways does the full heart reveal
> The presence of the love it would conceal;
> But in far more the estranged heart lets know
> The absence of the love, which yet it fain would show."

At length the news of his approaching marriage met her ear. Her head grew dizzy, and her heart fainted within her; but, with a strong effort at composure, she inquired all the particulars; and her pure mind at once took its resolution. Edward came that evening, and though she would have fain met him as usual, her heart was too full not to throw a deep sadness over her looks and tones. She had never complained of his decreasing tenderness, or of her own lonely hours; but he felt that the mute appeal of her heart-broken looks was more terrible than words. He kissed the hand she offered, and with a countenance almost as sad as her own, led her to a window in the recess, shadowed by a luxuriant Passion Flower. It was the same seat where they had spent the first evening in this beautiful cottage, consecrated to their youthful loves. The same calm, clear moonlight looked in through the trellis. The vine then planted had now a luxuriant growth; and many a time had Edward fondly twined its sacred blossoms with the glossy ringlets of her raven hair. The rush of memory almost overpowered poor Rosalie; and Edward felt too much oppressed and ashamed to break the long, deep silence. At length, in words scarcely audible, Rosalie said, "Tell me, dear Edward, are you to be married next week?" He dropped her hand, as if a rifle-ball had struck him; and it was not until after long hesitation, that he began to make some reply about the necessity of circumstances. Mildly, but earnestly, the poor girl begged him to spare apologies. It was enough that he no longer loved her, and that they must bid farewell. Trusting to the yielding tenderness of her character, he ventured, in the most soothing accents, to suggest that as he still loved her better than all the world, she would ever be his real wife, and they might see each other frequently. He was not prepared for the storm of indignant emotion his words excited. Hers was a passion too absorbing to admit of partnership; and her spirit was too pure and kind to enter into a selfish league against the happiness of the innocent young bride.

At length this painful interview came to an end. They stood together by the Gothic gate, where they had so often met and parted in the moonlight. Old remembrances melted their souls. "Farewell, dearest Edward," said Rosalie. "Give me a parting kiss." Her voice was choked for utterance, and the tears flowed freely, as she bent her lips toward him. He folded her convulsively in his arms, and imprinted a long, impassioned kiss on that mouth, which had never spoken to him but in love and blessing.

With effort like a death-pang, she at length raised her head from his heaving bosom, and turning from him with bitter sobs, she said, "It is our *last*. God bless you. I would not have you so miserable as I am. Farewell. A *last* farewell." "The *last!*" exclaimed he, with a wild shriek. "Oh, Rosalie, do not say that!" and covering his face with his hands, he wept like a child.

Recovering from his emotion, he found himself alone. The moon looked down upon him mild, but very sorrowful; as the Madonna seems to gaze on her worshipping children, bowed down with consciousness of sin. At that moment he would have given worlds to have disengaged himself from Charlotte; but he had gone so far, that blame, disgrace, and duels with angry relatives, would now attend any effort to obtain his freedom. Oh, how the moonlight oppressed him with its friendly sadness! It was like the plaintive eye of his forsaken one; like the music of sorrow echoed from an unseen world.

Long and earnestly he gazed at that dwelling, where he had so long known earth's purest foretaste of heavenly bliss. Slowly he walked away; then turned again to look on that charmed spot, the nestling-place of his young affections. He caught a glimpse of Rosalie, weeping beside a magnolia, which commanded a long view of the path leading to the public road. He would have sprung toward her, but she darted from him, and entered the cottage. That graceful figure, weeping in the moonlight, haunted him for years. It stood before his closing eyes, and greeted him with the morning dawn.

Poor Charlotte! had she known all, what a dreary lot would hers have been; but fortunately, she could not miss the impassioned tenderness she had never experienced; and Edward was the more careful in his kindness, because he was deficient in love. Once or twice she heard him murmur, "dear Rosalie," in his sleep; but the playful charge she brought was playfully answered, and the incident gave her no real uneasiness. The summer after their marriage, she proposed a residence at Sand-Hills; little aware what a whirlwind of emotion she excited in her husband's heart. The reasons he gave for rejecting the proposition appeared satisfactory; but she could not quite understand why he was never willing that their afternoon drives should be in the direction of those pleasant rural residences, which she had heard him praise so much. One day, as their barouche rolled along a winding road that skirted Sand-Hills, her attention was suddenly attracted by two figures among the trees by the way-side; and touching Edward's arm, she exclaimed, "Do look at that beautiful child!" He turned, and saw Rosalie and Xarifa. His lips quivered, and his face became deadly pale. His young wife looked at him intently, but said nothing. There were points of resemblance in the child, that seemed to account for his sudden emotion. Suspicion was awakened, and she soon learned that the mother of that lovely girl bore the name of Rosalie; with this information came recollections of the "dear Rosalie," murmured in uneasy slumbers. From gossiping tongues she soon learned more than she wished to know. She wept, but not as poor Rosalie had done; for she never had loved, and been beloved, like her, and her nature was more proud. Henceforth a change came over her feelings and her manners; and Edward had no further occasion to assume a tenderness in return for hers. Changed as he was by ambition, he felt the wintry chill of her polite propriety, and sometimes in agony of heart, compared it with the gushing love of her who was indeed his wife.

But these, and all his emotions, were a sealed book to Rosalie, of which she could only guess the contents. With remittances for her and her child's support, there sometimes came earnest pleadings that she would consent to see him again; but these she never answered, though her heart yearned to do so. She pitied his fair young bride, and would not be tempted to bring sorrow into their household by any fault of hers. Her earnest prayer was that she might never know of her existence. She had not looked on Edward since she watched him under the shadow of the magnolia, until his barouche passed her in her rambles some months after. She saw the deadly paleness of his countenance, and had he dared to look back, he would have seen her tottering with faintness. Xarifa brought water from a little rivulet, and sprinkled her face. When she revived, she clasped the beloved child to her heart with a vehemence that made her scream. Soothingly she kissed away her fears, and gazed into her beautiful eyes with a deep, deep sadness of expression, which Xarifa never forgot. Wild were the thoughts that pressed around her aching heart, and almost maddened her poor brain; thoughts which had almost driven her to suicide the night of that last farewell. For her child's sake she conquered the fierce temptation then; and for her sake, she struggled with it now. But the gloomy atmosphere of their once happy home overclouded the morning of Xarifa's life.

"She from her mother learnt the trick of grief,
And sighed among her playthings."

Rosalie perceived this; and it gave her gentle heart unutterable pain. At last, the conflicts of her spirit proved too strong for the beautiful frame in which it dwelt. About a year after Edward's marriage, she was found dead in her bed, one bright autumnal morning. She had often expressed to her daughter a wish to be buried under a spreading oak, that shaded a rustic garden-chair, in which she and Edward had spent many happy evenings. And there she was buried; with a small white cross at her head, twined with the cypress vine. Edward came to the funeral, and wept long, very long, at the grave. Hours after midnight, he sat in the recess-window, with Xarifa folded to his heart. The poor child sobbed herself to sleep on his bosom; and the convicted murderer had small reason to envy that wretched man, as he gazed on the lovely countenance, which so strongly reminded him of his early and his only love.

From that time, Xarifa was the central point of all his warmest affections. He hired an excellent old negress to take charge of the cottage, from which he promised his darling child that she should never be removed. He employed a music master, and dancing master, to attend upon her; and a week never passed without a visit from him, and a present of books, pictures, or flowers. To hear her play upon the harp, or repeat some favourite poem in her mother's earnest accents and melodious tones, or to see her pliant figure float in the garland-dance, seemed to be the highest enjoyment of his life. Yet was the pleasure mixed with bitter thoughts. What would be the destiny of this fascinating young creature, so radiant with life and beauty? She belonged to a proscribed race; and though the brown colour on her soft cheek was scarcely deeper than the sunny side of a golden pear, yet was it sufficient to exclude her from virtuous society. He thought of Rosalie's wish to carry her to France: and he would have fulfilled it, had he been unmarried. As it was, he inwardly resolved to make some arrangement to effect it in a few years, even if it involved separation from his darling child.

But alas for the calculations of man! From the time of Rosalie's death, Edward had sought relief for his wretched feelings in the free use of wine. Xarifa was scarcely fifteen, when her father was found dead by the road-side; having fallen from his horse, on his way to visit her. He left no will; but his wife, with kindness of heart worthy of a happier domestic fate, expressed a decided reluctance to change any of the plans he had made for the beautiful child at Sand-Hills.

Xarifa mourned her indulgent father; but not as one utterly desolate. True, she had lived "like a flower deep hid in rocky cleft;" but the sunshine of love had already peeped in upon her. Her teacher on the harp was a handsome and agreeable young man of twenty, the only son of an English widow. Perhaps Edward had not been altogether unmindful of the result, when he first invited him to the flowery cottage. Certain it is, he had more than once thought what a pleasant thing it would be, if English freedom from prejudice should lead him to offer legal protection to his graceful and winning child. Being thus encouraged, rather than checked, in his admiration, George Elliot could not be otherwise than strongly attracted toward his beautiful pupil. The lonely and unprotected state in which her father's death left her, deepened this feeling into tenderness. And lucky was it for her enthusiastic and affectionate nature; for she could not live without an atmosphere of love. In her innocence, she knew nothing of the dangers in her path; and she trusted George with an undoubting simplicity, that rendered her sacred to his noble and generous soul. It seemed as if that flower-embosomed nest was consecrated by the Fates to Love. The French have well named it *La Belle Passion*; for without it life were "a year without spring, or a spring without roses." Except the loveliness of infancy, what does earth offer so much like Heaven, as the happiness of two young, pure, and beautiful beings, living in each other's hearts?

Xarifa inherited her mother's poetic and impassioned temperament; and to her, above others, the first consciousness of these sweet emotions was like a golden sunrise on the sleeping flowers.

> "Thus stood she at the threshold of the scene
> Of busy life....
> How fair it lay in solemn shade and sheen!
> And he beside her, like some angel, posted
> To lead her out of childhood's fairy land,
> On to life's glancing summit, hand in hand."

Alas, the tempest was brooding over their young heads. Rosalie, though she knew it not, had been the daughter of a slave, whose wealthy master, though he remained attached to her to the end of her days, yet carelessly omitted to have papers of manumission recorded. His heirs had lately failed, under circumstances which greatly exasperated their creditors; and in an unlucky hour, they discovered their claim on Angelique's grand-child.

The gentle girl, happy as the birds in spring-time, accustomed to the fondest indulgence, surrounded by all the refinements of life, timid as a fawn, and with a soul full of romance, was ruthlessly seized by a sheriff, and placed on the public auction-stand in Savannah. There she stood, trembling, blushing, and weeping; compelled to listen to the grossest language, and shrinking from the rude hands that examined the graceful proportions of her beautiful frame. "Stop that!" exclaimed a stern voice. "I bid two thousand dollars for her, without asking any of their d——d questions." The speaker was probably about forty years of age, with handsome features, but a fierce and proud expression. An older man, who stood behind him, bid two thousand five hundred. The first bid higher; then a third, a dashing young man, bid three thousand; and thus they went on, with the keen excitement of gamblers, until the first speaker obtained the prize, for the moderate sum of five thousand dollars.

And where was George, during this dreadful scene? He was absent on a visit to his mother, at Mobile. But, had he been at Sand-Hills, he could not have saved his beloved from the wealthy profligate, who was determined to obtain her at any price. A letter of agonized entreaty from her brought him home on the wings of the wind. But what could he do? How could he ever obtain a sight of her, locked up as she was in the princely mansion of her master? At last, by bribing one of the slaves, he conveyed a letter to her, and received one in return. As yet, her purchaser treated her with respectful gentleness, and sought to win her favour, by flattery and presents; but she dreaded every moment, lest the scene should change, and trembled at the sound of every footfall. A plan was laid for escape. The slave agreed to drug his master's wine; a ladder of ropes was prepared, and a swift boat was in readiness. But the slave, to obtain a double reward, was treacherous. Xarifa had scarcely given an answering signal to the low cautious whistle of her lover, when the sharp sound of a rifle was followed by a deep groan, and a heavy fall on the pavement of the court-yard. With frenzied eagerness she swung herself down by the ladder of ropes, and, by the glancing light of lanthorns, saw George, bleeding and lifeless at her feet. One wild shriek, that pierced the brains of those who heard it, and she fell senseless by his side.

For many days she had a confused consciousness of some great agony, but knew not where she was, or by whom she was surrounded. The slow recovery of her reason settled into the most intense melancholy, which moved the compassion even of her cruel purchaser. The beautiful eyes, always pensive in expression, were now so heart-piercing in their sadness, that he could not endure to look upon them. For some months, he sought to win her smiles by lavish presents, and delicate attentions. He bought glittering chains of gold, and costly bands of pearl. His victim scarcely glanced at them, and her attendant slave laid them away, unheeded and forgotten. He purchased the furniture of the cottage at Sand-Hills, and one morning Xarifa found her harp at the bedside, and the room filled with her own books, pictures, and flowers. She gazed upon them with a pang unutterable, and burst into an agony of tears; but she gave her master no thanks, and her gloom deepened.

At last his patience was exhausted. He grew weary of her obstinacy, as he was pleased to term it; and threats took the place of persuasion.

In a few months more, poor Xarifa was a raving maniac. That pure temple was desecrated; that loving heart was broken; and that beautiful head fractured against the wall in the frenzy of despair. Her master cursed the useless expense she had cost him; the slaves buried her; and no one wept at the grave of her who had been so carefully cherished, and so tenderly beloved.

22

From *Georges*

Alexandre Dumas

Alexandre Dumas (1802–1870) enjoyed widespread acclaim for his plays, colorful historical novels, and three volumes of memoirs. His father, the biracial offspring of a French nobleman and a slave woman from Santo Domingo, was one of Napoleon's generals. Dumas's early theatrical successes included *Henri III et sa cour*, staged in 1829 by the Théâtre-Français, and the 1831 drama *Antony*, in which Dumas raised the topic of the adulterous wife in French theater for the first time. Among the best known of his novels are *Les Trois Mousquetaires* (1844) and *Le Comte de Monte-Cristo* (1844), which were written in collaboration with the historian Auguste Maquet and were wildly popular. Although these two novels (including their movie and television adaptations) are still enjoyed today, Dumas's earlier novel *Georges* (1843), of which one chapter follows in an anonymous nineteenth-century translation, remains little known. Its hero is the wealthy, mixed-race, and light-skinned Georges Munier, who leaves his native Indian Ocean island Île de France and is educated in Paris. Fourteen years later Georges returns incognito to the island and falls in love with the young Creole woman Sara de Malmédie; after her uncle refuses to give his consent to a marriage, Georges heads a slave rebellion.

Chapter III: Three Children

As may well be imagined, the English, though they had lost four vessels, had not abandoned their designs on the Isle of France; on the contrary, they had now both a fresh conquest to make and an old defeat to avenge. Accordingly, hardly three months after the events which we have just laid before the reader, a second struggle no less desperate, but destined to result very differently, had taken place at Port Louis itself, that is to say, at a spot in exactly the opposite direction to that where the former took place.

This time it was not a question of four ships or eighteen hundred men. Twelve frigates, eight corvettes and fifty transports had landed twenty or twenty-five thousand men on the coast, and the invading army was advancing on Port Louis, then called Port Napoléon. This was the capital of the island, and at the moment of being attacked by so large a force presented a spectacle difficult to describe. Everywhere the multitude, hurrying in from different quarters of the island and crowded together in the streets, showed signs of the greatest excitement; as nobody knew the real danger, every one invented some imaginary peril, and those which obtained most credence were the most exaggerated and unheard-of ones. From time to time some aide-de-camp of the General in command would appear suddenly, bringing an order and tossing to the crowd a proclamation intended to arouse the hatred which the Nationalists bore towards the English and to excite their patriotism. On its being read out, hats were raised on the points of bayonets; shouts of "Long live the Emperor" resounded; oaths to conquer or die were exchanged; a shiver of enthusiasm ran through the crowd, which passed from a state of noisy idleness to one of furious activity, and rushed headlong from all quarters, demanding to march upon the enemy.

But the real meeting-place was the Place d'Armes, that is to say, in the centre of the town. Thither were continually arriving, now an ammunition waggon dragged helter-skelter by two small horses of Timor or Pegu, now a gun brought in at full gallop by the National Artillery, young fellows of fifteen to sixteen years of age, for whom the powder that blackened their faces took the place of beards. There, too, assembled the Civic Guards in fighting trim, Volunteers in miscellaneous garments, who had added bayonets to their sporting guns; Negroes clothed in remnants of uniforms and armed with carbines, sabres and lances; all these mingling, colliding, crossing one another, upsetting one another, contributing each his share of noise to the insistent rumour which rose above the town, just as the hum of an innumerable swarm of bees ascends from a large hive.

Once arrived, however, at the Place, whether rushing in singly or in groups, these men assumed a more regular appearance and a calmer demeanour. At the Place d'Armes was stationed, while waiting for the order to march against the enemy, half of the garrison of the Island, composed of regular troops and forming a total of fifteen to eighteen hundred men, whose attitude, at once proud and nonchalant, was a silent reproach to the noise and confusion made by those who, less familiar with scenes of this kind, had nevertheless the courage and goodwill to take part in them. Accordingly, while the Negroes hurried pell-mell to one end of the great square, a regiment of national Volunteers, restraining themselves at sight of the military discipline of the Regulars, halted in front of the troops, forming in the same order as they, and trying, though without success, to imitate the regularity of their lines.

He who appeared to be the leader of this last body of men, and who, it must be said, gave himself infinite trouble to attain the result we have indicated, was a man from forty to forty-five years of age, wearing a Major's epaulettes, and endowed by nature with one of those insignificant faces to which no emotion can succeed in imparting signs of intelligence or character. For the rest, he was curled, shaved, smartly got up as if for parade; only, occasionally, he unfastened a clasp of his coat, originally buttoned from top to bottom but which gradually opening, displayed to view an embroidered vest, frilled shirt and white tie with embroidered ends. Near him, a pretty child of twelve, attended by a household Negro who stood some yards away, dressed in a suit of dimity, displayed, with that ease which the habit of being well-dressed imparts, his large scalloped collar, his jacket of green camlet with silver buttons, and his grey beaver adorned with a feather. At his side hung with his sabretache the scabbard of a little sword, the blade of which he held in his right hand, trying to copy, as well as he could, the martial bearing of the officer, whom he took care, from time to time to address very loudly as "Father," a title with which the Major seemed no less flattered than by the illustrious rank in the national militia to which the confidence of his fellow-citizens had raised him.

At a short distance from this group which swaggered so gaily, might be distinguished another, less brilliant no doubt, but certainly more remarkable. It consisted of a man from forty-five to forty-eight years of age, and two children, one aged fourteen and the other twelve.

The man was tall and thin, of bony frame, a little bent, not by age, since, as we have said, he was not more than forty-eight at the outside, but by the humility of a subservient position. From his copper tint and slightly woolly hair one could recognise at first glance one of those Mulattos whose fortunes, which are often enormous and the result of their own well-directed industry, avail nothing in the Colonies to excuse their colour. He was dressed with rich simplicity, held in his hand a carbine embossed with gold, armed with a long slender bayonet, and had at his side a cuirassier's sabre which, thanks to his great height, hung along his thigh like a sword. His pockets bulged with cartridges, in addition to those contained in his pouch.

The eldest of the two children who accompanied him was, as we have said, a tall lad of fourteen whose sporting pursuits, more than his Negro origin, had deepened his complexion. Thanks to the active life he had led he was as strong as a young man of eighteen, and thus had obtained his father's leave to share in the engagement which was soon to take place. He, on his side, was armed with a double-barrelled gun, the same which he used in his expeditions across the island, and with which, young as he was, he had already gained a reputation for skill which the most celebrated hunters envied him. But, at the present moment, his actual age overcame his apparent age; for having laid his gun down on the ground, he was rolling over and over with an enormous Madagascar hound, which seemed to have come there in case the English should have brought any of their bulldogs with them.

The young hunter's brother, younger son of the man of tall stature and humble mien, who completed the group we have endeavoured to describe, was a child of about twelve, whose slim and puny build bore no relation to his father's great height or the powerful frame of his brother, who seemed to have united in himself alone the vigour intended for both; in contrast therefore to Jacques, as the oldest was called, little Georges seemed two years younger than he really was, so far did his short stature, his pale, thin, and melancholy face, shaded by long dark hair, betoken a lack of the physical strength so common in the Colonies. But, to make up for this, you might read in his uneasy, penetrating look such an eager intelligence, and in the precocious knitting of the brows which was already habitual to him, such a manly reflection and such firmness of will, that you were amazed to meet with such insignificance and such vigour united in one and the same individual.

Having no weapons, he kept close by his father and grasped with all the strength of his little hand the barrel of the handsome embossed gun, turning his eager and inquiring eyes from his father to the Major, asking inwardly, no doubt, why his father, who was twice as rich and strong and clever as the other, did not also boast like him some honourable badge or individual mark of rank.

A Negro in waistcoat and trousers of blue cloth was waiting, as his comrade was for the child with the scalloped collar, till the time came for the men to march, for the boy would stay behind with him while his father and brother went to fight.

The noise of cannon had been heard since morning, for General Vandermaesen with the other half of the garrison had marched out to meet the enemy, so as to check them in the defiles of the Long Valley and at the crossing of the Pont-Rouge and La-taniers rivers. He had held on with tenacity the whole morning; but, not wishing to risk all his forces at one blow, and fearing besides that the attack which he met might be merely a feint during which the English would advance on Port-Louis by some other route, he had taken with him only eight hundred men, leaving the rest of the garrison, as has been said, and the national volunteers to defend the town. The result was that, after prodigies of courage, his small force, which had to deal with a body of four thousand English and two thousand sepoys, had been obliged to evacuate position after position, taking advantage of every accident of the ground, but soon forced to retire again; so that from the Place d'Armes, where the reserves were, it was possible, though the actual combatants were invisible, to calculate the progress the English were making by the increasing roar of the artillery drawing nearer and nearer every minute. Presently could be distinguished, between the thunders of the big guns, the crackling of musketry. But it must be confessed that this noise, instead of frightening those defenders of Port-Louis who, condemned to inaction by their General's orders, were stationed in the Great Square, only stimulated their bravery; so much so that, while the Regulars were content to bite their lips or swear beneath their moustaches, the Volunteers brandished their weapons, grumbling openly, and crying that, if the order to start was delayed any longer, they would break their ranks and go and fight as skirmishers.

At this moment there was a general shout, at the same time an aide-de-camp galloped up and, without even entering the Place, raising his hat to attract attention, shouted from the end of the street:—

"To your entrenchments; the enemy is here!"

Then he went off as fast as he had come.

At once the drum of the regulars sounded, and the soldiers, forming line with the quickness and precision of long habit, started off at the double.

Whatever rivalry might exist between the Volunteers and the Regulars, the former could not get away with so rapid a dash. Some moments elapsed before the ranks were formed; then as, when they were formed, some led off with the right foot, others with the left, there was a moment of confusion necessitating a halt.

At this moment, seeing a vacant place in the middle of the third file of volunteers, the tall man with the ornamented gun embraced the youngest of his children and, putting him into the arms of the Negro in the blue suit, ran with his eldest boy modestly to occupy the place which the false start of the Volunteers had left vacant.

But, at the approach of the two pariahs, their neighbours on the right and left turned aside, forcing the same movement upon the men next to them, so that the tall man and his son found themselves the centre of circles which went moving from them, just as circles of water retire from the spot at which a stone has been thrown in.

The stout man in Major's epaulettes, who had with great difficulty just got his first file in order, now perceived the disorder into which the third was being thrown; rising on his toes, he shouted to those who were executing the singular manœuvre which we have described:—

"To your ranks, my men! to your ranks!"

But at this repeated order, made in a tone that admitted no reply, a general shout arose:—

"No blacks! no blacks with us!"

This cry the entire battalion echoed with a universal roar.

Then the officer understood the cause of this disorder, and saw in the centre of a large circle the Mulatto who had remained at the "port arms," while his elder son, red with anger, had already fallen back two paces to get away from those who were pushing him back.

On seeing this, the Major passed through the two front ranks which opened to make way for him, and went straight for the insolent fellow who had dared, man of colour as he was, to mix with the whites. When in front of him he looked him up and down with an indignant stare, the man remaining before him upright and motionless as a post:—

"Well! Pierre Munier," said he, "can't you hear, or must you be told twice over, that this is not your place and that you are not wanted here?"

Pierre with his strong right hand might have crushed at a blow the man who spoke thus; but instead of this, he made no reply, only raised his head with a scared look, and, meeting the looks of his questioner, turned away his own in confusion.

This added fuel to the other's anger, and still further roused the man's insolence.

"Come! What are you doing there?" he asked, giving him a push with his open hand.

"Monsieur de Malmédie," answered Munier, "I had hoped that on a day like this difference of colour would disappear in face of the common danger."

"You hoped!" said the Major shrugging his shoulders with a loud chuckle. "You hoped! and what gave you this hope, if you please?"

"The desire that I have to die, if needs be, to save our Island."

"*Our* Island!" muttered the Major, "*our* Island. Because these fellows have plantations like us, they fancy the Island belongs to them."

"The Island belongs to us no more than to you white gentlemen, I am well aware," replied Munier in a timid voice, "but if we stay for such questions at the hour of fighting, it will soon be no longer either yours or ours."

"Enough!" said the Major, stamping his foot to impose silence both by gesture and voice on his interlocutor. "Enough! Are you in command of the National Guard?"

"No, sir, as you very well know," answered Munier; "for when I presented myself, you rejected me."

"Then what do you want?"

"I wanted to follow you as a volunteer."

"Impossible," said the Major.

"Why impossible? Ah! if you would only let me, Mons. de Malmédie."

"Impossible," repeated the Major, drawing himself up. "These gentlemen who are under my orders will have no Mulattos among them."

"No, no blacks," shouted the National Guards with one voice.

"But may I not fight them, sir?" said Munier, letting his arms fall dejectedly by his sides, and with difficulty keeping back the large tears which trembled on his eyelashes.

"Form a corps of coloured men and put yourself at their head, or join this detachment of blacks which is going to follow us."

"But—" murmured Pierre.

"I order you to quit the battalion; I order it," repeated M. de Malmédie, bridling up.

"Come, father, come, and leave these men who are insulting you," said a small voice trembling with anger. And Pierre felt himself pulled back with such force that he retreated a step.

"Yes! Jacques, yes, I will follow you," said he.

"It is not Jacques, father, it is I, Georges."

Munier turned in astonishment.

It was, in fact, the child who had got down from the Negro's arms, and come to give his father this lesson in dignity.

Munier let his head sink on his breast, and uttered a deep sigh. During this time the ranks of the National Guard had reformed, M. de Malmédie resumed his post at the head of the first file, and the regiment set off at increased speed.

Pierre Munier remained alone between his two children, one of whom was red as fire, the other pale as death. He glanced at the red face of Jacques and Georges' pale one, and as if these symptoms were a double reproach to him, exclaimed:—"What would you have, my poor children?—there is no help for it." Jacques was indifferent and philosophical. The first feeling had been painful to him, no doubt; but reflection had come quickly to his aid and consoled him.

"Bah!" he replied to his father, snapping his fingers. "What does it matter to us after all if this silly man despises us? We are richer than he, aren't we, father? And for myself," he added, casting a side glance at the child with the scalloped collar, "let me find his cub of a Henri at a lucky moment, and I will give him a drubbing which he will remember."

"Good, Jacques!" said Pierre Munier, thanking his eldest son for having in some degree relieved his shame by his careless attitude. Then he turned to his younger son, to see if the latter would take the matter as philosophically as the elder.

But Georges remained motionless: all that his father could discover in his stony countenance was an imperceptible smile which contracted his lips: still, imperceptible as it was, that smile had such a suggestion of contempt and pity that, as we sometimes reply to words that have not been uttered, Pierre answered to this smile:—

"But what do you want me to do then?"

And he waited for the child's answer, disquieted by that vague uneasiness which we never confess to ourselves, but which, however, disturbs us when we await, from an inferior, whom we fear in spite of ourselves, his opinion of something we have done.

Georges made no reply; but turning his head towards the extremity of the Great Square, said:—

"Father, the Negroes down there are waiting for a leader."

"Why, you are right, Georges!" cried Jacques joyously, already consoled for his humiliation by the consciousness of his strength, and reasoning, no doubt, as Cæsar did,—It is better to command these than to obey those.

And Munier, yielding to the advice given by his youngest son and the impetus imparted by the other, advanced towards the Negroes, who, engaged in discussing whom to choose as their leader, no sooner perceived the man whom all coloured people in the island looked up to as a father, than they grouped themselves round him as their natural chief, and begged him to lead them to battle.

Then a strange change took place in the man. That feeling of inferiority, which he could not overcome in presence of the whites, disappeared and gave way to a proper estimation of his own merit; his bowed frame drew itself up to its full height; his eyes, which he had kept humbly lowered or wandering vaguely before M. de Malmédie, darted fire; his voice, trembling a moment earlier, assumed an accent of formidable sternness, and it was with a gesture of noble energy that, throwing back his carbine slung over his shoulder, he drew his sword, and, extending his sinewy arm towards the enemy, cried "Forward!"

Then, taking a last look at his youngest child, who had returned to the protection of the Negro in the blue suit and, filled with pride and pleasure, was clapping his hands, Pierre disappeared with his black company round the corner of the same street by which the Regulars and National Guards had just disappeared, shouting once again to the Negro in the blue jacket:—"Télémaque, look after my son!"

The line of defence consisted of three divisions. On the left the Fanfaron bastion, situated on the edge of the sea and armed with eighteen cannon; in the centre the entrenchment, properly so called, lined with twenty-four field guns; and, on the right, the Dumas battery, protected by six guns only.

The victorious enemy, after having advanced at first in three columns on the three different points, abandoned the two first, the strength of which they perceived, so as to concentrate upon the third, which was not only, as has been said, the weakest, but which further was only defended by the National Artillery. However, contrary to all expectation, at the sight of the compact mass which marched on them with the terrible regularity of British discipline, this martial band of young men, instead of being alarmed, ran to their posts, manœuvring with the speed and the skill of veteran soldiers, with a fire so well maintained and directed that the enemy thought themselves mistaken as to the strength of the battery and the men who served it; still, they continued to advance, for the deadlier the battery became, the more imperative it was to silence its fire. But then the confounded battery got angry, and like a juggler who makes us forget one astounding trick by performing another still more astounding, it redoubled its volleys, making shot follow grape, and grape common shot, with such rapidity that disorder began to spread in the hostile ranks. At the same time, and as the British had come within musket-shot, the rifle discharge in its turn began to splutter, so that the enemy, seeing their ranks thinned by cannon shot and whole files swept away by musket fire, astonished by a resistance as vigorous as it was unexpected, wavered and drew back.

By order of the General in command the Regulars and the National Battalion who had combined on the threatened point now moved off, one to the left, the other to the right, and charged with fixed bayonets on the enemy's flanks, while the formidable battery continued to pound him in front. The Regulars carried out their manœuvre with their customary precision, fell upon the British, cut through their ranks and increased the disorder. But, whether carried away by their courage, or that they executed the given order clumsily, the National Guards, commanded by M. de Malmédie, instead of falling upon the left flank and making an attack parallel to that executed by the Regulars, made a wrong movement and encountered the British front. Consequently the battery was obliged to cease firing, and as it was this fire especially that frightened the enemy, who now had only to deal with men inferior in number to themselves, they regained courage and turned on the Nationals, who, to their credit be it said, sustained the shock without giving way a single yard. However, this resistance could not last on the part of these brave fellows placed between an enemy better disciplined than themselves and ten times superior in numbers, and the battery which was forced to be silent to avoid overwhelming them; at each moment they lost so many men that they began to give way. Soon, by a skilful movement, the British left outflanked the right of the National Battalion now on the point of being surrounded and who, too inexperienced to adopt the formation in square, were looked upon as lost. The British, in fact, continued their progressive movement and, like a rising tide were about to surround this island of men with their waves, when suddenly shouts of "France! France!" resounded in the rear of the enemy. This was followed by a fearful discharge, succeeded by a silence more dreadful than the discharge itself.

A strange undulation passed through the enemy's rear and was felt even in their front ranks; red-coats bent under a vigorous bayonet charge like ripe ears beneath the mower's sickle; it was now their turn to be surrounded, to have to face front, right and left. But the newly-arrived reinforcement gave them no respite, but kept on charging, so that at the end of ten minutes they had opened a path through a bloody gap to the unlucky battalion and extricated it. Then, seeing that they had accomplished their object, the new arrivals fell back, wheeled to the left with a circular movement, and charged the enemy's flank. Malmédie, on his side, imitating instinctively the same manœuvre, had given a similar impulse to his battalion, so that the battery, seeing itself unmasked, lost no time, and bursting forth once more aided the efforts of this triple attack, belching torrents of grape-shot on the enemy. From this point victory decided in favour of the French.

Then Malmédie, feeling himself out of danger, glanced at his liberators, whom he had already partly seen, but hesitated to acknowledge, so much did it go against the grain to owe his safety to such men. It was, indeed, the corps of blacks, so despised by him, that had followed in his wake and joined him at such an opportune moment, and at their head Pierre Munier, who, seeing Malmédie surrounded by the British who thus presented their backs to him, had with his three hundred men caught them in the rear and overthrown them; it was Munier who, after having planned this movement with the genius of a general, had carried it out with the courage of a soldier, and who at this moment finding himself in a position where he need fear nothing except death, fought in front of all, erect at his full height, his eyes flashing, his nostrils dilated, his forehead bare, his hair floating in the wind, enthusiastic, daring, sublime. In short, it was Munier's voice that was raised from time to time in the midst of the fighting, drowning all the noise of battle to shout "Forward!"

Then, as to follow him was to advance, and as the disorder in the British ranks increased, the cry was heard "Comrades, make for the flag!" He was seen to hurl himself into the midst of a group of British, fall, spring up again, plunge into their ranks, and after an instant reappear with torn clothes and bleeding forehead, but with the flag in his hand.

At this moment the General, fearing that the victors might advance too far in pursuit of the British and fall into a trap, gave the order to fall back. The Regulars obeyed first, bringing in the prisoners, the National Guard carrying away the dead; the black Volunteers in the rear, surrounding their flag.

The whole island had rushed to the port, crowding to see the victors, for the inhabitants of Port-Louis thought in their ignorance that the entire army of the enemy had been engaged, and hoped that the British, after being repulsed so vigorously, would not return to the charge, so, as each corps passed, they were greeted with fresh hurrahs!; all were proud, all victorious, all beside themselves. An unexpected happiness fills their hearts, an unhoped for success turns their heads; the inhabitants had expected to make some resistance, but not to gain a victory: so, when they saw victory so completely and entirely theirs, men, women, veterans and children swore with one mouth that they would work at the entrenchments and die, if needs be, for their defence. Excellent promises, no doubt, and made by all with the intention of keeping them, but not worth, by a great deal, an extra regiment, if an extra regiment could have arrived!

But, amid this general ovation, no object attracted so much notice as the British flag and the man who had taken it; there were endless cries of astonishment round Munier and his trophy, to which the blacks replied by blustering remarks, while their leader, becoming once more the humble Mulatto with whom we are acquainted, satisfied the questions put by each with a timid politeness. Standing near the conqueror, and leaning on his double-barrelled gun, which had not been dumb during the engagement and the bayonet of which was stained with blood, Jacques carried his head proudly, while Georges, who had escaped from Télémaque and joined his father at the port, convulsively clasped his powerful hand and vainly tried to check the tears of joy which fell from his eyes in spite of himself. Close by Munier was M. de Malmédie, no less curled and bedecked than when he started, but with his tie torn, his frill in rags and covered with sweat and dirt; he, too, was surrounded and congratulated by his family; but the congratulations he received were such as are offered to a man who has escaped a danger, not the praises lavished on a victor. So he appeared rather embarrassed by the chorus of affecting solicitude, and, to put a good face on it, was asking loudly where his son Henri and his Negro Bijou were, when he saw them both appear making their way through the crowd, Henri to throw himself into his father's arms, and Bijou to congratulate his master.

At this moment, some one came to tell Munier that a Negro who had fought under him and received a mortal wound, having been carried to a house near the port, wished to see him. Pierre looked round in search of Jacques to entrust him with his flag, but Jacques had discovered his friend the dog again, who in his turn had come with the rest to offer his compliments; he had placed his gun on the ground, and the child getting the better of the man, he and the dog were rolling over and over, some fifty yards off. Georges, seeing his father's difficulty, stretched out his hand, saying:—

"Give it me, father; I will take care of it for you."

Pierre smiled, and believing that none would dare to touch the glorious trophy which belonged to him alone, kissed Georges on the forehead, handed him the flag, which the child with great difficulty held upright by clasping his hands on his breast, and went off to the house where the sufferings of one of his Volunteers claimed his presence.

Georges remained alone; but the child felt instinctively that, though alone, he was not isolated; his father's fame protected him, and his eyes beaming with pride he looked at the crowd that surrounded him; this bright and happy glance then met that of the child with the embroidered collar, and became disdainful. The latter, on his part, eyed Georges with envy, asking himself no doubt why his father too had not taken a flag. This question naturally led him doubtless to say to himself, that, failing a flag of his own, he must monopolise another's. For, rudely approaching Georges, who, though he saw his hostile purpose, did not draw back a step, he said:—

"Give me that."

"What?" asked Georges.

"That flag," replied Henri.

"This flag is not yours, it's my father's."

"What has that got to do with me? I want it!"

"You shall not have it."

The child with the embroidered collar then put out his hand to snatch the staff of the flag, an action to which Georges only replied by tightening his lips, becoming paler than usual, and drawing back a step. But this act only encouraged Henri, who, like all spoilt children, thought he had but to ask to get; he stepped forward, and this time laid his plans so well that he grasped the stick, shouting loudly with his little angry voice:—

"I tell you I want it."

"And I tell you you shan't have it," repeated Georges, pushing him back with one hand, while with the other he continued to press the captured flag against his chest.

"Ah! you nigger, you! how dare you touch me?" cried Henri. "Well, you will see." And, drawing his little sword from the scabbard before Georges had time to defend himself, he struck him with all his strength on the top of the forehead. The blood at once gushed from the wound and trickled down the boy's face.

"Coward!" said Georges coldly.

Exasperated by this insult, Henri was about to repeat the blow, when Jacques, reaching his brother at one bound, sent the aggressor flying ten yards by a vigorous blow in the middle of his face, and, jumping on the sword which the latter had let fall in the struggle, broke it into three or four pieces, spat on it, and tossed the pieces at him.

It was now the turn of the boy with the embroidered collar to feel the blood run down his face, but *he* had lost his blood not from a sword blow, but from a blow with the fist.

All this had passed so rapidly that neither M. de Malmédie, who, as we have said, was engaged a few yards off in receiving the congratulations of his family, nor Munier, who was coming from the house where the Negro had just breathed his last, had time to anticipate it. They were merely spectators of the catastrophe, and ran up both at once; Pierre panting, troubled and trembling; Malmédie red with anger and choking with arrogance. They met in front of Georges.

"Did you see," cried M. de Malmédie, "what happened just now?"

"Alas! yes, M. de Malmédie," answered Pierre, "and, believe me, had I been there, this would not have taken place."

"Meanwhile, sir," cried M. de Malmédie, "your son laid his hand on mine. A Mulatto's son has dared to touch a white man's son."

"I am distressed at what has just taken place, M. de Malmédie," stammered the poor father, "and humbly offer my apologies."

"Your apologies, sir," replied the angry settler, bridling up as the other humbled himself; "do you think your apologies are sufficient?"

"What more can I do, sir?"

"What can you do?" repeated Malmédie, himself at a loss to name the satisfaction he wished to obtain; "you can have that wretch who struck my son whipped."

"Have me whipped?" said Jacques, picking up his double-barrelled gun and changing from child to man again. "Well, come and meddle with me yourself, M. de Malmédie."

"Hush! Jacques; hush, my son," cried Pierre.

"Excuse me, father," said Jacques, "but I am right, and I will not be silent. M. Henri struck my brother, who was doing nothing to him, with his sword; and I struck M. Henri with my fist. So M. Henri is wrong, and I am right."

"Struck my son with his sword, my Georges. Georges, dear child," cried Munier, going towards his son, "is it true that you are wounded?"

"It's nothing, father," said Georges.

"What! nothing?" cried Pierre Munier; "why! your forehead is cut open. Look, sir," he resumed, turning to M. de Malmédie, "Jacques spoke the truth; your son has almost killed mine."

Malmédie turned towards Henri, and, as there was no means of resisting the evidence, inquired:—

"Come, Henri, how did the thing happen?"

"Papa," said Henri, "it is not my fault; I wanted the flag to bring it to you, and that wretch wouldn't give it me."

"And why wouldn't you give my son the flag, you little rascal?" asked M. de Malmédie.

"Because the flag isn't yours, or your son's, or anybody's, but my father's."

"Well?" asked Malmédie, continuing to question his son.

"Well, when I saw he wouldn't give it me, I tried to take it. Then this brute came up and struck me in the face with his fist."

"Then that is what happened?"

"Yes, father."

"He is lying," said Jacques, "and I only struck him when I saw my brother's blood flowing; but for that, I should never have hit him."

"Silence, you villain!" cried M. de Malmédie. Then going up to Georges, he said:—

"Give me the flag."

But Georges, instead of obeying this order, stepped back once more, pressing the flag to his breast with all his might.

"Give me the flag," repeated Malmédie in a threatening tone which showed that, if his demand were not complied with, he would resort to the utmost extremities.

"But, sir," muttered Pierre, "it was I who took the flag from the British."

"I know it, sir, but it shall not be said that a Mulatto has coped with a man like me with impunity. Give me the flag."

"But, sir"—

"I will have it, I order it; obey your officer."

It entered Pierre's head to answer, "You are not my officer, sir, since you wouldn't have me as your soldier"; but the words died upon his lips; his habitual humility got the better of his courage. He sighed; and though obedience to such an unjust order grieved him, he himself took the flag from Georges, who ceased to offer any resistance, and handed it to the Major, who walked off laden with his stolen trophy.

It was incredible, strange, miserable, to see a man of a nature so rich, vigorous and determined, yield without resistance to that other nature so vulgar, dull, mean, common and poor, yet so it was; and, what is still more extraordinary, the thing surprised nobody, for it happened every day in the colonies, not in similar, but in parallel circumstances. So, accustomed from infancy to respect the white as men of a superior race, Munier had all his life let himself be crushed by that aristocracy of colour to which he had just yielded once more without even attempting to resist. He resembles those heroes who hold their heads high in the face of grape shot, and bend the knee to a prejudice. The lion attacks man, the terrestrial image of God, and flees in alarm when he hears the cock crow.

As for Georges, who had not shed a tear when he saw his blood trickling down, he burst into sobs on finding his hands empty in presence of his father, who looked at him sadly without even trying to comfort him.

Jacques, for his part, bit his fists with rage, and vowed to be avenged one day on Henri, M. de Malmédie and all the whites.

Scarcely ten minutes after the scene which we have just related, a messenger covered with dust rushed up announcing that the British, to the number of ten thousand, were advancing by the Williams plains and the Little River; then, almost immediately, the look-out signalled the arrival of a fresh British squadron which, anchoring in the bay of Grande-Rivière, landed five thousand men on the coast. Finally, it was ascertained at the same time that the division repulsed in the morning had rallied on the banks of the Rivière des Lataniers, and was ready to march again upon Port Louis, combining its movements with the two other invading corps who were advancing, one by Curtois Bay, the other by the Réduit. There were no means of resisting such a force; so, when some despairing voices, appealing to the oath taken in the morning to conquer or die, demanded fight, the Captain-General replied by disbanding the National Guard and the Volunteers, and declaring that, armed with full powers from his Majesty the Emperor Napoleon, he was about to treat with the British for the surrender of the town.

Only madmen could have tried to combat such a step; twenty-five thousand men surrounded less than four thousand; accordingly, on the order of the Captain-General every one went home, so that the town remained occupied only by the Regulars. On the night of the 2nd of December the capitulation was concluded and signed; at five a.m. it was approved and exchanged; the same day the enemy occupied the lines; on the morrow he took possession of the town and harbour.

Eight hours afterwards the captured French squadron left the harbour under full sail, carrying the whole of the garrison, like a poor family driven from the paternal roof; so long as the last flutter of the last flag could be seen, the crowd remained on the quay; but when the last frigate had disappeared, every one went home in gloom and silence. Two men remained alone and were the last to leave the harbour, the Mulatto Pierre Munier and the Negro Télémaque.

"M. Munier, we will climb the hill; we shall still be able to see Masters Jacques and Georges."

"Yes, you are right, my good Télémaque," cried Pierre Munier, "and if we do not see *them*, we shall at least see the ship that carries them."

And Pierre Munier, dashing off with the rapidity of a young man, in an instant had climbed the hill of the Discovery, from the height of which he could follow with his eyes, until it grew dark, not his *sons*, for the distance, as he had foreseen, was too great for him to distinguish them any longer, but the frigate *Bellona* on board which they had embarked.

In fact, Pierre Munier had resolved, cost him what it might, to sever himself from his children, and was sending them to France under the protection of the worthy General Decaen. Jacques and Georges started then for Paris with recommendations to two or three of the richest merchants in the capital, with whom Pierre Munier had for a long time had business relations. The pretext for their departure was to get their education. The real cause of their absence was the very evident hatred shown towards both of them by M. de Malmédie since the day of the flag incident, a hatred on account of which their poor father trembled, especially with their known disposition, lest they should become the victims.

As for Henri, his mother was too fond of him to part from him. Besides, what did he want to learn? unless it was that every coloured man was born to respect and obey him.

Well! as we have seen, that was a thing Henri had already learned by heart.

23

From Beyond the Seas

Theodor Storm

The German author Theodor Storm (1817–1888) practiced law and served as a magistrate while writing poetry and novellas that were imbued with a sense of yearning for an idyllic past and are still highly regarded for their realism and psychological insight. Storm's major works include the novellas *Immensee* (1850), *Aquis submersus* (1875), and *Der Schimmelreiter* (1888). His novella of interracial love, *From Beyond the Seas* (1863–64), is presented here in its first English translation by Judith Ryan. In a letter to Turgenev, Storm wondered whether the novella should not have a tragic ending, but never wrote one for it.

The hotel room had not been made more comfortable by the packed bags. My cousin, a young architect who had been living in the room for two days, paced silently up and down, smoking his cigar, like someone who is impatient to fill empty time.—It was a mild September night, and the stars shone through the open window; on the street below, the big city noise and rattling of carriages had died down, and we could hear the night air blowing through the mast-tops and the ropes of the ships in the harbor.

"When do you have to leave, Alfred?" I asked.

"The boat that takes me on board goes at 3 o'clock."

"Don't you want to rest for a few hours first?"

He shook his head.

"Then let me stay with you. I'll catch up on my sleep tomorrow on the carriage ride home. And if you'd like to, tell me—about her! I don't know her, you know—and tell me how everything came to pass."

Alfred closed the window and turned the lamplight higher until it was completely light in the room. "Sit down and be patient," he said, "and you shall know all."

"Even as a twelve-year-old boy," he began, once we had sat down opposite each other, "I lived with her in my parents' house. She was probably a few years younger than I. At the time, her father lived on one of the little islands in the West Indies, where, by luck and skill he had transformed himself from a penniless merchant into a rich plantation owner. He had sent his daughter to Germany a few years earlier to have her educated in the customs of his homeland; but the school she had been attending had been disbanded after the death of its headmistress, and until a new one was found, she was to stay in the care of my parents. Long before I set eyes on her, my fantasy was occupied with her, especially when my mother actually got a little room next to my parents' bedroom ready for her. For there was a mystery about the girl. Not just that she came from another part of the world and that she was the daughter of a planter, a group of people I knew from my picture books only as fabulously rich and very cruel masters;—I also knew that her mother was not married to her father. I hadn't been able to find out more about the mother, so I liked to imagine her as a beautiful, ebony black Negress with strands of pearls in her hair and bright metal bracelets on her arms.

"At last, one evening in February, a carriage stopped before the front steps of our house. A little old gentleman with white hair got out first; he was the clerk of a merchant company friendly with her father, the man who was to deliver her to her new guardians. Soon after, he lifted from the carriage a small girl, cloaked in many shawls and coats, and led her with a certain solemnity into our house, giving her, in an elegant little speech, into the protection of the senator and his wife.—But how amazed I was when she removed her veils; she was not black, not even brown; to my eyes, she seemed whiter than any other girl I knew. I can still see her looking around with the widest eyes as she let my mother take the fur-trimmed travel coat from her shoulders. When her hat and gloves had also been taken off and the delicate little figure now stood peeled of all her travel garb, she stretched out her hand to my mother and said somewhat timidly, "Are you my aunt?" But as my mother brushed the child's coal-black locks back from her forehead, took her in her arms and kissed her, I saw with astonishment how passionately the child responded to her fondling. Soon my mother drew me to her, too. "And that's my boy!" she said. "Look at him, Jenny; he has a kind face, but he's too wild, and so it's a good thing he's getting a girl for a playmate now."

Jenny looked around and gave me her hand; but at the same time, she gave me such a mischievous look, as if she wanted to say, "We understand each other. Good day, comrade!"

And so it turned out to be in the following days: no tree was too high, no leap too daring for this slight, delicate-limbed child. She was almost always part of our boyish games, and without our noticing it, she ruled over all of us, less, no doubt, because of her boldness than her beauty. Sometimes she swept us up in such a truly wild frenzy that my father was rousted out of his study by the noise, and put an end to all the fun with a pitiless command. While Jenny's dealings with my mother became closer and closer, she never attained an intimate relationship with him; he didn't know how to handle children; and he seemed to regard this strange being with a skeptical gaze. She had just as little success with Aunt Josephine, that honorable but somewhat stern old maid, who checked in a quite damnable way on whether we had finished our homework. And in this relationship, where Jenny was not kept in her place by too much respect, a continual little guerrilla war soon sprang up. At times, our dignified aunt could scarcely go ten paces without falling, to her horror, into one or another amusing practical joke.

But she didn't just do crazy things; the two of us could also talk together. She knew all kinds of stories and fairy-tales, which she recounted with shining eyes and lively gestures. Most of them she had probably learned at boarding school, but one or two, I now think, came from her old homeland. And so it was that we could often be seen sitting together in the evening dusk on the attic stairs or in the big travel trunk. The more secretly we created our fairy-tale hall, the more vividly all the wondrous, sweet figures, the enchanted monsters, Snow White or Frau Holle appeared before our imagination. Our preference for hidden story-telling spaces led us to discover one new hiding place after another; in fact, I recall that in the end we had chosen for this purpose a big empty barrel in a store-room not far from my father's study. In this most holy of places we huddled together as well as we could in the evening when I had finished work with my tutor. We held my little lamp, furnished with a few candle ends, on our laps and pushed a large board that had lain on top of the barrel over the opening from inside, so that we were sitting together as if in a closed parlor. When people who came to see my father in the evening heard murmuring coming from the barrel and saw, perhaps, a few rays of light coming from inside, our old clerk, whose room was opposite, hardly knew how to answer their questions about this peculiar phenomenon. When our candle ends had burned down or we heard the maid calling us from the gate of the yard, we climbed out of the barrel as stealthily as martens and slipped into our bedrooms before my father left his study.

We never spoke of her parents, though, especially not of her mother, except on one Sunday morning.—I was playing cops and robbers with my little friends. To the side of our house behind the garden was a whole row of factory buildings from my grandfather's time that now stood empty and were full of cellars and little rooms and layers of attics on top of each other. The other robbers had all hidden in this labyrinth; only I, who of course was one of them, was now standing indecisively in the garden. I thought of Jenny, who usually joined in this game and who, clambering over roofs and jumping through trapdoors, was no less wild than the wildest robbers. But today Aunt Josephine had forced her to write a school essay, and I knew that she was sitting there in the back room whose windows gave onto the garden. And while I could hear the leader of the cops haranguing his troops beneath the entrance gate to the yard, I carefully crept along the garden wall toward the house and, hidden by a jasmine bush, looked into the room.

Jenny was sitting over her composition book, her arms propped up on the table; but her thoughts didn't seem to be with her work; for, while one hand lay buried in her curly black hair, the other was smashing her poor goose quill against the table top.—Next to her writing utensils lay Aunt Josephine's familiar silver needle box and not far from it a fairly strong magnet that belonged to me. Suddenly, as she gazed out over it as if bored, a bold ray of light shot out from her dark eyes; the practical use of these two things seemed to take shape in her little head. Her lazy self-forgetfulness turned into the most diligent busy-ness. She shook the whole contents of Aunt Josephine's holy of holies out onto the table; then she took the magnet and began to stroke each needle with it assiduously. She sat there like a little black devil with her black eyes; she seemed to anticipate the angry astonishment of the old maid when she next pulled her genuine English sewing needles out of the box as a mysteriously united bundle. And as she worked more and more diligently at her maliciously gleeful task, a scarcely repressed laugh played continually about her lips, so that her little white teeth gleamed out between her red lips.

I knocked softly on the windowpane; for the signal horn of the soldiers marching off was sounding in the courtyard. She started; but when she recognized her old playmate, she nodded to me and hastily stuffed the whole mess into Aunt Josephine's needle box. Then she pushed her black hair behind her ears and came toward me on tiptoes. "Jenny," I said, "we're playing robbers!"

She opened the window cautiously. "Who are the robbers, Alfred?"

"You and I; the others are already in their hiding place."

"Wait a moment!" And she crept back quietly and pushed a bolt before the door that separated the room from the living room. "Farewell, Aunt Josephine!"—Soon she was back again, and with a light bound she stood outside.

It was a splendid spring day; garden and yard were full of sunshine. The old pear trees that stretched their branches out high up near the roofs of the buildings were covered with white blossoms, between which the young, light green leaves were emerging all over; but down here in the grove the leaves were sprouting only sparsely from the bushes. Jenny's white dress might betray us. I took her hand and pulled her through the bushes, close beside the garden wall, and while we heard the tramping of the cops dying away in a corridor on the front side of the factory building, we slipped through a door that led from the garden into the most remote annex, in the uppermost attic of which I had set up my dovecote. Once we were standing on the dimly lit steps, we took a breath for a moment; we had made a lucky escape. But we went up higher; into the first and then into the second attic; Jenny going ahead, with me hardly able to follow; but I was delighted—that I well remember—to see how her lithe little feet flew almost noiselessly ahead of me up the stairs. When we had reached the last attic, we let the trapdoor down carefully and shoved a large rectangular block of wood onto it that, for who knows what reason, had been left in the obscure attic. For a moment we heard the fluttering of the doves flying in and out of their cage next door; then we sat down together on our wooden block, and Jenny rested her little head in her hand, her curly hair hanging down over her face.

"You must be tired, Jenny," I asked.

She took my hand and laid it on her breast. "Just feel how it's beating!" she said.

As I looked down involuntarily at the slender white little fingers that held mine captive, something seemed different to me from usual. And suddenly, while I was reflecting on this, I saw what it was. The little crescent moons at the root of her fingernails were not lighter, as they are in the rest of us, but bluish and darker than the other part of the nail. At that time I hadn't yet read that this was a sign of those pariahs of the American states who are often so beautiful but in whose veins as little as a single drop of black slave blood flows; but it startled me, and I couldn't keep my eyes off it.

Finally, she must have noticed, for she asked me, "What are you staring at on my hands?"

I recall that I felt very embarrassed at this question. "Just look!" I said, placing her fingers next to one another so that the otherwise rose red nails looked like a string of pearls.

She didn't know what I meant.

"Why do you have those little dark moons?" I continued.

She looked closely at her hand and compared it with mine, which I held next to it. "I don't know," she said then; "in St. Croix everyone has that. My mother, I think, had even darker ones."—

From far away, out of the depth of some hidden cellar, we heard the noise of the cops and robbers, who must have begun to fight, but they were still very distant from our place of refuge. My thoughts took yet another turning. "Why didn't you stay with your mother?" I asked.

She rested her head in her hands again. "I think I was supposed to get an education," she said, indifferently.

"Couldn't you get one there?"

She shook her head. "Papa says that people speak so badly there."

It was very silent in our attic and almost dark, for the little windows were covered with spider webs; only in front of us, through a hole left by a roof tile that had been removed, a little sunshine broke through, as much as could steal in around a blossoming twig of the big pear tree. Jenny sat silently beside me; I observed her little face; it was very pale, but with strange dark shadows under her eyes.

Suddenly her lips parted and she laughed quite loudly to herself. I laughed too; but then I asked, "What are you laughing about?"

"She couldn't stand Papa!" she said.

"Who couldn't?"

"Mama's long-tailed monkey!"

"Wasn't your father kind to her?"

"Yes, he was!—I don't know.—She always stole his diamond tie pin from his jabot when he came to visit us."

"Didn't your papa live with you?"

She shook her head. "He often came to visit in the evening; he lived in a big house in town. Mama told me about it, but I was never in it."

"Well!—Where did you live, you and your mother?"

"We had a very beautiful place! Outside the city. The house was in a garden high above the large bay; a gallery with columns was in the front; I often sat on it with Mama: we could see all the ships come in."—She was silent for a moment. "Oh, she's very beautiful, my Mama!" she said proudly. Then her voice fell and she added, almost sadly, "She had such lovely black curls over her forehead!" And having said this, she broke into bitter tears.

After a while we could hear the noise and the tin bugles of the cops; they seemed to have stopped on the stairs to the first attic and to be taking counsel. I leaped up and looked down. We hadn't thought of that: there was no exit. "We'll have to defend ourselves," I said softly, "for we're trapped."

Jenny had soon dried her tears. "Not yet, Alfred!" And she pointed to the opening in the roof opposite us. "You have to go out that way, and then into the garden by means of the pear tree."

"That won't work; I can't leave you behind."

"Oh," she cried, "they mustn't catch me!" So saying, she looked up toward the darkest corner of the roof. "Quick, help me! I'll sit up there on the beam; then I'll see them racing around below!"

The idea was a good one; and after a few moments she had climbed up, with my help, on the studs and beams, and was sitting in the dark on the little crossbeam beneath the highest point of the roof. "Can you see me?" she called, as I stood below once more.

"Yes, I can see your white hand."

"Can you still see it?"

"No, now I can't see anything."

"Then make your getaway!"

But the opening was too narrow. I ripped another tile out and pushed my way through; for our pursuers were already crowding with loud cries beneath the trapdoor to our attic, and I could hear the heavy wooden block moving.

How it happened, I don't know, but scarcely was I outside than I felt the tiles slipping under me; I started to slide, the tree branches whipped against my face, there was a rustling sound all around me; as I slid unstoppably lower and lower, I caught hold of a branch at random, went down it in a rush while a few roof tiles fell down past me into the garden, and I finally fell to the ground with such a rude crash that I lay there almost as if unconscious.

When I looked up, I saw high up above me between the blossoming branches the large terrified eyes of the lovely child bending down to me from the damaged roof. To give her a sign of life, or perhaps rather of my courage, I let out a loud laugh, though not without effort; but then when I turned my head I was looking into the stern face of my father, who seemed to be looking at me more with anger than concern; Aunt Josephine, too, appeared in the distance, her inevitable knitting in hands frozen by fright. I still can't grasp how Jenny came down to us so quickly. She had thrown herself upon me and begun to stroke my hair diligently from face and temples; but at the same moment when my father stretched out his hand with a violent gesture, perhaps to help me up from the ground rather roughly, she leaped up as if on a spring. "No," she cried, raising her whole little body, "don't touch him!" She held her fist before his face; in the depths of her eyes something sparkling seemed about to shoot forth.

My father, stepping back a pace, pinched his lips together as he was accustomed to do and placed his hands behind his back; then he turned away and went back to his study mumbling to himself. It seemed to me as if he were saying, "we have to put an end to this." When my mother came into the garden, Jenny ran up to her and I saw the gentle woman press in both her arms the trembling body of the passionate child with quiet words that I couldn't hear.

From that day on—I thought—an unconscious feeling of belonging and reciprocal responsibility had arisen in both of us; a seed had been planted that slumbered for many years, but from which then, in the rays of a moonlit night, the blue flower of fairy tale rose up, the flower whose scent now intoxicates me.

How can I describe those small, intangible things! In the very first days after that, when my father asked me to summon the maid at lunch time, Jenny had most certainly already pulled the bell cord before he had quite finished uttering the request; just so that my limping gait would not recall the fatal incident.

But the beautiful days were over; the horrifying news came that a new boarding school had been found for Jenny, and soon the day of parting came.—I can still remember how, sitting in our big pear tree in a vague state of sadness and anger, I ripped off one unripe pear after another and threw them at the innocent attic windows of our neighbor until I heard a sound down below and, looking down, saw Jenny in her Nanking travel coat climbing up to me one branch after another. Once she had climbed up, she put her arm around a branch; then she took a little ring out of her pocket and put it on my hand. She didn't say a word, but simply looked at me extremely sadly with her large eyes. With the awkwardness of a growing boy, I let it happen, and while I was looking, half embarrassed, at my decorated finger, Jenny had disappeared again just as silently as she had come. Not until then did I get down from my tree so rapidly that I almost fell again. As I came out into the street from the house, however, the carriage was just driving off, and I saw only a little white handkerchief waving back at us.

There I stood, suddenly overwhelmed by sorrow and longing, and looked at my little souvenir. It was a ring of tortoise shell set in gold. I did not know that Jenny had given me the most cherished thing she possessed at that time.

While he was telling the story, Alfred had put away his cigar. "You're not smoking!" he said; "but I can't watch you sitting there so idly, you must have a distraction for your boredom." With these words he opened a small collection of bottles that was standing next to his suitcase; and soon I was holding in my hand a fine wine glass containing an aromatic drink. "Wine from Alicante!" said Alfred; "and here are figs, too, packed in wild thyme! I know that, along with the original inventor of hygiene, you love anything sweet and delicious. These are presents from Jenny's father; he packed them for me himself when I left his house a few days ago."

"You haven't mentioned your older brother," I observed, when Alfred had sat back down with me.

"My brother Hans," Alfred replied, "was away from home at an agricultural school; but he got to know Jenny later, as his wife was with her at a boarding school where Jenny stayed after she had finished her formal education.—I myself didn't see her again until ten years later.

It was last June. As you know, I had constructed the small basilica for that rich countess in her village and in the end had contracted the typhoid that was prevalent there. I was well cared for; but I was far from home, and the man with the long bony arms had stretched out sharply for me.—At the time, my mother was visiting my brother on his estate, leaving my father under Aunt Josephine's care; my mother had become ill herself and, to her own distress, had had to leave the care of her son to others. But now both of us were almost well again, and in the next days I was to begin my journey home. I had not yet seen my brother's estate. He had bought it shortly before his marriage from the property of a deceased man whose ancestor, a rich French immigrant, had built the manor house and laid out the park that surrounded it in the magnificent fashion of Lenôtre. As my mother wrote, a large part of it, what was known as the pleasure arbor, was in good condition; even some of those gracious statues for which the beautiful ladies of Louis XV's court had posed as models were still standing here and there beside ponds and in quiet corners between the high walls of greenery as if in bewitched solitude.

Shortly before my departure a letter came from my cheerful sister-in-law. "If you come soon," she wrote, "we can read children's stories together. I have living pictures to go with them; one of them depicts a robber bride: she has a beautiful pale face and raven black hair. Her head is bent, and she is looking at her ring finger, for that's where the ring used to be that she once gave the faithless robber." I leaped up, the letter in my hand, and rummaged among my things for a little ivory case in which I kept all kinds of small treasures. There was Jenny's ring. A black band was attached to it; for, as one can readily understand, I had kept the ring in the early time after that parting quite secretly next to my heart. Then it joined the other rarities I had long kept in the little case. Now, as if it could not be otherwise, I did what I had done as a boy; with a smile that laughed at myself and excused myself at the same time, I hung the ring once more around my neck.

"On your return trip"—Alfred interrupted himself—"you shouldn't fail to make the small detour! The estate is only a mile from here; and, as Hans tells me, you've promised to visit him for some time. You would find it, indeed, just as my mother described it.—"

It was an afternoon at the end of July when I drove out of the sun of the open road into the shade of the chestnut avenue that leads up to the main house; and soon the carriage stopped in front of a manor-like building built in what is known as the "commode" style, overlaid with an excess of ornamentation, but which in its protruding profiles and deep shadow-casting relief made an impression on me of magnificent ancient splendor. Hans and Greta greeted me on the steps. As we passed through the spacious hall, I was asked to speak softly, since our mother was having her afternoon rest.

We had entered a large, light room opposite the front door. Two open door panels led onto a terrace; below this, such an extensive lawn spread out that only a loud call could reach us from any of its sides. Everywhere in the green surface were lush groups of high bush and lower growing roses, which were now in full bloom and filled the air with pleasant scents. Behind it was a bushy part which, like the roses, had clearly been planted in recent times; beyond it, and fairly far off in the distance, rose the original owner's "pleasure arbor," with its steep leafy walls and regular shaping, extending the whole width of the garden. All this lay before me in the bright midday sun.

"What do you say to our paradise?" asked the young woman.

"What do I say, Greta?—How long has your husband owned the property?"

"I think since two years ago this May."

"And that practical farming man puts up with such a waste of space?"

"Go on, don't act as if you had the monopoly on poetry!"

My brother laughed. "But he's right, Greta!—The thing is, Alfred, I'm not allowed to alter these splendors; that's laid down in the contract."

"Thank goodness!"

"Not in my view.—In the middle of a small reflecting pond there's a Venus in the purest Louis XV style; I could have sold it for a goodly sum; but—as I said!"

At this moment, Greta took my hand. "Turn around!" she said.

And on the threshold opposite stood the figure of a girl in a white dress whom I couldn't fail to recognize. Those were the strange eyes of the West Indian planter's daughter; but her black hair, which used to be so hard to control, was now gathered into a shining bun that seemed almost too heavy for her delicate neck.

I went toward her; but before I could open my mouth, my merry sister-in-law had stepped between us. "Stop for a moment!" she cried. "I can see formal address, and 'Miss Jenny,' and all kinds of impossible titles on the tip of your tongue; and that disturbs my family feelings. So first of all, remember the old pear tree!"

Jenny put one hand over her friend's mouth and held the other out to me. "Welcome, Alfred!" she said.

I hadn't heard her voice for many years; so I was all the more struck by the peculiar accent with which she spoke my name, just as she had in the past. "Thank you, Jenny," I said, "that sounds just as it did in our childhood; but you must not have uttered that name for a long time."

"I have met no other Alfred," she replied, "and you have always avoided me."

Before I could respond to this reproach, Greta had separated us.

"That's enough," she exclaimed. "And now, Jenny, help me get the coffee; for he has had a long journey, and our mother will be here soon."

My reunion with the latter, when she appeared, was very moving. She had given up her son for lost; now she held him bodily in her arms, and fondled him and stroked his cheek as if he were a little child. As I straightened up to lead my mother to an easy chair, I saw Jenny leaning against a cupboard, pale and brimming with tears. As we went by, she started; a china bowl that she was holding fell onto the floor and broke. "Forgive me, forgive me, sweet Greta!" she cried and clasped her arms around her friend.

Greta led her gently out of the room.

My brother smiled. "Things will boil over in a minute!" he said.

"She has an empathetic heart, Hans," my mother observed, gazing tenderly after her.

Greta had come back in. "Let's leave her for a moment," she said; "the poor child was upset just now; her father has written to her; he will be here in the next few days, and then she is to go with him to Pyrmont."

I now discovered that the rich merchant who had lived until now without his own household, intended, now that he had finished his visits to various spas, to move into a newly built dwelling and to introduce his daughter there as lady of the house.— Greta did not exactly seem to be a friend of his. "It's Jenny's father," she said, "but— oh, I could hate him, this man who would give thousands for his daughter without a qualm, but from whom she would beg in vain for the tiniest thousandth of his own valuable personality.—Yes, Hans," she continued, as her husband stroked her blond hair teasingly and as if to appease her, "you should just see one of the answers Jenny usually gets to her letters; I for one can't distinguish them from receipts."

My mother took the young woman by both hands. "Now our Greta is boiling over," she said. "I knew the man; in earlier times, I mean. But he had to struggle with the hardships of life; and in cases like that, much becomes hard that in us is soft.—At least, so it seems to me at times."

When we gathered together again and I had to relate, in response to my family's questions everything that I had already written them in my letters, Jenny joined us and sat quietly by Greta's side.

In the evening, after a warm conversation, Hans led me to a bedroom on the upper floor.—Long after he had left me I lay awake, yet comfortably resting in the pillows; for the nightingales were singing overloudly in the bushes of the gardens onto which the windows gave.

When I woke up, my room was bright with the light of a summer morning. A feeling of growing health and fullness of life streamed through me in a way that I had never experienced before. I got dressed and opened the windows; the soft lawn below was still wet with dew, and the scent of the roses drifted up to me, fresh with morning coolness. My watch indicated six o'clock; there was still an hour before our common breakfast. So I looked once again around the room which, Greta had told me, had been the residence of my robber bride until my arrival. And indeed, in a drawer of the dressing table, when I pulled it open, lay a piece of pink silk in which a long, shining black hair had become so strangely intertwined that it could hardly be extricated without damage. Then, when I had succeeded in doing that, I found on a shelf above the bed a few books with Jenny's name in them, and I began to leaf through them. The first was an album, like those young girls have, full of all kinds of verses of rather undistinguished contents. Among them, however, were other poems like thistles among innocent clover. The very first that caught my eye:

> I'm a rose, pick me, don't pass by in vain;
> My roots lie bare in the wind and the rain.
>
> No, pass me by, leave me in repose;
> I'm not a blossom, I'm not a rose.
>
> My little coat flutters, the wind's blowing wild;
> I'm just a homeless and motherless child.

The last line was underlined twice; and there were more lines just like it.

I put the album down and picked up another book. I was very surprised. It was Sealsfield's *Life of a Planter*, the part that contains the vivid description of the colored people, those graceful creatures to whom the author hardly accords full membership in the human race but whose seductive beauty, according to his portrayal, derives from the evil spirits of Europeans who have emigrated there. In this book, too, individual passages were underlined in pencil, at times so sharply that the paper was torn. I recalled the conversation I had had many years ago with little Jenny on this topic; a sharp and painful light now fell on all the things that her imagination had retained so innocently.

When I stood up and looked out the window, Jenny was walking down below on the broad gravel garden paths. As she had yesterday, she was wearing a white dress; in those days I never saw her other than in white dresses.

A moment later I, too, was in the garden. She was walking ahead of me on the broad rising path that leads from the terrace around the lawn; she was walking rapidly as if in inner excitement, swinging her straw hat and its silk ribbons. I stopped and followed her with my gaze. Soon, when she turned to come back, I went to meet her. "Forgive me if I'm disturbing you," I said; "I haven't forgotten the little Jenny, but I'm impatient to get to know the big one."

She glanced at me rapidly with her black eyes. "That will be a bad exchange, Alfred!" she replied.

"I hope no exchange at all. You betrayed yourself yesterday; you're still exactly the warm, passionate Jenny of old; it seemed to me that your black hair was about to spring out of its bun and curl around your forehead again in wild little childish locks. And"—I continued—"let me tell you, too, how much that involuntary expression of your empathy moved me."

"I don't understand you," she said.

"Well, Jenny, what made you drop the bowl when my mother greeted her son?"

"That wasn't empathy, Alfred. You think I'm better than I am."

"Then what was it?" I asked.

"It was envy," she said, in a hard tone of voice.

"What are you saying, Jenny?"

She didn't answer; but as we walked side by side, I saw her shining teeth biting into her red lips. Then her feelings broke forth. "Oh!" she exclaimed, "you don't understand; you haven't yet lost a mother, and—oh, a mother who is still living!—That I was her child once makes me dizzy when I think of it; for it lies deep in an abyss below me. Again and again I struggle in vain to recall her lovely face from dull forgetfulness. I can only see her delicate figure kneeling beside my little bed; she's humming a strange song and looking at me with soft, velvet-black eyes, until sleep comes over me irresistibly."

She was silent. As we turned again toward the house, I saw my sister-in-law on the terrace waving her handkerchief to us. I grasped the girl's hand. "Do you think you still know me, Jenny?" I asked.

"Yes, Alfred; and that's a piece of great fortune for me."

As we stepped onto the terrace, Greta shook her finger at us laughingly. "If you still have need of earthly food, come to the tea table!"—With that, she showed us into the room where our mother was already sitting and talking to her eldest son. And in these friendly surroundings the shadows that had cast a bluish tone in that young face soon disappeared, or at least, they receded from the surface and were hidden inside her.

In the afternoon, I found a chance to reminisce with Jenny about our shared childhood stories, and she laughed brightly and warmly again. A few times I attempted to change the topic of our conversation from my mother to hers, but she either fell suddenly silent or talked of other things.

Later, as the sun's heat diminished, my brother called us and his wife to a badminton game on the large lawn. It was part of his regular Sunday entertainment and he insisted that it never be missed. He had an upholstered chair brought onto the terrace for our mother from which she watched the game.

Here Jenny was in her element. She followed the ball rapidly with her large, perceptive eyes, and her feet flew just as easily over the lawn, now backward, now sideways. Then at the right moment she would swing the racquet with her little hand and hit the downward shooting feathered ball so that it flew back into the air as if it were on wings. Once, too, as if enraptured in the excitement of the game, she threw the racquet away and, shouting, "How it flies! Let's follow it, let's follow it," she herself flew over the ground, snapping her fingers in the air as though in greeting.—Or whenever she bent down and picked up the ball, or when it once flew over her, hit by my brother's strong hand—one just had to see how she then threw back her head with her rich shining hair and how easily and quickly those supple hips followed the turn of her beautiful head. I could not take my eyes from her; in these strong, yet graceful movements there was something that was truly suggestive of the wilderness primeval. My dear sister-in-law also seemed completely enraptured by it. While Jenny chased the flying ball, Greta came running toward me and whispered: "You do see her, Alfred? You do have your eyes open?" And as I replied: "Ah, only too well, Greta!" she looked at me with her sisterly smile and said furtively: "I'll let only one person have her; do you hear me, only one single person in the world!"

Then our mother called us and said: "That's enough, children!" And Jenny knelt before her, and the old woman caressed her hot cheeks and called her "golden heart."

Later, after dinner, when the large lamp was already burning and after my mother had retired, I sat with the two young women in a dim corner of the room on the sofa. My brother had gone back to his room to take care of some business. The door panels to the terrace stood open and allowed free access to the cool of the evening; from our seat we could see, above the dark groups of trees, the stars in the deep blue night sky.

Greta and Jenny became absorbed in their memories of boarding school; their talk was lively, and I needed only to listen. So we sat for a long time. However, when Greta cried out, "That was such a happy time!" Jenny silently bowed her head; so deeply that I saw the parting of her shining hair.

Then she stood up and went to the open garden door, where she remained standing on the threshold; and since at this moment my brother called his wife into the next room, I went out to her. Meanwhile, the moonlit night had covered the garden outside in its soft scent; here and there roses gleamed forth from the twilight on the lawn, their cups turned toward the beams of the light that was just rising. Beyond the shrubbery, part of the high leafy walls of the pleasure grove appeared in bluish illumination, while the paths leading into it stood black and mysterious in between. Neither Jenny nor I attempted to converse, but I felt it sweet to stand silently beside her like that, gazing out into the night rich with intimations.

Only once did I say to her, "One thing I miss in you: where has your beautiful deviltry gone?"

And she replied, "Yes, Alfred"—and I could hear from her voice that she was smiling—"if only we had Aunt Josephine here! Perhaps"—she suddenly added, seriously—"I'm using my thought in other ways."

I didn't respond. As yesterday, the nightingales sang far and near; when they fell silent it was so quiet that I thought I could hear the dew falling from the stars onto the roses. How long that lasted, I don't know. But suddenly Jenny got up and saying "Good night, Alfred," gave me her hand.

I wanted to keep her there, but all I said was, "Give me your hand again.—No, here in my left hand."

"There it is. But why the left hand?"

"Why, Jenny?—I don't have to give that hand to other people."

And off she went; and in the bushes the nightingales were still singing.

The pearl string formed by those days had been interrupted; the next, in any event, had no luster for me; for—and that's how it was with me already—Jenny was gone; as she had said, to make a long-promised visit to a neighboring estate. She had gone early in the morning with the mail carriage which stopped there, as at my brother's house; her return was expected late in the evening.

I had spent the morning in my mother's room quietly communing with thoughts and plans for the future; in the afternoon I accompanied my brother into his fields, meadows, heaths and gravel pits; then Greta had told me the amusing story of her engagement; but in the evening, the darker it got the more I lost the composure needed to listen to my friends' words.—When my mother had gone to her bedroom, I leaned in the open door to the garden where I had stood yesterday with Jenny; and again I saw, across the lawn on the other side of the thicket the far-off beech wall of the pleasure arbor in the bluish scent of the moonlight. As it happened, I still hadn't gone in; but now the deep shadows that marked the entryways enticed me even more than yesterday.

It seemed to me as if in that labyrinth of shade and leafage lay hidden the sweetest secret of the summer's night. I looked back into the room to see if anyone had noticed me; then I stepped silently from the terrace into the garden. The moon had just climbed up from behind the oaks and chestnut trees that bordered the garden on its eastern side. I went around the lawn on this side, which still lay in total shadow; a rose that I plucked as I passed was still damp with dew. I reached the thicket opposite the house. Broad steps curved seemingly irregularly up between bushes and rose beds; here and there a jasmine bush glowed out of the dark with its white blossoms. After a while I entered a very broad path that lay at right angles before me and beyond which the leafy walls of the old garden architecture rose majestically, illuminated brightly by the moon. I stood for a moment and looked up at them; I could distinguish every leaf; from time to time a large beetle or a butterfly fluttered above me from the leafy confusion into the bright night. Opposite me, a path led into the interior; whether it was the same one whose darkness had enticed me from the terrace I couldn't decide, for the bushes obstructed my gaze back at the manor house.

On the steps that I now climbed was a solitude that filled me at moments with a dream-like anxiety, as if I mightn't know how to find my way back. The walls of leaves on either side were so dense and rose so high that I could see only a little piece of sky, as if cut out. When I came upon a somewhat freer spot where two paths crossed, it always seemed to me as if a powdered beauty in a hoop skirt and a pleated cloak from the year 1750 might step out into the moonlight on the arm of a supporter. But all was silent; only from time to time did the night air sigh through the leaves like a human breath.

After I had walked back and forth a few times, I found myself at the edge of a pond that, from the place where I was standing seemed to be about a hundred paces long and half as wide. It was separated from the leafy walls that surrounded it on all sides only by a broad path and several trees on the bank. White water lilies shone over its entire black depths; but among them, in the middle of the basin, on a pedestal that only just cleared the surface of the water, stood a silent and solitary marble Venus. There was a soundless silence at this spot. I went along the banks until I was as close as possible opposite the statue. It was obviously one of the loveliest statues from the period of Louis XV. She stretched out one bare foot just above the water as if to step into the pool; one hand rested on a rock, while the other held her garment, which had already been loosened, together over her breast. From this vantage point I couldn't see her face, for her head was turned as if she wanted to make sure there were no unbidden observers before she entrusted her unclothed body to the waves.

The expression of movement was so deceptively life-like, and at the same time, while the lower part of her figure was in shadow, the moonlight played with such soft gleaming around her marble shoulder that it seemed to me indeed as if I had crept into the innermost part of a forbidden sanctity. Behind me, against the wall of leaves, stood a wooden bench. From here I gazed at the lovely image for a long time; and—I don't know if it was just the mood into which I had been placed by the sight of this beauty, as I looked I had to keep thinking of Jenny.

Finally I stood up and wandered at random for a while in the dark passageways. Not far from the pond that I had just left I found the remains of a second statue on a marble base, standing in a spot overgrown with low bushes. It was a muscular male foot that might very well have belonged to Polyphemus; and so my cousin, the philologist, was probably not wrong when he was said to have declared the other marble statue to be Galatea, fleeing into the sea before the jealousy of the clumsy son of a god.

The artist side of me had been awoken. Whether Galatea or Venus—it delighted me to decide this question, too; and so I wanted to go back once more to look at it less dreamily than before. But however many paths I took, I didn't succeed in reaching the pond again; finally, when I turned out of a side path onto a broad leafy avenue, I saw the water glistening at the end, and soon I thought I was standing at the same spot where I had first stepped onto the bank. It was strange that I had missed the spot so many times. But I could hardly believe my eyes: there in the middle rose the pediment above the water; the water lilies, too, shone as before upon the black depths; but the marble statue that had stood there had disappeared. I couldn't understand it, and stared for a whole space of time at the empty spot. When I looked down across the length of the pond, I saw on the opposite bank in the shadow of the high wall of trees the white figure of a woman. She was leaning against a tree next to the water, and seemed to be gazing into the depths. And now she must have moved; for, while she had just now been in the shadow, now the moonlight played on her white garment.—Who was it? Were the ancient gods walking abroad? It was, no doubt, the right kind of night for that. The stars mirrored themselves in the water between the white flowers; the dew trickled from leaf to leaf in the bushes; from time to time a drop fell from one of the trees on the bank into the pond, making a gentle splash; from the garden, as if from very far away, sang the nightingale. I went around the pond on the shadowed side. As I approached, the figure lifted its head, and Jenny's beautiful pale face turned toward me; it was so brilliantly lit by the moon that I could see the bluish glaze of her teeth shining between her red lips.

"It's you, Jenny!" I cried.

"Yes, me, Alfred!" she replied and came to meet me.

"How did you get here?"

"I got out of the carriage behind there at the entrance to the park."

"I thought," I said quietly, "that it was the goddess who had stepped off her pedestal over there."

"She must have stepped down long ago, or fallen off perhaps; I've never seen her there."

"But I saw her just a quarter of an hour ago!"

She shook her head. "You were over on the other pond; there the marble statue is doubtless still standing. There are no gods here, Alfred; here is nothing but a poor human child in need of help."

"You, Jenny, in need of help?"

She nodded violently.

"If, as you said yesterday, you really still think you know me, then tell me: what is it you need?"

"Money," she said.

"You, money, Jenny!" And I stared in astonishment at this child of wealth.

"Don't ask me what for," she replied; "you will find out soon enough." Then she took her handkerchief out of her pocket and withdrew from it a piece of jewelry on which, as she held it out in the moonlight, I could see green stones twinkling in an artful setting. "I have no opportunity of selling it," she said; "will you try for me tomorrow?" and when I hesitated for a moment, she added hastily, "It's not anything that was given to me or that I inherited; I bought it one time for myself from my own pocket money."

"But, Jenny," I couldn't help saying, "why don't you turn to your father?"

She shook her head.

"I thought," I continued, "that he was taking good care of your needs."

"Yes, Alfred; he pays for me—generously!" Her voice resounding with the bitterest emotion, she added: "I can't beg the man."

She stepped back a pace and sat down on the bench that stood behind us against the wall of leaves. Then she put her head in both hands.

"Is it quite essential, then?" I asked.

She looked up at me and said, almost with devotion, "I have to fulfil a holy duty with it."

"And there's no other solution?"

"I don't know of any."

"Then give me the jewel."

She did so, and I took it with inward repugnance.—Jenny had leaned back silently; a strip of moonlight lit up her slender hand as it lay in her lap, and I saw once again, as I had years ago, the small dark crescents on her fingernails. I don't know why I almost started at the sight, as if my eyes had been bewitched. When Jenny noticed this, she moved her hand quietly into the shadow. "I have another request, Alfred!" she said.

"Tell me, Jenny!"

She bent her head a little. "Years ago, when we took leave of each other in our childhood, I gave you a little ring. Do you still remember it?"

"How can you doubt it?"

"If you still have that worthless jewel," she continued, "if you valued it enough to have it still, then I beg you, give it back to me!"

"If you ask for it back," I replied, not without a touch of irritation, "then I have no right to keep it any more."

"You misunderstand me, Alfred!" she cried. "Oh, it's the only souvenir I have of my mother!"

I had already pulled the ribbon with the ring from beneath my neckerchief. "Here it is, Jenny; but—forgive me, it hurts me all the same!"

She had stood up. I saw a slight flush creep over her face; but then, as if involuntarily, she reached for the ring and clasped it in her hand. I could not bring myself to give it to her; I held it fast. "A short while ago," I said, "it was nothing more to me than a remembrance of the charming playmate from my childhood.—Now it has become something else; with every day I spend here, more so."

But I paused, for she looked at me as if I had injured her. "Don't speak to me like that, Alfred," she said.

I paid no attention to these words; I grasped her hand, which she let lie calmly in mine. "Take the ring, Jenny," I said, "but give me your hand in exchange!"

Slowly she shook her head. "The hand of a colored person," she said tonelessly.

"*Your* hand, Jenny. What do we care about the rest?"

She stood without moving; only from the trembling of her hand, which still lay in mine, could I tell she was alive. "I know that we're beautiful," she said then, "seductively beautiful, like sin, which is our origin. But, Alfred—I won't seduce you."

And yet, as I stretched out my arms toward her, she suddenly lay on my breast and had clasped her hands firmly around my neck. She looked up at me; her big shining eyes were like an abyss beneath me. "Yes, Jenny," and it seemed to me as if a shudder went through me from the trees, "you are breathtakingly beautiful; she was no more beautiful, the demonic goddess who once confused men's hearts so that they forgot everything they once loved! Perhaps you are yourself the goddess and are just walking abroad on this blessed night to make those happy who believe in you.—No, don't tear yourself away; I know you're a child of the earth like myself, helplessly ensnared in your own spell; and just as the night air blows through the leaves—without trace—so you will also vanish.—But don't scold the mysterious night that has thrown us into each other's arms. Even if we must receive uninvited the foundation of our future here—the building that it will support one day is in our own hands."

I took her hands gently from my neck and laid my arm around her waist. Then I tore the ribbon from the ring and placed it on her finger. Still leaning on me like a comforted child, she let me lead her away.—When, after a time, we reached the other pond, there was indeed the statue of Venus still standing amid the white water lilies, and I knew for certain that I had an earthly woman in my arms.

Hesitating, we stepped, finally, out of the obscure shadowy paths into the thicket, and from the thicket into the free space opposite the house. Across the lawn through the open doors we saw my brother and his wife walking up and down as if in intimate conversation in the brightly lit room.

Jenny bent down and escaped from my arm before I realized what was happening; but just as quickly, she had taken hold of my hand again. "Do what you have promised, Alfred," she said; "and," she added almost inaudibly, "forget everything else."

At this moment Greta stepped into the open doorway and called out into the night, "Jenny, Alfred, is it you?" Jenny begged me urgently, "Don't speak of this; not even to your mother; we mustn't upset her."

"But I don't understand you, Jenny."

She only pressed my hand fervently. Then she left me and went to Greta on the terrace. Once we had gone into the bright room, Greta looked at us, one and the other, with a silent shake of her head.

The next morning I rode into town to fulfill my promise. There I had the jewel appraised by two different jewelers. Its value was high; but my pocketbook happened to be full at the time. So I could take care of the jewel for Jenny, and changed into coin a roll of gold of the appropriate worth from that which I had with me.—When that had been done, I walked up and down the beautiful harbor for a while. Out on the wharf, far away in the misty sunlight, I saw a large ship; a brig, as a sailor told me, ready to sail for the West Indies.—

"To her homeland!" I thought; and then my thoughts of her overwhelmed me so much and gave me no peace until I was on my way home again.

Shortly after noon I entered the garden room. No one was there; but from the door I saw Jenny standing with a skinny old gentleman some distance away. Shortly afterward, he gave her his arm with a certain formality of manner and led her toward the house. As they came closer, I saw that the man had almost white hair; but two sharp, masterful eyes gazed out from a dark face, and the abrupt movements of his head indicated that he was accustomed to command. The white neckerchief and large diamond pin in his ruffled jabot belonged quite naturally to his appearance. I knew right away that this was Jenny's father, the rich planter, my uncle through a cousin I had never yet met; but as he was, he was just as I had imagined in my boyhood. And now I could also hear his strangely accented voice; he spoke to his daughter in staccato words that I couldn't understand; she seemed just to be listening.

As I didn't feel prepared to meet him at this point, I left the room and went upstairs before the two of them had reached the terrace. The door to Jenny's room was open. I went in and, in accordance with our agreement, put the money for her jewel into a cupboard on the wall above the door. Then I went to my own room and flung myself, excited and yet exhausted, on the sofa.

Scarcely a few minutes had gone by than I heard footsteps on the stairs and soon heard two people go into the large room next to mine. Opposite my seat was a door that led from my room into the other one. At this point, it was closed, but there was a window hung on the other side with a thick white curtain.

From their voices I recognized that Jenny and her father were those who had entered, although, doubtless because they were at the other end of the room, I couldn't understand anything they said. When they came closer, I wanted to move quietly away; but the first words that clearly struck my ear had the effect of making me sit still in my place, forgetting everything else.

"You couldn't remain there!" I heard Jenny's father say, in the staccato tone previously mentioned.

"Why not?" asked Jenny.

I heard him pacing slowly up and down a few times. Then he stood still. "You may hear it," he said, "since you force me to say it. Given the family origins of your mother, you could never have shared the company of your father."

"And given my own," added Jenny. "I know that."

"You know that? Who told you these things?"

"No one; I read about them."

"Well, then you know why I had to send you to Europe. I think you should have thanked me for that."

"Yes," she said, "just as I have you to thank for my life."

To this, her father did not reply; but a window was opened, and from the sounds I heard I could tell that he stuck his head out into the open air and cleared his throat.— Jenny was leaning with her back against the door that separated the two rooms. Through the curtained window I could see the shadow of her head, and I could hear the rustling of her dress.

After some time her father seemed to have come back into the room. "I have done for you," he said, "what I could. Of course you have never uttered a wish; but I don't know either what you might have had to desire."

She rose and stepped slowly one pace toward him. "Where is my mother?" she asked.

"Your mother, Jenny!" exclaimed the man, as if he had expected anything other than a question about that woman. "You know she's alive; she is provided for."

"And," the girl continued persistently, "now your big new house is ready and furnished, you have taken steps to bring her over here so that she can live with us again?"

I heard him pacing firmly up and down the room several times. Then he approached his daughter again. "You're a child, Jenny," he said, with a muffled voice; but the words still sounded strongly accented. "You're not familiar with conditions over there in the land of your birth; you should not know them, either." And as if he, the old merchant, were suddenly overcome by the magic of recollection, he continued: "She was incredibly beautiful, that woman; incredibly!—when she swayed in her hammock, in her white clothes between the broad green leaves of the mangrove trees, below the bay in the bright sunlight, with the steel-blue tropical sky above; when she was playing with her birds or throwing her golden balls in the air!—But it wasn't good to hear her speak; her beautiful mouth stumbled along in the broken speech of the Negro; it was the babbling of a child.—That woman, Jenny, would have been no company for you, if you wanted to become what you have."

She was leaning against the door again. "And for that reason," she said, "you took the child away from her mother.—She cried; oh, she cried as you took me from her arms and took me over the gangplank on board ship. And that was the last sound I heard from my mother.—I had forgotten it for a long time; for I was a thoughtless child. God forgive me!—But now I hear it in my ears every night. What gave you the right to pay for my future with my mother's misery?" And I saw through the curtain how she straightened up as she said these words.

Her father seemed to clasp her hand. "Reflect, Jenny," he said; "I had only the choice between her and you;—but you were my child."

The soft, almost tender tone with which he uttered these last words seemed to make no impression on his daughter. "You haven't answered my question," she said; "the price you paid was not yours or mine; it must be repaid as far as it now can be. Answer me, yes or no, will my mother live in the new house with us?"

"No, Jenny; that's not possible."

These words were followed by a soundless pause. What was going on inside the girl during these moments, what may have been visible in her gestures or in some other way, I could not discern.

"I have one more request," she said at last.

"Tell me, Jenny," replied her father hastily; "just tell me; everything else that is within my power!"

"Then I request permission," she continued, "to remain here with our friends during your visit to Pyrmont."

He was silent for a moment. "If you don't find it more appropriate," he said then, "to accompany your father, I don't know of any objection."

She didn't respond, but merely asked, "May I go now?"

"If you have nothing more to say to me; I'll go downstairs too."

Thereupon the door opened, and I heard their footsteps moving along the corridor toward the stairs.—I stayed in my room until I was called to lunch.

When my brother introduced me to him, Jenny's father measured me with his alert eyes, so that I felt as if he were making a rough estimate of my person. Then he asked about my studies and travels, and if I had found the opportunity to use my knowledge at home. All this took place in a manner that was not unlike an exam. Finally, I was politely invited to give a specialist opinion of his newly built house as soon as he returned from his trip to the spa.—There was no trace of what had transpired between father and daughter in the man's formal manner.

At table he sat next to my mother and entertained her in the most attentive fashion; when she turned the conversation to the time they had spent together during their youth, he even managed to be jocular. He recalled his neighbor at various balls where she had danced in the public hall of their hometown and reminded her of a chubby little figure of Amor who had been depicted on the wallpaper there. "The young ladies," he said, "were so cautious of this figure that there was always a gap in the dance line at that point."

"And you, cousin," replied my mother, "were absolutely obsessed with leading your partner again and again in that direction."

He bowed to her gallantly. "I knew, of course, cousin," he said, "that with respect to me you didn't have to avoid the Amor."

At these words, I saw a delicate flush shoot across my mother's still attractive face; and involuntarily, I wondered whether, like their children, the two of them had once had bonds of affection between them. Jenny, too, who up to this point had sat there without a sign of involvement and scarcely touching her food, looked up at these words; perhaps she had never heard her father speak of such cheerful things. He himself did not address a word across the table to his daughter, but spoke once more to my brother about all kinds of travel connections. Later, however, over coffee, I heard him say to my mother, "Through the kindness of your children, Jenny will stay here a while longer; I'm traveling on alone tomorrow. We have known each other for many years, cousin; if you have a chance—tell her about those days.—Soon she will be living with the old man; it might be good if she got to know the young one first." And pressing his cousin's hand, he added as he stood up, "You'd be doing me a service, cousin."

The day passed without my managing to meet alone with Jenny; she was clearly avoiding it.

Greta, too, was mostly outdoors on the property.—The next morning, when she came out to me in the garden after the departure of our guest, she folded her hands across her breast and said with a deep sigh, "Now we're among ourselves again!"

To my distress, however, I soon discovered that Jenny was to go into town that morning for several days to take care of I know not what tasks with her father's housekeeper in the new house.

I was standing alone on the terrace when she came out to me in traveling costume. She gave me her hand; but I was annoyed that she could leave me at this moment. "Why are you doing this to me, Jenny?" I asked. "Are these tasks so urgent?"

Looking at me with large, quiet eyes, she shook her head. In her gaze was an expression, I can't put it otherwise, of noble idealism.

"And yet you're going?" I asked again, "and at this of all times?"

"I don't want to tell you a lie, Alfred," she said; "that's not it; but I must, I can't do otherwise."

"Then I'll come into town every day to help you."

She looked visibly startled. "No, no," she cried. "You mustn't do that!"

"Why not?"

"I don't know; don't ask me!—Oh, please believe me!"

"Can't you trust me, Jenny?"

She uttered a sound of agony, the most painful I had ever heard. Then she stretched her arms out to me, unconcerned who else might see it; and as once before in the secrecy of night, I held her to my heart now in the brightest sunlight. "Then don't stay too long!" I begged; "my father's waiting for me; my time here is coming to an end."

I looked at her beautiful pale face, as she remained silent. She had closed her eyes and was leaning her head on my shoulder as if she wanted to go to sleep there.

It was just a moment. She tore herself free, and we went to the front of the house where the carriage was already standing.—After Jenny had got in, I heard my mother say, clasping her hand, "Don't weep, child! You're weeping as if your heart would break."

Despite the bright sun, a series of gray days followed for me. It was lucky that my brother kept me busy with plans for a new administration building. It was no small task to combine his practical demands with the artistic ones I didn't want to neglect. Often, he marked my beautifully drawn plan pitilessly with his pencil; and we argued back and forth, until in the end the two women were called upon to decide.

On the fourth day after Jenny's departure I was sitting in my room occupied with this work. I wasn't having any success with it, however, and, blaming my poor sketching pen, I stood up to get another one out of my case. As I unpacked the laundry that was inside, a folded piece of paper fell into my hand. "From Jenny," it said. Inside lay the little tortoise-shell ring that I had placed on her finger, and plaited through it, a long lock of her shining black hair.

My first emotion was a shudder of delight, a feeling of immediate closeness to my loved one; but then a vague sense of worry overcame me. I looked at the paper from all sides; but there was no other letter or sign on it.

After I had tried in vain to work, I went down into the living room, where I found my brother talking to his wife about Jenny.

"But what eyes!" I heard Greta say as I came in.

Her husband seemed to be taking, in jest, the opposite point of view: for he replied: "Surely you don't find those wild eyes beautiful?"

"Wild, Hans? And not beautiful?—But of course, you're right, they're so beautiful that they call forth opposition. And this—!" She stopped and looked at her husband with a pitying smile.

"What, Greta?"

"Is nothing but the beginning of a defense. Honestly, Hans, you sense how dangerous she could be for you!"

"Yes, if I didn't have you!"

"Oh, even if you have me."

Laughing, he gave her both hands. "Hold them tight," he said, "and no pretty devil will seduce me."

But his wife wouldn't accept that. "The devil is in you men!" she cried. "Altogether, why are you constantly criticizing the innocent child, when you were always so gallant to her before?"

"Before, Greta, yes. But she has changed!" Then he thought for a moment. "I'm almost ashamed to tell you. But it's only too certain; the merchant's daughter has come to the fore in her—she's become miserly."

"Miserly!" exclaimed Greta. "That's too much! Jenny, who in her boarding school days could be restrained by the sternest of commands not to give away the clothes from her own body!"

"She's not giving away clothes any more," replied my brother, "she sells them to the old clothes man; and I can tell you that she negotiates the price for them very precisely."

Without intervening in their conversation, I had been listening attentively. At these last words a terrifying clarity overcame me.—My decision was quickly made. "Can I have your horse, Hans?" I asked.

"Of course; where do you want to go?"

"I want to ride into town."

His wife came right up to me. "Can't you stick it out any longer, Alfred?"

"No, Greta!"

"Well then, give Jenny my greetings; or better still, bring her back with you!"

I said nothing; but I was in the saddle right away; an hour later I was in town, and soon in the street where I knew Jenny's father's house was said to be situated. It was not hard to find, and after many rings, the door of the stately building was opened by an elderly woman. When I asked for Jenny, she answered dryly, "The young lady is not here."

"Not here?" I repeated; and my face must have expressed the distress I felt at these words; for the old woman did not ask my name. But when I had told her who I was and where I had come from, she added in an annoyed tone, "Why are you asking? The young lady went back again the other day."

I left the old woman standing there and ran from one street to another until I had reached the harbor. The sun had gone down and the far off wharf was glowing in the purple of a vivid sunset. There the brig had been anchored; now it was gone, and there was not a ship to be seen. I tried to start a conversation with the workers who were standing nearby, and found out the name of the shipping company owner and the ship, and that it had gone to sea three days ago. They knew nothing more; except for the place where the captain had stayed. I set out immediately, and there I discovered that a beautiful young lady with black hair had been on board. Then I went to the shipping office, where, as it happened, the old bookkeeper was still at his desk; but he could give me no more information, for the passengers were the captain's business alone.

I went back to the hotel and had my horse saddled. Faster than my brother would have permitted, we trotted back home. It was late already, and the sky was covered with clouds. As the night wind blew past me through the darkness, my thoughts flew with it, and I saw the ship that was carrying her away before my eyes as if it were a ghost; a tiny speck, drifting in the liquid element over the yawning abysses of the deeps, surrounded by night in the monstrous waste of the ocean.—Finally, the lights of the estate shone at me from the trees.

Here I found everything in sorrow and distress. A letter from Jenny had arrived, dated from on board the brig *Elizabeth*. She had gone over the sea to her mother; as she had told me, and as she repeated in the letter, in order to fulfill a sacred duty. In the most fervent, the sweetest words she begged us all to forgive her. My name was not mentioned in the letter; but I had already received my silent farewell. She did not mention her father, either.

The next day my brother and I were in town again; but only to receive the certain knowledge that the brig *Elizabeth* could no longer be reached.

Then, without first returning with Hans, I went straight to Pyrmont. A few moments after my arrival I met with Jenny's father and told him of his daughter's flight.—I had thought I would see the old man collapse beneath the weight of this news; but it was not pain, but a flash of sudden anger that came from his eyes. Clenching his fist on the table so that his thin knuckles stood out, he uttered curses against his daughter. "Let her go where she belongs!" he cried. "This race cannot be made better; cursed be the day when I believed it could!" But then he fell suddenly silent; he sat down and put his head in his hands. And as if to himself, he said, "What am I saying? It's my own blood; the other—it's my fault. How can the child help it! She wanted to go to her mother." And stretching out his arms, staring ahead, he cried aloud, "Oh, Jenny, my daughter, my child, what have I done to you!" He seemed to have forgotten my presence, and I let him remain undisturbed. "We are human beings," he continued; "you should have forgiven me; but I didn't know how to speak to you; that was it: we couldn't come together."

At that moment I ventured to gain his attention and to tell him that we loved each other. And the broken man grasped, as it were, at this straw and begged me to bring his child back to him.

What more can I say! The next day I left again; but before I did, he gave me a letter he had written to his daughter during the night. And believe me, this time it wasn't a receipt; anger and love, reproach and excuse will have alternated in this letter as they had during the long evening when we had sat together.

"The rest"—Alfred concluded his story—"is known to you. Here I am, equipped with full powers and fatherly consent, and am waiting for the bell to sound so that I can set forth on my wedding journey."

We were together for about another hour; then the bells struck three from the church tower, and a porter arrived to take Alfred's bags to the harbor.

I accompanied my young friend. It was a cool night; a sharp east wind ruffled the water and knocked the boat against the harbor steps. Alfred got in and held out his hand to me. "What do you think, Alfred," I said, veiling our parting in joke, "with Jenny or never?"

"No, no," he called back, as the boat steered out into the night, "with Jenny in any event!"

More than half a year has passed since that night. I still haven't come out to the estate; but just now, as the first breezes of May waft into my open window, a renewed invitation has arrived, and this time I won't let myself be begged in vain to come. Before me lie two letters; both dated from Christiansted in St. Croix; the one, from Jenny to Alfred, was opened in his absence by his sister-in-law. It reads:

"I have found my mother; without difficulty, for she has a large boarding house near the harbor. She is still beautiful and in the bloom of health; but in her features, whose outline I recognize very well, I look in vain for what I longed for all those long years.—I must tell you everything, Alfred; it is different from what I imagined. I feel reticent with this woman; I shudder when I think how she called me her daughter before a group of men at her lunch table. Right after that, in a mixture of every living language, she disclosed the story of her youth;—everything that had secretly gnawed at me, and what I would have wanted to bury in the darkest night.

"Most of her boarders and mealtime guests are colored people; but one of them, a rich Mulatto, seems to rule the whole household; he treats my mother with an intimacy that makes my blood rush hotly into my face. And this person, Alfred—he bares his teeth like a dog—desires to have me as his wife; and my mother herself urges me to accept, now by her uncontrolled fondling which almost stifles me, now in the presence of all kinds of other people by her shrieking threats and reproaches.—From time to time I have to stare, confused, into the woman's face; it seems to me as if I were looking at a mask that I would need to tear off to find the beautiful face beneath it that still gazes at me from my childhood; as if I would then hear the voice that once hummed me to sleep, as sweetly as the sound of a bee.—Oh, it's all horrible, everything all around me here! From early morning on, since my bedroom is situated on the harbor side, and the voices of the black workers and load carriers awaken me. You don't know such people over there; it's like howling, like the sound of animals; I tremble with horror when I hear it and bury my head in my pillows; for here in this country I'm one of them; I am of their blood; limb by limb, the chain extends from them to me. My father was right; and yet—I feel dizzy when I gaze into that abyss. I cast myself upon your breast; Alfred, help me, oh, help me!"

And help was not far off; the other letter is from Alfred to his sister-in-law, and the date is a few days later. The happy confidence with which he set out on his voyage helped him win the prize there as well.

"From on board ship"—he writes—"I was directed to Jenny's mother's house. Jenny herself was the first person I met when I stepped into the entryway; with a cry of joy, she ran into my arms.—Since then, I have got to know her mother well enough; she is a corpulent, still beautiful woman who rustles about in brightly colored silk dresses and speaks in a quite impossible language; according to whether she's speaking to her guest or her servants, in a gentle or else perhaps in a somewhat shrieking tone. She speaks of Jenny's father with grateful respect and calls him the 'good, noble man,' through whose generosity she has come into these comfortable circumstances. Nothing is further from her mind than to leave her home island or even to marry the distinguished father of her daughter. She is in her place here, and feels so at ease that it must have almost been a disappointment for Jenny to find, instead of the imagined misery, to cure which she ripped apart all the bonds of her old world, such a low-class realm in which such noble suffering cannot even flourish.—All the same, the arrival of her daughter has caused the lively woman great pleasure; and she has often enough heaped her up, before my eyes, with a wild, I might even say elemental tenderness. Since she wants to show off the lovely girl to her guests, she is constantly taking pains to deck her out in finery, and Jenny has to work hard to escape the burning colors her mother has picked out for her. But not enough; she has selected for Jenny's husband from among the guests of the house a rich man in whom circulates, it seems to me, a considerable measure of the blood that is so notorious here. And to that end she has already begun to take serious steps. At that point, I intervened, and the will and power of the 'good, noble man' smoothed everything over in the easiest manner.

"I sense very well that it was not a cry of joy but of relief with which Jenny greeted me. But that is well; she had to feel that first; for only as it has come about could she truly become mine; and if the backward gaze toward her family is missing, she will have a husband who is proud and happy to found a new house with her and see his future lineage blossom forth from her womb. For I am writing this on our wedding day.—You should have seen the glaring green silk the good, lively lady wore as she presided over the wedding table among the regular guests of her house, how proud she was of her wondrously beautiful daughter and—I can't deny it—of her son-in-law, and what incredible toasts she uttered in three languages to the health of the newly wed couple. We hope to arrive at your house in the first days of spring. And you, Greta, will not be jealous in your friendship when I confide in you what Jenny has just whispered to me: 'Now, Alfred, help me to come to my father!'"

These letters were included in the invitation from Hans and Greta. "So come"—it said in the latter, in Greta's hand—"Jenny's father is here already; Alfred's parents are arriving today; and even Aunt Josephine is coming, although she does express a few reservations from time to time about a person who behaved so inconsiderately with her English sewing needles.—We have just moved from our winter quarters into the bright garden room. The scent of the May lilies drifts from the lawn through the open windows, and over yonder in the pleasure grove beside the pond, where Venus stands, the banks are blue with violets."

And in the strong handwriting of my friend Hans follows:

"The brig *Elizabeth* passed Lisbon last Sunday; Jenny and Alfred are on board; in a few days they may be with us; for favorable winds are already blowing, bringing both of them and their good fortune."

TRANSLATED BY JUDITH RYAN

24

"The Quadroon Girl"

Henry Wadsworth Longfellow

Henry Wadsworth Longfellow (1807–1882) began publishing poetry while he was still an undergraduate. He was a gifted translator, became a professor of modern languages at Bowdoin and later Harvard, and published translations, works of literary scholarship, and travel essays as well as poetry. Many of his poems, including *The Song of Hiawatha* and "Paul Revere's Ride," enjoyed immense popularity in the United States. The poem "The Quadroon Girl," first published in Longfellow's *Poems on Slavery* (1842), attacks the institution of slavery, represented by the figure of a planter who sells his own mixed-race daughter to a slaver.

The Slaver in the broad lagoon
  Lay moored with idle sail;
He waited for the rising moon
  And for the evening gale.

Under the shore his boat was tied,
  And all her listless crew
Watched the gray alligator slide
  Into the still bayou.

Odors of orange-flowers and spice
  Reached them from time to time,
Like airs that breathe from Paradise
  Upon a world of crime.

The Planter, under his roof of thatch,
  Smoked thoughtfully and slow;
The Slaver's thumb was on the latch,
  He seemed in haste to go.

He said, "My ship at anchor rides
  In yonder broad lagoon;

I only wait the evening tides,
    And the rising of the moon."

Before them, with her face upraised,
    In timid attitude,
Like one half curious, half amazed,
    A Quadroon maiden stood.

Her eyes were large, and full of light,
    Her arms and neck were bare;
No garment she wore save a kirtle bright,
    And her own long, raven hair.

And on her lips there played a smile
    As holy, meek, and faint,
As lights in some cathedral aisle
    The features of a saint.

"The soil is barren,—the farm is old,"
    The thoughtful planter said;
Then looked upon the Slaver's gold,
    And then upon the maid.

His heart within him was at strife
    With such accursèd gains:
For he knew whose passions gave her life,
    Whose blood ran in her veins.

But the voice of nature was too weak;
    He took the glittering gold!
Then pale as death grew the maiden's cheek,
    Her hands as icy cold.

The Slaver led her from the door,
    He led her by the hand,
To be his slave and paramour
    In a strange and distant land!

25

"The Runaway Slave at Pilgrim's Point"

Elizabeth Barrett Browning

The English poet, essayist, and translator Elizabeth Barrett Browning (1806–1861) is best known for the love poems in her 1850 collection *Sonnets from the Portuguese*, but her writings often addressed philosophical and political themes as well. Her work was well received from the start, beginning with her first collection, *The Seraphim, and Other Poems* (1838), and including her book-length verse-novel *Aurora Leigh* (1857). She expressed her strong opposition to slavery in such poems as "A Curse for a Nation" (1860) and the poem reprinted here, "The Runaway Slave at Pilgrim's Point" (1848), which focuses on the black Medea figure of the slave mother who kills her own child.

I

I stand on the mark beside the shore
    Of the first white pilgrim's bended knee,
Where exile turned to ancestor,
    And God was thanked for liberty.
I have run through the night, my skin is as dark,
I bend my knee down on this mark:
    I look on the sky and the sea.

II

O pilgrim-souls, I speak to you!
    I see you come proud and slow
From the land of the spirits pale as dew
    And round me and round me ye go.
O pilgrims, I have gasped and run
All night long from the whips of one
    Who in your names works sin and woe!

III

And thus I thought that I would come
    And kneel here where ye knelt before,
And feel your souls around me hum

In undertone to the ocean's roar;
And lift my black face, my black hand,
Here, in your names, to curse this land
    Ye blessed in freedom's, evermore.

IV

I am black, I am black,
    And yet God made me, they say:
But if He did so, smiling back
    He must have cast His work away
Under the feet of His white creatures,
With a look of scorn, that the dusky features
    Might be trodden again to clay.

V

And yet He has made dark things
    To be glad and merry as light:
There's a little dark bird sits and sings,
    There's a dark stream ripples out of sight,
And the dark frogs chant in the safe morass,
And the sweetest stars are made to pass
    O'er the face of the darkest night.

VI

But we who are dark, we are dark!
    Ah God, we have no stars!
About our souls in care and cark
    Our blackness shuts like prison-bars:
The poor souls crouch so far behind
That never a comfort can they find
    By reaching through the prison-bars.

VII

Indeed we live beneath the sky,
    That great smooth Hand of God stretched out
On all his children fatherly,
    To save them from the dread and doubt
Which would be if, from this low place,
All opened straight up to his face
    Into the grand eternity.

VIII

And still God's sunshine and His frost,
    They make us hot, they make us cold,
As if we were not black and lost;

And the beasts and birds, in wood and fold,
Do fear and take us for very men:
Could the whip-poor-will or the cat of the glen
    Look into my eyes and be bold?

IX

I am black, I am black!
    But, once, I laughed in girlish glee,
For one of my colour stood in the track
    Where the drivers drove, and looked at me,
And tender and full was the look he gave—
Could a slave look *so* at another slave?—
    I look at the sky and the sea.

X

And from that hour our spirits grew
    As free as if unsold, unbought:
Oh, strong enough, since we were two,
    To conquer the world, we thought.
The drivers drove us day by day;
We did not mind, we went one way,
    And no better a freedom sought.

XI

In the sunny ground between the canes,
    He said "I love you" as he passed;
When the shingle-roof rang sharp with the rains,
    I heard how he vowed it fast:
While others shook he smiled in the hut,
As he carved me a bowl of the cocoa-nut
    Through the roar of the hurricanes.

XII

I sang his name instead of a song,
    Over and over I sang his name,
Upward and downward I drew it along
    My various notes,—the same, the same!
I sang it low, that the slave-girls near
Might never guess, from aught they could hear,
    It was only a name—a name.

XIII

I look on the sky and the sea.
    We were two to love, and two to pray:
Yes, two, O God, who cried to Thee,

Though nothing didst Thou say!
Coldly Thou sat'st behind the sun:
And now I cry who am but one,
    Thou wilt not speak to-day.

XIV

We were black, we were black,
    We had no claim to love and bliss,
What marvel if each went to wrack?
    They wrung my cold hands out of his,
They dragged him—where? I crawled to touch
His blood's mark in the dust … not much,
    Ye pilgrim-souls, though plain as this!

XV

Wrong, followed by a deeper wrong!
    Mere grief's too good for such as I:
So the white men brought the shame ere long
    To strangle the sob of my agony.
They would not leave me for my dull
Wet eyes!—it was too merciful
    To let me weep pure tears and die.

XVI

I am black, I am black!
    I wore a child upon my breast,
An amulet that hung too slack,
    And, in my unrest, could not rest:
Thus we went moaning, child and mother,
One to another, one to another,
    Until all ended for the best.

XVII

For hark! I will tell you low, low,
    I am black, you see,—
And the babe who lay on my bosom so,
    Was far too white, too white for me;
As white as the ladies who scorned to pray
Beside me at church but yesterday,
    Though my tears had washed a place for my knee.

XVIII

My own, own child! I could not bear
    To look in his face, it was so white;
I covered him up with a kerchief there,

I covered his face in close and tight:
And he moaned and struggled, as well might be,
For the white child wanted his liberty—
    Ha, ha! he wanted the master-right.

XIX

He moaned and beat with his head and feet,
    His little feet that never grew;
He struck them out, as it was meet,
    Against my heart to break it through:
I might have sung and made him mild,
But I dared not sing to the white-faced child
    The only song I knew.

XX

I pulled the kerchief very close:
    He could not see the sun, I swear,
More, then, alive, than now he does
    From between the roots of the mango … where?
I know where. Close! A child and mother
Do wrong to look at one another
    When one is black and one is fair.

XXI

Why, in that single glance I had
    Of my child's face, … I tell you all,
I saw a look that made me mad!
    The *master's* look, that used to fall
On my soul like his lash … or worse!
And so, to save it from my curse,
    I twisted it round in my shawl.

XXII

And he moaned and trembled from foot to head,
    He shivered from head to foot;
Till after a time, he lay instead
    Too suddenly still and mute.
I felt, beside, a stiffening cold:
I dared to lift up just a fold,
    As in lifting a leaf of the mango-fruit.

XXIII

But my fruit … ha, ha!—there, had been
    (I laugh to think on't at this hour!)
Your fine white angels (who have seen

Nearest the secret of God's power)
And plucked my fruit to make them wine,
And sucked the soul of that child of mine
  As the humming-bird sucks the soul of the flower.

XXIV

Ha, ha, the trick of the angels white!
  They freed the white child's spirit so.
I said not a word, but day and night
  I carried the body to and fro,
And it lay on my heart like a stone, as chill.
—The sun may shine out as much as he will:
  I am cold, though it happened a month ago.

XXV

From the white man's house, and the black man's hut,
  I carried the little body on;
The forest's arms did round us shut,
  And silence through the trees did run:
They asked no question as I went,
They stood too high for astonishment,
  They could see God sit on His throne.

XXVI

My little body, kerchiefed fast,
  I bore it on through the forest, on;
And when I felt it was tired at last,
  I scooped a hole beneath the moon:
Through the forest-tops the angels far,
With a white sharp finger from every star,
  Did point and mock at what was done.

XXVII

Yet when it was all done aright,—
  Earth, 'twixt me and my baby, strewed,—
All, changed to black earth,—nothing white,—
  A dark child in the dark!—ensued
Some comfort, and my heart grew young;
I sate down smiling there and sung
  The song I learnt in my maidenhood.

XXVIII

And thus we two were reconciled,
  The white child and black mother, thus;
For as I sang it soft and wild,

The same song, more melodious,
Rose from the grave whereon I sate:
It was the dead child singing that,
 To join the souls of both of us.

XXIX
I look on the sea and the sky.
 Where the pilgrims' ships first anchored lay
The free sun rideth gloriously,
 But the pilgrim-ghosts have slid away
Through the earliest streaks of the morn:
My face is black, but it glares with a scorn
 Which they dare not meet by day.

XXX
Ha!—in their stead, their hunter sons!
 Ha, ha! they are on me—they hunt in a ring!
Keep off! I brave you all at once,
 I throw off your eyes like snakes that sting!
You have killed the black eagle at nest, I think:
Did you ever stand still in your triumph, and shrink
 From the stroke of her wounded wing?

XXXI
(Man, drop that stone you dared to lift!—)
 I wish you who stand there five abreast,
Each, for his own wife's joy and gift,
 A little corpse as safely at rest
As mine in the mangoes! Yes, but *she*
May keep live babies on her knee,
 And sing the song she likes the best.

XXXII
I am not mad: I am black.
 I see you staring in my face—
I know you staring, shrinking back,
 Ye are born of the Washington-race,
And this land is the free America,
And this mark on my wrist—(I prove what I say)
 Ropes tied me up here to the flogging-place.

XXXIII
You think I shrieked then? Not a sound!
 I hung, as a gourd hangs in the sun;
I only cursed them all around

As softly as I might have done
My very own child: from these sands
Up to the mountains, lift your hands,
    O slaves, and end what I begun!

XXXIV
Whips, curses; these must answer those!
    For in this UNION you have set
Two kinds of men in adverse rows,
    Each loathing each; and all forget
The seven wounds in Christ's body fair,
While HE sees gaping everywhere
    Our countless wounds that pay no debt.

XXXV
Our wounds are different. Your white men
    Are, after all, not gods indeed,
Nor able to make Christs again
    Do good with bleeding. We who bleed
(Stand off!) we help not in our loss!
We are too heavy for our cross,
    And fall and crush you and your seed.

XXXVI
I fall, I swoon! I look at the sky.
    The clouds are breaking on my brain;
I am floated along, as if I should die
    Of liberty's exquisite pain.
In the name of the white child waiting for me
In the death-dark where we may kiss and agree,
White men, I leave you all curse-free
    In my broken heart's disdain!

26

"The Pilot's Story"

William Dean Howells

William Dean Howells (1837–1920) was an eminent American editor, literary critic, poet, and novelist, and a friend and supporter of writers like Mark Twain and Henry James. He published a campaign biography of Abraham Lincoln in 1860, for which he was rewarded with a consulship in Venice from 1861 to 1865. He became an assistant editor of the *Atlantic Monthly* in 1866, and then editor from 1871 to 1881. Howells transformed the *Atlantic Monthly* into a national magazine, introducing a fresh style, new features, and works by southern and western writers. He published a number of well-received realistic novels, including *A Modern Instance* (1882), *The Rise of Silas Lapham* (1885), and *A Hazard of New Fortunes* (1890). In his 1891 novel *An Imperative Duty* Howells explored race relations in America, a theme that also appears in the 1860 poem reprinted here.

I.

It was a story the pilot told, with his back to his hearers,—
Keeping his hand on the wheel and his eye on the globe of the jack-staff,
Holding the boat to the shore and out of the sweep of the current,
Lightly turning aside for the heavy logs of the drift-wood,
Widely shunning the snags that made us sardonic obeisance.

II.

All the soft, damp air was full of delicate perfume
From the young willows in bloom on either bank of the river,—
Faint, delicious fragrance, trancing the indolent senses
In a luxurious dream of the river and land of the lotus.
Not yet out of the west the roses of sunset were withered;
In the deep blue above light clouds of gold and crimson
Floated in slumber serene, and the restless river beneath them
Rushed away to the sea with a vision of rest in its bosom.
Far on the eastern shore lay dimly the swamps of the cypress;
Dimly before us the islands grew from the river's expanses,—
Beautiful, wood-grown isles;—with the gleam of the swart inundation
Seen through the swaying boughs and slender trunks of their willows;

And on the shore beside us the cotton-trees rose in the evening,
Phantom-like, yearningly, wearily, with the inscrutable sadness
Of the mute races of trees. While hoarsely the steam from the 'scape-pipes
Shouted, then whispered a moment, then shouted again to the silence,
Trembling through all her frame with the mighty pulse of her engines,
Slowly the boat ascended the swollen and broad Mississippi,
Bank-full, sweeping on, with nearing masses of drift-wood,
Daintily breathed about with hazes of silvery vapor,
Where in his arrowy flight the twittering swallow alighted,
And the belated blackbird paused on the way to its nestlings.

III.

It was the pilot's story:—"They both came aboard there, at Cairo,
From a New Orleans boat, and took passage with us for Saint Louis.
She was a beautiful woman, with just enough blood from her mother,
Darkening her eyes and her hair, to make her race known to a trader:
You would have thought she was white. The man that was with her,—you
    see such,—
Weakly good-natured and kind, and weakly good-natured and vicious,
Slender of body and soul, fit neither for loving nor hating.
I was a youngster then, and only learning the river,—
Not over-fond of the wheel. I used to watch them at *monte*,
Down in the cabin at night, and learned to know all of the gamblers.
So when I saw this weak one staking his money against them,
Betting upon the turn of the cards, I knew what was coming:
They never left their pigeons a single feather to fly with.
Next day I saw them together,—the stranger and one of the gamblers:
Picturesque rascal he was, with long black hair and moustaches,
Black slouch hat drawn down to his eyes from his villainous forehead:
On together they moved, still earnestly talking in whispers,
On toward the forecastle, where sat the woman alone by the gangway.
Roused by the fall of feet, she turned, and, beholding her master,
Greeted him with a smile that was more like a wife's than another's,
Rose to meet him fondly, and then, with the dread apprehension
Always haunting the slave, fell her eye on the face of the gambler,
Dark and lustful and fierce and full of merciless cunning.
Something was spoken so low that I could not hear what the words were;
Only the woman started, and looked from one to the other,
With imploring eyes, bewildered hands, and a tremor
All through her frame: I saw her from where I was standing, she shook so.
'Say! is it so?' she cried. On the weak, white lips of her master
Died a sickly smile, and he said,—'Louise, I have sold you.'
God is my judge! May I never see such a look of despairing,
Desolate anguish, as that which the woman cast on her master,
Griping her breast with her little hands, as if he had stabbed her,

Standing in silence a space, as fixed as the Indian woman,
Carved out of wood, on the pilot-house of the old Pocahontas!
Then, with a gurgling moan, like the sound in the throat of the dying,
Came back her voice, that, rising, fluttered, through wild incoherence,
Into a terrible shriek that stopped my heart while she answered:—
'Sold me? sold me? sold—And you promised to give me my freedom!—
Promised me, for the sake of our little boy in Saint Louis!
What will you say to our boy, when he cries for me there in Saint Louis?
What will you say to our God?—Ah, you have been joking! I see it!—
No? God! God! He shall hear it,—and all of the angels in heaven,—
Even the devils in hell!—and none will believe when they hear it!
Sold me!'—Fell her voice with a thrilling wail, and in silence
Down she sank on the deck, and covered her face with her fingers."

IV.

In his story a moment the pilot paused, while we listened
To the salute of a boat, that, rounding the point of an island,
Flamed toward us with fires that seemed to burn from the waters,—
Stately and vast and swift, and borne on the heart of the current.
Then, with the mighty voice of a giant challenged to battle,
Rose the responsive whistle, and all the echoes of island,
Swamp-land, glade, and brake replied with a myriad clamor,
Like wild birds that are suddenly startled from slumber at midnight;
Then we were at peace once more, and we heard the harsh cries of the
    peacocks
Perched on a tree by a cabin-door, where the white-headed settler's
White-headed children stood to look at the boat as it passed them,
Passed them so near that we heard their happy talk and their laughter.
Softly the sunset had faded, and now on the eastern horizon
Hung, like a tear in the sky, the beautiful star of the evening.

V.

Still with his back to us standing, the pilot went on with his story:—
"Instantly, all the people, with looks of reproach and compassion,
Flocked round the prostrate woman. The children cried, and
    their mothers
Hugged them tight to their breasts; but the gambler said to the captain,—
'Put me off there at the town that lies round the bend of the river.
Here, you! rise at once, and be ready now to go with me.'
Roughly he seized the woman's arm and strove to uplift her.
She—she seemed not to heed him, but rose like one that is dreaming,
Slid from his grasp, and fleetly mounted the steps of the gangway,
Up to the hurricane-deck, in silence, without lamentation.
Straight to the stern of the boat, where the wheel was, she ran, and
    the people

Followed her fast till she turned and stood at bay for a moment,
Looking them in the face, and in the face of the gambler.
Not one to save her,—not one of all the compassionate people!
Not one to save her, of all the pitying angels in heaven!
Not one bolt of God to strike him dead before her!
Wildly she waved him back, we waiting in silence and horror.
Over the swarthy face of the gambler a pallor of passion
Passed, like a gleam of lightning over the west in the night-time.
White, she stood, and mute, till he put forth his hand to secure her;
Then she turned and leaped,—in mid air fluttered a moment,—
Down, there, whirling, fell, like a broken-winged bird from a tree-top,
Down on the cruel wheel, that caught her, and hurled her, and
    crushed her,
And in the foaming water plunged her, and hid her forever."

VI.
Still with his back to us all the pilot stood, but we heard him
Swallowing hard, as he pulled the bell-rope to stop her. Then, turning,—
"This is the place where it happened," brokenly whispered the pilot.
"Somehow, I never like to go by here alone in the night-time."
Darkly the Mississippi flowed by the town that lay in the starlight,
Cheerful with lamps. Below we could hear them reversing the engines,
And the great boat glided up to the shore like a giant exhausted.
Heavily sighed her pipes. Broad over the swamps to the eastward
Shone the full moon, and turned our far-trembling wake into silver.
All was serene and calm, but the odorous breath of the willows
Smote like the subtile breath of an infinite sorrow upon us.

27

From *Mulatto:*
An Original Romantic Drama in Five Acts

Hans Christian Andersen

Although Hans Christian Andersen (1805–1875) arrived at his first public recognition as a romantic playwright and was awarded a royal stipend as the result of his dramatic work, his interesting 1840 play *Mulatten: Originalt romantisk Drama i Fem Akter* (Mulatto: An Original Romantic Drama in Five Acts), which Andersen adapted from a French novella, has never been translated into English. In the full play, the protagonist, Horatio, appears as a romantic genius figure, a Shakespeare-reading, scientifically minded man of a truly Christian spirit who is also handsome and close to nature. When, early in the play, the young Cecilie and the older Eleonore seek shelter in his cabin, both fall in love with Horatio. Eleonore's husband is driven to jealous rage when he learns of her secret, which she speaks out in a dream: she hates her husband and loves Horatio, the Mulatto!

The following scenes, translated by the editor with the help of Jesper Sørensen and Christoph Lohmann, convey a sense of the unusual features the Danish fairy tale teller added to the drama of interracial love, slavery, and revolution. When Andersen's *Mulatten* was first performed in 1840 (after only seven stage rehearsals), it received an overwhelmingly positive response from the audience and, on the whole, favorable notices in the Danish press, confirming Andersen's own feeling that his true poetic career had started with this play.

Dramatis Personae

HORATIO, a Mulatto
M. DE LA REBELLIÈRE, owner of several plantations on Martinique
ELEONORE, his wife
CECILIE, Countess of Ratél, his ward
PALÈME, Mulatto, escaped from La Rebellière's plantation
FEMI, black slave woman
PELAGI, peddlar woman
KADU, overseer of the countess's estate
AUCTIONEER

Market people. Servants. Male and female slaves.
The action takes place on Martinique.

II.ii

HORATIO *in hunting outfit.* PALÈME, *drinking from a coconut.*

HORATIO. Coconut milk is to your taste, I think!

PALÈME. Such milk I had when I was just a boy;
        It's real rum; wouldn't you like a drink?
        Your hunter's luck might grow with joy.

HORATIO. I thank you, no.

PALÈME. I never urge a soul.—
        There was a meeting here last night, of slaves
        Without masters, blacks who freed themselves,
        "The Avengers"! Look here, in those rocks, the coal
        Is still aglow they lit to brew their bane,
        As if vile poison were a sacrament!
        More slaves than I had ever hoped to see
        Were here, as one, to chant a magic melody.
        Snakelike they slithered, crawled, and schemed,
        To become "The Avengers" on their bloody fiend.
        What hellish tortures has devised the white
        To turn slaves' lives into one cry of misery, of plight.
        But now revenge of blood and fire turns things right.
        The mine the white man built will soon explode
        And red the bird of death fly o'er the scarlet road!

HORATIO. But were you just a silent witness to this plan?

PALÈME. No! I preached freedom's gospel here to every man,
        The freedom of the bird before the hunter's shots explode,
        Of forest trees before the axe cuts them to firewood.
        Soon freedom's banner we shall hoist on our shore,
        On roads and on plantations where slavery ruled before.
        Once blacks will be proud and dare to defy—
        It will be the end of white supremacy.
        Night follows day, that is the rule of Nature,
        Only by taking turns they govern earth.
        For too long now, white day has held the crown;
        But soon black night will take its rightful throne.

HORATIO. That will be a bloody coronation!

PALÈME. Hell itself will be our guest at celebration
        And happy, torchlight-like, will blaze every plantation.
        On scarlet carpets, dyed in deep red blood,
        Will trample the procession of the unshoe'd.
        Into my master's heart I'll plunge my knife
        After first raping what is sacred to his life.
        If I should fail, then God may damn us, one and all!
        Yet Europe's shores will hear our freedom's call!

HORATIO. Then all the whites must die?

PALÈME. Yes, all!
HORATIO. But when destroyed will be plantations and estates
            Will not the new masters be at pain?
            Who shall erect the burned-down house again?
            Who shall be slaves once there are no more whites?
PALÈME. Yes, that is true! Then not all whites must die!
HORATIO. The blacks will then be rulers of the isle;
            And who is strongest in his might and power
            Will force the weak ones to obey and cower.
            A black be king and in the throne be thrust—
            But will *you* bow before a Negro in the dust?
PALÈME. I'd rather whip myself with hardy reeds
            Or tear mine own eye from its socket as it bleeds!
            No, there must justice be and right,
            He who should rule both over black and white,
            Must be of color in between!
            Mulatto is the ideal king,
            None other must be governing!
HORATIO. Remember only that in tropic lands
            There is no dusk dividing day and night,
            No third time in between. Be careful with your plans!
            Silence your wish to govern black and white.
            Or have you preached to blacks your gospel true,
            As proudly you revealed it to me, too?
PALÈME. They would not dream what you so clearly see.
            Bastard trusts only bastard! Look at you and me:
            We are the same color, the same kind.
            The only difference: I had to flee from slavery's bind,
            While you are masterless and have a lighter lot;
            My path to happiness is slow and winding, yet I fought.
            —That I am still alive, however, is a gift
            I owe to you: my thanks will always be abiding.
            On rotting cane I lay in hiding,
            A modern Job, sick and bereft,
            A corpse whose faculty of thought was left!
            You freed me from the horde of evil ants,
            Revived me! How could I repay, if given a chance?
            The least is, trust in you till my last breath.
            Or—name an enemy: and he will meet his certain death!
HORATIO. An enemy I have; and he's my master:
            Heart's pride! No fiend is worse than he.
            His breath alone the rose of health makes wither,
            Turns restful sleep into a nightmare fever.
            His chant of triumph is heart's tragedy:
            Murder *this* fiend, it is the only remedy.

(Descends into the mountain crevice.)…

IV.vii

Sugar mill. HORATIO *is imprisoned in a vaulted chamber.* FEMI *enters*

FEMI. *(with a lamp in her hand)*
    How cold and damp it is in here! the canal's near by.
    —Tomorrow, when the sun shines brightest in the day,
    Is the appointed hour, when he'll be led away.
    How hard and cruel! Yet let us keep the memory
    Of Jesus, who was led to Calvary.
    (She approaches HORATIO.*)*
    Horatio! He does not hear me, deep asleep is he.
    (Holds the light closer to him.)
    How beautiful, yes, all too beautiful he is, though pale!
    His breathing, just like quiet sighing, tells a tale.
    Wait! I have a thought!—Must he not know
    His mother's name. Enambuk, long ago,
    Was father to him! Oh, how my forehead burns!
    Was he Biscuya's son? On this the whole tale turns
    I've heard a hundred times and more.—
    Wake up! My lady sends me to your door!

HORATIO. Who are you?

FEMI. Femi am I. This written note
    Is from my lady.

HORATIO. Give me what she wrote.
    (He reads it. His whole soul is moved.)

FEMI. *(Folds her hand and looks gently at him.)*

HORATIO. *(Lets his hand sink and repeats the conclusion of the letter.)*
    "No matter what should happen, always trust in God,
    Have faith in Him, for He will leave us not.
    What once you glanced at night, though as of sand,
    On solid rock in daylight it will stand."

FEMI. I do believe, I know—I see the saving port
    O tell me, say your mother's name!

HORATIO. Biscuya!

FEMI. What, Biscuya? Thank the Lord!

HORATIO. Biscuya was her name. Did you know her,
    My poor mother!

FEMI. Biscuya. Yes, I knew her,
    She carried herself like a princess proud.
    Ah, was she beautiful, as light in a cloud.
    Black like ebony, slim like a palm.
    Yet, only a child, I heard of the harm
    She suffered, was told how she was wounded.
    In Africa a thousand blacks surrounded
    Her father's tents, but the white foe

Robbed all her happiness, made it melt like snow:
A mere slave is the black in a foreign land!

HORATIO. A poor, sold woman was my mother!

FEMI. Sold into the last of the Enambuks' hand,
She won his heart, was loved by him, and,
As she was young, beautiful, proud like no other.
The first time that he pushed her away,
She fled and sought a hideaway
In the forest on my lady's property,
And in the cave she gave birth to a child.
Weeks went by; when the good Lord Ratél,
My lady's uncle, walked by and saw so well
The mother, seated by the palm tree,
Her head against the trunk, bent was her knee.
A child, the white man's, lay at her bosom still,
Yet she was dead, he saw the broken spirit in her face—!

HORATIO. My poor mother!

FEMI. He took the child,
You stayed with him.

HORATIO. Yes, I stayed in this place!

FEMI. Once in society it was said,
The last Enambuk, he made fun of this,
You were his son—!

HORATIO. His son!

FEMI. In the rooms of the house
It was often said. You were so beautiful, he thought!
Thus were you raised by Enambuk.

HORATIO. He my father! I am so deeply moved,
An austere master he so often proved!
As benefactor, all too much he gave, but rather
I wish he'd been more generous as a father!

FEMI. On my lady's estate, behind the hills,
In the caretaker's books, ledgers, and bills,
Carefully written is everyone's name,
Even that of Biscuya's son. Victory true!
You can't be sold, for my lady owns you....

V.vi

A small room. Church bells can be heard.

CECILIE. *(alone)*
Yes, he is knighted, knighted by God!
His ancestors: spirits of olden time.
What they have sung, what they have taught,
Make the banners and flags of a royal line.
The spirit alone rules and commands,
Oedipus-like in nature he stands.

The Sphinx's riddles he bravely explains,
Thus victory, true nobility, he obtains.
The noble coat of arms I wear
Is only a reflection of forefathers' deeds!
The spirit himself achieves triumph fair,
His heart's voice to permanent victory leads.
The bitter tears which flow with pity
One day will form a string of pearls.
Heart and mind make true nobility;
The spirit rules: vassal is everything else! …

V.viii

A wide open place.

(Here and there stands are being built; a fire is burning, on which food is being prepared. Coconuts and fruit are displayed; boxes and sacks are lying on the ground; flags are waving; a juggler's sign can be seen. The whole arrangement offers a picture of life in tropical climes. Whites, blacks, and colored people move about in a colorful crowd, the auctioneer and his scribe are seated behind a desk; a black slave, put up for sale, stands on a board which rests on two barrels; a number of blacks, all without chains, lie in picturesque groupings; in front among them is HORATIO, *with bare head and feet. As the scene opens, everything is in motion, many sounds and noises are heard.)*

AUCTIONEER. Order!

A PLANTER. My offer's a hundred times four!

AUCTIONEER. The black is yours!—Lead him before
      The circle's width.

LA REBELLIÈRE. The minutes pass!
      Precious is time; put the Mulatto up for bids.
      I'll buy him.

PELAGI. I want to buy him too!

LA REBELLIÈRE. Pelagi, you? Too dear this man
      Will be for you!

ANOTHER PLANTER. You'll soon learn why!

LA REBELLIÈRE. *(He has stepped over to* HORATIO.*)*
      Get up!—I'll make it come to pass!
      Get up and walk!—It's you I want to buy!

HORATIO. *(Looks contemptuously at him without answering.)*

LA REBELLIÈRE. My whip will teach you, powerless mite!

HORATIO. I'm free as my thoughts, free and proud!
      Only my body, not my spirit, can you dominate!—
      A lowly craftsman your father was; and loud
      Commonness speaks out of you; no spirit's flight
      Was ever in you! Baseness remains your fate.

LA REBELLIÈRE. *(Lifts his cane to hit him.)*
      Ha! I shall kill you!

HORATIO. *(Tears away the cane, breaks it in two, and throws the pieces at him.)*
      Contemptible man!

Come what may!
(Hides his face.)

LA REBELLIÈRE. The punishment
　　I shall choose! Yours will be full of pain!

AUCTIONEER. Bring the slave forward!

HORATIO. *(to himself)* Farewell, all hope!

V.ix

The previous, CECILIE, KADU.

CECILIE. He is my property. He is not for sale.

　KADU. He is owned by the Countess of Ratél.
　　On her estate this slave was born. His name
　　Is written here, his mother's name as well.
　　(Points to the book.)
　　On her behalf, I make the Countess's rightful claim.

AUCTIONEER. Yes! It is so!

LA REBELLIÈRE. Give me the slave!
　　It is my first request to you! Do not say no!
　　If I can't buy him, I shall pay in gold
　　His Slave chains' weight.

CECILIE. I cannot do that, no.

ELEONORE. Mother of God! You are benevolent to me and kind!

LA REBELLIÈRE. Just name a sum.

CECILIE. No, not for any price!
　　Where could a happiness like mine I find?
　　Stand up, Horatio! Since by law's decree
　　Command I must now over thee,
　　Obey my order, and it is: Be free!
　　Forget the nightmare, for this is its end,
　　The bleakest hours, they have disappeared.
　　Travel to France, and don't forget—your friend!

HORATIO. Yours I am, and will live for you alone,
　　My faith in God and world is firm as stone.
　　What you have built here, grow it must
　　For in Horatio you can put your trust!

LA REBELLIÈRE. You are freeing him? Is this in jest?

CECILIE. Free as his mind—which you could never dominate!

ELEONORE. *(to* CECILIE, *overwhelmed by her feelings)*
　　Oh, I could bow before you in the dust,
　　Blessed be you! *(to* LA REBELLIÈRE*)*
　　Did you not swear of late,
　　Before my eyes you'd whip him till he dies?

LA REBELLIÈRE. The Countess of Ratél is free to act:
　　The Law is on her side. Yet one must follow a legal tract
　　In all its points! It's also written in the Law,

As is most certainly and indisputably known:
The slave who against the white man raises his hand alone,
Shall die by flogging! And today everyone saw
How that slave treated me, as in a whim!
Hence he must die. On my side is the Law.
And not even an angel could now rescue him.

THE AUCTIONEER. *(repeating)*
"The slave who against whites raises his hand alone,
Shall die by flogging."

LA REBELLIÈRE. Yes! This Law is known.

CECILIE. That's what you want?

LA REBELLIÈRE. Thus speaks the Law!
(to ELEONORE)
Now shall come true what I have said,
Before your eyes I'll whip him till he is dead.
Broken his yoke on earth will lie.

ELEONORE. I hate you, tear apart the tie
That binds us!

LA REBELLIÈRE. Only fulfill
We must the Law!

CECILIE. Indeed! Yet there is still
Another law: and with the power it holds,
Both over life and death, it mercifully molds
Even a sentence of death. It reads:
When a freeborn dame marries a slave
Then he is *free*: Pardoned will be his deeds,
Revoked will be his punishment,
His fetters hung in the church's nave.
He is free. *Free*!

AUCTIONEER. Thus speaks the Law!

CECILIE. The Law is on my side. Let it be heeded!
(points to HORATIO)
No longer a slave, this man without a flaw,
He is my groom! The Countess of Ratél
Gives him her hand. He never was a slave
Whose soul is noble. Triumph the mind always must,
And blow the soulless form away like dust!

(to HORATIO) Will you be free?

HORATIO. Cecilie!

ELEONORE. May you live well. *(exits)*

THE CROWD. Viva! Long live the young masters of Ratél.
(The curtain falls quickly.)

TRANSLATED BY WERNER SOLLORS
WITH JESPER SØRENSEN AND CHRISTOPH LOHMANN

28

The Octoroon; or, Life in Louisiana: A Play in Five Acts

Dion Boucicault

The prolific playwright and actor Dion Boucicault (ca. 1820–1890) was born in Ireland and educated in England, and spent a good part of his professional life in New York City. Boucicault's output was prodigious: he wrote almost 150 plays, many of which were extremely successful and long-running, including *London Assurance* (1841) and *The Poor of New York* (1857). *The Octoroon, or Life in Louisiana* was first produced in 1859 at New York's Winter Garden. It was based on a novel by Mayne Reid and was one of the most popular nineteenth-century dramas. The American version is reprinted here in its entirety, followed by the revised happy ending from the British edition.

CAST

GEORGE PEYTON

SALEM SCUDDER

MR. SUNNYSIDE

JACOB M'CLOSKY

WAHNOTEE

CAPTAIN RATTS

COLONEL POINTDEXTER

JULES THIBODEAUX

JUDGE CAILLOU

LAFOUCHE

JACKSON

OLD PETE

PAUL (a boy slave)

SOLON

MRS. PEYTON

ZOE

DORA SUNNYSIDE

GRACE

MINNIE

DIDO

ACT I.

SCENE I.—*A view of the Plantation Terrebonne, in Louisiana.—A branch of the Mississippi is seen winding through the Estate.—A low built, but extensive Planter's Dwelling, surrounded with a veranda, and raised a few feet from the ground, occupies the* L. *side.— A table and chairs,* R. C.

GRACE *discovered sitting at breakfast-table with* CHILDREN.

Enter SOLON, *from house,* L.

SOLON. Yah! you bomn'ble fry—git out—a gen'leman can't pass for you.

GRACE. (*Seizing a fly whisk.*) Hee! ha—git out! (*Drives* CHILDREN *away: in escaping they tumble against and trip up* SOLON, *who falls with tray; the* CHILDREN *steal the bananas and rolls that fall about.*)

(*Enter* PETE, R. U. E. [*he is lame*]; *he carries a mop and pail.*)

PETE. Hey! laws a massey! why, clar out! drop dat banana! I'll murder this yer crowd. (*He chases* CHILDREN *about; they leap over railing at back.*)

(*Exit* SOLON, R. U. E.)

Dem little niggers is a judgment upon dis generation.

(*Enter* GEORGE, *from house,* L.)

GEORGE. What's the matter, Pete.

PETE. It's dem black trash, Mas'r George; dis ere property wants claring; dem's getting too numerous round: when I gets time I'll kill some on 'em, sure!

GEORGE. They don't seem to be scared by the threat.

PETE. Top, you varmin! top till I get enough of you in one place!

GEORGE. Were they all born on this estate?

PETE. Guess they nebber was born—dem tings! what, dem?—get away! Born here— dem darkies? What, on Terrebonne? Don't b'lieve it, Mas'r George; dem black tings never was born at all; dey swarmed one mornin' on a sassafras tree in the swamp: I cotched 'em; dey ain't no 'count. Don't b'lieve dey'll turn out niggers when dey're growed; dey'll come out sunthin else.

GRACE. Yes, Mas'r George, dey was born here; and old Pete is fonder on 'em dan he is of his fiddle on a Sunday.

PETE. What? dem tings—dem?—get away (*makes blow at the* CHILDREN.) Born here! dem darkies! What, on Terrebonne? Don't b'lieve it, Mas'r George,—no. One morning dey swarmed on a sassafras tree in de swamp, and I cotched 'em all in a sieve—dat's how dey come on top of dis yearth—git out, you,—ya, ya! (*Laughs.*)

(*Exit* GRACE, R. U. E.)

(*Enter* MRS. PEYTON, *from house.*)

MRS. P. So, Pete, you are spoiling those children as usual!

PETE. Dat's right, missus! gib it to ole Pete! he's allers in for it. Git away dere! Ya! if dey aint all lighted, like coons, on dat snake fence, just out of shot. Look dar! Ya! ya! Dem debils. Ya!

MRS. P. Pete, do you hear?

PETE. Git down dar! I'm arter you!

(*Hobbles off,* R. 1 E.)

MRS. P. You are out early this morning, George.

George. I was up before daylight. We got the horses saddled, and galloped down the shell road over the Piney Patch; then coasting the Bayou Lake, we crossed the long swamps, by Paul's Path, and so came home again.

Mrs. P. (*Laughing.*) You seem already familiar with the names of every spot on the estate.

(*Enter* Pete.—*Arranges breakfast, &c.*)

George. Just one month ago I quitted Paris. I left that siren city as I would have left a beloved woman.

Mrs. P. No wonder! I dare say you left at least a dozen beloved women there, at the same time.

George. I feel that I departed amid universal and sincere regret. I left my loves and my creditors equally inconsolable.

Mrs. P. George, you are incorrigible. Ah! you remind me so much of your uncle, the judge.

George. Bless his dear old handwriting, it's all I ever saw of him. For ten years his letters came every quarter-day, with a remittance and a word of advice in his formal cavalier style; and then a joke in the postscript, that upset the dignity of the foregoing. Aunt, when he died, two years ago, I read over those letters of his, and if I didn't cry like a baby——

Mrs. P. No, George; say you wept like a man. And so you really kept those foolish letters?

George. Yes; I kept the letters, and squandered the money.

Mrs. P. (*Embracing him.*) Ah! why were you not my son—you are so like my dear husband.

(*Enter* Salem Scudder, r.)

Scud. Ain't he! Yes—when I saw him and Miss Zoe galloping through the green sugar crop, and doing ten dollars' worth of damage at every stride, says I, how like his old uncle he do make the dirt fly.

George. O, aunt! what a bright, gay creature she is!

Scud. What, Zoe! Guess that you didn't leave anything female in Europe that can lift an eyelash beside that gal. When she goes along, she just leaves a streak of love behind her. It's a good drink to see her come into the cotton fields—the niggers get fresh on the sight of her. If she ain't worth her weight in sunshine you may take one of my fingers off, and choose which you like.

Mrs. P. She need not keep us waiting breakfast, though. Pete, tell Miss Zoe that we are waiting.

Pete. Yes, missus. Why, Minnie, why don't you run when you hear, you lazy crittur? (Minnie *runs off.*) Dat's de laziest nigger on dis yere property. (*Sits down.*) Don't do nuffin.

Mrs. P. My dear George, you are left in your uncle's will heir to this estate.

George. Subject to your life interest and an annuity to Zoe, is it not so?

Mrs. P. I fear that the property is so involved that the strictest economy will scarcely recover it. My dear husband never kept any accounts, and we scarcely know in what condition the estate really is.

SCUD. Yes, we do, ma'am; it's in a darned bad condition. Ten years ago the judge took as overseer a bit of Connecticut hardware called M'Closky. The judge didn't understand accounts—the overseer did. For a year or two all went fine. The judge drew money like Bourbon whiskey from a barrel, and never turned off the tap. But out it flew, free for everybody or anybody to beg, borrow, or steal. So it went, till one day the judge found the tap wouldn't run. He looked in to see what stopped it, and pulled out a big mortgage. "Sign that," says the overseer; "it's only a formality." "All right," says the judge, and away went a thousand acres; so at the end of eight years, Jacob M'Closky, Esquire, finds himself proprietor of the richest half of Terrebonne——

GEORGE. But the other half is free.

SCUD. No, it ain't; because, just then, what does the judge do, but hire another overseer—a Yankee—a Yankee named Salem Scudder.

MRS. P. O, no, it was——

SCUD. Hold on, now! I'm going to straighten this account clear out. What was this here Scudder? Well, he lived in New York by sittin' with his heels up in front of French's Hotel, and inventin'——

GEORGE. Inventing what?

SCUD. Improvements—anything, from a stay-lace to a fire-engine. Well, he cut that for the photographing line. He and his apparatus arrived here, took the judge's likeness and his fancy, who made him overseer right off. Well, sir, what does this Scudder do but introduces his inventions and improvements on this estate. His new cotton gins broke down, the steam sugar-mills burst up, until he finished off with his folly what Mr. M'Closky with his knavery began.

MRS. P. O, Salem! how can you say so? Haven't you worked like a horse?

SCUD. No, ma'am, I worked like an ass, an honest one, and that's all. Now, Mr. George, between the two overseers, you and that good old lady have come to the ground; that is the state of things, just as near as I can fix it. (ZOE *sings without*, L.)

GEORGE. 'Tis Zoe.

SCUD. O, I have not spoiled that anyhow. I can't introduce any darned improvement there. Ain't that a cure for old age; it kinder lifts the heart up, don't it?

MRS. P. Poor child! what will become of her when I am gone? If you haven't spoiled her, I fear I have. She has had the education of a lady.

GEORGE. I have remarked that she is treated by the neighbors with a kind of familiar condescension that annoyed me.

SCUD. Don't you know that she is the natural daughter of the judge, your uncle, and that old lady thar just adored anything her husband cared for; and this girl, that another woman would a hated, she loves as if she'd been her own child.

GEORGE. Aunt, I am prouder and happier to be your nephew and heir to the ruins of Terrebonne, than I would have been to have had half Louisiana without you.

(*Enter* ZOE, *from house*, L.)

ZOE. Am I late? Ah! Mr. Scudder, good morning.

SCUD. Thank'ye. I'm from fair to middlin', like a bamboo cane, much the same all the year round.

ZOE. No; like a sugar cane; so dry outside, one would never think there was so much sweetness within.

SCUD. Look here; I can't stand that gal! if I stop here, I shall hug her right off. (*Sees* PETE, *who has set his pail down* L. C. *up stage, and goes to sleep on it.*) If that old nigger ain't asleep, I'm blamed. Hillo! (*Kicks pail from under* PETE, *and lets him down.*)

(*Exit,* L. U. E.)

PETE. Hi! Debbel's in de pail! Whar's breakfass?

(*Enter* SOLON *and* DIDO *with coffee-pot, dishes, &c.,* R. U. E.)

DIDO. Bless'ee, Missey Zoe, here it be. Dere's a dish of penpans—jess taste, Mas'r George—and here's fried bananas; smell 'em, do, sa glosh.

PETE. Hole yer tongue, Dido. Whar's de coffee? (*Pours out.*) If it don't stain de cup, your wicked ole life's in danger, sure! dat right! black as nigger; clar as ice. You may drink dat, Mas'r George. (*Looks off.*) Yah! here's Mas'r Sunnyside, and Missey Dora, jist drov up. Some of you niggers run and hole de hosses: and take dis, Dido. (*Gives her coffee-pot to hold, and hobbles off, followed by* SOLON *and* DIDO, R. U. E.)

(*Enter* SUNNYSIDE *and* DORA, R. U. E.)

SUNNY. Good day, ma'am. (*Shakes hands with* GEORGE.) I see we are just in time for breakfast. (*Sits,* R.)

DORA. O, none for me; I never eat. (*Sits,* R. C.)

GEORGE. (*Aside.*) They do not notice Zoe.—(*Aloud.*) You don't see Zoe, Mr. Sunnyside.

SUNNY. Ah! Zoe, girl; are you there?

DORA. Take my shawl, Zoe. (ZOE *helps her.*) What a good creature she is.

SUNNY. I dare say, now, that in Europe you have never met any lady more beautiful in person, or more polished in manners, than that girl.

GEORGE. You are right, sir; though I shrank from expressing that opinion in her presence, so bluntly.

SUNNY. Why so?

GEORGE. It may be considered offensive.

SUNNY. (*Astonished.*) What? I say, Zoe, do you hear that?

DORA. Mr. Peyton is joking.

MRS. P. (L. C.) My nephew is not acquainted with our customs in Louisiana, but he will soon understand.

GEORGE. Never, aunt! I shall never understand how to wound the feelings of any lady; and, if that is the custom here, I shall never acquire it.

DORA. Zoe, my dear, what does he mean?

ZOE. I don't know.

GEORGE. Excuse me, I'll light a cigar. (*Goes up.*)

DORA. (*Aside to* ZOE.) Isn't he sweet! O, dear Zoe, is he in love with anybody?

ZOE. How can I tell?

DORA. Ask him, I want to know; don't say I told you to inquire, but find out. Minnie, fan me, it is so nice—and his clothes are French, ain't they?

ZOE. I think so; shall I ask him that too?

DORA. No, dear. I wish he would make love to me. When he speaks to one he does it so easy, so gentle; it isn't bar-room style; love lined with drinks, sighs tinged with tobacco—and they say all the women in Paris were in love with him, which I feel *I* shall be: stop fanning me; what nice boots he wears.

SUNNY. (*To* MRS. PEYTON.) Yes, ma'am, I hold a mortgage over Terrebonne; mine's a ninth, and pretty near covers all the property, except the slaves. I believe Mr. M'Closky has a bill of sale on them. O, here he is.

(*Enter* M'CLOSKY, R. U. E.)

SUNNY. Good morning, Mr. M'Closky.

M'CLOSKY. Good morning, Mr. Sunnyside; Miss Dora, your servant.

DORA. (*Seated*, R. C.) Fan me, Minnie.—(*Aside*.) I don't like that man.

M'CLOSKY. (*Aside*, C.) Insolent as usual.—(*Aloud*.) You begged me to call this morning. I hope I'm not intruding.

MRS. P. My nephew, Mr. Peyton.

M'CLOSKY. O, how d'ye do, sir? (*Offers hand*, GEORGE *bows coldly*, R. C., *aside*.) A puppy, if he brings any of his European airs here we'll fix him.—(*Aloud*.) Zoe, tell Pete to give my mare a feed, will ye?

GEORGE. (*Angrily*.) Sir.

M'CLOSKY. Hillo! did I tread on ye?

MRS. P. What is the matter with George?

ZOE. (*Takes fan from Minnie*.) Go, Minnie, tell Pete; run!

(*Exit* MINNIE, R.)

MRS. P. Grace, attend to Mr. M'Closky.

M'CLOSKY. A julep, gal, that's my breakfast, and a bit of cheese.

GEORGE. (*Aside to* MRS. PEYTON.) How can you ask that vulgar ruffian to your table?

MRS. P. Hospitality in Europe is a courtesy; here, it is an obligation. We tender food to a stranger, not because he is a gentleman, but because he is hungry.

GEORGE. Aunt, I will take my rifle down to the Atchafalaya. Paul has promised me a bear and a deer or two. I see my little Nimrod yonder, with his Indian companion. Excuse me ladies. Ho! Paul! (*Enters house*.)

PAUL. (*Outside*.) I'ss, Mas'r George.

(*Enter* PAUL, R. U. E., *with* INDIAN, *who goes up*.)

SUNNY. It's a shame to allow that young cub to run over the swamps and woods, hunting and fishing his life away instead of hoeing cane.

MRS. P. The child was a favorite of the judge, who encouraged his gambols. I couldn't bear to see him put to work.

GEORGE. (*Returning with rifle*.) Come, Paul, are you ready?

PAUL. I'ss, Mas'r George. O, golly! ain't that a pooty gun.

M'CLOSKY. See here, you imps; if I catch you, and your red skin yonder, gunning in my swamps, I'll give you rats, mind; them vagabonds, when the game's about, shoot my pigs.

(*Exit* GEORGE *into house*.)

PAUL. You gib me rattan, Mas'r Clostry, but I guess you take a berry long stick to Wahnotee; ugh, he make bacon of you.

M'CLOSKY. Make bacon of me, you young whelp. Do you mean that I'm a pig? Hold on a bit. (*Seizes whip, and holds* PAUL.)

ZOE. O, sir! don't, pray, don't.

M'CLOSKY. (*Slowly lowering his whip.*) Darn you, red skin, I'll pay you off some day, both of ye. (*Returns to table and drinks.*)

SUNNY. That Indian is a nuisance. Why don't he return to his nation out West.

M'CLOSKY. He's too fond of thieving and whiskey.

ZOE. No; Wahnotee is a gentle, honest creature, and remains here because he loves that boy with the tenderness of a woman. When Paul was taken down with the swamp fever the Indian sat outside the hut, and neither ate, slept, or spoke for five days, till the child could recognize and call him to his bedside. He who can love so well is honest—don't speak ill of poor Wahnotee.

MRS. P. Wahnotee, will you go back to your people.

WAHNOTEE. Sleugh.

PAUL. He don't understand; he speaks a mash-up of Indian, and Mexican. Wahnotee Patira na sepau assa wigiran.

WAHNOTEE. Weal Omenee.

PAUL. Says he'll go if I'll go with him. He calls me Omenee, the Pigeon, and Miss Zoe is Ninemoosha, the Sweetheart.

WAHNOTEE. (*Pointing to* ZOE.) Ninemoosha.

ZOE. No, Wahnotee, we can't spare Paul.

PAUL. If Omenee remain, Wahnotee will die in Terrebonne. (*During the dialogue* WAHNOTEE *has taken* GEORGE's *gun.*)

(*Enter* GEORGE, L.)

GEORGE. Now I'm ready. (GEORGE *tries to regain his gun;* WAHNOTEE *refuses to give it up;* PAUL *quietly takes it from him and remonstrates with him.*)

DORA. Zoe, he's going; I want him to stay and make love to me, that's what I came for to-day.

MRS. P. George, I can't spare Paul for an hour or two; he must run over to the landing; the steamer from New Orleans passed up the river last night, and if there's a mail they have thrown it ashore.

SUNNY. I saw the mail-bags lying in the shed this morning.

MRS. P. I expect an important letter from Liverpool; away with you, Paul; bring the mail-bags here.

PAUL. I'm 'most afraid to take Wahnotee to the shed, there's rum there.

WAHNOTEE. Rum!

PAUL. Come, then, but if I catch you drinkin', O, laws a mussey, you'll get snakes! I'll gib it you! now mind.

(*Exit with* INDIAN, R. U. E.)

GEORGE. Come, Miss Dora, let me offer you my arm.

DORA. Mr. George, I am afraid, if all we hear is true, you have led a dreadful life in Europe.

GEORGE. That's a challenge to begin a description of my feminine adventures.

DORA. You have been in love, then?

GEORGE. Two hundred and forty-nine times! Let me relate you the worst cases.

Dora. No! no!

George. I'll put the naughty parts in French.

Dora. I won't hear a word! O, you horrible man! go on.

(*Exit* George *and* Dora *to house.*)

M'Closky. Now, ma'am, I'd like a little business, if agreeable. I bring you news: your banker, old La Fouche, of New Orleans, is dead; the executors are winding up his affairs, and have foreclosed on all overdue mortgages, so Terrebonne is for sale. Here's the Picayune (*producing paper*) with the advertisement.

Zoe. Terrebonne for sale!

Mrs. P. Terrebonne for sale, and you, sir, will doubtless become its purchaser.

M'Closky. Well, ma'am, I spose there's no law agin my bidding for it. The more bidders, the better for you. You'll take care, I guess, it don't go too cheap.

Mrs. P. O, sir, I don't value the place for its price, but for the many happy days I've spent here: that landscape, flat and uninteresting though it may be, is full of charm for me; those poor people, born around me, growing up about my heart, have bounded my view of life; and now to lose that homely scene, lose their black, ungainly faces: O, sir, perhaps you should be as old as I am, to feel as I do, when my past life is torn away from me.

M'Closky. I'd be darned glad if somebody would tear my past life away from *me*. Sorry I can't help you, but the fact is, you're in such an all-fired mess that you couldn't be pulled out without a derrick.

Mrs. P. Yes, there is a hope left yet, and I cling to it. The house of Mason Brothers, of Liverpool, failed some twenty years ago in my husband's debt.

M'Closky. They owed him over fifty thousand dollars.

Mrs. P. I cannot find the entry in my husband's accounts; but you, Mr. M'Closky, can doubtless detect it. Zoe, bring here the judge's old desk; it is in the library.

(*Exit* Zoe *to house.*)

M'Closky. You don't expect to recover any of this old debt, do you?

Mrs. P. Yes; the firm has recovered itself, and I received a notice two months ago that some settlement might be anticipated.

Sunny. Why, with principal and interest this debt has been more than doubled in twenty years.

Mrs. P. But it may be years yet before it will be paid off, if ever.

Sunny. If there's a chance of it, there's not a planter round here who wouldn't lend you the whole cash, to keep your name and blood amongst us. Come, cheer up, old friend.

Mrs. P. Ah! Sunnyside, how good you are; so like my poor Peyton.

(*Exit* Mrs. Peyton *and* Sunnyside *to house.*)

M'Closky. Curse their old families—they cut me—a bilious, conceited, thin lot of dried up aristocracy. I hate 'em. Just because my grandfather wasn't some broken-down Virginia transplant, or a stingy old Creole, I ain't fit to sit down with the same meat with them. It makes my blood so hot I feel my heart hiss. I'll sweep these Peytons from this section of the country. Their presence keeps alive the reproach against me that I ruined them; yet, if this money should come. Bah! There's no chance of it. Then, if they go, they'll take Zoe—she'll follow them.

Darn that girl; she makes me quiver when I think of her; she's took me for all I'm worth.

(*Enter* Zoe *from house*, L., *with the desk.*)

O, here, do you know what annuity the old judge left you is worth to-day? Not a picayune.

Zoe. It's surely worth the love that dictated it; here are the papers and accounts. (*Putting it on the table,* R. C.)

M'Closky. Stop, Zoe; come here! How would you like to rule the house of the richest planter on Atchapalaga—eh? or say the word, and I'll buy this old barrack, and you shall be mistress of Terrebonne.

Zoe. O, sir, do not speak so to me!

M'Closky. Why not! look here, these Peytons are bust; cut 'em; I am rich, jine me; I'll set you up grand, and we'll give these first families here our dust, until you'll see their white skins shrivel up with hate and rage: what d'ye say?

Zoe. Let me pass! O, pray, let me go!

M'Closky. What, you won't, won't ye? If young George Peyton was to make you the same offer, you'd jump at it, pretty darned quick, I guess. Come, Zoe, don't be a fool; I'd marry you if I could, but you know I can't; so just say what you want. Here, then, I'll put back these Peytons in Terrebonne, and they shall know you done it; yes, they'll have you to thank for saving them from ruin.

Zoe. Do you think they would live here on such terms?

M'Closky. Why not? We'll hire out our slaves, and live on their wages.

Zoe. But I'm not a slave.

M'Closky. No; if you were I'd buy you, if you cost all I'm worth.

Zoe. Let me pass!

M'Closky. Stop.

(*Enter* Scudder, R.)

Scud. Let her pass.

M'Closky. Eh?

Scud. Let her pass! (*Takes out his knife.*) *Exit* Zoe *to house.*

M'Closky. Is that you, Mr. Overseer? (*Examines paper.*)

Scud. Yes, I'm here, somewhere, interferin'.

M'Closky. (*Sitting,* R. C.) A pretty mess you've got this estate in—

Scud. Yes—me and Co.—we done it; but, as you were senior partner in the concern, I reckon you got the big lick.

M'Closky. What d'ye mean.

Scud. Let me proceed by illustration. (*Sits,* R.) Look thar! (*Points with knife off,* R.) D'ye see that tree?—it's called a live oak, and is a native here; beside it grows a creeper; year after year that creeper twines its long arms round and round the tree—sucking the earth dry all about its roots—living on its life—overrunning its branches, until at last the live oak withers and dies out. Do you know what the niggers round here call that sight? they call it the Yankee hugging the Creole. (*Sits.*)

M'Closky. Mr. Scudder, I've listened to a great many of your insinuations, and now I'd like to come to an understanding what they mean. If you want a quarrel—

SCUDDER. No, I'm the skurriest crittur at a fight you ever see; my legs have been too well brought up to stand and see my body abused; I take good care of myself, I can tell you.

M'CLOSKY. Because I heard that you had traduced my character.

SCUD. Traduced! Whoever said so lied. I always said you were the darndest thief that ever escaped a white jail to misrepresent the North to the South.

M'CLOSKY. (*Raises hand to back of his neck.*) What!

SCUD. Take your hand down—take it down. (M'CLOSKY *lowers his hand.*) Whenever I gets into company like yours, I *always* start with the advantage on my side.

M'CLOSKY. What d'ye mean?

SCUD. I mean that before you could draw that bowie-knife, you wear down your back, I'd cut you into shingles. Keep quiet, and let's talk sense. You wanted to come to an understanding, and I'm coming thar as quick as I can. Now, Jacob M'Closky, you despise me because you think I'm a fool; I despise you because I know you to be a knave. Between us we've ruined these Peytons; you fired the judge, and I finished off the widow. Now, I feel bad about my share in the business. I'd give half the balance of my life to wipe out my part of the work. Many a night I've laid awake and thought how to pull them through, till I've cried like a child over the sum I couldn't do; and you know how darned hard 'tis to make a Yankee cry.

M'CLOSKY. Well, what's that to me?

SCUD. Hold on, Jacob, I'm coming to that—I tell ye, I'm such a fool—I can't bear the feeling, it keeps at me like a skin complaint, and if this family is sold up—

M'CLOSKY. What then?

SCUD. (*Rising.*) I'd cut my throat—or yours—yours I'd prefer.

M'CLOSKY. Would you now? why don't you do it?

SCUD. 'Cos I's skeered to try! I never killed a man in my life—and civilization is so strong in me I guess I couldn't do it—I'd like to, though!

M'CLOSKY. And all for the sake of that old woman and that young puppy—eh? No other cause to hate—to envy me—to be jealous of me—eh?

SCUD. Jealous! what for?

M'CLOSKY. Ask the color in your face: d'ye think I can't read you, like a book? With your New England hypocrisy, you would persuade yourself it was this family alone you cared for: it ain't—you know it ain't—'tis the "Octoroon;" and you love her as I do; and you hate me because I'm your rival—that's where the tears come from, Salem Scudder, if you ever shed any—that's where the shoe pinches.

SCUD. Wal, I do like the gal; she's a—

M'CLOSKY. She's in love with young Peyton; it made me curse, whar it made you cry, as it does now; I see the tears on your cheeks now.

SCUD. Look at 'em, Jacob, for they are honest water from the well of truth. I ain't ashamed of it—I do love the gal; but I ain't jealous of you, because I believe the only sincere feeling about you is your love for Zoe, and it does your heart good to have her image thar; but I believe you put it thar to spile. By fair means I don't think you can get her, and don't you try foul with her, 'cause if you do, Jacob, civilization be darned. I'm on you like a painter, and when I'm drawed out I'm pizin.

(*Exit* SCUDDER *to house,* L.)

M'CLOSKY. Fair or foul, I'll have her—take that home with you! (*Opens desk.*) What's here—judgments? yes, plenty of 'em; bill of costs; account with Citizens' Bank— what's this? "Judgment, 40,000, 'Thibodeaux against Peyton,'"—surely, that is the judgment under which this estate is now advertised for sale—(*takes up paper and examines it*): yes, "Thibodeaux against Peyton, 1838." Hold on! whew! this is worth taking to—in this desk the judge used to keep one paper I want—this should be it. (*Reads.*) "The free papers of my daughter, Zoe, registered February 4th, 1841." Why, judge, wasn't you lawyer enough to know that while a judgment stood against you it was a lien on your slaves? Zoe is your child by a quadroon slave, and you didn't free her; blood! if this is so, she's mine! this old Liverpool debt—that may cross me—if it only arrive too late—if it don't come by this mail—Hold on! this letter the old lady expects—that's it; let me only head off that letter, and Terrebonne will be sold before they can recover it. That boy and the Indian have gone down to the landing for the post-bags; they'll idle on the way as usual; my mare will take me across the swamp, and before they can reach the shed, I'll have purified them bags—ne'er a letter shall show this mail. Ha, ha!—(*Calls.*) Pete, you old turkey-buzzard, saddle my mare. Then, if I sink every dollar I'm worth in her purchase, I'll own that Octoroon. (*Stands with his hand extended towards the house, and tableau.*)
END OF THE FIRST ACT.

ACT II.

The Wharf—goods, boxes, and bales scattered about—a camera on stand, R.

SCUDDER, R., DORA, L., GEORGE *and* PAUL *discovered*; DORA *being photographed by* SCUDDER, *who is arranging photographic apparatus,* GEORGE *and* PAUL *looking on at back.*

SCUD. Just turn your face a leetle this way—fix your—let's see—look here.

DORA. So?

SCUD. That's right. (*Puts his head under the darkening apron.*) It's such a long time since I did this sort of thing, and this old machine has got so dirty and stiff, I'm afraid it won't operate. That's about right. Now don't stir.

PAUL. Ugh! she look as though she war gwine to have a tooth drawed!

SCUD. I've got four plates ready, in case we miss the first shot. One of them is pre-pared with a self-developing liquid that I've invented. I hope it will turn out better than most of my notions. Now fix yourself. Are you ready?

DORA. Ready!

SCUD. Fire!—one, two, three. (SCUDDER *takes out watch.*)

PAUL. Now it's cooking, laws mussey, I feel it all inside, as if it was at a lottery.

SCUD. So! (*Throws down apron.*) That's enough. (*Withdraws slide, turns and sees* PAUL.) What! what are you doing there, you young varmint! Ain't you took them bags to the house yet?

PAUL. Now, it ain't no use trying to get mad, Mas'r Scudder. I'm gwine! I only come back to find Wahnotee; whar is dat ign'ant Ingiun?

SCUD. You'll find him scenting round the rum store, hitched up by the nose.

(*Exit into room R.*)

PAUL. (*Calling at door.*) Say, Mas'r Scudder, take me in dat telescope?

SCUD. (*Inside room.*) Get out, you cub! clar out!

PAUL. You got four of dem dishes ready. Gosh, wouldn't I like to hab myself took! What's de charge, Mas'r Scudder? (*Runs off,* R. U. E.)

(*Enter* SCUDDER, *from room,* R.)

SCUD. Job had none of them critters on his plantation, else he'd never ha' stood through so many chapters. Well, that has come out clear, ain't it? (*Shows plate.*)

DORA. O, beautiful! Look, Mr. Peyton.

GEORGE. (*Looking.*) Yes, very fine!

SCUD. The apparatus can't mistake. When I travelled round with this machine, the homely folks used to sing out, "Hillo, mister, this ain't like me!" "Ma'am," says I, "the apparatus can't mistake." "But, mister, that ain't my nose." "Ma'am, your nose drawed it. The machine can't err—you may mistake your phiz but the apparatus don't." "But, sir, it ain't agreeable." "No, ma'am, the truth seldom is."

(*Enter* PETE, L. U. E., *puffing.*)

PETE. Mas'r Scudder! Mas'r Scudder!

SCUD. Hillo! what are you blowing about like a steamboat with one wheel for?

PETE. *You* blow, Mas'r Scudder, when I tole you: dere's a man from Noo Aleens just arriv' at de house, and he's stuck up two papers on de gates: "For sale—dis yer property," and a heap of oder tings—and he seen missus, and arter he shown some papers she burst out crying—I yelled; den de corious of little niggers dey set up, den de hull plantation children—de live stock reared up and created a purpiration of lamentation as did de ole heart good to har.

DORA. What's the matter?

SCUD. He's come.

PETE. Dass it—I saw'm!

SCUD. The sheriff from New Orleans has taken possession—Terrebonne is in the hands of the law.

(*Enter* ZOE, L. U. E.)

ZOE. O, Mr. Scudder! Dora! Mr. Peyton! come home—there are strangers in the house.

DORA. Stay, Mr. Peyton: Zoe, a word! (*Leads her forward—aside.*) Zoe, the more I see of George Peyton the better I like him; but he is too modest—that is a very impertinent virtue in a man.

ZOE. I'm no judge, dear.

DORA. Of course not, you little fool; no one ever made love to you, and you can't understand; I mean, that George knows I am an heiress; my fortune would release this estate from debt.

ZOE. O, I see!

DORA. If he would only propose to marry me I would accept him, but he don't know that, and he will go on fooling, in his slow European way, until it is too late.

ZOE. What's to be done?

DORA. You tell him.

ZOE. What? that he isn't to go on fooling in his slow—

DORA. No, you goose! twit him on his silence and abstraction—I'm sure it's plain enough, for he has not spoken two words to me all the day; then joke round the subject, and at last speak out.

SCUD. Pete, as you came here, did you pass Paul and the Indian with the letter-bags?

PETE. No, sar; but dem vagabonds neber take de 'specable straight road, dey goes by de swamp.

(*Exit up path*, L. U. E.)

SCUD. Come, sir!

DORA. (*To* ZOE.) Now's your time.—(*Aloud.*) Mr. Scudder, take us with you—Mr. Peyton is so slow, there's no getting him on.

(*Exit* DORA *and* SCUDDER, L. U. E.)

ZOE. They are gone!—(*Glancing at* GEORGE.) Poor fellow, he has lost all.

GEORGE. Poor child! how sad she looks now she has no resource.

ZOE. How shall I ask him to stay?

GEORGE. Zoe, will you remain here? I wish to speak to you.

ZOE. (*Aside.*) Well, that saves trouble.

GEORGE. By our ruin, you lose all.

ZOE. O, I'm nothing; think of yourself.

GEORGE. I can think of nothing but the image that remains face to face with me: so beautiful, so simple, so confiding, that I dare not express the feelings that have grown up so rapidly in my heart.

ZOE. (*Aside.*) He means Dora.

GEORGE. If I dared to speak!

ZOE. That's just what you must do, and do it at once, or it will be too late.

GEORGE. Has my love been divined?

ZOE. It has been more than suspected.

GEORGE. Zoe, listen to me, then. I shall see this estate pass from me without a sigh, for it possesses no charm for me; the wealth I covet is the love of those around me—eyes that are rich in fond looks, lips that breathe endearing words; the only estate I value is the heart of one true woman, and the slaves I'd have are her thoughts.

ZOE. George, George, your words take away my breath!

GEORGE. The world, Zoe, the free struggle of minds and hands, is before me; the education bestowed on me by my dear uncle is a noble heritage which no sheriff can seize; with that I can build up a fortune, spread a roof over the heads I love, and place before them the food I have earned; I will work—

ZOE. Work! I thought none but colored people worked.

GEORGE. Work, Zoe, is the salt that gives savor to life.

ZOE. Dora said you were slow: if she could hear you now—

GEORGE. Zoe, you are young; your mirror must have told you that you are beautiful. Is your heart free?

ZOE. Free? of course it is!

GEORGE. We have known each other but a few days, but to me those days have been worth all the rest of my life. Zoe, you have suspected the feeling that now commands an utterance—you have seen that I love you.

ZOE. Me! you love *me?*

GEORGE. As my wife,—the sharer of my hopes, my ambitions, and my sorrows; under the shelter of your love I could watch the storms of fortune pass unheeded by.

ZOE. *My* love! *My* love? George, you know not what you say. *I* the sharer of your sorrows—your wife. Do you know what I am?

GEORGE. Your birth—I know it. Has not my dear aunt forgotten it—she who had the most right to remember it? You are illegitimate, but love knows no prejudice.

ZOE. (*Aside.*) Alas! he does not know, he does not know! and will despise me, spurn me, loathe me, when he learns who, what, he has so loved.—(*Aloud.*) George, O, forgive me! Yes, I love you—I did not know it until your words showed me what has been in my heart; each of them awoke a new sense, and now I know how unhappy—how very unhappy I am.

GEORGE. Zoe, what have I said to wound you?

ZOE. Nothing; but you must learn what I thought you already knew. George, you cannot marry me; the laws forbid it!

GEORGE. Forbid it?

ZOE. There is a gulf between us, as wide as your love, as deep as my despair; but, O, tell me, say you will pity me! that you will not throw me from you like a poisoned thing!

GEORGE. Zoe, explain yourself—your language fills me with shapeless fears.

ZOE. And what shall I say? I—my mother was—no, no—not her! Why should I refer the blame to her? George, do you see that hand you hold? look at these fingers; do you see the nails are of a bluish tinge?

GEORGE. Yes, near the quick there is a faint blue mark.

ZOE. Look in my eyes; is not the same color in the white?

GEORGE. It is their beauty.

ZOE. Could you see the roots of my hair you would see the same dark, fatal mark. Do you know what that is?

GEORGE. No.

ZOE. That is the ineffaceable curse of Cain. Of the blood that feeds my heart, one drop in eight is black—bright red as the rest may be, that one drop poisons all the flood; those seven bright drops give me love like yours—hope like yours—ambition like yours—life hung with passions like dew-drops on the morning flowers; but the one black drop gives me despair, for I'm an unclean thing—forbidden by the laws—I'm an Octoroon!

GEORGE. Zoe, I love you none the less; this knowledge brings no revolt to my heart, and I can overcome the obstacle.

ZOE. But *I* cannot.

GEORGE. We can leave this country, and go far away where none can know.

ZOE. And our mother, she who from infancy treated me with such fondness, she who, as you said, had most reason to spurn me, can she forget what I am? Will she gladly see you wedded to the child of her husband's slave? No! she would revolt from it, as all but you would; and if I consented to hear the cries of my heart, if I did not crush out my infant love, what would she say to the poor girl on whom she had bestowed so much? No, no!

GEORGE. Zoe, must we immolate our lives on her prejudice?

ZOE. Yes, for I'd rather be black than ungrateful! Ah, George, our race has at least one virtue—it knows how to suffer!

GEORGE. Each word you utter makes my love sink deeper into my heart.

ZOE. And I remained here to induce you to offer that heart to Dora!

GEORGE. If you bid me do so I will obey you—

ZOE. No, no! if you cannot be mine, O, let me not blush when I think of you.

GEORGE. Dearest Zoe!

(*Exit* GEORGE *and* ZOE, R. U. E.)

(*As they exit,* M'CLOSKY *rises from behind rock,* R., *and looks after them.*)

M'CLOSKY. She loves him! I felt it—and how she can love! (*Advances.*) That one black drop of blood burns in her veins and lights up her heart like a foggy sun. O, how I lapped up her words, like a thirsty bloodhound! I'll have her, if it costs me my life! Yonder the boy still lurks with those mail-bags; the devil still keeps him here to tempt me, darn his yellow skin. I arrived just too late, he had grabbed the prize as I came up. Hillo! he's coming this way, fighting with his Injiun. (*Conceals himself.*)

(*Enter* PAUL, *wrestling with* WAHNOTEE, R. U. E.)

PAUL. It ain't no use now: you got to gib it up!

WAHNO. Ugh!

PAUL. It won't do! You got dat bottle of rum hid under your blanket—gib it up now, you—. Yar! (*Wrenches it from him.*) You nasty, lying Injiun! It's no use you putting on airs; I ain't gwine to sit up wid you all night and you drunk. Hillo! war's de crowd gone? And dar's de 'paratus—O, gosh, if I could take a likeness ob dis child! Uh—uh, let's have a peep. (*Looks through camera.*) O, golly! yar, you Wahnotee! you stan' dar, I see you, Ta demine usti. (*Goes* R., *and looks at* WAHNOTEE, L., *through the camera;* WAHNOTEE *springs back with an expression of alarm.*)

WAHNO. No tue Wahnotee.

PAUL. Ha, ha! he tinks it's a gun. You ign'ant Injiun, it can't hurt you! Stop, here's dem dishes—plates—dat's what he call 'em, all fix: I see Mas'r Scudder do it often—tink I can take likeness—stay dere, Wahnotee.

WAHNO. No, carabine tue.

PAUL. I must operate and take my own likeness too—how debbel I do dat? Can't be ober dar an' here too—I ain't twins. Ugh! ach! 'Top; you look, you Wahnotee; you see dis rag, eh? Well when I say go, den lift dis rag like dis, see! den run to dat pine tree up dar (*points,* L. U. E.) and back agin, and den pull down de rag so, d'ye see?

WAHNO. Hugh!

PAUL. Den you hab glass ob rum.

WAHNO. Rum!

PAUL. Dat wakes him up. Coute Wahnotee in omenee dit go Wahnotee, poina la fa, comb a pine tree, la revieut sala, la fa.

WAHNO. Fire-water!

PAUL. Yes, den a glass ob fire-water; now den. (*Throws mailbags down and sits on them,* L. C.) Pret, now den go. (WAHNOTEE *raises apron and runs off,* L. U. E. PAUL *sits for his picture*—M'CLOSKY *appears from* R. U. E.)

M'CLOSKY. Where are they? Ah, yonder goes the Indian!

PAUL. De time he gone just 'bout enough to cook dat dish plate.

M'CLOSKY. Yonder is the boy—now is my time! What's he doing; is he asleep? (*Advances.*) He is sitting on my prize! darn his carcass! I'll clear him off there—he'll never know what stunned him. (*Takes Indian's tomahawk and steals to* PAUL.)

PAUL. Dam dat Injiun! is dat him creeping dar? I daren't move fear to spile myself. (M'CLOSKY *strikes him on the head—he falls dead.*)

M'CLOSKY. Hooraw! the bags are mine—now for it!—(*Opens mail-bags.*) What's here? Sunnyside, Pointdexter, Jackson, Peyton; here it is—the Liverpool post-mark, sure enough!—(*Opens letter—reads.*) "Madam, we are instructed by the firm of Mason and Co., to inform you that a dividend of forty per cent. is payable on the 1st proximo, this amount in consideration of position, they send herewith, and you will find enclosed by draft to your order, on the Bank of Louisiana, which please acknowledge—the balance will be paid in full, with interest, in three, six, and nine months—your drafts on Mason Brothers at those dates will be accepted by La Palisse and Compagnie, N. O., so that you may command immediate use of the whole amount at once, if required Yours, &c., James Brown." What a find! this infernal letter would have saved all. (*During the reading of letter he remains nearly motionless under the focus of the camera.*) But now I guess it will arrive too late— these darned U. S. mails are to blame. The Injiun! he must not see me.

(*Exit rapidly*, L.)

(WAHNOTEE *runs on, pulls down apron—sees* PAUL *lying on ground—speaks to him— thinks he's shamming sleep—gesticulates and jabbers—goes to him—moves him with feet, then kneels down to rouse him—to his horror finds him dead—expresses great grief—raises his eyes—they fall upon the camera—rises with savage growl, seizes tomahawk and smashes camera to pieces, then goes to* PAUL—*expresses grief, sorrow, and fondness, and takes him in his arms to carry him away.—Tableau.*)

END OF THE SECOND ACT.

ACT III.

A Room in Mrs. Peyton's house; entrances, R. U. E. *and* L. U. E.—*An Auction Bill stuck up,* L.—*chairs,* C., *and tables,* R. *and* L.

SOLON *and* GRACE *discovered.*

PETE. (*Outside,* R. U. E.) Dis way—dis way.

(*Enter* PETE, POINTDEXTER, JACKSON, LAFOUCHE, *and* CAILLOU, R. U. E.)

PETE. Dis way, gen'l'men; now Solon—Grace—dey's hot and tirsty—sangaree, brandy, rum.

JACKSON. Well, what d'ye say, Lafouche—d'ye smile?

(*Enter* THIBODEAUX *and* SUNNYSIDE, R. U. E.)

THIBO. I hope we don't intrude on the family.

PETE. You see dat hole in dar, sar. (R. U. E.) I was raised on dis yar plantation—neber see no door in it—always open, sar, for stranger to walk in.

SUNNY. And for substance to walk out.

(*Enter* Ratts, r. u. e.)

Ratts. Fine southern style that, eh!

Lafouche. (*Reading bill.*) "A fine, well-built old family mansion, replete with every comfort."

Ratts. There's one name on the list of slaves scratched, I see.

Lafouche. Yes; No. 49, Paul, a quadroon boy, aged thirteen.

Sunny. He's missing.

Point. Run away, I suppose.

Pete. (*Indignantly.*) No, sar; nigger nebber cut stick on Terrebonne; dat boy's dead, sure.

Ratts. What, Picayune Paul, as we called him, that used to come aboard my boat?—poor little darkey, I hope not; many a picayune he picked up for his dance and nigger songs, and he supplied our table with fish and game from the Bayous.

Pete. Nebber supply no more, sar—nebber dance again. Mas'r Ratts, you hard him sing about de place where de good niggers go, de last time.

Ratts. Well!

Pete. Well, he gone dar hisself; why, I tink so—'cause we missed Paul for some days, but nebber tout nothin' till one night dat Injiun Wahnotee suddenly stood right dar 'mongst us—was in his war paint, and mighty cold and grave—he sit down by de fire. "Whar's Paul?" I say—he smoke and smoke, but nebber look out ob de fire; well knowing dem critters, I wait a long time—den he say, "Wahnotee, great chief;" den I say nothing—smoke anoder time—last, rising to go, he turn round at door, and say berry low—O, like a woman's voice, he say, "Omenee Pangeuk,"—dat is, Paul is dead—nebber see him since.

Ratts. That red-skin killed him.

Sunny. So we believe; and so mad are the folks around, if they catch the red-skin they'll lynch him sure.

Ratts. Lynch him! Darn his copper carcass, I've got a set of Irish deck-hands aboard that just loved that child; and after I tell them this, let them get a sight of the red-skin, I believe they would eat him, tomahawk and all. Poor little Paul!

Thibo. What was he worth?

Ratts. Well, near on five hundred dollars.

Pete. (*Scandalized.*) What, sar! You p'tend to be sorry for Paul, and prize him like dat. Five hundred dollars!—(*To* Thibodeaux.) Tousand dollars, Massa Thibodeaux.

(*Enter* Scudder, l. u. e.)

Scud. Gentlemen, the sale takes place at three. Good morning, Colonel. It's near that now, and there's still the sugar-houses to be inspected. Good day, Mr. Thibodeaux—shall we drive down that way? Mr. Lafouche, why, how do you do, sir? you're looking well.

Lafouche. Sorry I can't return the compliment.

Ratts. Salem's looking a kinder hollowed out.

Scud. What, Mr. Ratts, are you going to invest in swamps?

Ratts. No: I want a nigger.

Scud. Hush.

Pete. (r.) Eh! wass dat?

SCUD. Mr. Sunnyside, I can't do this job of showin' round the folks; my stomach goes agin it. I wan't Pete here a minute.

SUNNY. I'll accompany them certainly.

SCUD. (*Eagerly.*) Will ye? Thank ye; thank ye.

SUNNY. We must excuse Scudder, friends. I'll see you round the estate.

(*Enter* GEORGE *and* MRS. PEYTON, L. U. E.)

LAFOUCHE. Good morning, Mrs. Peyton. (*All salute.*)

SUNNY. This way, gentlemen.

RATTS. (*Aside to* SUNNYSIDE.) I say, I'd like to say summit soft to the old woman; perhaps it wouldn't go well, would it?

THIBO. No; leave it alone.

RATTS. Darn it, when I see a woman in trouble, I feel like selling the skin off my back.

(*Exit* THIBODEAUX, SUNNYSIDE, RATTS, POINTDEXTER, GRACE, JACKSON, LAFOUCHE, CAILLOU, SOLON, R. U. E.)

SCUD. (*Aside to* PETE.) Go outside, there; listen to what you hear, then go down to the quarters and tell the boys, for I can't do it. O, get out.

PETE. He said I wan't a nigger. Laws, mussey! What am goin' to cum ob us!

(*Exit slowly, as if concealing himself,* R. U. E.)

GEORGE. (C.) My dear aunt, why do you not move from this painful scene? Go with Dora to Sunnyside.

MRS. P. (R.) No, George; your uncle said to me with his dying breath, "Nellie, never leave Terrebonne," and I never *will* leave it, till the law compels me.

SCUD. (L.) Mr. George, I'm going to say somethin' that has been chokin' me for some time. I know you'll excuse it. Thar's Miss Dora—that girl's in love with you; yes, sir, her eyes are startin' out of her head with it: now her fortune would redeem a good part of this estate.

MRS. P. Why, George, I never suspected this!

GEORGE. I did, aunt, I confess, but—

MRS. P. And you hesitated from motives of delicacy?

SCUD. No, ma'am; here's the plan of it. Mr. George is in love with Zoe.

GEORGE. Scudder!

MRS. P. George!

SCUD. Hold on now! things have got so jammed in on top of us, we ain't got time to put kid gloves on to handle them. He loves Zoe, and has found out that she loves him. (*Sighing.*) Well, that's all right; but as he can't marry her, and as Miss Dora would jump at him—

MRS. P. Why didn't you mention this before?

SCUD. Why, because *I* love Zoe, too, and I couldn't take that young feller from her; and she's jist living on the sight of him, as I saw her do; and they so happy in spite of this yer misery around them, and they reproachin' themselves with not feeling as they ought. I've seen it, I tell you; and darn it, ma'am, can't you see that's what's been a hollowing me out so—I beg your pardon.

MRS. P. O, George,—my son, let me call you,—I do not speak for my own sake, nor for the loss of the estate, but for the poor people here: they will be sold, divided, and taken away—they have been born here. Heaven has denied me children; so all the strings of my heart have grown around and amongst them, like the fibres and roots of an old tree in its native earth. O, let all go, but save them! With them around us, if we have not wealth, we shall at least have the home that they alone can make—

GEORGE. My dear mother—Mr. Scudder—you teach me what I ought to do; if Miss Sunnyside will accept me as I am, Terrebonne shall be saved: I will sell myself, but the slaves shall be protected.

MRS. P. *Sell* yourself, George! Is not Dora worth any man's—

SCUD. Don't say that, ma'am; don't say that to a man that loves another gal. He's going to do an heroic act; don't spile it.

MRS. P. But Zoe is only an Octoroon.

SCUD. She's won this race agin the white, anyhow; it's too late now to start her pedigree.

(*Enter* DORA, L. U. E.)

SCUD. (*Seeing* DORA.) Come, Mrs. Peyton, take my arm. Hush! here's the other one: she's a little too thoroughbred—too much of the greyhound; but the heart's there, I believe.

(*Exit* SCUDDER *and* MRS. PEYTON, R. U. E.)

DORA. Poor Mrs. Peyton.

GEORGE. Miss Sunnyside, permit me a word: a feeling of delicacy has suspended upon my lips an avowal, which—

DORA. (*Aside.*) O, dear, has he suddenly come to his senses?

(*Enter* ZOE, L. U. E., *she stops at back.*)

GEORGE. In a word, I have seen and admired you!

DORA. (*Aside.*) He has a strange way of showing it. European, I suppose.

GEORGE. If you would pardon the abruptness of the question, I would ask you, Do you think the sincere devotion of my life to make yours happy would succeed?

DORA. (*Aside.*) Well, he has the oddest way of making love.

GEORGE. You are silent?

DORA. Mr. Peyton, I presume you have hesitated to make this avowal because you feared, in the present condition of affairs here, your object might be misconstrued, and that your attention was rather to my fortune than myself. (*A pause.*) Why don't he speak?—I mean, you feared I might not give you credit for sincere and pure feelings. Well, you wrong me. I don't think you capable of anything else than—

GEORGE. No, I hesitated because an attachment I had formed before I had the pleasure of seeing you had not altogether died out.

DORA. (*Smiling.*) Some of those sirens of Paris, I presume. (*Pause.*) I shall endeavor not to be jealous of the past; perhaps I have no right to be. (*Pause.*) But now that vagrant love is—eh? faded—is it not? Why don't you speak, sir?

GEORGE. Because, Miss Sunnyside, I have not learned to lie.

DORA. Good gracious—who wants you to?

GEORGE. I do, but I can't do it. No, the love I speak of is not such as you suppose,—it is a passion that has grown up here since I arrived; but it is a hopeless, mad, wild feeling, that must perish.

DORA. Here! since you arrived! Impossible: you have seen no one; whom can you mean?

ZOE. (*Advancing,* C.) Me.

GEORGE. (L.) Zoe!

DORA. (R.) You!

ZOE. Forgive him, Dora; for he knew no better until I told him. Dora, you are right. He is incapable of any but sincere and pure feelings—so are you. He loves me—what of that? You know you can't be jealous of a poor creature like me. If he caught the fever, were stung by a snake, or possessed of any other poisonous or unclean thing, you could pity, tend, love him through it, and for your gentle care he would love you in return. Well, is he not thus afflicted now? I am his love—he loves an Octoroon.

GEORGE. O, Zoe, you break my heart!

DORA. At college they said I was a fool—I must be. At New Orleans, they said, "She's pretty, very pretty, but no brains." I'm afraid they must be right; I can't understand a word of all this.

ZOE. Dear Dora, try to understand it with your heart. You love George; you love him dearly; I know it: and you deserve to be loved by him. He will love you—he must. His love for me will pass away—it shall. You heard him say it was hopeless. O, forgive him and me!

DORA. (*Weeping.*) O, why did he speak to me at all then? You've made me cry, then, and I hate you both!

(*Exit* L., *through room.*)

(*Enter* MRS. PEYTON *and* SCUDDER, M'CLOSKY *and* POINTDEXTER, R.)

M'CLOSKY. (C.) I'm sorry to intrude, but the business I came upon will excuse me.

MRS. PEY. Here is my nephew, sir.

ZOE. Perhaps I had better go.

M'CLOSKY. Wal, as it consarns you, perhaps you better had.

SCUD. Consarns Zoe?

M'CLOSKY. I don't know; she may as well hear the hull of it. Go on, Colonel—Colonel Pointdexter, ma'am—the mortgagee, auctioneer, and general agent.

POINT. (R. C.) Pardon me, madam, but do you know these papers? (*Hands papers to* MRS. PEYTON.)

MRS. PEY. (*Takes them.*) Yes, sir; they were the free papers of the girl Zoe; but they were in my husband's secretary. How came they in your possession?

M'CLOSKY. I—I found them.

GEORGE. And you purloined them?

M'CLOSKY. Hold on, you'll see. Go on, Colonel.

POINT. The list of your slaves is incomplete—it wants one.

SCUD. The boy Paul—we know it.

POINT. No, sir; you have omitted the Octoroon girl, Zoe.

MRS. PEY. Zoe!

ZOE. Me!

POINT. At the time the judge executed those free papers to his infant slave, a judgment stood recorded against him; while that was on record he had no right to make away with his property. That judgment still exists: under it and others this estate is sold to-day. Those free papers ain't worth the sand that's on 'em.

MRS. PEY. Zoe a slave! It is impossible!

POINT. It is certain, madam: the judge was negligent, and doubtless forgot this small formality.

SCUD. But the creditors will not claim the gal?

M'CLOSKY. Excuse me; one of the principal mortgagees has made the demand.

(*Exit* M'CLOSKY *and* POINTDEXTER, R. U. E.)

SCUD. Hold on yere, George Peyton; you sit down there. You're trembling so, you'll fall down directly. This blow has staggered me some.

MRS. PEY. O, Zoe, my child! don't think too hardly of your poor father.

ZOE. I shall do so if you weep. See, I'm calm.

SCUD. Calm as a tombstone, and with about as much life. I see it in your face.

GEORGE. It cannot be! It shall not be!

SCUD. Hold your tongue—it must. Be calm—darn the things; the proceeds of this sale won't cover the debts of the estate. Consarn those Liverpool English fellers, why couldn't they send something by the last mail? Even a letter, promising something—such is the feeling round amongst the planters. Darn me, if I couldn't raise thirty thousand on the envelope alone, and ten thousand more on the post-mark.

GEORGE. Zoe, they shall not take you from us while I live.

SCUD. Don't be a fool; they'd kill you, and then take her, just as soon as—stop: Old Sunnyside, he'll buy her! that'll save her.

ZOE. No, it won't; we have confessed to Dora that we love each other. How can she then ask her father to free me?

SCUD. What in thunder made you do that?

ZOE. Because it was the truth; and I had rather be a slave with a free soul, than remain free with a slavish, deceitful heart. My father gives me freedom—at least he thought so. May Heaven bless him for the thought, bless him for the happiness he spread around my life. You say the proceeds of the sale will not cover his debts. Let me be sold then, that I may free his name. I give him back the liberty he bestowed upon me; for I can never repay him the love he bore his poor Octoroon child, on whose breast his last sigh was drawn, into whose eyes he looked with the last gaze of affection.

MRS. PEY. O, my husband! I thank Heaven you have not lived to see this day.

ZOE. George, leave me! I would be alone a little while.

GEORGE. Zoe! (*Turns away overpowered.*)

ZOE. Do not weep, George. Dear George, you now see what a miserable thing I am.

GEORGE. Zoe!

SCUD. I wish they could sell *me!* I brought half this ruin on this family, with my all-fired improvements. I deserve to be a nigger this day—I feel like one, inside.

(*Exit* SCUDDER, L. U. E.)

ZOE. Go now, George—leave me—take her with you.

(*Exit* MRS. PEYTON *and* GEORGE, L. U. E.)

A slave! a slave! Is this a dream—for my brain reels with the blow? He said so. What! then I shall be sold!—sold! and my master—O! (*falls on her knees, with her face in her hands*) no—no master, but one. George—George—hush—they come! save me! No, (*looks off*, R.) 'tis Pete and the servants—they come this way. (*Enters inner room*, R. U. E.)

(*Enter* PETE, GRACE, MINNIE, SOLON, DIDO, *and all* NIGGERS, R. U. E.)

PETE. Cum yer now—stand round, cause I've got to talk to you darkies—keep dem chil'n quiet—don't make no noise, de missus up dar har us.

SOLON. Go on, Pete.

PETE. Gen'l'men, my colored frens and ladies, dar's mighty bad news gone round. Dis yer prop'ty to be sold—old Terrebonne—whar we all been raised, is gwine—dey's gwine to tak it away—can't stop here no how.

OMNES. O-o!—O-o!

PETE. Hold quiet, you trash o'niggers! tink anybody wants you to cry? Who's you to set up screeching?—be quiet! But dis ain't all. Now, my culled brethren, gird up your lines, and listen—hold on yer bref—it's a comin. We tought dat de niggers would belong to de ole missus, and if she lost Terrebonne, we must live dere allers, and we would hire out, and bring our wages to ole Missus Peyton.

OMNES. Ya! ya! Well—

PETE. Hush! I tell ye, 't'ain't so—we can't do it—we've got to be sold—

OMNES. Sold!

PETE. Will you hush? she will har you. Yes! I listen dar jess now—dar was ole lady cryin'—Mas'r George—ah! you seen dem big tears in his eyes. O, Mas'r Scudder, he didn't cry zackly; both ob his eyes and cheek look like de bad Bayou in low season—so dry dat I cry for him. (*Raising his voice.*) Den say de missus, "'Tain't for de land I keer, but for dem poor niggers—dey'll be sold—dat wot stagger me." "No," say Mas'r George, "I'd rather sell myself fuss; but dey shan't suffer, nohow,—I see 'em dam fuss."

OMNES. O, bless um! Bless Mas'r George.

PETE. Hole yer tongues. Yes, for you, for me, for dem little ones, dem folks cried. Now, den, if Grace dere wid her chil'n were all sold, she'll begin screechin' like a cat. She didn't mind how kind old judge was to her; and Solon, too, he'll holler, and break de ole lady's heart.

GRACE. No, Pete; no, I won't. I'll bear it.

PETE. I don't tink you will any more, but dis here will; 'cause de family spile Dido, dey has. She nebber was worth much 'a dat nigger.

DIDO. How dar you say dat, you black nigger, you? I fetch as much as any odder cook in Louisiana.

PETE. What's de use of your takin' it kind, and comfortin' de missus heart, if Minnie dere, and Louise, and Marie, and Julie is to spile it?

MINNIE. We won't, Pete; we won't.

PETE. (*To the men.*) Dar, do ye hear dat, ye mis'able darkies, dem gals is worth a boat load of kinder men dem is. Cum, for de pride of de family, let every darky look his best for the judge's sake—dat ole man so good to us, and dat ole woman—so dem strangers from New Orleans shall say, "Dem's happy darkies dem's a fine set of niggars"; every one say when he's sold, "Lor' bless dis yer family I'm gwine out of, and send me as good a home."

OMNES. We'll do it, Pete; we'll do it.

PETE. Hush! hark! I tell ye dar's somebody in dar. Who is it?

GRACE. It's Missy Zoe. See! see!

PETE. Come along; she har what we say, and she's cryin' for us. None o'ye ign'rant niggars could cry for yerselves like dat. Come here quite: now quite.

(*Exit* PETE *and all the* NEGROES, *slowly,* L. U. E.)

(*Enter* ZOE [*supposed to have overheard the last scene*], L. U. E.)

ZOE. O! must I learn from these poor wretches how much I owe, and how I ought to pay the debt? Have I slept upon the benefits I received, and never saw, never felt, never knew that I was forgetful and ungrateful? O, my father! my dear, dear father! forgive your poor child. You made her life too happy, and now these tears will flow. Let me hide them till I teach my heart. O, my—my heart!

(*Exit, with a low, wailing, suffocating cry,* L. U. E.)

(*Enter* M'CLOSKY, LAFOUCHE, JACKSON, SUNNYSIDE, *and* POINTDEXTER, R. U. E.)

POINT. (*Looking at watch.*) Come, the hour is past. I think we may begin business. Where is Mr. Scudder?

JACKSON. I want to get to Ophelensis to-night.

(*Enter* DORA, R.)

DORA. Father, come here.

SUNNY. Why, Dora, what's the matter? Your eyes are red.

DORA. Are they? thank you. I don't care, they were blue this morning, but it don't signify now.

SUNNY. My darling! who has been teasing you?

DORA. Never mind. I want you to buy Terrebonne.

SUNNY. Buy Terrebonne! What for?

DORA. No matter—buy it!

SUNNY. It will cost me all I'm worth. This is folly, Dora.

DORA. Is my plantation at Comptableau worth this?

SUNNY. Nearly—perhaps.

DORA. Sell it, then, and buy this.

SUNNY. Are you mad, my love?

DORA. Do you want *me* to stop here and *bid* for it?

SUNNY. Good gracious! no.

DORA. Then I'll do it, if you don't.

SUNNY. I will! I will! But for Heaven's sake go—here comes the crowd.

(*Exit* DORA, L. U. E.)

What on earth does that child mean or want?

(*Enter* SCUDDER, GEORGE, RATTS, CAILLOU, PETE, GRACE, MINNIE, *and all the* NEGROES. *A large table is in the* C., *at back.* POINTDEXTER *mounts the table with his hammer, his* CLERK *sits at his feet. The* NEGRO *mounts the table from behind* C. *The* COMPANY *sit.*)

POINT. Now, gentlemen, we shall proceed to business. It ain't necessary for me to dilate, describe, or enumerate; Terrebonne is known to you as one of the richest bits of sile in Louisiana, and its condition reflects credit on them as had to keep it. I'll trouble you for that piece of baccy, Judge—thank you—so, gentlemen, as life is short, we'll start right off. The first lot on here is the estate in block, with its sugar-houses, stock, machines, implements, good dwelling-houses and furniture. If there is no bid for the estate and stuff, we'll sell it in smaller lots. Come, Mr. Thibodeaux, a man has a chance once in his life—here's yours.

THIB. Go on. What's the reserve bid?

POINT. The first mortgagee bids forty thousand dollars.

THIB. Forty-five thousand.

SUNNY. Fifty thousand.

POINT. When you have done joking, gentlemen, you'll say one hundred and twenty thousand. It carried that easy on mortgage.

LAFOUCHE. (R.) Then why don't you buy it yourself, Colonel?

POINT. I'm waiting on your fifty thousand bid.

CAILLOU. Eighty thousand.

POINT. Don't be afraid: it ain't going for that, Judge.

SUNNY. (L.) Ninety thousand.

POINT. We're getting on.

THIB. One hundred—

POINT. One hundred thousand bid for this mag—

CAILLOU. One hundred and ten thousand—

POINT. Good again—one hundred and—

SUNNY. Twenty.

POINT. And twenty thousand bid. Squire Sunnyside is going to sell this at fifty thousand advance to-morrow.—(*Looks round.*) Where's that man from Mobile that wanted to give one hundred and eighty thousand?

THIB. I guess he ain't left home yet, Colonel.

POINT. I shall knock it down to the Squire—going—gone—for one hundred and twenty thousand dollars. (*Raises hammer.*) Judge, you can raise the hull on mortgage—going for half its value. (*Knocks.*) Squire Sunnyside, you've got a pretty bit o' land, Squire. Hillo, darkey, hand me a smash dar.

SUNNY. I got more than I can work now.

POINT. Then buy the hands along with the property. Now, gentlemen, I'm proud to submit to you the finest lot of field hands and house servants that was ever offered for competition: they speak for themselves, and do credit to their owners.— (*Reads.*) "No. 1, Solon, a guess boy, and good waiter."

PETE. (R. C.) That's my son—buy him, Mas'r Ratts; he's sure to sarve you well.

POINT. Hold your tongue!

RATTS. (L.) Let the old darkey alone—eight hundred for that boy.

CAILLOU. Nine.

RATTS. A thousand.

SOLON. Thank you, Mas'r Ratts: I die for you, sar; hold up for me, sar.

RATTS. Look here, the boy knows and likes me, Judge; let him come my way?

CAILLOU. Go on—I'm dumb.

POINT. One thousand bid. (*Knocks.*) He's yours, Captain Ratts, Magnolia steamer. (SOLON *goes down and stands behind* RATTS.) "No. 2, the yellow girl Grace, with two children.—Saul, aged four, and Victoria five." (*They get on table.*)

SCUD. That's Solon's wife and children, Judge.

GRACE. (*To* RATTS.) Buy me, Mas'r Ratts, do buy me, sar?

RATTS. What in thunder should I do with you and those devils on board my boat?

GRACE. Wash, sar—cook, sar—anyting.

RATTS. Eight hundred agin, then—I'll go it.

JACKSON. Nine.

RATTS. I'm broke, Solon—I can't stop the Judge.

THIB. What's the matter, Ratts? I'll lend you all you want. Go it, if you're a mind to.

RATTS. Eleven.

JACKSON. Twelve.

SUNNY. O, O!

SCUD. (*To* JACKSON.) Judge, my friend. The Judge is a little deaf. Hello! (*Speaking in his ar-trumpet.*) This gal and them children belong to that boy Solon there. You're bidding to separate them, Judge.

JACKSON. The devil I am! (*Rises.*) I'll take back my bid, Colonel.

POINT. All right, Judge; I thought there was a mistake. I must keep you, Captain, to the eleven hundred.

RATTS. Go it.

POINT. Eleven hundred—going—going—sold! "No. 3, Pete, a house servant."

PETE. Dat's me—yer, I'm comin'—stand around dar. (*Tumbles upon the table.*)

POINT. Aged seventy-two.

PETE. What's dat? A mistake, sar—forty-six.

POINT. Lame.

PETE. But don't mount to nuffin—kin work cannel. Come, Judge, pick up. Now's your time, sar.

JACKSON. One hundred dollars.

PETE. What, sar? me! for me—look ye here! (*Dances.*)

GEORGE. Five hundred.

PETE. Mas'r George—ah, no, sar—don't buy me—keep your money for some udder dat is to be sold. I ain't no count, sar.

POINT. Five hundred bid—it's a good price. (*Knocks.*) He's yours, Mr. George Peyton. (PETE *goes down.*) "No. 4, the Octoroon girl, Zoe."

(*Enter* ZOE, L. U. E., *very pale, and stands on table.—*M'CLOSKY *hitherto has taken no interest in the sale, now turns his chair.*)

SUNNY. (*Rising.*) Gentlemen, we are all acquainted with the circumstances of this girl's position, and I feel sure that no one here will oppose the family who desires to redeem the child of our esteemed and noble friend, the late Judge Peyton.

OMNES. Hear! bravo! hear!

POINT. While the proceeds of this sale promises to realize less than the debts upon it, it is my duty to prevent any collusion for the depreciation of the property.

RATTS. Darn ye! You're a man as well as an auctioneer, ain't ye?

POINT. What is offered for this slave?

SUNNY. One thousand dollars.

M'CLOSKY. Two thousand.

SUNNY. Three thousand.

M'CLOSKY. Five thousand.

GEORGE. (R.) Demon!

SUNNY. I bid seven thousand, which is the last dollar this family possesses.

M'CLOSKY. Eight.

THIBO. Nine.

OMNES. Bravo!

M'CLOSKY. Ten. It's no use, Squire.

SCUD. Jacob M'Closky, you shan't have that girl. Now, take care what you do. Twelve thousand.

M'CLOSKY. Shan't I! Fifteen thousand. Beat that any of ye.

POINT. Fifteen thousand bid for the Octoroon.

(*Enter* DORA, L. U. E.)

DORA. Twenty thousand.

OMNES. Bravo!

M'CLOSKY. Twenty-five thousand.

OMNES. (*Groan.*) O! O!

GEORGE. (L.) Yelping hound—take that. (*Rushes on* M'CLOSKY—M'CLOSKY *draws his knife.*)

SCUD. (*Darts between them.*) Hold on, George Peyton—stand back. This is your own house; we are under your uncle's roof; recollect yourself. And, strangers, ain't we forgetting there's a lady present. (*The knives disappear.*) If we can't behave like Christians, let's try and act like gentlemen. Go on, Colonel.

LAFOUCHE. He didn't ought to bid against a lady.

M'CLOSKY. O, that's it, is it? Then I'd like to hire a lady to go to auction and buy my hands.

POINT. Gentlemen, I believe none of us have two feelings about the conduct of that man; but he has the law on his side—we may regret, but we must respect it. Mr. M'Closky has bid twenty-five thousand dollars for the Octoroon. Is there any other bid? For the first time, twenty-five thousand—last time! (*Brings hammer down.*) To Jacob M'Closky, the Octoroon girl. Zoe, twenty-five thousand dollars. (*Tableaux.*)

END OF ACT THIRD.

ACT IV.

SCENE.—*The Wharf. The Steamer "Magnolia," alongside,* L. *a bluff rock,* R. U. E.

RATTS *discovered, superintending the loading of ship. Enter* LAFOUCHE *and* JACKSON, L.

JACKSON. How long before we start, captain?

RATTS. Just as soon as we put this cotton on board.

(*Enter* PETE, *with lantern, and* SCUDDER, *with note book,* R.)

SCUD. One hundred and forty-nine bales. Can you take any more?

RATTS. Not a bale. I've got engaged eight hundred bales at the next landing, and one hundred hogsheads of sugar at Patten's Slide—that'll take my guards under—hurry up thar.

VOICE. (*Outside.*) Wood's aboard.

Ratts. All aboard then.

(*Enter* M'Closky, r.)

Scud. Sign that receipt, captain, and save me going up to the clerk.

M'Closky. See here—there's a small freight of turpentine in the fore hold there, and one of the barrels leaks; a spark from your engines might set the ship on fire, and you'd go with it.

Ratts. You be darned! Go and try it, if you've a mind to.

Lafouche. Captain, you've loaded up here until the boat is sunk so deep in the mud she won't float.

Ratts. (*Calls off.*) Wood up thar, you Pollo—hang on to the safety valve—guess she'll crawl off on her paddles. (*Shouts heard,* r.)

Jackson. What's the matter?

(*Enter* Solon, r.)

Solon. We got him!

Scud. Who?

Solon. The Injiun!

Scud. Wahnotee? Where is he? D'ye call running away from a fellow catching him?

Ratts. Here he comes.

Omnes. Where? Where?

(*Enter* Wahnotee, r.: *they are all about to rush on him.*)

Scud. Hold on! stan' round thar! no violence—the critter don't know what we mean.

Jackson. Let him answer for the boy, then.

M'Closky. Down with him—lynch him.

Omnes. Lynch him!

(*Exit* Lafouche, r.)

Scud. Stay back, I say! I'll nip the first that lays a finger on him. Pete, speak to the red-skin.

Pete. Whar's Paul, Wahnotee? What's come ob de child?

Wahnotee. Paul wunce—Paul pangeuk.

Pete. Pangeuk—dead.

Wahnotee. Mort!

M'Closky. And you killed him? (*They approach again.*)

Scud. Hold on!

Pete. Um, Paul reste?

Wahnotee. Hugh vieu. (*Goes* l.) Paul reste ci!

Scud. Here, stay! (*Examines the ground.*) The earth has been stirred here lately.

Wahnotee. Weenee Paul. (*Points down, and shows by pantomime how he buried* Paul.)

Scud. The Injiun means that he buried him there! Stop! here's a bit of leather; (*draws out mail-bags*) the mail-bags that were lost! (*Sees tomahawk in* Wahnotee's *belt—draws it out and examines it.*) Look! here are marks of blood—look thar, red-skin, what's that?

Wahnotee. Paul! (*Makes sign that* Paul *was killed by a blow on the head.*)

M'Closky. He confesses it; the Indian got drunk, quarrelled with him, and killed him.

(*Re-enter* LAFOUCHE, R., *with smashed apparatus.*)

LAFOUCHE. Here are evidences of the crime; this rum-bottle half emptied—this photographic apparatus smashed—and there are marks of blood and footsteps around
the shed.

M'CLOSKY. What more d'ye want—ain't that proof enough? Lynch him!

OMNES. Lynch him! Lynch him!

SCUD. Stan' back, boys! He's an Injiun—fair play.

JACKSON. Try him, then—try him on the spot of his crime.

OMNES. Try him! Try him!

LAFOUCHE. Don't let him escape!

RATTS. I'll see to that. (*Draws revolver.*) If he stirs, I'll put a bullet through his skull,
mighty quick.

M'CLOSKY. Come, form a court then, choose a jury—we'll fix this varmin.

(*Enter* THIBODEAUX *and* CAILLOU, L.)

THIBO. What's the matter?

LAFOUCHE. We've caught this murdering Injiun, and are going to try him. (WAHNO-
TEE *sits* L., *rolled in blanket.*)

PETE. Poor little Paul—poor little nigger!

SCUD. This business goes agin me, Ratts—'tain't right.

LAFOUCHE. We're ready; the jury's impanelled—go ahead—who'll be accuser?

RATTS. M'Closky.

M'CLOSKY. Me?

RATTS. Yes; you was the first to hail Judge Lynch.

M'CLOSKY. (R.) Well, what's the use of argument whar guilt sticks out so plain; the
boy and Injiun were alone when last seen.

SCUD. (L. C.) Who says that?

M'CLOSKY. Everybody—that is, I heard so.

SCUD. Say what you know—not what you heard.

M'CLOSKY. I know then that the boy was killed with that tomahawk—the red-skin
owns it—the signs of violence are all round the shed—this apparatus smashed—
ain't it plain that in a drunken fit he slew the boy, and when sober concealed the
body yonder?

OMNES. That's it—that's it.

RATTS. Who defends the Injiun?

SCUD. I will; for it is agin my natur' to b'lieve him guilty; and if he be, this ain't the
place, nor you the authority to try him. How are we sure the boy is dead at all?
There are no witnesses but a rum bottle and an old machine. Is it on such evidence
you'd hang a human being?

RATTS. His own confession.

SCUD. I appeal against your usurped authority. This lynch law is a wild and lawless
proceeding. Here's a pictur' for a civilized community to afford: yonder, a poor,
ignorant savage, and round him a circle of hearts, white with revenge and hate,
thirsting for his blood: you call yourselves judges—you ain't—you're a jury of
executioners. It is such scenes as these that bring disgrace upon our Western
life.

M'CLOSKY. Evidence! Evidence! Give us evidence. We've had talk enough; now for proof.

OMNES. Yes, yes! Proof, proof.

SCUD. Where am I to get it? The proof is here, in my heart.

PETE. (*Who has been looking about the camera.*) Top, sar! Top a bit! O, laws-a-mussey, see dis: here's a pictur' I found stickin' in that yar telescope machine, sar! look sar!

SCUD. A photographic plate. (PETE *holds lantern up.*) What's this, eh? two forms! The child—'tis he! dead—and above him—Ah! ah! Jacob M'Closky, 'twas you murdered that boy!

M'CLOSKY. Me?

SCUD. You! You slew him with that tomahawk; and as you stood over his body with the letter in your hand, you thought that no witness saw the deed, that no eye was on you—but there was, Jacob M'Closky, there was. The eye of the Eternal was on you—the blessed sun in heaven, that, looking down, struck upon this plate the image of the deed. Here you are, in the very attitude of your crime!

M'CLOSKY. 'Tis false!

SCUD. 'Tis true! the apparatus can't lie. Look there, jurymen. (*Shows plate to jury.*) Look there. O, you wanted evidence—you called for proof—Heaven has answered and convicted you.

M'CLOSKY. What court of law would receive such evidence? (*Going.*)

RATTS. Stop; *this* would. You called it yourself; you wanted to make us murder that Injiun; and since we've got our hands in for justice, we'll try it on *you*. What say ye? shall we have one law for the red-skin and another for the white?

OMNES. Try him! Try him!

RATTS. Who'll be accuser?

SCUD. I will! Fellow-citizens, you are convened and assembled here under a higher power than the law. What's the law? When the ship's abroad on the ocean, when the army is before the enemy where in thunder's the law? It is in the hearts of brave men, who can tell right from wrong, and from whom justice can't be bought. So it is here, in the wilds of the West, where our hatred of crime is measured by the speed of our executions—where necessity is law! I say, then, air you honest men? air you true? Put your hands on your naked breasts, and let every man as don't feel a real American heart there, bustin' up with freedom, truth, and right, let that man step out—that's the oath I put to ye—and then say, Darn ye, go it!

OMNES. Go on. Go on.

SCUD. No! I won't go on; that man's down. I won't strike him, even with words. Jacob, your accuser is that picter of the crime—let that speak—defend yourself.

M'CLOSKY. (*Draws knife.*) I will, quicker than lightning.

RATTS. Seize him, then! (*They rush on* M'CLOSKY, *and disarm him.*) He can fight though he's a painter: claws all over.

SCUD. Stop! Search him, we may find more evidence.

M'CLOSKY. Would you rob me first, and murder me afterwards?

RATTS. (*Searching him.*) That's his programme—here's a pocketbook.

SCUD. (*Opens it.*) What's here? Letters! Hello! To "Mrs. Peyton, Terrebonne, Louisiana, United States." Liverpool post mark. Ho! I've got hold of the tail of a rat—come out. (*Reads.*) What's this? A draft for eighty-five thousand dollars, and credit on Palisse and Co., of New Orleans, for the balance. Hi! the rat's out. You killed the boy to steal this letter from the mail-bags—you stole this letter, that the money should not arrive in time to save the Octoroon; had it done so, the lien on the estate would have ceased, and Zoe be free.

OMNES. Lynch him! Lynch him! Down with him!

SCUD. Silence in the court: stand back, let the gentlemen of the jury retire, consult, and return their verdict.

RATTS. I'm responsible for the crittur—go on.

PETE. (*To* WAHNOTEE.) See Injiun; look dar (*shows him plate*), see dat innocent: look, dar's de murderer of poor Paul.

WAHNOTEE. Ugh! (*Examines plate.*)

PETE. Ya! as he? Closky tue Paul—kill de child with your tomahawk dar: 'twasn't you, no—ole Pete allus say so. Poor Injiun lub our little Paul. (WAHNOTEE *rises and looks at* M'CLOSKY—*he is in his war paint and fully armed.*)

SCUD. What say ye, gentlemen? Is the prisoner guilty, or is he not guilty?

OMNES. Guilty!

SCUD. And what is to be his punishment?

OMNES. Death! (*All advance.*)

WAHNOTEE. (*Crosses to* M'CLOSKY.) Ugh!

SCUD. No, Injiun; we deal out justice here, not revenge. 'Tain't you he has injured, 'tis the white man, whose laws he has offended.

RATTS. Away with him—put him down the aft hatch, till we rig his funeral.

M'CLOSKY. Fifty against one! O! if I had you one by one, alone in the swamp, I'd rip ye all. (*He is borne off in boat, struggling.*)

SCUD. Now then to business.

PETE. (*Re-enters from boat.*) O, law, sir, dat debil Closky, he tore hisself from de gen'lam, knock me down, take my light, and trows it on de turpentine barrels, and de shed's all afire! (*Fire seen,* R.)

JACKSON. (*Re-entering.*) We are catching fire forward: quick, cut free from the shore.

RATTS. All hands aboard there—cut the starn ropes—give her headway!

ALL. Ay, ay! (*Cry of "fire" heard—Engine bells heard—steam whistle noise.*)

RATTS. Cut all away for'ard—overboard with every bale afire.

(*The Steamer moves off—fire kept up—*M'CLOSKY *re-enters,* R., *swimming on.*)

M'CLOSKY. Ha! have I fixed ye? Burn! burn! that's right. You thought you had cornered me, did ye? As I swam down, I thought I heard something in the water, as if pursuing me—one of their darned alligators, I suppose—they swarm hereabout—may they crunch every limb of ye!

(*Exit,* L.)

(WAHNOTEE *swims on—finds trail—follows him. The Steamer floats on at back, burning. Tableaux.*)

CURTAIN.

END OF ACT FOURTH.

ACT V

SCENE I.—*Negroes' Quarters in* 1.

Enter ZOE, L. 1. E.

ZOE. It wants an hour yet to daylight—here is Pete's hut. (*Knocks.*) He sleeps—no; I
see a light.

DIDO. (*Enters from hut,* R. F.) Who dat?

ZOE. Hush, aunty! 'Tis I—Zoe.

DIDO. Missey Zoe! Why you out in de swamp dis time ob night, you catch de fever
sure—you is all wet.

ZOE. Where's Pete?

DIDO. He gone down to de landing last night wid Mas'r Scudder: not come back
since—kint make it out.

ZOE. Aunty, there is sickness up at the house: I have been up all night beside one who
suffers, and I remembered that when I had the fever you gave me a drink, a bitter
drink, that made me sleep—do you remember it?

DIDO. Didn't I? Dem doctors ain't no 'count; dey don't know nuffin.

ZOE. No; but you, aunty, you are wise—you know every plant, don't you, and what it
is good for?

DIDO. Dat you drink is fust rate for red fever. Is de folks head bad?

ZOE. Very bad, aunty; and the heart aches worse, so they can get no rest.

DIDO. Hold on a bit, I get you de bottle.

(*Exit,* L. R.)

ZOE. In a few hours that man, my master, will come for me: he has paid my price, and
he only consented to let me remain here this one night, because Mrs. Peyton
promised to give me up to him to-day.

DIDO. (*Re-enters with phial.*) Here 'tis—now you give one timble-full—dat's nuff.

ZOE. All there is there would kill one, wouldn't it?

DIDO. Guess it kill a dozen—nebber try.

ZOE. It's not a painful death, aunty, is it? You told me it produced a long, long sleep.

DIDO. Why you tremble so? Why you speak so wild? What you's gwine to do, missey?

ZOE. Give me the drink.

DIDO. No. Who dat sick at de house?

ZOE. Give it to me.

DIDO. No. You want to hurt yourself. O, Miss Zoe, why you ask ole Dido for dis pizen?

ZOE. Listen to me. I love one who is here, and he loves me—George. I sat outside his
door all night—I heard his sighs—his agony—torn from him by my coming fate;
and he said, "I'd rather see her dead than his!"

DIDO. Dead!

ZOE. He said so—then I rose up, and stole from the house, and ran down to the
bayou; but its cold, black, silent stream terrified me—drowning must be so horrible a death. I could not do it. Then, as I knelt there, weeping for courage, a snake

rattled beside me. I shrunk from it and fled. Death was there beside me, and I dared not take it. O! I'm afraid to die; yet I am more afraid to live.

DIDO. Die!

ZOE. So I came here to you; to you, my own dear nurse; to you, who so often hushed me to sleep when I was a child; who dried my eyes and put your little Zoe to rest. Ah! give me the rest that no master but One can disturb—the sleep from which I shall awake free! You can protect me from that man—do let me die without pain. (*Music.*)

DIDO. No, no—life is good for young ting like you.

ZOE. O! good, good nurse: you will, you will.

DIDO. No—g'way.

ZOE. Then I shall never leave Terrebonne—the drink, nurse; the drink; that I may never leave my home—my dear, dear home. You will not give me to that man? Your own Zoe, that loves you, aunty, so much, so much.—(*Gets phial.*) Ah! I have it.

DIDO. No, missey. O! no—don't.

ZOE. Hush!

(*Runs off,* L. 1 E.)

DIDO. Here, Solon, Minnie, Grace.

(*They enter.*)

ALL. Was de matter?

DIDO. Miss Zoe got de pizen.

(*Exit,* L.)

ALL. O! O!

(*Exeunt,* L.)

SCENE II.—*Cane-brake Bayou.—Bank,* C.—*Triangle Fire,* R. C.—*Canoe,* C.—M'CLOSKY *discovered asleep.*

M'CLOSKY. Burn, burn! blaze away! How the flames crack. I'm not guilty; would ye murder me? Cut, cut the rope—I choke—choke!—Ah! (*Wakes.*) Hello! where am I? Why, I was dreaming—curse it! I can never sleep now without dreaming. Hush! I thought I heard the sound of a paddle in the water. All night, as I fled through the cane-brake, I heard footsteps behind me. I lost them in the cedar swamp— again they haunted my path down the bayou, moving as I moved, resting when I rested—hush! there again!—no; it was only the wind over the canes. The sun is rising. I must launch my dug-out, and put for the bay, and in a few hours I shall be safe from pursuit on board of one of the coasting schooners that run from Galveston to Matagorda. In a little time this darned business will blow over, and I can show again. Hark! there's that noise again! If it was the ghost of that murdered boy haunting me! Well—I didn't mean to kill him, did I? Well, then, what has my all-cowardly heart got to skeer me so for? (*Music.*)

(*Gets in canoe and rows off,* L.—WAHNOTEE *paddles canoe on,* R.—*gets out and finds trail—paddles off after him,* L.)

SCENE III.—*Cedar Swamp.*

Enter SCUDDER *and* PETE, L. 1 E.

SCUD. Come on, Pete, we shan't reach the house before midday.

PETE. Nebber mind, sa, we bring good news—it won't spile for de keeping.

SCUD. Ten miles we've had to walk, because some blamed varmin onhitched our dugout. I left it last night all safe.

PETE. P'r'aps it floated away itself.

SCUD. No; the hitching line was cut with a knife.

PETE. Say, Mas'r Scudder, s'pose we go in round by de quarters and raise de darkies, den dey cum long wid us, and we 'proach dat ole house like Gin'ral Jackson when he took London out dar.

SCUD. Hello, Pete, I never heard of that affair.

PETE. I tell you, sa—hush!

SCUD. What? (*Music.*)

PETE. Was dat?—a cry out dar in de swamp—dar agin!

SCUD. So it is. Something forcing its way through the undergrowth—it comes this way—it's either a bear or a runaway nigger. (*Draws pistol*—M'CLOSKY *rushes on and falls at* SCUDDER's *feet.*)

SCUD. Stand off—what are ye?

PETE. Mas'r Clusky.

M'CLOSKY. Save me—save me! I can go no farther. I heard voices.

SCUD. Who's after you?

M'CLOSKY. I don't know, but I feel it's death! In some form, human, or wild beast, or ghost, it has tracked me through the night. I fled; it followed. Hark! there it comes—it comes—don't you hear a footstep on the dry leaves?

SCUD. Your crime has driven you mad.

M'CLOSKY. D'ye hear it—nearer—nearer—ah! (WAHNOTEE *rushes on, and at* M'CLOSKY, L. H.)

SCUD. The Injiun! by thunder.

PETE. You'se a dead man, Mas'r Clusky—you got to b'lieve dat.

M'CLOSKY. No—no. If I must die, give me up to the law; but save me from the tomahawk. You are a white man; you'll not leave one of your own blood to be butchered by the red-skin?

SCUD. Hold on now, Jacob; we've got to figure on that—let us look straight at the thing. Here we are on the selvage of civilization. It ain't our side, I believe, rightly; but Nature has said that where the white man sets his foot, the red man and the black man shall up sticks and stand around. But what do we pay for that possession? In cash? No—in kind—that is, in protection, forbearance, gentleness, in all them goods that show the critters the difference between the Christian and the savage. Now, what have you done to show them the distinction? for, darn me, if I can find out.

M'CLOSKY. For what I have done, let me be tried.

SCUD. You have been tried—honestly tried and convicted. Providence has chosen your executioner. I shan't interfere.

PETE. O, no; Mas'r Scudder, don't leave Mas'r Closky like dat—don't, sa—'tain't what good Christian should do.

SCUD. D'ye hear that, Jacob? This old nigger, the grandfather of the boy you murdered, speaks for you—don't that go through you? D'ye feel it? Go on, Pete, you've waked up the Christian here, and the old hoss responds. (*Throws bowie-knife to* M'CLOSKY.) Take that, and defend yourself.

(*Exit* SCUDDER *and* PETE, R. 1 E.—WAHNOTEE *faces him.—Fight—buss.—* M'CLOSKY *runs off,* L. 1 E.—WAHNOTEE *follows him.—Screams outside.*)

SCENE IV.—*Parlor at* TERREBONNE.

Enter ZOE, C. (*Music.*)

ZOE. My home, my home! I must see you no more. Those little flowers can live, but I cannot. To-morrow they'll bloom the same—all will be here as now, and I shall be cold. O! my life, my happy life, why has it been so bright?

(*Enter* MRS. PEYTON *and* DORA, C.)

DORA. Zoe, where have you been?

MRS. P. We felt quite uneasy about you.

ZOE. I've been to the negro quarters. I suppose I shall go before long, and I wished to visit all the places, once again, to see the poor people.

MRS. P. Zoe, dear, I'm glad to see you more calm this morning.

DORA. But how pale she looks, and she trembles so.

ZOE. Do I? (*Enter* GEORGE, C.) Ah! he is here.

DORA. George, here she is?

ZOE. I have come to say good-by, sir; two hard words—so hard, they might break many a heart; mightn't they?

GEORGE. O, Zoe! can you smile at this moment?

ZOE. You see how easily I have become reconciled to my fate—so it will be with you. You will not forget poor Zoe! but her image will pass away like a little cloud that obscured your happiness a while—you will love each other; you are both too good not to join your hearts. Brightness will return amongst you. Dora, I once made you weep; those were the only tears I caused any body. Will you forgive me?

DORA. Forgive you—(*Kisses her.*)

ZOE. I feel you do, George.

GEORGE. Zoe, you are pale. Zoe!—she faints!

ZOE. No; a weakness, that's all—a little water. (DORA *gets water.*) I have a restorative here—will you pour it in the glass? (DORA *attempts to take it.*) No; not you— George. (GEORGE *pours contents of phial in glass.*) Now, give it to me. George, dear George, do you love me?

GEORGE. Do you doubt it, Zoe?

ZOE. No! (*Drinks.*)

DORA. Zoe, if all I possess would buy your freedom, I would gladly give it.

ZOE. I am free! I had but one Master on earth, and he has given me my freedom!

DORA. Alas! but the deed that freed you was not lawful.

ZOE. Not lawful—no—but I am going to where there is no law—where there is only justice.

GEORGE. Zoe, you are suffering—your lips are white—your cheeks are flushed.

ZOE. I must be going—it is late. Farewell, Dora. (*Retires.*)

PETE. (*Outside*, R.) Whar's Missus—whar's Mas'r George?

GEORGE. They come.

(*Enter* SCUDDER.)

SCUD. Stand around and let me pass—room thar! I feel so big with joy, creation ain't wide enough to hold me. Mrs. Peyton, George Peyton, Terrebonne is yours. It was that rascal M'Closky—but he got rats, I swow—he killed the boy, Paul, to rob this letter from the mail-bags—the letter from Liverpool you know—he sot fire to the shed—that was how the steamboat got burned up.

MRS. P. What d'ye mean?

SCUD. Read—read that. (*Gives letter.*)

GEORGE. Explain yourself.

(*Enter* SUNNYSIDE.)

SUNNY. Is it true?

SCUD. Every word of it, Squire. Here, you tell it, since you know it. If I was to try, I'd bust.

MRS. P. Read, George. Terrebonne is yours.

(*Enter* PETE, DIDO, SOLON, MINNIE, *and* GRACE.)

PETE. Whar is she—whar is Miss Zoe?

SCUD. What's the matter?

PETE. Don't ax me. Whar's de gal? I say.

SCUD. Here she is—Zoe!—water—she faints.

PETE. No—no. 'Tain't no faint—she's a dying, sa: she got pison from old Dido here, this mornin'.

GEORGE. Zoe.

SCUD. Zoe! is this true?—no, it ain't—darn it, say it ain't. Look here, you're free, you know; nary a master to hurt you now: you will stop here as long as you're a mind to, only don't look so.

DORA. Her eyes have changed color.

PETE. Dat's what her soul's gwine to do. It's going up dar, whar dere's no line atween folks.

GEORGE. She revives.

ZOE. (*On sofa*, C.) George—where—where—

GEORGE. O, Zoe! what have you done?

ZOE. Last night I overheard you weeping in your room, and you said, "I'd rather see her dead than so!"

GEORGE. Have I then prompted you to this?

ZOE. No; but I loved you so, I could not bear my fate; and then I stood between your heart and hers. When I am dead she will not be jealous of your love for me, no laws will stand between us. Lift me; so—(GEORGE *raises her head*)—let me look at you, that your face may be the last I see of this world. O! George, you may, without a blush, confess your love for the Octoroon! (*Dies.*—GEORGE *lowers her head gently.—Kneels.—Others form picture.*)

(*Darken front of house and stage.*)

(*Light fires.—Draw flats and discover* PAUL's *grave.*—M'CLOSKY *dead on it*—WAH-NOTEE *standing triumphantly over him.*)

SLOW CURTAIN.

THE ENGLISH HAPPY ENDING
ACT FOUR

(WAHNOTEE *rises and looks at* M'CLOSKY—*he is in his war paint and fully armed.*)

SCUDDER. What say ye, gentlemen? Is the prisoner guilty, or is he not guilty?

OMNES. Guilty!

SCUDDER. And what is to be his punishment?

OMNES. Death!

WAHNOTEE. (*crosses to* M'CLOSKY). Ugh!

SCUDDER. The Inginn, by thunder!

PETE (*to* M'CLOSKY). You's a dead man, mas'r; you've got to b'lieve dat.

M'CLOSKY. No! If I must die, give me up to the laws, but save me from the tomahawk of the savage; you are a white man, you'll not leave one of your own blood to be butchered by the scalping knife of the redskin.

SCUDDER. Hold on now, Jacob, we've got to figure that out; let us look straight at the thing. Here we are on the confines of civilisation; it ain't our sile, I believe, rightly; Natur' has said that where the white mans sets his foot the red man and the black man shall up sticks and stan' round. Now, what do we pay for that possession? In cash? No—in kind—that is, in protection and forbearance, in gentleness, and in all them goods that show the critturs the difference between the Christian and the Savage. Now what have you done to show 'em the distinction? for darn me if I can find out.

M'CLOSKY. For what I've done let me be tried.

SCUDDER. Oh, you have been fairly and honestly tried, and convicted: Providence has chosen your executioner—I shan't interfere.

PETE. Oh! sar! hi, Mas'r Scudder, don't leave Mas'r 'Closky like dat—don't, sar—tain't what a good Christian would do.

SCUDDER. D'ye hear that, Jacob?—this old nigger, the grandfather of the boy you murdered, speaks for you—don't that go through ye—d'ye feel it? Go on, Pete, you've woke up the Christian here, and the old hoss responds.

WAHNOTEE (*placing his hand on* M'CLOSKY's *head*). Wahnotee!

SCUDDER. No, Inginn, we deal justice here, not revenge; tain't you he has injured, 'tis the white man, whose laws he has offended.

RATTS. Away with him! put him down the hatch till we rig his funeral.

M'CLOSKY. Fifty against one! Oh! if you were alone—if I had ye one by one in the swamp, I'd rip ye all.

Pete (*lighting him off*, R.) Dis way, Mas'r 'Closky, take care, sar.

(*Exit with* M'Closky *and* Jackson *to steamer.*)

Lafouche. Off with him quick—here come the ladies.

(*Enter* Mrs Claiborne, R 1 E.)

Mrs Claiborne. Shall we soon start, Captain?

Ratts. Yes, ma'am; we've only got a—Take my hand, ma'am, to steady you—a little account to square, and we're off.

Mrs Claiborne. A fog is rising.

Ratts. Swamp mist; soon clear off. (*Hands her to steamer.*)

Mrs Claiborne. Good night.

Ratts. Good night, ma'am—good night.

Scudder. Now to business.

(Pete *appears on deck.*)

Pete. Oh! law, sar. Dat debbel, 'Closky—he tore hisself from de gentleman—knock me down—take away my light, and throwed it on de turpentine barrels—de ship's on fire!

(*All hurry off to ship—alarm bell rings—loud shouts; a hatch in the deck is opened—a glare of red—and* M'Closky *emerges from the aperture; he is without his coat, and carries a bowie knife; he rushes down—*Wahnotee *alone is watching him from* R. U. E.)

M'Closky. Ha, ha, ha! I've given them something to remember how they treated Jacob M'Closky. Made my way from one end of the vessel to the other, and now the road to escape is clear before me—and thus to secure it! (*He goes to* R. C., *and is met by* Wahnotee, *who silently confronts him.*)

Wahnotee. Paul.

M'Closky. Devils!—you here!—stand clear!

Wahnotee. Paul.

M'Closky. You won't!—die, fool!

(*Thrusts at him—*Wahnotee, *with his tomahawk, strikes the knife out of his hand;* M'Closky *starts back;* Wahnotee *throws off his blanket, and strikes at* M'Closky *several times, who avoids him; at last he catches his arm, and struggles for the tomahawk, which falls; a violent struggle and fight takes place, ending with the triumph of* Wahnotee, *who drags* M'Closky *along the ground, takes up the knife and stabs him repeatedly;* George *enters, bearing* Zoe *in his arms—all the* Characters *rush on—noise increasing—the steam vessel blows up—grand Tableau, and*

CURTAIN

29

From *Black and White*:
A Drama in Three Acts

Wilkie Collins and Charles Fechter

The English writer and actor Wilkie Collins (1824–1889) was best known as the author of the novel *The Woman in White* (1860) and a pioneer in the mystery genre. He also collaborated with Charles Dickens in producing and writing plays. Charles Fechter (1824–1879), a member of the Théâtre Français, was a popular romantic actor in Paris before he moved to England; he enjoyed great success on the London stage as well. In 1869 Collins crafted the dialogue and characters of *Black and White* (selected scenes from which are reprinted here); Fechter had developed the plot and also acted in the production of the play. Obviously inspired by Boucicault's successful *Octoroon, Black and White* reverses the gender arrangement: while Boucicault's Zoe has always lived in a slave society, Collins and Fechter's Maurice is accustomed to European ways when he has to learn that, as the son of the slave woman Ruth, he is in danger of being sold as a slave. As did Cecilie in Andersen's *Mulatto*, Emily in *Black and White* ultimately attempts to rescue her beloved, no matter what his racial background might be. The language differentiation between heroic protagonists and buffoonish slaves and servants is so rigorously maintained in this play as to make possible the inclusion of minstrel acts, especially in the figure of Plato. *Black and White* opened in London to little fanfare or acclaim and appeared in Boston in 1870.

ACT I
CAST OF CHARACTERS.
Count Maurice de Leyrac (Lead)
Stephen Westeraft (Heavy Character)
David Michaelmas (Low Comedy or Old Man)
Plato (1st Low Comedy)
Provost Marshal (Utility)
Wolf (2d Heavy)
Slaves, Planters, Jailors, etc.
Miss Milburn (Lead)
Mrs. Pentold (Walking Lady)
Ruth, a Quadroon (Character)
Slave Girls, etc.

ACT I.

SCENE II.—*Forest*

Enter DAVID. *Enter* PLATO.

PLATO. Well, sah, you all alone? de Count not come?

DAVID. He will not be long. We will wait for him here, if you please.

PLATO. I consider 'um a pleasure to wait any whar wid you, sah.

DAVID. Indeed! May I have the honor to know whom I am addressing?

PLATO. I present my compliments and beg to present my card, sah. (*gives card.*)

DAVID. Ah!

(*Enter* SECRETARY, *sleepily.*)

PLATO. And allow me to present my secretary. (SECRETARY *goes* R. *of* DAVID)

DAVID. (*reads card*). Mr. Plato.

PLATO. Dat's me, sah.

DAVID. Then allow me to congratulate you on your name.

PLATO. (*bows*). It's 'um pretty good name, sah.

DAVID. (*reads card given by* SECRETARY). Mr. Horace, Mr. Washington, Mr. Spenser, Mr. Shakspeare, Mr. Milton. (SECRETARY *sits and prepares to go to sleep.*) All black, sir?

PLATO. All brack men, sah.

DAVID. Ah! They were all white the last time I heard of them. Might I ask you how you came by the names of Shakspeare and Milton, and so forth?

PLATO. We took 'um, sah. Saving your presence, sah, we don't see why de dam white man should hab all de good names to hisself, sah.

DAVID. That's a quite unanswerable reason, Mr. Plato.

PLATO. I t'ank you, sah. (SECRETARY *goes to sleep*) I respect you, sah! You am de white man dat we men ob color tinks de highest most ob on dis island.

DAVID. Thanks. Perhaps you can tell me why I deserve such a compliment. All I ever did was to run away from my plantation, which has returned the compliment by running away from me. It's going to be sold for the benefit of the mortgagees.

PLATO. Answer me, sah. Did you eber try to teach de niggahs on you' plantatium anyt'ing?

DAVID. Never.

PLATO. Berry well. Did you ever ax 'um to do any work onless dey agreed to it demselves.

DAVID. Never.

PLATO. Den, dar you hab it. You left de brains ob de nigger sleep in him 'kull; you left de han's ob de nigger sleep in him pocket. God bress you! you good man! I offer you my hand. (DAVID, *stepping aside, nearly stumbles over* SECRETARY.)

DAVID. Then I say, may ignorance flourish, and idleness be the best employment of human science. May I inquire if it was my words or yours that sent this worthy fellow off to sleep. (*touches* SECRETARY *with his foot.* SECRETARY *snores.*)

PLATO. My secrumtary, sah! he am waiting for my orders before he go to bed. I am oberwhelmed wid de brack business ob dis island. Oh! de dam white man will not hab his own way much longer.

DAVID. Looking at it from the blackest point of view, I am very glad to hear it!

PLATO. T'ank you, sah! We hab two great political parties on dis island.

DAVID. So have we at home.

PLATO. I am sorry to hear it, sah! Dar's de Conserbative Bracks an' de Liberal Bracks.

DAVID. Strange coincidence! we have the Conservative Whites and the Liberal Whites. May I inquire how these political parties differ?

PLATO. We hab all on'y de one design in view—dat is de sacred cause ob Freedom! but we hab two ways ob gittin' it. De Liberal idea am to git up early one fine mornin' an' kill all de white folks on de island.

DAVID. A truly liberal programme. But one can understand it, anyhow!

PLATO. De Conserbative idea am—

DAVID. Stop a minute. May I inquire—are you a Conservative?

PLATO. (*proudly*). I am de Conserbative chief, sah!

DAVID. Speaking as a white man, I am delighted to hear it!

PLATO. De Conserbative plan is not so bloodthirsty, dough it am much more slow. We found a club, sah! an' little by little we git all de black men on de island to join it, an' den, when all are in it, we demand de white fokes to quit.

DAVID. A charming prospect. As one of the white men, I shall be glad to leave at once. What is the name of the organization.

PLATO. De club am to be formed to-morrow night, and we propose to call 'um de Thickskull Club.

DAVID. The Thickskull Club? Why, even your most bitter enemies could not have hit upon a fitter name.

PLATO. Wait a lilly bit, sah! Dar's a reason for dat name. Answer me dis hyar? What am de most honorable part of de man's body? Why him head! Darfore de ticker him head, de more he hab ob de honorable part! See, sah? Dar you hab him!

DAVID. A very neat way of putting it, indeed. But a club to be constituted like this will be many months in progress.

PLATO. De longer time, sah, dat de officers ob de club will be enjoyin' deir salaries, sah!

DAVID. Hum! I see!

PLATO. Mr. Secretary! Mr. Secretary! Mr. Michaelmas, I present my compliments, an' would you please to kick de secretary?

DAVID. (*touches* SECRETARY, *who sits up.*) I present my compliments, Mr. Plato, and begs you not to mention it.

PLATO. Mr. Secretary, you have written down de performances for to-morrow night. In de fust place—de band ob music—dat is to say, two fifes an' a drum.

SEC. (*refers to book.*) Yes, massa.

PLATO. De banner wid de crest ob de club—a thick skull, wid de motto ob de club: "Dam all white men, an' down with labor!"

SEC. (*rises.*) Yes, massa.

PLATO. De refresherments for de six committee-men of the club—dat is to say, six bottles of rum punch (*smacks his lips*), an' six corkscrews, an' six glasses, to be carried by de committee-men demselves, two by two, one abreast? An' six chairs for the committee-men, to be carried by de grateful public. Hab you got dem all down?

SEC. Yes, massa. (*turns the book upside down, to write in it.*)

PLATO. Den, Missa Secrumtary, you can go to bed.

SEC. T'ank you, massa. (*to* DAVID) Your sarvint, sah!

(*Exit.*)

PLATO. Mr. Michaelmas, I would like to ax you to witness de foundation of de club, but dough you are de model white man ob dis island, you *are* a white man, an' dat am a fatal objection.

DAVID. Don't mention it. Besides, there might be one of the Liberals in the meeting, and the sight of me might lead to an objection even more *fatal* than that you allude to.

(*Voice of* LEYRAC). David! Michaelmas!

DAVID. This way, sir! this way!

(*Enter,* LEYRAC.)

LEY. Is she here?

DAVID. No, sir. She lives in a hut not far.

PLATO. (*bowing, hat in hand*). On'y a lilly bit of way, sir.

LEY. Who is that man?

DAVID. I present to you the Conservative chief, Mr. Plato! (*aside to* LEYRAC) They have Mr. Milton and Shakspeare here, and all the great men.

LEY. Ha, ha!

DAVID. He has come to show you the way to the house.

PLATO. Do you present your compliments, sah, and request me to lead de way.

LEY. (*lifting his hat*). With a thousand apologies for causing you the trouble.

PLATO. With two thousand thanks for have the honor of giving you so much trouble. (*aside, hat on*) No dam white man is gwine to be more polite dan me on dis island.

LEY. What's her name?

DAVID. Ruth, the quadroon. (LEYRAC *shakes his head.*)

LEY. You have seen her—do you know her?

DAVID. A perfect stranger.

LEY. She must be mad, or it's a mistake.

DAVID. No mistake, sir, I can assure you. She knew all about you, clearly enough.

LEY. I will see her.

DAVID. Shall I go with you?

LEY. You might see me to the place, and then go back to the hotel to wait for me.

(*Exit.*)

DAVID. (*to* PLATO). Come along, Mr. Plato!

(*Exeunt* PLATO *and* DAVID, *Music, tremolo. Gas down a little more.*)

(*Enter,* L., WESTCRAFT, *crossing to* R.; *pauses* R., *looking off* R., *and then exits* R., *as if following some one.*)

Scene changes to

SCENE III.—*Hut interior. Light on table.*

Discover RUTH *on couch and* GIRL *by table.*

RUTH. Time passes, and still he does not come. (*weak voice*) Look for him again, my dear. (GIRL *goes to door*) Look for him again. (GIRL *opens door.*)

(*Appear, outside door,* DAVID, LEYRAC *and* PLATO.)

PLATO. Dis am de place, sah. Dis, am Ruth's hut. (*bows and exits.*)

RUTH. Is he there?

LEY. (*on the threshold*). Are you speaking to me?

RUTH. (*eagerly*). Yes, yes, come in! (*sits up.*)

DAVID. Shall I wait for you here, sir?

LEY. No. Go back to the hotel and wait for me there. (DAVID *bows and exits.* GIRL *goes out the door, shutting it behind her after showing in* LEYRAC.) Look at me. Am I really the person you want to see? (*removes his hat.*)

RUTH. Yes. (LEYRAC *puts hat on table.*)

LEY. You know my name?

RUTH. Your name is Maurice de Leyrac. Will you move the light a little closer? (LEYRAC *moves table nearer head of bed.*) Thanks. (*leaning on one elbow, hoarsely, eagerly*) What has brought you to Trinidad?

LEY. What interest can you have in my movements? Oh, this is absurd. (*kindly*) I don't wish to speak harshly to you, my good woman, but you cannot expect me to stop here by your bed to hear your sick delusions.

RUTH. What evil wind brought you again to this accursed island?

LEY. The poor woman is wandering. (*gets his hat.*)

RUTH. Do you come to Trinidad of your own free will?

LEY. Of my own free will. Come, you are too ill—you are under some error. I—my time is precious. But—but, there—(*puts down his hat*)—is there anything I can do for you before I go?

RUTH. I want you to look back in your mind. What is the first thing that you remember, the first, first thing in your mind?

LEY. (*interested, but still a little careless of tone.*) The first thing I remember? (*thinking.*)

RUTH. Do I live in your mind? Look at me! yes, look at me! pray, oh, pray, look at me! (*leans forward.*)

LEY. (*shakes his head.*) The first thing that I remember? is—is being on board a ship with my father and mother.

RUTH. (*sighs disappointedly.*) Ah! (*sadly*) *My* memory goes back to a time farther than yours—when the Count and Countess de Leyrac adopted you for their own son.

LEY. *Adopted* me?

RUTH. Adopted.

LEY. (*incredulously*). I am *not* the son of the Count and Countess?

RUTH. You are not their son.

LEY. (*staggered*). Ah! (*quickly*) Oh! she is mad.

RUTH. I am not mad. Is this the truth or is it not? The Count and Countess had no other children, and brought you up in France.

LEY. Oh! you speak the truth so far.

RUTH. When you spoke to them of your infancy, were you not surprised that they should always change the conversation to another subject?

LEY. (*quickly*). Over and over again!

RUTH. Ah! and when they died and left you in charge of a guardian, did he not carefully keep from you the family papers?

LEY. Great heavens! yes!

RUTH. Am I mad now?

LEY. You say I was adopted. Then my parents, my real parents—do they still live?

RUTH. One is dead.

LEY. My mother?

RUTH. No! your father.

LEY. Then my mother lives!

RUTH. Yes. His name was Brentwood. His widow—

LEY. My mother!

RUTH. (*hanging her head*). Not your mother! his *wife!*

LEY. Then who was my mother?

RUTH. A slave-girl on your father's plantation.

LEY. A slave! Ah! (*bitterly*) It has been the one dream of my life to live worthy of my birth! And I was never so proud and glad of it as this day. And now!—(*sadly*) Is my mother living, say you?

RUTH. (*timidly*). Do you blame her?

LEY. (*forcibly*). God forbid!

RUTH. You are not ashamed?

LEY. It is not my fault. I am sure, not hers. You would not keep me in suspense unless you feared for her. Where is she?

RUTH. Oh! don't look at me! (*hides face with hands.*) Don't look at me!

LEY. Why not? You asked me to look at you an hour since, and now—Ah! (*forcibly*) you are—my mother! oh! mother! (*falls on knees by bedside.*) kiss me. (*they embrace.*)

(WESTCRAFT *appears on roof outside window, moonlight upon him.*)

WEST. (*aside*). The lamp is moved, I cannot see, but I can hear! I can hear!

LEY. (*rises*) Hark! There is something moving outside (*stands trembling with agitation, trying to recover his composure, dashes away a tear, etc.*)

RUTH. Nay, 'tis only the night wind coming down from the mountains, and rustling the dry leaves of the thatch.

LEY. Let me look and make sure. (*opens door and looks out. Moonlight on him. Music, piano, tremolo.*)

(*Enter remaining there,* MISS MILBURN.)

MISS M. (*aside*). What has brought him to Ruth's cottage? (*keeps herself hid, though seen from the front.*)

LEY. No, there is no one. (*closes door, retiring to bedside*). I see no living creature, I heard nothing but the wind.

RUTH. Come here to me, I have not said what I wanted to say.

LEY. (*tenderly*). You are too weak, mother. Not now; when you are stronger.

RUTH. My time is too short for me to linger. Listen. When your father was on his death bed, he thought of me, he wrote to me, but his jealous wife destroyed his letters. He wanted to see me, but his jealous wife stopped the messengers. He had, something to send to me, but thanks to his wife, I never received anything.

LEY. Go on, mother. (*holding her hand in his.*)

RUTH. His will left all his property, the plantations, houses, slaves and growing things to his widow. She hated me.

LEY. Ha!

RUTH. I don't complain. I deserved it. She was in her right. But she hated you, and you had never harmed her. She delayed in her vengeance until you were born, and then—then she sold us to the highest bidder in the market place!

LEY. Ah!

RUTH. Wait. She repented of this when her time came for her to die. She had destroyed nearly all things which your father had left to be given to me. But she had not destroyed everything! A pocket-book left among papers, as of no importance, had escaped her jealous eyes, and later, it fell into my hands.

LEY. Where is that pocket-book?

RUTH. Still in my possession. Search under my pillow, my son.

LEY. (*gets book from under pillow eagerly.*) Empty!

RUTH. No, a little scrap of writing—it is your father's hand.

LEY. My father's hand?

RUTH. Read it.

LEY. "The duplicate letter to the Provost-Marshal is hidden—my room—the old wing——" Mother, I cannot make out what follows? Can you?

RUTH. (*shaking her head*). No more than you can. All clue to the hiding place died with Mr. Brentwood's death. Keep that pocket-book. It proves that your father thought of me at the last. You were but a child when there came to the island a wealthy French noble, the Count, with the Countess de Leyrac. They took a fancy to you, and wished to adopt you. They promised to treat you like their own son.

LEY. Thank heaven! They did, mother, they did!

RUTH. (*tearfully*). I had to choose between parting with you and having you grow up on the plantation amongst the slaves.

LEY. Yes, mother!

RUTH. I tried hard to bear it. But it broke my heart! (*wandering, hand to forehead, to collect her thoughts*) I had something more to tell you. Did I say that we were sold in the market-place.

LEY. Yes.

RUTH. And the Count and Countess took you away—to—to England.

LEY. (*rises.*) To England, say you? God bless them! when my feet touched the soil of England, I became a free man! mother, a free man!

RUTH. But when you touched the soil of this island again, the laws of free England lost their hold, and you have become again what you were. Your old master that bought you can claim you for his own. You must leave me!

LEY. Leave you, mother! Never!

RUTH. Oh, why did you come back again? Go, go! While you remain here, you are under the shadow of the lash, you are a slave!

LEY. A slave! (*hides his face*, RUTH *falls back and dies*) Mother! (*bends over her*) She has fainted. Oh, God! her breath has ceased to come and go! her heart is still! Ah! dead! she is dead! (*falls upon* RUTH, *embracing her, kissing her hand.*)

MISS M. (*in disgust and pain, aside*). A slave! (*sobs and faints, supporting herself by the door post.*)

WEST. (*triumphantly, aside*). A slave! (*smiles, music, solemn.*)

QUICK CURTAIN.

ACT II.

SCENE III.

(*Enter* WESTCRAFT.)

WEST. The Frenchman is coming at last. Ah! (*in satisfaction*) I am glad of it. (*cane in hand*) Let her but come as I am correcting him, and it will be just the triumph I want.

(*Enter followed by* WOLF, LEYRAC. *Both come down.* SLAVES *and* PLANTERS *stroll on and off.*)

WEST. So you have come at last?

LEY. You have sent me a message relative to that whip which you hold in your hand. Do you want another lesson such as I taught you this morning? Are you responsible for the insolence of this man? (*meaning* WOLF.)

WEST. Settle it with the man! (WOLF *looks at* LEYRAC *and smiles defiantly*) What does it matter to me?

LEY. Hark ye, Mr. Planter, I gave you the option of settling our quarrel like a gentleman.

WEST. Are you so vain as to imagine that any friend of mine would take a message to *you*? (ALL *on for picture.*)

LEY. Is that your answer?

WEST. All my answer, yes.

LEY. (*drawing glove off*). Then, take mine! (*strikes* WESTCRAFT *across face with glove.*)

(*Excitement. Semi-circle formed of* SPECTATORS *behind* WOLF, LEYRAC *and* WESTCRAFT. *Pause.*)

WEST. Bear witness, all of ye, that he has struck me in the face with his glove.

LEY. What! do you call witnesses to your degradation? Is there no shame in you?

WEST. (*sternly, with suppressed passion*). Wait a bit. You shall see. Wolf.

WOLF. Master?

WEST. How many years' experience have you had in flogging my slaves?

WOLF. Four years!

WEST. (*gives* WOLF *cane*). Could you flog a slave with that cane?

WOLF. (*lays blow right and left with cane, making it whistle in the air*). Yes!

WEST. (*points to* LEYRAC.) Seize that man! (*confusion,* WOMEN *stand back affrighted.*)

VOICES. No, no! the French gentleman!

WEST. Who calls him a French gentleman? He is a slave!

LEY. What?

ALL. Oh! (*emotion.*)

WEST. (*to* LEYRAC, *tauntingly*). The wind on the leaves of the roof last night was I! (LEYRAC *falls back confounded*) Ha! you see! he cannot deny it! (*murmurs. The* PLANTERS *fall away from* LEYRAC *and side with* WESTCRAFT.) Stand back! would you break the laws? You know what is the penalty when a white man is struck by a slave. (WOLF *gets three or four* NEGROES *to prepare to rush on* LEYRAC.)

LEY. (*fiercely*). Wolf! if you want to see a coward, look at your master.

WOLF. Ha, ha! now, then, boys! (*they seize* LEYRAC, *struggle. Hurried music.*)

WEST. (*laughing*). Seize him up! That's right! Bear him to the whipping post. (LEYRAC *kneels to him.*)

(*Enter* MISS MILBURN. *Her hat falls off. She puts aside* WOLF *and* SLAVES *as they drag* LEYRAC *up* C.)

MISS M. Hold! (*embraces* LEYRAC, *who is kneeling, exhausted.*)

WEST. Are you mad! you are touching him?

MISS M. I am touching him.

WEST. You see the people around you?

MISS M. (*scornfully*). I see the people.

WEST. He is a slave!

MISS M. (*with great force*). I love him. (NEGROES *and the foreign merchants cheer.* Hurrah! *The* PLANTERS *silence the* NEGROES. ALL *form picture.*)

SLOW CURTAIN.

ACT III

SCENE II.—*Prison interior.*

Enter JAILOR. *Enter* MISS MILBURN.

MISS M. I want to speak to the Count de Leyrac. Here is the magistrate's order. (*gives paper.* JAILER *looks at paper, bows, crosses, unlocks door and then goes off.*)

(*Enter slowly* LEYRAC, *but seeing* MISS MILBURN, *approaches her eagerly.*)

LEY. Good-morning, my darling. You are most welcome!

MISS M. I bring you good news, Maurice.

LEY. You were sure to be the first to bring that. (*takes her hand.*)

MISS M. The sympathies of everybody on the island are with you. The magistrates themselves are all in your favor. There is proof that you insulted Mr. Westcraft in the market-place, but none that you are a slave. You are only known as the Count de Leyrac. Oh! what a charming thing Justice is—when it is on your own side! You will pass a formal examination, and leave the court as free as other men. But how you look at me. Do you so admire me?

LEY. I admire you, and I love you with all my heart and soul!

MISS M. You must have patience, my love. Come, come, my hand has nothing to do with it.

LEY. Is the day so far off when the hand will be mine?

MISS M. Ah! that may be nearer than you have expected. Mr. Westcraft insisted on my giving a definite answer to his pretensions. I shall find much pleasure in so doing.

LEY. I who am to stand as one of them amongst the slaves! can I concern myself with marriage?

MISS M. Now, I dislike you. Ah, hear me! I almost rejoice that your misfortunes have come. I can prove my esteem of you by saying: Slave or free, I love you! Maurice, will you take my hand?

LEY. As the hand of my wife?

MISS M. (*smiling*). If you have no objections, sir!

LEY. And when will we be married? To-day?

MISS M. You are in a great hurry, sir! Ah! it is not easy to say so, but I know you will not think the worse of me for it, but—but I have hastened the time of our marriage.

LEY. You! Ah, I understand. (*gloomily*). Your friends——

MISS M. No! You don't understand. My friends may suppose what they like, and say what they will. Marriage, in my eyes, is too sacred to be made a refuge from the opinion of the world. I have no parents—you are an orphan. To me you are the world. Slave or free, what is that to me? To-morrow there is a ship sails for France—will you go with it, and take me with you, as your wife?

LEY. Emily! (*embraces her.*) Does there a man live who is worthy of you?

MISS M. I think there does.

(*Enter, paper in hand,* PROVOST-MARSHAL.)

MARSHAL. Count Maurice de Leyrac, I regret that I have an unpleasant commission to perform.

LEY. (*with* MISS M. *on his left*). What is it, sir?

MAR. It is my official duty here to be present at the sale of slaves.

MISS M. My dear Provost-Marshal, that duty will be rendered less unpleasant by one exception to-day.

MAR. I am glad to hear it.

LEY. Stay, Emily. It is for me not to permit any thoughts injurious to my love of truth to be circulated. As far as regards me, your duty must be exercised.

MISS M. My darling, you are not bound to criminate yourself by revealing the secret of your birth.

MAR. You have only to remain silent. Mr. Westcraft has no written proof—and so matters will be in what is popularly termed a dead-lock.

LEY. I am not bound to volunteer any evidence that will injure me, but, if questions are directly put to me, I must not in honor permit my silence to pass for consent.

MAR. I must ask you certain leading questions, which will be registered in the records of the court.

LEY. Then, come what may I will not deny the mother that bore me! I am the son of Ruth the Quadroon! (MISS M. *tries to check his speaking.*)

MISS M. Oh! think of me! Don't speak of that.

MAR. Though the consequences may be of such grievous import to yourself.

LEY. Knowing far more of the consequences than you think!

MAR. Sir, I respect you! (*offers his hand which* LEYRAC *eagerly takes.*)

LEY. Ah! thank you!

MISS M. (*to* MARSHAL). I will not be behind my husband in truth and self-sacrifice! Slave or free, you shall have the hand that I promised you!

MAR. Miss Milburn, you are a woman in a thousand!

MISS M. No! (*embraces* LEYRAC.) I am only a woman who loves.

(*Enter, paper in hand,* WESTCRAFT.)

MISS M. What do you want here?

WEST. Ah! To tell you that the so-called Count de Laryac is included in the bill of sale. Does he deny he is a slave?

MAR. Alas! he will speak the truth.

WEST. You are wanted to attend the sale.

MAR. When?

WEST. In an hour.

MISS M. (*joyfully*). Then there is time to do what I wish for. Mr. Marshal, you were an old friend of my father's.

MAR. Yes.

MISS M. Well, will you do me a favor? I know you will. The rector is at my house, and all is ready for the ceremony; will you attend and give me away?

MAR. With the greatest pleasure!

WEST. Remember you are answerable for that man.

MISS M. (*tauntingly*). The Provost-Marshal shall not lose sight of him, sir!

WEST. I shall have the pleasure, Miss Milburn, of attending the sale and buying your husband.

MISS M. I shall attend and outbid you!

(*Exit* MARSHAL. MISS M. *and* LEYRAC.)

WEST. (C.). What! would you spend *all* your fortune on him?

MISS M. (*looking back.*) To the last mark!

(*Exit, with* LEYRAC, *affectionately.*)

WEST. (*alone*). Baffled! She meant what she said! And her fortune is more than mine. How shall I act? Let me see—(*reads paper.*) "All the property composing the Michaelmas estate, moveables, standing crops and in store and mill, cattle, slaves and buildings—" "To be sold at public auction, unless previously disposed of by private contract!" (*repeats excitedly.*) How did I come not to see that! by private sale! he's mine! he's mine at last!

(*Exit.*)

Scene changes to

SCENE III.—*Market-place in 5th grooves, same as Scene III., Act II. Groups and market-people as before.* PLANTERS, *some with rattans and cowhides, strolling about, note-books in hand, smoking, etc.*

FIRST PLANTER. What can all this mean? The first lot of the niggers hasn't yet arrived.

SECOND PLANTER. It begins to look like no sale.

FIRST P. Who'll come along of me around to the Provost-Marshal's. (*going up.*)

SECOND P. Oh! here comes the Provost-Marshal.

(*Enter* MARSHAL, MISS MILBURN *on* LEYRAC's *arm.* ALL *flock around them.*)

MAR. What does this all mean?

SECOND P. There's no sale.

FIRST P. It ought to have been begun half an hour ago.

MAR. I will go to my office and see what has caused the delay.

(*Enter* WESTCRAFT.)

WEST. The sale is stopped.

ALL. Stopped!

MISS M. (*to* LEYRAC). What does he mean? (*uneasy.* LEYRAC *tries to quiet her.*)

WEST. Yes. The notice has been sent to your office. (*to* MISS M.) It means that you rated your husband at the value of all your fortune, and I have rated my revenge at the whole value of mine. That is my slave! Take leave of your wife and come!

MISS M. (*clinging to* LEYRAC). He cannot part us! I will go with you! anywhere!

WEST. I forbid it! I forbid his wife to live on my plantation! He has married without his master's consent.

MISS M. (*to* MARSHAL). Oh! they cannot separate me from him?

MAR. (*affected*). I fear that the—the laws, in fact, he can.

WEST. Do you hear that?

LEY. Mr. Planter, *your slave* wishes a word with you on the subject of his wife.

WEST. Ha, ha! so you have found your tongue at last. You were silent enough the last time we met.

LEY. The last time that we met, and the other times that we have met, I was conscious that I came in between you, and the woman of your love. Besides, I was once or twice guilty of having given way to my passion towards you. Yet, I bore many an insult from you before I turned to chastise. I offered you the satisfaction of a gentleman, but you refused it. Then I insulted you in the public market place. Still you were the injured man.

WEST. I *was* the injured man (*loftily*). Pray, how is it that I am not so now?

LEY. Your conduct this day to me in the presence of my wife! If the wrong I had done you had been a thousand times what it is, what you have done would be exacting its requital ten-fold! You refused to meet me sword in hand, and waited till you might hold the slave-whip. Villain, you have taken the coward's vengeance! You strike at me through my wife's heart! Reptile! you forbore the sting until she was on my bosom. (PLANTERS *stand back from* WESTCRAFT. WOLF *enters and comes down to stay behind* WESTCRAFT) Tiger! you waited for this moment to tear her from me? (MISS MILBURN *sobs, clinging to* LEYRAC. *Tenderly*) What, tears! Don't cry! Your tears are a part of his vengeance! Look up! (*fiercely, as before*) Your slave defies you! Never can you sever what God and man have brought together! The prison is not strong enough to hold me! the whip is not twisted that can tame me! the laws not made that can keep me from her. Now, here she is! on her husband's breast! heart to heart! part us—part us, if you dare! and, by Heaven! you will do it at the peril of your life!

WEST. (*laughs*). Ha! my prison will hold you.

MISS M. (*sobbing*). No, no!

WEST. My lash will tame you! But I waste words on you. Wolf!

LEY. Try it!

WEST. For the last time, will you follow me? (*Business.* LEYRAC *tries to release himself from* MISS M. *in order to fight with* WOLF *and other* NEGROES.)

(*Enter, waving letter,* DAVID.)

DAVID. Oh, master! (ALL *fall back from* LEYRAC) I have found it! (*looks around, puzzled.*) What can have happened? You forget, sir—it is the letter that was hidden.

LEY. No matter! (*tries to restore* MISS M. *to consciousness out of her faint.*)

DAVID. But it may be of some importance. Oh! there is something wrong here!

LEY. Another time, good David! I cannot attend to it now.

DAVID. But it's the Brentwood letter! I found it by the instructions in the pocket-book of Ruth the quadroon.

WEST. What's that about Ruth the quadroon? If it concerns her son I claim an interest in it as his master. Let it be taken care of for me.

DAVID. (*to* MARSHAL). It is directed to you, sir.

MAR. (*takes letter*). To me! Mr. Brentwood's handwriting! Mention of a duplicate letter addressed to me—I never received any letter—could his jealous wife have suppressed it? Ah! (*opens letter.*)

WEST. There now, will you follow me? (*speaks to* WOLF *animatedly.*)

DAVID. (*aside*). I understand now! he is a slave on *his* plantation. Oh!

MAR. (*aside*). A few moments' delay will be a grace for his poor wife. (*reads letter and evinces surprise and joy*) What is this I see! can I credit it!

WEST. Come, don't read it to yourself, but read it aloud.

MAR. You wish me to read it aloud. Ha, ha! Thanks to your interference, Mr. Westcraft, I have read this now when I might otherwise have deferred it, and repented my delay all the rest of my life. I hold here in my hand a paper of manumission signed and sealed by Mr. Brentwood, in favor of the son of Ruth.

WEST. What's that you say? (*all are amazed.*)

MAR. I congratulate you, Mr. Westcraft. You have bought the Michaelmas estate, but you have not bought Maurice de Leyrac.

WEST. It's a forgery! I dispute it!

MAR. A man like you always disputes the truth! (PLANTERS *flock round* MARSHAL *to examine the papers.*)

WEST. I'll spend every penny I have to contest it.

DAVID. You can't! for you have spent every penny you have to buy my estate.

WEST. Oh! curse you all! (*they laugh at him. He and* WOLF *and several* NEGROES *go up and exeunt.*)

MISS M. I live again. You are free! (*takes* LEYRAC's *hand.*)

LEYRAC. No! (*kisses her hand.*) I am your slave!

CURTAIN.

30

From *Miscegenation*

The Theory of the Blending of the Races, Applied to the American White Man and Negro

David Goodman Croly and George Wakeman

The journalist David Goodman Croly (1829–1889), who was born in Ireland and raised in New York City, worked as a reporter for the *New York Evening Post* and an editor for the *New York Herald* before becoming managing editor of the *New York World*. The *World* was the leading pro-Democratic paper of its time and vehemently opposed the abolition of slavery and the re-election of Abraham Lincoln.

On December 25, 1863, an anonymous pamphlet entitled *Miscegenation: The Theory of the Blending of the Races, Applied to the American White Man and Negro* was distributed to abolitionist and other media. Its authors were Croly and George Wakeman, a *World* reporter. The pamphlet appeared to be written from an antislavery perspective and was endorsed by some prominent abolitionists, but its intention was to frighten readers with the prospect of rampant race-mixing to encourage them to vote against Lincoln. The pamphlet, which is excerpted here, ignited a firestorm of debate over interracial contact throughout the winter and spring. It was even read in congressional debates.

Lincoln secured reelection, but poor showings in New York City and Nassau County suggest that the *World* pamphlet did have some effect on New York voters' decisions. Croly and Wakeman's more lasting legacy was to coin the word that describes one of America's most contentious issues: "miscegenation," constructed from the Latin *miscere* (to mix) and *genus* (race or kind).

Introduction

The word is spoken at last. It is Miscegenation—the blending of the various races of men—the practical recognition of the brotherhood of all the children of the common father. While the sublime inspirations of Christianity have taught this doctrine, Christians so-called have ignored it in denying social equality to the colored man; while democracy is founded upon the idea that all men are equal, democrats have shrunk from the logic of their own creed, and refused to fraternize with the people of all nations; while science has demonstrated that the intermarriage of diverse races is indispensable to a progressive humanity, its votaries, in this country, at least, have never had the courage to apply that rule to the relations of the white and colored races. But Christianity, democracy, and science, are stronger than the timidity, prejudice, and pride of short-sighted men; and they teach that a people, to become great, must become composite. This involves what is vulgarly known as amalgamation, and those who dread that name, and the thought and fact it implies, are warned against reading these pages.

The author is aware that this book will call down upon itself a storm of contumely and abuse. He has withheld his name from the title page, not because he regrets any word in it, or is afraid to meet any argument against it; but because he prefers that a great truth should spread by the force of its own momentum against the heart of the world. He is patient, he is confident. He appeals from the imperfect American of to-day, to the more perfect race that is yet to appear upon this continent. "If God," said the great German Astronomer, "could wait six thousand years before he revealed to me the laws which govern the heavenly bodies, I too can wait until men accept them as true."

New Words Used in This Book

Miscegenation—from the Latin *Miscere*, to mix, and *Genus*, race, is used to denote the abstract idea of the mixture of two or more races.

Miscegen—is used to denote an offspring of persons of different races, with the plural form, Miscegens.

Miscegenate—is used as the verbal form of the first mentioned word; *e.g.* to *miscegenate, i.e.* to mingle persons of different races.

Miscegenetic—The adjective form.

But as the particular subject under discussion limits, in a certain view, the races that are to be intermingled, the following are suggested, to express the idea of the union of the white and black races.

Melaleukation—The abstract form.

Melaleukon (plural formed by adding *s* to the word)—Substantive form.

Melaleuketic—Adjective form.

These words are derived from two Greek words, viz.: *Melas*, (μέλας), black; and *Leukos* (λευκός), white. The word *Mignumi* (μίγνυμι), to mix, is understood, making the word Melamigleukation, which, aside from its difficulty of pronounciation, is ill adapted for popular use.

Reasons for coining these words—(1.) There is, as yet, no word in the language which expresses exactly the idea they embody. (2.) Amalgamation is a poor word, since it properly refers to the union of metals with quicksilver, and was, in fact, only borrowed for an emergency, and should now be returned to its proper signification. (3.) The words used above are just the ones wanted, for they express the ideas with which we are dealing, and, what is quite as important, they express nothing else.

I. Physiological Equality of the White and Colored Races

The teachings of physiology as well as the inspirations of Christianity settle the question that all the tribes which inhabit the earth were originally derived from one type. Whether or not the story of Adam and Eve is accepted by all as absolutely true, the fact which it represents has been demonstrated by history, and by the latest discoveries bearing upon the origin of the human family.

The form of the skull varies in different parts of the earth, from the prognathous to the elliptical, while the color is of all shades between ebony and white. There are structural peculiarities, also, from the short, squat Esquimaux to the tall, lithe Patagonian. But despite skull, color, structure, the race is essentially one, and the differences depend wholly upon climate and circumstances. The reader would not thank us if we should burden this work with physiological arguments, but by examining the most popular books upon the subject it will be seen that the most profound investigation has proved, conclusively, not merely the unity of the race but the equality of the black with the white under the same advantages of education and condition.

There is no fact better established in the physical history of man than that color depends primarily upon temperature. The inhabitant of a northern clime is always white; of an extreme southern clime always black. The varieties of color exist between the two extremes. The Jews, who are tawny in their own country, are white in Northern Europe, with blue eyes and red beards; while in Borneo and Sumatra they are almost black. The Englishman or American who goes to the East or West Indies soon has his liver affected, causing him in time to turn yellow. Indeed, Dr. Draper, of the New York University, attributes the change in the color of the skin entirely to the action of the liver. He accounts for the slight peculiarities of structure which distinguish the white from the black as being due to this important organ, and in his excellent work on Physiology explains the process minutely.

In reference to the general characteristics of races, he well says: "Submitted for a due time to a high temperature, any race, irrespective of its original color, will become dark, or if to a low temperature it will become fair. Under certain circumstances it will pass to the elliptical; under others, to the prognathous form of skull. No race is in a state of absolute equilibrium, or able successfully to maintain its present physiognomy, if the circumstances under which it lives undergo a change. It holds itself ready with equal facility to descend to a baser or rise to a more elevated state, in correspondence with those circumstances. We confound temporary equilibration with final equilibrium."

Camper, one of the first authorities among anatomists and naturalists, than whom few men have received in their lives so many marks of distinction, delivered a lecture to the public, while occupying the Chair of Anatomy and Medicine in the University of Groningen, on the color of the skin of the negro. He first proposes to show that God created only one man, Adam, to whom all mankind owe their origin, whatever may be the traits of their countenance, or the color of their skin. He then examines the cause of diversity of color as to the exact situation of the peculiarity. "Examine the skin of this negro. You see that the true skin is perfectly white; that over it is placed another membrane, called the reticular tissue, and that this is the membrane that is black; and, finally, that it is covered by a third membrane, the scarf skin, which has been compared to a fine varnish lightly extended over the colored membrane, and designed to protect it. Examine also this piece of skin, belonging to a very fair person. You perceive over the true white skin a membrane of a slightly brownish tint, and over that again, but quite distinct from it, a transparent membrane. In other words, it clearly appears that the whites and the copper-colored have a colored membrane which is placed under the scarf skin and immediately above the true skin, just as it is in the negro. The infant negroes are born white or rather reddish, like those of other people, but in two or three days the color begins to change; they speedily become copper-colored; and by the seventh or eighth day, though never exposed to the sun, they appear quite black." He mentions that it is known that negroes in some rare instances are born quite white or are true Albinos; sometimes, after being black for many years, they become piebald, or wholly white, without their general health suffering under the change. He also mentions another metamorphosis, which would not be agreeable to the prejudices of many amongst us; it is that of the white becoming piebald with black as deep as ebony. He had seen only one case himself, but refers to other instances which had occurred under the observation of others. He agrees with Aristotle and Galen among the ancients and with Buffon and others among the moderns, in thinking that temperature is the cause of color in the skin. With a long sojourn under a scorching sun, he says a white race would become black, and in opposite circumstances a black race become white. "Thus," he says, "I am satisfied with having proved by anatomical observation on our bodies and particularly on our skin, that there is no room for believing that the race of negroes does not descend from Adam, as our own. Take all these things into consideration and you will find no difficulty in considering them genuine descendants of the common father of our race as you yourselves, nor will you hesitate with me to tender to the negro a brother's hand."

In the measurement of the skull the greatest importance is fixed by anatomists, in the comparison of races, upon the position of the great occipital foramen. Dr. Prichard says: "I have carefully examined the situation of the foramen magnum in many negro skulls, and in all of them it is found in precisely the place which Mr. Owen has pointed out as the general position of the occipital hole in the human skull. In those negro skulls which have the alveolar process very protuberant, the anterior half of the line above described is lengthened in a slight degree by the circumstance. If allowance is made for it, no difference is perceptible.... If a line is let fall from the summit of the head at right-angles with the plane of the basis, the occipital foramen will be found to be situated immediately behind it; and this is precisely the case in negro and European heads."

It has been remarked also that there is only the difference in the degree of crispation and coloring matter between the hair of the negro and the white. Prichard remarks that in the skull of the more improved and civilized nations among the woolly-haired blacks of Africa, there is comparatively slight deviation from the form which may be looked upon as the common type of the human head.

Baron Larrey says that the Arabian race furnishes the most perfect type of the human head, and yet the negro, so much maligned, is far superior to the Arab in every attribute of manhood.

Professor Draper says:

"It must be observed how forcibly the doctrine here urged of the passage of man from one complexion to another, and through successively different forms of skull in the course of ages, is illustrated by the singular circumstance to which attention has of late years been directed, of the gradual disappearance of the red-haired and blue-eyed men from Europe. Less than two thousand years ago the Roman authors bear their concurrent testimony to the fact that the inhabitants of Britain, Gaul, and a large portion of Germany, were of this kind. But no one would accept such a description as correct in our own times.... The true reason is that the red-haired man has been slowly changing to get into correspondence with the conditions that have been introduced through the gradual spread of civilization—conditions of a purely physical kind, and with which the darker man was more in unison."

And upon the general subject of the unity of the race he comes to the following conclusions: "Wherever we look, man is the same. Stripped of exterior coverings, there is in every climate a common body and common mind. Are not all of us liable to the same diseases? Have not all a tendency to exist the same length of time? Is it the temperature of our body, the beat of our pulse, the respiration that we observe—are they not everywhere alike? Or, turning to the manifestations of the mind, is there not among all the tribes of our race a belief in the existence and goodness of God? in unseen agents intermediate between him and ourselves? and in a future life? Do we not all put a reliance in the efficacy of prayers, and all, in our youth, have a dread of ghosts? How many of us, in all parts of the world, attach a value to pilgrimages, sacrificial offerings, fastings, and unlucky days, and in our worldly proceedings are guided by codes of law and ideas of the nature of property! Have we not all the same fears, the same delights, the same aversions, and do we not resort to the use of fire, domestic animals, and weapons? Do we not all expect that the differences which surround us here will be balanced hereafter, and that there are rewards and punishments? Is there not a common interpretation of all the varied forms of funeral ceremonies? a common sentiment of the sacredness of the tomb? Have we not always, and do we not everywhere set apart a sacerdotal order who may mediate for us? In our less advanced civilization, do we not all believe in sorceries, witches, and charms? It signifies nothing in what particular form our mental conceptions are embodied; it is the conception that concerns us, and not the aspect it has assumed. Thus equally do the views of the various nations demonstrate their innate belief in a future world—the undisturbed hunting-ground of the American Indian, the voluptuous Paradise and society of Houris of the Arabian, or the snow hut of the Esquimaux, in which the righteous feed on the blubber of whales."

II. Superiority of Mixed Races

If any fact is well established in history, it is that the miscegenetic or mixed races are much superior, mentally, physically, and morally, to those pure or unmixed. Wherever on the earth's surface we find a community which has intermarried for generations, we also find evidences of decay both in the physical and mental powers. On the other hand, wherever, through conquest, colonization, or commerce, different nationalities are blended, a superior human product invariably results.

The English people are great, because they are a composite race. The French, notwithstanding that they are called Celtic, are also originally of many diverse bloods. But its people have intermarried for so many years only among themselves, that it has gone very far in decay. The two most brilliant writers it can boast of are the melaleukon, Dumas, and his son, a quadroon. Take most of the eminent French names in literature, statesmanship, or war, and it will be found that they are mixtures of the modern French with the Germans or Italians. The great Napoleon was of an Italian family, and the present Napoleon is known to be the son of a Dutch admiral. Germany also is made up of a wide mixture of nations and races. The Slavic, Teutonic, and Saxon are all of diverse bloods, and the German of to-day is consequently of composite origin. The real superiority of the German over the Swede and Dane is due to the so-called purity of the Scandinavian race. The effect of a mixture of bloods is shown in a remarkable degree in the comparison between Northern and Southern Italy. The Sardinian is the controlling power to-day on the Italian peninsula, and why? Simply because all Northern Italy has been frequently overrun by the French and Austrian powers. The blood of the people has been fed from France, from Italy, from Switzerland, and from the Germanic races, which have successively occupied their country, either as conquerors, allies, mercenaries, or emigrants. The people of Sicily and Naples have had no such chance of interchange of blood; and, as a consequence, they are probably the lowest people, except the Irish, in the scale of civilization in Europe. They are brutal, ignorant, and barbarous, lacking in everything which goes to make up a prosperous and enlightened community. The most promising nation in Europe is the Russian, and its future will be glorious, only because its people represents a greater variety of race than any other in Europe. The sources of power in its blood come not only from the Caucasian and European races, but also from the Asiatic. It would take pages to enumerate the tribes which are now known by the one generic name of Russian. That great empire includes every variety of race, with the exception of the extreme black. It is now the dominant, and is yet destined to be the master-power of Europe. The time is coming when the Russian dominion will stretch to the Atlantic ocean. Nor should such an event be dreaded. What the barbarians did for demoralized and degenerate Rome, the Russians will do for the effete and worn-out populations of Western Europe. These will be conquered. Their civilization, such as it is, will be overthrown; but the new infusion of a young and composite blood will regenerate the life of Europe, will give it a new and better civilization, because the German, French, Italian, Spanish, and English will be mixed with a miscegenetic and progressive people.

The evil of a pure and the benefit of a mixed race is strikingly shown in the history of Spain. When the Moors overran the Spanish peninsula and gave their blood to the Spanish people, it resulted in a civilization as remarkable of its kind as anything which has existed in Europe. The traces of art, the monuments of great deeds done on the Spanish peninsula, are connected with the Moors, or rather with the blended Moors and Spaniards. To this day we hear of the glories of the Alhambra; of the achievements in science, literature, and art, which resulted from the union between an Asiatic and a European people. The downfall of Spain dates from its cruel expulsion of the Moors from that peninsula. The pride of race, which led it to reject the rich blood of the Morisco, signaled the decadence of its power. Spain was once the greatest nation in Europe; but the intermarriages between its people, and especially among the nobility and leading classes, rapidly deprived it of vital energy, and its history, until within the last few years, has been one of steady decline.

Whatever of power and vitality there is in the American race is derived, not from its Anglo-Saxon progenitors, but from all the different nationalities which go to make up this people. All that is needed to make us the finest race on earth is to engraft upon our stock the negro element which providence has placed by our side on this continent. Of all the rich treasures of blood vouchsafed to us, that of the negro is the most precious, because it is the most unlike any other that enters into the composition of our national life....

III. The Blending of Diverse Bloods Essential to American Progress

As yet the law governing the rise and fall of races has not been definitely understood. That there is a law operating in all nations, and through all time, is evident to the most casual reader of history. We see races emerge from barbarism, flourish for a hundred or two hundred years, then become degenerate, and relapse into a condition worse than their former barbarism. The law in such cases may be stated thus: It is given to all created things to achieve a certain progress of their own, but a continuance of progress can only be obtained through a judicious crossing of diverse elements. Thus it was given to the Greeks, through a comparatively brief history, to develop a wonderful system of mythology, of philosophy, and of art; to create forms of government that we are to this day experimenting with; then when ripe with glory, to fall away, to lapse into a semi-barbarism, from which it appears impossible to rescue them. Their history is but the history of all other civilized nations which have succeeded them. France, to-day, is in its decline. The Gallic race, originally composed of diverse elements, has been blended into one for so many generations, that the Frenchman is losing in stature, his prolific powers are failing, his intellectual efforts show that finish, polish, precision, and effeminacy, as compared with the rude vigor of nature, which bespeak irreparable decay. The phenomenon has not been generally remarked, that of late years France has become stationary in population; that, in Paris, the number of deaths enormously exceeds the number of births; that the stature of the Frenchman of 1863, is at least three inches shorter than that of the Frenchman of a century since. England maintains its vitality much better. The prolific power of the numerous races which entered into the composition of the modern Englishman has not yet run out, enriched as it is with the Saxon, Celtic, Danish, and other bloods. The Englishman of to-day is of a composite race. The different characteristics (as has been said by a well-known author), may still be seen in different sections of the kingdom. "The Saxon may be found in Norfolk, Suffolk, and Essex, the Celtic in the western highlands, the Danish, with red hair, and the *burr*, in the north of England, the Norwegian further north, the Sclavonic, with cat-like faces, in Carthness." More recently the English people have again intermixed with the Irish and the Scotch. A striking instance of the decay of the races is shown in the history of the Irish. The parts of Ireland that are most habitable, and have the most thrifty population, are those in which Englishmen and Scotchmen have settled. In the north, and other portions of Ireland, the native race, by emigration, and by death, has been steadily decreasing, and will decrease until it blends with a separate people. The Irish, however, transplanted to our soil, become prolific again, because they mix with the American, the German, the Negro, all of whom are brought up under different climatic influences.

But, even the English race itself is beginning to decay. This is shown by the excessive number of females born in that country. They are known to exceed the number of males by over one million. It is a well-known law, that an increase of female population is a symptom of weakness and effeminacy. In the effete races of Northern Mexico, it is remarked that six or seven females are born to one male. The strongest species of animals are those which, like the lion, have a large number of male offspring; but the weaker animals, such as swine, rabbits, and fowl, have an excessive number of females. It is true of England to-day, and is proved by this and other facts, that its people are losing in vigor.

It is clear that no race can long endure without a commingling of its blood with that of other races. The condition of all human progress is miscegenation. The Anglo-Saxon should learn this in time for his own salvation. If we will not heed the demands of justice, let us, at least, respect the law of self-preservation. Providence has kindly placed on the American soil for his own wise purposes, four millions of colored people. They are our brothers, our sisters. By mingling with them we become powerful, prosperous, and progressive; by refusing to do so we become feeble, unhealthy, narrow-minded, unfit for the nobler offices of freedom, and certain of early decay.

IV. The March of the Dark Races Northward

The fact may be startling, but the student of ethnology will be willing to admit that in the course of time the dark races must absorb the white. It is demonstrable from the history of Europe, that the black-haired, black-eyed, swarthy-skinned races have been steadily and surely moving towards northern latitudes.

When Rome was in her pride, the vegetation of Italy, as we learn from the poems of Virgil and Horace, was similar to that which now prevails in Northern Germany and France, and its place has been taken by trees and plants of a more tropical character. The Romans were a lighter people than those which now exist on the shores of the Mediterranean. All the tribes north of the Apennines previous to the time of Cæsar,

were yellow-haired, red-bearded—perfect blondes, such as we even now see specimens of in portions of Northern Germany, Sweden, Norway, Denmark, and Scotland.
Since that time France has become inhabited almost entirely by brunettes. So, also,
has Southern Germany given evidence of a change in the type of its people, in the introduction of traces of the Tartar, in the long, coarse hair, the black eyes, and the yellow skin. England, today, is filled with specimens of the darker races. In the olden
times the yellow-haired Saxon prevailed over all the British Islands, but he has been
conquered by the darker Celt, or changed and improved by the gradual infusion from
the South of a richer and more tropical blood. Another thousand years will in all
probability see Southern Europe inhabited by a people darker than the Moors, while
Northern Europe, in the complexion of its inhabitants, will be similar to the Spain
and Italy of to-day.

All the noted ancient and modern wars of Europe may be traced to the yearning of
the brunette and blonde to mingle. The Romans conquered the Gauls, Britons, and
the Germanic races, to give them the laws and institutions of Rome, and to satisfy this
miscegenetic instinct. When Rome fell into decrepitude, the same instinct, as much as
the love of plunder and conquest, urged the Hun, Goth, Vandal, and the various tribes
of Scythia and Germany, to precipitate themselves upon the plains of southern Europe. Genseric with his yellow-haired Vandals conquered northern Africa to mingle
the blood of the two regions. The great wars of modern Europe, including the giant
conflicts of Napoleon, have had the effect of intermixing the treasures of different
bloods and complexions. Europe is becoming yearly more composite, at least as far as
the limit of its races will admit, and consequently more civilized. Thoroughly miscegenetic it cannot be until the Mongolian and African can be brought to its doors.

It will be our noble prerogative to set the example of this rich blending of blood. It
is idle to maintain that this present war is not a war for the negro. It is a war for the
negro. Not simply for his personal rights or his physical freedom—it is a war if you
please, of amalgamation, so called—a war looking, as its final fruit, to the blending of
the white and black. All attempts to end it without a recognition of the political, civil,
and social rights of the negro will only lead to still bloodier battles in the future. Let
us be wise and look to the end. Let the war go on until every black man and every
black woman is free. Let it go on until the pride of caste is done away. Let it go on
until church, and state, and society recognize not only the propriety but the necessity
of the fusion of the white and black—in short, until the great truth shall be declared
in our public documents and announced in the messages of our Presidents, that it is
desirable the white man should marry the black woman and the white woman the
black man—that the race should become melaleuketic before it becomes miscegenetic. The next step will be the opening of California to the teeming millions of eastern Asia. The patience, the industry, the ingenuity, the organizing power, the skill in
the mechanic arts, which characterize the Japanese and Chinese, must be transplanted
to our soil, not merely by the emigration of the inhabitants of those nations, but by
their incorporation with the composite race which will hereafter rule this continent.

It must be remembered that the Indians whom we have displaced were copper-colored, and no other complexion, physiologists affirm, can exist permanently in America. The white race which settled in New England will be unable to maintain its vital-

ity as a blonde people. The darker shades of color live and thrive, and the consumption so prevalent in our Eastern States is mainly confined to the yellow-haired and thin-blooded blondes.

They need the intermingling of the rich tropic temperament of the negro to give warmth and fullness to their natures. They feel the yearning, and do not know how to interpret it. The physician tells them they must travel to a warmer climate. They recognize in this a glimpse of the want they feel, though they are hopeless of its efficacy to fully restore the lost vitality. Still they feel the nameless longing.

> "Yet waft me from the harbor mouth,
> Wild Wind! I seek a warmer sky,
> And I will see before I die
> The palms and temples of the south."

It is only by the infusion into their very system of the vital forces of a tropic race that they may regain health and strength.

We must accept the facts of nature. We must become a yellow-skinned, black-haired people—in fine, we must become Miscegens, if we would attain the fullest results of civilization.

V. The Mystery of the Pyramids—The Sphynx Question Answered

The first instance given us in history of a highly cultivated state of society occurred in a miscegenetic community. We allude to Egypt. As the years roll by and new discoveries are made with regard to this remarkable people, tourists and archæologists are filled with amazement at the evidences of a state of civilization of which even we know nothing. Among the ancient Egyptians the conditions existed for the first time in the history of the world for a high condition of mental culture.

The first requisite is density of population. There must be the collision of mind with mind, and the personal contact of man with man, to intensify the faculties. But, another condition is also necessary. Variety of mental conception is essential to a high development of civilization. The more distant the springs which feed the fountains of knowledge, the richer is the draught supplied to the race. These conditions existed among the Egyptians. The early inhabitants, as has now been discovered, were of a great variety of tribes; some pure black, others red or copper-colored, and others again, almost white. The ancient Copts, or Quobtes, as M. Puguet calls them, were a miscegenetic people. Some came from the far south, or equatorial region, and were black and woolly-haired; others from the deserts of the West, and were copper-colored; from the East also came a red and yellow tribe, and from the North came the white Thracian or Grecian, all mingling their blood in the ancient Egyptian. Thus ancient historians have given us different accounts of the color of the Egyptians. Herodotus stated that they were black and woolly-haired; still other Greek writers have said that they were dark colored but with straight hair. Among the mummies are found all varieties except the pure white.

It is clear, therefore, that the Egyptians were a composite race. It was here that civilization dawned, because it was here that the first conditions for civilization existed. The great variety of development of different forms of knowledge brought from distant countries, and better than all, and richer than all, the judicious intermingling of divers tribes from different parts of the earth, produced an intelligent, brave, and progressive people, the like of which has probably never since appeared upon the planet. The arts which have made Greece famous were all undoubtedly of Egyptian origin; the philosophy that is still discussed in our schools, was first evolved from the miscegenetic mind developed upon the banks of the Nile. As for mechanic arts, it is admitted that with all our discoveries in the physical sciences, with all the marvels effected by steam, we are still far behind the ancient Copts. A pyramid could not be built by any modern people. The immense masses of stone were removed hundreds of miles from their original beds by machinery of which we know nothing. Mr. Wendell Phillips, in his famous lecture on the Lost Arts, shows how many different branches of human industry were known to the ancients, and even to the Egyptians, about which we are entirely ignorant. Even in painting they seem to have possessed a knowledge which the world has lost, for many of the pictures taken from the pyramids are untarnished by time, while those painted by Titian, Angelo, and Raphael, are chalky and discolored.

The Sphynx question is answered. Egypt calls to us from her tombs, telling us that the secret of progress and of a final perfected humanity lies in the principle of Miscegenation. If we would be raised to the full stature of manhood and womanhood; if we would be as gods, knowing good from evil; if we would fill our proper place in nature, we must mingle our blood with all the children of the common father of humanity. The great lesson of all religions is self-abnegation, the giving up of prejudice, the acknowledgment of our brother man, without regard to his complexion, or creed, or standing, as being dearer to us than our own selves. This is a lesson that America, strong in the pride of color and country, should lay well to heart.

Egypt decayed because her people forgot the lesson their own history should have taught them. After the race became thoroughly composite, they intermarried only with one another, and even carried the breeding in-and-in practice to such an extent that brothers married sisters, and mothers sons. Physical degeneracy and mental imbecility rapidly set in; the nation sank as swiftly as it had soared; and by the operation of the same great law.

VI. All Religions Derived from the Dark Races

It is a curious fact that the Caucasian or white race, which of late years has arrogated to itself all the civilization extant, has never yet developed a religious faith of its own. Let the reader peruse any work upon religious creeds and he will find that the whole human family derived their ideas of Deity and of the great hereafter from the earlier and darker races. It is enough to mention Buddhism, Brahmanism, Mahometanism, Judahism, and Christianity, to illustrate our meaning. The Caucasian race, it is true, are intellectual—the perceptive and reasoning organs are large; yet the sciences upon which we pride ourselves, and the arts which we call our own, are derived primarily from the Asiatics and Africans. Prof. Draper says: "The old white inhabitants of Europe were not able to commence their civilization from their own interior resources, but were thrown into that career by the example and aid of a more southern and darker people, whose climate was more favorable." The white race have originated nothing—they have improved upon many things. They are intellectual, artistic, scientific—in whatever relates to the material they are at home; but the glories of the Unseen World, the deeper mysteries of the human soul, the relations of humanity to the Omnipotent, the revelations of the hereafter, all there is of aspiration, of religious truth, we learn from the darker Asiatic races; in short, the whole emotional and spiritual part of our nature is fed by streams from

> "Shiloh's brook, which flows
> Fast by the oracles of God."

Enter a church in any part of Europe or America, and you will find carefully reproduced the religious creeds of prophets and priests who lived thousands of years ago in Egypt, Mesopotamia, or the land of the Orient, still further towards the rising sun. All the pure Caucasian race has been able to do has been to invent a cold skepticism, a denial of those religious truths without which the race cannot attain perfection.

May we not hope that in the happier hereafter of this continent, when the Mongolian from China and Japan and the negro from his own Africa, shall have blent their more emotional natures with ours, that here may be witnessed, at once, the most perfect religion, as well as the most perfect type of mankind the world has yet seen. Let us then embrace our black brother; let us give him the intellect, the energy, the nervous endurance of the cold North which he needs, and let us take from him his emotional power, his love of the spiritual, his delight in the wonders which we understand only through faith. In the beautiful words of Emerson:

> "He has the avenues to God
>   Hid from men of Northern brain,
> Far beholding, without cloud,
>   What these with slowest steps attain."

VII. The Type Man a Miscegen

The most recent physiological discoveries have demonstrated that the pale, fair, light hair, mild blue or grey eyes, and sandy, bleached complexions of the blonde or extreme white, are far from being indications of a healthy, refined, and perfected organization. It is among this class that scrofula, consumption, and the nervous diseases prevail. The ideal of the white race—the angels of our painters, the imaginary Christ of our sculptors and artists—is not the perfect ideal of manhood. The true ideal man can only be reached by blending the type man and woman of all the races of the earth. The highest conception of physical beauty possessed by the negro, by the Moor, by the Asiatic, is a model man and woman after their own race; the negro's Venus is black; his houris and gods are black; the divinity of the Hindoo is of the color of his own people; the Great Spirit of the Indian, if of any color, is copper-colored; and so through all the world, the highest conception of beauty and perfection is the noblest specimen of each particular community. Humanity's highest type, therefore, is not the white, which comprises only a comparatively small fraction of the people who inhabit the planet.

The ideal or type man of the future will blend in himself all that is passionate and emotional in the darker races, all that is imaginative and spiritual in the Asiatic races, and all that is intellectual and perceptive in the white races. He will also be composite as regards color. The purest Miscegen will be brown, with reddish cheeks, curly and waving hair, dark eyes, and a fullness and suppleness of form not now dreamed of by any individual people. Of course the old races will not be entirely lost sight of. Nature abhors uniformity, and while the highest and purest type will be such as we have described, there will be all shades of color, from white to black. It is to the credit of Professor Draper, of the New York University, that he has had the boldness to avow the physiological fact here announced. He comes to the conclusion, after discussing the question at some length, "That the extremes of humanity, which are represented by a prognathous aspect, and by a complexion either very dark or very fair, are equally unfavorable to intellect, which reaches its greatest perfection in the intermediate phase."

He further says, that "putting disturbances of civilization aside, and looking only to our natural state, we should be constrained to admit that the man of maximum intellectual capacity is of a brown hue."

It is not within the purpose of this book to prove physiological facts; but simply to state them. They are either true or false. If true, it matters little what critics may say with regard to them; if false, they fall to the ground.

Adam, the progenitor of the race, as his very name signifies, was made of red earth; and, like the inhabitants of Syria and Mesopotamia, must have been of a tawny or yellow color. The extreme white and black are departures from the original type. The Saviour is represented very falsely in paintings, as being light-haired and white-skinned, when, in truth, he must have been a man of very dark complexion, as were all the Palestine Jews. They were a tawny or yellow race. The fact has been noticed that the Amharic, the language of the Abyssinian, is remarkably analogous to the Hebrew, rendering it probable that the Jews were partly of Abyssinian or negro origin.

We urge upon white men and women no longer to glory in their color; it is no evidence of cultivation or of purity of blood. Adam and Christ, the type men of the world's great eras, were red or yellow, and to men of this color, above all others, must be communicated the higher inspirations which involve great spiritual truths, and which bring individuals of the human family into direct communion with supernatural agencies.

VIII. *Love of the Blonde for the Black*

Such of our readers as have attended anti-slavery meetings will have observed the large proportion of blondes in the assemblage. This peculiarity is also noticeable in the leading speakers and agitators in the great anti-slavery party. Mr. Horace Greeley, of the New York Tribune, known for his devotion to the negro race, is as opposite as a man possibly can be to the people to whom he has shown his attachment by long and earnest labor for their welfare. In color, complexion, structure, mental habits, peculiarities of all kinds, they are as far apart as the poles. The same is true of Mr. Wendell Phillips. He, too, is the very opposite of the negro. His complexion is reddish and sanguine; his hair in younger days was light; he is, in short, one of the sharpest possible contrasts to the pure negro. Mr. Theodore Tilton, the eloquent young editor of the Independent, who has already achieved immortality by advocating enthusiastically the doctrine of miscegenation, is a very pure specimen of the blonde, and when a young man was noted for his angelic type of feature—we mean angelic after the type of Raphael, which is not the true angelic feature, because the perfect type of the future will be that of the blended races, with the sunny hues of the South tinging the colorless complexion of the icy North. But it is needless further to particularize. The sympathy Mr. Greeley, Mr. Phillips, and Mr. Tilton feel for the negro is the love which the blonde bears for the black; it is a love of race, a sympathy stronger to them than the love they bear to woman. It is founded upon natural law. We love our opposites. It is in the nature of things that we should do so, and where nature has free course, men like those we have indicated, whether anti-slavery or pro-slavery, conservative or radical, democrat or republican, will marry and be given in marriage to the most perfect specimens of the colored race.

It is also remarkable that the anti-slavery agitation is confined to those climates and races that are the furthest removed from the natural home of the colored people. England and the Northern States of North America are strongly anti-slavery. The people of France are also anti-slavery after a fashion, but not so much so as the English. The Spanish people, with their dark hair and skin, have not the love for the negro which distinguishes the more northern races, and hence we never hear of an anti-slavery propaganda on the Spanish peninsula. The further south we go the less the sympathy for the negro; the further north, the greater.

Nor is it alone true that the blonde love the black. The black also love their opposites. Said Frederick Douglass, a noble specimen of the melaleuketic American, in one of his speeches: "We love the white man, and will remain with him. We like him too well to leave him but we must possess with him the rights of freemen." Our police courts give painful evidence that the passion of the colored race for the white is often so uncontrollable as to overcome the terror of the law. It has been so, too, upon the southern plantations. The only remedy for this is legitimate melaleuketic marriage. As Novalis wisely says: "The way to overcome nature, is to submit to her."

It is true that a few men of dark skin, and eyes, and hair are to be found among the anti-slavery leaders but it will be remarked by any careful observer that it is not so much the love of the negro that animates these men as hatred of the slaveholder. The case of Owen Lovejoy is one in point. He hates the South because the slaveholders murdered his brother. The bitterness manifested by these dark-skinned, dark-haired, dark eyed, saturnine northern men towards the southern man is due to the strong antipathy and opposition which always exists between males of a kindred type; but if the southern woman was a blonde, golden-haired, blue-eyed, and of sunny complexion, they would love her. The law therefore is that we love our opposites. Walker, in his work on Intermarriage, says: "In the vital systems the dry seek the humid; the meagre, the plump; the hard, the softer; the rough, the smoother; the warmer, the colder; the dark, the fairer, &c., upon the same principles.... In the mental system, the irritable seek the calm; the grave, the gay; the impassioned, the modest; the impetuous, the gentle, &c.; or in opposite cases the opposite. In all this it is not what we possess ourselves, it is something different, something new, something capable of exciting, which is sought for, and this conforms to the fundamental difference of the sexes."

IX. Present and Future of the Irish and the Negro

Notwithstanding the apparent antagonism which exists between the Irish and negroes on this continent, there are the strongest reasons for believing that the first movement towards a melaleuketic union will take place between these two races. Indeed, in very many instances it has already occurred. Wherever there is a poor community of Irish in the North, they naturally herd with the poor negroes, and as the result of the various offices of kindness which only the poor pay to one another, families become intermingled and connubial relations are formed between the black men and white Irish women. These matrimonial arrangements have generally been pleasant to both parties, and were it not for the unhappy prejudice which exists, such unions would be very much more frequent. The white Irishwoman loves the black man and in the old country, it has been stated, that the negro is sure of the handsomest among the poor white females. The very bitterness of feeling which exists on the part of the Irish in the large cities towards the negroes is an evidence that they will be the first to mingle. The disturbances created when brought into contact present the same phenomena as the attempted fusion of kindred electricities—repugnance and flying apart are followed by the closest of all unions. The fusion, whenever it takes place, will be of infinite service to the Irish. They are a more brutal race and lower in civilization than the negro. The latter is mild, spiritual, fond of melody and song, warm in his attachments, fervid in his passions but inoffensive and kind, and only apparently brutal when his warmest emotions are brought into play in his love for the white woman. The Irish are coarse-grained, revengeful, unintellectual, with very few of the finer instincts of humanity. Of course we speak of the laboring Irish as they appear in this country. The Milesian is a child of the sun. He was originally of a colored race, and has all the fervid emotional power which belongs to a people born in or near the tropics. His long habitation north, however, and the ignorance in which he has been kept by misgovernment, have sunk the Irishman below the level of the most degraded negro. Take an equal number of negroes and Irish from among the lowest communities of the city of New York, and the former will be found far superior to the latter in cleanliness, education, moral feelings, beauty of form and feature, and natural sense. One of the evidences of degeneracy which has been pointed out in certain of the negro races has been the prognathous skull, the projecting mouth, the flat and open nostril. Yet this is a characteristic as true of certain portions of the people of Ireland as of the Guinea African. The inhabitants of Sligo and Mayo, portions of Ireland under peculiarly bad government, have developed these precise types of feature. The people have become thin-legged, potbellied, with mouth projected, head sloped, nostril distended; in short they exhibit all the characteristics by which we have marked the lowest type of the negro. The blending of the Irish in this country with the negro will be a positive gain to the former. With education and an intermingling with the superior black, the Irish may be lifted up to something like the dignity of their ancestors, the Milesians. The poets who sang of the ancient Irish, of the wisdom of their rulers, of their bards and warriors, forgot, perhaps, that this noble old race was of a very dark complexion, and native of the far south. The red hair and beard so common in Ireland is a sure indication of the southern origin of its people. When a very dark people move to a northern climate the physiological change effected by the temperature is to convert the black into red hair. The red may change in the course of many generations into light or sandy, but the red which comes from a very dark people is not to be confounded with the blonde or light-brown which distinguishes a northern people.

The Irish-American press of this country have a duty to perform to their patrons in impressing these facts upon our Irish population. The black man is their brother in more senses than one, and, as in times past the Irish have shown themselves the most prejudiced and inhuman toward their dark-skinned fellow-laborers and friends, they should in the future set aside the prejudice which is the result of unfortunate education, and proclaim both by word and by the practice of intermarriage, their true relations with the negro....

XI. How the Anglo-American May Become Strong and Comely

The white people of America are dying for want of flesh and blood. They have bone and sinew, but they are dry and shriveled for lack of the healthful juices of life. The author has often sadly marked the contrast to be observed in social or intellectual gatherings of the negro and the white American. In the latter are seen unmistakably, the indications of physical decay. The cheeks are shrunken, the lips are thin and bloodless, the under jaw narrow and retreating, the teeth decayed and painful, the nose sharp and cold, the eyes small and watery, the complexion of a blue and yellow hue, the head and shoulders bent forward, the hair dry and straggling upon the men, the waists of the women thin and pinched, telling of sterility and consumption, the general appearance gaunt and cadaverous from head to foot. You will see bald heads upon young men. You will see eye-glasses and spectacles, false teeth, artificial color in the face, artificial plumpness to the form. The intercourse will be formal, ascetic, unemotional. You will see these characteristics so universal that they become rather the rule than the exception. Where the cheeks on one grown person will be rounded, and tinted with the healthy blood, ten persons will have them pale and hollow. Turn now to an assemblage of negroes. Every cheek is plump; the teeth are whiter than ivory; there are no bald heads, the eyes are large and bright, the head and shoulders are always up and back, every face wears a smile, every form is stalwart. The white man is going to seed; the black man is adding vigor and freshness to the trunk. The white child is born with full cheeks, but as he approaches manhood they fall away and are lank and thin. Nature did not intend that men's cheeks should be hollow. The dentists' signs in every locality only tell feebly of the sickness and racking pain that accompanies this weak and diseased condition of the jaws. Our professional men show more than any the lack of healthful association with their opposites of the other sex. They become thin, and gaunt, and old, when they should be strong and vigorous. They are told they need exercise; they take long walks in the morning air, and come back more cold and shriveled than ever. They need contact with healthy, loving, warm-blooded natures to fill up the lean interstices of their anatomy. Looking purely to physical benefits for themselves and their posterity, they might well form the resolve expressed in Tennyson's lines:

> "I will take some savage woman; she shall rear my dusky race;
> Iron-jointed, supple-sinewed, they shall dance and they shall run,
> Catch the wild goat by the hair, and hurl their lances in the sun;
> Whistle back the parrot's call, and leap the rainbows of the brooks,
> Not with blinded eyesight poring over miserable books."

XII. The Miscegenetic Ideal of Beauty in Woman

In what does beauty consist? In richness and brightness of color, and in gracefulness of curve and outline. What does the Anglo-Saxon, who assumes that his race monopolizes the beauty of the earth, look for in a lovely woman? Her cheeks must be rounded, and have a tint of the sun, her lips must be pouting, her teeth white and regular, her eyes large and bright; her hair must curl about her head, or descend in crinkling waves; she must be merry, gay, full of poetry and sentiment, fond of song, childlike and artless. But all these characteristics belong, in a somewhat exaggerated degree, to the negro girl. What color is beautiful in the human face? Is it the blank white? In paintings, the artist has never portrayed so perfect a woman to the fancy, as when choosing his subject from some other than the Caucasian race, he has been able to introduce the marvelous charm of the combination of colors in her face. Not alone to the white face, even when tinted with mantling blood, is the fascination of female loveliness imputed. The author may state—and the same experience can be witnessed to by thousands—that the most beautiful girl in form, feature, and every attribute of feminine loveliness he ever saw, was a mulatto. By crossing and improvement of different varieties, the strawberry, or other garden fruit, is brought nearest to perfection, in sweetness, size, and fruitfulness. This was a ripe and complete woman, possessing the best elements of two sources of parentage. Her complexion was warm and dark, and golden with the heat of tropical suns, lips full and luscious, cheeks perfectly moulded, and tinged with deep crimson, hair curling, and

> "Whose glossy black
> To shame might bring
> The plumage of the raven's wing."

For certain physiological reasons the mulattoes of this country are far from being true specimens of the results of miscegenetic reform; but occasionally there are combinations of circumstances which produce the superior of either of the parents. The "happy mean" between the physical characteristics of the white and black, forms the nearest approach to the perfect type of beauty in womanhood, and of strength and wisdom in manhood. The model of nature, will be one possessing in even balance all the characteristics of the various nations of the earth. Shakespeare, who said many things that in the light of after events seem almost prophetic, described briefly and completely the model representative of humanity:

> "The elements
> So mixed in him that nature might stand up,
> And say to all the world, 'This was a man.'"

Descriptions by travelers, of the beauty of negro and colored women, and of the stalwart and fine proportions of negro men, might be given here at length. It is sufficient that the colored girl may appear very beautiful in the eye of the white man. Adanson says of the negroes of Senegal: "Leur taille est pour l'ordinaire, au dessus de la mediocre, bien prise et sans défaut. Ils sont forts, robustes, et d'un temperament propre à la fatigue. Ils ont les traits du visage assez agréables." Of the women he says: "Leur visage est d'une douceur extrême. Elles ont yeux noirs bien fendus, la bouche et les lèvres petites et les traits du visage bien proportionnées. Il s'en trouve plusieurs d'une beauté parfaite."

Reynolds says, of the abstract question of beauty: "It is custom alone determines our preference of the color of the Europeans to the Ethiopians, and they, for the same reason, prefer their own color to ours. I suppose nobody will doubt, if one of their painters were to paint the Goddess of Beauty, but that he would represent her black, with thick lips, flat nose, and woolly hair; and it seems to me he would act very unnaturally if he did not, for by what criterion will any one dispute the propriety of his idea? We, indeed, say that the form and color of the European is preferable to that of the Ethiopian, but I know of no other reason we have for it, but that we are more accustomed to it."

He might have said that the criterion to beauty is the medium between all distinct models, and that such a criterion all the world would acknowledge.

Payne Knight says: "The sable Africans view with pity and contempt, the marked deformity of the Europeans, whose mouths are compressed, their noses pinched, their cheeks shrunk, their hair rendered lank and flimsy, their bodies lengthened and emaciated, and their skin unnaturally bleached by shade and seclusion, and the baneful influence of a cold, humid climate." These prejudices of the African against the European, are well-founded, but this is no reason why they should look upon us with "pity and contempt." For we have also our superiorities over the African, mostly intellectual, and these unnatural prejudices which destroy in the heart the sacred emotions of brotherhood, are the ruin of the races. There is in each race those elements which are needed to supply the deficiencies of the other. But these prejudices are dying out, and nature is asserting again the unity of all men. The negro now declares that he loves the white man, and the progressive party of the North assert the rights of the negro. The leaders of Progress—among whom we quote Phillips and Tilton—urge miscegenetic reform. The people are ripe to receive the truth. Through the fiery gate of war they are being led to deliverance from old prides and prejudices. And, indeed, the instinct of the white man responded to the call of the negro for fraternity. There were wants in his nature which only the negro could fill. There were defects in physical organization that only the negro could supply. There were cravings of the soul toward fraternity, that only the negro could comfort and satisfy. It is a mean pride, unworthy of a Christian or enlightened community, that should lead any to deny this. The success of the anti-slavery party has proved it, so that denial of the principle is denial of facts universally known. They have touched a chord that has vibrated with a sweet, strange, and marvelous music, awakening slumbering instincts in the heart of the nation and of the world. It has been felt alike by the free and the enslaved. When a deed is done for freedom and brotherhood, in the grand words of James Russell Lowell:

> "Through the earth's broad, aching breast,
> Runs a thrill of joy prophetic, trembling on from East to West,
> And the slave, where'er he cowers, feels the soul within him climb
> To the awful verge of manhood, as the energy sublime
> Of a century, bursts full blossomed on the thorny stem of time.
>
> Through the walls of hut and palace shoots the instantaneous throe,
> When the travail of the Ages wrings earth's systems to and fro;
> At the birth of each new Era, with a recognizing start,
> Nation wildly looks on nation, standing with mute lips apart,
> And glad truth's yet mightier man-child, leaps beneath the future's heart.
>
> For mankind are one in spirit, and an instinct bears along,
> Round the earth's electric circle, the swift flash of right or wrong,
> Whether conscious or unconscious, yet humanity's vast frame,
> Through its ocean-sundered fibers, feels the gush of joy or shame;
> In the gain or loss of *one* race, *all the rest* have equal claim."

XIII. *The Secret of Southern Success*

The North is wondering—the world is wondering—at the marvelous success of the Southern people in statesmanship and war. The discretion, endurance, energy, and heroism they have shown in sustaining for so long a time a rebellion supposed to be feeble and short-lived, have elicited the admiration even of their enemies; and Dr. Bellows, a gentleman than whom none can claim a more exalted and intense hate of slavery and of the rebellion, in an address before a Unitarian assemblage in Brooklyn, some time ago, paid a most eloquent and beautiful tribute to Southern chivalry, both as exhibited in the men and women. The truth may as well be understood, that the superiority of the slaveholding classes of the South arises from their intimate communication, from birth to death, with the colored race. Like Anteus, sent to his mother earth, they have risen reinvigorated. The unnatural separation of races which exists at the North, and the prejudice which keeps the poor whites of the South from the slave, have prevented a large portion of the American people from profiting by the presence of the negro in our midst. When this war opened, one of the leading English Reviews (the Edinburgh) had an article proving that the governing class at the South were superior men physically to those of the North; and it is true. The comments of the Northern press respecting the inferiority of the Southerners were true of the poor whites—of the sand-hillers and corncrackers, so well described in Mrs. Stowe's novels. But these people are kept apart, by their unwholesome prejudices, from the negro. Because they cannot mingle with him in the capacity of slaveholder, they shut themselves up in their unnatural pride, and shun the race that, even in its enslaved condition, is their superior. Their exclusiveness has been punished by their own physical inferiority. But it is otherwise with the so-called aristocratic classes of the South. The most intimate association exists. But the instinct here becomes a passion, and is often shameful and criminal.

On this point we might quote many pro and antislavery authorities, but the extracts would scarcely be fit for general reading. It is a notorious fact, however, that, for three generations back, the wealthy, educated, governing class of the South have mingled their blood with the enslaved race. These illicit unions, though sanctioned neither by law nor conscience, and which, therefore, are degrading morally, have helped to strengthen the vitality and add to the mental force of the Southerner. The emotional power, fervid oratory and intensity which distinguishes all thoroughbred slaveholders, is due to their intimate association with the most charming and intelligent of their slave girls. The local history of New Orleans, since its occupation by the Union army, proves what has often been suspected, that unions between the slaveholders and their slaves have often had, in the eyes of the parties themselves, all the sanctities of marriage. These facts give us an inkling of some of the sources of Southern power. The vigor to be derived from the contact with another race has never before been explained, because never suspected.

The idea that the Southerner has been benefited by his association with the black man is thus set forth, in a speech made by the Hon. Seth B. Cole, at a meeting of a

Loyal League Club in Brooklyn. It will be found reported in the Brooklyn *Eagle*, of June 20th, 1863:

"In accounting for the ability of the South successfully to cope with Union men, and maintain a persistence in the Cabinet, in battle, and on the sea, foreign to their character, and worthy of a better cause, the gentleman gave it as his belief, that the presence of the African in large numbers infused into the air a sort of barbaric malaria, a miasm of fierceness which, after long intercourse between the races, came to infect the white men and even the women also. On the contrary, the inferior race was made smoother, more, polished, and toned down by association with the superior. On this principle, therefore, he accounted for the wild, chivalrous spirit of the South; this combination of wild poison with the polish of the Southron made them great in many respects, and infusing itself into all grades of society, enabled the rebels for a time to overcome, or at least fairly contest with their Northern opponents. The realization of the fact, that this fierceness and fiery wildness of the negro was the real cause of the frequent success of Southern strategy and campaigning came slow, but the speaker thanked God that at last the nation understood it, and was already availing itself of it by putting the Africans, with all these traits developed, in the field against their most polished imitation. The black regiments in the field, and others to go, could compete with the wildness and recklessness of the rebels, and possessing this barbaric miasma in a greater degree could defeat them."

XIV. Heart-Histories of the White Daughters of the South

Nor are the Southern women indifferent to the strange magnetism of association with a tropical race. Far otherwise. The mothers and daughters of the aristocratic slave-holders are thrilled with a strange delight by daily contact with their dusky male servitors. These relations, though intimate and full of a rare charm to the passionate and impressible daughters of the South, seldom, if ever, pass beyond the bounds of propriety. A platonic love, a union of sympathies, emotions, and thoughts, may be the sweetness and grace of a woman's life, and without any formal human tie, may make her thoroughly happy.

And this is the secret of the strange infatuation of the Southern woman with the hideous barbarism of slavery. Freedom, she knows, would separate her forever from the colored man, while slavery retains him by her side. It is idle for the Southern woman to deny it; she loves the black man, and the raiment she clothes herself with is to please him. What are the distinguishing characteristics of a Southern woman's attire? Why, bright colors—a tendency to yellow and pale red, and those striking gold ornaments which make such a charming contrast to a dark skin, but are so out of place in the toilet of a blonde. Yes—the Southern beauty, as she parades her bright dresses and inappropriate colors in our Northern cities and watering-places, proclaims by every massive ornament in her shining hair, and by every yellow shade in the wavy folds of her dress, "I love the black man."

Nor, in view of the powerful attraction of the two races, is this frenzy of love in the white Southern woman for the negro, altogether inexplicable. The family is isolated on the plantations. The white young man is away at college, traveling in Europe, or practicing at his profession in the large cities, while the white girl, who matures early, is at her home, surrounded by the brightest and most intelligent of the young colored men on the estate. Passionate, full of sensibility, without the cold prudence of her Northern sister, who can wonder at the wild dreams of love which fire the hearts and fill the imagination of the impressible Southern maiden. The awkward, rude girl of yesterday, under the influence of the master passion of our common humanity, is changed in a day to the full measure of a glorious womanhood.

It is safe to say that the first heart experience of nearly every Southern maiden— the flowering sweetness and grace of her young life, is associated with a sad dream of some bondman lover. He may have been the waiter, or coachman, or the bright yellow lad who assisted the overseer; but to her he is a hero, blazing with all the splendors of imperial manhood. She treasures the looks from those dark eyes which made her pulses bound; every spot of earth, where he had awaited her coming, is, to her, holy ground.

The first bitter lesson of a woman's life—self-sacrifice—they learn when prejudice and pride of caste compels them to tear the loved image from their hearts. What wondrous romances are yet to be written on this sad but charming theme; what wealth of passional life is lost with all the heart-histories of the South blotted out by a blighting prejudice—a cruel pride of caste and color. The full mystery of sex—the sweet, wild dream of a perfect love, which will embrace all that is fervid and emotional in humanity, can never be generally known until men and women the world over are free to form unions with their opposites in color and race. The rule in love affinities is the same as in electrical affinities: unlike attract—like repel.

But while estimating the influence of the black upon the white race, we must not overlook the reverse action. The black race is also beneficially affected even when there is no intermarriage. On this point Dr. Hancock, the American traveler, says: "It has appeared to me that various obvious changes are produced in a few generations, from certain assimilations independently of intermarriage. We find, in negro families, which have long dwelt with those of the whites as domestics, that successive generations become less marked in their African features, in the thick lip and flat nose; and with skins of a shining black, they gradually acquire the European physiognomy." ...

XVI. *Progress of Public Opinion and National Policy towards Miscegenation*

The right of the negro to be free is now almost universally acknowledged. It is only those who are actuated by the meanest motives of personal interest who attempt to question it. The equality of the race is acknowledged far and wide. Its superiority in many of those characteristics which enter into the beau ideal of true manhood, is unquestionable. The necessity of the mingling of the race with ours as the only means of preserving us from the decay that inevitably follows the highest state of enlightenment and exclusiveness is beginning to be understood. The truth is dawning upon us. The light that glimmers along the horizon will soon break all over the sky.

In this war there has been seen the working of a marvellous Providence. The prejudices of many generations have been swept away in the tide of events. When we come to the dry land again we shall find ourselves across an ocean misty and stormy with old bigotries, superstitions, and passions. Let us pray that we rest our feet on no shoals or quicksands of compromise; but never cease our struggle, having saved this persecuted race from the waters, until we stand with them on the broad and solid ground of justice, equality, and fraternity.

No party in this country has yet dared, openly and unanimously, to speak the truth. But the times are big with hope. We see one party battling for the slave and another against him. We see in the North one party casting aside old prejudices; we see another clinging to them. It is only a question now when all will lose their hold. But we see progress more distinctly not in the defeat of one party by the other, so much as in the higher ground which both occupy. One presses forward and the other must follow it even to fight it. Yet the one the most advanced has not reached the *ultima thule* of its theories. Four years ago the Democrats, so-called, defended slavery, and the Republicans only dared to assert an opposition to the extension of slavery. The Republican party to-day boldly demands that every black man in the land shall be free; that he shall stand side by side with the white soldier in the defense of liberty and law; that the plantations of the South shall be transferred to him from his rebel master; that by the Government and people his services shall be recognized; that he shall receive from the white North the right hand of fellowship as the reward of his loyalty. The Democratic party hardly dares to oppose all this, but attempts to divert discussion to senseless side issues, such as peace, free speech, and personal and constitutional rights. In the olden time the master said, as loyal men say to-day, "He that is not with me is against me." When he cast out devils, as Burnside did in Ohio, and went about doing good as opportunity offered, to the poor and the oppressed, the hypocrites were horrified, and talked to him of the law and of the prophets, as the traitors of to-day talk of courts and constitutions. It is fitting that we should brand these men with the name of Copperheads, remembering how he addressed his audience of cavilers and hypocrites: "O! generation of vipers!"

The position of the Republican party to-day proves how far we are toward the truth. We have been driven. We have been carried in a whirlwind. It would have taken a thousand years in the old way to have come to this. But the party will not perform its whole mission till it throws aloft the standard of (so-called) Amalgamation. When the President proclaimed Emancipation he proclaimed also the mingling of the races. The one follows the other as surely as noonday follows sunrise. The party, as a whole, will not admit it yet. They move in the darkness, not knowing what the day will reveal to them. They denied that they were abolitionists. It was only at the commencement of this war that Congress, in its infinite stupidity, resolved that "neither the Federal Government, nor the people, nor the Governments of the non-slaveholding States have a purpose or constitutional right to legislate upon or interfere with slavery," and "that those persons in the North who do not subscribe to the foregoing proposition are too insignificant in numbers and influence to excite the serious attention or alarm of any portion of the people of the Republic, and that the increase of their numbers and influence does not keep pace with the increase of the aggregate population of the

Union." They were all conservatives then! But they had set their faces towards the light; they could not stand still; they could not go backward. And now, behold! the great Republican party has merged into the little abolition party. The drop has colored the bucket-full. There are only two parties now, the Abolition, which is, in effect, the party of miscegenation; and, behind them, that contemptible crowd who fear the South, and have no policy for the North but expediency. Why did abolitionism swallow Republicanism? Because it was founded on principles that approach nearer the truth. Because one man who is right is a majority against the world.

The people do not yet understand; but the old prejudices are being swept away. They say we must free the negroes. To free them is to recognize their equality with the white man. They are to compete with the white man in all spheres of labor. They are to receive wages. They are to provide for themselves. Therefore they will have the opportunity to rise to wealth and high position. Said a speaker at a Republican meeting at the Cooper Institute, in New York: "If the time ever comes when a majority of the people of this State desire a negro Governor, and elect him as such, I believe he ought to be Governor." It was a statement that commended itself to the common sense of the audience, and they did well to applaud. And the argument goes further. If a white woman shall prefer this black Governor, or any black man of wealth or distinction, for her husband, rather than an ignorant or drunken white man, she certainly ought to have him.

They dare to assert now, too, that the black man should be allowed to fight for us, maintaining that he will fight as well as the white man. So he will. If he may fight to protect our homes and firesides, why may he not enjoy a cordial association in our families and social circles? Shall the fair, whose smiles are the proverbial reward of bravery, discriminate as to color where merit is equal? The war is doing good in this, that our soldiers are mingling with the blacks now, as the whites of the south have mingled with them. But the association is more ennobling, because the black is now free, and may become, by industry and self-improvement, the equal of the white intellectually, as he is now physically and morally. The blacks that move with our regiments are beloved by their comrades; they perform the most valuable duties in the field—duties requiring courage and sagacity, with greater success than the white soldiers. There is a darker side to this picture which should be its brightest. The loves that have sprung up between the freed women and our soldiers have only been hinted at in public, though known by those who have followed our armies into slave regions to be universal and inevitable. The vacuum in the soldier's nature draws into itself the strength and the womanly fullness of the ripe and beautiful dark-skinned girl. The yearning instinct is satisfied at last, despite long-settled prejudices and blasphemous theories.

It is boldly announced now that the lands of rebel whites should be confiscated, and given to loyal negroes, in part payment of the debt of the nation toward them. They will then be peers in the land, able to educate and improve themselves. It is not contended here that the highly cultivated of any class should marry with the degraded. The elegant and refined gentleman would not find a congenial companion in the dirty, ignorant, and misformed Irish girl from the emigrant ships; the victim of poverty and despotism. So the influence of slavery must have been, in many instances, to degrade the negro far below his own standard in all the better attributes of man, and thus to render him unfit for marriage with the better classes. But there is an ideal of physical superiority to be found among the negro girls of the South that would give the incitement of warm and vigorous health to the chilly-blooded effeminacy that too often accompanies education and talent. The aristocrat of the South, for a century has gained strength by the association with his slaves. Let the poor and degraded whites of the South mingle with the negroes who have also partaken of the bitter fruits of slavery; let our soldiers occupy the plantations with those that are more fitted for their companionship, and the next generation will be a people worthy to occupy the sunny land that God has laid out there—a people who shall—

> "Walk in beauty like the night
>   Of cloudless climes and starry skies,
> And all that's best of dark and bright,
>   Meet in their aspect and their eyes."

Public opinion now acknowledges that the North is much to blame for slavery, because of the prejudice against the negro. But how is this prejudice to be removed? A separate race is always hated. The Jews have been the scoff and by-word of nations, simply because they were exclusive. The negro can only be respected and loved when he mingles with us, and becomes one of the elements of our race. The colonization scheme of the President has fallen stillborn from his pen.... The Republican party now wisely admits that we must let the negro remain with us, recognizing him as one of the great elements of our strength and prosperity. We have quoted the remark of Frederick Douglass concerning the love of the negro for the white. But it would be better for him to be transported to some foreign shore, to linger in poverty, and die in wretchedness, than to remain here isolated by prejudice from the white, persecuted, and hated. It has been the question always with the opponents of justice, "What will you do with the negro when he is free?" This is the answer, and the only answer: "We will take him into our societies, into our churches, into our schools, into our social circles, into our families; we will receive him as our younger brother." The Abolitionists did not answer thus in words; but their practice led to the true answer. They did not know, perhaps, the impulse that moved them. It was the sympathetic surging of the great heart of humanity towards the negro. As nature reveals the long-lost child to its mother, so the human heart went out towards its brother. It was a longing towards the realization of the common brotherhood, of the unity of the nations, which are the promise of all morality and of all Christianity. Might we hope that on this continent, at least, will be realized the vision of Tennyson:

> "Far along the world-wide whisper of the southwind rushing warm,
> With the standards of the peoples plunging through the thunder storm,
> Till the war-drums throbbed no longer, and the battle-flags were furl'd
> In the Parliament of man; the Federation of the world.
> There the common sense of most, shall hold a fretful realm in awe;
> And the kindly earth shall slumber, lapt in universal law."

XVII. *The Bloods of All Nations Find Their Level*

Whatever men may do, the immutable laws of nature are not subverted through the ages. For a brief period here, for a generation there, the great principles of equality may be ignored, and men may suffer. But not always. Man, though bent to the earth, surely becomes upright again. He holds in his hands the eternal years of God.

> "Through the ages one increasing purpose runs,
>   And the thoughts of men are widened
> With the process of the suns."

You may build cisterns, and canals, and levees; but some time, the water that you seek to confine will find its level again. Not the less so with the blood of man. As God made of one blood all nations of the earth, and as all are brothers from Adam; so, whatever artificial distinctions and barriers men may raise, the blood of humanity will at the end find its certain level.

There are nations that have built walls about themselves, as it were, so that their blood should not flow out, nor the blood of the nations outside flow in. They have said, "We will purify, and sweeten, and enrich the treasure of our veins. We will fill this nation full to the brim with gentle and noble blood, but will never let it overflow. And we will walk about on the turrets of our outside walls, and look upon all the other people of the earth, cold and lean below us." They denied the brotherhood of man; they failed to see the stamp of God on every brow. But the blood so confined became stagnant and fermented, so that before a century had passed it burst the bounds and ran out with wild force to mingle with that of barbarians outside. And the walls were torn down and again humanity was leveled. There are families that have hoarded their blood, as the miser his gold; and, as the gold cankers, so the blood has grown thick and muddy, losing its elements of health and vigor, and has only been rescued from death, if rescued at all, by the mingling with some purer streams in the lower strata of life. For as the waters are kept pure and sweet by perpetual motion, the blood of men is kept so by continual flowing through the veins of all the nations.

XVIII. *The Future—No White, No Black*

There are no insuperable difficulties in the way of this reform. The practice of melaleukation will be first openly adopted in the more thickly populated slave States. It is universal, now, throughout the South and only needs legitimatizing. The irregular alliances of to-day, will become the recognized unions of to-morrow. It has been well said that the slave of yesterday is the soldier of to-day and the citizen of to-morrow. He is to become the social and political equal of the white.

Under the ordinance of nature, confirmed by the solemn act of President Lincoln, in the emancipation proclamation, there are no slaves to-day in law at the South. Slavery is *de jure*, if not *de facto*, dead. This is the first step towards the redemption of the black and his absorption with the white. The second step is in making him a soldier of the United States. If he has fought beside the white, if he has spent his blood for the common country, the most ordinary sense of justice will revolt at the idea of remanding him back to slavery, or of denying him any opportunity or right accorded to his white comrade. If he has the ability in any sphere of industry, or in the development of any of the higher faculties of the mind to outstrip his white brother, he has also the right, and that theory which would deprive him of it is the plea of imbeciles and cowards. The only anomaly in our black army is that it has white officers. This will disappear as time passes by, and the black private and non-commissioned officer shows bravery and skill enough to lead not only men of his own race, but men of the white race. It will be a sad misfortune if this war should end without a battle being fought by a black general in command of a white or mixed body of troops. We want an American Toussaint L'Ouverture, to give the black his proper position on this continent, and the day is coming. People say the Rebellion is at an end, but this is not true. The South will fight to the last, but it is in the eternal fitness of things that they should finally be subdued by the black soldier. When the great armies of the Rebellion are destroyed, and the war resolves itself into guerrilla fighting, the black soldier, who is now in training, will be invaluable to seek out and put down the last remnants of organized force against the Government. It will then be due to the justice of history, that the Administration put the negro in supreme control of the South. The slave of yesterday not only is the soldier of to-day, but is destined to be the conqueror of to-morrow. The transition from this position to entire social equality will be very easy. The Southern whites will concede the full manhood of those who have met them in honorable conflict and defeated them. The Southern people, because of their intimate personal contact with the colored man, have never learned those prejudices against him which disgrace the North. They will disappear in the North, when the colored people become more numerous here.

It follows, therefore, that after the war is over, the American people will be compelled to apportion the great plantations of the South among their former slaves, who will have won the title by their valor in the field. They will be made not only landholders, but citizens. They will be eligible to office; to all the rights now possessed wholly by the white race. We shall then, in contested elections, see how eager the white candidate for office will be to prove not only that he is the black man's friend, but that he has black blood in his veins. Even in the last municipal election in New York, Mr. F. I. A. Boole, the candidate of the pro-slavery, Tammany, and Mozart organizations, for the Mayoralty, fearful of a defeat, called together a meeting of the black men, as reported in the Tribune of November 30 and 31 [*sic*], 1863, and besought their influence to elect him, promising to shield them in the exercise of their just rights and privileges, and placing himself on record as a friend of the colored man. During the same week a colored regiment passed through New York unmolested. The riot in that city was an expiring spasm of this prejudice, and had only the effect of increasing the public sentiment of respect and regard for the negroes. By the close of the war the pride of race, founded on an ignorant self-sufficiency, will be forgotten, and give place to a desire to secure his influence, and to become one with him in all the relations of life. The large cities of the South, New Orleans especially, even now swarm with mulattoes, quadroons, octoroons, and all shades of color. The unions producing these mixtures will be continued under the sanctions of public opinion, law, and religion.

Let no one, therefore, take trouble as to the possibility of effecting this great reform. It will work out itself. The course the Government has entered upon leads logically to this result. As the war has progressed, men's minds have been opened more and more to the true cause of our country's difficulties. Human nature is imperfect; it can ordinarily take in only half or quarter truths. It was a great step in the advance when the country willingly accepted the truth that all men should be free. But it might not have been seen by many that further along in the path of Progress we should recognize the great doctrine of human brotherhood, and that human brotherhood comprehended not merely the personal freedom, but the acknowledgment of the political and social rights of the negro, and the provision for his entrance into those family relations which form the dearest and strongest ties that bind humanity together. Once place the races upon a footing of perfect equality, and these results will surely follow.

History presents some curious instances of the effect of law and public opinion in keeping separate or in absorbing a distinct people. The Jews are a peculiar example. Since the time of the destruction of Jerusalem, they have been a marked race upon the earth, and both in Christian and Mahommedan countries have been under the pale of the law and of public opinion. As a consequence they have remained a peculiar people by themselves. Their customs and habits have been different, their very features different, from the masses of people about them. They have come to be hated and despised. America is the first country that has done the Jews justice, and what has been the result? They are equal here socially and politically with other sects, and the Jews in America, as a distinct nation, are dying out. They occupy our public offices, they are lecturers, actors, journalists. The American Jew of the second and third generation cannot be distinguished either by feature or habits from other American citizens. They have already commenced to intermarry, and soon the American Jew will be no more peculiar than the American Methodist or Presbyterian.

The wandering Gipsies or Bohemians, are another instance of the separation and subsequent absorption of a people. During the Middle Ages, and down almost to our time, the Gipsies were a peculiar people—made so by laws and public opinion. George Borrow, in his famous book on the Zincali of Spain, has traced their history for several generations. He shows that they began to disappear in Spain just so soon as the laws in relation to them were abrogated. From that time forth, they mingled with the Spanish people, and are to-day scarcely distinguishable from the other inhabitants of that peninsula. English Gipsies are also fast being absorbed, and in this country they are not known from the rest of the population. In England the Irish are a separate class, degraded as the negro is in the Northern States. But the Irishman who emigrates to America is lost in our population after the first generation. He has here perfect social and political rights, and, as a consequence, is an American citizen, and loses all the peculiarities which render him so disagreeable to the Anglo-Saxon on the other side of the ocean.

Once let the negro become the equal before the law, and the equal in social rights with the white, and he will disappear as a peculiar man, as the Jews and

Irish disappear by absorption in America, and as the Gipsies are disappearing under the enlightened public opinion of modern Europe.

Let it be understood, then, that equality before the law, for the negro, secures to him freedom, privilege to secure property and public position, and above all, carries with it the ultimate fusion of the negro and white races. When this shall be accomplished by the inevitable influences of time, all the troubles that loom up now in the future of our country, will have passed away. It is the true solution of our difficulties, and he is blind who does not see it. The President of the United States, fortunately for the country, has made a great advance in the right direction. His first thought in connection with the enfranchisement of the slaves, was to send them from the country. He discovered first, that this was physically impossible, and second that the labor alone which would be lost to America and the world, would amount in value to more than the debts of all the nations of the earth. The negro is rooted on this continent; we cannot remove him; we must not hold him in bondage. The wisest course is to give him his rights, and let him alone; and by the certain influence of our institutions, he will become a component element of the American Man.

XIX. Miscegenation in the Presidential Contest

The question of miscegenetic reform should enter into the approaching presidential contest. It is our duty as Americans, as Christians, as humanitarians, to take advantage of the circumstances which Providence has brought about, to introduce a new and improved life on this continent. Slavery no longer exists, but the black man is not yet an equal, before the law, of the white man, nor does custom give him the same social rights. But the times are propitious. If the progressive party of this country have courage, have faith in humanity and in their own doctrines, they can solve the problem which has perplexed our Statesmen since the establishment of the Government. That problem is, What to do with the black race. The slaveholder himself concedes that we require the labor of that race, that we want the thews and sinews of the black man for the cotton he grows, the sugar he produces, the tobacco he reaps, and all the thousand products of the Southern States, which go to fill the coffers of the nation. The mere value of the slave as a laborer, judged by the standard of the ox or horse, was estimated before the war as high as two thousand millions of dollars. His value as a moral and intellectual being is infinitely higher. The value of his blood with the mingled bloods which go to make up the American people, can never be estimated by money. Let the Republican party, then, rise to the height of the great argument; let them recognize the full equality of the negro before the law; let them ordain that, as a matter of simple justice, the man whose toil has enriched the Southern plantations should own them. For three or four generations, the profits of the labor of the slaves of the South have been spent in idleness by a few thousand white families. This great crime against the black man, thanks to the President's proclamation, the confiscation act, and the growing humanity of public opinion at the North, is no longer possible. As a matter of justice, the lands of the South must be divided among the negroes, who are its only loyal population. The work has commenced well at Port Royal, where the negroes are buying from the Government the farms that used to be their masters', and it must be continued throughout the rebel States.

But the negroes have another claim which is indisputable in law or justice—the claim of hereditary descent. Three-fourths of the four millions of the former slaves of the South have the blood of white aristocrats in their veins. They are, as the direct descendents of owners of plantations, entitled to share the property of their fathers, with their white brothers and sisters. It will be a crime for which history will never forgive the American people, if, after the slave oligarchy of the South has raised its hand to strike down the Constitution of the country, and obliterate nearly half of the stars which cluster upon its flag, they should restore it to its old place and power, and turn their backs upon the millions of loyal Africans whose prayers by day and by night have gone up for the success of the banner of Union and Liberty. The platform of the Chicago Convention—how meagre, how mean does it look beside the great result which followed the election of Abraham Lincoln. Let the Republican party go into the next contest with a platform worthy of itself; worthy of the events which have occurred during the last three years; worthy of America, worthy of the great future. Let the motto then of the great progressive party of this country be Freedom, Political and Social Equality; Universal Brotherhood. Let it send a message to all the nations of the earth, "Come hither with your means, come hither in the strength of your manhood, come hither with the wealth of your varied bloods. Let us establish here a nation founded on the principles of eternal justice, and upon the application of the doctrine of human brotherhood." These are questions, we are aware, that alarm those timid men, that always deprecate any movement toward Reform. They will dread the old prejudices which these subjects will awaken into new activity. But the promulgation of anti-slavery principles excited far more intense opposition than these are likely to receive; because, as time has passed by, and the questions affecting the colored race have been discussed, men have perceived that the hatred of race they indulged in was unworthy of their manhood, and that the negro, if not up to the level of the best specimens of the Caucasian, had all the qualifications which would fit him to be the companion of his white brother.

XX. An Omen

The statue of Liberty which has just crowned the capitol at Washington, stands as a symbol of the future American of this continent. It was meet and proper that while slavery exercised its baneful sway at the seat of Government, that the great dome of the capitol should have been unfinished, and that the figure of Liberty should not have unveiled its awful form upon the topmost summit. The maker of that statue has "builded better than he knew." In order to insure it against the storms and variable temperature of a Virginia atmosphere, it has been washed with an acid which has caused a slight oxidation, producing a rich and uniform bronze tint, which no rains can discolor and no sun bleach. When the traveler approaches the city of magnificent distances, the seat of what is destined to be the greatest and most beneficent power on earth, the first object that will strike his eye will be the figure of Liberty surmounting the capitol; not white, symbolizing but one race, nor black typifying another, but a statue representing the composite race, whose sway will extend from the Atlantic to the Pacific ocean, from the Equator to the North Pole—the Miscegens of the Future.

Conclusions

In the preceding pages the author has endeavored to make plain the following propositions:

1. That as by the teaching of science, religion, and democracy, the whole human race is of one family, it follows that there should be no distinction in political or social rights on account of color, race, or nativity, in a republic.
2. That the doctrine of human brotherhood should be accepted in its entirety in the United States, and that it implies the right of white and black to intermarry, should they so desire.
3. That the solution of the negro problem will not have been reached in this country, until public opinion sanctions a union of the two races.
4. That, as the negro cannot be driven out of the country, or exterminated, as for a wise purpose he has been placed side by side with the white in the Southern States, there should be no impediment to the absorption of the one race in the other.
5. That whereas, this mingling of races has been going on illegitimately for over a hundred years at the South, without any evil effect, legitimate unions between whites and blacks could not possibly have any worse result than the present system.
6. That the mingling of diverse races is a positive benefit to the progeny, as is proven by the history of all nations, from that of Egypt to the present day.
7. That as the rebellion has been caused not so much by slavery, as the base prejudice resulting from a distinction of color, and that perfect peace cannot be restored to our country until that distinction shall measurably cease, by a general absorption of the black race by the white.
8. That it is the duty of anti-slavery men everywhere to advocate miscegenation, or the mingling of all the races on this continent. It is well to make the negro free, it is better still to make him a soldier, but it is best of all to share with him our hearts and homes.
9. That whereas, the result of the last Presidential election has given the colored race on this continent its freedom, the next Presidential election should secure to every black man and woman the rest of their social and political rights; that the progressive party must rise to the height of the great argument, and not flinch from the conclusions to which they are brought by their own principles.
10. That in the millennial future, the most perfect and highest type of manhood will not be white or black, but brown, or colored, and that whoever helps to unite the various races of men, helps to make the human family the sooner realize its great destiny.

Realism and Local Color

Realistic features in interracial literature increased in the second half of the nineteenth century and included more psychological depth in character and more attention to historic and topographic detail, providing the fullest sense of the locale. For example, George Washington Cable's Louisiana is a great deal more vivid than Boucicault's. There are also fresh departures in telling by now familiar-seeming tales: for example, both Guy de Maupassant and Charles W. Chesnutt employ comic strategies, James Edwin Campbell's verse transforms an interracial romance into a national allegory, and Kate Chopin intensifies an explicitly female point of view. Among the targets of attack are narrowness, provincialism, prejudice, and hypocrisy, but also the sentimental expectations that readers may bring to these plot lines.

31

Madame Delphine

George Washington Cable

George Washington Cable (1844–1925) served in the Confederate army from 1863 to 1865, but he went on to write short stories, novels, and essays that criticized slavery and post-Emancipation discrimination against blacks. Cable's first short story appeared in *Scribner's Monthly* in 1873. A collection of stories, *Old Creole Days*, was published in 1879, followed by a novel, *The Grandissimes*, in 1880. Both books, which featured life in Creole New Orleans, were well received. Cable was harshly criticized, however, for his opposition to segregation and white supremacy, expressed in essay collections such as *The Silent South* (1885), which included the famous essay "The Freedman's Case in Equity," and *The Negro Question* (1888). Among his tales with centrally represented interracial themes are "Tite Poulette" (1879) and "Attalie Brouillard" (1889). Cable's novella *Madame Delphine* (1881), reprinted here, also appeared in later editions of *Old Creole Days*.

Chapter I. An Old House

A few steps from the St. Charles Hotel, in New Orleans, brings you to and across Canal Street, the central avenue of the city, and to that corner where the flower-women sit at the inner and outer edges of the arcaded sidewalk, and make the air sweet with their fragrant merchandise. The crowd—and if it is near the time of the carnival it will be great—will follow Canal Street.

But you turn, instead, into the quiet, narrow way which a lover of Creole antiquity, in fondness for a romantic past, is still prone to call the Rue Royale. You will pass a few restaurants, a few auction-rooms, a few furniture warehouses, and will hardly realize that you have left behind you the activity and clatter of a city of merchants before you find yourself in a region of architectural decrepitude, where an ancient and foreign-seeming domestic life, in second stories, overhangs the ruins of a former commercial prosperity, and upon every thing has settled down a long sabbath of decay. The vehicles in the street are few in number, and are merely passing through; the stores are shrunken into shops; you see here and there, like a patch of bright mould, the stall of that significant fungus, the Chinaman. Many great doors are shut and clamped and grown gray with cobweb; many street windows are nailed up; half the balconies are begrimed and rust-eaten, and many of the humid arches and alleys which characterize the older Franco-Spanish piles of stuccoed brick betray a squalor almost oriental.

Yet beauty lingers here. To say nothing of the picturesque, sometimes you get sight of comfort, sometimes of opulence, through the unlatched wicket in some *porte-cochère*—red-painted brick pavement, foliage of dark palm or pale banana, marble or granite masonry and blooming parterres; or through a chink between some pair of heavy batten window-shutters, opened with an almost reptile wariness, your eye gets a glimpse of lace and brocade upholstery, silver and bronze, and much similar rich antiquity.

The faces of the inmates are in keeping; of the passengers in the street a sad proportion are dingy and shabby; but just when these are putting you off your guard, there will pass you a woman—more likely two or three—of patrician beauty.

Now, if you will go far enough down this old street, you will see, as you approach its intersection with———. Names in that region elude one like ghosts.

However, as you begin to find the way a trifle more open, you will not fail to notice on the right-hand side, about midway of the square, a small, low, brick house of a story and a half, set out upon the sidewalk, as weather-beaten and mute as an aged beggar fallen asleep. Its corrugated roof of dull red tiles, sloping down toward you with an inward curve, is overgrown with weeds, and in the fall of the year is gay with the yellow plumes of the golden-rod. You can almost touch with your cane the low edge of the broad, overhanging eaves. The batten shutters at door and window, with hinges like those of a postern, are shut with a grip that makes one's knuckles and nails feel lacerated. Save in the brick-work itself there is not a cranny. You would say the house has the lockjaw. There are two doors, and to each a single chipped and battered marble step. Continuing on down the sidewalk, on a line with the house, is a garden masked from view by a high, close board-fence. You may see the tops of its fruit-trees—pomegranate, peach, banana, fig, pear, and particularly one large orange, close by the fence, that must be very old.

The residents over the narrow way, who live in a three-story house, originally of much pretension, but from whose front door hard times have removed almost all vestiges of paint, will tell you:

"Yass, de 'ouse is in'abit; 'tis live in."

And this is likely to be all the information you get—not that they would not tell, but they cannot grasp the idea that you wish to know—until, possibly, just as you are turning to depart, your informant, in a single word and with the most evident non-appreciation of its value, drops the simple key to the whole matter:

"Dey's quadroons."

He may then be aroused to mention the better appearance of the place in former years, when the houses of this region generally stood farther apart, and that garden comprised the whole square.

Here dwelt, sixty years ago and more, one Delphine Carraze; or, as she was commonly designated by the few who knew her, Madame Delphine. That she owned her home, and that it had been given her by the then deceased companion of her days of beauty, were facts so generally admitted as to be, even as far back as that sixty years ago, no longer a subject of gossip. She was never pointed out by the denizens of the quarter as a character, nor her house as a "feature." It would have passed all Creole powers of guessing to divine what you could find worthy of inquiry concerning a retired quadroon woman; and not the least puzzled of all would have been the timid and restive Madame Delphine herself.

Chapter II. Madame Delphine

During the first quarter of the present century, the free quadroon caste of New Orleans was in its golden age. Earlier generations—sprung, upon the one hand, from the merry gallants of a French colonial military service which had grown gross by affiliation with Spanish-American frontier life, and, upon the other hand, from comely Ethiopians culled out of the less negroidal types of African live goods, and bought at the ship's side with vestiges of quills and cowries and copper wire still in their headdresses,—these earlier generations, with scars of battle or private rencontre still on the fathers, and of servitude on the manumitted mothers, afforded a mere hint of the splendor that was to result from a survival of the fairest through seventy-five years devoted to the elimination of the black pigment and the cultivation of hyperian excellence and nymphean grace and beauty. Nor, if we turn to the present, is the evidence much stronger which is offered by the *gens de couleur* whom you may see in the quadroon quarter this afternoon, with "Ichabod" legible on their murky foreheads through a vain smearing of toilet powder, dragging their chairs down to the narrow gateway of their close-fenced gardens, and staring shrinkingly at you as you pass, like a nest of yellow kittens.

But as the present century was in its second and third decades, the *quadroones* (for we must contrive a feminine spelling to define the strict limits of the caste as then established) came forth in splendor. Old travellers spare no terms to tell their praises, their faultlessness of feature, their perfection of form, their varied styles of beauty,—for there were even pure Caucasian blondes among them,—their fascinating manners, their sparkling vivacity, their chaste and pretty wit, their grace in the dance, their modest propriety, their taste and elegance in dress. In the gentlest and most poetic sense they were indeed the sirens of this land, where it seemed "always afternoon"—a momentary triumph of an Arcadian over a Christian civilization, so beautiful and so seductive that it became the subject of special chapters by writers of the day more original than correct as social philosophers.

The balls that were got up for them by the male *sang-pur* were to that day what the carnival is to the present. Society balls given the same nights proved failures through the coincidence. The magnates of government,—municipal, state, federal,—those of the army, of the learned professions and of the clubs,—in short, the white male aristocracy in every thing save the ecclesiastical desk,—were there. Tickets were high-priced to insure the exclusion of the vulgar. No distinguished stranger was allowed to miss them. They were beautiful! They were clad in silken extenuations from the throat to the feet, and wore, withal, a pathos in their charm that gave them a family likeness to innocence.

Madame Delphine, were you not a stranger, could have told you all about it; though hardly, I suppose, without tears.

But at the time of which we would speak (1821–22) her day of splendor was set, and her husband—let us call him so for her sake—was long dead. He was an American, and, if we take her word for it, a man of noble heart and extremely handsome; but this is knowledge which we can do without.

Even in those days the house was always shut, and Madame Delphine's chief occupation and end in life seemed to be to keep well locked up in-doors. She was an excellent person, the neighbors said,—a very worthy person; and they were, maybe, nearer correct then they knew. They rarely saw her save when she went to or returned from church; a small, rather tired-looking, dark quadroone of very good features and a gentle thoughtfulness of expression which would take long to describe: call it a widow's look.

In speaking of Madame Delphine's house, mention should have been made of a gate in the fence on the Royal-street sidewalk. It is gone now, and was out of use then, being fastened once for all by an iron staple clasping the cross-bar and driven into the post.

Which leads us to speak of another person.

Chapter III. Capitaine Lemaitre

He was one of those men that might be any age,—thirty, forty, forty-five; there was no telling from his face what was years and what was only weather. His countenance was of a grave and quiet, but also luminous, sort, which was instantly admired and ever afterward remembered, as was also the fineness of his hair and the blueness of his eyes. Those pronounced him youngest who scrutinized his face the closest. But waiving the discussion of age, he was odd, though not with the oddness that he who had reared him had striven to produce.

He had not been brought up by mother or father. He had lost both in infancy, and had fallen to the care of a rugged old military grandpa of the colonial school, whose unceasing endeavor had been to make "his boy" as savage and ferocious a holder of unimpeachable social rank as it became a pure-blooded French Creole to be who would trace his pedigree back to the god Mars.

"Remember, my boy," was the adjuration received by him as regularly as his waking cup of black coffee, "that none of your family line ever kept the laws of any government or creed." And if it was well that he should bear this in mind, it was well to reiterate it persistently, for, from the nurse's arms, the boy wore a look, not of docility so much as of gentle, *judicial* benevolence. The domestics of the old man's house used to shed tears of laughter to see that look on the face of a babe. His rude guardian addressed himself to the modification of this facial expression; it had not enough of majesty in it, for instance, or of large dare-deviltry; but with care these could be made to come.

And, true enough, at twenty-one (in Ursin Lemaitre), the labors of his grandfather were an apparent success. He was not rugged, nor was he loud-spoken, as his venerable trainer would have liked to present him to society; but he was as serenely terrible as a well-aimed rifle, and the old man looked upon his results with pride. He had cultivated him up to that pitch where he scorned to practise any vice, or any virtue, that did not include the principle of self-assertion. A few touches only were wanting here and there to achieve perfection, when suddenly the old man died. Yet it was his proud satisfaction, before he finally lay down, to see Ursin a favored companion and the peer, both in courtesy and pride, of those polished gentlemen famous in history, the brothers Lafitte.

The two Lafittes were, at the time young Lemaitre reached his majority (say 1808 or 1812), only merchant-blacksmiths, so to speak, a term intended to convey the idea of blacksmiths who never soiled their hands, who were men of capital, stood a little higher than the clergy, and moved in society among its autocrats. But they were full of possibilities, men of action, and men, too, of thought, with already a pronounced disbelief in the custom-house. In these days of big carnivals they would have been patented as the dukes of Little Manchac and Barataria.

Young Ursin Lemaitre (in full the name was Lemaitre-Vignevielle) had not only the hearty friendship of these good people, but also a natural turn for accounts; and as his two friends were looking about them with an enterprising eye, it easily resulted that he presently connected himself with the blacksmithing profession. Not exactly at the forge in the Lafittes' famous smithy, among the African Samsons, who, with their shining black bodies bared to the waist, made the Rue St. Pierre ring with the stroke of their hammers; but as a—there was no occasion to mince the word in those days—smuggler.

Smuggler—patriot—where was the difference? Beyond the ken of a community to which the enforcement of the revenue laws had long been merely so much out of every man's pocket and dish, into the all-devouring treasury of Spain. At this date they had come under a kinder yoke, and to a treasury that at least echoed when the customs were dropped into it; but the change was still new. What could a man be more than Capitaine Lemaitre was—the soul of honor, the pink of courtesy, with the courage of the lion, and the magnanimity of the elephant; frank—the very exchequer of truth! Nay, go higher still: his paper was good in Toulouse Street. To the gossips in the gaming-clubs he was the culminating proof that smuggling was one of the sublimer virtues.

Years went by. Events transpired which have their place in history. Under a government which the community by and by saw was conducted in their interest, smuggling began to lose its respectability and to grow disreputable, hazardous, and debased. In certain onslaughts made upon them by officers of the law, some of the smugglers became murderers. The business became unprofitable for a time until the enterprising Lafittes—thinkers—bethought them of a corrective—"privateering."

Thereupon the United States Government set a price upon their heads. Later yet it became known that these outlawed pirates had been offered money and rank by Great Britain if they would join her standard, then hovering about the water-approaches to their native city, and that they had spurned the bribe; wherefore their heads were ruled out of the market, and, meeting and treating with Andrew Jackson, they were received as lovers of their country, and as compatriots fought in the battle of New Orleans at the head of their fearless men, and—here tradition takes up the tale—were never seen afterward.

Capitaine Lemaitre was not among the killed or wounded, but he was among the missing.

Chapter IV. Three Friends

The roundest and happiest-looking priest in the city of New Orleans was a little man fondly known among his people as Père Jerome. He was a Creole and a member of one of the city's leading families. His dwelling was a little frame cottage, standing on high pillars just inside a tall, close fence, and reached by a narrow out-door stair from the green batten gate. It was well surrounded by crape myrtles, and communicated behind by a descending stair and a plank-walk with the rear entrance of the chapel over whose worshippers he daily spread his hands in benediction. The name of the street—ah! there is where light is wanting. Save the Cathedral and the Ursulines, there is very little of record concerning churches at that time, though they were springing up here and there. All there is certainty of is that Père Jerome's frame chapel was some little new-born "down-town" thing, that may have survived the passage of years, or may have escaped "Paxton's Directory" "so as by fire." His parlor was dingy and carpetless; one could smell distinctly there the vow of poverty. His bed-chamber was bare and clean, and the bed in it narrow and hard; but between the two was a dining-room that would tempt a laugh to the lips of any who looked in. The table was small, but stout, and all the furniture of the room substantial, made of fine wood, and carved just enough to give the notion of wrinkling pleasantry. His mother's and sister's doing, Père Jerome would explain; they would not permit this apartment—or department—to suffer. Therein, as well as in the parlor, there was odor, but of a more epicurean sort, that explained interestingly the Père Jerome's rotundity and rosy smile.

In this room, and about this miniature round table, used sometimes to sit with Père Jerome two friends to whom he was deeply attached—one, Evariste Varrillat, a playmate from early childhood, now his brother-in-law; the other, Jean Thompson, a companion from youngest manhood, and both, like the little priest himself, the regretful rememberers of a fourth comrade who was a comrade no more. Like Père Jerome, they had come, through years, to the thick of life's conflicts,—the priest's brother-in-law a physician, the other an attorney, and brother-in-law to the lonely wanderer,—yet they loved to huddle around this small board, and be boys again in heart while men in mind. Neither one nor another was leader. In earlier days they had always yielded to him who no longer met with them a certain chieftainship, and they still thought of him and talked of him, and, in their conjectures, groped after him, as one of whom they continued to expect greater things than of themselves.

They sat one day drawn thus close together, sipping and theorizing, speculating upon the nature of things in an easy, bold, sophomoric way, the conversation for the most part being in French, the native tongue of the doctor and priest, and spoken with facility by Jean Thompson the lawyer, who was half Américain; but running sometimes into English and sometimes into mild laughter. Mention had been made of the absentee.

Père Jerome advanced an idea something like this:

"It is impossible for any finite mind to fix the degree of criminality of any human act or of any human life. The Infinite One alone can know how much of our sin is chargeable to us, and how much to our brothers or our fathers. We all participate in one another's sins. There is a community of responsibility attaching to every misdeed. No human since Adam—nay, nor Adam himself—ever sinned entirely to himself. And so I never am called upon to contemplate a crime or a criminal but I feel my conscience pointing at me as one of the accessories."

"In a word," said Evariste Varrillat, the physician, "you think we are partly to blame for the omission of many of your Paternosters, eh?"

Father Jerome smiled.

"No; a man cannot plead so in his own defence; our first father tried that, but the plea was not allowed. But, now, there is our absent friend. I tell you truly this whole community ought to be recognized as partners in his moral errors. Among another people, reared under wiser care and with better companions, how different might he not have been! How can *we* speak of him as a law-breaker who might have saved him from that name?" Here the speaker turned to Jean Thompson, and changed his speech to English. "A lady sez to me to-day: 'Père Jerome, 'ow dat is a dreadfool dat 'e gone at de coas' of Cuba to be one corsair! Ain't it?' 'Ah, madame,' I sez, ''tis a terrible! I 'ope de good God will fo'give me an' you fo' dat!'"

Jean Thompson answered quickly:

"You should not have let her say that."

"*Mais,* fo' w'y?"

"Why, because, if you are partly responsible, you ought so much the more to do what you can to shield his reputation. You should have said,"—the attorney changed to French,—"'He is no pirate; he has merely taken out letters of marque and reprisal under the flag of the republic of Carthagena!'"

"*Ah, bah!*" exclaimed Doctor Varrillat, and both he and his brother-in-law, the priest, laughed.

"Why not?" demanded Thompson.

"Oh!" said the physician, with a shrug, "say id thad way iv you wand."

Then, suddenly becoming serious, he was about to add something else, when Père Jerome spoke.

"I will tell you what I could have said. I could have said: 'Madame, yes; 'tis a terrible fo' him. He stum'le in de dark; but dat good God will mek it a *mo' terrible* fo' dat man oohever he is, w'at put 'at light out!'"

"But how do you know he is a pirate?" demanded Thompson, aggressively.

"How do we know?" said the little priest, returning to French. "Ah! there is no other explanation of the ninety-and-nine stories that come to us, from every port where ships arrive from the north coast of Cuba, of a commander of pirates there who is a marvel of courtesy and gentility"—[1]

---

1. See gazettes of the period.

"And whose name is Lafitte," said the obstinate attorney.

"And who, nevertheless, is not Lafitte," insisted Père Jerome.

"Daz troo, Jean," said Doctor Varrillat. "We hall know daz troo."

Père Jerome leaned forward over the board and spoke, with an air of secrecy, in French.

"You have heard of the ship which came into port here last Monday. You have heard that she was boarded by pirates, and that the captain of the ship himself drove them off."

"An incredible story," said Thompson.

"But not so incredible as the truth. I have it from a passenger. There was on the ship a young girl who was very beautiful. She came on deck, where the corsair stood, about to issue his orders, and, more beautiful than ever in the desperation of the moment, confronted him with a small missal spread open, and, her finger on the Apostles' Creed, commanded him to read. He read it, uncovering his head as he read, then stood gazing on her face, which did not quail; and then with a low bow, said: 'Give me this book and I will do your bidding.' She gave him the book and bade him leave the ship, and he left it unmolested."

Père Jerome looked from the physician to the attorney and back again, once or twice, with his dimpled smile.

"But he speaks English, they say," said Jean Thompson.

"He has, no doubt, learned it since he left us," said the priest.

"But this ship-master, too, says his men called him Lafitte."

"Lafitte? No. Do you not see? It is your brother-in-law, Jean Thompson! It is your wife's brother! Not Lafitte, but" (softly) "Lemaitre! Lemaitre! Capitaine Ursin Lemaitre!"

The two guests looked at each other with a growing drollery on either face, and presently broke into a laugh.

"Ah!" said the doctor, as the three rose up, "you juz kip dad cog-an'-bull fo' yo' negs summon."

Père Jerome's eyes lighted up—

"I goin' to do it!"

"I tell you," said Evariste, turning upon him with sudden gravity, "iv dad is troo, I tell you w'ad is sure-sure! Ursin Lemaitre din kyare nut'n fo' doze creed; *he fall in love!*"

Then, with a smile, turning to Jean Thompson, and back again to Père Jerome:

"But anny'ow you tell it in dad summon dad 'e kyare fo' dad creed."

Père Jerome sat up late that night, writing a letter. The remarkable effects upon a certain mind, effects which we shall presently find him attributing solely to the influences of surrounding nature, may find for some a more sufficient explanation in the fact that this letter was but one of a series, and that in the rover of doubted identity and incredible eccentricity Père Jerome had a regular correspondent.

Chapter V. The Cap Fits

About two months after the conversation just given, and therefore somewhere about the Christmas holidays of the year 1821, Père Jerome delighted the congregation of his little chapel with the announcement that he had appointed to preach a sermon in French on the following sabbath—not there, but in the cathedral.

He was much beloved. Notwithstanding that among the clergy there were two or three who shook their heads and raised their eyebrows, and said he would be at least as orthodox if he did not make quite so much of the Bible and quite so little of the dogmas, yet "the common people heard him gladly." When told, one day, of the unfavorable whispers, he smiled a little and answered his informant,—whom he knew to be one of the whisperers himself,—laying a hand kindly upon his shoulder:

"Father Murphy,"—or whatever the name was,—"your words comfort me."

"How is that?"

"Because—'*Væ quum benedixerint mihi homines!*'"[2]

The appointed morning, when it came, was one of those exquisite days in which there is such a universal harmony, that worship rises from the heart like a spring.

"Truly," said Père Jerome to the companion who was to assist him in the mass, "this is a sabbath day which we do not have to make holy, but only to *keep* so."

Maybe it was one of the secrets of Père Jerome's success as a preacher, that he took more thought as to how he should feel, than as to what he should say.

The cathedral of those days was called a very plain old pile, boasting neither beauty nor riches; but to Père Jerome it was very lovely; and before its homely altar, not homely to him, in the performance of those solemn offices, symbols of heaven's mightiest truths, in the hearing of the organ's harmonies, and the yet more eloquent interunion of human voices in the choir, in overlooking the worshipping throng which knelt under the soft, chromatic lights, and in breathing the sacrificial odors of the chancel, he found a deep and solemn joy; and yet I guess the finest thought of his soul the while was one that came thrice and again:

"Be not deceived, Père Jerome, because saintliness of feeling is easy here; you are the same priest who overslept this morning, and over-ate yesterday, and will, in some way, easily go wrong to-morrow and the day after."

He took it with him when—the *Veni Creator* sung—he went into the pulpit. Of the sermon he preached, tradition has preserved for us only a few brief sayings, but they are strong and sweet.

"My friends," he said,—this was near the beginning,—"the angry words of God's book are very merciful—they are meant to drive us home; but the tender words, my friends, they are sometimes terrible! Notice these, the tenderest words of the tenderest prayer that ever came from the lips of a blessed martyr—the dying words of the holy Saint Stephen, 'Lord, lay not this sin to their charge.' Is there nothing dreadful in that? Read it thus: 'Lord, lay not this sin to *their* charge.' Not to the charge of them who stoned him? To whose charge then? Go ask the holy Saint Paul. Three years afterward,

---

2. "Woe unto me when all men speak well of me!"

praying in the temple at Jerusalem, he answered that question: 'I stood by and consented.' He answered for himself only; but the Day must come when all that wicked council that sent Saint Stephen away to be stoned, and all that city of Jerusalem, must hold up the hand and say: 'We, also, Lord—we stood by.' Ah! friends, under the simpler meaning of that dying saint's prayer for the pardon of his murderers is hidden the terrible truth that we all have a share in one another's sins."

Thus Père Jerome touched his key-note. All that time has spared us beside may be given in a few sentences.

"Ah!" he cried once, "if it were merely my own sins that I had to answer for, I might hold up my head before the rest of mankind; but no, no, my friends—we cannot look each other in the face, for each has helped the other to sin. Oh, where is there any room, in this world of common disgrace, for pride? Even if we had no common hope, a common despair ought to bind us together and forever silence the voice of scorn!"

And again, this:

"Even in the promise to Noë, not again to destroy the race with a flood, there is a whisper of solemn warning. The moral account of the antediluvians was closed off and the balance brought down in the year of the deluge; but the account of those who come after runs on and on, and the blessed bow of promise itself warns us that God will not stop it till the Judgment Day! O God, I thank thee that that day must come at last, when thou wilt destroy the world, and stop the interest on my account!"

It was about at this point that Père Jerome noticed, more particularly than he had done before, sitting among the worshippers near him, a small, sad-faced woman, of pleasing features, but dark and faded, who gave him profound attention. With her was another in better dress, seemingly a girl still in her teens, though her face and neck were scrupulously concealed by a heavy veil, and her hands, which were small, by gloves.

"Quadroones," thought he, with a stir of deep pity.

Once, as he uttered some stirring word, he saw the mother and daughter (if such they were), while they still bent their gaze upon him, clasp each other's hand fervently in the daughter's lap. It was at these words:

"My friends, there are thousands of people in this city of New Orleans to whom society gives the ten commandments of God with all the *nots* rubbed out! Ah! good gentlemen! if God sends the poor weakling to purgatory for leaving the right path, where ought some of you to go who strew it with thorns and briers!"

The movement of the pair was only seen because he watched for it. He glanced that way again as he said:

"O God, be very gentle with those children who would be nearer heaven this day had they never had a father and mother, but had got their religious training from such a sky and earth as we have in Louisiana this holy morning! Ah! my friends, nature is a big-print catechism!"

The mother and daughter leaned a little farther forward, and exchanged the same spasmodic hand-pressure as before. The mother's eyes were full of tears.

"I once knew a man," continued the little priest, glancing to a side aisle where he had noticed Evariste and Jean sitting against each other, "who was carefully taught, from infancy to manhood, this single only principle of life: defiance. Not justice, not righteousness, not even gain; but defiance: defiance to God, defiance to man, defiance to nature, defiance to reason; defiance and defiance and defiance."

"He is going to tell it!" murmured Evariste to Jean.

"This man," continued Père Jerome, "became a smuggler and at last a pirate in the Gulf of Mexico. Lord, lay not that sin to his charge alone! But a strange thing followed. Being in command of men of a sort that to control required to be kept at the austerest distance, he now found himself separated from the human world and thrown into the solemn companionship with the sea, with the air, with the storm, the calm, the heavens by day, the heavens by night. My friends, that was the first time in his life that he ever found himself in really good company."

"Now, this man had a great aptness for accounts. He had kept them—had rendered them. There was beauty, to him, in a correct, balanced, and closed account. An account unsatisfied was a deformity. The result is plain. That man, looking out night after night upon the grand and holy spectacle of the starry deep above and the watery deep below, was sure to find himself, sooner or later, mastered by the conviction that the great Author of this majestic creation keeps account of it; and one night there came to him, like a spirit walking on the sea, the awful, silent question: 'My account with God—how does it stand?' Ah! friends, that is a question which the book of nature does not answer."

"Did I say the book of nature is a catechism? Yes. But, after it answers the first question with 'God,' nothing but questions follow; and so, one day, this man gave a ship full of merchandise for one little book which answered those questions. God help him to understand it! and God help you, monsieur, and you, madame, sitting here in your *smuggled clothes*, to beat upon the breast with me and cry, 'I, too, Lord—I, too, stood by and consented.'"

Père Jerome had not intended these for his closing words; but just there, straight away before his sight and almost at the farthest door, a man rose slowly from his seat and regarded him steadily with a kind, bronzed, sedate face, and the sermon, as if by a sign of command, was ended. While the *Credo* was being chanted he was still there; but when, a moment after its close, the eye of Père Jerome returned in that direction, his place was empty.

As the little priest, his labor done and his vestments changed, was turning into the Rue Royale and leaving the cathedral out of sight, he just had time to understand that two women were purposely allowing him to overtake them, when the one nearer him spoke in the Creole *patois*, saying, with some timid haste:

"Good-morning, Père—Père Jerome; Père Jerome, we thank the good God for that sermon."

"Then, so do I," said the little man. They were the same two that he had noticed when he was preaching. The younger one bowed silently; she was a beautiful figure, but the slight effort of Père Jerome's kind eyes to see through the veil was vain. He would presently have passed on, but the one who had spoken before said:

"I thought you lived in the Rue des Ursulines."

"Yes; I am going this way to see a sick person."

The woman looked up at him with an expression of mingled confidence and timidity.

"It must be a blessed thing to be so useful as to be needed by the good God," she said.

Père Jerome smiled:

"God does not need me to look after his sick; but he allows me to do it, just as you let your little boy in frocks carry in chips." He might have added that he loved to do it, quite as much.

It was plain the woman had somewhat to ask, and was trying to get courage to ask it.

"You have a little boy?" asked the priest.

"No, I have only my daughter;" she indicated the girl at her side. Then she began to say something else, stopped, and with much nervousness asked:

"Père Jerome, what was the name of that man?"

"His name?" said the priest. "You wish to know his name?"

"Yes, Monsieur" (or *Miché*, as she spoke it); "it was such a beautiful story." The speaker's companion looked another way.

"His name," said Father Jerome,—"some say one name and some another. Some think it was Jean Lafitte, the famous; you have heard of him? And do you go to my church, Madame——?"

"No, Miché; not in the past; but from this time, yes. My name"—she choked a little, and yet it evidently gave her pleasure to offer this mark of confidence—"is Madame Delphine—Delphine Carraze."

Chapter VI. A Cry of Distress

Père Jerome's smile and exclamation, as some days later he entered his parlor in response to the announcement of a visitor, were indicative of hearty greeting rather than surprise.

"Madame Delphine!"

Yet surprise could hardly have been altogether absent, for though another Sunday had not yet come around, the slim, smallish figure sitting in a corner, looking very much alone, and clad in dark attire, which seemed to have been washed a trifle too often, was Delphine Carraze on her second visit. And this, he was confident, was over and above an attendance in the confessional, where he was sure he had recognized her voice.

She rose bashfully and gave her hand, then looked to the floor, and began a faltering speech, with a swallowing motion in the throat, smiled weakly and commenced again, speaking, as before, in a gentle, low note, frequently lifting up and casting down her eyes, while shadows of anxiety and smiles of apology chased each other rapidly across her face. She was trying to ask his advice.

"Sit down," said he; and when they had taken seats she resumed, with downcast eyes:

"You know,—probably I should have said this in the confessional, but"—

"No matter, Madame Delphine; I understand; you did not want an oracle, perhaps; you want a friend."

She lifted her eyes, shining with tears, and dropped them again.

"I"—she ceased. "I have done a"—she dropped her head and shook it despondingly—"a cruel thing." The tears rolled from her eyes as she turned away her face.

Père Jerome remained silent, and presently she turned again, with the evident intention of speaking at length.

"It began nineteen years ago—by"—her eyes, which she had lifted, fell lower than ever, her brow and neck were suffused with blushes, and she murmured—"I fell in love."

She said no more, and by and by Père Jerome replied:

"Well, Madame Delphine, to love is the right of every soul. I believe in love. If your love was pure and lawful I am sure your angel guardian smiled upon you; and if it was not, I cannot say you have nothing to answer for, and yet I think God may have said: 'She is a quadroone; all the rights of her womanhood trampled in the mire, sin made easy to her—almost compulsory,—charge it to account of whom it may concern.'"

"No, no!" said Madame Delphine, looking up quickly, "some of it might fall upon"—Her eyes fell, and she commenced biting her lips and nervously pinching little folds in her skirt. "He was good—as good as the law would let him be—better, indeed, for he left me property, which really the strict law does not allow. He loved our little daughter very much. He wrote to his mother and sisters, owning all his error and asking them to take the child and bring her up. I sent her to them when he died, which was soon after, and did not see my child for sixteen years. But we wrote to each other all the time, and she loved me. And then—at last"—Madame Delphine ceased speaking, but went on diligently with her agitated fingers, turning down foolish hems lengthwise of her lap.

"At last your mother-heart conquered," said Père Jerome.

She nodded.

"The sisters married, the mother died; I saw that even where she was she did not escape the reproach of her birth and blood, and when she asked me to let her come"—The speaker's brimming eyes rose an instant. "I know it was wicked, but—I said, come."

The tears dripped through her hands upon her dress.

"Was it she who was with you last Sunday?"

"Yes."

"And now you do not know what to do with her?"

"*Ah! c'est ça oui!*—that is it."

"Does she look like you, Madame Delphine?"

"Oh, thank God, no! you would never believe she was my daughter; she is white and beautiful!"

"You thank God for that which is your main difficulty, Madame Delphine."

"Alas! yes."

Père Jerome laid his palms tightly across his knees with his arms bowed out, and fixed his eyes upon the ground, pondering.

"I suppose she is a sweet, good daughter?" said he, glancing at Madame Delphine, without changing his attitude.

Her answer was to raise her eyes rapturously.

"Which gives us the dilemma in its fullest force," said the priest, speaking as if to the floor. "She has no more place than if she had dropped upon a strange planet." He suddenly looked up with a brightness which almost as quickly passed away, and then he looked down again. His happy thought was the cloister; but he instantly said to himself: "They cannot have overlooked that choice, except intentionally—which they have a right to do." He could do nothing but shake his head.

"And suppose you should suddenly die," he said; he wanted to get at once to the worst.

The woman made a quick gesture, and buried her head in her handkerchief, with the stifled cry:

"Oh, Olive, my daughter!"

"Well, Madame Delphine," said Père Jerome, more buoyantly, "one thing is sure: we *must* find a way out of this trouble."

"Ah!" she exclaimed, looking heavenward, "if it might be!"

"But it must be!" said the priest.

"But how shall it be?" asked the desponding woman.

"Ah!" said Père Jerome, with a shrug, "God knows."

"Yes," said the quadroone, with a quick sparkle in her gentle eye; "and I know, if God would tell anybody, He would tell you!"

The priest smiled and rose.

"Do you think so? Well, leave me to think of it. I will ask Him."

"And He will tell you!" she replied. "And He will bless you!" She rose and gave her hand. As she withdrew it she smiled. "I had such a strange dream," she said, backing toward the door.

"Yes?"

"Yes. I got my troubles all mixed up with your sermon. I dreamed I made that pirate the guardian of my daughter."

Père Jerome smiled also, and shrugged.

"To you, Madame Delphine, as you are placed, every white man in this country, on land or on water, is a pirate, and of all pirates, I think that one is, without doubt, the best."

"Without doubt," echoed Madame Delphine, wearily, still withdrawing backward. Père Jerome stepped forward and opened the door.

The shadow of some one approaching it from without fell upon the threshold, and a man entered, dressed in dark blue cottonade, lifting from his head a fine Panama hat, and from a broad, smooth brow, fair where the hat had covered it, and dark below, gently stroking back his very soft, brown locks. Madame Delphine slightly started aside, while Père Jerome reached silently, but eagerly, forward, grasped a larger hand than his own, and motioned its owner to a seat. Madame Delphine's eyes ventured no higher than to discover that the shoes of the visitor were of white duck.

"Well, Père Jerome," she said, in a hurried undertone, "I am just going to say Hail Marys all the time till you find that out for me!"

"Well, I hope that will be soon, Madame Carraze. Good-day, Madame Carraze."

And as she departed, the priest turned to the newcomer and extended both hands, saying, in the same familiar dialect in which he had been addressing the quadroone:

"Well-a-day, old playmate! After so many years!"

They sat down side by side, like husband and wife, the priest playing with the other's hand, and talked of times and seasons past, often mentioning Evariste and often Jean.

Madame Delphine stopped short half-way home and returned to Père Jerome's. His entry door was wide open and the parlor door ajar. She passed through the one and with downcast eyes was standing at the other, her hand lifted to knock, when the door was drawn open and the white duck shoes passed out. She saw, besides, this time the blue cottonade suit.

"Yes," the voice of Père Jerome was saying, as his face appeared in the door—"Ah! Madame"—

"I lef' my para*sol*," said Madame Delphine, in English.

There was this quiet evidence of a defiant spirit hidden somewhere down under her general timidity, that, against a fierce conventional prohibition, she wore a bonnet instead of the turban of her caste, and carried a parasol.

Père Jerome turned and brought it.

He made a motion in the direction in which the late visitor had disappeared.

"Madame Delphine, you saw dat man?"

"Not his face."

"You couldn' billieve me iv I tell you w'at dat man pur*pose* to do!"

"Is dad so, Père Jerome?"

"He's goin' to hopen a bank!"

"Ah!" said Madame Delphine, seeing she was expected to be astonished.

Père Jerome evidently longed to tell something that was best kept secret; he repressed the impulse, but his heart had to say something. He threw forward one hand and looking pleasantly at Madame Delphine, with his lips dropped apart, clenched his extended hand and thrusting it toward the ground, said in a solemn undertone:

"He is God's own banker, Madame Delphine."

Chapter VII. *Miché Vignevielle*

Madame Delphine sold one of the corner lots of her property. She had almost no revenue, and now and then a piece had to go. As a consequence of the sale, she had a few large bank-notes sewed up in her petticoat, and one day—maybe a fortnight after her tearful interview with Père Jerome—she found it necessary to get one of these changed into small money. She was in the Rue Toulouse, looking from one side to the other for a bank which was not in that street at all, when she noticed a small sign hanging above a door, bearing the name "Vignevielle." She looked in. Père Jerome had told her (when she had gone to him to ask where she should apply for change) that if she could only wait a few days, there would be a new concern opened in Toulouse Street,—it really seemed as if Vignevielle was the name, if she could judge; it looked to be, and it was, a private banker's,—"U. L. Vignevielle's," according to a larger inscription which met her eyes as she ventured in. Behind the counter, exchanging some last words with a busy-mannered man outside, who, in withdrawing, seemed bent on running over Madame Delphine, stood the man in blue cottonade, whom she had met in Père Jerome's doorway. Now, for the first time, she saw his face, its strong, grave, human kindness shining softly on each and every bronzed feature. The recognition was mutual. He took pains to speak first, saying, in a re-assuring tone, and in the language he had last heard her use:

"'Ow I kin serve you, Madame?"

"Iv you pliz, to mague dad bill change, Miché."

She pulled from her pocket a wad of dark cotton handkerchief, from which she began to untie the imprisoned note. Madame Delphine had an uncommonly sweet voice, and it seemed so to strike Monsieur Vignevielle. He spoke to her once or twice more, as he waited on her, each time in English, as though he enjoyed the humble melody of its tone, and presently, as she turned to go, he said:

"Madame Carraze!"

She started a little, but bethought herself instantly that he had heard her name in Père Jerome's parlor. The good father might even have said a few words about her after her first departure; he had such an overflowing heart. "Madame Carraze," said Monsieur Vignevielle, "doze kine of note wad you 'an' me juz now is bein' contrefit. You muz tek kyah from doze kine of note. You see"—He drew from his cash-drawer a note resembling the one he had just changed for her, and proceeded to point out certain tests of genuineness. The counterfeit, he said, was so and so.

"Bud," she exclaimed, with much dismay, "dad was de manner of my bill! Id muz be—led me see dad bill wad I give you,—if you pliz, Miché."

Monsieur Vignevielle turned to engage in conversation with an employé and a new visitor, and gave no sign of hearing Madame Delphine's voice. She asked a second time, with like result, lingered timidly, and as he turned to give his attention to a third visitor, reiterated.

"Miché Vignevielle, I wizh you pliz led"—

"Madame Carraze," he said, turning so suddenly as to make the frightened little woman start, but extending his palm with a show of frankness, and assuming a look of benignant patience, "'ow I kin fine doze note now, mongs' all de rez? Iv you pliz nod to mague me doze troub."

The dimmest shadow of a smile seemed only to give his words a more kindly authoritative import, and as he turned away again with a manner suggestive of finality, Madame Delphine found no choice but to depart. But she went away loving the ground beneath the feet of Monsieur U. L. Vignevielle.

"Oh, Père Jerome!" she exclaimed in the corrupt French of her caste, meeting the little father on the street a few days later, "you told the truth that day in your parlor. *Mo conné li à c't heure.* I know him now; he is just what you called him."

"Why do you not make him *your* banker, also, Madame Delphine?"

"I have done so this very day!" she replied, with more happiness in her eyes than Père Jerome had ever before seen there.

"Madame Delphine," he said, his own eyes sparkling, "make *him* your daughter's guardian; for myself, being a priest, it would not be best; but ask him; I believe he will not refuse you."

Madame Delphine's face grew still brighter as he spoke.

"It was in my mind," she said.

Yet to the timorous Madame Delphine many trifles became, one after another, an impediment to the making of this proposal, and many weeks elapsed before further delay was positively without excuse. But at length, one day in May, 1822, in a small private office behind Monsieur Vignevielle's banking-room,—he sitting beside a table, and she, more timid and demure than ever, having just taken a chair by the door,—she said, trying, with a little bashful laugh, to make the matter seem unimportant, and yet with some tremor of voice:

"Miché Vignevielle, I bin maguing my will." (Having commenced their acquaintance in English, they spoke nothing else.)

"'Tis a good idy," responded the banker.

"I kin mague you de troub' to kib dad will fo' me, Miché Vignevielle?"

"Yez."

She looked up with grateful re-assurance; but her eyes dropped again as she said:

"Miché Vignevielle"—Here she choked, and began her peculiar motion of laying folds in the skirt of her dress, with trembling fingers. She lifted her eyes, and as they met the look of deep and placid kindness that was in his face, some courage returned, and she said:

"Miché."

"Wad you wand?" asked he, gently.

"If it arrive to me to die"—

"Yez?"

Her words were scarcely audible:

"I wand you teg kyah my lill' girl."

"You 'ave one lill' gal, Madame Carraze?"

She nodded with her face down.

"An' you godd some mo' chillen?"

"No."

"I nevva know dad, Madame Carraze. She's a lill' small gal?"

Mothers forget their daughters' stature. Madame Delphine said:

"Yez."

For a few moments neither spoke, and then Monsieur Vignevielle said:

"I will do dad."

"Lag she been you' h-own?" asked the mother, suffering from her own boldness.

"She's a good lill' chile, eh?"

"Miché, she's a lill' hangel!" exclaimed Madame Delphine, with a look of distress.

"Yez; I teg kyah 'v 'er, lag my h-own. I mague you dad promise."

"But"—There was something still in the way, Madame Delphine seemed to think. The banker waited in silence.

"I suppose you will want to see my lill' girl?"

He smiled; for she looked at him as if she would implore him to decline.

"Oh, I tek you' word fo' hall dad, Madame Carraze. It mague no differend wad she loog lag; I don' wan' see 'er."

Madame Delphine's parting smile—she went very shortly—was gratitude beyond speech.

Monsieur Vignevielle returned to the seat he had left, and resumed a newspaper,—the *Louisiana Gazette* in all probability,—which he had laid down upon Madame Delphine's entrance. His eyes fell upon a paragraph which had previously escaped his notice. There they rested. Either he read it over and over unwearyingly, or he was lost in thought. Jean Thompson entered.

"Now," said Mr. Thompson, in a suppressed tone, bending a little across the table, and laying one palm upon a package of papers which lay in the other, "it is completed. You could retire from your business any day inside of six hours without loss to anybody." (Both here and elsewhere, let it be understood that where good English is given the words were spoken in good French.)

Monsieur Vignevielle raised his eyes and extended the newspaper to the attorney, who received it and read the paragraph. Its substance was that a certain vessel of the navy had returned from a cruise in the Gulf of Mexico and Straits of Florida, where she had done valuable service against the pirates—having, for instance, destroyed in one fortnight in January last twelve pirate vessels afloat, two on the stocks, and three establishments ashore.

"United States brig *Porpoise*," repeated Jean Thompson. "Do you know her?"

"We are acquainted," said Monsieur Vignevielle.

Chapter VIII. She

A quiet footstep, a grave new presence on financial sidewalks, a neat garb slightly out of date, a gently strong and kindly pensive face, a silent bow, a new sign in the Rue Toulouse, a lone figure with a cane, walking in meditation in the evening light under the willows of Canal Marigny, a long-darkened window re-lighted in the Rue Conti—these were all; a fall of dew would scarce have been more quiet than was the return of Ursin Lemaitre-Vignevielle to the precincts of his birth and early life.

But we hardly give the event its right name. It was Capitaine Lemaitre who had disappeared; it was Monsieur Vignevielle who had come back. The pleasures, the haunts, the companions, that had once held out their charms to the impetuous youth, offered no enticements to Madame Delphine's banker. There is this to be said even for the pride his grandfather had taught him, that it had always held him above low indulgences; and though he had dallied with kings, queens, and knaves through all the mazes of Faro, Rondeau, and Craps, he had done it loftily; but now he maintained a peaceful estrangement from all. Evariste and Jean, themselves, found him only by seeking.

"It is the right way," he said to Père Jerome, the day we saw him there. "Ursin Lemaitre is dead. I have buried him. He left a will. I am his executor."

"He is crazy," said his lawyer brother-in-law, impatiently.

"On the contr-y," replied the little priest, "'e 'as come ad hisse'f."

Evariste spoke.

"Look at his face, Jean. Men with that kind of face are the last to go crazy."

"You have not proved that," replied Jean, with an attorney's obstinacy. "You should have heard him talk the other day about that newspaper paragraph. 'I have taken

Ursin Lemaitre's head; I have it with me; I claim the reward, but I desire to commute it to citizenship.' He is crazy."

Of course Jean Thompson did not believe what he said; but he said it, and, in his vexation, repeated it, on the *banquettes* and at the clubs; and presently it took the shape of a sly rumor, that the returned rover was a trifle snarled in his top-hamper.

This whisper was helped into circulation by many trivial eccentricities of manner, and by the unaccountable oddness of some of his transactions in business.

"My dear sir!" cried his astounded lawyer, one day, "you are not running a charitable institution!"

"How do you know?" said Monsieur Vignevielle. There the conversation ceased.

"Why do you not found hospitals and asylums at once," asked the attorney, at another time, with a vexed laugh, "and get the credit of it?"

"And make the end worse than the beginning," said the banker, with a gentle smile, turning away to a desk of books.

"Bah!" muttered Jean Thompson.

Monsieur Vignevielle betrayed one very bad symptom. Wherever he went he seemed looking for somebody. It may have been perceptible only to those who were sufficiently interested in him to study his movements; but those who saw it once saw it always. He never passed an open door or gate but he glanced in; and often, where it stood but slightly ajar, you might see him give it a gentle push with his hand or cane. It was very singular.

He walked much alone after dark. The *guichinangoes* (garroters, we might say), at those times the city's particular terror by night, never crossed his path. He was one of those men for whom danger appears to stand aside.

One beautiful summer night, when all nature seemed hushed in ecstasy, the last blush gone that told of the sun's parting, Monsieur Vignevielle, in the course of one of those contemplative, uncompanioned walks which it was his habit to take, came slowly along the more open portion of the Rue Royale, with a step which was soft without intention, occasionally touching the end of his stout cane gently to the ground and looking upward among his old acquaintances, the stars.

It was one of those southern nights under whose spell all the sterner energies of the mind cloak themselves and lie down in bivouac, and the fancy and the imagination, that cannot sleep, slip their fetters and escape, beckoned away from behind every flowering bush and sweet-smelling tree, and every stretch of lonely, half-lighted walk, by the genius of poetry. The air stirred softly now and then, and was still again, as if the breezes lifted their expectant pinions and lowered them once more, awaiting the rising of the moon in a silence which fell upon the fields, the roads, the gardens, the walls, and the suburban and half-suburban streets, like a pause in worship. And anon she rose.

Monsieur Vignevielle's steps were bent toward the more central part of the town, and he was presently passing along a high, close, board-fence, on the right-hand side of the way, when, just within this enclosure, and almost overhead, in the dark boughs of a large orange-tree, a mocking-bird began the first low flute-notes of his all-night song. It may have been only the nearness of the songster that attracted the passer's attention, but he paused and looked up.

And then he remarked something more,—that the air where he had stopped was filled with the overpowering sweetness of the night-jasmine. He looked around; it could only be inside the fence. There was a gate just there. Would he push it, as his wont was? The grass was growing about it in a thick turf, as though the entrance had not been used for years. An iron staple clasped the cross-bar, and was driven deep into the gate-post. But now an eye that had been in the blacksmithing business—an eye which had later received high training as an eye for fastenings—fell upon that staple, and saw at a glance that the wood had shrunk from it, and it had sprung from its hold, though without falling out. The strange habit asserted itself; he laid his large hand upon the cross-bar; the turf at the base yielded, and the tall gate was drawn partly open.

At that moment, as at the moment whenever he drew or pushed a door or gate, or looked in at a window, he was thinking of one, the image of whose face and form had never left his inner vision since the day it had met him in his life's path and turned him face about from the way of destruction.

The bird ceased. The cause of the interruption, standing within the opening, saw before him, much obscured by its own numerous shadows, a broad, ill-kept, many-flowered garden, among whose untrimmed rose-trees and tangled vines, and often, also, in its old walks of pounded shell, the coco-grass and crab-grass had spread riotously, and sturdy weeds stood up in bloom. He stepped in and drew the gate to after him. There, very near by, was the clump of jasmine, whose ravishing odor had tempted him. It stood just beyond a brightly moonlit path, which turned from him in a curve toward the residence, a little distance to the right, and escaped the view at a point where it seemed more than likely a door of the house might open upon it. While he still looked, there fell upon his ear, from around that curve, a light footstep on the broken shells—one only, and then all was for a moment still again. Had he mistaken? No. The same soft click was repeated nearer by, a pale glimpse of robes came through the tangle, and then, plainly to view, appeared an outline—a presence—a form—a spirit—a girl!

From throat to instep she was as white as Cynthia. Something above the medium height, slender, lithe, her abundant hair rolling in dark, rich waves back from her brows and down from her crown, and falling in two heavy plaits beyond her round, broadly girt waist and full to her knees, a few escaping locks eddying lightly on her graceful neck and her temples,—her arms, half hid in a snowy mist of sleeve, let down to guide her spotless skirts free from the dewy touch of the grass,—straight down the path she came!

Will she stop? Will she turn aside? Will she espy the dark form in the deep shade of the orange, and, with one piercing scream, wheel and vanish? She draws near. She approaches the jasmine; she raises her arms, the sleeves falling like a vapor down to the shoulders; rises upon tiptoe, and plucks a spray. O Memory! Can it be? *Can it be?* Is this his quest, or is it lunacy? The ground seems to Monsieur Vignevielle the unsteady sea, and he to stand once more on a deck. And she? As she is now, if she but turn toward the orange, the whole glory of the moon will shine upon her face. His heart stands still; he is waiting for her to do that. She reaches up again; this time a bunch for her mother. That neck and throat! Now she fastens a spray in her hair. The mocking-bird cannot withhold; he breaks into song—she turns—she turns her face—it is she, it is she! Madame Delphine's daughter is the girl he met on the ship.

Chapter IX. Olive

She was just passing seventeen—that beautiful year when the heart of the maiden still beats quickly with the surprise of her new dominion, while with gentle dignity her brow accepts the holy coronation of womanhood. The forehead and temples beneath her loosely bound hair were fair without paleness, and meek without languor. She had the soft, lack-lustre beauty of the South; no ruddiness of coral, no waxen white, no pink of shell; no heavenly blue in the glance; but a face that seemed, in all its other beauties, only a tender accompaniment for the large, brown, melting eyes, where the openness of child-nature mingled dreamily with the sweet mysteries of maiden thought. We say no color of shell on face or throat; but this was no deficiency, that which took its place being the warm, transparent tint of sculptured ivory.

This side doorway which led from Madame Delphine's house into her garden was over-arched partly by an old remnant of vine-covered lattice, and partly by a crape-myrtle, against whose small, polished trunk leaned a rustic seat. Here Madame Delphine and Olive loved to sit when the twilights were balmy or the moon was bright.

"*Chérie*," said Madame Delphine on one of those evenings, "why do you dream so much?"

She spoke in the *patois* most natural to her, and which her daughter had easily learned.

The girl turned her face to her mother, and smiled, then dropped her glance to the hands in her own lap, which were listlessly handling the end of a ribbon. The mother looked at her with fond solicitude. Her dress was white again; this was but one night since that in which Monsieur Vignevielle had seen her at the bush of night-jasmine. He had not been discovered, but had gone away, shutting the gate, and leaving it as he had found it.

Her head was uncovered. Its plaited masses, quite black in the moonlight, hung down and coiled upon the bench, by her side. Her chaste drapery was of that revived classic order which the world of fashion was again laying aside to re-assume the mediæval bondage of the staylace; for New Orleans was behind the fashionable world, and Madame Delphine and her daughter were behind New Orleans. A delicate scarf, pale blue, of lightly netted worsted, fell from either shoulder down beside her hands. The look that was bent upon her changed perforce to one of gentle admiration. She seemed the goddess of the garden.

Olive glanced up. Madame Delphine was not prepared for the movement, and on that account repeated her question:

"What are you thinking about?"

The dreamer took the hand that was laid upon hers between her own palms, bowed her head, and gave them a soft kiss.

The mother submitted. Wherefore, in the silence which followed, a daughter's conscience felt the burden of having withheld an answer, and Olive presently said, as the pair sat looking up into the sky:

"I was thinking of Père Jerome's sermon."

Madame Delphine had feared so. Olive had lived on it ever since the day it was preached. The poor mother was almost ready to repent having ever afforded her the opportunity of hearing it. Meat and drink had become of secondary value to her daughter; she fed upon the sermon.

Olive felt her mother's thought and knew that her mother knew her own; but now that she had confessed, she would ask a question:

"Do you think, *maman*, that Père Jerome knows it was I who gave that missal?"

"No," said Madame Delphine, "I am sure he does not."

Another question came more timidly:

"Do—do you think he knows *him?*"

"Yes, I do. He said in his sermon he did."

Both remained for a long time very still, watching the moon gliding in and through among the small dark-and-white clouds. At last the daughter spoke again.

"I wish I was Père—I wish I was as good as Père Jerome."

"My child," said Madame Delphine, her tone betraying a painful summoning of strength to say what she had lacked the courage to utter,—"my child, I pray the good God you will not let your heart go after one whom you may never see in this world!"

The maiden turned her glance, and their eyes met. She cast her arms about her mother's neck, laid her cheek upon it for a moment, and then, feeling the maternal tear, lifted her lips, and, kissing her, said:

"I will not! I will not!"

But the voice was one, not of willing consent, but of desperate resolution.

"It would be useless, anyhow," said the mother, laying her arm around her daughter's waist.

Olive repeated the kiss, prolonging it passionately.

"I have nobody but you," murmured the girl; "I am a poor quadroone!"

She threw back her plaited hair for a third embrace, when a sound in the shrubbery startled them.

"*Qui ci ça?*" called Madame Delphine, in a frightened voice, as the two stood up, holding to each other.

No answer.

"It was only the dropping of a twig," she whispered, after a long holding of the breath. But they went into the house and barred it everywhere.

It was no longer pleasant to sit up. They retired, and in course of time, but not soon, they fell asleep, holding each other very tight, and fearing, even in their dreams, to hear another twig fall.

Chapter X. Birds

Monsieur Vigneville looked in at no more doors or windows; but if the disappearance of this symptom was a favorable sign, others came to notice which were especially bad,—for instance, wakefulness. At well-nigh any hour of the night, the city guard, which itself dared not patrol singly, would meet him on his slow, unmolested, sky-gazing walk.

"Seems to enjoy it," said Jean Thompson; "the worst sort of evidence. If he showed distress of mind, it would not be so bad; but his calmness,—ugly feature."

The attorney had held his ground so long that he began really to believe it was tenable.

By day, it is true, Monsieur Vignevielle was at his post in his quiet "bank." Yet here, day by day, he was the source of more and more vivid astonishment to those who held preconceived notions of a banker's calling. As a banker, at least, he was certainly out of balance; while as a promenader, it seemed to those who watched him that his ruling idea had now veered about, and that of late he was ever on the quiet alert, not to find, but to evade, somebody.

"Olive, my child," whispered Madame Delphine one morning, as the pair were kneeling side by side on the tiled floor of the church, "yonder is Miché Vignevielle! If you will only look at once—he is just passing a little in—Ah, much too slow again; he stepped out by the side door."

The mother thought it a strange providence that Monsieur Vignevielle should always be disappearing whenever Olive was with her.

One early dawn, Madame Delphine, with a small empty basket on her arm, stepped out upon the *banquette* in front of her house, shut and fastened the door very softly, and stole out in the direction whence you could faintly catch, in the stillness of the daybreak, the songs of the Gascon butchers and the pounding of their meat-axes on the stalls of the distant market-house. She was going to see if she could find some birds for Olive,—the child's appetite was so poor; and, as she was out, she would drop an early prayer at the cathedral. Faith and works.

"One must venture something, sometimes, in the cause of religion," thought she, as she started timorously on her way. But she had not gone a dozen steps before she repented her temerity. There was some one behind her.

There should not be any thing terrible in a footstep merely because it is masculine; but Madame Delphine's mind was not prepared to consider that. A terrible secret was haunting her. Yesterday morning she had found a shoe-track in the garden. She had not disclosed the discovery to Olive, but she had hardly closed her eyes the whole night.

The step behind her now might be the fall of that very shoe. She quickened her pace, but did not leave the sound behind. She hurried forward almost at a run; yet it was still there—no farther, no nearer. Two frights were upon her at once—one for herself, another for Olive, left alone in the house; but she had but the one prayer—"God protect my child!" After a fearful time she reached a place of safety, the cathedral. There, panting, she knelt long enough to know the pursuit was, at least, suspended, and then arose, hoping and praying all the saints that she might find the way clear for her return in all haste to Olive.

She approached a different door from that by which she had entered, her eyes in all directions and her heart in her throat.

"Madame Carraze."

She started wildly and almost screamed, though the voice was soft and mild. Monsieur Vignevielle came slowly forward from the shade of the wall. They met beside a bench, upon which she dropped her basket.

"Ah, Miché Vignevielle, I thang de good God to mid you!"

"Is dad so, Madame Carraze? Fo' w'y dad is?"

"A man was chase me all dad way since my 'ouse!"

"Yes, Madame, I sawed him."

"You sawed 'im? Oo it was?"

"'Twas only one man wad is a foolizh. De people say he's crezzie. *Mais*, he don' goin' to meg you no 'arm."

"But I was scare' fo' my lill' girl."

"Noboddie don' goin' trouble you' lill' gal, Madame Carraze."

Madame Delphine looked up into the speaker's strangely kind and patient eyes, and drew sweet re-assurance from them.

"Madame," said Monsieur Vignevielle, "wad pud you hout so hearly dis morning?"

She told him her errand. She asked if he thought she would find any thing.

"Yez," he said, "it was possible—a few lill' *bécassines-de-mer*, ou somezin' ligue. But fo' w'y you lill' gal lose doze hapetide?"

"Ah, Miché,"—Madame Delphine might have tried a thousand times again without ever succeeding half so well in lifting the curtain upon the whole, sweet, tender, old, old-fashioned truth,—"Ah, Miché, she wone tell me!"

"Bud, anny'ow, Madame, wad you thing?"

"Miché," she replied, looking up again with a tear standing in either eye, and then looking down once more as she began to speak, "I thing—I thing she's lonesome."

"You thing?"

She nodded.

"Ah! Madame Carraze," he said, partly extending his hand, "you see? 'Tis impossible to mague you' owze shud so tighd to priv-en dad. Madame, I med one mizteg."

"Ah, *non*, Miché!"

"Yez. There har nod one poss'bil'ty fo' me to be dad guardian of you' daughteh!"

Madame Delphine started with surprise and alarm.

"There is ondly one wad can be," he continued.

"But oo, Miché?"

"God."

"Ah, Miché Vignevielle"—She looked at him appealingly.

"I don' goin' to dizzerd you, Madame Carraze," he said.

She lifted her eyes. They filled. She shook her head, a tear fell, she bit her lip, smiled, and suddenly dropped her face into both hands, sat down upon the bench and wept until she shook.

"You dunno wad I mean, Madame Carraze?"

She did not know.

"I mean dad guardian of you' daughteh godd to fine 'er now one 'uzban'; an' no-boddie are hable to do dad egceb de good God 'imsev. But, Madame, I tell you wad I do."

She rose up. He continued:

"Go h-open you' owze; I fin' you' daughteh dad uzban'."

Madame Delphine was a helpless, timid thing; but her eyes showed she was about to resent this offer. Monsieur Vignevielle put forth his hand—it touched her shoulder—and said, kindly still, and without eagerness:

"One w'ite man, Madame: 'tis prattycabble. I *know* 'tis prattycabble. One w'ite jantleman, Madame. You can truz me. I goin' fedge 'im. H-ondly you go h-open you' owze."

Madame Delphine looked down, twining her handkerchief among her fingers.

He repeated his proposition.

"You will come firz by you'se'f?" she asked.

"Iv you wand."

She lifted up once more her eye of faith. That was her answer.

"Come," he said, gently, "I wan' sen' some bird ad you' lill' gal."

And they went away, Madame Delphine's spirit grown so exaltedly bold that she said as they went, though a violent blush followed her words:

"Miché Vignevielle, I thing Père Jerome mighd be ab'e to tell you someboddie."

Chapter XI. Face to Face

Madame Delphine found her house neither burned nor rifled.

"*Ah! ma piti sans popa!* Ah! my little fatherless one!" Her faded bonnet fell back between her shoulders, hanging on by the strings, and her dropped basket, with its "few lill' *bécassines-de-mer*" dangling from the handle, rolled out its okra and soup-joint upon the floor. "*Ma piti!* kiss!—kiss!—kiss!"

"But is it good news you have, or bad?" cried the girl, a fourth or fifth time.

"*Dieu sait, ma cère; mo pas conné!*"—God knows, my darling; I cannot tell!

The mother dropped into a chair, covered her face with her apron, and burst into tears, then looked up with an effort to smile, and wept afresh.

"What have you been doing?" asked the daughter, in a long-drawn, fondling tone. She leaned forward and unfastened her mother's bonnet-strings. "Why do you cry?"

"For nothing at all, my darling; for nothing—I am such a fool."

The girl's eyes filled. The mother looked up into her face and said:

"No, it is nothing, nothing, only that"—turning her head from side to side with a slow, emotional emphasis, "Miché Vignevielle is the best—*best* man on the good Lord's earth!"

Olive drew a chair close to her mother, sat down and took the little yellow hands into her own white lap, and looked tenderly into her eyes. Madame Delphine felt herself yielding; she must make a show of telling something:

"He sent you those birds!"

The girl drew her face back a little. The little woman turned away, trying in vain to hide her tearful smile, and they laughed together, Olive mingling a daughter's fond kiss with her laughter.

"There is something else," she said, "and you shall tell me."

"Yes," replied Madame Delphine, "only let me get composed."

But she did not get so. Later in the morning she came to Olive with the timid yet startling proposal that they would do what they could to brighten up the long-neglected front room. Olive was mystified and troubled, but consented, and thereupon the mother's spirits rose.

The work began, and presently ensued all the thumping, the trundling, the lifting and letting down, the raising and swallowing of dust, and the smells of turpentine, brass, pumice and woollen rags that go to characterize a housekeeper's *émeute*; and still, as the work progressed, Madame Delphine's heart grew light, and her little black eyes sparkled.

"We like a clean parlor, my daughter, even though no one is ever coming to see us, eh?" she said, as entering the apartment she at last sat down, late in the afternoon. She had put on her best attire.

Olive was not there to reply. The mother called but got no answer. She rose with an uneasy heart, and met her a few steps beyond the door that opened into the garden, in a path which came up from an old latticed bower. Olive was approaching slowly, her face pale and wild. There was an agony of hostile dismay in the look, and the trembling and appealing tone with which, taking the frightened mother's cheeks between her palms, she said:

"*Ah! ma mère, qui vini 'ci ce soir?*"—Who is coming here this evening?

"Why, my dear child, I was just saying, we like a clean"—

But the daughter was desperate:

"Oh, tell me, my mother, *who* is coming?"

"My darling, it is our blessed friend, Miché Vignevielle!"

"To see me?" cried the girl.

"Yes."

"Oh, my mother, what have you done?"

"Why, Olive, my child," exclaimed the little mother, bursting into tears, "do you forget it is Miché Vignevielle who has promised to protect you when I die?"

The daughter had turned away, and entered the door; but she faced around again, and extending her arms toward her mother, cried:

"How can—he is a white man—I am a poor"—

"Ah! *chérie*," replied Madame Delphine, seizing the outstretched hands, "it is there—it is there that he shows himself the best man alive! He sees that difficulty; he proposes to meet it; he says he will find you a suitor!"

Olive freed her hands violently, motioned her mother back, and stood proudly drawn up, flashing an indignation too great for speech; but the next moment she had uttered a cry, and was sobbing on the floor.

The mother knelt beside her and threw an arm about her shoulders.

"Oh, my sweet daughter, you must not cry! I did not want to tell you at all! I did not want to tell you! It isn't fair for you to cry so hard. Miché Vignevielle says you shall have the one you wish, or none at all, Olive, or none at all."

"None at all! none at all! None, none, none!"

"No, no, Olive," said the mother, "none at all. He brings none with him to-night, and shall bring none with him hereafter."

Olive rose suddenly, silently declined her mother's aid, and went alone to their chamber in the half-story.

Madame Delphine wandered drearily from door to window, from window to door, and presently into the newly-furnished front room which now seemed dismal beyond degree. There was a great Argand lamp in one corner. How she had labored that day to prepare it for evening illumination! A little beyond it, on the wall, hung a crucifix. She knelt under it, with her eyes fixed upon it, and thus silently remained until its outline was indistinguishable in the deepening shadows of evening.

She arose. A few minutes later, as she was trying to light the lamp, an approaching step on the sidewalk seemed to pause. Her heart stood still. She softly laid the phosphorus-box out of her hands. A shoe grated softly on the stone step, and Madame Delphine, her heart beating in great thuds, without waiting for a knock, opened the door, bowed low, and exclaimed in a soft perturbed voice:

"Miché Vignevielle!"

He entered, hat in hand, and with that almost noiseless tread which we have noticed. She gave him a chair and closed the door; then hastened, with words of apology, back to her task of lighting the lamp. But her hands paused in their work again,— Olive's step was on the stairs; then it came off the stairs; then it was in the next room, and then there was the whisper of soft robes, a breath of gentle perfume, and a snowy figure in the door. She was dressed for the evening.

"Maman?"

Madame Delphine was struggling desperately with the lamp, and at that moment it responded with a tiny bead of light.

"I am here, my daughter."

She hastened to the door, and Olive, all unaware of a third presence, lifted her white arms, laid them about her mother's neck, and, ignoring her effort to speak, wrested a fervent kiss from her lips. The crystal of the lamp sent out a faint gleam; it grew; it spread on every side; the ceiling, the walls lighted up; the crucifix, the furniture of the room came back into shape.

"Maman!" cried Olive, with a tremor of consternation.

"It is Miché Vignevielle, my daughter"—

The gloom melted swiftly away before the eyes of the startled maiden, a dark form stood out against the farther wall, and the light, expanding to the full, shone clearly upon the unmoving figure and quiet face of Capitaine Lemaitre.

Chapter XII. The Mother Bird

One afternoon, some three weeks after Capitaine Lemaitre had called on Madame Delphine, the priest started to make a pastoral call and had hardly left the gate of his cottage, when a person, overtaking him, plucked his gown:

"Père Jerome"—

He turned.

The face that met his was so changed with excitement and distress that for an instant he did not recognize it.

"Why, Madame Delphine"—

"Oh, Père Jerome! I wan' see you so bad, so bad! *Mo oulé dit quiç'ose,*—I godd some' to tell you."

The two languages might be more successful than one, she seemed to think.

"We had better go back to my parlor," said the priest, in their native tongue.

They returned.

Madame Delphine's very step was altered,—nervous and inelastic. She swung one arm as she walked, and brandished a turkey-tail fan.

"I was glad, yass, to kedge you," she said, as they mounted the front, outdoor stair; following her speech with a slight, unmusical laugh, and fanning herself with unconscious fury.

"*Fé chaud,*" she remarked again, taking the chair he offered and continuing to ply the fan.

Père Jerome laid his hat upon a chest of drawers, sat down opposite her, and said, as he wiped his kindly face:

"Well, Madame Carraze?"

Gentle as the tone was, she started, ceased fanning, lowered the fan to her knee, and commenced smoothing its feathers.

"Père Jerome"—She gnawed her lip and shook her head.

"Well?"

She burst into tears.

The priest rose and loosed the curtain of one of the windows. He did it slowly—as slowly as he could, and, as he came back, she lifted her face with sudden energy, and exclaimed:

"Oh, Père Jerome, de law is brogue! de law is brogue! I brogue it! 'Twas me! 'Twas me!"

The tears gushed out again, but she shut her lips very tight, and dumbly turned away her face. Père Jerome waited a little before replying; then he said, very gently:

"I suppose dad muss 'ave been by accyden', Madame Delphine?"

The little father felt a wish—one which he often had when weeping women were before him—that he were an angel instead of a man, long enough to press the tearful cheek upon his breast, and assure the weeper God would not let the lawyers and judges hurt her. He allowed a few moments more to pass, and then asked:

"*N'est-ce-pas,* Madame Delphine? Daz ze way, ain't it?"

"No, Père Jerome, no. My daughter—oh, Père Jerome, I bethroath my lill' girl—to a w'ite man!" And immediately Madame Delphine commenced savagely drawing a thread in the fabric of her skirt with one trembling hand, while she drove the fan with the other. "Dey goin' git marry."

On the priest's face came a look of pained surprise. He slowly said:

"Is dad possib', Madame Delphine?"

"Yass," she replied, at first without lifting her eyes; and then again, "Yass," looking full upon him through her tears, "yaas, 'tis tru."

He rose and walked once across the room, returned, and said, in the Creole dialect:

"Is he a good man—without doubt?"

"De bez in God's world!" replied Madame Delphine, with a rapturous smile.

"My poor, dear friend," said the priest, "I am afraid you are being deceived by somebody."

There was the pride of an unswerving faith in the triumphant tone and smile with which she replied, raising and slowly shaking her head:

"Ah-h, no-o-o, Miché! Ah-h, no, no! Not by Ursin Lemaitre-Vignevielle!"

Père Jerome was confounded. He turned again, and, with his hands at his back and his eyes cast down, slowly paced the floor.

"He *is* a good man," he said, by and by, as if he thought aloud. At length he halted before the woman.

"Madame Delphine"—

The distressed glance with which she had been following his steps was lifted to his eyes.

"Suppose dad should be true w'at doze peop' say 'bout Ursin."

"*Qui ci ça?* What is that?" asked the quadroone, stopping her fan.

"Some peop' say Ursin is crezzie."

"Ah, Père Jerome!" She leaped to her feet as if he had smitten her, and putting his words away with an outstretched arm and wide-open palm, suddenly lifted hands and eyes to heaven, and cried: "I wizh to God—*I wizh to God*—de whole worl' was crezzie dad same way!" She sank, trembling, into her chair. "Oh, no, no," she continued, shaking her head, "'tis not Miché Vignevielle w'at's crezzie." Her eyes lighted with sudden fierceness. "'Tis dad *law!* Dad *law* is crezzie! Dad law is a fool!"

A priest of less heart-wisdom might have replied that the law is—the law; but Père Jerome saw that Madame Delphine was expecting this very response. Wherefore he said, with gentleness:

"Madame Delphine, a priest is not a bailiff, but a physician. How can I help you?"

A grateful light shone a moment in her eyes, yet there remained a piteous hostility in the tone in which she demanded:

"*Mais, pou'quoi yé fé cette méchanique là?*"—What business had they to make that contraption?

His answer was a shrug with his palms extended and a short, disclamatory "Ah." He started to resume his walk, but turned to her again and said:

"Why did they make that law? Well, they made it to keep the two races separate."

Madame Delphine startled the speaker with a loud, harsh, angry laugh. Fire came from her eyes and her lip curled with scorn.

"Then they made a lie, Père Jerome! Separate! No-o-o! They do not want to keep us separated; no, no! But they *do* want to keep us despised!" She laid her hand on her heart, and frowned upward with physical pain. "But, very well! from which race do they want to keep my daughter separate? She is seven parts white! The law did not stop her from being that; and now, when she wants to be a white man's good and honest wife, shall that law stop her? Oh, no!" She rose up. "No; I will tell you what that law is made for. It is made to—punish—my—child—for—not—choosing—her—father! Père Jerome—my God, what a law!" She dropped back into her seat. The tears came in a flood, which she made no attempt to restrain.

"No," she began again—and here she broke into English—"fo' me I don' kyare; but, Père Jerome,—'tis fo' dat I came to tell you,—dey *shall not* punizh my daughter!" She was on her feet again, smiting her heaving bosom with the fan. "She shall marrie oo she want!"

Père Jerome had heard her out, not interrupting by so much as a motion of the hand. Now his decision was made, and he touched her softly with the ends of his fingers.

"Madame Delphine, I want you to go at 'ome. Go at 'ome."

"Wad you goin' mague?" she asked.

"Nottin'. But go at 'ome. Kip quite; don' put you'se'f sig. I goin' see Ursin. We trah to figs dat law fo' you."

"You kin figs dad!" she cried, with a gleam of joy.

"We goin' to try, Madame Delphine. Adieu!"

He offered his hand. She seized and kissed it thrice, covering it with tears, at the same time lifting up her eyes to his and murmuring:

"De bez man God evva mague!"

At the door she turned to offer a more conventional good-by; but he was following her out, bareheaded. At the gate they paused an instant, and then parted with a simple adieu, she going home and he returning for his hat, and starting again upon his interrupted business.

Before he came back to his own house, he stopped at the lodgings of Monsieur Vignevielle, but did not find him in.

"Indeed," the servant at the door said, "he said he might not return for some days or weeks."

So Père Jerome, much wondering, made a second detour toward the residence of one of Monsieur Vignevielle's employés.

"Yes," said the clerk, "his instructions are to hold the business, as far as practicable, in suspense, during his absence. Every thing is in another name." And then he whispered:

"Officers of the Government looking for him. Information got from some of the prisoners taken months ago by the United States brig *Porpoise*. But"—a still softer whisper—"have no fear; they will never find him: Jean Thompson and Evariste Varrillat have hid him away too well for that."

Chapter XIII. Tribulation

The Saturday following was a very beautiful day. In the morning a light fall of rain had passed across the town, and all the afternoon you could see signs, here and there upon the horizon, of other showers. The ground was dry again, while the breeze was cool and sweet, smelling of wet foliage and bringing sunshine and shade in frequent and very pleasing alternation.

There was a walk in Père Jerome's little garden, of which we have not spoken, off on the right side of the cottage, with his chamber window at one end, a few old and twisted, but blossom-laden, crape-myrtles on either hand, now and then a rose of some unpretending variety and some bunches of rue, and at the other end a shrine, in whose blue niche stood a small figure of Mary, with folded hands and uplifted eyes. No other window looked down upon the spot, and its seclusion was often a great comfort to Père Jerome.

Up and down this path, but a few steps in its entire length, the priest was walking, taking the air for a few moments after a prolonged sitting in the confessional. Penitents had been numerous this afternoon. He was thinking of Ursin. The officers of the Government had not found him, nor had Père Jerome seen him; yet he believed they had, in a certain indirect way, devised a simple project by which they could at any time "figs dad law," providing only that these Government officials would give over their search; for, though he had not seen the fugitive, Madame Delphine had seen him, and had been the vehicle of communication between them. There was an orange-tree, where a mocking-bird was wont to sing and a girl in white to walk, that the detectives wot not of. The law was to be "figs" by the departure of the three frequenters of the jasmine-scented garden in one ship to France, where the law offered no obstacles.

It seemed moderately certain to those in search of Monsieur Vignevielle (and it was true) that Jean and Evariste were his harborers; but for all that the hunt, even for clews, was vain. The little banking establishment had not been disturbed. Jean Thompson had told the searchers certain facts about it, and about its gentle proprietor as well, that persuaded them to make no move against the concern, if the same relations did not even induce a relaxation of their efforts for his personal discovery.

Père Jerome was walking to and fro, with his hands behind him, pondering these matters. He had paused a moment at the end of the walk farthest from his window, and was looking around upon the sky, when, turning, he beheld a closely veiled female figure standing at the other end, and knew instantly that it was Olive.

She came forward quickly and with evident eagerness.

"I came to confession," she said, breathing hurriedly, the excitement in her eyes shining through her veil, "but I find I am too late."

"There is no too late or too early for that; I am always ready," said the priest. "But how is your mother?"

"Ah!"—

Her voice failed.

"More trouble?"

"Ah, sir, I have *made* trouble. Oh, Père Jerome, I am bringing so much trouble upon my poor mother!"

Père Jerome moved slowly toward the house, with his eyes cast down, the veiled girl at his side.

"It is not your fault," he presently said. And after another pause: "I thought it was all arranged."

He looked up and could see, even through the veil, her crimson blush.

"Oh, no," she replied, in a low, despairing voice, dropping her face.

"What is the difficulty?" asked the priest, stopping in the angle of the path, where it turned toward the front of the house.

She averted her face, and began picking the thin scales of bark from a crape-myrtle.

"Madame Thompson and her husband were at our house this morning. *He* had told Monsieur Thompson all about it. They were very kind to me at first, but they tried"—She was weeping.

"What did they try to do?" asked the priest.

"They tried to make me believe he is insane."

She succeeded in passing her handkerchief up under her veil.

"And I suppose then your poor mother grew angry, eh?"

"Yes; and they became much more so, and said if we did not write, or send a writing, to *him*, within twenty-four hours, breaking the"—

"Engagement," said Père Jerome.

"They would give him up to the Government. Oh, Père Jerome, what shall I do? It is killing my mother!"

She bowed her head and sobbed.

"Where is your mother now?"

"She has gone to see Monsieur Jean Thompson. She says she has a plan that will match them all. I do not know what it is. I begged her not to go; but oh, sir, *she is crazy*,—and I am no better."

"My poor child," said Père Jerome, "what you seem to want is not absolution, but relief from persecution."

"Oh, father, I have committed mortal sin,—I am guilty of pride and anger."

"Nevertheless," said the priest, starting toward his front gate, "we will put off your confession. Let it go until to-morrow morning; you will find me in my box just before mass; I will hear you then. My child, I know that in your heart, now, you begrudge the time it would take; and that is right. There are moments when we are not in place even on penitential knees. It is so with you now. We must find your mother. Go you at once to your house; if she is there, comfort her as best you can, and *keep her in, if possible,* until I come. If she is not there, stay; leave me to find her; one of you, at least, must be where I can get word to you promptly. God comfort and uphold you. I hope you may find her at home; tell her, for me, not to fear,"—he lifted the gate-latch,—"that she and her daughter are of more value than many sparrows; that God's priest sends her that word from Him. Tell her to fix her trust in the great Husband of the Church, and she shall yet see her child receiving the grace-giving sacrament of matrimony. Go; I shall, in a few minutes, be on my way to Jean Thompson's, and shall find her, either there or wherever she is. Go; they shall not oppress you. Adieu!"

A moment or two later he was in the street himself.

Chapter XIV. By an Oath

Père Jerome, pausing on a street-corner in the last hour of sunlight, had wiped his brow and taken his cane down from under his arm to start again, when somebody, coming noiselessly from he knew not where, asked, so suddenly as to startle him:

"*Miché, commin yé pellé la rie ici?*—how do they call this street here?"

It was by the bonnet and dress, disordered though they were, rather than by the haggard face which looked distractedly around, that he recognized the woman to whom he replied in her own *patois*:

"It is the Rue Burgundy. Where are you going, Madame Delphine?"

She almost leaped from the ground.

"Oh, Père Jerome! *mo pas conné,*—I dunno. You know w'ere's dad 'ouse of Miché Jean Tomkin? *Mo courri 'ci, mo courri là,—mo pas capabe li trouvé.* I go (run) here— there—I cannot find it," she gesticulated.

"I am going there myself," said he; "but why do you want to see Jean Thompson, Madame Delphine?"

"I *'blige'* to see 'im!" she replied, jerking herself half around away, one foot planted forward with an air of excited pre-occupation; "I godd some' to tell 'im wad I *'blige'* to tell 'im!"

"Madame Delphine"—

"Oh! Père Jerome, fo' de love of de good God, show me dad way to de 'ouse of Jean Tomkin!"

Her distressed smile implored pardon for her rudeness.

"What are you going to tell him?" asked the priest.

"Oh, Père Jerome,"—in the Creole *patois* again,—"I am going to put an end to all this trouble—only I pray you do not ask me about it now; every minute is precious!"

He could not withstand her look of entreaty.

"Come," he said, and they went.

Jean Thompson and Doctor Varrillat lived opposite each other on the Bayou road, a little way beyond the town limits as then prescribed. Each had his large, white-columned, four-sided house among the magnolias,—his huge live-oak overshadowing either corner of the darkly shaded garden, his broad, brick walk leading down to the tall, brick-pillared gate, his square of bright, red pavement on the turf-covered side-walk, and his railed platform spanning the draining-ditch, with a pair of green benches, one on each edge, facing each other crosswise of the gutter. There, any sunset hour, you were sure to find the householder sitting beside his cool-robed matron, two or three slave nurses in white turbans standing at hand, and an excited throng of fair children, nearly all of a size.

Sometimes, at a beckon or call, the parents on one side of the way would join those on the other, and the children and nurses of both families would be given the liberty of the opposite platform and an ice-cream fund! Generally the parents chose the Thompson platform, its outlook being more toward the sunset.

Such happened to be the arrangement this afternoon. The two husbands sat on one bench and their wives on the other, both pairs very quiet, waiting respectfully for the day to die, and exchanging only occasional comments on matters of light moment as they passed through the memory. During one term of silence Madame Varrillat, a pale, thin-faced, but cheerful-looking lady, touched Madame Thompson, a person of two and a half times her weight, on her extensive and snowy bare elbow, directing her attention obliquely up and across the road.

About a hundred yards distant, in the direction of the river, was a long, pleasantly shaded green strip of turf, destined in time for a sidewalk. It had a deep ditch on the nearer side, and a fence of rough cypress palisades on the farther, and these were over-hung, on the one hand, by a row of bitter-orange-trees inside the enclosure, and, on the other, by a line of slanting china-trees along the outer edge of the ditch. Down this cool avenue two figures were approaching side by side. They had first attracted Madame Varrillat's notice by the bright play of sunbeams which, as they walked, fell upon them in soft, golden flashes through the chinks between the palisades.

Madame Thompson elevated a pair of glasses which were no detraction from her very good looks, and remarked, with the serenity of a reconnoitring general:

"*Père Jerome et cette milatraise.*"

All eyes were bent toward them.

"She walks like a man," said Madame Varrillat, in the language with which the conversation had opened.

"No," said the physician, "like a woman in a state of high nervous excitement."

Jean Thompson kept his eyes on the woman, and said:

"She must not forget to walk like a woman in the State of Louisiana,"—as near as the pun can be translated. The company laughed. Jean Thompson looked at his wife, whose applause he prized, and she answered by an asseverative toss of the head, leaning back and contriving, with some effort, to get her arms folded. Her laugh was musical and low, but enough to make the folded arms shake gently up and down.

"Père Jerome is talking to her," said one. The priest was at that moment endeavoring, in the interest of peace, to say a good word for the four people who sat watching his approach. It was in the old strain:

"Blame them one part, Madame Delphine, and their fathers, mothers, brothers, and fellow-citizens the other ninety-nine."

But to every thing she had the one amiable answer which Père Jerome ignored:

"I am going to arrange it to satisfy everybody, all together. *Tout à fait.*"

"They are coming here," said Madame Varrillat, half articulately.

"Well, of course," murmured another; and the four rose up, smiling courteously, the doctor and attorney advancing and shaking hands with the priest.

No—Père Jerome thanked them—he could not sit down.

"This, I believe you know, Jean, is Madame Delphine"—

The quadroone courtesied.

"A friend of mine," he added, smiling kindly upon her, and turning, with something imperative in his eye, to the group. "She says she has an important private matter to communicate."

"To me?" asked Jean Thompson.

"To all of you; so I will—Good-evening." He responded nothing to the expressions of regret, but turned to Madame Delphine. She murmured something.

"Ah! yes, certainly." He addressed the company: "She wishes me to speak for her veracity; it is unimpeachable. Well, good-evening." He shook hands and departed.

The four resumed their seats, and turned their eyes upon the standing figure.

"Have you something to say to us?" asked Jean Thompson, frowning at her law-defying bonnet.

"Oui," replied the woman, shrinking to one side, and laying hold of one of the benches, "*mo oulé di' tou' ç'ose*"—I want to tell every thing. "*Miché Vignevielle la plis bon homme di moune*"—the best man in the world; "*mo pas capabe li fé tracas*"—I cannot give him trouble. "*Mo pas capabe, non; m'olé di' tous ç'ose.*" She attempted to fan herself, her face turned away from the attorney, and her eyes rested on the ground.

"Take a seat," said Doctor Varrillat, with some suddenness, starting from his place and gently guiding her sinking form into the corner of the bench. The ladies rose up; somebody had to stand; the two races could not both sit down at once—at least not in that public manner.

"Your salts," said the physician to his wife. She handed the vial. Madame Delphine stood up again.

"We will all go inside," said Madame Thompson, and they passed through the gate and up the walk, mounted the steps, and entered the deep, cool drawing-room.

Madame Thompson herself bade the quadroone be seated.

"Well?" said Jean Thompson, as the rest took chairs.

"*C'est drole*"—it's funny—said Madame Delphine, with a piteous effort to smile, "that nobody thought of it. It is so plain. You have only to look and see. I mean about Olive." She loosed a button in the front of her dress and passed her hand into her bosom. "And yet, Olive herself never thought of it. She does not know a word."

The hand came out holding a miniature. Madame Varrillat passed it to Jean Thompson.

"*Ouala so popa*," said Madame Delphine. "That is her father."

It went from one to another, exciting admiration and murmured praise.

"She is the image of him," said Madame Thompson, in an austere undertone, returning it to her husband.

Doctor Varrillat was watching Madame Delphine. She was very pale. She had passed a trembling hand into a pocket of her skirt, and now drew out another picture, in a case the counterpart of the first. He reached out for it, and she handed it to him. He looked at it a moment, when his eyes suddenly lighted up and he passed it to the attorney.

"*Et là*"—Madame Delphine's utterance failed—"*et là ouala sa moman*. That is her mother."

The three others instantly gathered around Jean Thompson's chair. They were much impressed.

"It is true beyond a doubt!" muttered Madame Thompson.

Madame Varrillat looked at her with astonishment.

"The proof is right there in the faces," said Madame Thompson.

"Yes! yes!" said Madame Delphine, excitedly; "the proof is there! You do not want any better! I am willing to swear to it! But you want no better proof! That is all any-body could want! My God! you cannot help but see it!"

Her manner was wild.

Jean Thompson looked at her sternly.

"Nevertheless you say you are willing to take your solemn oath to this."

"Certainly"—

"You will have to do it."

"Certainly, Miché Thompson, *of course* I shall; you will make out the paper and I will swear before God that it is true! Only"—turning to the ladies—"do not tell Olive; she will never believe it. It will break her heart! It"—

A servant came and spoke privately to Madame Thompson, who rose quickly and went to the hall. Madame Delphine continued, rising unconsciously:

"You see, I have had her with me from a baby. She knows no better. He brought her to me only two months old. Her mother had died in the ship, coming out here. He did not come straight from home here. His people never knew he was married!"

The speaker looked around suddenly with a startled glance. There was a noise of excited speaking in the hall.

"It is not true, Madame Thompson!" cried a girl's voice.

Madame Delphine's look became one of wildest distress and alarm, and she opened her lips in a vain attempt to utter some request, when Olive appeared a mo-ment in the door, and then flew into her arms.

"My mother! my mother! my mother!"

Madame Thompson, with tears in her eyes, tenderly drew them apart and let Madame Delphine down into her chair, while Olive threw herself upon her knees, continuing to cry:

"Oh, my mother! Say you are my mother!"

Madame Delphine looked an instant into the upturned face, and then turned her own away, with a long, low cry of pain, looked again, and laying both hands upon the suppliant's head, said:

"*Oh, chère piti à moin, to pa' ma fie!*"—Oh, my darling little one, you are not my daughter!—Her eyes closed, and her head sank back; the two gentlemen sprang to her assistance, and laid her upon a sofa unconscious.

When they brought her to herself, Olive was kneeling at her head silently weeping.

"*Maman, chère maman!*" said the girl softly, kissing her lips.

"*Ma courri c'ez moin*"—I will go home—said the mother, drearily.

"You will go home with me," said Madame Varrillat, with great kindness of man-ner—"just across the street here; I will take care of you till you feel better. And Olive will stay here with Madame Thompson. You will be only the width of the street apart."

But Madame Delphine would go nowhere but to her home. Olive she would not allow to go with her. Then they wanted to send a servant or two to sleep in the house with her for aid and protection; but all she would accept was the transient service of a messenger to invite two of her kinspeople—man and wife—to come and make their dwelling with her.

In course of time these two—a poor, timid, helpless pair—fell heir to the premises. Their children had it after them; but, whether in those hands or these, the house had its habits and continued in them; and to this day the neighbors, as has already been said, rightly explain its close-sealed, uninhabited look by the all-sufficient statement that the inmates "is quadroons."

Chapter XV. Kyrie Eleison

The second Saturday afternoon following was hot and calm. The lamp burning before the tabernacle in Père Jerome's little church might have hung with as motionless a flame in the window behind. The lilies of St. Joseph's wand, shining in one of the half opened panes, were not more completely at rest than the leaves on tree and vine without, suspended in the slumbering air. Almost as still, down under the organ-gallery, with a single band of light falling athwart his box from a small door which stood ajar, sat the little priest, behind the lattice of the confessional, silently wiping away the sweat that beaded on his brow and rolled down his face. At distant intervals the shadow of some one entering softly through the door would obscure, for a moment, the band of light, and an aged crone, or a little boy, or some gentle presence that the listening confessor had known only by the voice for many years, would kneel a few moments beside his waiting ear, in prayer for blessing and in review of those slips and errors which prove us all akin.

The day had been long and fatiguing. First, early mass; a hasty meal; then a business call upon the archbishop in the interest of some projected charity; then back to his cottage, and so to the banking-house of "Vignevielle," in the Rue Toulouse. There all was open, bright, and re-assured, its master virtually, though not actually, present. The search was over and the seekers gone, personally wiser than they would tell, and officially reporting that (to the best of their knowledge and belief, based on evidence, and especially on the assurances of an unexceptionable eye-witness, to wit, Monsieur Vignevielle, banker) Capitaine Lemaitre was dead and buried. At noon there had been a wedding in the little church. Its scenes lingered before Père Jerome's vision now— the kneeling pair: the bridegroom, rich in all the excellences of man, strength and kindness slumbering interlocked in every part and feature; the bride, a saintly weariness on her pale face, her awesome eyes lifted in adoration upon the image of the Saviour; the small knots of friends behind: Madame Thompson, large, fair, self-contained; Jean Thompson, with the affidavit of Madame Delphine showing through his tightly buttoned coat; the physician and his wife, sharing one expression of amiable consent; and last—yet first—one small, shrinking female figure, here at one side, in faded robes and dingy bonnet. She sat as motionless as stone, yet wore a look of apprehension, and in the small, restless black eyes which peered out from the pinched and wasted face, betrayed the peacelessness of a harrowed mind; and neither the recollection of bride, nor of groom, nor of potential friends behind, nor the occupation of the present hour, could shut out from the tired priest the image of that woman, or the sound of his own low words of invitation to her, given as the company left the church—"Come to confession this afternoon."

By and by a long time passed without the approach of any step, or any glancing of light or shadow, save for the occasional progress from station to station of some one over on the right who was noiselessly going the way of the cross. Yet Père Jerome tarried.

"She will surely come," he said to himself; "she promised she would come."

A moment later, his sense, quickened by the prolonged silence, caught a subtle evidence or two of approach, and the next moment a penitent knelt noiselessly at the window of his box, and the whisper came tremblingly, in the voice he had waited to hear:

"*Bénissez-moin, mo' Père, pa'ce que mo péché.*" (Bless me, father, for I have sinned.)

He gave his blessing.

"*Ainsi soit-il*—Amen," murmured the penitent, and then, in the soft accents of the Creole *patois*, continued:

"'I confess to Almighty God, to the blessed Mary, ever Virgin, to blessed Michael the Archangel, to blessed John the Baptist, to the holy Apostles Peter and Paul, and to all the saints, that I have sinned exceedingly in thought, word, and deed, *through my fault, through my fault, through my most grievous fault.*' I confessed on Saturday, three weeks ago, and received absolution, and I have performed the penance enjoined. Since then"—There she stopped.

There was a soft stir, as if she sank slowly down, and another as if she rose up again, and in a moment she said:

"Olive *is* my child. The picture I showed to Jean Thompson is the half-sister of my daughter's father, dead before my child was born. She is the image of her and of him; but, O God! Thou knowest! Oh, Olive, my own daughter!"

She ceased, and was still. Père Jerome waited, but no sound came. He looked through the window. She was kneeling, with her forehead resting on her arms—motionless.

He repeated the words of absolution. Still she did not stir.

"My daughter," he said, "go to thy home in peace." But she did not move.

He rose hastily, stepped from the box, raised her in his arms, and called her by name:

"Madame Delphine!" Her head fell back in his elbow; for an instant there was life in the eyes—it glimmered—it vanished, and tears gushed from his own and fell upon the gentle face of the dead, as he looked up to heaven and cried:

"Lord, lay not this sin to her charge!"

32

From *"The Pariah"*

James Edwin Campbell

James Edwin Campbell (1867–1895) was a poet and educator whose poetry inspired Afro-American poets of the Harlem Renaissance and beyond. Campbell worked as a teacher in his hometown, Pomeroy, Ohio, before moving to West Virginia, where he became the principal of Langston School and then the president of the new Afro-American agricultural and mechanical Collegiate Institute. Campbell contributed poems and articles to the *Chicago Times-Herald* and other publications, and his collected poems were published in two volumes, *Driftings and Gleanings* (1887) and *Echoes from the Cabin and Elsewhere* (1895), in which "The Pariah" appeared.

Owned her father all the fact'ries
    Which their black'ning smoke sent up,
Miles and miles all 'round the country,
    From the town by hills pent up.
Traced he back his proud ancestry
    To the Rock on Plymouth's shore,
Traced I mine to Dutch ship landing
    At Jamestown, one year before.
Thus was she of haughty lineage,
    I of mongrel race had sprung;
O'er my fathers in the workfield
    Whips of scorpions had been swung.
Years of freedom were her race's,
    Years of cruel slavery mine;
Years of culture were her race's,
    Years of darkest ign'rance mine.
She a lily sought by all men,
    I a thistle shunned by all;
She the Brahmin, I the Pariah
    Who must e'er before her crawl.
Fair was I as her complexion,
    Honest came my fairness, too,

For my father and my mother
    Were in wedlock banded true.
Yes, this mixing of the races
    Had been years, long years ago,
That you could not trace the streamlet
    To the fountain whence the flow....

And she comes and stands before me
    As I gaze into the stream,
And I see her, I behold her
    As some vision in a dream,
And the waves of love come surging
    And they sweep my will away,
For I love her, O I love her—
    Aye, forever and a day!
And I called her: "Edie! Edie!"
    As I'd called her oft before,
When as little guileless children
    We plucked lilies from this shore.
Oh my voice sobbed like a harp string
    When the rough hand breaks a chord,
And it wailed and moaned as sadly
    As some broken-hearted bard.
And she came up to me quickly
    When I thus wailed out her name,
All her soul rose in her blue eyes
    There was ne'er a look of shame,
And she threw her arms up to me
    And I caught her to my heart,
While the whole earth reeled beneath me
    And the heavens fell apart!

Faint and trembling then I asked her
    What the cruel world would say,
While she blushed but spoke out bravely:
    "We'll forget the World to-day.
This I only know, I love you,
    I have loved you all the while;
What care I then for your lineage
    Or the harsh world's frown or smile.
Men are noble from *their* actions,
    From *their* deeds and theirs alone,
Father's deeds are *not* their children's—
    Reap not that by others sown.
They are naught but dwarfish pigmies

Who would scorn you for your birth;
Who would scorn you for your lineage,
    Raise they not their eyes from Earth.
What is blood? The human body?
    Trace it back, it leads to dust,
Trace it forward, same conclusion,
    Naught but vile dust find you must.
But the *soul* is sent from heaven
    And the Sculptor-Hand is God's
Part and parcel of his being,
    While our bodies are but clods!"

33

"Boitelle"

Guy de Maupassant

Guy de Maupassant (1850–1893) was considered France's greatest short story writer. As a young man he volunteered for military duty in the Franco-Prussian War, and then held various positions in the civil service while honing his writing talent under the tutelage of Gustave Flaubert, a friend of Maupassant's mother. His short story "Boule de suif" (Ball of Fat) was published in 1880 and brought him immediate success. Tolstoy considered Maupassant's first novel, *Une vie* (1883), on a par with *Les Misérables*. The years between 1880 and 1890 were extraordinarily productive for Maupassant: he published plays, articles, poetry, and travel books in addition to six novels and around three hundred short stories. He developed an ironic voice that examines human motives, often in the context of erotic attachments, as in the 1889 story "Boitelle," which follows here in an anonymous translation.

Father Boitelle (Antoine) made a specialty of undertaking dirty jobs all through the countryside. Whenever there was a ditch or a cesspool to be cleaned out, a dunghill removed, a sewer cleansed, or any dirt hole whatever, he was always employed to do it.

He would come with the instruments of his trade, his sabots covered with dirt, and set to work, complaining incessantly about his occupation. When people asked him then why he did this loathsome work, he would reply resignedly:

"Faith, 'tis for my children, whom I must support. This brings me in more than anything else."

He had, indeed, fourteen children. If any one asked him what had become of them, he would say with an air of indifference:

"There are only eight of them left in the house. One is out at service and five are married."

When the questioner wanted to know whether they were well married, he replied vivaciously:

"I did not oppose them. I opposed them in nothing. They married just as they pleased. We shouldn't go against people's likings, it turns out badly. I am a night scavenger because my parents went against my likings. But for that I would have become a workman like the others."

Here is the way his parents had thwarted him in his likings:

He was at the time a soldier stationed at Havre, not more stupid than another, or sharper either, a rather simple fellow, however. When he was not on duty, his greatest pleasure was to walk along the quay, where the bird dealers congregate. Sometimes alone, sometimes with a soldier from his own part of the country, he would slowly saunter along by cages containing parrots with green backs and yellow heads from the banks of the Amazon, or parrots with gray backs and red heads from Senegal, or enormous macaws, which look like birds reared in hot-houses, with their flower-like feathers, their plumes and their tufts. Parrots of every size, who seem painted with minute care by the miniaturist, God Almighty, and the little birds, all the smaller birds hopped about, yellow, blue and variegated, mingling their cries with the noise of the quay, and adding to the din caused by unloading the vessels, as well as by passengers and vehicles, a violent clamor, loud, shrill and deafening, as if from some distant forest of monsters.

Boitelle would pause, with wondering eyes, wide-open mouth, laughing and enraptured, showing his teeth to the captive cockatoos, who kept nodding their white or yellow topknots toward the glaring red of his breeches and the copper buckle of his belt. When he found a bird that could talk he put questions to it, and if it happened at the time to be disposed to reply and to hold a conversation with him he would carry away enough amusement to last him till evening. He also found heaps of amusement in looking at the monkeys, and could conceive no greater luxury for a rich man than to own these animals as one owns cats and dogs. This kind of taste for the exotic he had in his blood, as people have a taste for the chase, or for medicine, or for the priesthood. He could not help returning to the quay every time the gates of the barracks opened, drawn toward it by an irresistible longing.

On one occasion, having stopped almost in ecstasy before an enormous macaw, which was swelling out its plumes, bending forward and bridling up again as if making the court curtseys of parrot-land, he saw the door of a little café adjoining the bird dealer's shop open, and a young Negress appeared, wearing on her head a red silk handkerchief. She was sweeping into the street the corks and sand of the establishment.

Boitelle's attention was soon divided between the bird and the woman, and he really could not tell which of these two beings he contemplated with the greater astonishment and delight.

The Negress, having swept the rubbish into the street, raised her eyes, and, in her turn, was dazzled by the soldier's uniform. There she stood facing him with her broom in her hands as if she were bringing him a rifle, while the macaw continued bowing. But at the end of a few seconds the soldier began to feel embarrassed at this attention, and he walked away quietly so as not to look as if he were beating a retreat.

But he came back. Almost every day he passed before the Café des Colonies, and often he could distinguish through the window the figure of the little black-skinned maid serving "bocks" or glasses of brandy to the sailors of the port. Frequently, too, she would come out to the door on seeing him; soon, without even having exchanged a word, they smiled at one another like acquaintances; and Boitelle felt his heart touched when he suddenly saw, glittering between the dark lips of the girl, a shining row of white teeth. At length, one day he ventured to enter, and was quite surprised to find that she could speak French like every one else. The bottle of lemonade, of which she was good enough to accept a glassful, remained in the soldier's recollection memorably delicious, and it became a custom with him to come and absorb in this little tavern on the quay all the agreeable drinks which he could afford.

For him it was a treat, a happiness, on which his thoughts dwelt constantly, to watch the black hand of the little maid pouring something into his glass while her teeth laughed more than her eyes. At the end of two months they became fast friends, and Boitelle, after his first astonishment at discovering that this Negress had as good principles as honest French girls, that she exhibited a regard for economy, industry, religion and good conduct, loved her more on that account, and was so charmed with her that he wanted to marry her.

He told her his intentions, which made her dance with joy. She had also a little money, left her by a female oyster dealer, who had picked her up when she had been left on the quay at Havre by an American captain. This captain had found her, when she was only about six years old, lying on bales of cotton in the hold of his ship, some hours after his departure from New York. On his arrival in Havre he abandoned to the care of this compassionate oyster dealer the little black creature, who had been hidden on board his vessel, he knew not why or by whom.

The oyster woman having died, the young Negress became a servant at the Colonial Tavern.

Antoine Boitelle added: "This will be all right if my parents don't oppose it. I will never go against them, you understand, never! I'm going to say a word or two to them the first time I go back to the country."

On the following week, in fact, having obtained twenty-four hours' leave, he went to see his family, who cultivated a little farm at Tourteville, near Yvetot.

He waited till the meal was finished, the hour when the coffee baptized with brandy makes people more open-hearted, before informing his parents that he had found a girl who satisfied his tastes, all his tastes, so completely that there could not exist any other in all the world so perfectly suited to him.

The old people, on hearing this, immediately assumed a cautious manner and wanted explanations. He had concealed nothing from them except the color of her skin.

She was a servant, without much means, but strong, thrifty, clean, well-conducted and sensible. All these things were better than money would be in the hands of a bad housewife. Moreover, she had a few sous, left her by a woman who had reared her, a good number of sous, almost a little dowry, fifteen hundred francs in the savings bank. The old people, persuaded by his talk, and relying also on their own judgment, were gradually weakening, when he came to the delicate point. Laughing in rather a constrained fashion, he said:

"There's only one thing you may not like. She is not a white slip."

They did not understand, and he had to explain at some length and very cautiously, to avoid shocking them, that she belonged to the dusky race of which they had only seen samples in pictures at Épinal. Then they became restless, perplexed, alarmed, as if he had proposed a union with the devil.

The mother said: "Black? How much of her is black? Is the whole of her?"

He replied: "Certainly. Everywhere, just as you are white everywhere."

The father interposed: "Black? Is it as black as the pot?"

The son answered: "Perhaps a little less than that. She is black, but not disgustingly black. The curé's cassock is black, but it is not uglier than a surplice, which is white."

The father said: "Are there more black people besides her in her country?"

And the son, with an air of conviction, exclaimed: "Certainly!"

But the old man shook his head.

"That must be unpleasant."

And the son:

"It isn't more disagreeable than anything else when you get accustomed to it."

The mother asked:

"It doesn't soil the underwear more than other skins, this black skin?"

"Not more than your own, as it is her proper color."

Then, after many other questions, it was agreed that the parents should see this girl before coming to any decision, and that the young fellow, whose term of military service would be over in a month, should bring her to the house in order that they might examine her and decide by talking the matter over whether or not she was too dark to enter the Boitelle family.

Antoine accordingly announced that on Sunday, the 22d of May, the day of his discharge, he would start for Tourteville with his sweetheart.

She had put on, for this journey to the house of her lover's parents, her most beautiful and most gaudy clothes, in which yellow, red and blue were the prevailing colors, so that she looked as if she were adorned for a national festival.

At the terminus, as they were leaving Havre, people stared at her, and Boitelle was proud of giving his arm to a person who commanded so much attention. Then, in the third-class carriage, in which she took a seat by his side, she aroused so much astonishment among the country folks that the people in the adjoining compartments stood up on their benches to look at her over the wooden partition which divides the compartments. A child, at sight of her, began to cry with terror, another concealed his face in his mother's apron. Everything went off well, however, up to their arrival at their destination. But when the train slackened its rate of motion as they drew near Yvetot, Antoine felt ill at ease, as he would have done at a review when he did not know his drill practice. Then, as he leaned his head out, he recognized in the distance his father, holding the bridle of the horse harnessed to a carryall, and his mother, who had come forward to the grating, behind which stood those who were expecting friends.

He alighted first, gave his hand to his sweetheart, and holding himself erect, as if he were escorting a general, he went to meet his family.

The mother, on seeing this black lady in variegated costume in her son's company, remained so stupefied that she could not open her mouth, and the father found it hard to hold the horse, which the engine or the Negress caused to rear continuously. But Antoine, suddenly filled with unmixed joy at seeing once more the old people, rushed forward with open arms, embraced his mother, embraced his father, in spite of the nag's fright, and then turning toward his companion, at whom the passengers on the platform stopped to stare with amazement, he proceeded to explain:

"Here she is! I told you that, at first sight, she is not attractive; but as soon as you know her, I can assure you there's not a better sort in the whole world. Say good-morning to her so that she may not feel badly."

Thereupon Mère Boitelle, almost frightened out of her wits, made a sort of curtsy, while the father took off his cap, murmuring:

"I wish you good luck!"

Then, without further delay, they climbed into the carryall, the two women at the back, on seats which made them jump up and down as the vehicle went jolting along the road, and the two men in front on the front seat.

Nobody spoke. Antoine, ill at ease, whistled a barrack-room air; his father whipped the nag; and his mother, from where she sat in the corner, kept casting sly glances at the Negress, whose forehead and cheekbones shone in the sunlight like well-polished shoes.

Wishing to break the ice, Antoine turned round.

"Well," said he, "we don't seem inclined to talk."

"We must have time," replied the old woman.

He went on:

"Come! Tell us the little story about that hen of yours that laid eight eggs."

It was a funny anecdote of long standing in the family. But, as his mother still remained silent, paralyzed by her emotion, he undertook himself to tell the story, laughing as he did so at the memorable incident. The father, who knew it by heart, brightened at the opening words of the narrative; his wife soon followed his example; and the Negress herself, when he reached the drollest part of it, suddenly gave vent to a laugh, such a loud, rolling torrent of laughter that the horse, becoming excited, broke into a gallop for a while.

This served to cement their acquaintance. They all began to chat.

They had scarcely reached the house and had all alighted, when Antoine conducted his sweetheart to a room, so that she might take off her dress, to avoid staining it, as she was going to prepare a nice dish, intended to win the old people's affections through their stomachs. He drew his parents outside the house, and, with beating heart, asked:

"Well, what do you say now?"

The father said nothing. The mother, less timid, exclaimed:

"She is too black. No, indeed, this is too much for me. It turns my blood."

"You will get used to it," said Antoine.

"Perhaps so, but not at first."

They went into the house, where the good woman was somewhat affected at the spectacle of the Negress engaged in cooking. She at once proceeded to assist her, with petticoats tucked up, active in spite of her age.

The meal was an excellent one, very long, very enjoyable. When they were taking a turn after dinner, Antoine took his father aside.

"Well, dad, what do you say about it?"

The peasant took care never to compromise himself.

"I have no opinion about it. Ask your mother."

So Antoine went back to his mother, and, detaining her behind the rest, said:

"Well, mother, what do you think of her?"

"My poor lad, she is really too black. If she were only a little less black, I would not go against you, but this is too much. One would think it was Satan!"

He did not press her, knowing how obstinate the old woman had always been, but he felt a tempest of disappointment sweeping over his heart. He was turning over in his mind what he ought to do, what plan he could devise, surprised, moreover, that she had not conquered them already as she had captivated himself. And they, all four, walked along through the wheat fields, having gradually relapsed into silence. Whenever they passed a fence they saw a countryman sitting on the stile, and a group of brats climbed up to stare at them, and every one rushed out into the road to see the "black" whom young Boitelle had brought home with him. At a distance they noticed people scampering across the fields just as when the drum beats to draw public attention to some living phenomenon. Père and Mère Boitelle, alarmed at this curiosity, which was exhibited everywhere through the country at their approach, quickened their pace, walking side by side, and leaving their son far behind. His dark companion asked what his parents thought of her.

He hesitatingly replied that they had not yet made up their minds.

But on the village green people rushed out of all the houses in a flutter of excitement; and, at the sight of the gathering crowd, old Boitelle took to his heels, and regained his abode, while Antoine, swelling with rage, his sweetheart on his arm, advanced majestically under the staring eyes, which opened wide in amazement.

He understood that it was at an end, and there was no hope for him, that he could not marry his Negress. She also understood it; and as they drew near the farmhouse they both began to weep. As soon as they had got back to the house, she once more took off her dress to aid the mother in the household duties, and followed her everywhere, to the dairy, to the stable, to the hen house, taking on herself the hardest part of the work, repeating always: "Let me do it, Madame Boitelle," so that, when night came on, the old woman, touched but inexorable, said to her son: "She is a good girl, all the same. It's a pity she is so black; but indeed she is too black. I could not get used to it. She must go back again. She is too, too black!"

And young Boitelle said to his sweetheart:

"She will not consent. She thinks you are too black. You must go back again. I will go with you to the train. No matter—don't fret. I am going to talk to them after you have started."

He then took her to the railway station, still cheering her with hope, and, when he had kissed her, he put her into the train, which he watched as it passed out of sight, his eyes swollen with tears.

In vain did he appeal to the old people. They would never give their consent.

And when he had told this story, which was known all over the country, Antoine Boitelle would always add:

"From that time forward I have had no heart for anything—for anything at all. No trade suited me any longer, and so I became what I am—a night scavenger."

People would say to him:

"Yet you got married."

"Yes, and I can't say that my wife didn't please me, seeing that I have fourteen children; but she is not the other one, oh, no—certainly not! The other one, mark you, my Negress, she had only to give me one glance, and I felt as if I were in Heaven."

34

"The Father of Désirée's Baby"

Kate Chopin

Kate Chopin (1851–1904) is best known for her 1899 novel *The Awakening*, a controversial tale of one woman's quest for sexual and emotional autonomy. Chopin was born into a wealthy family in St. Louis and began writing seriously only after she was widowed in her early thirties. Her first story, published in 1889, was followed by a novel, *At Fault* (1890), and the story collections *Bayou Folk* (1894) and *A Night in Acadie* (1897). In many of her stories Chopin portrayed Creole life in New Orleans and rural Louisiana, where she had spent much of her married life; she also subtly critiqued conventional marriage and questioned race and class distinctions, as in the following story, published in *Vogue* in 1893.

As the day was pleasant, Madame Valmondé drove over to L'Abri to see Désirée and the baby.

It made her laugh to think of Désirée with a baby. Why, it seemed but yesterday that Désirée was little more than a baby herself; when Monsieur in riding through the gateway of Valmondé had found her lying asleep in the shadow of the big stone pillar.

The little one awoke in his arms and began to cry for "Dada." That was as much as she could do or say. Some people thought she might have strayed there of her own accord, for she was of the toddling age. The prevailing belief was that she had been purposely left by a party of Texans, whose canvas-covered wagon, late in the day, had crossed the ferry that Coton Maïs kept, just below the plantation. In time Madame Valmondé abandoned every speculation but the one that Désirée had been sent to her by a beneficent Providence to be the child of her affection, seeing that she was without child of the flesh. For the girl grew to be beautiful and gentle, affectionate and sincere,—the idol of Valmondé.

It was no wonder, when she stood one day against the stone pillar in whose shadow she had lain asleep, eighteen years before, that Armand Aubigny riding by and seeing her there, had fallen in love with her. That was the way all the Aubignys fell in love, as if struck by a pistol shot. The wonder was that he had not loved her before; for he had known her since his father brought him home from Paris, a boy of eight, after his mother died there. The passion that awoke in him that day, when he saw her at the gate, swept along like an avalanche, or like a prairie fire, or like anything that drives headlong over all obstacles.

Monsieur Valmondé grew practical and wanted things well considered: that is, the girl's obscure origin. Armand looked into her eyes and did not care. He was reminded that she was nameless. What did it matter about a name when he could give her one of the oldest and proudest in Louisiana? He ordered the *corbeille* from Paris, and contained himself with what patience he could until it arrived; then they were married.

Madame Valmondé had not seen Désirée and the baby for four weeks. When she reached L'Abri she shuddered at the first sight of it, as she always did. It was a sad looking place, which for many years had not known the gentle presence of a mistress, old Monsieur Aubigny having married and buried his wife in France, and she having loved her own land too well ever to leave it. The roof came down steep and black like a cowl, reaching out beyond the wide galleries that encircled the yellow stuccoed house. Big, solemn oaks grew close to it, and their thick-leaved, far-reaching branches shadowed it like a pall. Young Aubigny's rule was a strict one, too, and under it his negroes had forgotten how to be gay, as they had been during the old master's easy-going and indulgent lifetime.

The young mother was recovering slowly, and lay full length, in her soft white muslins and laces, upon a couch. The baby was beside her, upon her arm, where he had fallen asleep, at her breast. The yellow nurse woman sat beside a window fanning herself.

Madame Valmondé bent her portly figure over Désirée and kissed her, holding her an instant tenderly in her arms. Then she turned to the child.

"This is not the baby!" she exclaimed, in startled tones. French was the language spoken at Valmondé in those days.

"I knew you would be astonished," laughed Désirée, "at the way he has grown. The little *cochon de lait!* Look at his legs, mamma, and his hands and fingernails,—real finger-nails. Zandrine had to cut them this morning. Is n't it true, Zandrine?"

The woman bowed her turbaned head majestically, "Mais si, Madame."

"And the way he cries," went on Désirée, "is deafening. Armand heard him the other day as far away as La Blanche's cabin."

Madame Valmondé had never removed her eyes from the child. She lifted it and walked with it over to the window that was lightest. She scanned the baby narrowly, then looked as searchingly at Zandrine, whose face was turned to gaze across the fields.

"Yes, the child has grown, has changed," said Madame Valmondé, slowly, as she replaced it beside its mother. "What does Armand say?"

Désirée's face became suffused with a glow that was happiness itself.

"Oh, Armand is the proudest father in the parish, I believe, chiefly because it is a boy, to bear his name; though he says not,—that he would have loved a girl as well. But I know it is n't true. I know he says that to please me. And mamma," she added, drawing Madame Valmondé's head down to her, and speaking in a whisper, "he has n't punished one of them—not one of them—since baby is born. Even Négrillon, who pretended to have burnt his leg that he might rest from work—he only laughed, and said Négrillon was a great scamp. Oh, mamma, I'm so happy; it frightens me."

What Désirée said was true. Marriage, and later the birth of his son, had softened Armand Aubigny's imperious and exacting nature greatly. This was what made the gentle Désirée so happy, for she loved him desperately. When he frowned she trembled, but loved him. When he smiled, she asked no greater blessing of God. But Armand's dark, handsome face had not often been disfigured by frowns since the day he fell in love with her.

When the baby was about three months old, Désirée awoke one day to the conviction that there was something in the air menacing her peace. It was at first too subtle to grasp. It had only been a disquieting suggestion; an air of mystery among the blacks; unexpected visits from far-off neighbors who could hardly account for their coming. Then a strange, an awful change in her husband's manner, which she dared not ask him to explain. When he spoke to her, it was with averted eyes, from which the old love-light seemed to have gone out. He absented himself from home; and when there, avoided her presence and that of her child, without excuse. And the very spirit of Satan seemed suddenly to take hold of him in his dealings with the slaves. Désirée was miserable enough to die.

She sat in her room, one hot afternoon, in her *peignoir*, listlessly drawing through her fingers the strands of her long, silky brown hair that hung about her shoulders. The baby, half naked, lay asleep upon her own great mahogany bed, that was like a sumptuous throne, with its satin-lined half-canopy. One of La Blanche's little quadroon boys—half naked too—stood fanning the child slowly with a fan of peacock feathers. Désirée's eyes had been fixed absently and sadly upon the baby, while she was striving to penetrate the threatening mist that she felt closing about her. She looked from her child to the boy who stood beside him, and back again; over and over. "Ah!" It was a cry that she could not help; which she was not conscious of having uttered. The blood turned like ice in her veins, and a clammy moisture gathered upon her face.

She tried to speak to the little quadroon boy; but no sound would come, at first. When he heard his name uttered, he looked up, and his mistress was pointing to the door. He laid aside the great, soft fan, and obediently stole away, over the polished floor, on his bare tiptoes.

She stayed motionless, with gaze riveted upon her child, and her face the picture of fright.

Presently her husband entered the room, and without noticing her, went to a table and began to search among some papers which covered it.

"Armand," she called to him, in a voice which must have stabbed him, if he was human. But he did not notice. "Armand," she said again. Then she rose and tottered towards him. "Armand," she panted once more, clutching his arm, "look at our child. What does it mean? tell me."

He coldly but gently loosened her fingers from about his arm and thrust the hand away from him. "Tell me what it means!" she cried despairingly.

"It means," he answered lightly, "that the child is not white; it means that you are not white."

A quick conception of all that this accusation meant for her nerved her with unwonted courage to deny it. "It is a lie; it is not true, I am white! Look at my hair, it is brown; and my eyes are gray, Armand, you know they are gray. And my skin is fair," seizing his wrist. "Look at my hand; whiter than yours, Armand," she laughed hysterically.

"As white as La Blanche's," he returned cruelly; and went away leaving her alone with their child.

When she could hold a pen in her hand, she sent a despairing letter to Madame Valmondé.

"My mother, they tell me I am not white. Armand has told me I am not white. For God's sake tell them it is not true. You must know it is not true. I shall die. I must die. I cannot be so unhappy, and live."

The answer that came was as brief:

"My own Désirée: Come home to Valmondé; back to your mother who loves you. Come with your child."

When the letter reached Désirée she went with it to her husband's study, and laid it open upon the desk before which he sat. She was like a stone image: silent, white, motionless after she placed it there.

In silence he ran his cold eyes over the written words. He said nothing. "Shall I go, Armand?" she asked in tones sharp with agonized suspense.

"Yes, go."

"Do you want me to go?"

"Yes, I want you to go."

He thought Almighty God had dealt cruelly and unjustly with him; and felt, somehow, that he was paying Him back in kind when he stabbed thus into his wife's soul. Moreover he no longer loved her, because of the unconscious injury she had brought upon his home and his name.

She turned away like one stunned by a blow, and walked slowly towards the door, hoping he would call her back.

"Good-by, Armand," she moaned.

He did not answer her. That was his last blow at fate.

Désirée went in search of her child. Zandrine was pacing the sombre gallery with it. She took the little one from the nurse's arms with no word of explanation, and descending the steps, walked away, under the live-oak branches.

It was an October afternoon; the sun was just sinking. Out in the still fields the negroes were picking cotton.

Désirée had not changed the thin white garment nor the slippers which she wore. Her hair was uncovered and the sun's rays brought a golden gleam from its brown meshes. She did not take the broad, beaten road which led to the far-off plantation of Valmondé. She walked across a deserted field, where the stubble bruised her tender feet, so delicately shod, and tore her thin gown to shreds.

She disappeared among the reeds and willows that grew thick along the banks of the deep, sluggish bayou; and she did not come back again.

Some weeks later there was a curious scene enacted at L'Abri. In the centre of the smoothly swept back yard was a great bonfire. Armand Aubigny sat in the wide hallway that commanded a view of the spectacle; and it was he who dealt out to a half dozen negroes the material which kept this fire ablaze.

A graceful cradle of willow, with all its dainty furbishings, was laid upon the pyre, which had already been fed with the richness of a priceless *layette*. Then there were silk gowns, and velvet and satin ones added to these; laces, too, and embroideries; bonnets and gloves; for the *corbeille* had been of rare quality.

The last thing to go was a tiny bundle of letters; innocent little scribblings that Désirée had sent to him during the days of their espousal. There was the remnant of one back in the drawer from which he took them. But it was not Désirée's; it was part of an old letter from his mother to his father. He read it. She was thanking God for the blessing of her husband's love:—

"But, above all," she wrote, "night and day, I thank the good God for having so arranged our lives that our dear Armand will never know that his mother, who adores him, belongs to the race that is cursed with the brand of slavery."

35

"Uncle Wellington's Wives"

Charles W. Chesnutt

Charles W. Chesnutt (1858–1932), a preeminent figure in African American letters, wrote novels, short stories, and essays that used subtle irony and psychological realism to critique social injustice. Chesnutt, the son of free blacks, both of interracial parentage, was raised in Fayetteville, North Carolina, and became a school principal at the Normal School there before moving to Cleveland, where he established a legal stenography business. His 1887 story "The Goophered Grapevine" was the first work by an African American author to be published in the *Atlantic Monthly*. His 1899 story collection *The Conjure Woman* introduced a white audience to Afro-American hoodoo and dialect, and ultimately to a more human, dignified portrait of African Americans themselves. William Dean Howells praised Chesnutt's short stories and compared him to James, Turgenev, and Maupassant. Chesnutt's collection *The Wife of His Youth and Other Stories of the Color Line*, also published in 1899, took a more controversial direction as it unapologetically examined taboo interracial issues. "Uncle Wellington's Wives" represents a rare instance of a humorous treatment of such subject matter.

I

Uncle Wellington Braboy was so deeply absorbed in thought as he walked slowly homeward from the weekly meeting of the Union League, that he let his pipe go out, a fact of which he remained oblivious until he had reached the little frame house in the suburbs of Patesville, where he lived with aunt Milly, his wife. On this particular occasion the club had been addressed by a visiting brother from the North, Professor Patterson, a tall, well-formed mulatto, who wore a perfectly fitting suit of broadcloth, a shiny silk hat, and linen of dazzling whiteness,—in short, a gentleman of such distinguished appearance that the doors and windows of the offices and stores on Front Street were filled with curious observers as he passed through that thoroughfare in the early part of the day. This polished stranger was a traveling organizer of Masonic lodges, but he also claimed to be a high officer in the Union League, and had been invited to lecture before the local chapter of that organization at Patesville.

The lecture had been largely attended, and uncle Wellington Braboy had occupied a seat just in front of the platform. The subject of the lecture was "The Mental, Moral, Physical, Political, Social, and Financial Improvement of the Negro Race in America," a theme much dwelt upon, with slight variations, by colored orators. For to this struggling people, then as now, the problem of their uncertain present and their doubtful future was the chief concern of life. The period was the hopeful one. The Federal Government retained some vestige of authority in the South, and the newly emancipated race cherished the delusion that under the Constitution, that enduring rock on which our liberties are founded, and under the equal laws it purported to guarantee, they would enter upon the era of freedom and opportunity which their Northern friends had inaugurated with such solemn sanctions. The speaker pictured in eloquent language the state of ideal equality and happiness enjoyed by colored people at the North: how they sent their children to school with the white children; how they sat by white people in the churches and theatres, ate with them in the public restaurants, and buried their dead in the same cemeteries. The professor waxed eloquent with the development of his theme, and, as a finishing touch to an alluring picture, assured the excited audience that the intermarriage of the races was common, and that he himself had espoused a white woman.

Uncle Wellington Braboy was a deeply interested listener. He had heard something of these facts before, but his information had always come in such vague and questionable shape that he had paid little attention to it. He knew that the Yankees had freed the slaves, and that runaway negroes had always gone to the North to seek liberty; any such equality, however, as the visiting brother had depicted, was more than uncle Wellington had ever conceived as actually existing anywhere in the world. At first he felt inclined to doubt the truth of the speaker's statements; but the cut of his clothes, the eloquence of his language, and the flowing length of his whiskers, were so far superior to anything uncle Wellington had ever met among the colored people of his native State, that he felt irresistibly impelled to the conviction that nothing less than the advantages claimed for the North by the visiting brother could have produced such an exquisite flower of civilization. Any lingering doubts uncle Wellington may have felt were entirely dispelled by the courtly bow and cordial grasp of the hand with which the visiting brother acknowledged the congratulations showered upon him by the audience at the close of his address.

The more uncle Wellington's mind dwelt upon the professor's speech, the more attractive seemed the picture of Northern life presented. Uncle Wellington possessed in large measure the imaginative faculty so freely bestowed by nature upon the race from which the darker half of his blood was drawn. He had indulged in occasional daydreams of an ideal state of social equality, but his wildest flights of fancy had never located it nearer than heaven, and he had felt some misgivings about its practical working even there. Its desirability he had never doubted, and the speech of the evening before had given a local habitation and a name to the forms his imagination had bodied forth. Giving full rein to his fancy, he saw in the North a land flowing with milk and honey,—a land peopled by noble men and beautiful women, among whom colored men and women moved with the ease and grace of acknowledged right. Then he placed himself in the foreground of the picture. What a fine figure he would have made in the world if he had been born at the free North! He imagined himself dressed like the professor, and passing the contribution-box in a white church; and most pleasant of his dreams, and the hardest to realize as possible, was that of the gracious white lady he might have called wife. Uncle Wellington was a mulatto, and his features were those of his white father, though tinged with the hue of his mother's race; and as he lifted the kerosene lamp at evening, and took a long look at his image in the little mirror over the mantelpiece, he said to himself that he was a very good-looking man, and could have adorned a much higher sphere in life than that in which the accident of birth had placed him. He fell asleep and dreamed that he lived in a two-story brick house, with a spacious flower garden in front, the whole inclosed by a high iron fence; that he kept a carriage and servants, and never did a stroke of work. This was the highest style of living in Patesville, and he could conceive of nothing finer.

Uncle Wellington slept later than usual the next morning, and the sunlight was pouring in at the open window of the bedroom, when his dreams were interrupted by the voice of his wife, in tones meant to be harsh, but which no ordinary degree of passion could rob of their native unctuousness.

"Git up f'm dere, you lazy, good-fuh-nuffin' nigger! Is you gwine ter sleep all de mawnin'? I's ti'ed er dis yer runnin' 'roun' all night an' den sleepin' all day. You won't git dat tater patch hoed ovuh ter-day 'less'n you git up f'm dere an' git at it."

Uncle Wellington rolled over, yawned cavernously, stretched himself, and with a muttered protest got out of bed and put on his clothes. Aunt Milly had prepared a smoking breakfast of hominy and fried bacon, the odor of which was very grateful to his nostrils.

"Is breakfus' done ready?" he inquired, tentatively, as he came into the kitchen and glanced at the table.

"No, it ain't ready, an' 't ain't gwine ter be ready 'tel you tote dat wood an' water in," replied aunt Milly severely, as she poured two teacups of boiling water on two table-spoonfuls of ground coffee.

Uncle Wellington went down to the spring and got a pail of water, after which he brought in some oak logs for the fireplace and some lightwood for kindling. Then he drew a chair towards the table and started to sit down.

"Wonduh what's de matter wid you dis mawnin' anyhow," remarked aunt Milly. "You must 'a' be'n up ter some devilment las' night, fer yo' recommemb'ance is so po' dat you fus' fergit ter git up, an' den fergit ter wash yo' face an' hands fo' you set down ter de table. I don' 'low nobody ter eat at my table dat a-way."

"I don' see no use 'n washin' 'em so much," replied Wellington wearily. "Dey gits dirty ag'in right off, an' den you got ter wash 'em ovuh ag'in; it 's jes' pilin' up wuk what don' fetch in nuffin'. De dirt don' show nohow, 'n' I don' see no advantage in bein' black, ef you got to keep on washin' yo' face 'n' han's jes' lack w'ite folks." He nevertheless performed his ablutions in a perfunctory way, and resumed his seat at the breakfast-table.

"Ole 'oman," he asked, after the edge of his appetite had been taken off, "how would you lack ter live at de Norf?"

"I dunno nuffin' 'bout de Norf," replied aunt Milly. "It's hard 'nuff ter git erlong heah, whar we knows all erbout it."

"De brother what 'dressed de meetin' las' night say dat de wages at de Norf is twicet ez big ez dey is heah."

"You could make a sight mo' wages heah ef you 'd 'ten' ter yo' wuk better," replied aunt Milly.

Uncle Wellington ignored this personality, and continued, "An' he say de cullud folks got all de privileges er de w'ite folks,—dat dey chillen goes ter school tergedder, dat dey sets on same seats in chu'ch, an' sarves on jury, 'n' rides on de kyars an' steamboats wid de w'ite folks, an' eats at de fus' table."

"Dat 'u'd suit you," chuckled aunt Milly, "an' you 'd stay dere fer de secon' table, too. How dis man know 'bout all dis yer foolis'ness?" she asked incredulously.

"He come f'm de Norf," said uncle Wellington, "an' he 'speunced it all hisse'f."

"Well, he can't make me b'lieve it," she rejoined, with a shake of her head.

"An' you would n' lack ter go up dere an' 'joy all dese privileges?" asked uncle Wellington, with some degree of earnestness.

The old woman laughed until her sides shook. "Who gwine ter take me up dere?" she inquired.

"You got de money yo'se'f."

"I ain' got no money fer ter was'e," she replied shortly, becoming serious at once; and with that the subject was dropped.

Uncle Wellington pulled a hoe from under the house, and took his way wearily to the potato patch. He did not feel like working, but aunt Milly was the undisputed head of the establishment, and he did not dare to openly neglect his work. In fact, he regarded work at any time as a disagreeable necessity to be avoided as much as possible.

His wife was cast in a different mould. Externally she would have impressed the casual observer as a neat, well-preserved, and good-looking black woman, of middle age, every curve of whose ample figure—and her figure was all curves—was suggestive of repose. So far from being indolent, or even deliberate in her movements, she was the most active and energetic woman in the town. She went through the physical exercises of a prayer-meeting with astonishing vigor. It was exhilarating to see her wash a shirt, and a study to watch her do it up. A quick jerk shook out the dampened garment; one pass of her ample palm spread it over the ironing-board, and a few well-directed strokes with the iron accomplished what would have occupied the ordinary laundress for half an hour.

To this uncommon, and in uncle Wellington's opinion unnecessary and unnatural activity, his own habits were a steady protest. If aunt Milly had been willing to support him in idleness, he would have acquiesced without a murmur in her habits of industry. This she would not do, and, moreover, insisted on his working at least half the time. If she had invested the proceeds of her labor in rich food and fine clothing, he might have endured it better; but to her passion for work was added a most detestable thrift. She absolutely refused to pay for Wellington's clothes, and required him to furnish a certain proportion of the family supplies. Her savings were carefully put by, and with them she had bought and paid for the modest cottage which she and her husband occupied. Under her careful hand it was always neat and clean; in summer the little yard was gay with bright-colored flowers, and woe to the heedless pickaninny who should stray into her yard and pluck a rose or a verbena! In a stout oaken chest under her bed she kept a capacious stocking, into which flowed a steady stream of fractional currency. She carried the key to this chest in her pocket, a proceeding regarded by uncle Wellington with no little disfavor. He was of the opinion—an opinion he would not have dared to assert in her presence—that his wife's earnings were his own property; and he looked upon this stocking as a drunkard's wife might regard the saloon which absorbed her husband's wages.

Uncle Wellington hurried over the potato patch on the morning of the conversation above recorded, and as soon as he saw aunt Milly go away with a basket of clothes on her head, returned to the house, put on his coat, and went uptown.

He directed his steps to a small frame building fronting on the main street of the village, at a point where the street was intersected by one of the several creeks meandering through the town, cooling the air, providing numerous swimming-holes for the amphibious small boy, and furnishing water-power for grist-mills and saw-mills. The rear of the building rested on long brick pillars, built up from the bottom of the steep bank of the creek, while the front was level with the street. This was the office of Mr. Matthew Wright, the sole representative of the colored race at the bar of Chinquapin County. Mr. Wright came of an "old issue" free colored family, in which, though the negro blood was present in an attenuated strain, a line of free ancestry could be traced beyond the Revolutionary War. He had enjoyed exceptional opportunities, and enjoyed the distinction of being the first, and for a long time the only colored lawyer in North Carolina. His services were frequently called into requisition by impecunious people of his own race; when they had money they went to white lawyers, who, they shrewdly conjectured, would have more influence with judge or jury than a colored lawyer, however able.

Uncle Wellington found Mr. Wright in his office. Having inquired after the health of the lawyer's family and all his relations in detail, uncle Wellington asked for a professional opinion.

"Mistah Wright, ef a man's wife got money, whose money is dat befo' de law—his'n er her'n?"

The lawyer put on his professional air, and replied:—

"Under the common law, which in default of special legislative enactment is the law of North Carolina, the personal property of the wife belongs to her husband."

"But dat don' jes' tech de p'int, suh. I wuz axin' 'bout money."

"You see, uncle Wellington, your education has not rendered you familiar with legal phraseology. The term 'personal property' or 'estate' embraces, according to Blackstone, all property other than land, and therefore includes money. Any money a man's wife has is his, constructively, and will be recognized as his actually, as soon as he can secure possession of it."

"Dat is ter say, suh—my eddication don' quite 'low me ter understan' dat—dat is ter say"—

"That is to say, it's yours when you get it. It isn't yours so that the law will help you get it; but on the other hand, when you once lay your hands on it, it is yours so that the law won't take it away from you."

Uncle Wellington nodded to express his full comprehension of the law as expounded by Mr. Wright, but scratched his head in a way that expressed some disappointment. The law seemed to wobble. Instead of enabling him to stand up fearlessly and demand his own, it threw him back upon his own efforts; and the prospect of his being able to overpower or outwit aunt Milly by any ordinary means was very poor.

He did not leave the office, but hung around awhile as though there were something further he wished to speak about. Finally, after some discursive remarks about the crops and politics, he asked, in an offhand, disinterested manner, as though the thought had just occurred to him:—

"Mistah Wright, w'ile 's we're talkin' 'bout law matters, what do it cos' ter git a defoce?"

"That depends upon circumstances. It isn't altogether a matter of expense. Have you and aunt Milly been having trouble?"

"Oh no, suh; I was jes' a-wond'rin'."

"You see," continued the lawyer, who was fond of talking, and had nothing else to do for the moment, "a divorce is not an easy thing to get in this State under any circumstances. It used to be the law that divorce could be granted only by special act of the legislature; and it is but recently that the subject has been relegated to the jurisdiction of the courts."

Uncle Wellington understood a part of this, but the answer had not been exactly to the point in his mind.

"S'pos'n', den, jes' fer de argyment, me an' my ole 'oman sh'd fall out en wanter separate, how could I git a defoce?"

"That would depend on what you quarreled about. It's pretty hard work to answer general questions in a particular way. If you merely wished to separate, it would n't be necessary to get a divorce; but if you should want to marry again, you would have to be divorced, or else you would be guilty of bigamy, and could be sent to the penitentiary. But, by the way, uncle Wellington, when were you married?"

"I got married 'fo' de wah, when I was livin' down on Rockfish Creek."

"When you were in slavery?"

"Yas, suh."

"Did you have your marriage registered after the surrender?"

"No, suh; never knowed nuffin' 'bout dat."

After the war, in North Carolina and other States, the freed people who had sustained to each other the relation of husband and wife as it existed among slaves, were required by law to register their consent to continue in the marriage relation. By this simple expedient their former marriages of convenience received the sanction of law, and their children the seal of legitimacy. In many cases, however, where the parties lived in districts remote from the larger towns, the ceremony was neglected, or never heard of by the freedmen.

"Well," said the lawyer, "if that is the case, and you and aunt Milly should disagree, it wouldn't be necessary for you to get a divorce, even if you should want to marry again. You were never legally married."

"So Milly ain't my lawful wife, den?"

"She may be your wife in one sense of the word, but not in such a sense as to render you liable to punishment for bigamy if you should marry another woman. But I hope you will never want to do anything of the kind, for you have a very good wife now."

Uncle Wellington went away thoughtfully, but with a feeling of unaccustomed lightness and freedom. He had not felt so free since the memorable day when he had first heard of the Emancipation Proclamation. On leaving the lawyer's office, he called at the workshop of one of his friends, Peter Williams, a shoemaker by trade, who had a brother living in Ohio.

"Is you hearn f'm Sam lately?" uncle Wellington inquired, after the conversation had drifted through the usual generalities.

"His mammy got er letter f'm 'im las' week; he 's livin' in de town er Groveland now."

"How 's he gittin' on?"

"He says he gittin' on monst'us well. He 'low ez how he make five dollars a day w'ite-washin', an' have all he kin do."

The shoemaker related various details of his brother's prosperity, and uncle Wellington returned home in a very thoughtful mood, revolving in his mind a plan of future action. This plan had been vaguely assuming form ever since the professor's lecture, and the events of the morning had brought out the detail in bold relief.

Two days after the conversation with the shoemaker, aunt Milly went, in the afternoon, to visit a sister of hers who lived several miles out in the country. During her absence, which lasted until nightfall, uncle Wellington went uptown and purchased a cheap oilcloth valise from a shrewd son of Israel, who had penetrated to this locality with a stock of notions and cheap clothing. Uncle Wellington had his purchase done up in brown paper, and took the parcel under his arm. Arrived at home he unwrapped the valise, and thrust into its capacious jaws his best suit of clothes, some underwear, and a few other small articles for personal use and adornment. Then he carried the valise out into the yard, and, first looking cautiously around to see if there was any one in sight, concealed it in a clump of bushes in a corner of the yard.

It may be inferred from this proceeding that uncle Wellington was preparing for a step of some consequence. In fact, he had fully made up his mind to go to the North; but he still lacked the most important requisite for traveling with comfort, namely, the money to pay his expenses. The idea of tramping the distance which separated him from the promised land of liberty and equality had never occurred to him. When a slave, he had several times been importuned by fellow servants to join them in the attempt to escape from bondage, but he had never wanted his freedom badly enough to walk a thousand miles for it; if he could have gone to Canada by stage-coach, or by rail, or on horseback, with stops for regular meals, he would probably have undertaken the trip. The funds he now needed for his journey were in aunt Milly's chest. He had thought a great deal about his right to this money. It was his wife's savings, and he had never dared to dispute, openly, her right to exercise exclusive control over what she earned; but the lawyer had assured him of his right to the money, of which he was already constructively in possession, and he had therefore determined to possess himself actually of the coveted stocking. It was impracticable for him to get the key of the chest. Aunt Milly kept it in her pocket by day and under her pillow at night. She was a light sleeper, and, if not awakened by the abstraction of the key, would certainly have been disturbed by the unlocking of the chest. But one alternative remained, and that was to break open the chest in her absence.

There was a revival in progress at the colored Methodist church. Aunt Milly was as energetic in her religion as in other respects, and had not missed a single one of the meetings. She returned at nightfall from her visit to the country and prepared a frugal supper. Uncle Wellington did not eat as heartily as usual. Aunt Milly perceived his want of appetite, and spoke of it. He explained it by saying that he did not feel very well.

"Is you gwine ter chu'ch ter-night?" inquired his wife.

"I reckon I'll stay home an' go ter bed," he replied. "I ain' be'n feelin' well dis evenin', an' I'spec' I better git a good night's res'."

"Well, you kin stay ef you mineter. Good preachin' 'u'd make you feel better, but ef you ain't gwine, don' fergit ter tote in some wood an' lighterd 'fo' you go ter bed. De moon is shinin' bright, an' you can't have no 'scuse 'bout not bein' able ter see."

Uncle Wellington followed her out to the gate, and watched her receding form until it disappeared in the distance. Then he re-entered the house with a quick step, and taking a hatchet from a corner of the room, drew the chest from under the bed. As he applied the hatchet to the fastenings, a thought struck him, and by the flickering light of the pine-knot blazing on the hearth, a look of hesitation might have been seen to take the place of the determined expression his face had worn up to that time. He had argued himself into the belief that his present action was lawful and justifiable. Though this conviction had not prevented him from trembling in every limb, as though he were committing a mere vulgar theft, it had still nerved him to the deed. Now even his moral courage began to weaken. The lawyer had told him that his wife's property was his own; in taking it he was therefore only exercising his lawful right. But at the point of breaking open the chest, it occurred to him that he was taking this money in order to get away from aunt Milly, and that he justified his desertion of her by the lawyer's opinion that she was not his lawful wife. If she was not his wife, then he had no right to take the money; if she was his wife, he had no right to desert her, and would certainly have no right to marry another woman. His scheme was about to go to shipwreck on this rock, when another idea occurred to him.

"De lawyer say dat in one sense er de word de ole 'oman is my wife, an' in anudder sense er de word she ain't my wife. Ef I goes ter de Norf an' marry a w'ite 'oman, I ain't commit no brigamy, 'caze in dat sense er de word she ain't my wife; but ef I takes dis money, I ain't stealin' it, 'caze in dat sense er de word she is my wife. Dat 'splains all de trouble away."

Having reached this ingenious conclusion, uncle Wellington applied the hatchet vigorously, soon loosened the fastenings of the chest, and with trembling hands extracted from its depths a capacious blue cotton stocking. He emptied the stocking on the table. His first impulse was to take the whole, but again there arose in his mind a doubt—a very obtrusive, unreasonable doubt, but a doubt, nevertheless—of the absolute rectitude of his conduct; and after a moment's hesitation he hurriedly counted the money—it was in bills of small denominations—and found it to be about two hundred and fifty dollars. He then divided it into two piles of one hundred and twenty-five dollars each. He put one pile into his pocket, returned the remainder to the stocking, and replaced it where he had found it. He then closed the chest and shoved it under the bed. After having arranged the fire so that it could safely be left burning, he took a last look around the room, and went out into the moonlight, locking the door behind him, and hanging the key on a nail in the wall, where his wife would be likely to look for it. He then secured his valise from behind the bushes, and left the yard. As he passed by the wood-pile, he said to himself:—

"Well, I declar' ef I ain't done fergot ter tote in dat lighterd; I reckon de ole 'oman, 'll ha' ter fetch it in herse'f dis time."

He hastened through the quiet streets, avoiding the few people who were abroad at that hour, and soon reached the railroad station, from which a North-bound train left at nine o'clock. He went around to the dark side of the train, and climbed into a second-class car, where he shrank into the darkest corner and turned his face away from the dim light of the single dirty lamp. There were no passengers in the car except one or two sleepy negroes, who had got on at some other station, and a white man who had gone into the car to smoke, accompanied by a gigantic bloodhound.

Finally the train crept out of the station. From the window uncle Wellington looked out upon the familiar cabins and turpentine stills, the new barrel factory, the brickyard where he had once worked for some time; and as the train rattled through the outskirts of the town, he saw gleaming in the moonlight the white headstones of the colored cemetery where his only daughter had been buried several years before.

Presently the conductor came around. Uncle Wellington had not bought a ticket, and the conductor collected a cash fare. He was not acquainted with uncle Wellington, but had just had a drink at the saloon near the depot, and felt at peace with all mankind.

"Where are you going, uncle?" he inquired carelessly.

Uncle Wellington's face assumed the ashen hue which does duty for pallor in dusky countenances, and his knees began to tremble. Controlling his voice as well as he could, he replied that he was going up to Jonesboro, the terminus of the railroad, to work for a gentleman at that place. He felt immensely relieved when the conductor pocketed the fare, picked up his lantern, and moved away. It was very unphilosophical and very absurd that a man who was only doing right should feel like a thief, shrink from the sight of other people, and lie instinctively. Fine distinctions were not in uncle Wellington's line, but he was struck by the unreasonableness of his feelings, and still more by the discomfort they caused him. By and by, however, the motion of the train made him drowsy; his thoughts all ran together in confusion; and he fell asleep with his head on his valise, and one hand in his pocket, clasped tightly around the roll of money.

II

The train from Pittsburg drew into the Union Depot at Groveland, Ohio, one morning in the spring of 187–, with bell ringing and engine puffing; and from a smoking-car emerged the form of uncle Wellington Braboy, a little dusty and travel-stained, and with a sleepy look about his eyes. He mingled in the crowd, and, valise in hand, moved toward the main exit from the depot. There were several tracks to be crossed, and more than once a watchman snatched him out of the way of a baggage-truck, or a train backing into the depot. He at length reached the door, beyond which, and as near as the regulations would permit, stood a number of hackmen, vociferously soliciting patronage. One of them, a colored man, soon secured several passengers. As he closed the door after the last one he turned to uncle Wellington, who stood near him on the sidewalk, looking about irresolutely.

"Is you goin' uptown?" asked the hackman, as he prepared to mount the box.

"Yas, suh."

"I'll take you up fo' a quahtah, ef you want ter git up here an' ride on de box wid me."

Uncle Wellington accepted the offer and mounted the box. The hackman whipped up his horses, the carriage climbed the steep hill leading up to the town, and the passengers inside were soon deposited at their hotels.

"Whereabouts do you want to go?" asked the hackman of uncle Wellington, when the carriage was emptied of its last passengers.

"I want ter go ter Brer Sam Williams's," said Wellington.

"What's his street an' number?"

Uncle Wellington did not know the street and number, and the hackman had to explain to him the mystery of numbered houses, to which he was a total stranger.

"Where is he from?" asked the hackman, "and what is his business?"

"He is f'm Norf Ca'lina," replied uncle Wellington, "an' makes his livin' w'ite-washin'."

"I reckon I knows de man," said the hackman. "I 'spec' he 's changed his name. De man I knows is name' Johnson. He b'longs ter my chu'ch. I'm gwine out dat way ter git a passenger fer de ten o'clock train, an' I'll take you by dere."

They followed one of the least handsome streets of the city for more than a mile, turned into a cross street, and drew up before a small frame house, from the front of which a sign, painted in white upon a black background, announced to the reading public, in letters inclined to each other at various angles, that whitewashing and kalsomining were "dun" there. A knock at the door brought out a slatternly looking colored woman. She had evidently been disturbed at her toilet, for she held a comb in one hand, and the hair on one side of her head stood out loosely, while on the other side it was braided close to her head. She called her husband, who proved to be the Patesville shoemaker's brother. The hackman introduced the traveler, whose name he had learned on the way out, collected his quarter, and drove away.

Mr. Johnson, the shoemaker's brother, welcomed uncle Wellington to Groveland, and listened with eager delight to the news of the old town, from which he himself had run away many years before, and followed the North Star to Groveland. He had changed his name from "Williams" to "Johnson," on account of the Fugitive Slave Law, which, at the time of his escape from bondage, had rendered it advisable for runaway slaves to court obscurity. After the war he had retained the adopted name. Mrs. Johnson prepared breakfast for her guest, who ate it with an appetite sharpened by his journey. After breakfast he went to bed, and slept until late in the afternoon.

After supper Mr. Johnson took uncle Wellington to visit some of the neighbors who had come from North Carolina before the war. They all expressed much pleasure at meeting "Mr. Braboy," a title which at first sounded a little odd to uncle Wellington. At home he had been "Wellin'ton," "Brer Wellin'ton," or "uncle Wellin'ton;" it was a novel experience to be called "Mister," and he set it down, with secret satisfaction, as one of the first fruits of Northern liberty.

"Would you lack ter look 'roun' de town a little?" asked Mr. Johnson at breakfast next morning. "I ain' got no job dis mawnin', an' I kin show you some er de sights."

Uncle Wellington acquiesced in this arrangement, and they walked up to the corner to the street-car line. In a few moments a car passed. Mr. Johnson jumped on the moving car, and uncle Wellington followed his example, at the risk of life or limb, as it was his first experience of street cars.

There was only one vacant seat in the car and that was between two white women in the forward end. Mr. Johnson motioned to the seat, but Wellington shrank from walking between those two rows of white people, to say nothing of sitting between the two women, so he remained standing in the rear part of the car. A moment later, as the car rounded a short curve, he was pitched sidewise into the lap of a stout woman magnificently attired in a ruffled blue calico gown. The lady colored up, and uncle Wellington, as he struggled to his feet amid the laughter of the passengers, was absolutely helpless with embarrassment, until the conductor came up behind him and pushed him toward the vacant place.

"Sit down, will you," he said; and before uncle Wellington could collect himself, he was seated between the two white women. Everybody in the car seemed to be looking at him. But he came to the conclusion, after he had pulled himself together and reflected a few moments, that he would find this method of locomotion pleasanter when he got used to it, and then he could score one more glorious privilege gained by his change of residence.

They got off at the public square, in the heart of the city, where there were flowers and statues, and fountains playing. Mr. Johnson pointed out the court-house, the post-office, the jail, and other public buildings fronting on the square. They visited the market near by, and from an elevated point, looked down upon the extensive lumber yards and factories that were the chief sources of the city's prosperity. Beyond these they could see the fleet of ships that lined the coal and iron ore docks of the harbor. Mr. Johnson, who was quite a fluent talker, enlarged upon the wealth and prosperity of the city; and Wellington, who had never before been in a town of more than three thousand inhabitants, manifested sufficient interest and wonder to satisfy the most exacting *cicerone*. They called at the office of a colored lawyer and member of the legislature, formerly from North Carolina, who, scenting a new constituent and a possible client, greeted the stranger warmly, and in flowing speech pointed out the superior advantages of life at the North, citing himself as an illustration of the possibilities of life in a country really free. As they wended their way homeward to dinner uncle Wellington, with quickened pulse and rising hopes, felt that this was indeed the promised land, and that it must be flowing with milk and honey.

Uncle Wellington remained at the residence of Mr. Johnson for several weeks before making any effort to find employment. He spent this period in looking about the city. The most commonplace things possessed for him the charm of novelty, and he had come prepared to admire. Shortly after his arrival, he had offered to pay for his board, intimating at the same time that he had plenty of money. Mr. Johnson declined to accept anything from him for board, and expressed himself as being only too proud to have Mr. Braboy remain in the house on the footing of an honored guest, until he had settled himself. He lightened in some degree, however, the burden of obligation under which a prolonged stay on these terms would have placed his guest, by soliciting from the latter occasional small loans, until uncle Wellington's roll of money began to lose its plumpness, and with an empty pocket staring him in the face, he felt the necessity of finding something to do.

During his residence in the city he had met several times his first acquaintance, Mr. Peterson, the hackman, who from time to time inquired how he was getting along. On one of these occasions Wellington mentioned his willingness to accept employment. As good luck would have it, Mr. Peterson knew of a vacant situation. He had formerly been coachman for a wealthy gentleman residing on Oakwood Avenue, but had resigned the situation to go into business for himself. His place had been filled by an Irishman, who had just been discharged for drunkenness, and the gentleman that very day had sent word to Mr. Peterson, asking him if he could recommend a competent and trustworthy coachman.

"Does you know anything erbout hosses?" asked Mr. Peterson.

"Yas, indeed, I does," said Wellington. "I wuz raise' 'mongs' hosses."

"I tol' my ole boss I 'd look out fer a man, an' ef you reckon you kin fill de 'quirements er de situation, I 'll take yo' roun' dere termorrer mornin'. You wants ter put on yo' bes' clothes an' slick up, fer dey 're partic'lar people. Ef you git de place I 'll expec' you ter pay me fer de time I lose in 'tendin' ter yo' business, fer time is money in dis country, an' folks don't do much fer nuthin'."

Next morning Wellington blacked his shoes carefully, put on a clean collar, and with the aid of Mrs. Johnson tied his cravat in a jaunty bow which gave him quite a sprightly air and a much younger look than his years warranted. Mr. Peterson called for him at eight o'clock. After traversing several cross streets they turned into Oakwood Avenue and walked along the finest part of it for about half a mile. The handsome houses of this famous avenue, the stately trees, the widespreading lawns, dotted with flower beds, fountains and statuary, made up a picture so far surpassing anything in Wellington's experience as to fill him with an almost oppressive sense of its beauty.

"Hit looks lack hebben," he said softly.

"It 's a pootty fine street," rejoined his companion, with a judicial air, "but I don't like dem big lawns. It's too much trouble ter keep de grass down. One er dem lawns is big enough to pasture a couple er cows."

They went down a street running at right angles to the avenue, and turned into the rear of the corner lot. A large building of pressed brick, trimmed with stone, loomed up before them.

"Do de gemman lib in dis house?" asked Wellington, gazing with awe at the front of the building.

"No, dat 's de barn," said Mr. Peterson with good-natured contempt; and leading the way past a clump of shrubbery to the dwelling-house, he went up the back steps and rang the door-bell.

The ring was answered by a buxom Irish-woman, of a natural freshness of complexion deepened to a fiery red by the heat of a kitchen range. Wellington thought he had seen her before, but his mind had received so many new impressions lately that it was a minute or two before he recognized in her the lady whose lap he had involuntarily occupied for a moment on his first day in Groveland.

"Faith," she exclaimed as she admitted them, "an' it 's mighty glad I am to see ye ag'in, Misther Payterson! An' how hev ye be'n, Misther Payterson, sence I see ye lahst?"

"Middlin' well, Mis' Flannigan, middlin' well, 'ceptin' a tech er de rheumatiz. S'pose you be'n doin' well as usual?"

"Oh yis, as well as a dacent woman could do wid a drunken baste about the place like the lahst coachman. O Misther Payterson, it would make yer heart bleed to see the way the spalpeen cut up a-Saturday! But Misther Todd discharged 'im the same avenin', widout a charachter, bad 'cess to 'im, an' we 've had no coachman sence at all, at all. An' it 's sorry I am"—

The lady's flow of eloquence was interrupted at this point by the appearance of Mr. Todd himself, who had been informed of the men's arrival. He asked some questions in regard to Wellington's qualifications and former experience, and in view of his recent arrival in the city was willing to accept Mr. Peterson's recommendation instead of a reference. He said a few words about the nature of the work, and stated his willingness to pay Wellington the wages formerly allowed Mr. Peterson, thirty dollars a month and board and lodging.

This handsome offer was eagerly accepted, and it was agreed that Wellington's term of service should begin immediately. Mr. Peterson, being familiar with the work, and financially interested, conducted the new coachman through the stables and showed him what he would have to do. The silver-mounted harness, the variety of carriages, the names of which he learned for the first time, the arrangements for feeding and watering the horses,—these appointments of a rich man's stable impressed Wellington very much, and he wondered that so much luxury should be wasted on mere horses. The room assigned to him, in the second story of the barn, was a finer apartment than he had ever slept in; and the salary attached to the situation was greater than the combined monthly earnings of himself and aunt Milly in their Southern home. Surely, he thought, his lines had fallen in pleasant places.

Under the stimulus of new surroundings Wellington applied himself diligently to work, and, with the occasional advice of Mr. Peterson, soon mastered the details of his employment. He found the female servants, with whom he took his meals, very amiable ladies. The cook, Mrs. Katie Flannigan, was a widow. Her husband, a sailor, had been lost at sea. She was a woman of many words, and when she was not lamenting the late Flannigan's loss,—according to her story he had been a model of all the virtues,—she would turn the batteries of her tongue against the former coachman. This gentleman, as Wellington gathered from frequent remarks dropped by Mrs. Flannigan, had paid her attentions clearly susceptible of a serious construction. These attentions had not borne their legitimate fruit, and she was still a widow unconsoled,—hence Mrs. Flannigan's tears. The housemaid was a plump, good-natured German girl, with a pronounced German accent. The presence on washdays of a Bohemian laundress, of recent importation, added another to the variety of ways in which the English tongue was mutilated in Mr. Todd's kitchen. Association with the white women drew out all the native gallantry of the mulatto, and Wellington developed quite a helpful turn. His politeness, his willingness to lend a hand in kitchen or laundry, and the fact that he was the only male servant on the place, combined to make him a prime favorite in the servants' quarters.

It was the general opinion among Wellington's acquaintances that he was a single man. He had come to the city alone, had never been heard to speak of a wife, and to personal questions bearing upon the subject of matrimony had always returned evasive answers. Though he had never questioned the correctness of the lawyer's opinion in regard to his slave marriage, his conscience had never been entirely at ease since his departure from the South, and any positive denial of his married condition would have stuck in his throat. The inference naturally drawn from his reticence in regard to the past, coupled with his expressed intention of settling permanently in Groveland, was that he belonged in the ranks of the unmarried, and was therefore legitimate game for any widow or old maid who could bring him down. As such game is bagged easiest at short range, he received numerous invitations to tea-parties, where he feasted on unlimited chicken and pound cake. He used to compare these viands with the plain fare often served by aunt Milly, and the result of the comparison was another item to the credit of the North upon his mental ledger. Several of the colored ladies who smiled upon him were blessed with good looks, and uncle Wellington, naturally of a susceptible temperament, as people of lively imagination are apt to be, would probably have fallen a victim to the charms of some woman of his own race, had it not been for a strong counter-attraction in the person of Mrs. Flannigan. The attentions of the lately discharged coachman had lighted anew the smouldering fires of her widowed heart, and awakened longings which still remained unsatisfied. She was thirty-five years old, and felt the need of some one else to love. She was not a woman of lofty ideals; with her a man was a man—

> "For a' that an' a' that;"

and, aside from the accident of color, uncle Wellington was as personable a man as any of her acquaintance. Some people might have objected to his complexion; but then, Mrs. Flannigan argued, he was at least half white; and, this being the case, there was no good reason why he should be regarded as black.

Uncle Wellington was not slow to perceive Mrs. Flannigan's charms of person, and appreciated to the full the skill that prepared the choice tidbits reserved for his plate at dinner. The prospect of securing a white wife had been one of the principal inducements offered by a life at the North; but the awe of white people in which he had been reared was still too strong to permit his taking any active steps toward the object of his secret desire, had not the lady herself come to his assistance with a little of the native coquetry of her race.

"Ah, Misther Braboy," she said one evening when they sat at the supper table alone,—it was the second girl's afternoon off, and she had not come home to supper,—"it must be an awful lonesome life ye 've been afther l'adin', as a single man, wid no one to cook fer ye, or look afther ye."

"It are a kind er lonesome life, Mis' Flannigan, an' dat's a fac'. But sence I had de privilege er eatin' yo' cookin' an' 'joyin' yo' society, I ain' felt a bit lonesome."

"Yer flatthrin' me, Misther Braboy. An' even if ye mane it"—

"I means eve'y word of it, Mis' Flannigan."

"An' even if ye mane it, Misther Braboy, the time is liable to come when things 'll be different; for service is uncertain, Misther Braboy. An' then you 'll wish you had some nice, clean woman, 'at knowed how to cook an' wash an' iron, ter look afther ye, an' make yer life comfortable."

Uncle Wellington sighed, and looked at her languishingly.

"It 'u'd all be well ernuff, Mis' Flannigan, ef I had n' met you; but I don' know whar I's ter fin' a colored lady w'at 'll begin ter suit me after habbin' libbed in de same house wid you."

"Colored lady, indade! Why, Misther Braboy, ye don't nade ter demane yerself by marryin' a colored lady—not but they 're as good as anybody else, so long as they behave themselves. There 's many a white woman 'u'd be glad ter git as fine a lookin' man as ye are."

"Now *you're* flattrin' *me*, Mis' Flannigan," said Wellington. But he felt a sudden and substantial increase in courage when she had spoken, and it was with astonishing ease that he found himself saying:—

"Dey ain' but one lady, Mis' Flannigan, dat could injuce me ter want ter change de lonesomeness er my singleness fer de 'sponsibilities er matermony, an' I'm feared she'd say no ef I 'd ax her."

"Ye 'd better ax her, Misther Braboy, an' not be wastin' time a-wond'rin'. Do I know the lady?"

"You knows 'er better 'n anybody else, Mis' Flannigan. *You* is de only lady I 'd be satisfied ter marry after knowin' you. Ef you casts me off I'll spen' de rest er my days in lonesomeness an' mis'ry."

Mrs. Flannigan affected much surprise and embarrassment at this bold declaration.

"Oh, Misther Braboy," she said, covering him with a coy glance, "an' it's rale 'shamed I am to hev b'en talkin' ter ye ez I hev. It looks as though I'd b'en doin' the coortin'. I did n't drame that I'd b'en able ter draw yer affections to mesilf."

"I's loved you ever sence I fell in yo' lap on de street car de fus' day I wuz in Groveland," he said, as he moved his chair up closer to hers.

One evening in the following week they went out after supper to the residence of Rev. Cæsar Williams, pastor of the colored Baptist church, and, after the usual preliminaries, were pronounced man and wife.

III

According to all his preconceived notions, this marriage ought to have been the acme of uncle Wellington's felicity. But he soon found that it was not without its drawbacks. On the following morning Mr. Todd was informed of the marriage. He had no special objection to it, or interest in it, except that he was opposed on principle to having husband and wife in his employment at the same time. As a consequence, Mrs. Braboy, whose place could be more easily filled than that of her husband, received notice that her services would not be required after the end of the month. Her husband was retained in his place as coachman.

Upon the loss of her situation, Mrs. Braboy decided to exercise the married woman's prerogative of letting her husband support her. She rented the upper floor of a small house in an Irish neighborhood. The newly wedded pair furnished their rooms on the installment plan and began housekeeping.

There was one little circumstance, however, that interfered slightly with their enjoyment of that perfect freedom from care which ought to characterize a honeymoon. The people who owned the house and occupied the lower floor had rented the upper part to Mrs. Braboy in person, it never occurring to them that her husband could be other than a white man. When it became known that he was colored, the landlord, Mr. Dennis O'Flaherty, felt that he had been imposed upon, and, at the end of the first month, served notice upon his tenants to leave the premises. When Mrs. Braboy, with characteristic impetuosity, inquired the meaning of this proceeding, she was informed by Mr. O'Flaherty that he did not care to live in the same house "wid naygurs." Mrs. Braboy resented the epithet with more warmth than dignity, and for a brief space of time the air was green with choice specimens of brogue, the altercation barely ceasing before it had reached the point of blows.

It was quite clear that the Braboys could not longer live comfortably in Mr. O'Flaherty's house, and they soon vacated the premises, first letting the rent get a couple of weeks in arrears as a punishment to the too fastidious landlord. They moved to a small house on Hackman Street, a favorite locality with colored people.

For a while, affairs ran smoothly in the new home. The colored people seemed, at first, well enough disposed toward Mrs. Braboy, and she made quite a large acquaintance among them. It was difficult, however, for Mrs. Braboy to divest herself of the consciousness that she was white, and therefore superior to her neighbors. Occasional words and acts by which she manifested this feeling were noticed and resented by her keen-eyed and sensitive colored neighbors. The result was a slight coolness between them. That her few white neighbors did not visit her, she naturally and no doubt correctly imputed to disapproval of her matrimonial relations.

Under these circumstances, Mrs. Braboy was left a good deal to her own company. Owing to lack of opportunity in early life, she was not a woman of many resources, either mental or moral. It is therefore not strange that, in order to relieve her loneliness, she should occasionally have recourse to a glass of beer, and, as the habit grew upon her, to still stronger stimulants. Uncle Wellington himself was no teetotaler, and did not interpose any objection so long as she kept her potations within reasonable limits, and was apparently none the worse for them; indeed, he sometimes joined her in a glass. On one of these occasions he drank a little too much, and, while driving the ladies of Mr. Todd's family to the opera, ran against a lamp-post and overturned the carriage, to the serious discomposure of the ladies' nerves, and at the cost of his situation.

A coachman discharged under such circumstances is not in the best position for procuring employment at his calling, and uncle Wellington, under the pressure of need, was obliged to seek some other means of livelihood. At the suggestion of his friend Mr. Johnson, he bought a whitewash brush, a peck of lime, a couple of pails, and a handcart, and began work as a whitewasher. His first efforts were very crude, and for a while he lost a customer in every person he worked for. He nevertheless managed to pick up a living during the spring and summer months, and to support his wife and himself in comparative comfort.

The approach of winter put an end to the whitewashing season, and left uncle Wellington dependent for support upon occasional jobs of unskilled labor. The income derived from these was very uncertain, and Mrs. Braboy was at length driven, by stress of circumstances, to the washtub, that last refuge of honest, able-bodied poverty, in all countries where the use of clothing is conventional.

The last state of uncle Wellington was now worse than the first. Under the soft firmness of aunt Milly's rule, he had not been required to do a great deal of work, prompt and cheerful obedience being chiefly what was expected of him. But matters were very different here. He had not only to bring in the coal and water, but to rub the clothes and turn the wringer, and to humiliate himself before the public by emptying the tubs and hanging out the wash in full view of the neighbors; and he had to deliver the clothes when laundered.

At times Wellington found himself wondering if his second marriage had been a wise one. Other circumstances combined to change in some degree his once rose-colored conception of life at the North. He had believed that all men were equal in this favored locality, but he discovered more degrees of inequality than he had ever perceived at the South. A colored man might be as good as a white man in theory, but neither of them was of any special consequence without money, or talent, or position. Uncle Wellington found a great many privileges open to him at the North, but he had not been educated to the point where he could appreciate them or take advantage of them; and the enjoyment of many of them was expensive, and, for that reason alone, as far beyond his reach as they had ever been. When he once began to admit even the possibility of a mistake on his part, these considerations presented themselves to his mind with increasing force. On occasions when Mrs. Braboy would require of him some unusual physical exertion, or when too frequent applications to the bottle had loosened her tongue, uncle Wellington's mind would revert, with a remorseful twinge of conscience, to the *dolce far niente* of his Southern home; a film would come over his eyes and brain, and, instead of the red-faced Irishwoman opposite him, he could see the black but comely disk of aunt Milly's countenance bending over the washtub; the elegant brogue of Mrs. Braboy would deliquesce into the soft dialect of North Carolina; and he would only be aroused from this blissful reverie by a wet shirt or a handful of suds thrown into his face, with which gentle reminder his wife would recall his attention to the duties of the moment.

There came a time, one day in spring, when there was no longer any question about it: uncle Wellington was desperately homesick.

Liberty, equality, privileges,—all were but as dust in the balance when weighed against his longing for old scenes and faces. It was the natural reaction in the mind of a middle-aged man who had tried to force the current of a sluggish existence into a new and radically different channel. An active, industrious man, making the change in early life, while there was time to spare for the waste of adaptation, might have found in the new place more favorable conditions than in the old. In Wellington age and temperament combined to prevent the success of the experiment; the spirit of enterprise and ambition into which he had been temporarily galvanized could no longer prevail against the inertia of old habits of life and thought.

One day when he had been sent to deliver clothes he performed his errand quickly, and boarding a passing street car, paid one of his very few five-cent pieces to ride down to the office of the Hon. Mr. Brown, the colored lawyer whom he had visited when he first came to the city, and who was well known to him by sight and reputation.

"Mr. Brown," he said, "I ain' gitt'n' 'long very well wid my ole 'oman."

"What's the trouble?" asked the lawyer, with business-like curtness, for he did not scent much of a fee.

"Well, de main trouble is she doan treat me right. An' den she gits drunk, an' wuss'n dat, she lays vi'lent han's on me. I kyars de marks er dat 'oman on my face now."

He showed the lawyer a long scratch on the neck.

"Why don't you defend yourself?"

"You don' know Mis' Braboy, suh; you don' know dat 'oman," he replied, with a shake of the head. "Some er dese yer w'ite women is monst'us strong in de wris'."

"Well, Mr. Braboy, it's what you might have expected when you turned your back on your own people and married a white woman. You were n't content with being a slave to the white folks once, but you must try it again. Some people never know when they've got enough. I don't see that there's any help for you; unless," he added suggestively, "you had a good deal of money."

"'Pears ter me I heared somebody say sence I be'n up heah, dat it wuz 'gin de law fer w'ite folks an' colored folks ter marry."

"That was once the law, though it has always been a dead letter in Groveland. In fact, it was the law when you got married, and until I introduced a bill in the legislature last fall to repeal it. But even that law did n't hit cases like yours. It was unlawful to make such a marriage, but it was a good marriage when once made."

"I don' jes' git dat th'oo my head," said Wellington, scratching that member as though to make a hole for the idea to enter.

"It's quite plain, Mr. Braboy. It's unlawful to kill a man, but when he's killed he's just as dead as though the law permitted it. I'm afraid you have n't much of a case, but if you'll go to work and get twenty-five dollars together, I'll see what I can do for you.

We may be able to pull a case through on the ground of extreme cruelty. I might even start the case if you brought in ten dollars."

Wellington went away sorrowfully. The laws of Ohio were very little more satisfactory than those of North Carolina. And as for the ten dollars,—the lawyer might as well have told him to bring in the moon, or a deed for the Public Square. He felt very, very low as he hurried back home to supper, which he would have to go without if he were not on hand at the usual supper-time.

But just when his spirits were lowest, and his outlook for the future most hopeless, a measure of relief was at hand. He noticed, when he reached home, that Mrs. Braboy was a little preoccupied, and did not abuse him as vigorously as he expected after so long an absence. He also perceived the smell of strange tobacco in the house, of a better grade than he could afford to use. He thought perhaps some one had come in to see about the washing; but he was too glad of a respite from Mrs. Braboy's rhetoric to imperil it by indiscreet questions.

Next morning she gave him fifty cents.

"Braboy," she said, "ye've be'n helpin' me nicely wid the washin', an' I'm going ter give ye a holiday. Ye can take yer hook an' line an' go fishin' on the breakwater. I'll fix ye a lunch, an' ye need n't come back till night. An' there's half a dollar; ye can buy yerself a pipe er terbacky. But be careful an' don't waste it," she added, for fear she was overdoing the thing.

Uncle Wellington was overjoyed at this change of front on the part of Mrs. Braboy; if she would make it permanent he did not see why they might not live together very comfortably.

The day passed pleasantly down on the breakwater. The weather was agreeable, and the fish bit freely. Towards evening Wellington started home with a bunch of fish that no angler need have been ashamed of. He looked forward to a good warm supper; for even if something should have happened during the day to alter his wife's mood for the worse, any ordinary variation would be more than balanced by the substantial addition of food to their larder. His mouth watered at the thought of the finny beauties sputtering in the frying-pan.

He noted, as he approached the house, that there was no smoke coming from the chimney. This only disturbed him in connection with the matter of supper. When he entered the gate he observed further that the window-shades had been taken down.

"'Spec' de ole 'oman's been house-cleanin'," he said to himself. "I wonder she did n' make me stay an' he'p 'er."

He went round to the rear of the house and tried the kitchen door. It was locked. This was somewhat of a surprise, and disturbed still further his expectations in regard to supper. When he had found the key and opened the door, the gravity of his next discovery drove away for the time being all thoughts of eating.

The kitchen was empty. Stove, table, chairs, wash-tubs, pots and pans, had vanished as if into thin air.

"Fo' de Lawd's sake!" he murmured in open-mouthed astonishment.

He passed into the other room,—they had only two,—which had served as bedroom and sitting-room. It was as bare as the first, except that in the middle of the floor were piled uncle Wellington's clothes. It was not a large pile, and on the top of it lay a folded piece of yellow wrapping-paper.

Wellington stood for a moment as if petrified. Then he rubbed his eyes and looked around him.

"W'at do dis mean?" he said. "Is I erdreamin', er does I see w'at I 'pears ter see?" He glanced down at the bunch of fish which he still held. "Heah 's de fish; heah 's de house; heah I is; but whar's de ole 'oman, an' whar's de fu'niture? *I* can't figure out w'at dis yer all means."

He picked up the piece of paper and unfolded it. It was written on one side. Here was the obvious solution of the mystery,—that is, it would have been obvious if he could have read it; but he could not, and so his fancy continued to play upon the subject. Perhaps the house had been robbed, or the furniture taken back by the seller, for it had not been entirely paid for.

Finally he went across the street and called to a boy in a neighbor's yard.

"Does you read writin', Johnnie?"

"Yes, sir, I'm in the seventh grade."

"Read dis yer paper fuh me."

The youngster took the note, and with much labor read the following:—

"Mr. Braboy:
"In lavin' ye so suddint I have ter say that my first husban' has turned up unixpected, having been saved onbeknownst ter me from a wathry grave an' all the money wasted I spint fer masses fer ter rist his sole an' I wish I had it back I feel it my dooty ter go an' live wid 'im again. I take the furnacher because I bought it yer close is yors I leave them and wishin' yer the best of luck I remane oncet yer wife but now agin
"Mrs. Katie Flannigan.

"N. B. I'm lavin town terday so it won't be no use lookin' fer me."

On inquiry uncle Wellington learned from the boy that shortly after his departure in the morning a white man had appeared on the scene, followed a little later by a moving-van, into which the furniture had been loaded and carried away. Mrs. Braboy, clad in her best clothes, had locked the door, and gone away with the strange white man.

The news was soon noised about the street. Wellington swapped his fish for supper and a bed at a neighbor's, and during the evening learned from several sources that the strange white man had been at his house the afternoon of the day before. His neighbors intimated that they thought Mrs. Braboy's departure a good riddance of bad rubbish, and Wellington did not dispute the proposition.

Thus ended the second chapter of Wellington's matrimonial experiences. His wife's departure had been the one thing needful to convince him, beyond a doubt, that he had been a great fool. Remorse and homesickness forced him to the further conclusion that he had been knave as well as fool, and had treated aunt Milly shamefully. He was not altogether a bad old man, though very weak and erring, and his better nature now gained the ascendency. Of course his disappointment had a great deal to do with his remorse; most people do not perceive the hideousness of sin until they begin to reap its consequences. Instead of the beautiful Northern life he had dreamed of, he found himself stranded, penniless, in a strange land, among people whose sympathy he had forfeited, with no one to lean upon, and no refuge from the storms of life. His outlook was very dark, and there sprang up within him a wild longing to get back to North Carolina,—back to the little whitewashed cabin, shaded with china and mulberry trees; back to the woodpile and the garden; back to the old cronies with whom he had swapped lies and tobacco for so many years. He longed to kiss the rod of aunt Milly's domination. He had purchased his liberty at too great a price.

The next day he disappeared from Groveland. He had announced his departure only to Mr. Johnson, who sent his love to his relations in Patesville.

It would be painful to record in detail the return journey of uncle Wellington—Mr. Braboy no longer—to his native town; how many weary miles he walked; how many times he risked his life on railroad trucks and between freight cars; how he depended for sustenance on the grudging hand of backdoor charity. Nor would it be profitable or delicate to mention any slight deviations from the path of rectitude, as judged by conventional standards, to which he may occasionally have been driven by a too insistent hunger; or to refer in the remotest degree to a compulsory sojourn of thirty days in a city where he had no references, and could show no visible means of support. True charity will let these purely personal matters remain locked in the bosom of him who suffered them.

IV

Just fifteen months after the date when uncle Wellington had left North Carolina, a weather-beaten figure entered the town of Patesville after nightfall, following the railroad track from the north. Few would have recognized in the hungry-looking old brown tramp, clad in dusty rags and limping along with bare feet, the trim-looking middle-aged mulatto who so few months before had taken the train from Patesville for the distant North; so, if he had but known it, there was no necessity for him to avoid the main streets and sneak around by unfrequented paths to reach the old place on the other side of the town. He encountered nobody that he knew, and soon the familiar shape of the little cabin rose before him. It stood distinctly outlined against the sky, and the light streaming from the half-opened shutters showed it to be occupied. As he drew nearer, every familiar detail of the place appealed to his memory and to his affections, and his heart went out to the old home and the old wife. As he came nearer still, the odor of fried chicken floated out upon the air and set his mouth to watering, and awakened unspeakable longings in his half-starved stomach.

At this moment, however, a fearful thought struck him; suppose the old woman had taken legal advice and married again during his absence? Turn about would have been only fair play. He opened the gate softly, and with his heart in his mouth approached the window on tiptoe and looked in.

A cheerful fire was blazing on the hearth, in front of which sat the familiar form of aunt Milly—and another, at the sight of whom uncle Wellington's heart sank within him. He knew the other person very well; he had sat there more than once before uncle Wellington went away. It was the minister of the church to which his wife belonged. The preacher's former visits, however, had signified nothing more than pastoral courtesy, or appreciation of good eating. His presence now was of serious portent; for Wellington recalled, with acute alarm, that the elder's wife had died only a few weeks before his own departure for the North. What was the occasion of his presence this evening? Was it merely a pastoral call? or was he courting? or had aunt Milly taken legal advice and married the elder?

Wellington remembered a crack in the wall, at the back of the house, through which he could see and hear, and quietly stationed himself there.

"Dat chicken smells mighty good, Sis' Milly," the elder was saying; "I can't fer de life er me see why dat low-down husban' er yo'n could ever run away f'm a cook like you. It's one er de beatenis' things I ever heared. How he could lib wid you an' not 'preciate you *I* can't understan', no indeed I can't."

Aunt Milly sighed. "De trouble wid Wellin'ton wuz," she replied, "dat he did n' know when he wuz well off. He wuz alluz wishin' fer change, er studyin' 'bout somethin' new."

"Ez fer me," responded the elder earnestly, "I likes things what has be'n prove' an' tried an' has stood de tes', an' I can't 'magine how anybody could spec' ter fin' a better housekeeper er cook dan you is, Sis' Milly. I'm a gittin' mighty lonesome sence my wife died. De Good Book say it is not good fer man ter lib alone, en it 'pears ter me dat you an' me mought git erlong tergether monst'us well."

Wellington's heart stood still, while he listened with strained attention. Aunt Milly sighed.

"I ain't denyin', elder, but what I've be'n kinder lonesome myse'f fer quite a w'ile, an' I doan doubt dat w'at de Good Book say 'plies ter women as well as ter men."

"You kin be sho' it do," averred the elder, with professional authoritativeness; "yas'm, you kin be cert'n sho'."

"But, of co'se," aunt Milly went on, "havin' los' my ole man de way I did, it has tuk me some time fer ter git my feelin's straighten' out like dey oughter be."

"I kin 'magine yo' feelin's Sis' Milly," chimed in the elder sympathetically, "w'en you come home dat night an' foun' yo' chist broke open, an' yo' money gone dat you had wukked an' slaved fuh f'm mawnin' 'tel night, year in an' year out, an' w'en you foun' dat no-'count nigger gone wid his clo's an' you lef' all alone in de worl' ter scuffle 'long by yo'self."

"Yas, elder," responded aunt Milly, "I wa'n't used right. An' den w'en I heared 'bout his goin' ter de lawyer ter fin' out 'bout a defoce, an' w'en I heared w'at de lawyer said 'bout my not bein' his wife 'less he wanted me, it made me so mad, I made up my min' dat ef he ever put his foot on my do'-sill ag'in, I'd shet de do' in his face an' tell 'im ter go back whar he come f'm."

To Wellington, on the outside, the cabin had never seemed so comfortable, aunt Milly never so desirable, chicken never so appetizing, as at this moment when they seemed slipping away from his grasp forever.

"Yo' feelin's does you credit, Sis' Milly," said the elder, taking her hand, which for a moment she did not withdraw. "An' de way fer you ter close yo' do' tightes' ag'inst 'im is ter take me in his place. He ain' got no claim on you no mo'. He tuk his ch'ice 'cordin' ter w'at de lawyer tol' 'im, an' 'termine' dat he wa'n't yo' husban'. Ef he wa'n't yo' husban', he had no right ter take yo' money, an' ef he comes back here ag'in you kin hab 'im tuck up an' sent ter de penitenchy fer stealin' it."

Uncle Wellington's knees, already weak from fasting, trembled violently beneath him. The worst that he had feared was now likely to happen. His only hope of safety lay in flight, and yet the scene within so fascinated him that he could not move a step.

"It 'u'd serve him right," exclaimed aunt Milly indignantly, "ef he wuz sent ter de penitenchy fer life! Dey ain't nuthin' too mean ter be done ter 'im. What did I ever do dat he should use me like he did?"

The recital of her wrongs had wrought upon aunt Milly's feelings so that her voice broke, and she wiped her eyes with her apron.

The elder looked serenely confident, and moved his chair nearer hers in order the better to play the rôle of comforter. Wellington, on the outside, felt so mean that the darkness of the night was scarcely sufficient to hide him; it would be no more than right if the earth were to open and swallow him up.

"An' yet aftuh all, elder," said Milly with a sob, "though I knows you is a better man, an' would treat me right, I wuz so use' ter dat ole nigger, an' libbed wid 'im so long, dat ef he 'd open dat do' dis minute an' walk in, I 'm feared I 'd be foolish ernuff an' weak ernuff to forgive 'im an' take 'im back ag'in."

With a bound, uncle Wellington was away from the crack in the wall. As he ran round the house he passed the wood-pile and snatched up an armful of pieces. A moment later he threw open the door.

"Ole 'oman," he exclaimed, "here's dat wood you tol' me ter fetch in! Why, elder," he said to the preacher, who had started from his seat with surprise, "w'at 's yo' hurry? Won't you stay an' hab some supper wid us?"

Harlem Renaissance and Modernism

The first half of the twentieth century witnessed a flourishing of interracial themes, especially in American literature. The figure of the Mulatto is explored in the poetry by Joseph Seamon Cotter, Jr., Georgia Douglas Johnson, Countée Cullen, Langston Hughes, Claude McKay, and Gwendolyn Brooks; prose tales about passing proliferate in the period and are here represented by McKay and Caroline Bond Day; and exemplary modern race dramas were written by Eugene O'Neill and Hughes. William Pickens tells a fresh version of a tale of switched babies. And Jean Toomer, who propagated a racially mixed definition of "American," his friend Waldo Frank, and his wife, Margery Latimer, participated fully in the experimental mode that was so characteristic of the modernist period.

"The Mulatto to His Critics"

Joseph Seamon Cotter, Jr.

Joseph Seamon Cotter, Jr. (1895–1919) was a journalist and experimental poet who focused his energies on new forms like free verse and variations on traditional forms. He pointedly avoided the Afro-American dialect used by his father, the poet Joseph Cotter, and their family friend Paul Laurence Dunbar. His best-known collection, *The Band of Gideon* (1918), contained the poem included here, "The Mulatto to His Critics," which influenced the sociologist Robert E. Park in his development of the notion of the "marginal man."

> Ashamed of my race?
> And of what race am I?
> I am many in one.
> Through my veins there flows the blood
> Of Red Man, Black Man, Briton, Celt and Scot,
> In warring clash and tumultuous riot.
> I welcome all,
> But love the blood of the kindly race
> That swarthes my skin, crinkles my hair,
> And puts sweet music into my soul.

"The Octoroon"
"Cosmopolite"
"The Riddle"

Georgia Douglas Johnson

Georgia Douglas Johnson (1880–1966) was a major poet of the Harlem Renaissance. She was raised in Atlanta, worked as a teacher, and pursued music studies while writing poetry and short stories. When Johnson and her husband moved to Washington, D.C., in 1910, she opened her home to black writers and intellectuals, including Langston Hughes and Zora Neale Hurston. When her first poetry collection, *The Heart of a Woman*, was published in 1918, Johnson was praised for her skill as a romantic poet but criticized for emphasizing not race but the role of love in women's lives. She responded with the more race-conscious *Bronze: A Book of Verse* in 1922. Johnson also focused on interracial themes in her poems, including the three reprinted here, "The Octoroon," "Cosmopolite," and "The Riddle," the last of which echoed a phrase from a speech by Theodore Tilton that also appeared in an appendix to David Goodman Croly and George Wakeman's *Miscegenation* pamphlet. Johnson returned to her earlier love themes in her collections *An Autumn Love Cycle* (1928) and *Share My World* (1962).

The Octoroon

One drop of midnight in the dawn of life's pulsating stream
Marks her an alien from her kind, a shade amid its gleam;
Forevermore her step she bends insular, strange, apart—
And none can read the riddle of her wildly warring heart.

The stormy current of her blood beats like a mighty sea
Against the man-wrought iron of her captivity.
For refuge, succor, peace and rest, she seeks that humble fold
Whose every breath is kindliness, whose hearts are purest gold.

Cosmopolite

Not wholly this or that,
But wrought
Of alien bloods am I,
A product of the interplay
Of traveled hearts.
Estranged, yet not estranged, I stand
All comprehending;
From my estate
I view earth's frail dilemma;
Scion of fused strength am I,
All understanding,
Nor this nor that
Contains me.

The Riddle

White men's children spread over the earth—
A rainbow suspending the drawn swords of birth,
Uniting and blending the races in one
The world man—cosmopolite—everyman's son!

He channels the stream of the red blood and blue,
Behold him! A Triton—the peer of the two;
Unriddle this riddle of "outside in"
White men's children in black men's skin.

38

From *The Vengeance of the Gods*

William Pickens

William Pickens (1881–1954) was an essayist, fiction writer, and lifelong activist for black civil rights. The son of ex-slave tenant farmers, Pickens grew up in Arkansas and attended Talladega College in Alabama before transferring to Yale, from which he graduated in 1904. He returned to Talladega as a professor and became vice president of Morgan College in Baltimore. In his later work as an organizer for the NAACP, Pickens played an important role in expanding NAACP membership throughout the South. From 1901 on, his fiery essays appeared in such publications as the *Voice of the Negro*, and he became known for his active support of the struggle for equal justice and his criticism of contemporaries. His novella *The Vengeance of the Gods*, of which chapters 1, 2, and 4 are reprinted here, appeared in the collection *The Vengeance of the Gods and Other Stories of Real American Color Line Life* (1922).

Chapter I. "Two Twins"

There is an old unsettled war 'twixt blood and chance. Heredity or environment? Which has the major influence on the destinies of men?

The unnatural social and the illegitimate sex relations of white and colored people in the United States furnish the best body of material through which to investigate this problem. One of the best illustrations of the power of environment and at the same time the persistency of blood, hails from the river lands of the State of Arkansas.

John Elliot was a wealthy plantation owner. He held title to many thousand acres of fertile cotton lands of eastern Arkansas in the last decade of the nineteenth century. His farms were worked by scores of Negro families, most of whom had migrated from the Carolinas and Georgia in the eighties. Elliot had advanced the railroad fares to these families through his labor agents who operated in the older states. The heads of these families had "made their mark" or signed their names to contracts for their entire families to "work out" these debts on Elliot's estate. These contracts were made and signed through agents in the older states, and the "parties of the second part" had no knowledge of the conditions of the work to be required, beyond the general understanding that it was farm labor.

Of course, Elliot had to furnish these "newcomers" their "rations." For most of them came west in the winter, after the close of the farming season in the east; and accordingly they had to be supplied with food and clothing at the expense of the new landlord even before steady work should begin in the spring. This caused the debt against them to mount rapidly, for the landlord charged these supplies to their account at a profit to himself of one hundred per cent or more. And although he was party to the contract, he was sole keeper of all records; and it was not necessary to tell the consumer what he was being charged for a gallon of molasses till the final settlement next fall or Christmas,—and not necessary then.

This system was the successor and heir of the slave system. Elliot lived in "the Big House" on a long and ample hill near the center of his estates, while the Negroes lived in cabins of one or two rooms, all over the great plantations, each cabin being situated on or near the little farm that was assigned or allotted to its occupants. Once each month, on the regular "rationing day," all the heads of these various tenant or peon families came to the Big House to claim as much molasses, salt pork, meal, dark-brown sugar, coffee and rice as was deemed necessary to keep their respective families alive for thirty days more. This system kept them tied close to their master and periodically reminded of their dependence upon him.

The landlord was perfectly secure in these advanced outlays: the tenant was bound by this debt and local law would enforce it against his very person, spite of the Thirteenth Amendment. If he sought to escape, any justice of the peace could fine him and then jail him in default of payment of fine. But of course the fine would be paid by his magnanimous and benevolent (?) landlord and added to his former debt,—thus binding him the closer. In fact it was better for the landlord when a peon attempted to escape and failed, for after the matter was reviewed by the "court" or justice, it gave the aggrieved landlord a better claim, a sort of adjudicated title to this Negro's brawn.

Thus the original "cost of transportation" from South Carolina to Arkansas became an octopus with ever increasing bulk and multiplying suckers. Despair broke many a heart. Even the doctor and his medicines had to be secured through this system. Chills and fevers attacked the unacclimated new-comers and they had to summon the plantation doctor, who got his pay, not from the tenant, but from the great land-baron, who in turn charged this account against the tenant's account at the Big House,—with the usual profits. This doctor who was not at all accountable to the tenant, naturally gave himself the least trouble: he might ride to the door of a cabin where black people lay fevered and delirious within, and without dismounting from his saddle make a few inquiries, write a prescription for medicine, hand it down and ride away.

Small wonder that under circumstances such as these some of the more thrifty and determined immigrants would try auxiliary means to break the bonds of this gripping debt-slavery,—even allowing their women folk to serve as cooks or maids or washerwomen to the white folk in the Big House and elsewhere.

And this is how "Aunt Katy," now a woman of middle age, had come into the family of John Elliot as a maid-of-all-work. Twenty years before, when she was a slim black girl of twenty, she and her father and mother and younger sisters and brothers had become the debt-slaves of John Elliot. They were of those wonderfully virile black folk of South Carolina, whose mark can be found everywhere in America today. They escaped from the barren poverty of their native state to find themselves in the rich cotton lands of the great Arkansas "bottoms," but also in the coils of the octopus. All hands worked with a will, even the little children being deprived of most of their schooling. The oldest sister, Katy, was hired out as house girl to the Elliots, lords of the estate. "Aunt Katy," a title which the dignity and the burden of more years had finally won for her, was now a matronly-looking black woman with a bit of gray about her temples. She had that clear and beautiful black skin through which the red blood was visible on the more prominent features of the face.

Aunt Katy had a daughter, Essie, who should not be described as yellow, but as of a rich cream color decorated with vanishing rose tints, which sometimes appear in the sun-lit eddies when the powerful streams of black and white run into the same channel.

And Essie, only nineteen years old, had a baby, with dark hair, dark eyes, and skin—*white*.

Three generations: mother, daughter, grandson—black, light, white. And yet, in law, they were all black; and in the wisdom of the same law Essie, Aunt Katy's daughter, had no father, and Essie's baby was fatherless.

And yet the stranger, to whom resemblances are always more discernible, might have noticed that although these two normal human creatures were legally akin to nobody, they very much resembled some of their neighbors. Essie was enough like Mrs. Elliot, the wife of the landlord, to be her daughter; and Mrs. Elliot's baby looked like the twin of Essie's baby. These little baby boys were six months old and just ten days apart in their birth, the Elliot baby being the older. And they were indeed so indistinguishably alike that one day Mrs. Elliot, seeing Essie's baby clad in the cast-off clothes of her own child, seized it in her arms, and pressing it to her heart she inquired of Aunt Katy pettishly: "Why have you put my little angel into these old rags? I told you to throw them away."

"That's Essie's—not your'n!" said Aunt Katy, in a tone not altogether kind. Mrs. Elliot almost dropped the child into Aunt Katy's arms. Mrs. Elliot had heard all about this child and knew well the circumstances of its being. But this moment of realization seemed to arouse the jungle woman. She looked wrathfully toward John Elliot, who sat in his easy chair, spying upon the scene through the smoke screen of his pipe. He was the picture of self-satisfaction and conscious mastery. And when his angry mate turned upon him, all the threatening storm of her sex gathered itself in this one harmless bolt:

"As God lives, no good will ever come of this!" To which John Elliot replied with a new cloud of smoke, as if to thicken the screen and dodge any second shot.

Then, as too frequently happens in such cases, this indignant wife turned all her anger and fury away from the really guilty party and upon his helpless victims:

"And this is *thanks*, is it, Katy?" forgetting the mollifying Southern term of "Aunt."—"We gave you work and bread when my only brother was here,—and there is Essie. And now *this* from her, and she my brother's own———!"

She stopped short and shook with wrath. The code of honor of her group forbade to speak plainly and honorably her relationship to these people. But Essie was her natural niece, her own brother's child; and Essie's baby was the half-brother and apparently the very twin of her own child. These plain things her proud tongue could not utter, but the following came natural to her:

"You niggers all! Take those clothes off that brat, and never bring your daughter or this thing near my house again. Let Essie work on the farm, and we have plenty of coarse cloth for nigger children."

With that she swept proudly away. John Elliot had already withdrawn to the porch.

Meanwhile dark rage and the images of darker resolves were sweeping the dusky breast of Aunt Katy, like the shadows of storm clouds. She remembered how twenty years ago she was practically trapped and assaulted by this woman's pampered brother, and how this very woman had excused and connived, and was certainly an accomplice after the fact. And now Essie, the fruit and one of the victims of the previous wrong, had told her mother how this white woman's own husband had at first attempted to take advantage of her through bribery and persuasion and coercion; and failing in that, had finally used force to do this thing.

And yet, continued Aunt Katy's memory, this woman had kept her and her child Essie for twenty years in the Big House. A few weeks before Essie's baby was born, Mrs. Elliot had ordered Aunt Katy to put the prospective mother into one of the servant's cabins; whereupon Aunt Katy had also moved out to live with Essie although she still performed her daily tasks at the Elliots. The baby had been born, and everybody had remarked that it was "the very spit an' image uv ole man Elliot." The colored people said that Essie's baby and Mrs. Elliot's baby were as much alike "as two black-eyed peas."

Time had passed, and Essie began again to go back and forth from the cabin to the Big House to assist in the work. Aunt Katy who spent most of her time in and near the kitchen and dining room, kept the little grandchildren with her. Under the strange power which the evils we tolerate seem to acquire over us, Mrs. Elliot had apparently become reconciled to all this, and Essie was as formerly her hair-dresser and maid. But the mistress was less communicative, somewhat less condescending and much more formal in her relations with this beautiful outcaste creature, and always dismissed her now as soon as the work was finished.

In a few moments all this record unrolled itself in Aunt Katy's heated brain. And it would not have comforted the Elliots, had they remained to observe the fire of her dark deep African eyes. She hugged passionately the little nameless grandchild, which, though frightened for the moment by the storm that had passed with Mrs. Elliot, was still unconscious of its own situation and immune against the deeper significance of all these clashing forces, and was now pressing its soft baby cheek against the dark face of its grandmother and patting her neck with a tiny hand.

"No!" exclaimed Aunt Katy, in apostrophizing defiance, "my Essie will not work in your fields." Then hugging the baby closer: "You will not be put among strangers. You an' Essie can stay in the cabin; I will support you." And looking in the direction toward which Mrs. Elliot had gone: "What can *she* do without me? I have cared for her house for twenty years.—Yes, long as I live, he will support you, and Essie too. For if they refuse to support you in the cabin————" Her tongue refused to utter the awful thought which seemed to find it difficult to express itself even in the sudden demon look of her face. This terrible inspiration ran into a dry, jerky, inhuman laugh, which so frightened the child that it clung the closer about her neck.

Chapter II. The Tattoo and the Scar

The Tattoo

Miss Ollie Price, Mrs. Elliot's younger sister, who since her school-days had led the life of a social "climber," and almost that of an adventuress in the east, had at last become engaged to some French sportsman, and was now back at her sister's home in Arkansas to prepare for the wedding. She needed a maid, she must have a maid. That was what everybody had in New York and Washington. Mrs. Elliot told her that on all the Elliot plantations there was but one person qualified for the position,—Aunt Katy's daughter Essie. Then she related to her sister all the circumstances connected with Essie's banishment to the cabin. Miss Price who had experienced some liberalizing contact with the outside world, replied that it was "too bad," and even referred to Essie as "the poor thing." But then she "must have a suitable maid."

Essie was accordingly recalled from her exile to serve again at the Big House. Expedience is master of many of our emotions and author of many of our decisions.

Curiosity led "Miss Ollie" to seek an opportunity to see Essie's baby. One day while Essie was arranging her new Mistress' hair, Miss Price was contemplating the face and figure of the beautiful mulatto in her mirror. And perhaps tenderness was vying with curiosity when she said: "It must be hard to leave your baby so long. Bring him with you tomorrow, and I think—you will work better."

"But, Miss Ollie, Mis' Elliot————."

"O, that's all right," anticipated Miss Price, "It'll be all right in my rooms." And then with a tone almost of command: "Bring him tomorrow."

The next day Miss Price was surprised almost into speechlessness by the closeness of resemblance between this child and her own little nephew. She was agitated. By a strange fascination we often seek after what will not comfort us. "What is his name?" she asked Essie, as the little fellow traced with his finger the figures in the wall paper opposite her.

"We call him Jim," said Essie, blushing and uncomfortable.

"Jim!" called Miss Price, as if to test the matter or to destroy a possible illusion. The little fellow shrank at the strange voice, turned timidly and moved around in the direction of its mother. Her own nephew would run to her at the slightest invitation.

The sure instincts of the mother caught the meaning of all this curious interest. She was pensive and pale and silent as she worked all that morning, and little Jim also gave the stranger lady a wide berth when he moved about the room, as if sympathetic with his mother's spirit. When she went away at noon she did not bring him back, and she remarked that he was right out in the kitchen with "Aunt Katy," as she called her own mother, where she could see him when necessary. It did not escape her notice that Miss Price now made no protest against his absence, and never asked to see him and never even mentioned the child again. It is hard to be consistent in a false attitude.

Miss Price talked much about this child, however, to her sister, Mrs. Elliot: "Suppose something should happen! How could you make sure? Only their clothes make it possible to tell one from the other."

"Nonsense!" retorted the proud white mother, "because you have been staying in the North, you forget the difference between a white person and a nigger. If the nails or the hair of the neck don't tell, the very spirit will tell. Blood will tell! Why, if they were lost till they were grown, you could tell the white man and the nigger when you found them."

But Miss Price was nonetheless skeptic. She disclosed to her sister that she had learned from a sailor associate in the east the art of tattooing, and shocked that lady's honor and offended her pride of race by proposing to tattoo little nephew William as a distinguishing mark. As proof of her skill she showed on her left arm a small tattoo which she herself had done. The haughty wife and proud mother rejected this proposal with an air that was truly impressive of her faith in racial superiority and "blood."

But that one sight of little Jim had stuck like poison in Miss Price's soul. She could be seen often brooding and gazing into the far-away when playing with nephew William. She was trying to prevail upon her sister to permit her to take the child to France after the wedding. Meanwhile Mrs. Elliot and her husband were summoned to the bedside of her brother, the natural father of Essie, who was dying in Atlanta. Miss Price readily consented to assume the responsibility for the household and the care of her little nephew. The Elliots were gone for several weeks, what with funeral arrangements and what with looking after the brother's estate.

If Mrs. Elliot had ever bathed and dressed her own baby instead of leaving it entirely to the servants, she might have noticed, when she returned from Atlanta, a mark under its arm up near the body. This mark was irregular in shape but might have passed for an M or a W, accordingly as one looked at it. But with her sublime confidence in herself and her kind, she noticed nothing. And the servants, who had been glad to have "Miss Ollie" to relieve them of all service to little "Willyum" for several weeks, saw nothing—and cared not.

The Scar

The wedding came to pass. The Elliots were persuaded to take the trip to France with the bride and groom. It was arranged to take Essie along as maid to the whole party. She would return with the Elliots, who would stay about three months. Mrs. Elliot had consented to go only after her sister in New Orleans agreed to come and be the head of the place in their absence and take care of the child. And Essie had been reconciled to going only after it was agreed that her own mother, Aunt Katy, should have entire care of "Jimmie." The Elliots also had every confidence in Aunt Katy, but then it "would look better to have some white person in charge here." That is a religion in the South. Aunt Katy would be the real head and the chief reliance. Indeed nothing could have induced Mrs. Elliot to leave her child or her house in the care of even her own sister without the help of Aunt Katy. But altho a colored person may be the *defacto* head, the *de jure* headship must reside in a "white person."

This New Orleans sister could not come, however, until some time after the wedding party had left, and before the Elliots and Duprees set sail from New York, they received the anxiously awaited news of her arrival. She reported that all was well at the Big House and that Aunt Katy had taken excellent care of the interests of the Elliots. She had met the new arrival and brought little William in her arms, who was "the very picture of health, and, O, so fond of Aunt Katy," as the letter went on to say.

What had really happened was this: when this strange aunt arrived, the child in Aunt Katy's arms would have nothing to do with the newcomer but clung with both arms tight around the black woman's neck, its cheek against her cheek. The child seemed frightened when the stranger touched it and showed no disposition to respond to her repeated invitations to "my dearest little nephew William." The chagrined aunt did not relate all this in her letter, for indeed she felt ashamed to tell in detail of the very cold reception accorded her by the heir to the Elliot estate. Pride deals in half truths and camouflage. She went on to say that she hoped soon to win the entire confidence and affection of the little master of the place, altho they were strangers for the present and she was allowing him to sleep with Aunt Katy.

At this point in the letter, the former Miss Price who was now Madame Dupree, parted her lips and gasped and was about to make some earnest comment,—but subsided when the next line went on to say:

"Do not tell Essie that a little accident happened to Jimmie. He was burned the next day after you left. He was not seriously hurt, but the doctor says it will leave a large scar on his leg."

"Aunt Katy says it happend in the kitchen. The child pulled a hot stove lid down. Fortunately William was not around, as Aunt Katy had sent him out for a ride with the new nurse who came that same day."

The letter repeated and emphasized it as a request from Aunt Katy "not to tell Essie about it," and said that the grandmother was much distressed. This last statement seemed to produce a complete calm in Madame Dupree's features, and she only remarked: "Aunt Katy always would have that young one hanging to her apron in the kitchen." Then, as if to reassure herself: "And did she say that it is the doctor's opinion that the scar on the leg will last for life?" ...

Chapter IV. The Power of Circumstance

No; environment is not omnipotent, but it is so almost all-powerful that it deserves the major consideration in the making of a man on earth. Here are two babies. Three-fourths of the blood of the one is from the same sources as three-fourths of the blood of the other. And that other fourth of blood is just—human blood. In physical feature they are like duplicates. But the divergence of their ways on earth will carry them to differing destinies.

And which is which? Why did Aunt Katy hug little William so passionately, when alone with him? And when alone with little Jimmie, why did she croon so wierdly and almost compassionately over him, and treat him with all the indulgent pity of her race? William's aunt remarked the strange fascination with which Jimmie seemed to hold his grandmother.

And why had Aunt Katy done this thing which "Miss Ollie" feared would be done, and which the reader of this history must by this time suspect to have been done? Partly for fear and partly for revenge.

For fear: because she had often heard John Elliot tell, with approval, of the terrible vengeance wreaked by one of his brothers on "a little nigger gal." It seemed that the little colored girl was not much older than his brother's child whom she was supposed to nurse and take care of; and that by carelessness or childish neglect she had allowed the little white child to come too near a boiling pot in which soap was being made. The child stumbled, overturned the pot and scalded itself to death. The angry and brutal father then seized the little nurse and "cut both ears off that little nigger." All the other colored people had fled at the sight, so that "nobody ever knew what became of the rest of the little nigger gal," for not even the parents of the colored child had dared to address any inquiries to the infuriated demon who was responsible for her unrevealed fate. Aunt Katy recalled this oft repeated story and remembered that as John Elliot was leaving on the previous day, he had said to her concerning William: "Take good care of him,—for hell will be too good for any nigger if he gets hurt." And so, as the stove lid fell on that little leg, what was Aunt Katy to do when there was another pair of little legs just like them, close at hand and perfectly sound?

For revenge: because in the innermost of her soul she had always resented with deepest human hate the outrage which John Elliot had committed upon the innocence of her little Essie. Every slight and every act of neglect or contempt which Essie and Essie's child had suffered from the Elliots and their kin, had deepened this hate and fed this desire for revenge. Whenever John Elliot was the offender, the inspiration to this deed had spoken in her ear like a tempting devil.

So—well—when the Elliots returned from Europe, William had become quite fond of his New Orleans aunt, but looked strangely upon his parents, which was "perfectly natural." He had to be won over by his mother and father, but that was soon done with a multitude of playthings and goodies.

What did the babies care?

We next see these two children when they are seven years old. How swift is the passage of childhood,—to the eye of the observer. But to the child it seems longer, the longest period of life,—like great oceans of time.

In outward appearances these two little boys had become less alike, so that now there was no mistaking the one for the other. But if one disregarded the illusions and veneer of this world's fortunes and saw only their essential features, they were still enough alike to be twins. Clothing and the care of their bodies clearly distinguished them. Besides, each had now a personality which could never be confounded with the other. William was generally well-dressed, well-shod, pampered and autocratic. Essie's "little nigger Jim" was clad in home-made things or cast-offs, and had a temper to fight and a disposition to carry away the playthings of the little autocrat. The last named trait was "proof of his sect," as the colloquialism used by Mrs. Elliot would have it. She often pointed to the differences between these two little spirits, especially in the presence of John Elliot, in support of her theories about "blood,"—as if indeed that was the only difference,—as if they were otherwise circumstanced alike,—when as a matter of fact they were more nearly equally endowed with "blood" than with any other thing.

But while William was an autocrat, Jimmie was a revolutionist, a radical. Ever and anon was the autocrat forced to call loudly for aid from the greater powers against this unsubduable revolutionist. Aunt Katy, Essie and others of the servants had often to succor the titled possessor of the throne. Some of these encounters were naturally provoked by the arrogance of the little autocrat, who was beginning to overhear the conversations of his elders, and to understand that between him and Jimmie there was some sort of a gulf fixed—a gulf which he himself might cross and recross at will, but which forever shut Jimmie out.

The Russo-Japanese war was going on, and when a great naval battle was imminent, John Elliot had remarked to guests at table that the Japanese could never win because they were "too much like niggers." This unpremised conclusion about "niggers" went unchallenged, as usual. William had listened closely to this table-talk. And so in the afternoon, when he carried his bean-shooting cannon and his uniformed card-board soldiers into the kitchen yard to play war with Jimmie, he insisted that his side must be the "Rushins" and that Jimmie's side must be the "nigger Japs." This was finally agreed to by Jimmie, as nationalities were not so important to him. For Jimmie's army consisted of soldiers of different sizes and shapes and colors, which with the help of Aunt Katy he had recruited with a pair of scissors from old paper boxes, and a few faded, battered and crippled, limbless or headless "Rushins" which the opposing general magnanimously loaned him on the eve of battle. And while Jimmie was setting his motley army in battle array, it seems that the "Rushin" general had the nerve to fire a shot at them before the "nigger Jap" general "wuz ready to give orders to shoot." In the heated parley which followed from these oddly conflicting notions of the laws of war, the commanders came to blows. And when John Elliot rushed from the house with reinforcement for the distressed and vociferous "Rushin," the opposing general had discarded the conventional weapons of warfare, and winding his left fingers in the curls of his antagonist, was pounding him with his right fist and with the regularity of drumfire. At sight of this savage attack, John Elliot, one of the great powers, rushed forward, seized the barbarian in the back, gave him two hard spanks, then dropped him and turned to console the rescued party. But instead of yielding tamely, the little Afro-Asiatic, catching the great power for a moment off guard, kicked him violently on the shin and retreated at top speed. Whereupon that infuriated superman, tho more insulted than injured, uttered this fearful prophecy: "The little devil! that nigger will die with his boots on."

Jimmie was now completely outlawed; all diplomatic and commercial intercourse was forbidden, and never again was he to be tolerated on the premises of the Big House, the stronghold of the powerful land-baron, John Elliot.

39

"Hope"

Waldo Frank

Though his popularity declined precipitously later in his life, at the height of his career the writer Waldo Frank (1889–1967) was one of America's foremost intellectuals. Frank, the son of an attorney, was raised in New York City and graduated from Yale. He wrote for the *New York Times*, the *New York Evening Post*, and the *New Yorker*, cofounded the short-lived journal *Seven Arts*, and was a longtime contributing editor of the *New Republic*. In addition to numerous literary and political essays, he wrote novels, short stories, plays, and well-received books of social history. Frank developed a philosophy that stressed a consciousness of the Whole and a belief in the interdependence of all people, in contrast to the materialism and individualism he saw plaguing America. He expressed this philosophy in his essays and fiction, including his novels *The Unwelcome Man* (1917) and *Holiday* (1923) and in his first book of criticism, *Our America* (1919). The short story "Hope," which is reprinted here, was published in 1922.

He was walking a long time. It seemed to him he was walking always .. walking toward no thing .. walking away. He had the sense of himself very white, very dim yet sharp: white thin throat weary with breathing, white brow weary with pressing through black air, white legs weary with walking away. He had the sense of himself a white thing walking forever from the dark, through dark....

He had no thoughts. His past was the wake behind his feet. He sensed it arching up behind him to a black horizon, arching beyond horizon, the wake of his past .. a thing that was not he and was not the darkness: was the stain of his white passing along upon the dark that passed never....

His past was beingless and thoughtless. He was moving whiteness, his past was where he had moved. Yet certain knowings went with him. They were without dimension. They were impalpable like odors. He moved, a white moving, and with him emanations .. things he knew about himself and the world .. frail pitiful things, impalpable like odors.

One knowing: he was lonely. One knowing: his loneliness was not a birth of his leaving his beloved, but his leaving her was birth of his being lonely. They loved each other. There, between them, growing like a tree, his loneliness. Like a tree clefting a rock, his loneliness: as they clove together, as his arms were about her body, as his mouth was upon her mouth .. his loneliness clefting them asunder. It spread. It blossomed. It spread up until its branches were sky, until its roots were earth .. until its trunk was life between earth and sky. His loneliness blotted out his beloved. His loneliness blotted out himself. He was moving whiteness, moved by loneliness to walk forever away.

He stood at the corner of a street and tried to change himself into a thing that thought.

He tried hard: his legs hurt: he tried to think of that. There was an empty whiteness in his stomach. He tried to think of that and of the simple way .. there was money .. whereby he could recolor his stomach red. Against his brow black fumes of people moved .. slow, tragically, men and women in black shoes pushing white faces away, moving against each other forever away through black.

Long lost strokes .. white soot in blackness streaking from before his eyes into the pregnant past .. men, women. Little balls of tremulous commotion .. black all about their whiteness, moulding their whiteness .. children. Above his hat, the Elevated Road .. a balance in sonorous black where all that was over it and under was contained. The structure so immediate above him, so infinite beyond him, was a Word. Its recurrent meaningless boom had meaning for him. He stood, white upright wisp, and listened to the word of the murmuring, pounding, failing trains, to the refrain before and after of long black beams parting the dwellings of men, swung between mists.

He took this, satisfied, in place of thought.

The odors of self were free to touch him. He knew now for long he was wandering the City. Long, he had no thought of his beloved, no care. He knew that soon he would stop. His whiteness .. because he needed so, so hoped .. was going to stop.

The street corner where he stood was sharp. Blackness still. But each particle in his eyes stood up: each particle like iron dust was suddenly within the sway of a hid Magnet so that each particle stood up, yet otherwise did not move.

A saloon with garish yellow light and yellow wood. Gray pavement. Desolate forms of men like lamp-soot on the yellow wood, on the yellow light. Grey pavement.

Then in the foreground of his eye a sudden force upon him, a slow thin form.— She is a negress! He saw her big awkward hat, her shoes stuck out from the wooden stiffness of her coat. He saw her wrists stuck out from the stiff wool arms: two hands, luminous sinuous, flexed .. hands moving in air. The air that her hands moved wreathed in volumnear curves like the curves of a slender stem of a flower, to her head. This he saw also. He saw within the black of her stupid hat a smile toward him. He felt her throat.

He left the yellow light. The grey pavement here was gaseous, clouded beyond. In the dim, he knew the woman beside him.

She walked. Her parting the blackness left a wake that sucked him subtly, slowly. Not horizontal but in true measure with her was their way: the spirallic leap and dip of an uneven hoop. There was a heavy door and a room .. he quiet beside her.

He was aware of quiet. The gas jet spat light with a rasping breath. It and his breathing and her breathing were encased in quiet. The room was thick and muffled. Foul walls that were thick, the heavy scarlet cover on the bed, the painted door ..

made the quiet. These were a fabulous womb of her breathing and his and the gaslight.

She took off her hat. She took off her brown-wooden coat. She turned her eyes upon him .. the white of her eyes. Then her hands uprose, they swam upon her like fish deep in dark waters. She took off her tawdry one-piece dress. She took off her heavy shoes and her coarse stockings. She ripped soiled flannel, sparking from her skin. She lifted the scarlet cover and her black body slid within the bed.

He flung away the cover. Her black body lay on the white sheet. He looked at her body. She looked at her body. It was a black still thing, flowing forever within itself, moveless beyond its boundaries which were white. And within its blackness a glowing cloud of white, making it blue, making it yellow and blue, making it blackness alive.

He said to himself: "Now I had better think."

He took off his clothes. He let the room close in him, touch him everywhere .. at his throat, under his armpits, at his thighs .. the foulpadded room. He lay beside her. Her bloated lips touched like the room on his.

He lay still, stiffly. Her lips worked on him, her arms shuttled at his flanks. He lay still, stiffly. She seemed to hear him, now. She relaxed beside him. She lay flexed. Barely her skin in the narrow bed touched his.

So they lay: gaze threading upward like untroubled smoke; he stiff, she undulous easeful, black like a buried sea: both still.

The wave of her was measurelessly long as if some tiding force .. no wind .. with infinite stroke caused it. He felt himself white. He felt this blackness beside her. He was not stiff. He was not moving away. He knew in her blackness, the white mist running through: saturate white, invisible from the blackness of her body, making it alive.

A great need filled him. He .. separate white, pushing through black .. felt the need and felt the power to be merged in her, to join the white mist making her black alive.

Passion, pure beyond object and beyond self, lifted him so. He took her body: it was body: black dead body she was. So he took her. So he made her alive. He was impress of life upon her substance: song.

Before his eyes was dark Void. Falling through it threads of white, globules of white: in his eyes this woman's body, falling through it himself.

He lay smiling with shut eyes on his back.

She left the bed and knelt on the floor beside him.

She kissed his feet. She kissed his knees. She took his fingers, pressed each finger one by one, on her eyes. His fingers were cold.

She beat her brow, dashed her brow and her breast against the iron bed....

40

"Withered Skin of Berries"

Jean Toomer

When his first book, *Cane*, appeared in 1923, Jean Toomer (1894–1967) was hailed as the fore-most black race writer of the Harlem Renaissance. Ironically, Toomer later preferred not to be labeled a black author (he was of mixed-race origins and simply called himself an American), and *Cane* was his last foray into race writing. His later fiction, poetry, and essays reflected his interest in Eastern philosophy and spiritual self-development, especially the mysticism of Georges Gurdjieff in the 1920s and 1930s, and his subsequent involvement with the Society of Friends.

Toomer was the son of Georgia farmers and was raised in Washington, D.C., by his mother and maternal grandparents; his grandfather, former Louisiana governor P. B. S. Pinchback, was the first state governor of African American descent. After finishing high school Toomer traveled widely and attended a number of colleges, though he did not graduate. In 1921 he accepted a temporary job as principal of the Sparta Agricultural and Industrial Institute in Sparta, Georgia. Here, during Toomer's first extended sojourn south, he was exposed to the Afro-American oral and folk cultures that inspired him to write *Cane*. A collection of poetry, short stories, and drama, *Cane* enjoyed critical success and endures as one of the most powerful texts of the Harlem Renaissance. The short story "Withered Skin of Berries," which is reprinted here, was written at the same time as *Cane* and published posthumously.

I

Men listen to her lispings and murmurs. Black souls steal back to Georgia canefields, soft and misty, underneath a crescent moon. The mystery of their whispered promises seems close to revelation, seems tangibly incarnate in her. Black souls, tropic and fiery, dream of love. Sing joyful codas to forgotten folk-songs. Spin love to the soft weaving of her arms. Men listen to her lispings and murmurs. White souls awake to adolescent fantasies they thought long buried with the dead leaves along the summer streets of mid-western towns. Solvents of melancholy burn through their bitten modes of pioneer aggressiveness to a southern repose. They too spin love to the soft weaving of her arms. White men, black men, only in retrospective kisses, know the looseness of her lips .. pale withered skin of berries...

Departmental buildings are grey gastronomic structures, innocuously coated with bile. They pollute the breath of Washington. Washington's breath is sickish and stale because of them. With the slow, retarded process of dyspeptics, they suck the life of mediocrities. They secrete a strange preservative that keeps flesh and bones intact after the blood is dry.. Vera is a typist. She is a virgin. A virgin whose notion of purity tape-worms her. Men sense her corporeal virginity. Her slim body, her olive skin, clear as white grapes held to the sun, are pure. Sandalwood odor of her thick brown hair, the supplication of her eyes, her lifeless lips, all pure. Men like to paw pure bodies. They adore them. So Vera came to find out. "They only want to paw me." She blamed the beast in men, black men especially. Pure bodies tease. So the men found out. "Vera is a tease." The thought found its way to her. She set up her creed: Tease the beast.. Vera is a typist. She is neither more nor less palatable than the other morsels that come in from South Carolina, Illinois, or Oregon. But there is a condiment-like irritability in the process of her digestion. Unquestionably, Vera is white. Routine segregates niggers. Black life seems more soluble in lump. White life, pitiably agitated to superiority, is more palatable. Black life is pepper to the salt of white. Pepper in the nose of white. Sneezes are first-rate aids to digestion. Unquestionably, Vera is white. Her fellow workers sneeze about the niggers. Niggers are all right as janitors, as messengers; in fact, anywhere where they keep their place. Niggers, despite their smell and flat feet, aren't so bad. They are good to joke about. Sneezes over colored girls using powder and straightening their kinky hair to look like white. But it is a different thing when niggers try to pass for white. They are slick at it. Youve got to watch out. But there is always a way of telling: finger-nails, and eyes, and odor, and oh, any number of things. Vera listens to them, smiles, jokes, laughs, sometimes with a curious gurgle-like flutter, says goodby to them of evenings outside the office door, and rides uptown to the respite of a Negro home.

Carl. A fellow in the office. From a small town across the lake from Chicago where his father is an independent dealer in oil. Carl got in the government service to earn a little money against the coming of a dream he had. He would be rich some day—when his uncle died. He had plans for the conquest of the Argentine. He had studied agriculture at Wisconsin. He read books, and even took a correspondence course in foreign trade. Spanish he was learning from Cortina. He went out of his way to pick acquaintances with South Americans, Spaniards, and Portuguese. This trait it was that first led him to Vera. She looked Spanish. Casual remarks led to their having lunch together. Carl was sincere. He held roseate and chivalrous notions of womanhood. His enthusiasm bid well to hold out, for a time, against the stale utilitarian atmosphere of governmental Washington. In the office, and during the brief strolls they had after lunch, the inward anemia of Vera fed on it. She liked him. She established a sort of moral equilibrium and dulled a growing sense of deceit by resolving not to tease him. Carl wanted to take her home, to call on her, to take her to the movies, to Penn Gardens, to the dances the office gave. She put him off. Her soft reticence and sly evasions implied purity, evoked an aura of desirability and charm. Carl was buying a car, a Dodge. One afternoon in early spring the departments were given a holiday. It was unexpected. Vera could not possibly have any plans for it, and Carl told her so. He insisted on the falsity of the reasons she gave for refusing to drive with him. Vera was more than usually nervous that day. Carl's stubbornness irritated her. She felt herself getting hot, as if her nerves were heated pins and needles pricking her. That would not do. Carl's friendship made the office tolerable. He took hold her arm. Vera went with him.

Driving down Seventeenth Street, Carl only spoke to call the name of buildings. That was the Corcoran Gallery of Art, that, the Pan-American building. Negroes were working on the basin of an artificial lake that was to spread its smooth glass surface before Lincoln's Memorial. The shadow of their emancipator stirred them neither to bitterness nor awe. The scene was a photograph on Vera's eye-balls. Carl was concentrated on the road. He squirmed skillfully in the traffic that was getting dense. The exotic fragrance of cherry blossoms reached them, slightly rancid as it mingled with the odor of exploded gasoline. As they passed the crescent line of blossomed trees, a group of Japanese, hats off, were seen reverently lost in race memories of reed lutes, jet black eyebrows, and jeweled palanquins. Consciously, the episode meant nothing to Vera. But an unprecedented nostalgia, a promise of awakening, making her feel faint, clutched her throat almost to stricture, and made her swallow hard. Her face was pallid. Carl noticed it and said he guessed it was the heat from the engine and the motion of the car.. A word was struggling with her throat.. They swung into the speedway. Potomac's water was muddy, streaked with sea-weed. A tug, drawing a canal barge from miles in the interior, blew its whistle for the bridge to turn and let it by. Across the river, the green, and white marble splotches of Virginia's hills. Curious for her, lines of a poem came unbidden to her mind:

> far-off trees
> Whose gloom is rounded like the hives of bees
> All humming peace to soldiers who have gone.

She was trying to think where she had heard them. They hadnt impressed her at the time. No poems ever did. She would not let them. A word was struggling with her throat.. Carl called her attention to the superb grace of a Pierce Arrow that glided by. They had reached the point. A hydroplane was humming high above the War College.—That man, what was his name? Who Arthur Bond introduced to me the other night. Who hardly noticed me, he was so stuck up. Whom Art called a genius, and the poet of Washington. The lines, she felt sure, were his. Yes, Art had recited them.—What was his name? He had irritated her. He was closed up in himself. She had felt she could not tease him.—Well, so much the worse for Art Bond. What was his name? Men were fishing, casting their lines from the river wall. Straight ahead, between low banks of trees, the Potomac rolled its muddy course, and, miles away, emptied into the Chesapeake. Smoke from Alexandria was blown up-stream by the river breeze.

"What do you say we run out the Conduit road to Cabin John's and make a day of it?"

Vera answered automatically.

"Sorry I cant to-day. I have an engagement at eight."

"Youve broken what should have been mine enough to break one date with him."

The almost perfect white of his skin was flushed, and rubbed to glowing by the wind. The hair he brushed so smooth was free and rumpled. His grey eyes were eagerly expectant. Vera's seemed to be glowing with prana. The coils of her hair threatened to uncurl and stream out backward like loose waves of silken bunting. Her skirt, rustling and flapping, was pressed close to her thighs.

"What do you say? We'll have dinner there, and afterwards go on to Great Falls. It would be a crime to waste a day like this."

Bud of a word was bursting in her throat.

"Beautiful!"

"Good. I knew youd go. Come on, lets get on our way."

"It is a word I've never said before."

"You bet it is. But youve said it now—no more holding off like you used to do. 'Yes' is a word that once said can be said again. Oh I knew you would someday, Vera, but what made you wait so long? Look at the good times we have already missed. Come on. Lets make up for lost time."

Carl held her hand and was propelling her. A little startled, she looked at him.

"Where are you pulling me, Carl?"

That was a good move on Vera's part. Carl had never seen her playful. Good. He'd play the game.

"To the sand-dunes of Lake Michigan where two loves build a bungalow."

"Really, Carl, I mean it. Where are you pulling me to?"

A fly-like shadow of doubt lit on Carl. He tossed his head, and drove it off.

"Just where I said: to the sand-dunes, where rippling waves make music all the time."

Vera realized that she must have promised something. Well, why not. She let herself be pulled. She'd cover herself with play. Her hair uncurled.

"Beautiful Michigan's azure waves—"

"Fine! Sweet! O poetess of Benton Harbor!"

"How many rooms will the bungalow be?"

Carl was completely red.

"Three."

Shadows of clouds, lazy-like, were gliding over the canopy-trees of the Potomac palisades. Below, the river, eddying in shallows, churning to a cream foam against mud-colored rocks, was carrying the brown burden of a wasted sediment … John Brown's body … from Harper's Ferry to the Chesapeake and the sea. Carl and Vera spun along the smooth asphalt of Conduit Road. The country beside the pike was dotted now and then by clustered shanties—poor white homes. Carl was quite happily absorbed in the handling of his car. It was vaguely good to have her there beside him. Vera, since she had come with him, would have been hurt to know her temporary relegation to the position of a pleasant accessory. Silence released her for the uncertain attempt at recapturing a mood which, save as an unreal memory, was new and strange to her. Art Bond.. What was his name? What dreams she had had, always swerved up from the concrete image of a man. The mood that had struggled to a hesitant and spattered ecstasy, that had forced some unused crevice of her soul to a vocalization of beauty, came from—What was his ..? She could not tease him. That hurt her. She had thrust him from her mind. Even his image would not come. The mood lay fallow before the unfound symbol of its evocation.

Carl was chatting over his cigarettes and cheese and coffee.

"You are sympathetic, Vera, and you'll understand. America, now the war is over, dont give a young fellow with push and brains and energy half a chance. Of course you can make money with a million. It makes itself. But what I want is not to loaf around and see it grow, or get tied down to some machine where even if you are a captain of industry youre no more than a petty officer in the army. Thats not what America stands for; but its what it is. And going to be more so in the future. The spirit of the country is one of individual enterprise. But unless it be in the oil-fields—and there the Standard gets you—its dying out, or, rather, its passing on to new lands. Now the Argentine is virginal. Or if not the Argentine, then some of those smaller countries. Theyre now just where this country was when Vanderbilt and Carnegie and Rockefeller first came up. Why a young fellow with go can go down there and clean up. But he's got to be quick about it. Ford and other men are pushing out over the world.. It sounds hard to say it, but I wish the Uncle would hurry up—and do whatever he's going to do. I'm studying hard—and say, Vera, heres where you can help me if you will. Lets talk Spanish when we're together. I dont know so much yet, but you can help me."

"I'd like to Carl, but I dont know any more Spanish than you do."

"But I thought—"

"If someone has told you that I am of Spanish descent, its true. My great grandfather was a Spaniard, but I was born in America, just like you. English is the only language that I know. Except for the smattering of others that I've picked up in school."

"I didnt think that you acted like a foreigner. Theyre all right, you know. I'm not prejudiced against them like I am against the niggers. A couple of them are friends of mine. Foreigners, I mean. But they do act a little different."

"Why do you hate niggers?"

"Hang if I know. Dont you?"

"Sometimes."

"Of course I dont hate them like these southern fellows do. And not as much as I hate Jews. The kikes are spreading all over the country; you see their names everywhere. There was one I remember at Wisconsin. He went out for football. We tried to break him up. And then there was Bugger—thats what we called the nigger—he was a good sort of fellow, and we had good fun with him. A good linesman—tackle he was—but he didnt make the team. Ever been to Madison, Vera? Swell place. Ideal location for a college town. A few snobs like there are everywhere, but most of the men came from the middle-west—good fellows, Vera. Youd like them. And there was one colored fellow I remember—say, did you ever see Sang Osmond run? Conference quarter miler from Chicago. I ran against him once. Clean cut fellow, good sport—I liked him. Niggers arent so bad, if only they didnt look so."

"All colored people arent disagreeable—"

"No, of course not. Theres Osmond. But you cant judge people by their exceptions. Look what we would have come to if we'd tried to believe that all Germans toed the mark of a man, say, like Beethoven."

"Why judge at all?"

"Good lord, Vera, youve got to have something to go by. Take me, when I go down into South America. I'll feel superior to those greasers—all Americans do. And thats the reason why we're running things.... Come on, lets get out of here and run up to the falls before it gets too dark."

"Dont forget that I have an engagement at eight."

"Hang it, Vera, I thought youd broken it."

"That wouldnt be right, Carl. You wouldnt want me to break one with you. I've been with you all day. And there are other times."

She had meant to make this the first and last.

"All right. Its a go. We'll make it Friday. Dance some place, and then take a drive. Thats closed. Come on, lets hurry up."

Carl paid the waiter.

The Dodge was purring along towards Great Falls.

Parked. They crossed a narrow springy toll-bridge into the clump of wood that vibrates like a G-string to the deep bass of the falls. Dusk, subtly scented violet, sprayed through the scant foliage of clustered trees. Carl's skin was of a greenish pallor. Vera's, almost as purple as the dusk. The agitation of the ground, the falls' thunder, conjured the sense of an impending lightning. Vera shivered. Carl drew her close to him. As they walked, she began to fancy she saw things behind the trunks and rocks, hiding in the bushes. A twig cracked. Vera's jumping upset Carl. But only for a moment. The heavy pounding of the falls was getting nearer. Quarter heaven in the west, the evening star. She pressed his arm. He was holding her waist. Slender, supple waist, trembling at unseen terrors in the forest. Carl would walk in many forests. Across great wastes and plains. The pampa grass, great stationary sea. Villages of untamed Indians. Stealthy marauding savages. This little wood near Washington was tame. Vera, for no reason, vaguely thought of Africa. She shivered. Carl stopped in their now winding path, and kissed her. Her lips were cool. Carl did not think of them as pale withered skin of berries. They reached the high-piled rocks. Footing was insecure. Vera stumbled. Carl lifted her in his arms. Carrying her, he almost fell over lovers hidden in the alcove of a giant boulder. With apologies, he moved on some paces, and set her down. The falls were below them. The foam, the dark suggestion of whirlpools, were weird, wildly arush. One's shouting voice was barely heard above a whisper. Vera leaned against him. Her mind was blank. It was just good to be held in his arms. A flickering light, a torch perhaps, flared up on the other bank. An intangibly phosphorescent glow gave light. Sandalwood odor of hair. Carl's conscious mind had not planned on love. With a million coming, things could wait. It came. Love was a tender joy, protective-like, that gave soft scents of sandalwood above the din of churning waters, beneath the chaste fire of the evening star.

. . .

They too had found a boulder. One's voice could be heard. Vera seated Indian fashion, responding, perhaps, to some folk persuasion of the place, rested Carl's head in her lap. Carl had been talking brokenly, trying to tell himself just how he felt. Her holding him made it easier to think. If it was love, it was curiously without passion. Passion was not love; but it was a part of it. One should pretend not to feel too much until one was married. But hiding it, and not feeling it at all, were two different things. "Once at Madison," he said aloud to Vera, "I felt like this." Her mind wanted Vera to listen. She must not tease or play with him.—Tease Art Bond though. Its almost time, it must be time, for my date with him. What was his name? O wont you come to me. Poet. I will not admit that he ever did or ever could hurt me. Oh yes and just you wait, I'll tease him too. Him whom I cannot tease. Who put beauty, a senseless warm thing like a sucking baby, in my mouth.

"I have never said it before."

"Said what, Vera?"

"Oh, nothing."

"As I was saying, he was an odd sort of chap. Peculiar, and most of the fellows resented it. It wasnt that he was stuck up. We couldnt see any reason why he should be. Enough money, but not too much at that. And I dont guess his folks were anything to brag about. He never mentioned them. In fact he never mentioned anything unless you sort of forced him to it. It looked as though he was acting up to mystery, and all that sort of thing. And then he was dark, and that made some difference. I gave him the duck until it came to summer school and myself and two other fellows from the frat moved over to the Y and on the sleeping porch I found myself in the bed next to him. We got to talking, and walking up the hill together. One day he asked me if I'd like to sail with him, him and two girls. He was strong for girls. That started it. And say, you should have seen him with that boat, as neat as I can handle a six-horse plow. We went to dances, and swam around a bit. One night he took me in his canoe. Just him and I. The moon was shining. When we got out in the middle of the lake, he slid down on the bottom, on the cushions, and began to hum. Yodels and singing were coming from canoes all over the water. I didnt notice him at first. And then, something like a warm finger seemed to touch my heart. I cant just explain it. I looked around and saw him. His eyes, set in that dark face, looked like two stars. 'Put the paddle in,' he said, 'we'll drift.' I did. 'Turn around and slide over the bar, theres a cushion on the bottom for you,' he then said. He saw me try, tip the canoe, and hesitate. 'Come on, dont be afraid, youre with an Indian, pale-face friend.' Saying that, way out in the middle of the lake, surrounded by shores that were once the home of Indians, made me feel strange and queer, you bet. Lights gleaming from the boat-house were far to shore. I made it, and again he started humming. 'Are you an Indian, really?' I asked. He kept on humming. And God if it didnt raise a lump the size of an apple in my throat. 'Whats that?' I asked. 'A negro folk-song,' he stopped long enough to say. 'God, I didnt know niggers could sing like that.' An answer, I guess, wasnt necessary. Abruptly he stopped singing, and I could feel him quiver-like—"

—He does not paw me. His arms embrace the shadow of a dream. I cannot tease him. His dream is a solvent of my resolution. He has taken something from me. It will be harder to face the office. I'd like to hate him for it. Easier to face the office because I share his dream. Will it melt something in me? Why cant I feel? If Art Bond should dream, I could not tease him. Time to go. What was his name? Will no one ever awake a dream in me? Poet. He must be like the fellow Carl is talking about. Him whom I cannot tease. What is his name? Who put beauty, a senseless warm thing like a sucking baby, in my mouth.

"I have never said that before."

"There you go again. Said what, Vera? Youre not listening."

"Oh nothing. Yes I am. Go on, Carl."

"I could feel him quiver-like. 'Carl,' he said, his eyes were gleaming, 'the wonder and mystery of it.' I had a quick foolish notion that he was trying to play up to the role we'd given him. Then I think I began to feel like he did. 'Dead leaves of northern Europe, Carl, have decayed for roots tangled here in America. Roots thrusting up a stark fresh life. Thats you. Multi-colored leaves, tropic, temperate, have decayed for me. We meet here where a race has died for both of us. Only a few years ago, forests and fields, this lake, Mendota, heard the corn and hunting songs of a vanished people. They have resolved their individualism to the common stream. We live on it. We live on them. And we are growing. Life lives on itself and grows.. The mystery and wonder of it.' He paused. And then, 'Deep River spreads over Mendota. Whirl up and dance above them new world soul!' God if he hadnt stirred me. Songs, and young girls' voices yodeling, criss-crossed on the waters. He turned to me and asked, 'Carl, you are a field man, have you ever felt overpowered by the sum of something, of which plowed fields, blue sky, and sunset were a part, overpowered till you sank choking with wonder and reverence?' I had, almost, once. I told him. He closed his hand over mine. Me, a football man, holding hands with a man on the lake. If that had ever got out it would have done for me. But it never did. I could never tell it. Only to you. You are the first. And thats the point of all I've told you. I feel like that with you, here by the falls, in the shadow of a boulder where some Indian made love."

Carl's words were strange to him.

Vera shivered.

"Chilly?"

"A little."

Carl shifted positions and took her in his arms. He kissed her lips .. pale withered skin of berries, puckered a little tight .. and drew her to him with a tension that was more muscular than passionate...

> John Brown's body, rumbles in the river,
> John Brown's body, thunders down the falls..

"What was that Carl?"

"I didnt hear a thing, sweetheart."

It would be good to fall in love with Carl, really. With anybody. Tease? Her mind said that because no man torrential enough—but there had been men, men with swift brutal passions—they didnt love. They bruised her with their instincts, bruised and frightened and disgusted her .. she must keep her body pure.. Carl didnt paw. He loved as she had long wanted men to. Why couldnt she feel? She recalled that she had not had a genuine emotion in the presence of a man .. at night, when she was alone .. since her last affair at home. Ugly. Why were men so callous? Brutal in insisting on her sacrifice. Then they wouldnt want her .. she must keep her body pure. Why couldnt she feel? This was pure love. Why couldnt she feel to return it? Feel for him the emotion that had spattered in "beautiful." Perhaps—Vera, lead in her heart, faced the possibility, that, for some unknown reason, maybe she really couldnt love. Some shameful defect made her incapable of it. She pressed Carl close to her. Held him to her lips. Tensioned thighs. Her heart beat faster. She strained. Carl's strength was tender. Why couldnt she feel? Something in her felt like it was empty. Men poured themselves into her because she was empty..

"Its time to go, now, Carl."

"I had forgotten. Of course, sweetheart."

Deep bass of the falls seemed coming from a throat that had been turned the other way... John Brown's body... They crossed the toll-bridge and found their car.

As Carl swung into S Street from Sixteenth, Vera saw Art Bond come out of her gate, and walk their way. The car passed. He did not see them. With a hasty goodby she ran up the steps and waited in the vestibule until Carl had gone. Coming down, Vera called to Art who was standing, undecided, on the corner. He seemed impersonalized, a shadow, beneath the great bulk of the Masonic Temple.

"I had a car, and everything," Art was irritably saying.

"I'm sorry Art, I tried to be on time. Is it so very late?"

"How'd you get in anyway? Was that you in that car?"

"I dropped from the stars."

"It was a Dodge. Whose was it? Dave Teyy's?"

"What a simple name!"

Her eyes were sparkling.

"I dont guess its too late yet; that is, if you really want to go."

"And I have been searching, Oh how I have been searching all afternoon."

Vera seemed talking to the apex of the Temple.

"Now whats the use of lying, Vera? You could have found me easy enough if you wanted to."

"David Teyy."

"Oh hang him, Vera. Youre with me now. That is, if you want to go."

Vera looked down into a dark serious face, mobile and expressive, like shifting, sun-shot dusk.

"Of course I want to go, Art. Where's the car?"

"Can I use your phone a minute?"

Vera was hard to talk to, hard to touch to-night. It was to lead her into a mood for loving when they reached the park that Art had hired a car. The Cadillac had hummed up Sixteenth Street, like a shuttle, between the Castle and Meridian Hill, past the portentous embassies. Turning, it had followed the curve of Park Road, across the broad bridge blanketed in a chill vapor. Down the hill, hemmed in by the quickening life of Rock Creek Park. The driver had been dismissed and told to return within an hour. During the whole ride Vera seemed absorbed in herself, and kept to her corner of the car. The wind whistled on the sharp edge of an invisible partition that was between them. Now they sat, Vera hugging her knees, on the slope of a knoll within earshot of the purling of the creek. Great curved massy trees in sharp planes of shadow and moonlight. Mountain clouds, fleecy silver. Massive undulations, barely perceptible—earth's respiration, earth breathing to life. Vera felt dwarfed. She felt that Art could be of no aid to her. Dwarfed by the great heaving blocks of nature. By the shadow of a man. David Teyy. He should be riding the backs of trees, spurring them to swing up and trumpet. Him whom she could not tease. Who put beauty, a senseless warm thing like a sucking baby—Suppose I cannot love him? The thought gave her a sinking feeling, and made her shiver.

"Chilly."

"A little."

Art tucked a robe around her shoulder. He stretched out, lit a cigarette. Women were like that; you had to wait for them. Vera was thankful for the glow of Art's cigarette. It was a small point one could look at. Narrowing her eyes, Art's face looked like a far-off mountain, faintly ruddy, beneath the supernal glowing of a red star. Black man, white man, lips seeking love, souls dreaming.. Man of the multi-colored leaves, dreaming, will your lips seek love? Vera raised her hand, delicate, tapering olive fingers, and pressed it against her lips .. pale withered skin of berries.. The contact was loose and cool. Her heart sank. She shivered. Art reached up and pulled her down beside him.

"Whats the matter, sugar?"

"Nothing, only I dont feel so well to-night."

"Driving all afternoon should have done better for you than that. And with Dave Teyy."

"I wasnt with him, Art."

"Now whats the use of lying, Vera?"

"I tell you I wasnt."

"Oh well, dont lets scrap about it. He's my friend. But I've got to bar him with my girls. He doesnt believe in letting them out."

"What do you mean?"

"You know what I mean."

"Well, he let me out."

"I thought you wasnt with him."

"Art, you are so stupid when you fuss. Why dont you sing, or .. love me?"

"You irritate me. You wont let me."

"There, there. Thats a good sweet boy."

Vera, softly weaving arms. Sandalwood odor of hair. Murmurs. Lispings. Art's arms tightened around her. Vera averted her lips. He kissed her throat. Caught a soft fold in his teeth and bit it.

"You mustnt Art."

"Mustnt love you?"

"Not that way ... O cant you see I'm empty.. Art, Art I'm empty, fill me with dreams."

"With love."

"No, with dreams. Dreams of how life grows, feeding on itself. Dreams of dead leaves, multi-colored leaves. Dreams of leaves decaying for a vernal stalk, phosphorescent in the dusk, flaming in dawn. O Art, in that South from which you come, under its hates and lynchings, have you no lake, no river, no falls to sit beside and dream .. dream?"

"Red dust roads are our rivers, the swishing of the cane, our falls. I am an inland man."

"Then you have choked with the sum—O tell me, Art, tell me, I know you have."

"Beside the syrup-man?"

"Beside the syrup-man."

"He comes to boil the cane when the harvest is through. He pitches camp in a clearing of the wood. You smell only the pines at first, and saw-dust smoke. Then a mule, circling with a beam, begins to grind. The syrup, toted in a barrel, is poured on the copper boiling stove. Then you begin to smell the cane. It goes to your head like wine. Men are seated round. Some chewing cane-stalk, some with snuff. They tell tales, gossip about the white folks, and about moonshine licker. The syrup-man (his clothes look like a crazy-quilt and smell sweetish) with his ladle is the center of them. His face is lit by the glow. He is the ju-ju man. Sometimes he sings, and then they all commence to singing. But after a while you dont notice them. Your soul rises with the smoke and songs above the pine-trees. Once mine rose up, and, instead of travelling about the heavens, looked down. I saw my body there, seated with the other men. As I looked, it seemed to dissolve, and melt with the others that were dissolving too. They were a stream. They flowed up-stream from Africa and way up to a height where the light was so bright I could hardly see, burst into a multi-colored spraying fountain. My throat got tight. I guess it was that that pulled me back into myself—"

—This black man from the South has choked with beauty. He does not paw me. His arms embrace the shadow of a dream. I cannot tease him. Why cant I feel? David Teyy. Can I love him? Vera shivered. Art drew her closer to him. Her arms tightened like strong slender vines across his back. Lips met. Something was tautening her lip-strings to the firmness of a bow. Their thighs were vines. Her heart beat faster. She strained. Art was a wedge .. she tried to push loose .. a black wedge of hot red life, cleaving. Arms strained against his chest. Wedge .. cleaving.. Trees whirl! Stab. Stampede. Spinning planes, shadow, silver. Night thrust back before a burning light. They were rolling, over, over, down the hill.. Trees stand still, glowering, in a stationary sky. Trees continuing to whirl. Art's lips still clung to her. She clawed his face. Pushed at his eye. Her face was wet and grass streaked. Weeds tangled in her uncurled hair. She clawed his face.

"You are a beast. O let me go."

Wedge trying to cleave her.

"Black nigger beast."

Art swung loose, and as if a lash had cut him, groaned. Whip him lash! Art groaned, choked, groaned. Shrinking on a slave-block black man groan! His head swung loose as if his neck had been wrenched... Vera couldnt think what she had done to him. Her eyes were dizzy pendulums of her soul.

"Art.."

"...Go way .. go way .. ohhh."

"Art, what have I—"

"Go way, .. go way .. ohhh.. Go way... O why dont you go way..."

"Art, Art, have I hurt you so? O Art have I hurt you so?"

He sprang to his feet. Vera hoped he would hit her. Swung off across the road, crashed through the bushes, going towards the creek. John Brown's body .. she heard him splashing through the creek .. thunders down the falls.

Vera buried her teeth in the ground to steady the convulsions of her sobbing.

II

Vera was walking down Sixteenth Street to work. Young green leaves looked yellow in the thick flood of sunlight. Morning, clover-sweet and ruddy; melancholy morning. Vera's buoyancy seemed to rest on a nervous and slightly unreal basis. She tried to rid herself of this curious haze by walking. The muscles of her limbs were firm, the skin of her face, flushed and tight. Men passing in sleek expensive cars turned to look at her. Memory of Art was a stinging insect, aflutter, pinned down .. that it was not dead denied by her will. Carl. Carl had proposed to her. She'd put him off. Vera tried to write to her mother. That she could not bring herself to do it gave her a sense of isolation so swift and intolerable that she had rushed from the house, impotently dreading, as in a bad dream. She hid from herself in desperately trivial details of office work. And then, a vicarious peace was vouchsafed her by the innocent loveliness of external Washington. The well-paved streets, the rows of comfortable, inconspicuous houses, the men and women that walked and lived in them, established a perfect sympathy with her in her attempt to defer a settlement with life. If life would only let her alone—save when she beckoned to it. Vera was too aware of her physical loveliness to desire a complete negation. Walking to work helped her to put off. Moving pictures, dances, men whom she could handle. David Teyy. She feared to see him. As a dream, he could be evoked, a final recourse, in dispelling the evil of a too-insistent nightmare. This morning, Vera had no need of David Teyy. The young green leaves looked yellow. The air was sweet with clover. The Masonic Temple, receding over her left shoulder, was a granite chrysalis that had emerged from the mystery of moonlight and shadow into the solid implications of day. A car, full of young girls in brilliant scarfs and sport shoes, drew up to the curb. Vera heard someone call her name. One or two, she slightly recognized. Just a bunch driving to [the] office. Would she go along? They were happy about nothing. Vera caught their spirit. She reached the office tingling and aglow. Anemic thin odor of stale tobacco. She went from sash to sash, throwing up the windows. A digested fellow came in, changed his street-coat for one that had been worn glossy and thread-bare, grumbled at the draft that was coming in, cancelled Vera's efforts for fresh air with quick successive bangs, went to his desk, opened a drawer from which exuded a musty smell, drew out some papers, sharpened his pencils, and, with an habitual show of infinite diligence, virtue, and purpose, started work. Younger voices greeted her upon their arrival. Carl entered, flushed as if just from a shower-bath. He threw up the windows. He and the digested fellow had a fuss. Ingloriously routed, he whispered something into the dark coil that covered Vera's ear. She laughed. The gong rang. Flutter of those almost late. A few stragglers. Tick, tick, tick, tick, pounding of typewriters, metallic slide of files, rustle of starched paper, and the day began. Young girls who worked all month to imitate leisure class flappers. Young girls from South Carolina, Illinois, Oregon, waiting. Widows of improvident men who had been somebody in their day. Boys who had left school. Men dreaming of marriage and bungalows in Chevy Chase. Old digested fellows. Negro messengers. Something was up. The girls were whispering. A group gathered around Vera. The head-clerk looked up uneasily and scowled at them.

"What do you know about it?" one was saying.

"Shows you how slick they are."

"How'd they find out?"

"Oh she left a note-book in her desk. Somebody was looking for papers and came across it."

"What was in it?"

"Nothing, except a date she had to go to the Howard Theatre. Thats a nigger place, you know. It looked suspicious. So somebody followed her home, and saw her go out with a nigger. The chief was told, and he had her up about it. And they say she stood there brazen as anything, and said yes she was a nigger and proud of it. What do you think of that?"

"You could never have told."

"Oh yes you could. Some of them had been suspicious for a long time. And nigger blood will out. Its like Lincoln said, you can fool some of the people some of the time, but you cant fool all of the people all the time."

"But they are slick at it."

"I dont see what they want to be white for anyway. The way they boast about progress and all that youd think theyd be satisfied with their own race. But theyre not, theyre always trying to push into ours."

"Its because these northern politicians—I dont mean the President of course—coddle them. Theyd never even think of having such notions down South. In the South they know where their place is, and they keep it."

"Well, its good we caught her. It'll be a lesson to others."

"Oh, we always do. Sometimes its long, sometimes its short, but we catch up to them. You cant fool all of the people all of the time. I wonder if they know that saying of Lincoln's? Somebody ought to write it on a slip of paper and put it in their desks."

"Lets do."

"Here, Vera, you make some carbon copies."

"Are there as many as that?"

"Well, you cant tell. We've got our eyes on any number."

"Oh I cant see how anyone can be so deceitful."

Carl had drifted up.

"Whats all the row about?"

"Oh just another nigger we caught passing."

"What is it? A game or something?"

"You wouldnt think it was a game if you had been deceived and imposed upon."

"Serious as all that?"

"They'll think so by the time we get through with them."

Carl winked at Vera. The head-clerk came up, smiling behind his scowl.

"And now whats occupying the governments time?"

"Oh, nothing, just something about that Preston person."

"Yes, well, um, well better settle that at lunch. Run along now."

"Yes, Mr. Darby."

"Just as you say, Mr. Darby."

"Aurwewar, Mr. Darby."

Vera, left to herself plunged into work. Carl took her out to lunch. He insisted that she go out with him that night. Vera knew that he wanted an answer. Pressure was becoming intense, almost to suffocation. Not tonight, Carl, she had managed to say only by promising the next evening. He assured her that if she didnt give an answer to him, he would come after her. The afternoon, hugely unreal, ticked away. Reaching home, she plunged into a hot bath and tried to vaporize herself, one with its fumes. The towel but accentuated life. She had a banal observation: now I see why men drink. She tried to sleep. She exhausted herself with the tangled covers. Tossed out of bed and ran down to the phone. Yes, David Teyy would come around to see her; fortunately, he had no date. Vera, dressed, a trifle drawn, but with eyes brilliant in their searching sparkle, compounded of pain and hope and wistfulness, had the sincere impression that for the first time in her life she was really beautiful.

Something from David Teyy ran down the steering-gear, down the brakes and clutches, and gave flesh and blood life to the car. Vera was curled, as if she was in the dark enclosure of a womb. She could drive on forever. Covered by life that flowed up the blue veins of the city. Up Sixteenth Street. David was a red blood center flowing down. She sucked his blood. Go on forever with David flowing down. He had hardly spoken to her. She wished he would never speak. Life flowed away from her to gestate his words.

"What is that, Vera?"

His face, a bronze plate engrossed in sharp lines and curves, emerged from a blood-shot dusk. His words tasted of blood and copper. Why could he not let her be?

"The Masonic Temple, David."

"I mean to you."

"To me?"

"Who live under the shadow of it."

"I have never thought."

"Who live under the shadow of it. Under life."

"How do you know?"

"I have been told that you tease—"

"Men who are not strong enough—"

"—yourself."

"I am pure."

"You are a living profanation of the procreative principle of Deity."

Smile, which she could not see in the dusk.

"Because black children are repulsive to me?"

"Because you hold a phallus to the eye, and tease yourself."

"I do not understand."

"That is a rite of profanation."

"Your words cannot make me bad."

"My words were not used in your making."

Smile, she feels.

"You give me sarcasm when what I need is love."

"The necessary complement of giving is the capacity to take."

Smile.

"I cannot understand your words. Let me be."

"You wanted me?"

"After a while. O dont talk now. Please. Let me be."

…David flowing down. Vera had wanted to pass the cherry trees. And on out to the point. A word might struggle with her throat.

"Look, the cherry trees. I have seen them bloom. I have seen Japanese in reverence beneath them."

—Would it come?

"Lafcadio Hearn—"

"'Lafcadio,' that is a soft word, David."

"You are sensitive—"

"Oh to so many things if I would only let myself be."

"Lafcadio Hearn tells of how the Japanese visit regions where the trees are blooming, much as we go to the mountains or the sea, drawn by their fragrance. It is hard to think of them succumbing to gaudy show and blare like our Americans at Atlantic City."

"You do not like Americans, David?"

"Do you feel Americans apart from you?"

"Answer my question first."

"One does not dislike when one is living. Life is inconceivable except in relation to its surrounding forms. I love."

"People?"

"The process and mystery of life. Life feeding on itself. ."

Deep River, Mendota. Vera saw souls drifting to the rhythm of forgotten cadences, whirled up … and growing. The inexplicable wonder of it! And our scientists, who can name more strangely minute exceptions than anyone, believing that they have caught it in a formula. Churchmen and scientists contending over formulas, over beliefs! Could anything be more militantly superstitious, more doggedly naive??

…David flowing down. David flowing out. David like mass undulations of shadow-silver trees. She wished he would light a cigarette. They were curving into the Potomac Speedway.

—Would it come?

far-off trees
Whose gloom is rounded like the hives of bees
All humming peace to soldiers who have gone

"Echoes."

"They are yours?"

"Mine two years ago. Now, more yours than mine? Where did you hear them?"

Potomac swishes and gurgles in the crevices of the river wall. Cars parked beneath the willows are more frequent. Lovers, swift receding oval faces, float in the gloom of back seats.

"Art Bond. He is a friend of yours?"

Vera, restless.

"One of the best. The best, here, perhaps, except for his habit of fastening on the ghosts of my dead selves. Ghosts, the spiritualists tell us, should be allowed to depart, with a bon voyage for the way. That is a serviceable truth that should be brought from the cheap tappings and illogic of the seance room to the practice of broad day."

Smile; serious.

"You believe in ghosts?"

"Your meaning of the word is beside the question. Things die, transmute. Their memory lingers. A preoccupation with them clogs creative life. People who are forever fastening on them give tangibility to the clogs. They can very easily slip from friends to nuisances."

"But do you believe in the ghosts I mean?"

"In the ghosts of hysterical women, their fortune-tellers, ouija-boards, and cards? Perfectly valid as symptoms."

"I do not understand."

"Apis, steer god, cock your ears and listen to the rite of profanation. Vera, you wanted me?"

"I do not understand your words. Let me be. After a while. Lets stop here and run out to the point.—And plunge in the river. Lord, I want to cross over into camp ground."

Mobile river, scintillant beneath the moon.. John Brown's Body.. River flowing from Harper's Ferry to the Chesapeake and the sea. Open ocean for brown sediment of the river. Tide in, send your tang. Resistant ripples. Wave in, send your waves. Wash back. John Brown's body rumbles in the sea. Mobile river, scintillant beneath the moon... Lights twinkle on the wharves of Seventh Street. Wash red blood. Search-lights play on Lincoln Memorial and the Monument. Wash red blood. Blue blood clots in the veins of Washington. Wash red blood. John Brown's body.. Mobile river, carrying brown sediment, scintillant beneath the moon.

They were standing on the point. David's face seemed unreal, and high above her. The line of his nose was a thin rim of silver. You have teased me. Your easy phrases when they turned on me, were teasing. Yours is a sin. Not mine. I cannot help it. You whom I turn to, tease me. Whom I love. Who carry solution within you. Who could, but by a touch, make me feel the world not so utterly dreadful, so sinking, without bottom, so utterly outside, and me alone. You tease me. O you do not know my need. It is not in you to sin callously. You are here .. why will you not touch me?.: the dream vanishes, the floor slips, and I dangle, dangle. O you do not know my need. Tease you? You know I cannot, and you play with me. O dreamer of Life why do you tease your dream? Do you not see that I have never wanted to tease? You place my compulsions to your eye, and play with me. What vision is it that lets you be blinded by the eye? You sing of rivers. O cant you see? Beneath the scum I am a river. You who plunge and cause stale drifts to stampede, releasing the river, will you not even touch me? You cannot sin so. O Christ forgive him if he sins. Virgin Mother, you will understand if I drown in the river. Forgive him, Christ. O God, I dangle. Lord God, I want to cross over into the camp ground.

David was humming.

"David, it would be a Godsend for the river to overflow and sweep me under."

…David flowing down.—Was that his hand that touched me? Are these his eyes bending over mine? Christ eyes, do not let me cry for loving you.

"Emptiness desires Nirvana. At best, I thought that that was what you would want."

—Words, do not take him from his eyes. Glow, Christ eyes.

"Living from herself."

—Christ eyes, do not let me cry for loving you.

Perfect within yourself, incarnate mystery.

"I kneel in reverence before the wonder of it."

David's hand was almost crushing hers. It must have been a tear she felt, so hot it was. Her free hand tingled to the electric of his bent head.

"I am not worthy that you should kneel to me."

Vera shivered. Shook with a strange convulsion.

Roll river!

Something so complete and overpowering came over her that she sank, almost senseless, to her knees on the grass beside him.

"David," she was leaning against him, trembling, "what was it?"

Mobile river, scintillant, flowing to the sea.

"You ask me, who could but kneel before it?"

"I almost sinned, and then God struck me."

They were rolling over the smooth asphalt of Conduit Road, going towards the Falls. Head-lights of approaching cars glared at them. Rushed swiftly by. Across the river, Potomac palisades, great wavy outlined masses, glided leisurely with them. John Brown's body rumbles up the river…

"I have nothing to say to him but 'No'."

"People, Vera, unless you insult them, are insistent for reasons of refusal. Now Art—"

"It is unkind of you to remind me of him—after to-night."

"Ghosts of our dead selves—"

"And yet, if I have gained any strength at all, I should be able to face him. That wont be a ghost until it has been faced. I will sometime. But it will be purely selfish.

People cant really forgive. Yet in this case there is nothing to forgive. I dont know how I shall meet him."

"Carl, first. He will want reasons."

"That I love you."

"Will that satisfy your own integrity? It was a half-truth up till tonight."

"It has been a whole truth, always."

"But you see, sweetheart—"

"You do not say that like you would say it if you loved me."

"—your tendency is to make of love a sort of sublimated postponement. Love solves inner complications for a while. It holds little or no solution for the outside world. Perhaps in a better day... Especially is this true of the two worlds you dangle over. Love is inoperative here."

"Then what is?"

"A burning integrity of vision."

"You have it, man of the multi-colored leaves.. O I knew it was you Carl dreamed about. I seemed to love him when the dreams he poured into me were you. I could not feel—"

Vera looked at David, and grew frightened.

"—not with him. I guess I led him on. But it was you who were struggling to birth in a word beneath the cherry trees, you along the river, at the point, above the falls, you. David, David, I love you... You have it, man of the multi-colored leaves, but I? .."

"When you knelt beside me at the point?"

"I saw only a wonderful glow that I was too afraid to really look at."

"You have never, not once, succeeded in facing yourself?"

"I have run."

"Where?"

"What is it you say? Nirvana. To you."

"Before me?"

"Men's arms, up to a point. And my bed at night."

"Before that?"

"Before my father died, his arms. Before him, mother's."

"And now mine?"

"Now yours, .. if you will let me."

"I seem then, to be in the direct descent of varied and sundry prehensiles—"

"How can you joke?"

"Once learn to laugh at arms and you will find that they will release you. Hasnt your experience taught you that?"

"You are cruel, cruel. Why do you torment me so?"

"Art's spirit working through me, perhaps."

"David."

Tears, by the motion of the car, were shaken from her eyes.

"Seriously, I want you to see this thing through. Answer Carl, and his look will lead you to an answer for the world."

"That I love you."

. . .

Clump of wood that vibrates like a G-string to the deep bass of the falls. Night, furtive and shifting where shafts of moonlight stab in quick succession through the veering leaves. Ground trembles to the storm and lightning from clouds of trees. John Brown's body .. John Brown's body thunders up the falls ...

"I always feel nervous and unreal in these woods."

"They are under a spell."

"Hold me, David."

David slipped his arm around her, and, bending over, chanted:

> Court-house tower,
> Bell-buoy of the Whites,
> Charting the white-man's channel,
> Bobs on the agitated crests of pines
> And sends its mellow monotone,
> Satirically sweet,
> To guide the drift of barges..
> Black barges...
> African Guardian of Souls,
> Drunk with rum,
> Feasting on a strange cassava,
> Yielding to new words and a weak palabra
> Of a white-faced sardonic God—

"Oh dont, David."

"You who would mate with me—"

"Not that way, David."

"—quail at such a simple evocation? What would you do, if a whole troupe of souls who love the earth-sphere too well to go away, were to suddenly materialize before you? You who are still neither in nor out yourself."

"You are only trying to frighten me."

"Well, so I am. Here, see the good fairy beckoning to you from my lips? Do you wish her?"

"David."

Lips that but a few moments ago were the pale withered skin of berries, who tautened you with dew? Brushed you with the sweet scent of cane?

"Now—let us hurry to the falls, David."

John Brown's body was below them... Lovers let your dreams fly out the moon.. The golden flare of torches was diluted by the cold white light. Torches flare! It was wonderful to be in his arms.

"Do you know what I say of you, David?"

"I cannot hear you."

"Come, I know a rock."

David smiled at this girl leading him to secret places in his boulders.

"Carl will come to this place."

"How do you know, David? Oh lets not think of him. Tell me, do you know what I say of you? I will tell you. I say that you, man of the multicolored leaves, put beauty, a senseless warm thing like a sucking baby, in my mouth."

"How did that come to you?"

"It just came, O man, who knows better yet cant help seeking solutions of mysteries. Wouldnt you love, sometimes, to get rid of your mind?"

"Ask me if I would love to postpone."

"Must you ever refer to it?"

"The western world demands of us that we not escape. The implication of fresh life is its use. Monasteries and sepulchres are the habitats of shades."

"Not even in love? O David I love you."

"For yourself; for me?"

"Your questions chill me. Your words. O do not talk to me David. Love."

Lips that but a few moments ago were the pale withered skin of berries, who tautened you with dew? Brushed you with the sweet scent of cane? Sandalwood odor of hair. Murmurs. Lispings. Love spinning to the tight pressure of tensioned arms. David .. wedge .. cleaving. Bronze sun, hammered to a sharp wedge .. cleaving .. His lips tasted of copper and blood.

"O David, David, not that. Not that, David. How could you—after to-night, your kneeling at the point?"

"Passion?"

"No, David, O no—love."

"Young girl asking for the moon."

"What do you mean? O David, you cannot sin so. Love."

"Young girl asking for the moon."

"David, you are killing something in me. You cannot sin so. Mother of Christ, forgive him."

Hands that tautened with dew, brushed with the sweet scent of cane, you are Indian-givers.

Vera lay, a limp, damp thing, like a young bird fallen from its nest, found in the morning, in David's arms. John Brown's body rumbles in the river ...

"Cry."

"I cant, David. I want to go home."

A shadowy shape was silhouetted above them.

"Beg pardon," it said.

"Carl."

"Is that you, Vera? I cant see. What are you doing here? Oh, beg pardon."

"Its all right, Carl. Sit with us. He is a friend of yours."

"Hello, Carl."

"I cant quite see—well I'll be damned if it isnt David Teyy. Where did you come from? I didnt know that you were in town. Vera, you didnt tell me you knew Dave Teyy. How long you been here? Working? Well I'll be damned. Pardon, Vera. And out here at the falls. What on earth ever brought you out here? This is a surprise. Damn. Pardon, Vera."

"Sit down, Carl. I have something I want to tell you."

Carl crouched down, Indian fashion. The three of them seemed as though gathered round an improbable fire.

"Dave Teyy. Old man, I havent seen you since that summer at Wisconsin. But I've thought of you. Havent I, Vera? Its good to see you. Recalls old days, and everything. Hows the world using you? Piled up a fortune I bet. But no, as I remember it, that wasnt your line. Man of the multi-colored leaves. What was that you used to get off about faces that chiseled dreams? From American marble? Or something like that? Like the fellows used to say, you were a queer duck, but they couldnt help liking you. Damn."

"Carl, this is as good a time as any other. I want to tell you that I cannot marry you."

"But not here, Vera. You cant mean it. Wait till another time. Hell's bells."

"But I do mean it, Carl. And I want to get it over with."

"Cant marry me? Oh this is an h of a time to tell a feller. Pardon, Dave. But it sort of upsets a feller."

"Deep down in your heart you really dont care, Carl. You think you do. But some-day you'll find the right girl. Then you'll see."

"You dont love me. Thats it. But thats no reason—what is it Vera, tell me. I thought you did—up till to-night. What is it?"

David was trying to whip her with his will.

"I love David Teyy."

"Oh—well—congratulations, Dave. Hell's bells. Pardon. Guess I'd better be running on."

Something held him.

"Vera, Carl, both of you will sit as you are."

Life was thrashing in David. He would stampede these pale ghost people. He gathered wood, built a fire. Its flare disturbed nearby lovers who grumbled at it and moved away. Carl and Vera could not believe themselves. Fingers pulled down their stomachs. They shivered. Drew nearer the flames. David, holding them with his eyes, was crouching.

"Know you, people, that you sit beside the boulder where Tiacomus made love. Made love, do you understand me? Know you, people, that you are above a river, spattered with blood. John Brown's blood. With blood, do you understand me? White red blood. Black red blood. Know you, people, that you are beneath the stars of wonder, of reverence, of mystery. Know you that you are boulders of love, rivers spattered with blood, stars of wonder and mystery. Roll river. Flow river. Roll river. Flow river. River, river, roll, Roll!"

> The river was empty, flowing to the sea,
> From Harper's Ferry to the Chesapeake and the sea—
> …They hung John Brown..

> The river was empty, flowing to the sea,
> From Harper's Ferry to the Chesapeake and the sea—
> …They hung John Brown.. Roll river..

River was empty, flowing to the sea,
From Harper's Ferry to the Chesapeake and the sea—
...They hung John Brown.. Roll river roll!

John Brown's body, rumbles in the river,
John Brown's body, thunders down the falls—
...Roll river roll!

"Know you, people, that you sit beside the boulder where Tiacomus made love. Made love, you understand me? Know you, people, that you are above a river, spattered with blood. With blood, you understand me? John Brown's blood. Know you, people, that you are beneath the stars of wonder, of reverence, of mystery. Know you that you are boulders of love, rivers spattered with blood, white red blood, black red blood, that you are stars of wonder and mystery. Roll river! Flow river! Roll river! Flow river! River, river, roll, Roll!!"

The boulder seemed cleft by a clap of thunder. As if the falls had risen and were thundering its fragments away ...

Tick, tick, tick, tick, pounding of typewriters, metallic slide of files, rustle of starched paper. Young girls who work all month to imitate leisure-class flappers. Young girls from South Carolina, Illinois, Oregon, waiting. Widows of improvident men who had been somebody in their day. Boys who have left school. Men dreaming of marriage and bungalows in Chevy Chase. Old digested fellows. Negro messengers. Carl but little changed. The slow process of digestion. Black life pepper to the salt of white. Sneezes. Tick, tick, tick, tick. Vera listless, nervous ...

Men listen to her lispings and murmurs. Black souls steal back to Georgia canefields, soft and misty, underneath a crescent moon. The mystery of their whispered promises seems close to revelation, seems tangibly incarnate in her. Black souls, tropic and fiery, dream of love. Sing joyful codas to forgotten folk-songs. Spin love to the soft weaving of her arms. Men listen to her lispings and murmurs. White souls awake to adolescent fantasies they thought long buried with the dead leaves along the summer streets of mid-western towns. Solvents of melancholy burn through their bitten modes of pioneer aggressiveness to a southern repose. They too spin love to the soft weaving of her arms. White men, black men, only in retrospective kisses, know the looseness of her lips .. pale withered skin of berries ...

41

"Confession"

Margery Latimer

In the decades following her death, Margery Latimer (1899–1932) was recognized as a significant modernist who laid the foundation for many later feminist writers. Latimer, a protégée of the feminist journalist Zona Gale, was raised in Wisconsin and in 1924 moved to New York City, where she wrote book reviews for the *New York Herald* and the *New York World*, and published two novels and a number of short stories. Her first novel, *We Are Incredible*, appeared in 1928; it was followed by the story collection *Nellie Bloom and Other Stories* in 1929 and the novel *This Is My Body* in 1930. Latimer's work featured challenges to social structures, the liberation and sensualization of the female body, and experimentation with points of view. Through her interest in Gurdjieffian philosophy she met the writer Jean Toomer, also a student of Gurdjieff; they married in 1931. Because Latimer was white and Toomer was of mixed-race origins, their marriage generated a great deal of negative publicity. Latimer died in childbirth in 1932. A posthumous collection of short stories, *Guardian Angel and Other Stories*, appeared later that year. The story reprinted here, "Confession," was published in 1929.

What do I care for the years that pass when I am not moving? Why should I bother about morning, then noon, then night, and weeks, months and years when I am not moving? My bones are changing, my face is slipping, my skin is opening its pores and tanning. But I am not growing as weeks and months and years grow. Something inside me is strong and steady, like a body there beyond my ribs. Perhaps it looks out through my ribs sometimes, seeing through the minute blood cells and skin cells into outdoors. Perhaps it doesn't care to look outdoors.

But this is what I want to say. I do not grow. My body grows. Weeks and months grow to years but I, this curled, deaf I, does not grow. It is not a presence. It is not like the pressure of air moving in colored folds about me. It is not something that can be seen or smelled or touched. I only know it is there and I imagine it lies curled up and demands food and I hate it, I hate it, I hate it. Its food is not bread and wine or flesh. It has other food.

I must tell you about this deep rotten knot in me because now my blood and my skin cells and my tears are revolving in remorse. I can feel a straining through my legs up to my shoulders and my head, beyond my eyes, in my ears, to see and hear this monster and drive it out so that I may inhabit my body and make it my own house and be at peace in all its intricate rooms and halls.

I tell you I am not to blame. This curled up thing makes me act. The first time I realized it was not myself that did the work I felt happy, then when I saw that I couldn't push the monster out I pounded my head. Let me show you what it does to me. If you can imagine a girl twenty-eight years old with large, set eyes and bright hair and a small mouse-mouth you will have something of me from the outside. Now pretend you are in a basement room with a boarded up fireplace, an India rug on the floor with the tree of life in amber and jade birds flying in the branches. Imagine too, a Persian screen and beyond it a green glass bottle hanging from the wall. See the couch with a striped silk cover and the spoke of a bannister in a corner, left by a drunken friend. See the little white duck floating on the wooden stretch of bookcase top; her feathers are purple and red and green. Behind her is a tea set with lost ships rocking in a snowy sea. There are two chairs that have shiny seats and glossy bodies. Their legs are thin and bulging at the knee-cap. One expects them to hop across the room.

Now feel at home in this room and look around at the people, most of them men. It is ten o'clock. Outside is snow and cats are using their paws like hands at the shutters, pushing and clattering to get in. Carlo is sitting upright in a camp chair. He is small and his black suit is too large for him. His face is beautiful and ecstatic, no matter what is being said, and when he talks he pushes out his red lips and pauses before a large word which he always pronounces wrong. His face is in perpetual wonderment. I like Carlo. On the floor near the door sits Evan. He has light hair that makes his head in some lights look like a polished egg. His hands are long and white and he wears glasses without bows. Sometimes the light catches his glasses and then he looks very odd, like an aluminum man in his grey suit and glittering head and eyes. Gertrude I won't describe because I don't like her. She is one of those harsh people who laughs like this, "a-a-a-a-a" quickly like sheep or a train. She thinks I'm a hypocrite. I don't like Gertrude, she has no imagination.

Come to the other side of the room. In a red chair is Robin. He is twenty-two. He is very small. His tiny hands and feet and his small head, like a glossy acorn, make me very happy. Robin is a seven months child. He came out too soon. I'm always trying to make it up to him as if I were to blame. Florida is sitting on the floor with his head against the jade curtains. He looks very beautiful, I think. You may not like him. He is colored and his face and eyes look as if he were standing on a mountain top singing, "Little David Play On Your Harp." I think he believes that angels live in the sky even though he has several degrees. He feels at home now but when he first came he talked about how educated he was and how many colleges he had been vice-president of and how many lectures he gave. He thought they didn't accept him. He thought right. Max Gold—I suppose you can tell he's Jewish. Once he got drunk and put his head on the table and cried, "I'm a Jew. God, God, they all hate me." There's the Armenian. He had a beautiful name and he changed it to John. His family were all murdered and his village was burned. Once he said, "Even if I had money to go back nobody would be there and no houses, not even the store."

Perhaps now you begin to see what I'm driving at. But look at me. Please look at me. I am walking toward the percolator that bubbles behind the screen on a shining white table. My hair is straight across my forehead and under the light it looks like gold. My ears show and the back of my hair is like a golden bush. From the side and with imagination I might be Alice in Wonderland. My dress is blue with sad white flowers and bands of blue velvet. I walk across the room on velvet slippers with slanting heels. I hear the slish of my skirts and I nod my head a little and feel quite-quite.

No one has seen the monster yet. No one even suspects that it lies curled up between my ribs, looking out with its dreadful eyes, reaching with its arms, its manifold arms. I serve the coffee. I try to decide which shall have the largest cup. Florida because he is colored or John because his parents were slaughtered and his village destroyed. Carlo has just mispronounced gigantic, automaton, and adamant, all in the same sentence. Everyone is laughing at Carlo so I give him the largest cup. He keeps on talking and mispronounces Spengler, Epicurus, Ulysses and rococo. Now he is going on just because they are laughing and he calls horizon wrong and occurs something very strange. They are all shrieking and the dreadful, unimaginative Gertrude is going "a-a-a-a-a-a."

I am ashamed to describe what happened inside me. It hurts to think I am not rare and wonderful, as unique as the golden bush of hair at the back of my head and the quite-quite walk on velvet heels. Perhaps Gertrude saw me truly and that was why she shrugged and pulled her horrid mouth down at the corner. Now I am telling, now I am revealing myself. When I looked at Carlo I heard his brave voice challenging those wolves in snow, those beasts that were laughing at him. A gash opened between my breasts and then I seemed to be all breasts, millions of them up and down, great warm breasts for him to hide his face between and they were filled with myself and with the living substance of trees and flowers and earth. It was as if I was in blossom. I hadn't said anything or done anything but as I looked at Carlo it seemed to me that he knew what I was feeling and then when Max said something cutting and brutal I felt that I had gathered him into me and that he was lying safe behind my ribs.

They call me Angelica. My real name is Hertha. They call me Angelica for some unfathomable reason. They are none of them sentimental and they all seem to know their position and importance on this earth and the position of this earth among planets. I know that they like me and yet sometimes I feel that in the farthest corner of themselves they despise me as Gertrude despises me. And here I am with eyes that see waves of snow and in the next instant clouds of fruit blossoms and always the faces of people moving over this earth with all its changes, moving over the body of earth, eating and being eaten.

Let me show you another night. Florida suddenly begins to talk about how important he is. His dark face is strange against the Persian screen and his teeth are kitty-white. I ache with shame and torture for him as he expands and insists upon his importance, demands attention and homage from the white faces all around, those wolves in snow, ready to tear him to pieces. I cannot bear it. I can see him hiding behind his talk, frightened, small. I can see him on a mountain top singing, "Little David Play On Your Harp." I despise the way Carlo shrugs and turns his back. I hate Gertrude for her "a-a-a-a-a-a" and Max and John and Evan, aluminum again in the light. There were distances between them and this colored boy who was trying to prove his equality. Rivers and walls and houses and rocks were between. Impenetrable substances, invisible and infinite, shut off their bodies. Then his blood was my blood and I wanted him to see that between us there were no stones or rivers or walls or death-substances. I went over to him, before them all. I looked into his face and put my hands on his black cheeks. He was shining, rich singing filled my ears. I leaned over and kissed his mouth lightly so that he could know there were no walls between. I was in flaming sun, I was wrapped in rich, deep music, my stomach was a rose.

Some one said, "You're a good sport, Angelica."

Another said, "I didn't know Angelica drank."

And another, "God, I'm tired."

Evan yawned, "I always wanted to see Angelica tight."

Their voices were soft and solemn. I saw them look at me covertly as if they considered me treacherous. Gertrude's "a-a-a-a-a" cracked like a whip in my ears. Florida ran from the house.

Look into this beautiful day. It isn't winter any more. It is spring and the park is full of babies and stomachs resting on spread knees and every one is smelling and tasting and hearing spring-air, spring substance from earth and branches and birds. The curtains blow into my room on sun and wind and Robin is on the couch. His glossy, acorn face is sober and his hair makes a little fringe around his head. Robin is a seven months child you remember. He came out of his mother's body too soon and he has never felt at home here except with me. Suddenly he screwed up his forehead and said, "People get so old and tattered after you've known them a while." For some reason he began to talk about his childhood. He told me about his father and how he would come home drunk and fall on his bed and lie until Sunday morning. On Sunday he would be up early, bathing and shaving, filling the house with hymns. He would put on his fine black clothes, kiss the children that he had beaten, kneel before his wife, and then pick up his stick and stroll to church in the warm sun. One day he bought a plaid suit for Robin and then on Sunday mornings he would make him put it on and wear it to Sunday School. Robin hated the suit. As he told about it his mouth fell at the corners, "I despise anything conspicuous." But he made him wear it and Robin would feel crying in him all day and crying with the memory of it and with the anticipation of that hideous plaid suit.

Suddenly I knew that I didn't want to be listening and suffering with Robin or making him suffer by my big gaunt look. I knew that I wanted to lead him out of that ugly knot into the outdoors, into clouds of fruit bloom and clear sky and let him feel the breathing and flowing of the body of earth, our life, our God. I wanted to lead him out of those stagnant layers of pity. "That is not you any more, Robin," I wanted to say. "Leave the little sad boy, let him die, let him be buried like a boy in a book."

But all the time I was walking slowly toward Robin and suddenly I sat down and put my arms around him and pressed his head, that glossy acorn head, between my breasts, and then I was holding him on my lap and my flesh was spreading over and around him, like feathers over an egg and I was singing something down in my throat.

Days are making weeks, and months, and years, but I am not growing. I am not letting others grow. I am making them drain off their poisons and now they like it, they like to tell about their miseries and the cruelties and violence of their childhood. I am not showing them that their poison is food for my ugly black knot, the curled I lying behind my ribs, the monster. I am not making them see that they should move up out of death and stagnation-mud into light and do the mysterious and magical things that men can do.

Examine my name. Angelica. Look into my face. See the large, set eyes, the white cheeks, the mouse-mouth. I am twenty-eight years old but that means no more to me than four or six or fifty. I do not grow. See the folds of my cashmere dress and look at the lilac sprays all over it and the sandals on my feet. My hair is like gold wires, fine wires, all blurring together in sun and it makes a fantastic bush behind my white ears and my forehead is covered with hair to my brows. Don't let me tell what happened with Max and Evan and John. It is the same story, all the same story, all my life the same. I need not tell.

Finally I met blackness. I was deep in its soundless, infinite roar, far in its mouth filling sorrow. It was as if I must push away bolts of black. I must struggle as I had never struggled and push away black bars miles high and deep as the ocean and wide as our earth, this body we move upon. I put my head in my hands. I lay down on my bed and pressed my face into the pillow and my body into the mattress. I was all blackness, wrapped tight in blackness. I had no thoughts. Suddenly I had no emotions. My pores opened and let the darkness in and it spread inside and moved through me. And then I seemed to turn into earth, and then I was clay and then a monster. Tiny wings, wings the size of a fly's or a mosquito's rose from the neck.

I opened my eyes and looked at the monster. I saw the face. It grew smaller and smaller as I watched. Blackness rolled away from me like ocean water. Then I seemed to be in tight clothes. I was strangling, without air, sick. The monster grew smaller and smaller and suddenly tears poured out of me, out of my pores, but it was not I who cried—I don't know who was crying. Images wrenched out of me. I was a little girl again in body. I was sliding around on a pond. A boy came. He picked up a black frozen branch and beat me with it. His snarls flung around my head. I felt no pain, only dumbness and wonder. I felt no pain the day I looked up and saw what looked like a strange, revolving bird in the air and was struck in the eye with it and knocked unconscious. A teacher grabbed my long hair and shook me back and forth by it in front of the whole school. I was rising into the sky. I was looking at clouds. I was on the back of a soft white bird. I was looking into the face of Christ. Then I felt blows on my cheeks and my head revolved and I fell against my desk and cut my chin. "a-a-a-a-" came from the children. It burned me with wounds inside. I did not cry. Days later at dinner I was given a dish of steamed dates and cream. I got down from my chair and ran upstairs into the dark end of the clothes closet. There I wound myself up and began to cry, there my body awoke and throbbed with sores. Then the butcher-boy, an ogre, the ice-man a terrifying oufe, Mary in the grocery a glittering cruel witch, my parents ice-images who never met my hopes, my sister, my sister. This is what she said to me one day, "Other girls have nice little sisters. But you—you're impossible. Scared of every one. And you don't know anything. You can't even tell time yet even though Papa did buy you that nice watch."

It was that little girl who lay curled up behind my ribs. It was she who kept me feeding her from the wounds of others and kept myself and others young while time was mixing with my curtains and my walls and my body but not with me, while days were making weeks and months and years. It was not Evan's sorrow that I arched over,

or John's burned village, or Florida, or Robin or Max or any of them. It was this en-
tombed child who had never been happy or praised or had a friend. It was this baby,
curled behind my ribs, who was making me all breasts, all tenderness and sorrow. It
was she who filled my body so that I could not inhabit it and it was she who kept
those others from their bodies and this is my confession and this is my shame. My
body does not do my bidding. Haven't I proven to you that I am not to blame? And
days are making weeks and months and years. Robin and Evan and the others are
here. I am not old and neither are they. Time is rolling up our lives while we sit,
pouched over living children with arms that stretch out and mouths that are hungry
and hopes that have never been fulfilled.

42

All God's Chillun Got Wings

Eugene O'Neill

Eugene O'Neill (1888–1953), the most important American dramatist of the twentieth century, was the only U.S. playwright to be awarded the Nobel Prize for literature. He was born in New York City and spent his childhood touring the country with his father, a successful theater actor. Influenced by his readings of the Greek tragedies and the works of Ibsen and Strindberg, O'Neill began writing plays in 1913. In 1916 he joined the experimental Provincetown Players, first as a writer and later as a director. Performance of his plays and receipt of the 1920 Pulitzer Prize (the first of four he would receive) for *Beyond the Horizon* established O'Neill as America's foremost playwright. His 1924 play *All God's Chillun Got Wings* caused much controversy for representing an interracial marriage—then prohibited in the majority of the United States. Though he hardly offered an idyllic portrait of the marriage, O'Neill received threats from the Ku Klux Klan for the opening production.

CHARACTERS

JIM HARRIS

MRS. HARRIS, *his mother*

HATTIE, *his sister*

ELLA DOWNEY

SHORTY

JOE

MICKEY

Whites and Negroes

ACT ONE

SCENE ONE—*A corner in lower New York. Years ago. End of an afternoon in Spring.*

SCENE TWO—*The same. Nine years later. End of an evening in Spring.*

SCENE THREE—*The same. Five years later. A night in Spring.*

SCENE FOUR—*The street before a church in the same ward. A morning some weeks later.*

ACT TWO

SCENE ONE—*A flat in the same ward. A morning two years later.*

SCENE TWO—*The same. At twilight some months later.*
SCENE THREE—*The same. A night some months later.*

ACT I

Scene 1

A corner in lower New York, at the edge of a colored district. Three narrow streets converge. A triangular building in the rear, red brick, four-storied, its ground floor a grocery. Four-story tenements stretch away down the skyline of the two streets. The fire escapes are crowded with people. In the street leading left, the faces are all white; in the street leading right, all black. It is hot Spring. On the sidewalk are eight children, four boys and four girls. Two of each sex are white, two black. They are playing marbles. One of the black boys is JIM HARRIS. *The little blonde girl, her complexion rose and white, who sits behind his elbow and holds his marbles is* ELLA DOWNEY. *She is eight. They play the game with concentrated attention for a while. People pass, black and white, the Negroes frankly participants in the spirit of Spring, the whites laughing constrainedly, awkward in natural emotion. Their words are lost. One only hears their laughter. It expresses the difference in race. There are street noises—the clattering roar of the Elevated, the puff of its locomotives, the ruminative lazy sound of a horse-car, the hooves of its team clacking on the cobbles. From the street of the whites a high-pitched, nasal tenor sings the chorus of "Only a Bird in a Gilded Cage." On the street of the blacks a Negro strikes up the chorus of: "I Guess I'll Have to Telegraph My Baby." As this singing ends, there is laughter, distinctive in quality, from both streets. Then silence. The light in the street begins to grow brilliant with the glow of the setting sun. The game of marbles goes on.*

WHITE GIRL. (*Tugging at the elbow of her brother*) Come on, Mickey!

HER BROTHER. (*Roughly*) Aw, gwan, youse!

WHITE GIRL. Aw right, den. You kin git a lickin' if you wanter. (*Gets up to move off.*)

HER BROTHER. Aw, git off de eart!

WHITE GIRL. De old woman'll be madder'n hell!

HER BROTHER. (*Worried now*) I'm comin', ain't I? Hold your horses.

BLACK GIRL. (*To a black boy*) Come on, you Joe. We gwine git frailed too, you don't hurry.

JOE. Go long!

MICKEY. Bust up de game, huh? I gotta run! (*Jumps to his feet.*)

OTHER WHITE BOY. Me, too! (*Jumps up.*)

OTHER BLACK GIRL. Lawdy, it's late!

JOE. Me for grub!

MICKEY. (*To* JIM HARRIS) You's de winner, Jim Crow. Yeh gotta play tomorrer.

JIM. (*Readily*) Sure ting, Mick. Come one, come all! (*He laughs.*)

OTHER WHITE BOY. Me too! I gotta git back at yuh.

JIM. Aw right, Shorty.

LITTLE GIRLS. Hurry! Come on, come on! (*The six start off together. Then they notice that* JIM *and* ELLA *are hesitating, standing awkwardly and shyly together. They turn to mock.*)

JOE. Look at dat Jim Crow! Land sakes, he got a gal! (*He laughs. They all laugh.*)

JIM. (*Ashamed*) Ne'er mind, you Chocolate!

MICKEY. Look at de two softies, will yeh! Mush! Mush! (*He and the two other boys take this up.*)

LITTLE GIRLS. (*Pointing their fingers at Ella*) Shame! Shame! Everybody knows your name! Painty Face! Painty Face!

ELLA. (*Hanging her head*) Shut up!

LITTLE WHITE GIRL. He's been carrying her books!

COLORED GIRL. Can't you find nuffin better'n him, Ella? Look at de big feet he got! (*She laughs. They all laugh.* JIM *puts one foot on top of the other, looking at* ELLA.)

ELLA. Mind yer own business, see! (*She strides toward them angrily. They jump up and dance in an ecstasy, screaming and laughing.*)

ALL. Found yeh out! Found yeh out!

MICKEY. Mush-head! Jim Crow de Sissy! Stuck on Painty Face!

JOE. Will Painty Face let you hold her doll, boy?

SHORTY. Cissy! Softy! (ELLA *suddenly begins to cry. At this they all howl.*)

ALL. Cry-baby! Cry-baby! Look at her! Painty Face!

JIM. (*Suddenly rushing at them, with clenched fists, furiously*) Shut yo' moufs! I kin lick de hull of you! (*They all run away, laughing, shouting, and jeering, quite triumphant now that they have made him, too, lose his temper. He comes back to* ELLA, *and stands beside her sheepishly, stepping on one foot after the other. Suddenly he blurts out:*) Don't bawl no more. I done chased 'em.

ELLA. (*Comforted, politely*) T'anks.

JIM. (*Swelling out*) It was a cinch. I kin wipe up de street wid any one of dem. (*He stretches out his arms, trying to bulge out his biceps*) Feel dat muscle!

ELLA. (*Does so gingerly—then with admiration*) My!

JIM. (*Protectingly*) You mustn't never be scared when I'm hanging round, Painty Face.

ELLA. Don't call me that, Jim—please!

JIM. (*Contritely*) I didn't mean nuffin'. I didn't know you'd mind.

ELLA. I do—more'n anything.

JIM. You oughtn't to mind. Dey's jealous, dat's what.

ELLA. Jealous? Of what?

JIM. (*Pointing to her face*) Of dat. Red 'n' white. It's purty.

ELLA. I hate it!

JIM. It's purty. Yes, it's—it's purty. It's—outa sight!

ELLA. I hate it. I wish I was black like you.

JIM. (*Sort of shrinking*) No you don't. Dey'd call you Crow, den—or Chocolate—or Smoke.

ELLA. I wouldn't mind.

JIM. (*Somberly*) Dey'd call you nigger sometimes, too.

ELLA. I wouldn't mind.

JIM. (*Humbly*) You wouldn't mind?

ELLA. No, I wouldn't mind. (*An awkward pause.*)

JIM. (*Suddenly*) You know what, Ella? Since I been tuckin' yo' books to school and back, I been drinkin' lots o' chalk 'n' water tree times a day. Dat Tom, de barber, he tole me dat make me white, if I drink enough. (*Pleadingly*) Does I look whiter?

ELLA. (*Comfortingly*) Yes—maybe—a little bit—

JIM. (*Trying a careless tone*) Reckon dat Tom's a liar, an' de joke's on me! Dat chalk only makes me feel kinder sick inside.

ELLA. (*Wonderingly*) Why do you want to be white?

JIM. Because—just because—I lak dat better.

ELLA. I wouldn't. I like black. Let's you and me swap. I'd like to be black. (*Clapping her hands*) Gee, that'd be fun, if we only could!

JIM. (*Hesitatingly*) Yes—maybe—

ELLA. Then they'd call me Crow, and you'd be Painty Face!

JIM. They wouldn't never dast call you nigger, you bet! I'd kill 'em! (*A long pause. Finally she takes his hand shyly. They both keep looking as far away from each other as possible.*)

ELLA. I like you.

JIM. I like you.

ELLA. Do you want to be my feller?

JIM. Yes.

ELLA. Then I'm your girl.

JIM. Yes. (*Then grandly*) You kin bet none o' de gang gwine call you Painty Face from dis out! I lam' em' good! (*The sun has set. Twilight has fallen on the street. An organ grinder comes up to the corner and plays "Annie Rooney." They stand hand-in-hand and listen. He goes away. It is growing dark.*)

ELLA. (*Suddenly*) Golly, it's late! I'll git a lickin'!

JIM. Me, too.

ELLA. I won't mind it much.

JIM. Me nuther.

ELLA. See you going to school tomorrow.

JIM. Sure.

ELLA. I gotta skip now.

JIM. Me, too.

ELLA. I like you, Jim.

JIM. I like you.

ELLA. Don't forget.

JIM. Don't you.

ELLA. Good-by.

JIM. So long. (*They run away from each other—then stop abruptly, and turn as at a signal.*)

ELLA. Don't forget.

JIM. I won't, you bet!

ELLA. Here! (*She kisses her hand at him, then runs off in frantic embarrassment.*)

JIM. (*Overcome*) Gee! (*Then he turns and darts away, as*

THE CURTAIN FALLS

Scene 2

The same corner. Nine years have passed. It is again late Spring at a time in the evening which immediately follows the hour of Scene 1. Nothing has changed much. One street is still all white, the other all black. The fire escapes are laden with drooping human beings. The grocery-store is still at the corner. The street noises are now more rhythmically mechanical, electricity having taken the place of horse and steam. People pass, white and black. They laugh as in Scene 1. From the street of the whites the high-pitched nasal tenor sings: "Gee, I Wish That I Had a Girl," and the Negro replies with "All I Got Was Sympathy." The singing is followed again by laughter from both streets. Then silence. The dusk grows darker. With a spluttering flare the arc-lamp at the corner is lit and sheds a pale glare over the street. Two young roughs slouch up to the corner, as tough in manner as they can make themselves. One is the SHORTY *of Scene 1; the other the Negro,* JOE. *They stand loafing. A boy of seventeen or so passes by, escorting a girl of about the same age. Both are dressed in their best, the boy in black with stiff collar, the girl in white.*

SHORTY. (*Scornfully*) Hully cripes! Pipe who's here! (*To the girl, sneeringly*) Wha's matter, Liz? Don't yer recernize yer old fr'ens?

GIRL. (*Frightenedly*) Hello, Shorty.

SHORTY. Why de glad rags? Goin' to graduation? (*He tries to obstruct their way but, edging away from him, they turn and run.*)

JOE. Har-har! Look at dem scoot, will you! (SHORTY *grins with satisfaction.*)

SHORTY. (*Looking down other street*) Here comes Mickey.

JOE. He won de semi-final last night easy?

SHORTY. Knocked de bloke out in de thoid.

JOE. Dat boy's suah a-comin'! He'll be de champeen yit.

SHORTY. (*Judicially*) Got a good chanct—if he leaves de broads alone. Dat's where he's wide open. (*Mickey comes in from the left. He is dressed loudly, a straw hat with a gaudy band cocked over one cauliflower ear. He has acquired a typical "pug's" face, with the added viciousness of a natural bully. One of his eyes is puffed, almost closed, as a result of his battle the night before. He swaggers up.*)

BOTH. Hello, Mickey.

MICKEY. Hello.

JOE. Hear you knocked him col'.

MICKEY. Sure. I knocked his block off. (*Changing the subject*) Say. Seen 'em goin' past to de graduation racket?

SHORTY. (*With a wink*) Why? You int'rested?

JOE. (*Chuckling*) Mickey's gwine roun' git a good conduct medal.

MICKEY. Sure. Dey kin pin it on de seat o' me pants. (*They laugh*) Listen. Seen Ella Downey goin'?

SHORTY. Painty Face? No, she ain't been along.

MICKEY. (*With authority*) Can dat name, see! Want a bunch o' fives in yer kisser? Den nix! She's me goil, understan'?

JOE. (*Venturing to joke*) Which one? Yo' number ten?

MICKEY. (*Flattered*) Sure. De real K.O. one.

SHORTY. (*Pointing right—sneeringly*) Gee! Pipe Jim Crow all dolled up for de racket.

JOE. (*With disgusted resentment*) You mean tell me dat nigger's graduatin'?

SHORTY. Ask him. (JIM HARRIS *comes in. He is dressed in black, stiff white collar, etc.—a quiet-mannered Negro boy with a queerly-baffled, sensitive face.*)

JIM. (*Pleasantly*) Hello, fellows. (*They grunt in reply, looking over him scornfully.*)

JOE. (*Staring resentfully*) Is you graduatin' tonight?

JIM. Yes.

JOE. (*Spitting disgustedly*) Fo'Gawd's sake! You *is* gittin' high-falutin'!

JIM. (*Smiling deprecatingly*) This is my second try. I didn't pass last year.

JOE. What de hell does it git you, huh? Whatever is you gwine do wid it now you gits it? Live lazy on yo' ol' woman?

JIM. (*Assertively*) I'm going to study and become a lawyer.

JOE. (*With a snort*) Fo' Chris' sake, nigger!

JIM. (*Fiercely*) Don't you call me that—not before them!

JOE. (*Pugnaciously*) Does you deny you's a nigger? I shows you—

MICKEY. (*Gives them both a push—truculently*) Cut it out, see! I'm runnin' dis corner. (*Turning to* JIM *insultingly*) Say, you! Painty Face's gittin' her ticket tonight, ain't she?

JIM. You mean Ella—

MICKEY. Painty Face Downey, dat's who I mean! I don't have to be perlite wit' her. She's me goil!

JIM. (*Glumly*) Yes, she's graduating.

SHORTY. (*Winks at Mickey*) Smart, huh?

MICKEY. (*Winks back—meaningly*) Willin' to loin, take it from me! (JIM *stands tensely as if a struggle were going on in him.*)

JIM. (*Finally blurts out*) I want to speak to you, Mickey—alone.

MICKEY. (*Surprised—insultingly*) Aw, what de hell—!

JIM. (*Excitedly*) It's important, I tell you!

MICKEY. Huh? (*Stares at him inquisitively—then motions the others back carelessly and follows* JIM *down front.*)

SHORTY. Some noive!

JOE. (*Vengefully*) I gits dat Jim alone, you wait!

MICKEY. Well, spill de big news. I ain't got all night. I got a date.

JIM. With—Ella?

MICKEY. What's dat to you?

JIM. (*The words tumbling out*) What—I wanted to say! I know—I've heard—all the stories—what you've been doing around the ward—with other girls—it's none of my business, with them—but she—Ella—it's different—she's not that kind—

MICKEY. (*Insultingly*) Who told yuh so, huh?

JIM. (*Draws back his fist threateningly*) Don't you dare—! (MICKEY *is so paralyzed by this effrontery that he actually steps back.*)

MICKEY. Say, cut de comedy! (*Beginning to feel insulted*) Listen, you Jim Crow! Ain't you wise I could give yuh one poke dat'd knock yuh into next week?

JIM. I'm only asking you to act square, Mickey.

MICKEY. What's it to yuh? Why, yuh lousy goat, she wouldn't spit on yuh even! She hates de sight of a coon.

JIM. (*In agony*) I—I know—but once she didn't mind—we were kids together—

MICKEY. Aw, ferget dat! Dis is *now!*

JIM. And I'm still her friend always—even if she don't like colored people—

MICKEY. *Coons*, why don't yuh say it right! De trouble wit' you is yuh're gittin' stuck up, dat's what! Stay where yeh belong, see! Yer old man made coin at de truckin' game and yuh're tryin' to buy yerself white—graduatin' and law, fer Hell's sake! Yuh're gittin' yerself in Dutch wit' everyone in de ward—and it ain't cause yer a coon neider. Don't de gang all train wit' Joe dere and lots of others? But yuh're tryin' to buy white and it won't git yuh no place, see!

JIM. (*Trembling*) Some day—I'll show you—

MICKEY. (*Turning away*) Aw, gwan!

JIM. D'you think I'd change—be you—your dirty white—!

MICKEY. (*Whirling about*) What's dat?

JIM. (*With hysterical vehemence*) You act square with her—or I'll show you up—I'll report you—I'll write to the papers—the sporting writers—I'll let them know how white you are!

MICKEY. (*Infuriated*) Yuh damn nigger, I'll bust yer jaw in! (*Assuming his ring pose he weaves toward* JIM, *his face set in a cruel scowl.* JIM *waits helplessly but with a certain dignity.*)

SHORTY. Cheese it! A couple bulls! And here's de Downey skoit comin', too.

MICKEY. I'll get yuh de next time! (ELLA DOWNEY *enters from the right. She is seventeen, still has the same rose and white complexion, is pretty but with a rather repelling bold air about her.*)

ELLA. (*Smiles with pleasure when she sees* MICKEY) Hello, Mick. Am I late? Say, I'm so glad you won last night. (*She glances from one to the other as she feels something in the air*) Hello! What's up?

MICKEY. Dis boob. (*He indicates* JIM *scornfully.*)

JIM. (*Diffidently*) Hello, Ella.

ELLA. (*Shortly, turning away*) Hello. (*Then to* MICKEY) Come on, Mick. Walk down with me. I got to hurry.

JIM. (*Blurts out*) Wait—just a second. (*Painfully*) Ella, do you hate—colored people?

MICKEY. Aw, shut up!

JIM. Please answer.

ELLA. (*Forcing a laugh*) Say! What is this—another exam?

JIM. (*Doggedly*) Please answer.

ELLA. (*Irritably*) Of course I don't! Haven't I been brought up alongside—Why, some of my oldest—the girls I've been to public school the longest with—

JIM. Do you hate me, Ella?

ELLA. (*Confusedly and more irritably*) Say, is he drunk? Why should I? I don't hate anyone.

JIM. Then why haven't you ever hardly spoken to me—for years?

ELLA. (*Resentfully*) What would I speak about? You and me've got nothing in common any more.

JIM. (*Desperately*) Maybe not any more—but—right on this corner—do you remember once—?

ELLA. I don't remember nothing! (*Angrily*) Say! What's got into you to be butting into my business all of a sudden like this? Because you finally managed to graduate, has it gone to your head?

JIM. No, I—only want to help you, Ella.

ELLA. Of all the nerve! You're certainly forgetting your place! Who's asking you for help, I'd like to know? Shut up and stop bothering me!

JIM. (*Insistently*) If you ever need a friend—a true friend—

ELLA. I've got lots of friends among my own—kind, I can tell you. (*Exasperatedly*) You make me sick! Go to—hell! (*She flounces off. The three men laugh.* MICKEY *follows her.* JIM *is stricken. He goes and sinks down limply on a box in front of the grocery-store.*)

SHORTY. I'm going to shoot a drink. Come on, Joe, and I'll blow yuh.

JOE. (*Who has never ceased to follow every move of* JIM'S *with angry, resentful eyes*) Go long. I'se gwine stay here a secon'. I got a lil' argyment. (*He points to* JIM.)

SHORTY. Suit yerself. Do a good job. See yuh later. (*He goes, whistling.*)

JOE. (*Stands for a while glaring at* JIM, *his fierce little eyes peering out of his black face. Then he spits on his hands aggressively and strides up to the oblivious* JIM. *He stands in front of him, gradually working himself into a fury at the other's seeming indifference to his words*) Listen to me, nigger: I got a heap to whisper in yo' ear! Who is you, anyhow? Who does you think you is? Don't yo' old man and mine work on de docks togidder befo' yo' old man gits his own truckin' business? Yo' ol' man swallers his nickels, my ol' man buys him beer wid dem and swallers dat—dat's de on'y diff'rence. Don't you'n'me drag up togidder?

JIM. (*Dully*) I'm your friend, Joe.

JOE. No, you isn't! I ain't no fren o' yourn! I don't even know who you is! What's all dis schoolin' you doin'? What's all dis dressin' up and graduatin' an' sayin' you gwine study be a lawyer? What's all dis fakin' an' pretendin' and swellin' out grand an' talkin' soft and perlite? What's all dis denyin' you's a nigger—an' wid de white boys listenin' to you say it! Is you aimin' to buy white wid yo' ol' man's dough like Mickey say? What is you? (*In a rage at the other's silence*) You don't talk? Den I takes it out o' yo' hide! (*He grabs* JIM *by the throat with one hand and draws the other fist back*) Tell me befo' I wrecks yo' face in! Is you a nigger or isn't you? (*Shaking him*) Is you a nigger, Nigger? Nigger, is you a nigger?

JIM. (*Looking into his eyes—quietly*) Yes. I'm a nigger. We're both niggers. (*They look at each other for a moment.* JOE'S *rage vanishes. He slumps onto a box beside* JIM'S. *He offers him a cigarette.* JIM *takes it.* JOE *scratches a match and lights both their cigarettes.*)

JOE. (*After a puff, with full satisfaction*) Man, why didn't you 'splain dat in de fust place?

JIM. We're both niggers. (*The same hand-organ man of Scene 1 comes to the corner. He plays the chorus of "Bon Bon Buddie, the Chocolate Drop." They both stare straight ahead listening. Then the organ man goes away. A silence.* JOE *gets to his feet.*)

JOE. I'll go get me a cold beer. (*He starts to move off—then turns*) Time you was graduatin', ain't it? (*He goes.* JIM *remains sitting on his box staring straight before him as*

THE CURTAIN FALLS

Scene 3

The same corner five years later. Nothing has changed much. It is a night in Spring. The arc-lamp discovers faces with a favorless cruelty. The street noises are the same but more intermittent and dulled with a quality of fatigue. Two people pass, one black and one white. They are tired. They both yawn, but neither laughs. There is no laughter from the two streets. From the street of the whites the tenor, more nasal than ever and a bit drunken, wails in high barber-shop falsetto the last half of the chorus of "When I Lost You." The Negro voice, a bit maudlin in turn, replies with the last half of "Waitin' for the Robert E. Lee." Silence. SHORTY *enters. He looks tougher than ever, the typical gangster. He stands waiting, singing a bit drunkenly, peering down the street.*

SHORTY. (*Indignantly*) Yuh bum! Ain't yuh ever comin'? (*He begins to sing: "And sewed up in her yeller kimona, She had a blue-barrelled forty-five gun, For to get her man Who'd done her wrong." Then he comments scornfully*) Not her, dough! No gat for her. She ain't got de noive. A little sugar. Dat'll fix her. (ELLA *enters. She is dressed poorly, her face is pale and hollow-eyed, her voice cold and tired.*)

SHORTY. Yuh got de message?

ELLA. Here I am.

SHORTY. How yuh been?

ELLA. All right. (*A pause. He looks at her puzzledly.*)

SHORTY. (*A bit embarrassedly*) Well, I s'pose yuh'd like me to give yuh some dope on Mickey, huh?

ELLA. No.

SHORTY. Mean to say yuh don't wanter know where he is or what he's doin'?

ELLA. No.

SHORTY. Since when?

ELLA. A long time.

SHORTY. (*After a pause—with a rat-like viciousness*) Between you'n me, kid, you'll get even soon—you'n all de odder dames he's tossed. I'm on de inside. I've watched him trainin'. His next scrap, watch it! He'll go! It won't be de odder guy. It'll be all youse dames he's kidded—and de ones what's kidded him. Youse'll all be in de odder guy's corner. He won't need no odder seconds. Youse'll trow water on him, and sponge his face, and take de kinks out of his socker—and Mickey'll catch it on de button—and he won't be able to take it no more—'cause all your weight—you and de odders—'ll be behind dat punch. Ha ha! (*He laughs an evil laugh*) And Mickey'll go—down to his knees first—(*He sinks to his knees in the attitude of a groggy boxer.*)

ELLA. I'd like to see him on his knees!

SHORTY. And den—flat on his pan—dead to de world—de boidies singin' in de trees—ten—out! (*He suits his action to the words, sinking flat on the pavement, then rises and laughs the same evil laugh.*)

ELLA. He's been out—for me—a long time. (*A pause*) Why did you send for me?

SHORTY. He sent me.

ELLA. Why?

SHORTY. To slip you dis wad o' dough. (*He reluctantly takes a roll of bills from his pocket and holds it out to her.*)

ELLA. (*Looks at the money indifferently*) What for?

SHORTY. For you.

ELLA. No.

SHORTY. For de kid den.

ELLA. The kid's dead. He took diptheria.

SHORTY. Hell yuh say! When?

ELLA. A long time.

SHORTY. Why didn't you write Mickey—?

ELLA. Why should I? He'd only be glad.

SHORTY. (*After a pause*) Well—it's better.

ELLA. Yes.

SHORTY. You made up wit yer family?

ELLA. No chance.

SHORTY. Livin' alone?

ELLA. In Brooklyn.

SHORTY. Workin'?

ELLA. In a factory.

SHORTY. You're a sucker. There's lots of softer snaps fer you, kid—

ELLA. I know what you mean. No.

SHORTY. Don't yuh wanter step out no more—have fun—live?

ELLA. I'm through.

SHORTY. (*Mockingly*) Jump in de river, huh? T'ink it over, baby. I kin start yuh right in my stable. No one'll bodder yuh den. I got influence.

ELLA. (*Without emphasis*) You're a dirty dog. Why doesn't someone kill you?

SHORTY. Is dat so! What're you? They say you been travelin' round with Jim Crow.

ELLA. He's been my only friend.

SHORTY. A nigger!

ELLA. The only white man in the world! Kind and white. You're all black—black to the heart!

SHORTY. Nigger-lover! (*He throws the money in her face. It falls to the street*) Listen, you! Mickey says he's off of yuh for keeps. Dis is de finish! Dat's what he sent me to tell you. (*Glances at her searchingly—a pause*) Yuh won't make no trouble?

ELLA. Why should I? He's free. The kid's dead. I'm free. No hard feelings—only—I'll be there in spirit at his next fight, tell him! I'll take your tip—the other corner—second the punch—nine—ten—out! He's free! That's all. (*She grins horribly at Shorty*) Go away, Shorty.

SHORTY. (*Looking at her and shaking his head—maudlinly*) Groggy! Groggy! We're all groggy! Gluttons for punishment! Me for a drink. So long. (*He goes. A Salvation Army band comes toward the corner. They are playing and singing "Till We Meet at Jesus' Feet." They reach the end as they enter and stop before* ELLA. THE CAPTAIN *steps forward.*)

CAPTAIN. Sister—

ELLA. (*Picks up the money and drops it in his hat—mockingly*) Here. Go save yourself. Leave me alone.

A WOMAN SALVATIONIST. Sister—

ELLA. Never mind that. I'm not in your line—yet. (*As they hesitate, wonderingly*) I want to be alone. (*To the thud of the big drum they march off.* ELLA *sits down on a box, her hands hanging at her sides. Presently* JIM HARRIS *comes in. He has grown into a quietly-dressed, studious-looking Negro with an intelligent yet queerly-baffled face.*)

JIM. (*With a joyous but bewildered cry*) Ella! I just saw Shorty—

ELLA. (*Smiling at him with frank affection*) He had a message from Mickey.

JIM. (*Sadly*) Ah!

ELLA. (*Pointing to the box behind her*) Sit down. (*He does so. A pause—then she says indifferently*) It's finished. I'm free, Jim.

JIM. (*wearily*) We're never free—except to do what we have to.

ELLA. What are you getting gloomy about all of a sudden?

JIM. I've got the report from the school. I've flunked again.

ELLA. Poor Jim.

JIM. Don't pity me. I'd like to kick myself all over the block. Five years—and I'm still plugging away where I ought to have been at the end of two.

ELLA. Why don't you give it up?

JIM. No!

ELLA. After all, what's being a lawyer?

JIM. A lot—to me—what it means. (*Intensely*) Why, if I was a Member of the Bar right now, Ella, I believe I'd almost have the courage to—

ELLA. What?

JIM. Nothing. (*After a pause—gropingly*) I can't explain—just—but it hurts like fire. It brands me in my pride. I swear I know more'n any member of my class. I ought to, I study harder. I work like the devil. It's all in my head—all fine and correct to a T. Then when I'm called on—I stand up—all the white faces looking at me—and I can feel their eyes—I hear my own voice sounding funny, trembling—and all of a sudden it's all gone in my head—there's nothing remembered—and I hear myself stuttering—and give up—sit down—They don't laugh, hardly ever. They're kind. They're good people. (*In a frenzy*) They're considerate, damn them! But I feel branded!

ELLA. Poor Jim!

JIM. (*Going on painfully*) And it's the same thing in the written exams. For weeks before I study all night. I can't sleep anyway. I learn it all, I see it, I understand it. Then they give me the paper in the exam room. I look it over, I know each answer—perfectly. I take up my pen. On all sides are white men starting to write. They're so sure—even the ones that I know know nothing. But I know it all—but I can't remember any more—it fades—it goes—it's gone. There's a blank in my head—stupidity—I sit like a fool fighting to remember a little bit here, a little bit there—not enough to pass—not enough for anything—when I know it all!

ELLA. (*Compassionately*) Jim. It isn't worth it. You don't need to—

JIM. I need it more than anyone ever needed anything. I need it to live.

ELLA. What'll it prove?

JIM. Nothing at all much—but everything to me.

ELLA. You're so much better than they are in every other way.

JIM. (*Looking up at her*) Then—you understand?

ELLA. Of course. (*Affectionately*) Don't I know how fine you've been to me! You've been the only one in the world who's stood by me—the only understanding person—and all after the rotten way I used to treat you.

JIM. But before that—way back so high—you treated me good. (*He smiles.*)

ELLA. You've been white to me, Jim. (*She takes his hand.*)

JIM. White—to you!

ELLA. Yes.

JIM. All love is white. I've always loved you. (*This with the deepest humility.*)

ELLA. Even now—after all that's happened!

JIM. Always.

ELLA. I like you, Jim—better than anyone else in the world.

JIM. That's more than enough, more than I ever hoped for. (*The organ grinder comes to the corner. He plays the chorus of "Annie Laurie." They sit listening, hand in hand.*)

JIM. Would you ever want to marry me, Ella?

ELLA. Yes, Jim.

JIM. (*As if this quick consent alarmed him*) No, no, don't answer now. Wait! Turn it over in your mind! Think what it means to you! Consider it—over and over again! I'm in no hurry, Ella. I can wait months—years—

ELLA. I'm alone. I've got to be helped. I've got to help someone—or it's the end—one end or another.

JIM. (*Eagerly*) Oh, I'll help—I know I can help—I'll give my life to help you—that's what I've been living for—

ELLA. But can I help you? Can I help you?

JIM. Yes! Yes! We'll go abroad where a man is a man—where it don't make that difference—where people are kind and wise to see the soul under skins. I don't ask you to love me—I don't dare to hope nothing like that! I don't want nothing—only to wait—to know you like me—to be near you—to keep harm away—to make up for the past—to never let you suffer any more—to serve you—to lie at your feet like a dog that loves you—to kneel by your bed like a nurse that watches over you sleeping—to preserve and protect and shield you from evil and sorrow—to give my life and my blood and all the strength that's in me to give you peace and joy—to become your slave!—yes, be your slave!—your black slave that adores you as sacred! (*He has sunk to his knees. In a frenzy of self-abnegation, as he says the last words he beats his head on the flagstones.*)

ELLA. (*Overcome and alarmed*) Jim! Jim! You're crazy! I want to help you, Jim—I want to help—

CURTAIN

Scene 4

Some weeks or so later. A street in the same ward in front of an old brick church. The church sets back from the sidewalk in a yard enclosed by a rusty iron railing with a gate at center. On each side of this yard are tenements. The buildings have a stern, forbidding look. All the shades on the windows are drawn down, giving an effect of staring, brutal eyes that pry callously at human beings without acknowledging them. Even the two tall, narrow church windows on either side of the arched door are blanked with dull green shades. It is a bright, sunny morning. The district is unusually still, as if it were waiting, holding its breath.

From the street of the blacks to the right a Negro tenor sings in a voice of shadowy richness—the first stanza with a contented, childlike melancholy—

Sometimes I feel like a mourning dove,
Sometimes I feel like a mourning dove,
    I feel like a mourning dove.

The second with a dreamy, boyish exultance—

Sometimes I feel like an eagle in the air,
Sometimes I feel like an eagle in the air,
    I feel like an eagle in the air.

The third with a brooding, earthbound sorrow—

Sometimes I wish that I'd never been born,
Sometimes I wish that I'd never been born,
    I wish that I'd never been born.

As the music dies down there is a pause of waiting stillness. This is broken by one startling, metallic clang of the church-bell. As if it were a signal, people—men, women, children—pour from the two tenements, whites from the tenement to the left, blacks from the one to the right. They hurry to form into two racial lines on each side of the gate, rigid and unyielding, staring across at each other with bitter hostile eyes. The halves of the big church door swing open and Jim *and* Ella *step out from the darkness within into the sunlight. The doors slam behind them like wooden lips of an idol that has spat them out.* Jim *is dressed in black,* Ella *in white, both with extreme plainness. They stand in the sunlight, shrinking and confused. All the hostile eyes are now concentrated on them. They become aware of the two lines through which they must pass; they hesitate and tremble; then stand there staring back at the people as fixed and immovable as they are. The organ grinder comes in from the right. He plays the chorus of "Old Black Joe." As he finishes the bell of the church clangs one more single stroke, insistently dismissing.*

Jim. (*As if the sound had awakened him from a trance, reaches out and takes her hand*) Come. Time we got to the steamer. Time we sailed away over the sea. Come, Honey! (*She tries to answer but her lips tremble; she cannot take her eyes off the eyes of the people; she is unable to move. He sees this and, keeping the same tone of profound, affectionate kindness, he points upward in the sky, and gradually persuades her eyes to look up*) Look up, Honey! See the sun! Feel his warm eye lookin' down! Feel how kind he looks! Feel his blessing deep in your heart, your bones! Look up, Honey! (*Her eyes are fixed on the sky now. Her face is calm. She tries to smile bravely back at the sun. Now he pulls her by the hand, urging her gently to walk with him down through the yard and gate, through the lines of people. He is maintaining an attitude to support them through the ordeal only by a terrible effort, which manifests itself in the hysteric quality of ecstasy which breaks into his voice.*) And look at the sky! Ain't it kind and blue! Blue for hope! Don't they say blue's for hope? Hope! That's for us, Honey. All those blessings in the sky! What's it the Bible says? Falls on just and unjust alike? No, that's the sweet rain. Pshaw, what am I saying? All mixed up.

There's no unjust about it. We're all the same—equally just—under the sky—under the sun—under God—sailing over the sea—to the other side of the world—the side where Christ was born—the kind side that takes count of the soul—over the sea—the sea's blue, too—. Let's not be late—let's get that steamer! (*They have reached the curb now, passed the lines of people. She is looking up to the sky with an expression of trancelike calm and peace. He is on the verge of collapse, his face twitching, his eyes staring. He calls hoarsely:*) Taxi! Where is he? Taxi!

CURTAIN

ACT II

Scene 1

Two years later. A flat of the better sort in the Negro district near the corner of Act 1. This is the parlor. Its furniture is a queer clash. The old pieces are cheaply ornate, naïvely, childishly gaudy—the new pieces give evidence of a taste that is diametrically opposed, severe to the point of somberness. On one wall, in a heavy gold frame, is a colored photograph—the portrait of an elderly Negro with an able, shrewd face but dressed in outlandish lodge regalia, a get-up adorned with medals, sashes, a cocked hat with frills—the whole effect as absurd to contemplate as one of Napoleon's Marshals in full uniform. In the left corner, where a window lights it effectively, is a Negro primitive mask from the Congo—a grotesque face, inspiring obscure, dim connotations in one's mind, but beautifully done, conceived in a true religious spirit. In this room, however, the mask acquires an arbitrary accentuation. It dominates by a diabolical quality that contrast imposes upon it.

There are two windows on the left looking out in the street. In the rear, a door to the hall of the building. In the right, a doorway with red and gold portières leading into the bedroom and the rest of the flat. Everything is cleaned and polished. The dark brown wall paper is new, the brilliantly figured carpet also. There is a round mahogany table at center. In a rocking chair by the table MRS. HARRIS *is sitting. She is a mild-looking, gray-haired Negress of sixty-five, dressed in an old-fashioned Sunday-best dress. Walking about the room nervously is* HATTIE, *her daughter,* JIM's *sister, a woman of about thirty with a high-strung, defiant face—an intelligent head showing both power and courage. She is dressed severely, mannishly.*

It is a fine morning in Spring. Sunshine comes through the windows at the left.

MRS. HARRIS. Time dey was here, ain't it?

HATTIE. (*Impatiently*) Yes.

MRS. H. (*Worriedly*) You ain't gwine ter kick up a fuss, is you—like you done wid' Jim befo' de weddin'?

HATTIE. No. What's done is done.

MRS. H. We mustn't let her see we hold it agin her—de bad dat happened to her wid dat no-count fighter.

HATTIE. I certainly never give that a thought. It's what she's done to Jim—making him run away and give up his fight—!

MRS. H. Jim loves her a powerful lot, must be.

HATTIE. (*After a pause—bitterly*) I wonder if she loves Jim!

Mrs. H. She must, too. Yes, she must, too. Don't you forget dat it was hard for her—mighty, mighty hard—harder for de white dan for de black!

Hattie. (*Indignantly*) Why should it be?

Mrs. H. (*Shaking her head*) I ain't talkin' of shoulds. It's too late for shoulds. Dey's o'ny one should. (*Solemnly*) De white and de black shouldn't mix dat close. Dere's one road where de white goes on alone; dere's anudder road where de black goes on alone—

Hattie. Yes if they'd only leave us alone!

Mrs. H. Dey leaves your Pa alone. He comes to de top till he's got his own business, lots o' money in de bank, he owns a building even befo' he die. (*She looks up proudly at the picture.* Hattie *sighs impatiently—then her mother goes on*) Dey leaves me alone. I bears four children into dis worl', two dies, two lives, I helps you two grow up fine an' healthy and eddicated wid schoolin' and money fo' yo' comfort—

Hattie. (*Impatiently*) Ma!

Mrs. H. I does de duty God set for me in dis worl'. Dey leaves me alone. (Hattie *goes to the window to hide her exasperation. The mother broods for a minute—then goes on*) The worl' done change. Dey ain't no satisfaction wid nuffin' no more.

Hattie. Oh! (*Then after a pause*) They'll be here any minute now.

Mrs. H. Why didn't you go meet 'em at de dock like I axed you?

Hattie. I couldn't. My face and Jim's among those hundreds of white faces—(*With a harsh laugh*) It would give her too much advantage!

Mrs. H. (*Impatiently*) Don't talk dat way! What makes you so proud? (*Then after a pause—sadly*) Hattie.

Hattie. (*Turning*) Yes, Ma.

Mrs. H. I want to see Jim again—my only boy—but—all de same I'd ruther he stayed away. He say in his letter he's happy, she's happy, dey likes it dere, de folks don't think nuffin' but what's natural at seeing 'em married. Why don't dey stay?

Hattie. (*Vehemently*) No! They were cowards to run away. If they believe in what they've done, then let them face it out, live it out here, be strong enough to conquer all prejudice!

Mrs. H. Strong? Dey ain't many strong. Dey ain't many happy neider. Dey was happy ovah yondah.

Hattie. We don't deserve happiness till we've fought the fight of our race and won it! (*In the pause that follows there is a ring from back in the flat*) It's the door bell! You go, Ma. I—I—I'd rather not. (*Her mother looks at her rebukingly and goes out agitatedly through the portières.* Hattie *waits, nervously walking about, trying to compose herself. There is a long pause. Finally the portières are parted and* Jim *enters. He looks much older, graver, worried.*)

Jim. Hattie!

Hattie. Jim! (*They embrace with great affection.*)

Jim. It's great to see you again! You're looking fine.

Hattie. (*Looking at him searchingly*) You look well, too—thinner maybe—and tired. (*Then as she sees him frowning*) But where's Ella?

Jim. With Ma. (*Apologetically*) She sort of—broke down—when we came in. The trip wore her out.

Hattie. (*Coldly*) I see.

Jim. Oh, it's nothing serious. Nerves. She needs a rest.

Hattie. Wasn't living in France restful?

Jim. Yes, but—too lonely—especially for her.

Hattie. (*Resentfully*) Why? Didn't the people there want to associate—?

Jim. (*Quickly*) Oh, no indeedy, they didn't think anything of that. (*After a pause*) But—she did. For the first year it was all right. Ella liked everything a lot. She went out with French folks and got so she could talk it a little—and I learned it—a little. We were having a right nice time. I never thought then we'd ever want to come back here.

Hattie. (*Frowning*) But—what happened to change you?

Jim. (*After a pause—haltingly*) Well—you see—the first year—she and I were living around—like friends—like a brother and sister—like you and I might.

Hattie. (*Her face becoming more and more drawn and tense*) You mean—then—? (*She shudders—then after a pause*) She loves you, Jim?

Jim. If I didn't know that I'd have to jump in the river.

Hattie. Are you sure she loves you?

Jim. Isn't that why she's suffering?

Hattie. (*Letting her breath escape through her clenched teeth*) Ah!

Jim. (*Suddenly springs up and shouts almost hysterically*) Why d'you ask me all those damn questions? Are you trying to make trouble between us?

Hattie. (*Controlling herself—quietly*) No, Jim.

Jim. (*After a pause—contritely*) I'm sorry, Hattie. I'm kind of on edge today. (*He sinks down on his chair—then goes on as if something forced him to speak*) After that we got to living housed in. Ella didn't want to see nobody, she said just the two of us was enough. I was happy then—and I really guess she was happy too—in a way—for a while. (*Again a pause*) But she never did get to wanting to go out any place again. She got to saying she felt she'd be sure to run into someone she knew—from over here. So I moved us out to the country where no tourist ever comes—but it didn't make any difference to her. She got to avoiding the French folks the same as if they were Americans and I couldn't get it out of her mind. She lived in the house and got paler and paler, and more and more nervous and scarey, always imagining things—until I got to imagining things, too. I got to feeling blue. Got to sneering at myself that I wasn't any better than a quitter because I sneaked away right after getting married, didn't face nothing, gave up trying to become a Member of the Bar—and I got to suspecting Ella must feel that way about me too—that I wasn't a *real man!*

Hattie. (*Indignantly*) She couldn't!

Jim. (*With hostility*) You don't need to tell me! All this was only in my own mind. We never quarreled a single bit. We never said a harsh word. We were as close to each other as could be. We were all there was in the world to each other. We were alone together! (*A pause*) Well, one day I got so I couldn't stand it. I could see she couldn't stand it. So I just up and said: Ella, we've got to have a plain talk, look everything straight in the face, hide nothing, come out with the exact truth of the way we feel.

HATTIE. And you decided to come back!

JIM. Yes. We decided the reason we felt sort of ashamed was we'd acted like cowards. We'd run away from the thing—and taken it with us. We decided to come back and face it and live it down in ourselves, and prove to ourselves we were strong in our love—and then, and that way only, by being brave we'd free ourselves, and gain confidence, and be really free inside and able then to go anywhere and live in peace and equality with ourselves and the world without any guilty uncomfortable feeling coming up to rile us. (*He has talked himself now into a state of happy confidence.*)

HATTIE. (*Bending over and kissing him*) Good for you! I admire you so much, Jim! I admire both of you! And are you going to begin studying right away and get admitted to the Bar?

JIM. You bet I am!

HATTIE. You must, Jim! Our race needs men like you to come to the front and help— (*As voices are heard approaching she stops, stiffens, and her face grows cold.*)

JIM. (*Noticing this—warningly*) Remember Ella's been sick! (*Losing control—threateningly*) You be nice to her, you hear! (Mrs. HARRIS *enters, showing* ELLA *the way. The colored woman is plainly worried and perplexed.* ELLA *is pale, with a strange, haunted expression in her eyes. She runs to* JIM *as to a refuge, clutching his hands in both of hers, looking from* MRS. HARRIS *to* HATTIE *with a frightened defiance.*)

MRS. H. Dere he is, child, big's life! She was afraid we'd done kidnapped you away, Jim.

JIM. (*Patting her hand*) This place ought to be familiar, Ella. Don't you remember playing here with us sometimes as a kid?

ELLA. (*Queerly—with a frown of effort*) I remember playing marbles one night—but that was on the street.

JIM. Don't you remember Hattie?

HATTIE. (*Coming forward with a forced smile*) It was a long time ago—but I remember Ella. (*She holds out her hand.*)

ELLA. (*Taking it—looking at* HATTIE *with the same queer defiance*) I remember. But you've changed so much.

HATTIE. (*Stirred to hostility by* ELLA's *manner—condescendingly*) Yes, I've grown older, naturally. (*Then in a tone which, as if in spite of herself, becomes bragging*) I've worked so hard. First I went away to college, you know—then I took up postgraduate study—when suddenly I decided I'd accomplish more good if I gave up learning and took up teaching. (*She suddenly checks herself, ashamed, and stung by* ELLA's *indifference*) But this sounds like stupid boasting. I don't mean that. I was only explaining—

ELLA. (*Indifferently*) I didn't know you'd been to school so long. (*A pause*) Where are you teaching? In a colored school, I suppose. (*There is an indifferent superiority in her words that is maddening to* HATTIE.)

HATTIE. (*Controlling herself*) Yes. A private school endowed by some wealthy members of our race.

ELLA. (*Suddenly—even eagerly*) Then you must have taken lots of examinations and managed to pass them, didn't you?

HATTIE. (*Biting her lips*) I always passed with honors!

ELLA. Yes, we both graduated from the same High School, didn't we? That was dead easy for me. Why I hardly even looked at a book. But Jim says it was awfully hard for him. He failed one year, remember? (*She turns and smiles at* JIM—*a tolerant, superior smile but one full of genuine love.* HATTIE *is outraged, but* JIM *smiles.*)

JIM. Yes, it was hard for me, Honey.

ELLA. And the law school examinations Jim hardly ever could pass at all. Could you? (*She laughs lovingly.*)

HATTIE. (*Harshly*) Yes, he could! He can! He'll pass them now—if you'll give him a chance!

JIM. (*Angrily*) Hattie!

MRS. HARRIS. Hold yo' fool tongue!

HATTIE. (*Sullenly*) I'm sorry. (ELLA *has shrunk back against* JIM. *She regards* HATTIE *with a sort of wondering hatred. Then she looks away about the room. Suddenly her eyes fasten on the primitive mask and she gives a stifled scream.*)

JIM. What's the matter, Honey?

ELLA. (*Pointing*) That! For God's sake, what is it?

HATTIE. (*Scornfully*) It's a Congo mask. (*She goes and picks it up*) I'll take it away if you wish. I thought you'd like it. It was my wedding present to Jim.

ELLA. What is it?

HATTIE. It's a mask which used to be worn in religious ceremonies by my people in Africa. But, aside from that, it's beautifully made, a work of Art by a real artist—as real in his way as your Michael Angelo. (*Forces* ELLA *to take it*) Here. Just notice the workmanship.

ELLA. (*Defiantly*) I'm not scared of it if you're not. (*Looking at it with disgust*) Beautiful? Well, some people certainly have queer notions! It looks ugly to me and stupid—like a kid's game—making faces! (*She slaps it contemptuously*) Pooh! You needn't look hard at me. I'll give you the laugh. (*She goes to put it back on the stand.*)

JIM. Maybe, if it disturbs you, we better put it in some other room.

ELLA. (*Defiantly aggressive*) No. I want it here where I can give it the laugh! (*She sets it there again—then turns suddenly on* HATTIE *with aggressive determination*) Jim's not going to take any more examinations! I won't let him!

HATTIE. (*Bursting forth*) Jim! Do you hear that? There's white justice!—their fear for their superiority!—

ELLA. (*With a terrified pleading*) Make her go away, Jim!

JIM. (*Losing control—furiously to his sister*) Either you leave here—or we will!

MRS. H. (*Weeping—throws her arms around* HATTIE) Let's go, chile! Let's go!

HATTIE. (*Calmly now*) Yes, Ma. All right. (*They go through the portières. As soon as they are gone,* JIM *suddenly collapses into a chair and hides his head in his hands.*

ELLA *stands beside him for a moment. She stares distractedly about her, at the portrait, at the mask, at the furniture, at* JIM. *She seems fighting to escape from some weight on her mind. She throws this off and, completely her old self for the moment, kneels by* JIM *and pats his shoulder.*)

ELLA. (*With kindness and love*) Don't, Jim! Don't cry, please! You don't suppose I really meant that about the examinations, do you? Why, of course, I didn't mean a word! I couldn't mean it! I want you to take the examinations! I want you to pass! I want you to be a lawyer! I want you to be the best lawyer in the country! I want you to show 'em—all the dirty sneaking, gossiping liars that talk behind our backs—what a man I married. I want the whole world to know you're the whitest of the white! I want you to climb and climb—and step on 'em, stamp right on their mean faces! I love you, Jim. You know that!

JIM. (*Calm again—happily*) I hope so, Honey—and I'll make myself worthy.

HATTIE. (*Appears in the doorway—quietly*) We're going now, Jim.

ELLA. No. Don't go.

HATTIE. We were going to anyway. This is your house—Mother's gift to you, Jim.

JIM. (*Astonished*) But I can't accept—Where are you going?

HATTIE. We've got a nice flat in the Bronx—(*With bitter pride*) in the heart of the Black Belt—the Congo—among our own people!

JIM. (*Angrily*) You're crazy—I'll see Ma—(*He goes out.* HATTIE *and* ELLA *stare at each other with scorn and hatred for a moment, then* HATTIE *goes.* ELLA *remains kneeling for a moment by the chair, her eyes dazed and strange as she looks about her. Then she gets to her feet and stands before the portrait of* JIM's *father—with a sneer.*)

ELLA. It's his Old Man—all dolled up like a circus horse! Well, they can't help it. It's in the blood, I suppose. They're ignorant, that's all there is to it. (*She moves to the mask—forcing a mocking tone*) Hello, sport! Who d'you think you're scaring. Not me! I'll give you the laugh. He won't pass, you wait and see. Not in a thousand years! (*She goes to the window and looks down at the street and mutters*) All black! Every one of them! (*Then with sudden excitement*) No, there's one. Why, it's Shorty! (*She throws the window open and calls*) Shorty! Shorty! Hello, Shorty! (*She leans out and waves—then stops, remains there for a moment looking down, then comes back into the room suddenly as if she wanted to hide—her whole face in an anguish*) Say! Say! I wonder?—No, he didn't hear you. Yes, he did too! He must have! I yelled so loud you could hear me in Jersey! No, what are you talking about? How would he hear with all kids yelling down there? He never heard a word, I tell you! He did too! He didn't want to hear you! He didn't want to let anyone know he knew you! Why don't you acknowledge it? What are you lying about? I'm not! Why shouldn't he? Where does he come in to—For God's sake, who is Shorty anyway? A pimp! Yes, and a dope-peddler, too! D'you mean to say he'd have the nerve to hear me call him and then deliberately—? Yes, I mean to say it! I do say it! And it's true, and you know it, and you might as well be honest for a change and admit it! He heard you but he didn't want to hear you! He doesn't want to know you any more. No, not even him! He's afraid it'd get him in wrong with the old gang. Why? You know well enough! Because you married a—a—a—well, I won't say it, but you know without my mentioning names! (ELLA *springs to her feet in horror and shakes off her obses-*

sion with a frantic effort) Stop! (*Then whimpering like a frightened child*) Jim! Jim!
Jim! Where are you? I want you, Jim! (*She runs out of the room as*

THE CURTAIN FALLS

Scene 2

The same. Six months later. It is evening. The walls of the room appear shrunken in, the ceiling lowered, so that the furniture, the portrait, the mask look unnaturally large and domineering. JIM *is seated at the table studying, law books piled by his elbows. He is keeping his attention concentrated only by a driving physical effort which gives his face the expression of a runner's near the tape. His forehead shines with perspiration. He mutters one sentence from Blackstone over and over again, tapping his forehead with his fist in time to the rhythm he gives the stale words. But, in spite of himself, his attention wanders, his eyes have an uneasy, hunted look, he starts at every sound in the house or from the street. Finally, he remains rigid, Blackstone forgotten, his eyes fixed on the portières with tense grief. Then he groans, slams the book shut, goes to the window and throws it open and sinks down beside it, his arms on the sill, his head resting wearily on his arms, staring out into the night, the pale glare from the arc-lamp on the corner throwing his face into relief. The portières on the right are parted and* HATTIE *comes in.*

HATTIE. (*Not seeing him at the table*) Jim! (*Discovering him*) Oh, there you are. What're you doing?

JIM. (*Turning to her*) Resting. Cooling my head. (*Forcing a smile*) These law books certainly are a sweating proposition! (*Then, anxiously*) How is she?

HATTIE. She's asleep now. I felt it was safe to leave her for a minute. (*After a pause*) What did the doctor tell you, Jim?

JIM. The same old thing. She must have rest, he says, her mind needs rest—(*Bitterly*) But he can't tell me any prescription for that rest—leastways not any that'd work.

HATTIE. (*After a pause*) I think you ought to leave her, Jim—or let her leave you—for a while, anyway.

JIM. (*Angrily*) You're like the doctor. Everything's so simple and easy. Do this and that happens. Only it don't. Life isn't simple like that—not in this case, anyway—no, it isn't simple a bit. (*After a pause*) I can't leave her. She can't leave me. And there's a million little reasons combining to make one big reason why we can't. (*A pause*) For her sake—if it'd do her good—I'd go—I'd leave—I'd do anything—because I love her. I'd kill myself even—jump out of this window this second—I've thought it over, too—but that'd only make matters worse for her. I'm all she's got in the world! Yes, that isn't bragging or fooling myself. I know that for a fact! Don't you know that's true? (*There is a pleading for the certainty he claims.*)

HATTIE. Yes, I know she loves you, Jim. I know that now.

JIM. (*Simply*) Then we've got to stick together to the end, haven't we, whatever comes—and hope and pray for the best. (*A pause—then hopefully*) I think maybe this is the crisis in her mind. Once she settles this in herself, she's won to the other side. And me—once I become a Member of the Bar—then I win, too! We're both free—by our own fighting down our own weakness! We're both really, truly free! Then we can be happy with ourselves here or anywhere. She'll be proud then! Yes, she's told me again and again, she says she'll be actually proud!

HATTIE. (*Turning away to conceal her emotion*) Yes, I'm sure—but you mustn't study too hard, Jim! You mustn't study too awfully hard!

JIM. (*Gets up and goes to the table and sits down wearily*) Yes, I know. Oh, I'll pass easily. I haven't got any scarey feeling about that any more. And I'm doing two years' work in one here alone. That's better than schools, eh?

HATTIE. (*Doubtfully*) It's wonderful, Jim.

JIM. (*His spirit evaporating*) If I can only hold out! It's hard! I'm worn out. I don't sleep. I get to thinking and thinking. My head aches and burns like fire with thinking. Round and round my thoughts go chasing like crazy chickens hopping and flapping before the wind. It gets me crazy mad—'cause I can't stop!

HATTIE. (*Watching him for a while and seeming to force herself to speak*) The doctor didn't tell you all, Jim.

JIM. (*Dully*) What's that?

HATTIE. He told me you're liable to break down too, if you don't take care of yourself.

JIM. (*Abjectly weary*) Let'er come! I don't care what happens to me. Maybe if I get sick she'll get well. There's only so much bad luck allowed to one family, maybe. (*He forces a wan smile.*)

HATTIE. (*Hastily*) Don't give in to that idea, for the Lord's sake!

JIM. I'm tired—and blue—that's all.

HATTIE. (*After another long pause*) I've got to tell you something else, Jim.

JIM. (*Dully*) What?

HATTIE. The doctor said Ella's liable to be sick like this a very long time.

JIM. He told me that too—that it'd be a long time before she got back her normal strength. Well, I suppose that's got to be expected.

HATTIE. (*Slowly*) He didn't mean convalescing—what he told me. (*A long pause.*)

JIM. (*Evasively*) I'm going to get other doctors in to see Ella—specialists. This one's a damn fool.

HATTIE. Be sensible, Jim. You'll have to face the truth—sooner or later.

JIM. (*Irritably*) I know the truth about Ella better'n any doctor.

HATTIE. (*Persuasively*) She'd get better so much sooner if you'd send her away to some nice sanitarium—

JIM. No! She'd die of shame there!

HATTIE. At least until after you've taken your examinations—

JIM. To hell with me!

HATTIE. Six months. That wouldn't be long to be parted.

JIM. What are you trying to do—separate us? (*He gets to his feet—furiously*) Go on out! Go on out!

HATTIE. (*Calmly*) No, I won't. (*Sharply*) There's something that's got to be said to you and I'm the only one with the courage—(*Intensely*) Tell me, Jim, have you heard her raving when she's out of her mind?

JIM. (*With a shudder*) No!

HATTIE. You're lying, Jim. You must have—if you don't stop your ears—and the doctor says she may develop a violent mania, dangerous for you—get worse and worse until—Jim, you'll go crazy too—living this way. Today she raved on about "Black!

Black!" and cried because she said her skin was turning black—that you had poisoned her—

JIM. (*In anguish*) That's only when she's out of her mind.

HATTIE. And then she suddenly called me a dirty nigger.

JIM. No! She never said that ever! She never would!

HATTIE. She did—and kept on and on! (*A tense pause*) She'll be saying that to you soon.

JIM. (*Torturedly*) She don't mean it! She isn't responsible for what she's saying!

HATTIE. I know she isn't—yet she is just the same. It's deep down in her or it wouldn't come out.

JIM. Deep down in her people—not deep in her.

HATTIE. I can't make such distinctions. The race in me, deep in me, can't stand it. I can't play nurse to her any more, Jim,—not even for your sake. I'm afraid—afraid of myself—afraid sometime I'll kill her dead to set you free! (*She loses control and begins to cry.*)

JIM. (*After a long pause—somberly*) Yes, I guess you'd better stay away from here. Good-by.

HATTIE. Who'll you get to nurse her, Jim,—a white woman?

JIM. Ella'd die of shame. No, I'll nurse her myself.

HATTIE. And give up your studies?

JIM. I can do both.

HATTIE. You can't! You'll get sick yourself! Why, you look terrible even as it is—and it's only beginning!

JIM. I can do anything for her! I'm all she's got in the world! I've got to prove I can be all to her! I've got to prove worthy! I've got to prove she can be proud of me! I've got to prove I'm the whitest of the white!

HATTIE. (*Stung by this last—with rebellious bitterness*) Is that the ambition she's given you? Oh, you soft, weak-minded fool, you traitor to your race! And the thanks you'll get—to be called a dirty nigger—to hear her cursing you because she can never have a child because it'll be born black—!

JIM. (*In a frenzy*) Stop!

HATTIE. I'll say what must be said even though you kill me, Jim. Send her to an asylum before you both have to be sent to one together.

JIM. (*With a sudden wild laugh*) Do you think you're threatening me with something dreadful now? Why, I'd like that. Sure, I'd like that! Maybe she'd like it better, too. Maybe we'd both find it all simple then—like you think it is now. Yes. (*He laughs again.*)

HATTIE. (*Frightenedly*) Jim!

JIM. Together! You can't scare me even with hell fire if you say she and I go together. It's heaven then for me! (*With sudden savagery*) You go out of here! All you've ever been aiming to do is to separate us so we can't be together!

HATTIE. I've done what I did for your own good.

JIM. I have no own good. I only got a good together with her. I'm all she's got in the world! Let her call me nigger! Let her call me the whitest of the white! I'm all she's got in the world, ain't I? She's all I've got! You with your fool talk of the black race and the white race! Where does the human race get a chance to come in? I suppose that's simple for you. You lock it up in asylums and throw away the key! (*With fresh violence*) Go along! There isn't going to be no more people coming in here to separate—excepting the doctor. I'm going to lock the door and it's going to stay locked, you hear? Go along, now!

HATTIE. (*Confusedly*) Jim!

JIM. (*Pushes her out gently and slams the door after her—vaguely*) Go along! I got to study. I got to nurse Ella, too. Oh, I can do it! I can do anything for her! (*He sits down at the table and, opening the book, begins again to recite the line from Blackstone in a meaningless rhythm, tapping his forehead with his fist.* ELLA *enters noiselessly through the portières. She wears a red dressing-gown over her night-dress but is in her bare feet. She has a carving-knife in her right hand. Her eyes fasten on* JIM *with a murderous mania. She creeps up behind him. Suddenly he senses something and turns. As he sees her he gives a cry, jumping up and catching her wrist. She stands fixed, her eyes growing bewildered and frightened.*)

JIM. (*Aghast*) Ella! For God's sake! Do you want to murder me? (*She does not answer. He shakes her.*)

ELLA. (*Whimperingly*) They kept calling me names as I was walking along—I can't tell you what, Jim—and then I grabbed a knife—

JIM. Yes! See! This! (*She looks at it frightenedly.*)

ELLA. Where did I—? I was having a nightmare—Where did they go—I mean, how did I get here? (*With sudden terrified pleading—like a little girl*) O Jim—don't ever leave me alone! I have such terrible dreams, Jim—promise you'll never go away!

JIM. I promise, Honey.

ELLA. (*Her manner becoming more and more childishly silly*) I'll be a little girl—and you'll be old Uncle Jim who's been with us for years and years—Will you play that?

JIM. Yes, Honey. Now you better go back to bed.

ELLA. (*Like a child*) Yes, Uncle Jim. (*She turns to go. He pretends to be occupied by his book. She looks at him for a second—then suddenly asks in her natural woman's voice*) Are you studying hard, Jim?

JIM. Yes, Honey. Go to bed now. You need to rest, you know.

ELLA. (*Stands looking at him, fighting with herself. A startling transformation comes over her face. It grows mean, vicious, full of jealous hatred. She cannot contain herself but breaks out harshly with a cruel, venomous grin*) You dirty nigger!

JIM. (*Starting as if he'd been shot*) Ella! For the good Lord's sake!

ELLA. (*Coming out of her insane mood for a moment, aware of something terrible, frightened*) Jim! Jim! Why are you looking at me like that?

JIM. What did you say to me just then?

ELLA. (*Gropingly*) Why, I—I said—I remember saying, are you studying hard, Jim? Why? You're not mad at that, are you?

JIM. No, Honey. What made you think I was mad? Go to bed now.

ELLA. (*Obediently*) Yes, Jim. (*She passes behind the portières.* JIM *stares before him. Suddenly her head is thrust out at the side of the portières. Her face is again that of a vindictive maniac*) Nigger! (*The face disappears—she can be heard running away, laughing with cruel satisfaction.* JIM *bows his head on his outstretched arms but he is too stricken for tears.*)

CURTAIN

Scene 3

The same, six months later. The sun has just gone down. The Spring twilight sheds a vague, gray light about the room, picking out the Congo mask on the stand by the window. The walls have shrunken in still more, the ceiling now barely clears the people's heads, the furniture and the characters appear enormously magnified. Law books are stacked in two great piles on each side of the table. ELLA *comes in from the right, the carving-knife in her hand. She is pitifully thin, her face is wasted, but her eyes glow with a mad energy, her movements are abrupt and spring-like. She looks stealthily about the room, then advances and stands before the mask, her arms akimbo, her attitude one of crazy mockery, fear and bravado. She is dressed in the red dressing-gown, grown dirty and ragged now, and is in her bare feet.*

ELLA. I'll give you the laugh, wait and see! (*Then in a confidential tone*) He thought I was asleep! He called, Ella, Ella—but I kept my eyes shut, I pretended to snore. I fooled him good. (*She gives a little hoarse laugh*) This is the first time he's dared to leave me alone for months and months. I've been wanting to talk to you every day but this is the only chance—(*With sudden violence—flourishing her knife*) What're you grinning about, you dirty nigger, you? How dare you grin at me? I guess you forget what you are! That's always the way. Be kind to you, treat you decent, and in a second you've got a swelled head, you think you're somebody, you're all over the place putting on airs, why, it's got so I can't even walk down the street without seeing niggers, niggers everywhere. Hanging around, grinning, grinning—going to school—pretending they're white—taking examinations—(*She stops, arrested by the word, then suddenly*) That's where he's gone—down to the mail-box—to see if there's a letter from the Board—telling him—But why is he so long? (*She calls pitifully*) Jim! (*Then in a terrified whimper*) Maybe he's passed! Maybe he's passed! (*In a frenzy*) No! No! He can't! I'd kill him! I'd kill myself! (*Threatening the Congo mask*) It's you who're to blame for this! Yes, you! Oh, I'm on to you! (*Then appealingly*) But why d'you want to do this to us? What have I ever done wrong to you? What have you got against me? I married you, didn't I? Why don't you let Jim alone? Why don't you let him be happy as he is—with me? Why don't you let me be happy? He's white, isn't he—the whitest man that ever lived? Where do you come in to interfere? Black! Black! Black as dirt! You've poisoned me! I can't wash myself clean! Oh, I hate you! I hate you! Why don't you let Jim and I be happy? (*She sinks down in his chair, her arms outstretched on the table. The door from the hall is slowly opened and* JIM *appears. His bloodshot, sleepless eyes stare from deep hollows. His expression is one of crushed numbness. He holds an open letter in his hand.*)

JIM. (*Seeing* ELLA—*in an absolutely dead voice*) Honey—I thought you were asleep.

ELLA. (*Starts and wheels about in her chair*) What's that? You got—you got a letter—?

JIM. (*Turning to close the door after him*) From the Board of Examiners for admission to the Bar, State of New York—God's country! (*He finishes up with a chuckle of ironic self-pity so spent as to be barely audible.*)

ELLA. (*Writhing out of her chair like some fierce animal, the knife held behind her—with fear and hatred*) You didn't—you didn't—you didn't pass, did you?

JIM. (*Looking at her wildly*) Pass? Pass? (*He begins to chuckle and laugh between sentences and phrases, rich, Negro laughter, but heart-breaking in its mocking grief*) Good Lord, child, how come you can ever imagine such a crazy idea? Pass? Me? Jim Crow Harris? Nigger Jim Harris—become a full-fledged Member of the Bar! Why the mere notion of it is enough to kill you with laughing! It'd be against all natural laws, all human right and justice. It'd be miraculous, there'd be earthquakes and catastrophes, the seven Plagues'd come again and locusts'd devour all the money in the banks, the second Flood'd come roaring and Noah'd fall overboard, the sun'd drop out of the sky like a ripe fig, and the Devil'd perform miracles, and God'd be tipped head first right out of the Judgment seat! (*He laughs, maudlinly uproarious.*)

ELLA. (*Her face beginning to relax, to light up*) Then you—you didn't pass?

JIM. (*Spent—giggling and gasping idiotically*) Well, I should say not! I should certainly say not!

ELLA. (*With a cry of joy, pushes all the lawbooks crashing to the floor—then with childish happiness she grabs* JIM *by both hands and dances up and down*) Oh Jim, I knew it! I knew you couldn't! Oh, I'm so glad, Jim! I'm so happy! You're still my old Jim—and I'm so glad! (*He looks at her dazedly, a fierce rage slowly gathering on his face. She dances away from him. His eyes follow her. His hands clench. She stands in front of the mask—triumphantly*) There! What did I tell you? I told you I'd give you the laugh! (*She begins to laugh with wild unrestraint, grabs the mask from its place, sets it in the middle of the table and plunging the knife down through it pins it to the table*) There! Who's got the laugh now?

JIM. (*His eyes bulging—hoarsely*) You devil! You white devil woman! (*In a terrible roar, raising his fists above her head*) You devil!

ELLA. (*Looking up at him with a bewildered cry of terror*) Jim! (*Her appeal recalls him to himself. He lets his arms slowly drop to his sides, bowing his head.* ELLA *points tremblingly to the mask*) It's all right, Jim! It's dead. The devil's dead. See! It couldn't live—unless you passed. If you'd passed it would have lived in you. Then I'd have had to kill you, Jim, don't you see—or it would have killed me. But now I've killed it. (*She pats his hand*) So you needn't ever be afraid any more, Jim.

JIM. (*Dully*) I've got to sit down, Honey. I'm tired. I haven't had much chance for sleep in so long—(*He slumps down in the chair by the table.*)

ELLA. (*Sits down on the floor beside him and holds his hand. Her face is gradually regaining an expression that is happy, childlike and pretty*) I know, Jim! That was my fault. I wouldn't let you sleep. I couldn't let you. I kept thinking if he sleeps good then he'll be sure to study good and then he'll pass—and the devil'll win!

JIM. (*With a groan*) Don't, Honey!

ELLA. (*With a childish grin*) That was why I carried that knife around—(*She frowns—puzzled*)—one reason—to keep you from studying and sleeping by scaring you.

JIM. I wasn't scared of being killed. I was scared of what they'd do to you after.

ELLA. (*After a pause—like a child*) Will God forgive me, Jim?

JIM. Maybe He can forgive what you've done to me; and maybe He can forgive what I've done to you; but I don't see how He's going to forgive—Himself.

ELLA. I prayed and prayed. When you were away taking the examinations and I was alone with the nurse, I closed my eyes and pretended to be asleep but I was praying with all my might: O, God, don't let Jim pass!

JIM. (*With a sob*) Don't, Honey, don't! For the good Lord's sake! You're hurting me!

ELLA. (*Frightenedly*) How, Jim? Where? (*Then after a pause—suddenly*) I'm sick, Jim. I don't think I'll live long.

JIM. (*Simply*) Then I won't either. Somewhere yonder maybe—together—our luck'll change. But I wanted—here and now—before you—we—I wanted to prove to you—to myself—to become a full-fledged Member—so you could be proud—(*He stops. Words fail and he is beyond tears.*)

ELLA. (*Brightly*) Well, it's all over, Jim. Everything'll be all right now. (*Chattering along*) I'll be just your little girl, Jim—and you'll be my little boy—just as we used to be, remember, when we were beaux; and I'll put shoe blacking on my face and pretend I'm black and you can put chalk on your face and pretend you're white just as we used to do—and we can play marbles—Only you mustn't all the time be a boy. Sometimes you must be my old kind Uncle Jim who's been with us for years and years. Will you, Jim?

JIM. (*With utter resignation*) Yes, Honey.

ELLA. And you'll never, never, never, never leave me, Jim?

JIM. Never, Honey.

ELLA. 'Cause you're all I've got in the world—and I love you, Jim. (*She kisses his hand as a child might, tenderly and gratefully.*)

JIM. (*Suddenly throws himself on his knees and raises his shining eyes, his transfigured face*) Forgive me, God—and make me worthy! Now I see Your Light again! Now I hear Your Voice! (*He begins to weep in an ecstasy of religious humility*) Forgive me, God, for blaspheming You! Let this fire of burning suffering purify me of selfishness and make me worthy of the child You send me for the woman You take away!

ELLA. (*Jumping to her feet—excitedly*) Don't cry, Jim! You mustn't cry! I've got only a little time left and I want to play. Don't be old Uncle Jim now. Be my little boy Jim. Pretend you're Painty Face and I'm Jim Crow. Come and play!

JIM. (*Still deeply exalted*) Honey, Honey, I'll play right up to the gates of Heaven with you! (*She tugs at one of his hands, laughingly trying to pull him up from his knees as*

THE CURTAIN FALLS

43

"Near White"
"Two Who Crossed a Line"

Countée Cullen

His ability to maintain a racial consciousness while following traditional verse forms made Countée Cullen (1903–1946) the most popular Afro-American literary figure of the mid-1920s. Raised in New York City, Cullen was adopted by Reverend Frederick Cullen, pastor of Harlem's Salem Methodist Episcopal Church, and his wife, Carolyn. Cullen excelled in academics, distinguishing himself as a poet at De Witt Clinton High School, then at New York University, then at Harvard, where he received an M.A. in French and English in 1926. In 1925 Cullen's first verse collection, *Color*, was published; *Color* and later volumes won Cullen critical acclaim, a popular audience, and numerous prizes from sources black and white. In 1928 he became the second Afro-American to receive a Guggenheim Fellowship. His career declined after the 1928 publication of *The Black Christ and Other Poems*, which was poorly received; nevertheless Cullen continued to write, if less prolifically. In 1934 he published a new version of Euripides' *Medea*, set to music by Virgil Thomson. Declining offers from black colleges in the South, Cullen taught French and English at New York's Frederick Douglass Junior High School. He also published children's books. His poems "Near White" and "Two Who Crossed a Line," reprinted here, are representative of the Harlem Renaissance interest in themes of racial "passing."

Near White

Ambiguous of race they stand,
    By one disowned, scorned of another,
Not knowing where to stretch a hand,
    And cry, "My sister" or "My brother."

Two Who Crossed a Line

(She Crosses)

From where she stood the air she craved
    Smote with the smell of pine;
It was too much to bear; she braved
    Her gods and crossed the line.

And we were hurt to see her go,
    With her fair face and hair,
And veins too thin and blue to show
    What mingled blood flowed there.

We envied her a while, who still
    Pursued the hated track;
Then we forgot her name, until
    One day her shade came back.

Calm as a wave without a crest,
    Sorrow-proud and sorrow-wise,
With trouble sucking at her breast,
    With tear-disdainful eyes,

She slipped into her ancient place,
    And, no word asked, gave none;
Only the silence in her face
    Said seats were dear in the sun.

Two Who Crossed a Line

(He Crosses)

He rode across like a cavalier,
    Spurs clicking hard and loud;
And where he tarried dropped his tear
    On heads he left low-bowed.

But, "Even Stephen," he cried, and struck
    His steed an urgent blow;
He swore by youth he was a buck
    With savage oats to sow.

To even up some standing scores,
    From every flower bed
He passed, he plucked by threes and fours
    Till wheels whirled in his head.

But long before the drug could tell,
    He took his anodyne;
With scornful grace, he bowed farewell
    And retraversed the line.

44

"Cross"
"Mulatto"
Mulatto: A Tragedy of the Deep South

Langston Hughes

The prolific author Langston Hughes (1902–1967) holds a prominent place in the literary canons of both black and white America. Hughes was born in Missouri and spent much of his childhood in Lawrence, Kansas. His first poem, "The Negro Speaks of Rivers," was published in the *Crisis* in 1921, just after his graduation from a Cleveland high school. He moved to New York City and attended Columbia University from 1921 to 1922, then supported himself with menial jobs until 1926, the year he won a prestigious literary award, a scholarship to Lincoln University, and a book contract with Knopf for his first poetry collection, *The Weary Blues*. Hughes experimented in his poetry with folk dialect and free verse patterned after blues and jazz. Interracial themes appear in a number of his works, including those reprinted here, the poems "Cross" (1925) and "Mulatto" (1927), and the play *Mulatto: A Tragedy of the Deep South*, which opened on Broadway in 1935 and became the longest-running play by a black writer until *A Raisin in the Sun*. Hughes was drawn to the themes explored in *Mulatto* by an episode in his maternal great-uncle John Mercer Langston's autobiography, and he also adapted the play to serve as libretto for the opera *The Barrier* composed by Jan Meyerowitz. Hughes, who settled in Harlem for good in 1947, added to his list of publications sixty-six short stories (including a 1934 short story version of *Mulatto*, entitled "Father and Son"), novels, children's books, libretti, anthologies, a history of the NAACP, and an essay on Mark Twain's interracial novel, *Pudd'n-head Wilson*. His 1940 autobiography, *The Big Sea*, provides a detailed firsthand recollection of Hughes's days in the Harlem Renaissance and has been one of his most valuable works.

Cross

My old man's a white old man
And my old mother's black.
If ever I cursed my white old man
I take my curses back.

If ever I cursed my black old mother
And wished she were in hell,
I'm sorry for that evil wish
And now I wish her well.

My old man died in a fine big house.
My ma died in a shack.
I wonder where I'm gonna die,
Being neither white nor black?

Mulatto

    I am your son, white man!

Georgia dusk
And the turpentine woods.
One of the pillars of the temple fell.

    You are my son!
    Like hell!

The moon over the turpentine woods.
The Southern night
Full of stars,
Great big yellow stars.
    What's a body but a toy?
        Juicy bodies
        Of nigger wenches
        Blue black
        Against black fences.
        O, you little bastard boy,
        What's a body but a toy?
The scent of pine wood stings the soft night air.
        What's the body of your mother?
Silver moonlight everywhere.
        What's the body of your mother?
Sharp pine scent in the evening air.
        A nigger night,
        A nigger joy,
        A little yellow
        Bastard boy.

    Naw, you ain't my brother.
    Niggers ain't my brother.

Not ever.
Niggers ain't my brother.

The Southern night is full of stars,
Great big yellow stars.
          O, sweet as earth,
          Dusk dark bodies
          Give sweet birth
To little yellow bastard boys.

          Git on back there in the night,
          You ain't white.

The bright stars scatter everywhere.
Pine wood scent in the evening air.
          A nigger night,
          A nigger joy.

I am your son, white man!

          A little yellow
          Bastard boy.

Mulatto: A Tragedy of the Deep South

Characters

COLONEL THOMAS NORWOOD. *Plantation owner, a still vigorous man of about sixty, nervous, refined, quick-tempered, and commanding; a widower who is the father of four living mulatto children by his Negro housekeeper*

CORA LEWIS. *A brown woman in her forties who has kept the house and been the mistress of Colonel Norwood for some thirty years*

WILLIAM LEWIS. *The oldest son of Cora Lewis and the Colonel; a fat, easy-going, soft-looking mulatto of twenty-eight; married*

SALLIE LEWIS. *The seventeen-year-old daughter, very light with sandy hair and freckles, who could pass for white*

ROBERT LEWIS. *Eighteen, the youngest boy; strong and well-built; a light mulatto with ivory-yellow skin and proud thin features like his father's; as tall as the Colonel, with the same gray-blue eyes, but with curly black hair instead of brown; of a fiery, impetuous temper—immature and willful—resenting his blood and the circumstances of his birth*

FRED HIGGINS. *A close friend of Colonel Norwood; a county politician; fat and elderly, conventionally Southern*

SAM. *An old Negro retainer, a personal servant of the Colonel*

BILLY. *The small son of William Lewis; a chubby brown kid about five*

TALBOT. *The overseer*
MOSE. *An elderly Negro, chauffeur for Mr. Higgins*
A STOREKEEPER.
AN UNDERTAKER.
UNDERTAKER'S HELPER. *Voice off-stage only*
THE MOB.

ACT ONE

TIME: *An afternoon in early fall.*

THE SETTING: *The living room of the Big House on a plantation in Georgia. Rear center of the room, a vestibule with double doors leading to the porch; at each side of the doors, a large window with lace curtains and green shades; at left a broad flight of stairs leading to the second floor; near the stairs, downstage, a doorway leading to the dining room and kitchen; opposite, at right of stage, a door to the library. The room is furnished in the long out-dated horsehair and walnut style of the nineties; a crystal chandelier, a large old-fashioned rug, a marble-topped table, upholstered chairs. At the right there is a small cabinet. It is a very clean, but somewhat shabby and rather depressing room, dominated by a large oil painting of* NORWOOD's *wife of his youth on the center wall. The windows are raised. The afternoon sunlight streams in.*

ACTION: *As the curtain rises, the stage is empty. The door at the right opens and* COLONEL NORWOOD *enters, crossing the stage toward the stairs, his watch in his hand. Looking up, he shouts:*

NORWOOD. Cora! Oh, Cora!
CORA. (*Heard above*) Yes, sir, Colonel Tom.
NORWOOD. I want to know if that child of yours means to leave here this afternoon?
CORA. (*At head of steps now*) Yes, sir, she's goin' directly. I's gettin' her ready now, packin' up an' all. 'Course, she wants to tell you goodbye 'fore she leaves.
NORWOOD. Well, send her down here. Who's going to drive her to the railroad? The train leaves at three—and it's after two now. You ought to know you can't drive ten miles in no time.
CORA. (*Above*) Her brother's gonna drive her. Bert. He ought to be back here most any time now with the Ford.
NORWOOD. (*Stopping on his way back to the library*) Ought to be *back* here? Where's he gone?
CORA. (*Coming downstairs nervously*) Why, he driv in town 'fore noon, Colonel Tom. Said he were lookin' for some tubes or somethin' 'nother by de mornin' mail for de radio he's been riggin' up out in de shed.
NORWOOD. Who gave him permission to be driving off in the middle of the morning? I bought that Ford to be used when I gave orders for it to be used, not ...
CORA. Yes, sir, Colonel Tom, but ...
NORWOOD. But what? (*Pausing. Then deliberately*) Cora, if you want that hardheaded yellow son of yours to get along around here, he'd better listen to me. He's no more than any other black buck on this plantation—due to work like the rest of 'em. I

don't take such a performance from nobody under me—driving off in the middle
of the day to town, after I've told him to bend his back in that cotton. How's Talbot
going to keep the rest of those darkies working right if that boy's allowed to set that
kind of an example? Just because Bert's your son, and I've been damn fool enough
to send him off to school for five or six years, he thinks he has a right to privileges,
acting as if he owned this place since he's been back here this summer.

CORA. But, Colonel Tom ...

NORWOOD. Yes, I know what you're going to say. I don't give a damn about him!
There's no nigger-child of mine, yours, ours—no darkie—going to disobey me. I
put him in that field to work, and he'll stay on this plantation till I get ready to let
him go. I'll tell Talbot to use the whip on him, too, if he needs it. If it hadn't been
that he's yours, he'd-a had a taste of it the other day. Talbot's a damn good overseer,
and no saucy, lazy Nigras stay on this plantation and get away with it. (*To* CORA)
Go on back upstairs and see about getting Sallie out of here. Another word from
you and I won't send your (*Sarcastically*) pretty little half-white daughter anywhere, either. Schools for darkies! Huh! If you take that boy of yours for an example, they do 'em more harm than good. He's learned nothing in college but impudence, and he'll stay here on this place and work for me awhile before he gets back
to any more schools. (*He starts across the room*)

CORA. Yes, sir, Colonel Tom. (*Hesitating*) But he's just young, sir. And he was mighty
broke up when you said last week he couldn't go back to de campus. (COLONEL
NORWOOD *turns and looks at* CORA *commandingly. Understanding, she murmurs*)
Yes, sir. (*She starts upstairs, but turns back*) Can't I run and fix you a cool drink,
Colonel Tom?

NORWOOD. No, damn you! Sam'll do it.

CORA. (*Sweetly*) Go set down in de cool, then, Colonel. 'Taint good for you to be
going on this way in de heat. I'll talk to Robert maself soon's he comes in. He don't
mean nothing—just smart and young and kinder careless, Colonel Tom, like ma
mother said you used to be when you was eighteen.

NORWOOD. Get on upstairs, Cora. Do I have to speak again? Get on! (*He pulls the cord
of the servants' bell*)

CORA. (*On the steps*) Does you still be in the mind to tell Sallie good-bye?

NORWOOD. Send her down here as I told you. (*Impatiently*) Where's Sam? Send him
here first. (*Fuming*) Looks like he takes his time to answer that bell. You colored
folks are running the house to suit yourself nowadays.

CORA. (*Coming downstairs again and going toward door under the steps*) I'll get Sam
for you.

(CORA *exits left.* NORWOOD *paces nervously across the floor. Goes to the window and
looks out down the road. Takes a cigar from his pocket, sits in a chair with it unlighted,
scowling. Rises, goes toward servants' bell and rings it again violently as* SAM *enters, out
of breath*)

NORWOOD. What the hell kind of a tortoise race is this? I suppose you were out in the
sun somewhere sleeping?

SAM. No, sah, Colonel Norwood. Just tryin' to get Miss Sallie's valises down to de yard
so's we can put 'em in de Ford, sah.

NORWOOD. (*Out of patience*) Huh! Darkies waiting on darkies! I can't get service in my own house. Very well. (*Loudly*) Bring me some whiskey and soda, and ice in a glass. Is that damn Frigidaire working right? Or is Livonia still too thickheaded to know how to run it? Any ice cubes in the thing?

SAM. Yes, sah, Colonel, yes, sah. (*Backing toward door left*) 'Scuse me, please sah, but (*as* NORWOOD *turns toward library*) Cora say for me to ask you is it all right to bring that big old trunk what you give Sallie down by de front steps. We ain't been able to tote it down them narrer little back steps, sah. Cora, say, can we bring it down de front way through here?

NORWOOD. No other way? (*Sam shakes his head*) Then pack it on through to the back, quick. Don't let me catch you carrying any of Sallie's baggage out of that front door here. You-all'll be wanting to go in and out the front way next. (*Turning away, complaining to himself*) Darkies have been getting mighty fresh in this part of the country since the war. The damn Germans should've … (*To* SAM) Don't take that trunk out that front door.

SAM. (*Evilly, in a cunning voice*) I's seen Robert usin' de front door—when you ain't here, and he comes up from de cabin to see his mammy.

(SALLIE, *the daughter, appears at the top of the stairs, but hesitates about coming down*)

NORWOOD. Oh, you have, have you? Let me catch him and I'll break his young neck for him. (*Yelling at* SAM) Didn't I tell you some whiskey and soda an hour ago?

(SAM *exits left.* SALLIE *comes shyly down the stairs and approaches her father. She is dressed in a little country-style coat-suit ready for traveling. Her features are Negroid, although her skin is very fair.* COLONEL NORWOOD *gazes down at her without saying a word as she comes meekly toward him, half-frightened*)

SALLIE. I just wanted to tell you goodbye, Colonel Norwood, and thank you for letting me go back to school another year, and for letting me work here in the house all summer where mama is. (NORWOOD *says nothing. The girl continues in a strained voice as if making a speech*) You mighty nice to us colored folks certainly, and mama says you the best white man in Georgia. (*Still* NORWOOD *says nothing. The girl continues*) You been mighty nice to your—I mean to us colored children, letting my sister and me go off to school. The principal says I'm doing pretty well and next year I can go to Normal and learn to be a teacher. (*Raising her eyes*) You reckon I can, Colonel Tom?

NORWOOD. Stand up straight and let me see how you look. (*Backing away*) Hum-m-m! Getting kinder grown, ain't you? Do they teach you in that school to have good manners, and not be afraid of work, *and to respect white folks?*

SALLIE. Yes, sir, I been taking up cooking and sewing, too.

NORWOOD. Well, that's good. As I recall it, that school turned your sister out a right smart cook. Cora tells me she's got a good job in some big hotel in Chicago. I'm thinking about you going on up North there with her in a year or two. You're getting too old to be around here, and too womanish. (*He puts his hands on her arms as if feeling her flesh*)

SALLIE. (*Drawing back slightly*) But I want to live down here with mama. I want to teach school in that there empty school house by the Cross Roads what hasn't had a teacher for five years.

(SAM *has been standing with the door cracked, overhearing the conversation. He enters with the drink and places it on the table, right.* NORWOOD *sits down, leaving the girl standing, as* SAM *pours out a drink*)

NORWOOD. Don't get that into your head, now. There's been no teacher there for years—and there won't be any teacher there, either. Cotton teaches these pickaninnies enough around here. Some of 'em's too smart as it is. The only reason I did have a teacher there once was to get you young ones o' Cora's educated. I gave you all a chance and I hope you appreciate it. (*He takes a long drink*) Don't know why I did it. No other white man in these parts ever did it, as I know of. (*To* SAM) Get out of here! (SAM *exits left*) Guess I couldn't stand to see Cora's kids working around here dumb as the rest of these no good darkies—need a dozen of 'em to chop one row of cotton, or to keep a house clean. Or maybe I didn't want to see Talbot eyeing you gals. (*Taking another drink*) Anyhow, I'm glad you and Bertha turned out right well. Yes, hum-m-m! (*Straightening up*) You know I tried to do something for those brothers of yours, too, but William's stupid as an ox—good for work, though—and that Robert's just an impudent, hardheaded, yellow young fool. I'm gonna break his damn neck for him if he don't watch out. Or else put Talbot on him.

SALLIE. (*Suddenly frightened*) Please, sir, don't put the overseer on Bert, Colonel Tom. He was the smartest boy at school, Bert was. On the football team, too. Please, sir, Colonel Tom. Let brother work here in the house, or somewhere else where Talbot can't mistreat him. He ain't used …

NORWOOD. (*Rising*) Telling me what to do, heh? (*Staring at her sternly*) I'll use the back of my hand across your face if you don't hush. (*He takes another drink. The noise of a Ford is heard outside*) That's Bert now, I reckon. He's to take you to the railroad line, and while you're riding with him, you better put some sense into his head. And tell him I want to see him as soon as he gets back here. (CORA *enters left with a bundle and an umbrella.* SAM *and* WILLIAM *come downstairs with a big square trunk, and exit hurriedly, left*)

SALLIE. Yes, sir, I'll tell him.

CORA. Colonel Tom, Sallie ain't got much time now. (*To the girl*) Come on, chile. Bert's here. Yo' big brother and Sam and Livonia and everybody's all waiting at de back door to say goodbye. And your baggage is being packed in. (*Noise of another car is heard outside*) Who else is that there coming up de drive? (CORA *looks out the window*) Mr. Higgins' car, Colonel Tom. Reckon he's coming to see you … Hurry up out o' this front room, Sallie. Here, take these things of your'n (*Hands her the bundle and parasol*) while I opens de door for Mr. Higgins. (*In a whisper*) Hurry up, chile! Get out! (NORWOOD *turns toward the front door as* CORA *goes to open it*)

SALLIE. (*Shyly to her father*) Goodbye, Colonel Tom.

NORWOOD. (*His eyes on the front door, scarcely noticing the departing* SALLIE, *he motions*) Yes, yes, goodbye! Get on now! (CORA *opens the front door as her daughter exits left*) Well, well! Howdy do, Fred. Come in, come in! (CORA *holds the outer door of the vestibule wide as* FRED HIGGINS *enters with rheumatic dignity, supported on the arm of his chauffeur,* MOSE, *a very black Negro in a slouchy uniform.* CORA *closes the door and exits left hurriedly, following* SALLIE)

NORWOOD. (*Smiling*) How's the rheumatiz today? Women or licker or heat must've made it worse—from the looks of your speed!

HIGGINS. (*Testily, sitting down puffing and blowing in a big chair*) I'm in no mood for fooling, Tom, not now. (To MOSE) All right. (*The* CHAUFFEUR *exits front.* HIGGINS *continues angrily*) Norwood, that damned yellow nigger buck of yours that drives that new Ford tried his best just now to push my car off the road, then got in front of me and blew dust in my face for the last mile coming down to your gate, trying to beat me in here—which he did. Such a deliberate piece of impudence I don't know if I've ever seen out of a nigger before in all the sixty years I've lived in this county. (*The noise of the Ford is heard going out the drive, and the cries of the* NEGROES *shouting farewells to* SALLIE. HIGGINS *listens indignantly*) What kind of crazy coons have you got on your place, anyhow? Sounds like a black Baptist picnic to me. (*Pointing to the window with his cane*). Tom, listen to that.

NORWOOD. (*Flushing*) I apologize to you, Fred, for each and every one of my darkies. (SAM *enters with more ice and another glass*) Permit me to offer you a drink. I realize I've got to tighten down here.

HIGGINS. Mose tells me that was Cora's boy in that Ford—and that young black fool is what I was coming here to talk to you about today. That boy! He's not gonna be around here long—not the way he's acting. The white folks in town'll see to that. Knowing he's one of your yard niggers, Norwood, I thought I ought to come and tell you. The white folks at the Junction aren't intending to put up with him much longer. And I don't know what good the jail would do him once he got in there.

NORWOOD. (*Tensely*) What do you mean, Fred—jail? Don't I always take care of the folks on my plantation without any help from the Junction's police force? Talbot can do more with an unruly black buck than your marshal.

HIGGINS. Warn't lookin' at it that way, Tom. I was thinking how weak the doors to that jail is. They've broke 'em down and lynched four niggers to my memory since it's been built. After what happened this morning, you better keep that yellow young fool out o' town from now on. It might not be safe for him around there—today, nor no other time.

NORWOOD. What the hell? (*Perturbed*) He went in just now to take his sister to the depot. Damn it, I hope no ruffians'll break up my new Ford. What was it, Fred, about this morning?

HIGGINS. You haven't heard? Why, it's all over town already. He sassed out Miss Gray in the post office over a box of radio tubes that come by mail.

NORWOOD. He did, heh?

HIGGINS. Seems like the stuff was sent C. O. D. and got here all smashed up, so he wouldn't take it. Paid his money first before he saw the box was broke. Then wanted the money order back. Seems like the post office can't give money orders back—rule against it. Your nigger started to argue, and the girl at the window— Miss Gray—got scared and yelled for some of the mail clerks. They threw Bert out of the office, that's all. But that's enough. Lucky nothing more didn't happen. (*Indignantly*) That Bert needs a damn good beating—talking back to a white woman—and I'd like to give it to him myself, the way he kicked the dust up in my eyes all the way down the road coming out here. He was mad, I reckon. That's one yellow buck don't know his place, Tom, and it's your fault he don't—sending 'em off to be educated.

NORWOOD. Well, by God, I'll show him. I wish I'd have known it before he left here just now.

HIGGINS. Well, he's sure got mighty aggravating ways for a buck his color to have. Drives down the main street and don't stop for nobody, white or black. Comes in my store and if he ain't waited on as quick as the white folks are, he walks out and tells the clerk his money's as good as a white man's any day. Said last week standing out on my store front that he wasn't *all* nigger no how; said his name was Norwood—not Lewis, like the rest of his family—and part of your plantation here would be his when you passed out—and all that kind of stuff, boasting to the walleyed coons listening to him.

NORWOOD. (*Astounded*) Well, I'll be damned!

HIGGINS. Now, Tom, you know that don't go 'round these parts 'o Georgia, nor nowhere else in the South. A darkie's got to keep in his place down here. Ruinous to other niggers hearing that talk, too. All this postwar propaganda on the radio about freedom and democracy—why the niggers think it's meant for them! And that Eleanor Roosevelt, she ought to been muzzled. She's driving our niggers crazy—your boy included! Crazy! Talking about civil rights. Ain't been no race trouble in our country for three years—since the Deekin's lynching—but I'm telling you, Norwood, you better see that that buck of yours goes away from here. I'm speaking on the quiet, but I can see ahead. And what happened this morning about them radio tubes wasn't none too good.

NORWOOD. (*Beside himself with rage*) A black ape! I——I ...

HIGGINS. You been too decent to your darkies, Norwood. That's what's the matter with you. And then the whole county suffers from a lot of impudent bucks who take lessons from your crowd. Folks been kicking about that, too. Guess you know it. Maybe that's the reason you didn't get that nomination for committeeman a few years back.

NORWOOD. Maybe 'tis, Higgins. (*Rising and pacing the room*) God damn niggers! (*Furiously*) Everything turns on niggers, niggers, niggers! No wonder Yankees call this the Black Belt! (*He pours a large drink of whiskey*)

HIGGINS. (*Soothingly*) Well, let's change the subject. Hand me my glass, there, too.

NORWOOD. Pardon me, Fred. (*He puts ice in his friend's glass and passes him the bottle*)

HIGGINS. Tom, you get excited too easy for warm weather ... Don't ever show black folks they got you going, though. I think sometimes that's where you make your mistake. Keep calm, keep calm—and then you command. Best plantation manager I ever had never raised his voice to a nigger—and they were scared to death of him.

NORWOOD. Have a smoke. (*Pushes cigars toward* HIGGINS)

HIGGINS. You ought've married again, Tom—brought a white woman out here on this damn place o' yours. A woman could help you run things. Women have soft ways, but they can keep things humming. Nothing but blacks in the house—a man gets soft like niggers are inside. (*Puffing at cigar*) And living with a colored woman! Of course, I know we all have 'em—I didn't know you could make use of a white girl till I was past twenty. Thought too much o' white women for that—but I've given many a yellow gal a baby in my time. (*Long puff at cigar*) But for a man's own house you need a wife, not a black woman.

NORWOOD. Reckon you're right, Fred, but it's too late to marry again now. (*Shrugging his shoulders*) Let's get off of darkies and women for awhile. How's crops? (*Sitting down*) How's politics going?

HIGGINS. Well, I guess you know the Republicans is trying to stir up trouble for us in Washington. I wish the South had more men like Bilbo and Rankin there. But, say, by the way, Lawyer Hotchkiss wants to see us both about that budget money next week. He's got some real Canadian stuff at his office, in his filing case, too—brought back from his vacation last summer. Taste better'n this old mountain juice we get around here. Not meaning to insult your drinks, Tom, but just remarking. I serve the same as you myself, label and all.

NORWOOD. (*Laughing*) I'll have you know, sir, that this is prewar licker, sir!

HIGGINS. Hum-m-m! Well, it's got me feelin' better'n I did when I come in here—whatever it is. (*Puffs at his cigar*) Say, how's your cotton this year?

NORWOOD. Doin' right well, specially down in the south field. Why not drive out that road when you leave and take a look at it? I'll ride down with you. I want to see Talbot, anyhow.

HIGGINS. Well, let's be starting. I got to be back at the Junction by four o'clock. Promised to let that boy of mine have the car to drive over to Thomasville for a dance tonight.

NORWOOD. One more shot before we go. (*He pours out drinks*) The young ones must have their fling, I reckon. When you and I grew up down here it used to be a carriage and the best pair of black horses when you took the ladies out—now it's an automobile. That's a good lookin' new car of yours, too.

HIGGINS. Right nice.

NORWOOD. Been thinking about getting a new one myself, but money's been kinder tight this year, and conditions are none too good yet, either. Reckon that's why everybody's so restless. (*He walks toward stairs calling*) Cora! Oh, Cora! . . . If I didn't have a few thousand put away, I'd feel the pinch myself. (*As* CORA *appears on the stairs*) Bring me my glasses up there by the side of my bed … Better whistle for Mose, hadn't I, Higgins? He's probably 'round back with some of his women. (*Winking*) You know I got some nice black women in this yard.

HIGGINS. Oh, no, not Mose. I got my servants trained to stay in their places—right where I want 'em—while they're working for me. Just open the door and tell him to come in here and help me out. (NORWOOD *goes to the door and calls the* CHAUFFEUR. MOSE *enters and assists his master out to the car.* CORA *appears with the glasses, goes to the vestibule and gets the* COLONEL's *hat and cane which she hands him*)

NORWOOD. (*To* CORA) I want to see that boy o' yours soon as I get back. That won't be long, either. And tell him to put up that Ford of mine and don't touch it again.

CORA. Yes, sir, I'll have him waiting here. (*In a whisper*) It's hot weather, Colonel Tom. Too much of this licker makes your heart upset. It ain't good for you, you know. (NORWOOD *pays her no attention as he exits toward the car. The noise of the departing motor is heard.* CORA *begins to tidy up the room. She takes a glass from a side table. She picks up a doily that was beneath the glass and looks at it long and lovingly. Suddenly she goes to the door left and calls toward the kitchen)* William, you William! Com'ere, I want to show you something. Make haste, son. *(As* CORA *goes back toward the table, her eldest son,* WILLIAM *enters carrying a five-year-old boy)* Look here at this purty doily yo' sister made this summer while she been here. She done learned all about sewing and making purty things at school. Ain't it nice, son?

WILLIAM. Sho' is. Sallie takes after you, I reckon. She's a smart little crittur, ma. *(Sighs)* De Lawd knows, I was dumb at school. *(To his child)* Get down, Billy, you's too heavy. *(He puts the boy on the floor)* This here sewin's really fine.

BILLY. *(Running toward the big upholstered chair and jumping up and down on the spring seat)* Gityap! I's a mule driver. Haw! Gee!

CORA. You Billy, get out of that chair 'fore I skins you alive. Get on into de kitchen, sah.

BILLY. I'm playin' horsie, grandma. *(Jumps up in the chair)* Horsie! Horsie!

CORA. Get! That's de Colonel's favorite chair. If he knows any little darkie's been jumpin' on it, he raise sand. Get on, now.

BILLY. Ole Colonel's ma grandpa, ain't he? Ain' he ma white grandpa?

WILLIAM. *(Snatching the child out of the chair)* Boy, I'm gonna fan your hide if you don't hush!

CORA. Shs-ss-s! You Billy, hush yo' mouth! Chile, where you hear that? *(To her son)* Some o' you all been talking too much in front o' this chile. *(To the boy)* Honey, go on in de kitchen till yo' daddy come. Get a cookie from 'Vonia and set down on de back porch. *(Little* BILLY *exits left)*

WILLIAM. Ma, you know it 'twarn't me told him. Bert's the one been goin' all over de plantation since he come back from Atlanta remindin' folks right out we's Colonel Norwood's chilluns.

CORA. *(Catching her breath)* Huh!

WILLIAM. He comes down to my shack tellin' Billy and Marybell they got a white man for grandpa. He's gonna get my chilluns in trouble sho'—like he got himself in trouble when Colonel Tom whipped him.

CORA. Ten or 'leven years ago, warn't it?

WILLIAM. And Bert's *sho'* in trouble now. Can't go back to that college like he could-a if he'd-a had any sense. You can't fool with white folks—and de Colonel ain't never really liked Bert since that there first time he beat him, either.

CORA. No, he ain't. Leastwise, he ain't understood him. *(Musing sadly in a low voice)* Time Bert was 'bout seven, warn't it? Just a little bigger'n yo' Billy.

WILLIAM. Yes.

CORA. Went runnin' up to Colonel Tom out in de horse stables when de Colonel was showin' off his horses—I 'members so well—to fine white company from town. Lawd, that boy's always been foolish! He went runnin' up and grabbed a-holt de Colonel and yelled right in front o' de white folks' faces, "O, papa, Cora say de dinner's ready, papa!" Ain't never called him papa before, and I don't know where he got it from. And Colonel Tom knocked him right backwards under de horse's feet.

WILLIAM. And when de company were gone, he beat that boy unmerciful.

CORA. I thought sho' he were gonna kill ma chile that day. And he were mad at me, too, for months. Said I was teaching you chilluns who they pappy were. Up till then Bert had been his favorite little colored child round here.

WILLIAM. Sho' had.

CORA. But he never liked him no more. That's why he sent him off to school so soon to stay, winter and summer, all these years. I had to beg and plead to have him home this summer—but I's sorry now I ever got that boy back here again.

WILLIAM. He's sho' growed more like de Colonel all de time, ain't he? Bert thinks he's a real white man hisself now. Look at de first thing he did when he come home, he ain't seen de Colonel in six years—and Bert sticks out his hand fo' to shake hands with him!

CORA. Lawd! That chile!

WILLIAM. Just like white folks! And de Colonel turns his back and walks off. Can't blame him. He ain't used to such doings from colored folks. God knows what's got into Bert since he come back. He's acting like a fool—just like he was a boss man round here. Won't even say "Yes, sir" and "No, sir" no more to de white folks. Talbot asked him warn't he gonna work in de field this mornin'. Bert say "No!" and turn and walk away. White man so mad, I could see him nearly foam at de mouth. If he warn't yo' chile, ma, he'd been knocked in de head fo' now.

CORA. You's right.

WILLIAM. And you can't talk to him. I tried to tell him something the other day, but he just laughed at me, and said we's all just scared niggers on this plantation. Says he ain't no nigger, no how. He's a Norwood. He's half-white, and he's gonna act like it. (*In amazement at his brother's daring*) And this is Georgia, too!

CORA. I's scared to death for de boy, William. I don't know what to do. De Colonel says he won't send him off to school no mo'. Says he's mo' sassy and impudent now than any nigger he ever seed. Bert never has been like you was, and de girls, quiet and sensible like you knowed you had to be. (*She sits down*) De Colonel say he's gonna make Bert stay here now and work on this plantation like de rest of his niggers. He's gonna show him what color he is. Like that time when he beat him for callin' him "papa." He say he's gwine to teach him his place and make de boy know where he belongs. Seems like me or you can't show him. Colonel Tom has to take him in hand, or these white folks'll kill him around here and then—oh, My God!

WILLIAM. A nigger's just got to know his place in de South, that's all, ain't he, ma?

CORA. Yes, son. That's all, I reckon.

WILLIAM. And ma brother's one damn fool nigger. Don't seems like he knows nothin'. He's gonna ruin us all round here. Makin' it bad for everybody.

CORA. Oh, Lawd, have mercy! (*Beginning to cry*) I don't know what to do. De way he's acting up can't go on. Way he's acting to de Colonel can't last. Somethin's gonna happen to ma chile. I had a bad dream last night, too, and I looked out and seed de moon all red with blood. I seed a path o' living blood across this house, I tell you, in my sleep. Oh, Lawd, have mercy! (*Sobbing*) Oh, Lawd, help me in ma troubles. (*The noise of the returning Ford is heard outside.* CORA *looks up, rises, and goes to the window*) There's de chile now, William. Run out to de back door and tell him I wants to see him. Bring him in here where Sam and Livonia and de rest of 'em won't hear ever'thing we's sayin'. I got to talk to ma boy. He's ma baby boy, and he don't know de way.

(*Exit* WILLIAM *through the door left.* CORA *is wiping her eyes and pulling herself together when the front door is flung open with a bang and* ROBERT *enters*)

ROBERT. (*Running to his mother and hugging her teasingly*) Hello, ma! Your daughter got off, and I've come back to keep you company in the parlor! Bring out the cookies and lemonade. *Mister* Norwood's here!

CORA. (*Beginning to sob anew*) Take yo' hands off me, boy! Why don't you mind? Why don't you mind me?

ROBERT. (*Suddenly serious, backing away*) Why, mamma, what's the matter? Did I scare you? Your eyes are all wet! Has somebody been telling you 'bout this morning?

CORA. (*Not heeding his words*) Why don't you mind me, son? Ain't I told you and told you not to come in that front door, never? (*Suddenly angry*) Will somebody have to beat it into you? What's got wrong with you when you was away at that school? What am I gonna do?

ROBERT. (*Carelessly*) Oh, I knew that the Colonel wasn't here. I passed him and old man Higgins on the road down by the south patch. He wouldn't even look at me when I waved at him. (*Half playfully*) Anyhow, isn't this my old man's house? Ain't I his son and heir? (*Grandly, strutting around*) Am I not Mr. Norwood, Junior?

CORA. (*Utterly serious*) I believes you goin' crazy, Bert. I believes you wants to get us all killed or run away or something awful like that. I believes … (WILLIAM *enters left*)

WILLIAM. Where's Bert? He ain't come round back——(*Seeing his brother in the room*) How'd you get in here?

ROBERT. (*Grinning*) Houses have front doors.

WILLIAM. Oh, usin' de front door like de white folks, heh? You gwine do that once too much.

ROBERT. Yes, like de white folks. What's a front door for, you rabbit-hearted coon?

WILLIAM. Rabbit-hearted coon's better'n a dead coon any day.

ROBERT. I wouldn't say so. Besides you and me's only half-coons, anyhow, big boy. And I'm gonna act like my white half, not my black half. Get me, kid?

WILLIAM. Well, you ain't gonna act like it long here in de middle o' Georgy. And you ain't gonna act like it when de Colonel's around, either.

ROBERT. Oh, no? My stay down here'll be short and sweet, boy, short and sweet. The old man won't send me away to college no more—so you think I'm gonna stick around and work in the fields? Like fun? I might stay here awhile and teach some o' you darkies to think like men, maybe—till it gets too much for the old Colonel— but no more bowing down to white folks for me—not Robert Norwood.

CORA. Hush, son!

ROBERT. Certainly not right on my own old man's plantation—Georgia or no Georgia.

WILLIAM. (*Scornfully*) I hears you.

ROBERT. *You* can do it if you want to, but I'm ashamed of you. I've been away from here six years. (*Boasting*) I've learned something, seen people in Atlanta, and Richmond, and Washington where the football team went—real colored people who don't have to take off their hats to white folks or let 'em go to bed with their sisters—like that young Higgins boy, asking me what night Sallie was comin' to town. A damn cracker! (*To* CORA) 'Scuse me, ma. (*Continuing*) Back here in these woods maybe Sam and Livonia and you and mama and everybody's got their places fixed for 'em, but not me. (*Seriously*) Nobody's gonna fix a place for me. I'm old man Norwood's son. Nobody fixed a place for him. (*Playfully again*) Look at me. I'm a 'fay boy. (*Pretends to shake his hair back*) See these gray eyes? I got the right to everything everybody else has. (*Punching his brother in the belly*). Don't talk to me, old slavery-time Uncle Tom.

WILLIAM. (*Resentfully*) I ain't playin', boy. (*Pushes younger brother back with some force*) I ain't playin' a-tall.

CORA. All right, chilluns, stop. Stop! And William, you take Billy and go on home. 'Vonia's got to get supper and she don't like no young-uns under her feet in de kitchen. I wants to talk to Bert in here now 'fore Colonel Tom gets back. (*Exit* WILLIAM *left*. CORA *continues to* BERT) Sit down, child, right here a minute, and listen.

ROBERT. (*Sitting down*) All right, ma.

CORA. Hard as I's worked and begged and humbled maself to get de Colonel to keep you chilluns in school, you comes home wid yo' head full o' stubbornness and yo' mouth full o' sass for me an' de white folks an' everybody. You know can't no colored boy here talk like you's been doin' to no white folks, let alone to de Colonel and that old devil of a Talbot. They ain't gonna stand fo' yo' sass. Not only you, but I 'spects we's all gwine to pay fo' it, every colored soul on this place. I was scared to death today fo' yo' sister, Sallie, scared de Colonel warn't gwine to let her go back to school, neither, 'count o' yo' doins, but he did, thank Gawd—and then you come near makin' her miss de train. Did she have time to get her ticket and all?

ROBERT. Sure! Had to drive like sin to get there with her, though. I didn't mean to be late getting back here for her, ma, but I had a little run-in about them radio tubes in town.

CORA. (*Worried*) What's that?

ROBERT. The tubes was smashed when I got 'em, and I had already made out my money order, so the woman in the post office wouldn't give the three dollars back to me. All I did was explain to her that we could send the tubes back—but she got hot because there were two or three white folks waiting behind me to get stamps, I guess. So she yells at me to move on and not give her any of my "educated nigger talk." So I said, "I'm going to finish showing you these tubes before I move on"— and then she screamed and called the mail clerk working in the back, and told him to throw me out. (*Boasting*) He didn't do it by himself, though. Had to call all the white loafers out in the square to get me through that door.

CORA. (*Fearfully*) Lawd have mercy!

ROBERT. Guess if I hadn't-a had the Ford then, they'd've beat me half-to-death, but when I saw how many crackers there was, I jumped in the car and beat it on away.

CORA. Thank God for that!

ROBERT. Not even a football man (*Half-boasting*) like me could tackle the whole junction. 'Bout a dozen colored guys standing around, too, and not one of 'em would help me—the dumb jiggaboos! They been telling me ever since I been here, (*Imitating darky talk*) "You can't argue wid whut folks, man. You better stay out o' this Junction. You must ain't got no sense, nigger! You's a fool" ... Maybe I am a fool, ma—but I didn't want to come back here nohow.

CORA. I's sorry I sent for you.

ROBERT. Besides you, there ain't nobody in this country but a lot of evil white folks and cowardly niggers. (*Earnestly*) I'm no nigger, anyhow, am I, ma? I'm half-white. The Colonel's my father—the richest man in the county—and I'm not going to take a lot of stuff from nobody if I do have to stay here, not from the old man either. He thinks I ought to be out there in the sun working, with Talbot standing over me like I belonged in the chain gang. Well, he's got another thought coming! (*Stubbornly*) I'm a Norwood—not a field-hand nigger.

CORA. You means you ain't workin' no mo'?

ROBERT. (*Flaring*) No, I'm not going to work in the fields. What did he send me away to school for—just to come back here and be his servant, or pick his hills of cotton?

CORA. He sent you away to de school because *I* asked him and begged him, and got down on my knees to him, that's why. (*Quietly*) And now I just wants to make you see some sense, if you can. I knows, honey, you reads in de books and de papers, and you knows a lot more'n I do. But, chile, you's in Georgy—and I don't see how it is you don't know where you's at. This ain't up North—and even up yonder where we hears it's so fine, yo' sister has to pass for white to get along good.

ROBERT. (*Bitterly*) I know it.

CORA. She ain't workin' in no hotel kitchen like de Colonel thinks. She's in a office typewriting. And Sallie's studyin' de typewriter, too, at de school, but yo' pappy don't know it. I knows we ain't s'posed to study nothin' but cookin' and hard workin' here in Georgy. That's all I ever done, or knowed about. I been workin' on this very place all ma life—even 'fore I come to live in this Big House. When de Colonel's wife died, I come here, and borned you chilluns. And de Colonel's been real good to me in his way. Let you all sleep in this house with me when you was little, and sent you all off to school when you growed up. Ain't no white man in this county done that with his cullud chilluns before, far as I can know. But you—Robert, be awful, awful careful! When de Colonel comes back, in a few minutes, he wants to talk to you. Talk right to him, boy. Talk like you was colored, 'cause you ain't white.

ROBERT. (*Angrily*) And I'm not black, either. Look at me, mama. (*Rising and throwing up his arms*) Don't I look like my father? Ain't I as light as he is? Ain't my eyes gray like his eyes are? (*The noise of a car is heard outside*) Ain't this our house?

CORA. That's him now. (*Agitated*) Hurry, chile, and let's we get out of this room. Come on through yonder to the kitchen. (*She starts toward the door left*) And I'll tell him you're here.

ROBERT. I don't want to run into the kitchen. Isn't this our house? (*As* CORA *crosses hurriedly left,* ROBERT *goes toward the front door*) The Ford is parked out in front, anyway.

CORA. (*At the door left to the rear of the house*) Robert! Robert! (*As ROBERT nears the front door, COLONEL NORWOOD enters, almost runs into the boy, stops at the threshold and stares unbelievingly at his son. CORA backs up against the door left*)

NORWOOD. Get out of here! (*He points toward the door to rear of the house where CORA is standing*)

ROBERT. (*Half-smiling*) Didn't you want to talk to me?

NORWOOD. Get out of here!

ROBERT. Not that way. (*The COLONEL raises his cane to strike the boy. CORA screams. BERT draws himself up to his full height, taller than the old man and looking very much like him, pale and proud. The man and the boy face each other. NORWOOD does not strike*)

NORWOOD. (*In a hoarse whisper*) Get out of here. (*His hand is trembling as he points*)

CORA. Robert! Come on, son, come on! Oh, my God, come on. (*Opening the door left*)

ROBERT. Not that way, ma. (*ROBERT walks proudly out the front door. NORWOOD, in an impotent rage, crosses the room to a small cabinet right, opens it nervously with a key from his pocket, takes out a pistol, and starts toward the front door. CORA overtakes him, seizes his arm, stops him*)

CORA. He's our son, Tom. (*She sinks slowly to her knees, holding his body*) Remember, he's our son.

CURTAIN

ACT TWO

SCENE ONE

TIME: *After supper. Sunset.*

SETTING: *The same.*

ACTION: *As the curtain rises, the stage is empty. Through the windows the late afternoon sun makes two bright paths toward the footlights. SAM, carrying a tray bearing a whiskey bottle and a bowl of ice, enters left and crosses toward the library. He stoops at the door right, listens a moment, knocks, then opens the door and goes in. In a moment SAM returns. As he leaves the library, he is heard replying to a request of NORWOOD's.*

SAM. Yes, sah, Colonel! Sho' will, sah! Right away, sah! Yes, sah, I'll tell him. (*He closes the door and crosses the stage muttering to himself*) Six o'clock. Most nigh that now. Better tell Cora to get that boy right in here. Can't nobody else do nothin' with that fool Bert but Cora. (*He exits left. Can be heard calling*) Cora! You, Cora …

(*Again the stage is empty. Off stage, outside, the bark of a dog is heard, the sound of Negroes singing down the road, the cry of a child. The breeze moves the shadows of leaves and tree limbs across the sunlit paths from the windows. The door left opens and CORA enters, followed by ROBERT*)

CORA. (*Softly to* ROBERT *behind her in the dining room*) It's all right, son. He ain't
   come out yet, but it's nearly six, and that's when he said he wanted you, but I was
   afraid maybe you was gonna be late. I sent for you to come up here to de house and
   eat supper with me in de kitchen. Where'd you eat yo' vittuals at, chile?
ROBERT. Down at Willie's house, ma. After the old man tried to hit me you still want
   me to hang around and eat up here?
CORA. I wanted you to be here on time, honey, that's all. (*She is very nervous*) I kinder
   likes to have you eat with me sometimes, too, but you ain't et up here more'n once
   this summer. But this evenin' I just wanted you to be here when de Colonel sent
   word for you, 'cause we's done had enough trouble today.
ROBERT. He's not here on time, himself, is he?
CORA. He's in de library. Sam couldn't get him to eat no supper tonight, and I ain't
   seen him a-tall.
ROBERT. Maybe he wants to see me in the library, then.
CORA. You know he don't 'low no colored folks in there 'mongst his books and things
   'cept Sam. Some o' his white friends goes in there, but none o' us.
ROBERT. Maybe he wants to see *me* in there, though.
CORA. Can't you never talk sense, Robert? This ain't no time for foolin' and jokin.'
   Nearly thirty years in this house and I ain't never been in there myself, not once,
   'mongst de Colonel's papers. (*The clock strikes six*) Stand over yonder and wait till
   he comes out. I's gwine on upstairs now, so's he can talk to you. And don't aggravate him no mo' fo' God's sake. Agree to whatever he say. I's scared fo' you, chile, de
   way you been actin,' and de fool tricks you done today, and de trouble about de
   post office besides. Don't aggravate him. Fo' yo' sake, honey, 'cause I loves you—
   and fo' all de po' colored folks on this place what has such a hard time when his
   humors get on him—agree to whatever he say, will you, Bert?
ROBERT. All right, ma. (*Voice rising*) But he better not start to hit me again.
CORA. Shs-ss-s! He'll hear you. He's right in there.
ROBERT. (*Sullenly*) This was the day I ought to have started back to school—like my
   sister. I stayed my summer out here, didn't I? Why didn't he keep his promise to
   me? You said if I came home I could go back to college again.
CORA. Shs-ss-s! He'll be here now. Don't say nothin', chile. I's done all I could.
ROBERT. All right, ma.
CORA. (*Approaching the stairs*) I'll be in ma room, honey, where I can hear you when
   you goes out. I'll come down to de back door and see you 'fore you goes back to de
   shack. Don't aggravate him, chile.
(*She ascends the stairs. The boy sits down sullenly, left, and stares at the door opposite
from which his father must enter. The clock strikes the quarter after six. The shadows of
the window curtains have lengthened on the carpet. The sunshine has deepened to a
pale orange, and the light paths grow less distinct across the floor. The boy sits up
straight in his chair. He looks at the library door. It opens.* NORWOOD *enters. He is
bent and pale. He looks across the room and sees the boy. Suddenly he straightens up.
The old commanding look comes into his face. He strides directly across the room toward his son. The boy, half afraid, half defiant, yet sure of himself, rises. Now that*
ROBERT *is standing, the white man turns, goes back to a chair near the table, right,*

and seats himself. He takes out a cigar, cuts off the end and lights it, and in a voice of mixed condescension and contempt, he speaks to his son. ROBERT *remains standing near the chair)*

NORWOOD. I don't want to have to beat you another time as I did when you were a child. The next time I might not be able to control myself. I might kill you if I touched you again. I been runnin' this plantation for thirty-five years, and I never had to beat a Nigra as old as you are. I never had to beat one of Cora's children either—but you. The rest of 'em had sense 'nough to keep out of my sight, and to speak to me like they should ... I don't have any trouble with my colored folks. Never have trouble. They do what I say, or what Mr. Talbot says, and that's all there is to it. I give 'em a chance. If they turn in crops they get paid. If they're workin' for wages, they get paid. If they want to spend their money on licker, or buy an old car, or fix up their cabins, they can. Do what they choose long as they know their places and it don't hinder their work. And to Cora's young ones I give all the chances any colored folks ever had in these parts. More'n many a white child's had. I sent you all off to school. Let Bertha go on up North when she got grown and educated. Intend to let Sallie do the same. Gave your brother William that house he's living in when he got married, pay him for his work, help him out if he needs it. None of my darkies suffer. Sent you to college. Would have kept on, would have sent you back today, but I don't intend to pay for no darky, or white boy either if I had one, that acts the way you've been acting. And certainly for no black fool. Now I want to know what's wrong with you? I don't usually talk about what I'm going to do with anybody on this place. It's my habit to tell people *what to do*, not discuss it with 'em. But I want to know what's the matter with you—whether you're crazy or not. In that case, you'll have to be locked up. And if you aren't, you'll have to change your ways a damn sight or it won't be safe for you here, and you know it—venting your impudence on white women, parking the car in front of my door, driving like mad through the Junction, and going, everywhere, just as you please. Now, I'm going to let you talk to me, but I want you to talk right.

ROBERT. (*Still standing*) What do you mean, "talk right?"

NORWOOD. I mean talk like a nigger should to a white man.

ROBERT. Oh! But I'm not a nigger, Colonel Tom. I'm your son.

NORWOOD. (*Testily*) You're Cora's boy.

ROBERT. Women don't have children by themselves.

NORWOOD. Nigger women don't know the fathers. You're a bastard.

(ROBERT *clenches his fist.* NORWOOD *turns toward the drawer where the pistol is, takes it out, and lays it on the table. The wind blows the lace curtains at the windows, and sweeps the shadows of falling leaves across the paths of sunlight on the floor)*

ROBERT. I've heard that before. I've heard it from Negroes, and I've heard it from white folks. Now I hear it from you. (*Slowly*) You're talking about my mother.

NORWOOD. I'm talking about Cora, yes. Her children are bastards.

ROBERT. (*Quickly*) And you're their father. (*Angrily*) How come I look like you, if you're not my father?

NORWOOD. Don't shout at me, boy. I can hear you. (*Half-smiling*) How come your skin is yellow and your elbows rusty? How come they threw you out of the post office today for talking to a white woman? How come you're the crazy young buck you are?

ROBERT. They had no right to throw me out. I asked for my money back when I saw the broken tubes. Just as you had no right to raise that cane today when I was standing at the door of this house where *you* live, while *I* have to sleep in a shack down the road with the field hands. (*Slowly*) But my mother sleeps with you.

NORWOOD. You don't like it?

ROBERT. No, I don't like it.

NORWOOD. What can you do about it?

ROBERT. (*After a pause*) I'd like to kill all the white men in the world.

NORWOOD. (*Starting*) Niggers like you are hung to trees.

ROBERT. I'm not a nigger.

NORWOOD. You don't like your own race? (ROBERT *is silent*) Yet you don't like white folks either?

ROBERT. (*Defiantly*) You think I ought to?

NORWOOD. You evidently don't like me.

ROBERT. (*Boyishly*) I used to like you, when I first knew you were my father, when I was a little kid, before that time you beat me under the feet of your horses. (*Slowly*) I liked you until then.

NORWOOD. (*A little pleased*) So you did, heh? (*Fingering his pistol*) A pickaninny calling me "papa." I should've broken your young neck for that first time. I should've broken your head for you today, too—since I didn't then.

ROBERT. (*Laughing scornfully*) You should've broken my head?

NORWOOD. Should've gotten rid of you before this. But you was Cora's child. I tried to help you. (*Aggrieved*) I treated you decent, schooled you. Paid for it. But tonight you'll get the hell off this place and stay off. Get the hell out of this county. (*Suddenly furious*) Get out of this state. Don't let me lay eyes on you again. Get out of here now. Talbot and the storekeeper are coming up here this evening to talk cotton with me. I'll tell Talbot to *see* that you go. That's all. (NORWOOD *motions toward the door, left*) Tell Sam to come in here when you go out. Tell him to make a light here.

ROBERT. (*Impudently*) Ring for Sam—I'm not going through the kitchen. (*He starts toward the front door*) I'm not your servant. You're not going to tell me what to do. You're not going to have Talbot run me off the place like a field hand you don't want to use any more.

NORWOOD. (*Springing between his son and the front door, pistol in hand*) You black bastard! (ROBERT *goes toward him calmly, grasps his father's arm and twists it until the gun falls to the floor. The older man bends backward in startled fury and pain*) Don't you dare put your …

ROBERT. (*Laughing*) Why don't you shoot, papa? (*Louder*) Why don't you shoot?

NORWOOD. (*Gasping as he struggles, fighting back*) … black … hands … on … you …

ROBERT. (*Hysterically, as he takes his father by the throat*) Why don't you shoot, papa? (NORWOOD's *hands claw the air helplessly.* ROBERT *chokes the struggling white man until his body grows limp*) Why don't you shoot! (*Laughing*) Why don't you shoot? Huh? Why?

(CORA *appears at the top of the stairs, hearing the commotion. She screams*)

CORA. Oh, my God! (*She rushes down.* ROBERT *drops the body of his father at her feet in a path of flame from the setting sun.* CORA *starts and stares in horror*)

ROBERT. (*Wildly*) Why didn't he shoot, mama? He didn't want *me* to live. Why didn't he shoot? (*Laughing*) He was the boss. Telling me what to do. Why didn't he shoot, then? He was the white man.

CORA. (*Falling on the body*) Colonel Tom! Colonel Tom! Tom! Tom! (*Gazes across the corpse at her son*) He's yo' father, Bert.

ROBERT. He's dead. The white man's dead. My father's dead. (*Laughing*) I'm living.

CORA. Tom! Tom! Tom!

ROBERT. Niggers are living. He's dead. (*Picks up the pistol*) This is what he wanted to kill me with, but he's dead. I can use it now. Use it on all the white men in the world, because they'll be coming looking for me now. (*Stuffs the pistol into his shirt*) They'll want me now.

CORA. (*Rising and running toward her boy*) Quick, chile, out that way, (*Pointing toward the front door*) so they won't see you in de kitchen. Make for de swamp, honey. Cross de fields fo' de swamp. Go de crick way. In runnin' water, dogs can't smell no tracks. Hurry, chile!

ROBERT. Yes, mama. I can go out the front way now, easy. But if I see they gonna get me before I can reach the swamp, I'm coming back here, mama, and (*Proudly*) let them take me out of my father's house—if they can. (*Pats the gun under his shirt*) They're not going to string me up to some roadside tree for the crackers to laugh at.

CORA. (*Moaning aloud*) Oh, O-o-o! Hurry! Hurry, chile!

ROBERT. I'm going, ma. (*He opens the door. The sunset streams in like a river of blood*)

CORA. Run, chile!

ROBERT. Not out of my father's house. (*He exits slowly, tall and straight against the sun*)

CORA. Fo' God's sake, hurry, chile! (*Glancing down the road*) Lawd have mercy! There's Talbot and de storekeeper in de drive. They sees my boy! (*Moaning*) They sees ma boy. (*Relieved*) But thank God, they's passin' him! (CORA *backs up against the wall in the vestibule. She stands as if petrified as* TALBOT *and the* STOREKEEPER *enter*)

TALBOT. Hello, Cora. What's the matter with you? Where's that damn fool boy o' your'n goin', coming out the front door like he owned the house? What's the matter with you, woman? Can't you talk? Can't you talk? Where's Norwood? Let's have some light in this dark place. (*He reaches behind the door and turns on the lights.* CORA *remains backed up against the wall, looking out into the twilight, watching* ROBERT *as he goes across the field*) Good God, Jim! Look at this! (*The* TWO WHITE MEN *stop in horror before the sight of* NORWOOD's *body on the floor*)

STOREKEEPER. He's blue in the face. (*Bends over the body*) That nigger we saw walking out the door! (*Rising excitedly*) That nigger bastard of Cora's ... (*Stooping over the body again*) Why the Colonel's dead!

TALBOT. That nigger! (*Rushes toward the door*) He's running toward the swamp now ... We'll get him ... Telephone town—there, in the library. Telephone the sheriff. Get men, white men, after that nigger.

(STOREKEEPER *rushes into the library. He can be heard talking excitedly on the phone*)

STOREKEEPER. Sheriff! Sheriff! Is this the sheriff? I'm calling from Norwood's plantation. That nigger, Bert, has just killed Norwood—and run, headed for the swamp.
Notify the gas station at the crossroads! Tell the boys at the sawmill to head him off
at the creek. Warn everybody to be on the lookout. Call your deputies! Yes! Yes!
Spread a dragnet. Get out the dogs. Meanwhile we'll start after him. (*He slams the
phone down and comes back into the room*) Cora, where's Norwood's car? In the
barn? (CORA does *not answer*)

TALBOT. Talk, you black bitch!

(*She remains silent.* TALBOT *runs, yelling and talking, out into the yard, followed by the*
STOREKEEPER. *Sounds of excited shouting outside, and the roar of a motor rushing
down the drive. In the sky the twilight deepens into early night.* CORA *stands looking into
the darkness*)

CORA. My boy can't get to de swamp now. They's telephoned the white folks down
that way. So he'll come back home now. Maybe he'll turn into de crick and follow
de branch home directly. (*Protectively*) But they shan't get him. I'll make a place for
to hide him. I'll make a place upstairs down under de floor, under ma bed. In a
minute ma boy'll be runnin' from de white folks with their hounds and their ropes
and their guns and everything they uses to kill po' colored folks with. (*Distressed*)
Ma boy'll be out there runnin'. (*Turning to the body on the floor*) Colonel Tom, you
hear me? Our boy, out there runnin'. (*Fiercely*) You said he was ma boy—*ma* bastard boy. I heard you … but he's yours too … but yonder in de dark runnin'—runnin' from yo' people, from white people. (*Pleadingly*) Why don't you get up and
stop 'em? He's *your* boy. His eyes is gray—like your eyes. He's tall like you's tall.
He's proud like you's proud. And he's runnin'—runnin' from po' white trash what
ain't worth de little finger o' nobody what's got your blood in 'em, Tom. (*Demand-
ingly*) Why don't you get up from there and stop 'em, Colonel Tom? What's that
you say? He ain't your chile? He's ma bastard chile? My yellow bastard chile?
(*Proudly*) Yes, he's mine. But don't call him that. Don't you touch him. Don't you
put your white hands on him. You's beat him enough, and cussed him enough.
Don't you touch him now. He *is* ma boy, and no white folks gonna touch him now.
That's finished. I'm gonna make a place for him upstairs under ma bed. (*Backs
away from the body toward the stairs*) He's ma chile. Don't you come in ma bedroom while he's up there. Don't you come to my bed no mo'. I calls you to help me
now, and you just lays there. I calls you for to wake up, and you just lays there.
Whenever you called me, in de night, I woke up. When you called for me to love, I
always reached out ma arms fo' you. I borned you five chilluns and now one of 'em
is out yonder in de dark runnin' from yo' people. Our youngest boy out yonder in
de dark runnin'. (*Accusingly*) He's runnin' from you, too. You said he warn't
your'n—he's just Cora's po' little yellow bastard. But he *is* your'n, Colonel Tom.
(*Sadly*) And he's runnin' from you. You are out yonder in de dark, (*Points toward
the door*) runnin' our chile, with de hounds and de gun in yo' hand, and Talbot's
followin' 'hind you with a rope to hang Robert with. (*Confidently*) I been sleepin'
with you too long, Colonel Tom, not to know that this ain't you layin' down there
with yo' eyes shut on de floor. You can't fool me—you ain't never been so still like

this before—you's out yonder runnin' ma boy. (*Scornfully*) Colonel Thomas Norwood, runnin' ma boy through de fields in de dark, runnin' ma poor little helpless Bert through de fields in de dark to lynch him … Damn you, Colonel Norwood! (*Backing slowly up the stairs, staring at the rigid body below her*) Damn you, Thomas Norwood! God damn you!

CURTAIN

SCENE TWO

TIME: *One hour later. Night.*

SETTING: *The same.*

ACTION: *As the curtain rises, the* UNDERTAKER *is talking to* SAM *at the outer door. All through this act the approaching cries of the man hunt are heard.*

UNDERTAKER. Reckon there won't be no orders to bring his corpse back out here, Sam. None of us ain't seen Talbot or Mr. Higgins, but I'm sure they'll be having the funeral in town. The coroner told us to bring the body into the Junction. Ain't nothin' but niggers left out here now.

SAM. (*Very frightened*) Yes, sah! Yes, sah! You's right, sah! Nothin' but us niggers, sah!

UNDERTAKER. The Colonel didn't have no relatives far as you know, did he, Sam?

SAM. No, sah. Ain't had none. No, sah! You's right, sah!

UNDERTAKER. Well, you got everything o' his locked up around here, ain't you? Too bad there ain't no white folks about to look after the Colonel's stuff, but every white man that's able to walk's out with the posse. They'll have that young nigger swingin' before ten.

SAM. (*Trembling*) Yes, sah, yes, sah! I 'spects so. Yes, sah!

UNDERTAKER. Say, where's that woman the Colonel's been living with—where's that black housekeeper, Cora, that murderin' bastard's mother?

SAM. She here, sah! She's up in her room.

UNDERTAKER. (*Curiously*) I'd like to see how she looks. Get her down here. Say, how about a little drink before we start that ride back to town, for me and my partner out there with the body?

SAM. Cora got de keys to all de licker, sah!

UNDERTAKER. Well, get her down here then, double quick! (SAM *goes up the stairs. The* UNDERTAKER *leans in the front doorway talking to his partner outside in the wagon*) Bad business, a white man having saucy nigger children on his hands, and his black woman living in his own house.

VOICE OUTSIDE. Damn right, Charlie.

UNDERTAKER. Norwood didn't have a gang o' yellow gals, though, like Higgins and some o' these other big bugs. Just this one bitch far's I know, livin' with him damn near like a wife. Didn't even have much company out here. And they tell me ain't been a white woman stayed here overnight since his wife died when I was a baby.

(Sam's *shuffle is heard on the stairs*) Here comes a drink, I reckon, boy. You needn't get down off the ambulance. I'll have Sam bring it out there to you. (Sam *descends followed by* Cora *who comes down the stairs. She says nothing. The* Undertaker *looks up grinning at* Cora) Well, so you're the Cora that's got these educated nigger children? Hum-m! Well, I guess you'll see one of 'em swinging full of bullet holes when you wake up in the morning. They'll probably hang him to that tree down here by the Colonel's gate—'cause they tell me he strutted right out the front gate past that tree after the murder. Or maybe they'll burn him. How'd you like to see him swinging there roasted in the morning when you wake up, girlie?

Cora. (*Calmly*) Is that all you wanted to say to me?

Undertaker. Don't get smart! Maybe you think there's nobody to boss you now. We gonna have a little drink before we go. Get out a bottle of rye.

Cora. I takes ma orders from Colonel Norwood, sir.

Undertaker. Well, you'll take no more orders from him. He's dead out there in my wagon—so get along and get the bottle.

Cora. He's out yonder with de mob, not in your wagon.

Undertaker. I tell you he's in my wagon!

Cora. He's out there with de mob.

Undertaker. God damn! (*To his partner outside*) I believe this black woman's gone crazy in here. (*To* Cora) Get the keys out for that licker, and be quick about it! (Cora *does not move.* Sam *looks from one to the other, frightened*)

Voice Outside. Aw, to hell with the licker, Charlie. Come on, let's start back to town. We want to get in on some of that excitement, too. They should've found that nigger by now—and I want to see 'em drag him out here.

Undertaker. All right, Jim. (*To* Cora *and* Sam) Don't you all go to bed until you see that bonfire. You niggers are getting besides yourselves around Polk County. We'll burn a few more of you if you don't be careful. (*He exits, and the noise of the dead-wagon going down the road is heard*)

Sam. Oh, Lawd, hab mercy on me! I prays, Lawd hab mercy! O, ma Lawd, ma Lawd, ma Lawd! Cora, is you a fool? *Is you a fool?* Why didn't you give de mens de licker, riled as these white folks is? In ma old age is I gonna be burnt by de crackers? Lawd, is I sinned? Lawd, what has I done? (*Suddenly stops moaning and becomes schemingly calm*) I don't have to stay here tonight, does I? I done locked up de Colonel's library, and he can't be wantin' nothin'. No, ma Lawd, he won't want nothin' now. He's with Jesus—or with de devil, one. (*To* Cora) I's gwine on away from here. Sam's gwine in town to his chilluns' house, and I ain't gwine by no road either. I gwine through de holler where I don't have to pass no white folks.

Cora. Yes, Samuel, you go on. De Colonel can get his own drinks when he comes back tonight.

Sam. (*Bucking his eyes in astonishment at* Cora) Lawd God Jesus!

(*He bolts out of the room as fast as his old legs will carry him.* Cora *comes down stairs, looks for a long moment out into the darkness, then closes the front door and draws the blinds. She looks down at the spot where the* Colonel's *body lay*)

Cora. All de colored folks are runnin' from you tonight. Po' Colonel Tom, you too old now to be out with de mob. You got no business goin', but you had to go, I reckon. I 'members that time they hung Luke Jordon, you sent yo' dogs out to hunt him. The next day you killed all de dogs. You were kinder softhearted. Said you didn't like that kind of sport. Told me in bed one night you could hear them dogs howlin' in yo' sleep. But de time they burnt de courthouse when that po' little cullud boy was locked up in it cause they said he hugged a white girl, you was with 'em again. Said you had to go help 'em. Now you's out chasin' ma boy. (*As she stands at the window, she sees a passing figure*) There goes yo' other woman, Colonel Tom, Livonia is runnin' from you too, now. She would've wanted you last night. Been wantin' you again ever since she got old and fat and you stopped layin' with her and put her in the kitchen to cook. Don't think I don't know, Colonel Tom. Don't think I don't remember them nights when you used to sleep in that cabin down by de spring. I knew 'Vonia was there with you. I ain't no fool, Colonel Tom. But she ain't bore you no chilluns. I'm de one that bore 'em. (*Musing*) White mens, and colored womens, and little bastard chilluns—that's de old way of de South— but it's ending now. Three of your yellow brothers yo' father had by Aunt Sallie Deal—what had to come and do your laundry to make her livin'—you got colored relatives scattered all over this county. Them de ways o' de South—mixtries, mixtries. (WILLIAM *enters left, silently, as his mother talks. She is sitting in a chair now. Without looking up*) Is that you, William?

WILLIAM. Yes, ma, it's me.

CORA. Is you runnin' from him, too?

WILLIAM. (*Hesitatingly*) Well, ma, you see … don't you think kinder … well, I reckon I ought to take Libby and ma babies on down to de church house with Reverend Martin and them, or else get 'long to town if I can hitch up them mules. They's scared to be out here, my wife and her ma. All de folks done gone from de houses down yonder by de branch, and you can hear de hounds a bayin' off yonder by de swamp, and cars is tearin' up that road, and de white folks is yellin' and hollerin' and carryin' on somethin' terrible over toward de brook. I done told Robert 'bout his foolishness. They's gonna hang him sure. Don't you think you better be comin' with us, ma. That is, do you want to? 'Course we can go by ourselves, and maybe you wants to stay here and take care o' de big house. I don't want to leave you, ma, but I … I …

CORA. Yo' brother'll be back, son, then I won't be by myself.

WILLIAM. (*Bewildered by his mother's sureness*) I though Bert went … I thought he run … I thought …

CORA. No, honey. He went, but they ain't gonna get him out there. I sees him comin' back here now, to be with me. I's gwine to guard him 'till he can get away.

WILLIAM. Then de white folks'll come here, too.

CORA. Yes, de Colonel'll come back here sure. (*The deep baying of the hounds is heard at a distance through the night*) Colonel Tom will come after his son.

WILLIAM. My God, ma! Come with us to town.

CORA. Go on, William, go on! Don't wait for them to get back. You never was much like neither one o' them—neither de Colonel or Bert—you's mo' like de field hands. Too much o' ma blood in you, I guess. You never liked Bert much, neither, and you always was afraid of de Colonel. Go on, son, and hide yo' wife and her ma and your chilluns. Ain't nothin' gonna hurt you. You never did go against nobody. Neither did I, till tonight. Tried to live right and not hurt a soul, white or colored. (*Addressing space*) I tried to live right, Lord. (*Angrily*) Tried to live right, Lord. (*Throws out her arms resentfully as if to say, "and this is what you give me."*) What's de matter, Lawd, you ain't with me?

(*The hounds are heard howling again*)

WILLIAM. I'm gone, ma. (*He exits fearfully as his mother talks*)

CORA. (*Bending over the spot on the floor where the* COLONEL *has lain. She calls*) Colonel Tom! Colonel Tom! Colonel Tom! Look! Bertha and Sallie and William and Bert, all your chilluns, runnin' from you, and you layin' on de floor there, dead! (*Pointing*) Out yonder with the mob, dead. And when you come home, upstairs in my bed on top of my body, dead. (*Goes to the window, returns, sits down, and begins to speak as if remembering a far-off dream*) Colonel Thomas Norwood! I'm just poor Cora Lewis, Colonel Norwood. Little black Cora Lewis, Colonel Norwood. I'm just fifteen years old. Thirty years ago, you put your hands on me to feel my breasts, and you say, "You a pretty little piece of flesh, ain't you? Black and sweet, ain't you?" And I lift up ma face, and you pull me to you, and we laid down under the trees that night, and I wonder if your wife'll know when you go back up the road into the big house. And I wonder if my mama'll know it, when I go back to our cabin. Mama said she nursed you when you was a baby, just like she nursed me. And I loved you in the dark, down there under that tree by de gate, afraid of you and proud of you, feelin' your gray eyes lookin' at me in de dark. Then I cried and cried and told ma mother about it, but she didn't take it hard like I thought she'd take it. She said fine white mens like de young Colonel always took good care o' their colored womens. She said it was better than marryin' some black field hand and workin' all your life in de cotton and cane. Better even than havin' a job like ma had, takin' care o' de white chilluns. Takin' care o' you, Colonel Tom. (*As* CORA *speaks the sounds of the approaching mob gradually grow louder and louder. Auto horns, the howling of dogs, the far-off shouts of men, full of malignant force and power, increase in volume*) And I was happy because I liked you, 'cause you was tall and proud, 'cause you said I was sweet to you and called me purty. And when yo' wife died—de Mrs. Norwood (*Scornfully*) that never bore you any chilluns, the pale beautiful Mrs. Norwood that was like a slender pine tree in de winter frost … I knowed you wanted me. I was full with child by you then—William, it was—our first boy. And ma mammy said, go up there and keep de house for Colonel Tom, sweep de floors and make de beds, and by and by, you won't have to sweep de floors and make no beds. And what ma mammy said was right. It all come true. Sam and Rusus and 'Vonia and Lucy did de waitin' on you and me, and de washin' and de cleanin' and de cookin'. And all I did was a little sewin' now and then, and a little preservin' in de summer and a little makin' of pies and sweet cakes and things you like to eat on Christmas. And de years went by. And I was always ready for you when you come to me in de night. And we had them chilluns, your chilluns and mine, Tom Norwood, all of 'em! William, born dark like me, dumb like me, and then Baby John what died; then Bertha, white and smart like you; and then Bert with your eyes and your ways and your temper, and mighty nigh your color; then

Sallie, nearly white, too, and smart, and purty. But Bert was yo' chile! He was always yo' child … Good-looking, and kind, and headstrong, and strange, and stubborn, and proud like you, and de one I could love most 'cause he needed de most lovin'. And he wanted to call you "papa," and I tried to teach him no, but he did it anyhow and (*Sternly*) you beat him, Colonel Thomas Norwood. And he growed up with de beatin' in his heart, and your eyes in his head, and your ways, and your pride. And this summer he looked like you that time I first knowed you down by de road under them trees, young and fiery and proud. There was no touchin' Bert, just like there was no touchin' you. I could only love him, like I loved you. I could only love him. But I couldn't talk to him, because he hated you. He had your ways—and you beat him! After you beat that chile, then you died, Colonel Norwood. You died here in this house, and you been living dead a long time. You lived dead. (*Her voice rises above the nearing sounds of the mob*) And when I said this evenin', "Get up! Why don't you help me?" You'd done been dead a long time—a long time before you laid down on this floor, here, with the breath choked out o' you—and Bert standin' over you living, living, living. That's why you hated him. And you want to kill him. Always, you wanted to kill him. Out there with de hounds and de torches and de cars and de guns, you want to kill ma boy. But you won't kill him! He's comin' home first. He's comin' home to me. He's comin' home! (*Outside the noise is tremendous now, the lights of autos flash on the window curtains, there are shouts and cries.* CORA *sits, tense, in the middle of the room*) He's comin' home!

A MAN'S VOICE. (*Outside*) He's somewhere on this lot.

ANOTHER VOICE. Don't shoot, men. We want to get him alive.

VOICE. Close in on him. He must be in them bushes by the house.

FIRST VOICE. Porch! Porch! Porch! There he is yonder—running to the door!

(*Suddenly shots are heard. The door bursts open and* ROBERT *enters, firing back into the darkness. The shots are returned by the mob, breaking the windows. Flares, lights, voices, curses, screams*)

VOICES. Nigger! Nigger! Nigger! Get the nigger!

(CORA *rushes toward the door and bolts it after her son's entrance*)

CORA. (*Leaning against the door*) I was waiting for you, honey. Yo' hiding place is all
    ready, upstairs, under ma bed, under de floor. I sawed a place there fo' you. They
    can't find you there. Hurry—before yo' father comes.

ROBERT. (*Panting*) No time to hide, ma. They're at the door now. They'll be coming
    up the back way, too. (*Sounds of knocking and the breaking of glass*) They'll be coming in the windows. They'll be coming in everywhere. And only one bullet left, ma.
    It's for me.

CORA. Yes, it's fo' you, chile. Save it. Go upstairs in mama's room. Lay on ma bed and
    rest.

ROBERT. (*Going slowly toward the stairs with the pistol in his hand*) Goodnight, ma.
    I'm awful tired of running, ma. They been chasing me for hours.

CORA. Goodnight, son.

(CORA *follows him to the foot of the steps. The door begins to give at the forcing of the mob. As* ROBERT *disappears above, it bursts open. A great crowd of white men pour into the room with guns, ropes, clubs, flashlights, and knives.* CORA *turns on the stairs, facing them quietly.* TALBOT, *the leader of the mob, stops*)

TALBOT. Be careful, men. He's armed. (*To* CORA) Where is that yellow bastard of yours—upstairs?

CORA. Yes, he's going to sleep. Be quiet, you all. Wait. (*She bars the way with outspread arms*)

TALBOT. (*Harshly*) Wait, hell! Come on, boys, let's go! (*A single shot is heard upstairs*) What's that?

CORA. (*Calmly*) My boy … is gone … to sleep!

(TALBOT *and some of the men rush up the stairway,* CORA *makes a final gesture of love toward the room above. Yelling and shouting, through all the doors and windows, a great crowd pours into the room. The roar of the mob fills the house, the whole night, the whole world. Suddenly* TALBOT *returns at the top of the steps and a hush falls over the crowd*)

TALBOT. Too late, men. We're just a little too late.

(*A sigh of disappointment rises from the mob.* TALBOT *comes down the stairs, walks up to* CORA *and slaps her once across the face. She does not move. It is as though no human hand can touch her again*)

CURTAIN

45

"The Mulatto"
"Near-White"

Claude McKay

The Jamaican-born writer Claude McKay (1890–1948) is widely recognized as one of the har-bingers of the Harlem Renaissance. He published his first poetry collection, *Songs of Jamaica*, in 1912, and became the first black person to win a medal from the Jamaican Institute of Arts and Sciences. In that same year McKay moved to the United States, where he briefly studied agriculture at the Tuskegee Institute and at Kansas State University before moving to Harlem. From 1914 to 1919 McKay was active in radical political and literary circles while supporting himself with a series of menial jobs. In July 1919 he gained wide acclaim when his poem "If We Must Die" was published in the *Liberator*. McKay traveled across Europe from 1920 to 1934, writing for leftist publications in London, touring the Soviet Union as a communist sympa-thizer, and visiting Africa. While living in France McKay published his most famous novel, *Home to Harlem* (1928), a skilled, provocative portrayal of black life in Harlem; it was the first novel by an African American to become a best-seller. The poem and short story reprinted here, "The Mulatto" (1925) and "Near-White" (1932), are examples of McKay's treatment of in-terracial themes.

The Mulatto

Because I am the white man's son—his own,
Bearing his bastard birth-mark on my face,
I will dispute his title to his throne,
Forever fight him for my rightful place.
There is a searing hate within my soul,
A hate that only kin can feel for kin,
A hate that makes me vigorous and whole,
And spurs me on unceasingly to win.
Because I am my cruel father's child,
My love of justice stirs me up to hate,
A warring Ishmaelite, unreconciled,
When falls the hour I shall not hesitate,
Into my father's heart to plunge the knife
To gain the utmost freedom that is life.

Near-White

I

The Butterfly craze had hit the Belt hard. Some Yank or Yid had launched the song and it was riding the waves of public enthusiasm. It was hard to tell why, for the words were banal to the point of senselessness and the tune was not catchy. But by one of those gestures inexplicable to intelligence, New York had chosen to make it the song and dance of the season, all America had followed suit, and Harlem had gone quite crazy.

Every cabaret and every casino was playing it. There were Butterfly fancy-dress balls and Butterfly parties where each dark damsel tried to outshine each in butterfly radiance. A new tony tearoom was opened and called Butterfly.

Harlem journalism profited when the *Colored World* started a "Butterfly" column in which it maliciously chronicled the imaginary doings of the colored butterflies on Broadway.

The craze was a little like that that started boosting Madam Prosperina's hair-and-skin business and continued until it made her a rich woman and a leader of the social set of Harlem. Before that Madam Prosperina was an ignorant black woman whose name was popular only among the servant girls of the Belt who patronized her Kink-no-more process.

Then the light-brown Harlem actress, Chauncy Keating, returned from Europe after her great artistic and social success there. She brought back a ton of notices. Her charming figure and her style had received as much praise as her achievements.

Chauncy gave the *Colored World* an interview in which she said that for her social success she had to thank Madam Prosperina's hair and skin preparations which she had used all the time she was abroad. In the same number of the *Colored World* there was a full-page advertisement of all of Madam Prosperina's hair and skin preparations, in the center of which was an expensive photograph of Chauncy done by the famous photographer of the Avenue de l'Opéra.

That started the madness of the beauty craze in the Belt. Chauncy was one of Harlem's smart set, and the élite and the best folk followed her in making such a noise about Madam Prosperina's beauty stuff, that it finally outrivaled all others and became the most famous business of Harlem.

Angie woke up to the tune of Butterfly wailing out of a phonograph. Wrapping a peacock-blue kimono around her, she went to the window looking out on the large court, and fed her canary.

Butterfly, jazz-moaning Butterfly. So early in the day. That phonograph across the way was always grinding away. They ought to cut it out, she thought. She glanced upwards. The sky was gloriously blue, with long thin streaks of cloud-white. Curious and pretty, a crowd of white butterflies drifted timidly down as if they were frightened of the vast void. White moths in September floating in the exquisite dry air of New York.

Butterfly! Stupid irritating tune! Butterfly or butterflies did not interest her right then. She was interested only in herself; wrapped up in herself. She repeated her name to herself and liked the sound of it, Angie, Angie Dove. A much nicer thing than Butterfly, poor or rich.

It was rather late. She was hungry. The savory smell of food came from the kitchen. Yet there was another sort of hunger mingled with her desire for food. A hunger that had crept into her veins, gnawing and gnawing there for so many weeks and disturbing her normal taste for food.

She was the most attractive girl, she knew, at the casino last night. There had been sharp competition between the smartest fellows to dance with her. She had not missed a number. She overheard the girls talking about the loveliness of her frock. She knew how to dress with effect, knew what colors went with her rich creamy complexion. If only other colored girls like her had her taste in clothes! But there was her black chum, Hilda Forbes, who would wear old-rose because she wore it. And there was Emmie Ranger who over-powdered until her dark-brown skin was ashy gray.

She was different and she knew it. She had good taste, and an indulgent stepfather to humor it. She was pretty, she was twenty. She was Angie Dove. All Harlem admired her.

And up until last winter she had been contented with that. Proud of the fact of being *the* beauty of the Belt and that one day she would marry the chocolate hero, William Graves, the famous sprinter of the New England University, whose splendid photographs adorned the Negro journals and even the big white newspapers.

Harlem had provided for her a bigger way of living than might have come to her in the Virginia town where she was born. It was nine years since she had moved from there, when her mother was married to the black dentist from New York. Her mother belonged to one of those equivocal near-white families of Virginia, socially better than the common colored families but not considered as good as the commonest white. Her first marriage had been with an octoroon school-teacher.

Angie grew up in Negro Harlem with her black stepfather and octoroon mother, her colored playmates of all shades, living the intensive existence of cultivated colored people in a white city, conscious of her pretty curls, her nice creamy skin, and yet never conscious of how really white she was. She was never conscious that actually it was the fact of her stepfather and of her living in the Belt alone that made her Negro. She had often gone downtown in the fashionable white district to shop with her parents, but as a stranger into an unfriendly place. She had often gone with them to the Nigger Heaven of the theaters, without realizing that no tangible thing separated her from the respectable white audience down below, her features being whiter and more regular than many persons' who moved boldly and freely in the privileged circles of the Great Majority.

It was meeting Eugene Vincent that shocked her into a realization of her unused assets. Angie had met him at Emmie Ranger's party in Flatbush. He was dapper-dressed in a dark-green sports suit and yellow spats. He stood high and attractive on his feet. He played tantalizing blues on the piano, putting in them those strange slurring inimitable accents peculiar to Negro musicians. He was octoroon and blue-eyed, and insisted that his name should be pronounced in the French way.

Vincent's color and bonhomie were easy enough passports into the better circles of Harlem. Nobody seemed certain about where he came from or how he lived. Some

Harlemites gossiped about his being Louisianan and creole; and the young men who were jealous of him whispered nasty things. After the party he saw Angie home, and during the ensuing weeks he was a frequent caller at her stepfather's.

From his first sight of her, Vincent had felt that Angie was precisely the sort of girl that he would like to play round with in New York. He invited her out. The first night they went to the Palace Vaudeville. Vincent bought orchestra seats and Angie gasped and almost exclaimed at that. She sat down excited and flushed in the fourth row and anxiously glanced at him as he tipped the usher with elegant sangfroid. As if it were natural to him to play the part of the fine white man! Sitting so close to the stage she could see distinctly the paint on the actors' faces, and distinguished the girls' flesh from the pink tights.

And when the show was ended Vincent took her for ice-cream and cake to a fashionable Broadway tearoom.

"It's all right," he had said, noticing that she was hesitant about going in.

"How could you get away with it like that," she had asked as they rode in the Subway train to Harlem. She was excited, pleased, confused, astonished.

"*Get away* with it?" he had repeated. "Why, *get away* with nothing! You and I, why, we are as white as any of them. Am I not white like any white man you've seen? And you're prettier, Angie, than any of those six girls with wings in that Butterfly song act."

She pinched his arm and pouted prettily.

"But I couldn't do it with father and mother."

"No, for *he* is very real colored. He's black and belongs in Harlem."

"But mother," she objected, "she's just like me and we've been alone together and she only goes to places where colored people can go. Why?"

"Why?" said Vincent. "Because she's timid, because she's beaten, and she's accepted the worse without making any effort for better." He spoke harshly.

"Oh, don't talk like that about mother," she said, sharply.

"It's true, though," he answered. "But don't mind that, don't mind me now. I'll take you to lots better places. I'll show you things."

And she was pleased again as she tried to visualize more of that new world that she had just glimpsed.

The next morning Angie told her mother where Vincent had taken her, and met with another surprise when Mrs. Miller commented in a matter-of-fact way, "That must have been very nice." Was her mother aware, then, that light-skinned colored people out of Harlem often went downtown to act white rôles in the smart establishments? Perhaps!

And then her romance of a new world began. It was as if Vincent had pressed the button of a magic panel and enchanted vistas opened up to her view. They had orchestra seats for two of New York's thundering melodramas; dinner at a French-style-and-name restaurant with obsequious French waiters fiddling around them; tea at an English-style-and-name house, dancing at the Spanish cabaret El Toro. All the fashionable places with those exotic names that New York delights in were opened to her. Vincent went everywhere and spent money without thought. How did he make it and where had he learned all those gentlemanly gestures? Angie wondered. Sometimes they went from a dinner on Broadway to a house party in Harlem, and in those days they moved among colored Harlem with a halo around them. They went about in a high state of excitement, hugging the secret of their double social life. Vincent, apparently always dapper, quiet, and suave, inwardly felt and responded to Angie's frank, childlike pleasure in their adventures.

One evening he went to the limit in entertaining Angie. They dined at the German Garden on Broadway, went to the Follies afterwards, and later to El Toro's, where the orchestra was dressed up in picturesque Spanish costumes, and Angie had the satisfaction of hearing members of her own sex praise her figure and her frock.

From there they went to the Arabian Café, which was really an Armenian affair. They had a quiet corner to themselves, and there Vincent announced that he was going away the next day—that very day, in reality, for it was already four o'clock.

"Going away!" said Angie. "And you never told me!"

"I only knew yesterday and I didn't want to mention it this evening before we had our fun."

"Will you come back soon?"

"I don't know; hardly think so," he said, evasively.

"Will you send me a card?"

"Sure."

"I'll be awful lonely."

The magic portal swung suddenly back into place, shutting Angie out of her new world. Again she became entirely a girl of the Belt. Again she went to parties with Hilda Forbes and Emmie Ranger; to Nigger Heavens of the downtown movies with her parents. But she was no longer contented within the Belt. The city held a vast pleasure-world to which she felt she was entitled like any of the white thousands, entitled by right of feeling, of birth, and by right of color. Why should she be sacrificed to the prejudices of the city and settle down to the narrow life of Harlem, marry, perhaps, a William Graves, and be trapped forever, when by going with a Eugene Vincent she could escape to freedom? Why should she not seek escape?

She had not cared personally for Vincent. He had not shown himself much of a lover. They had both been more absorbed in the romance of their adventure. But now she was no more just a pretty, irresponsible girl of the Belt. In a few weeks she had developed into a very discontented woman.

II

Butterfly! That terrible song again! Harlem was crazy with a thousand phonographs and pianolas grinding out sentimental jazz. Butterfly! Would it never stop? Wish something would snap in the damned box. Butterfly! ... Oh, the Belt and its ragtime and jazz! The dark, close, suffocating Belt!

Angie closed the windows on the court to deaden the sound. She flopped in the easy-chair, covering her eyes, and saw a great ring floating before her packed with a mass of dark objects among which was herself and a few other yellow specks floating restless hither and thither. The Belt!

Oh, if she were a man like Vincent she would cut loose from it all and enter triumphantly the new world that she had tasted, the world of her dreams! But in a man-fashioned world a woman could not cut herself off from home and relations to make her way alone. Few men even had the courage to do it, and the strength to succeed. Her fascinating frock, a soft, glistening length of orange, lay on her white bed. It was a stunning thing. Draped in it she would be *the* attraction at the Colored Elks' ball at the Casino. That she knew, and once upon a time that feeling would have thrilled her—the startling effect she created among Harlem folk and voices whispering audibly, "That's Angelina Dove!"

Now she regarded her lovely frock indifferently. An Elks' ball, that was all. Merely another affair of the Belt. She was sick, pining, wilting, dying of that tight-roped-in life of the Belt.... She rose, finished her toilet and went into the sitting-room.

"Mother, if Hilda Forbes telephones, please tell her I'll meet her at the Casino."

"All right, Angie. But are you going somewhere else?"

"Somewhere else, mother?" she asked in a startled tone. "What could put that into your head? Where else could I go besides the Casino?"

"Why, Angie, I only meant if you were going first to some other friend's house."

"No, mother," she answered, absentmindedly, "I really don't know where I'm going."

Outside, instead of walking towards 135th Street, she crossed over to 142nd and took the Elevated train for downtown. Getting out at Fiftieth Street, she walked over into the flaring brilliance of Broadway. She mixed with the merry, pushing, pale, powder-faced Broadwayites. She liked them; she was one of them. She stopped before the great Vaudeville House. She bought a seat in the orchestra and entered.

"If only Vincent were here," she thought, "I would be very happy. What's the good of life in a city if one can't enjoy the best of it?"

During the intermission she missed a glove and became aware of a smartly-tuxedoed young man beside her. He found the glove under the seat.

"Thank you," she said. "Sorry for the trouble."

"None at all, none at all," he replied. "Rather poor pieces tonight, don't you think?"

"Yes," she agreed, without knowing whether it was a bad show or not.

"Yes, very poor," he continued. "I can't account for the big applause. New York applauds everything. That fat, hoarse-voiced woman got as much applause as Galli-Curci received at the Hippodrome last Sunday. Did you hear her?"

"No, I've never heard Galli-Curci."

He told her about the great singer and then changed the subject abruptly.

"If I had a partner, I would go dancing. This show gives me a headache. I wish I had some one to go along with me."

He looked questioningly at her in a challenging way.

"Do you dance?"

"Yes," she murmured.

"I wonder if you'd mind ... if I asked you? Would you? Suppose we go to the Pyramid together. There's a splendid dancing-floor there."

"I don't know that I should ..." She hesitated. She was quivering with sweet excitement.

"Oh, it's informal and all that, but if you don't mind, I'd love to take you."

She liked his profile, liked the tone of his voice, and felt quite confident.

"I'll go …" she said.

The Pyramid went straight to her head. That was the place to show her frock. Here was the desired place where vanity was charming and right among elegant women whose sole joy in living was to make a rich display of lovely dresses and jewels. A Spanish valse was in progress as they entered, and Angie's heart melted to the castanets, and the tipsy-colored skirts that swirled like waves away and away round the room, against the sober-black pantaloons.

They glided in among the crowd and Angie floated happily in the arms of her strange companion. She surrendered to the strong touch of him and felt as if those delicious delights of her escapades with Vincent, that had been fading out of her blood, leaving her pale and discontented, were being pumped from a great swell into her again. She felt a terribly delicious throbbing in her brain, and herself mounting upwards like a feather, like a lovely dream, on waves upon waves of exaltation. Her exhilaration transferred itself to her companion. He caught the precise spirit of his partner's ecstasy. He knew girls, knew that what he felt in her was not merely a momentary passion. This girl was ripe and weighted down under a deep emotion.

"You dance beautifully," he said, watching her twirl the straw through the thickly-iced crême-de-menthe.

"Do I?"

"Yes, you do. You love dancing, too; don't have enough of it, I guess."

"Yes, I …"

She checked herself and sucked at her straw without actually swallowing any of the liquor. She blushed, and the young man eyed her with the frankest admiration. She had suddenly thought of the Casino in Harlem, and dark waves following and breaking against dark waves of dancers, with ripples of mulattoes and, like foam in the sea, a few octoroons.

Oh, she had danced a great deal! But the life that fascinated her was the life that she had tasted outside of the Belt. She felt more at home in the world of Greater New York. Her features possessed no trace of the stigmata of Africa. By the very sensations that pulsed in her blood that greater world was hers. Even the accent of her dancing had made her partner aware.

"We must see one another again if you don't mind," he said. "This is the greatest pleasure of my life."

"Yes," she answered, in tragic tone.

"And will you tell me your name?"

"Angie—Angelina Dove."

"A heavenly one," he smiled.

She wanted to take the Subway train, but he insisted on calling a taxicab.

"You live far uptown? Then I'll see you home. I also live halfway up."

"No, no," she said in a frightened voice.

"You mustn't go with me. I live so far … way up Morningside.…"

"That's nothing, really. I know it's not regular and all that, but after such an evening together I feel as if I've known you a long time. Well, to the corner of your street then, if you object to me going any farther."

"Oh, I couldn't let you come!"

"If you're afraid that anybody should see us together …"

"Oh, please don't!" said Angie. "You make it worse. I … I … But you couldn't understand. I *must* go home now."

"And never see each other again!" exclaimed the young man. "Can't we be some sort of friends? Didn't you enjoy it this evening?"

"Yes, I did. Don't think for a moment I didn't. If only you could understand. But you mustn't ask questions. You couldn't come to my house. I'm so unhappy there. I just ran away alone tonight, when I should have been at a party, because I felt if I didn't … if I didn't, something in me would snap. There!"

She was actually weeping in the shadows of a line of taxicabs. She stopped, took a perfumed handkerchief from a mesh bag and dabbed her eyes. He could not speak. He could not think what right thing to say. But she felt his sympathy and said:

"I would like to go out with you again, but I can go only on certain conditions."

"Any conditions will be all right," he said, eagerly. "I think it is awful that your people should make your life so miserable."

"My parents are good enough to me," she answered, "but they don't understand me, either, so I'm wretched, wretched. Nobody understands, nobody can."

"I might if you'll let me," he assured her.

He was turning different ideas over in his mind and wondering which was nearer the right one. He was not long in concluding that it was a matter of love. Perhaps she was by way of getting tied up with somebody she didn't care for any more and did not know how to pull out of it. She was so sweet-natured.

Finally Angie consented that he should take her in a taxicab to the corner of 116th Street and Seventh Avenue. A rendezvous was arranged for the next Saturday evening at a tea place in the theatrical district. Before he left her he gave her his card. "If you should change your mind or anything," he said, "you might let me know."

As she walked away she read it: "John West—a nice name," she thought.

"John, John," she repeated.

III

Before her mother should find out from some one else and entertain any suspicion, Angie told her that she had gone to the vaudeville house instead of the Star Casino.

"I sat in the orchestra, mother. I get a feeling for that sort of thing since I used to go around with Eugene."

"Did he never write?"

"Not a word to a soul. He just vanished. Well, I had some fun with him. He showed me so many things."

"If you want to go out like that sometimes, why not go with Marie Taylor. I think she goes everywhere."

"Don't like her, mother. She's a gossip. About everybody, and herself, too. And malicious. She'd tell it around that we were playing white downtown, and have me written up in the Butterfly column of the *Colored World*."

She did not tell her mother, however, of her strange encounter. Her secret filled her with a perpetual sharp, sweet thrill. But she was also afraid. After the first evening with John West she lived through a week of dark, delicious purgatory until she saw him again. She had asked herself a thousand questions without finding answers. Had he thought her actions very strange? Was he perhaps suspicious? Did he believe that she lived on Morningside Heights? Oh, God! Had he watched her, perhaps—seen her double back to Lenox Avenue and take the Subway train for the Belt?

She could not shake off the feeling that she had done something dishonest and her conscience would not let her see herself in a simple light. She could not imagine that her new friend, also dreaming about her during the whole week, had only thought of her as an extraordinarily nice girl whose home life was unhappy and whom he felt a desire to help.

But the second meeting gave her confidence. West was extremely attentive to her smallest needs and very considerate of her feelings. She could go home as she preferred, by the Subway or by taxicab.

In three weeks they had seen each other many times. She visited his bachelor apartment in the East Fifties, and one night, instead of going any place, they spent an intimate evening together until the cabaret closing hours.

One evening at the Spanish Cabaret they ran into a business associate of West's. The young broker was accompanied by two actresses. The prettier one was especially charming to Angie. She remarked: "You should be on the stage, my dear. You've got just the right face and figure. Do come and see me sometime. Won't you bring her, Mr. West?"

But when they were alone in the taxicab, Angie declared she could not go.

"Oh, I just can't pay visits like that!" she said, almost crying, "I couldn't ask them to my home.... I'm so miserable."

"Well, we won't go, then, little timid," West consoled her. "They're nothing to you. Only a couple of cheap actresses."

"You won't mind, will you?" she asked, slipping her arm through his and pressing it.

"Mind? No! I only mind about you.... Poor girl! Who's the boob you don't want to marry?"

"Me? Marry? I couldn't marry William ..."

Abruptly she checked herself and trembled through a wild moment of fear. It was such a sudden, unexpected question. Oh, had he found anything out?

"So!" he cried, triumphantly. "I thought I was right. But this is a modern world, Angie. You don't have to marry anyone you don't like.... You don't *have* to do *anything* ... nothing. I wish you'd let me tell your people that."

She relaxed herself with a sigh and leaned confidently, expectantly against him. He drew his hand up to her breast, pressed her to him, and turned her face up for a long kiss.

But as she walked home alone and thought about the rencontre, she became panic-stricken.

Supposing I had met Hilda Forbes or Emmie Ranger just like that on Broadway.... Oh, I'd hold my head so haughty—haughty, they wouldn't dare speak to me. But if it were mother and Uncle Robert, what would I do? Oh, what? ... Not likely, not likely, though. And if I did meet mother and Uncle Robert they would surely understand right away and pass me without saying a word. Gee! I was frightened, though, tonight!

The next morning, late, after her stepfather had left for his office, she sat listlessly in the big leather chair by the radiator, wrapped in her peacock-blue kimono. Her mother was cutting to pattern a house dress spread out on the large sitting-room table.

"If you're a good girl, you'll stitch this off for me today," said Mrs. Miller.

Angie did not reply nor show any signs of unwillingness. She glanced at the Singer in the opposite corner burdened with a basket of spools of thread, balls of wool, scraps of cloth, bits of embroidery, and half-covered with an old torn silk skirt of her mother's.

"Mother! Do you think there are many colored people, the real light ones, going in among white folks and staying white?"

"I guess so. There's all sorts of talk about that, some true, some gossip only."

"But what happens, mother, with those who cross over? Do they forget altogether about color, marry among the whites and become happy, real happy, mother?"

"I don't know about happiness, Angie. But I guess if the light-colored ones cross over, it's better if they stay over. Some say that there's a big white lawyer right here in New York with a light-colored wife, and there's a big vaudeville actor that's colored, too. They claim that two Southern Congressmen have a streak, also, and that they spit more nigger-hating talk than anybody in Washington. I don't know. There's plenty of nigger gossip going round, although if you see smoke, there must be fire."

"But if some colored people are light enough to live like white, mother, why should there be such a fuss? ... Why should they live colored when they could be happier living white?"

"Angie, I don't know. You've got education to think for yourself. Did you read of a light-colored man somewhere out in Indiana? His wife divorced him after being married eleven years, *because she found out he had a little color in him?* And they'd had two children. And then it turned out she'd known all along he was colored! But she was tired of him; she just used that as a blind to get quit of him. It's the same way some colored folks hold down places as whites, and as soon as it's known they're colored, they lose out.... Let those who want to live white—do it if they can. But what's the use of selling your birth-mark for a mess of pottage that might turn bitter-gall in your mouth afterwards?"

Mrs. Miller ran her scissors through a long length of the cloth.

"But, mother, isn't it terrible that we—that light-colored people—should live away from the white, when we are just like them in everything? We, we can't hate them as if we were black, mother."

"O Lord, child! What're you saying now?"

Mrs. Miller dropped her needle and plumped into the leather-seated oak chair.

"Listen to me, Angie. Our people come from an old Virginian family that always held white folks at their distance. We come from a line of stewards. There's a story about our family, how our women resisted against the life that the slave-owners tried to force upon them. And how they also scorned the idea of marrying black plantation hands. It's a long story. How we tried to make the light-colored natives of Virginia stand together. How we fought to marry among ourselves ... and succeeded. How we reared our children. How the slave-owners pursued us. How the poor whites persecuted us. How the blacks reviled us. It's a long story.

"Your grandfather was a judge under Reconstruction. It was we light-colored ones who were first in politics. For we'd had more education, more opportunities, than the dark-skinned. And when the Crackers got control again, your grandfather was shot down dead in his tracks because he tried to organize a general provision store for colored people. That was *my* father, Angie, and your grandfather.

"And today, white folks treat us just the same as forty-five years gone when they shot down my father. You know what they say about us light-colored, what they *write* about us. That we're degenerate, that we're criminal—and their biggest bare-faced lie, that we can't propagate our own stock. They hate us even more than they do the blacks. For they're never sure about us, they can't place us.

"And you say we can't hate the whites, because we are not blacks! Why, we hate them more because we are so close to them and yet so far from them. We hate them more because we are *not* black."

"And do you love Uncle Robert, then, mother? I mean, love him as much as you did my father?"

Angie had always called her stepfather Uncle Robert.

"Indeed I do, child. Your Uncle Robert was my first deep-down love. When I married him and came up here, I kinder cut myself off from the rest of the family. It was the second time that one of us Claremonts married a black man. But black men are making good and doing big things for themselves now in America, and I'm proud of Robert.

"I don't know why you ask me such questions, Angie. Perhaps your head was sort of turned going around with that Vincent. But we belong to the colored race. Our feelings and our ties are colored. We will find more contentment being ourselves than in trying to climb in among the lily-whites who've done us all sorts of dirt."

Butterfly! Butterfly!

Over across the court the damned machine was wailing and whining:

"Butterfly! Butterfly!"

"Seems those folks over there don't have nothing to do but play the phonograph all day and all night," said Mrs. Miller.

Angie's whole body burned with feeling against her pitiful position. She could not share her mother's traditional hatred for white folks. She liked white people. She preferred their fashionable world to the Belt. She did not want to hate anybody. For she was in love! And her first real desire for a lover was fixed upon a white youth. Oh, what would she do about it?

She cleared the things off the sewing machine and placed the dress under the spindle. By-r-r-r-h! ... By-r-r-r-h! ... BY-r-r-r-H! ... The needle tore through the cloth with a roar. By-r-r-r-h! ... By-r-r-r-h! ... The noise of the Singer filled the flat like a little locomotive. By-r-r-r-h! ... Deafening! She endeavored to drown her mother's words that were echoing in her ears. For she was in love, sweet love! By-r-r-rh!

But despite the tumult, her mother's words would not be stifled and drowned and die out of her ears. They continued to boom there like a drum! We hate them more because we are *not* black.

"Oh, hatred is a terrible thing! Why should I, so young, so hopeful, why should I be sucked into this dark, narrow world of hate? Mother can't be right; mother must be wrong. I can't bear this secret any longer. I can't! Somebody must help me. I'll tell John. I will trust him. I must trust somebody. He's so keen, so fine. He understands everything. He'll understand that, too. Prejudice is not stronger than love. O God, help me!"

She got her elbow onto the machine and covered her face with her hands. And from across the court the brassy voice of the phonograph assaulted her ears with Butterfly, Butterfly.

IV

John West waited for Angie on the Subway platform. It was thirty minutes later than the appointed hour, but he remained expectant and unimpatient. He amused himself by beating his stick against his unbuttoned gray Raglan, like a person keeping time to pretty music.

At last she arrived, agitated, with apologies that made her prettier in his eyes. Her stepfather had bought tickets for a downtown theater. She had excused herself from going by telling her parents she had a special engagement with a girl friend. But while she was dressing, and just before her parents left, her friend called. And she had had to use all of her wits to escape.

She was so pretty there explaining everything that West felt an overpowering desire to gather her up in his arms for a long embrace. But he was deterred by the vast electric flare in the heart of the city, no little back alleys, no shadowy corners nor dim entrances but enormous eyes burning into you from all the vertical angles.

"Let's taxi around a little in Central Park," he suggested.

"I'd love it!"

"But perhaps you'd like an orange drink first!"

"No, I prefer the Park."

The taxicab sailed round and round the great Park, passing other vehicles that were, perhaps, engaged for the same purpose. It was a long while before they spoke....

Once she murmured close to his lips: "If I were a different person, quite different person from what I am, would you like me all the same, John?"

"I'd love you no matter what you were."

"But if I were very different from what you think?"

"What makes you ask such funny questions? I can only think you're a dear, funny, timid little girl."

"But if I were very bad, not frank, not nice."

"You'd always be the nicest, whitest little girl in the world for me."

"But if I was not as white as you think?"

"I'd love you if you were even Chinese!"

Chinese! That was the lowest thing he could imagine.

They swung out of the Park down to the Spanish Cabaret. There was nothing of much interest there. A group of girl entertainers sitting together stared insolently at them. Angie was uneasy, depressed.

"I don't seem to care for it tonight."

"No. Let's go," he assented. "They're just a set of cheap butterflies."

They dallied along the street until they reached a big dance-hall with the sign Moonland blazing in front. It reminded Angie of similar places in the Belt.

"Might go in here for a dance," she suggested.

"It's a cheap old barn," he said, "but we can try it for a change."

"It's an East Side crowd," he said, looking round the hall, "but they have a good dance-floor."

They fox-trotted round the hall. West felt that Angie was not in her usual form; her rhythm was halting, wilting.

"Awful bad music for such a good floor," he said.

Upon leaving the hall they caught sight of a dapper colored man and a white girl just being turned away from the ticket-office.

"Damned buck nigger," they heard the ticket-seller say as they passed by, "thought he could get in here because he's got a white street-walker with him."

"She looked a lot nicer than those things at the cabaret," Angie said to West.

"Yes, but how could she show her face in the street with a nigger?"

Angie felt as if a hot flat-iron had been clapped on her face.

"Perhaps she wasn't white ..."

"As white as you and me," interrupted West.

"But I knew a colored girl in high school who was whiter than I. You couldn't tell the difference. And she was so refined, John. I don't see that it matters if respectable colored people go to places where white people amuse themselves."

"For Christ's sake, Angie dear, don't talk as if you were the daughter of an Abolitionist."

"No, I'm not pleading any cause. I only feel as if it couldn't hurt us any ... if colored people were given a chance ... public rights like other people, I mean."

"Oh, well, little girlie. Don't take *me* for a Southerner. I think colored folks should have their chance, all right. There was a chap at my university that was awfully clever, valedictorian for his class. But what's the use of trying to force niggers on a public that won't stand for it?"

"Perhaps you're right, John. But if some colored folk are very white like ... very white, why should they suffer so when they are white like us?"

"Don't cry about it, Angie dear. You're so tender about everything. I guess you feel for the niggers more than they do for themselves. Life is an awful mix-up already. And it's better, I think, to leave it as it is. Suppose we were all mixed up in America.... And suppose, for instance, you should meet a fellow, and you both got to like each other, and then you found out afterwards that he had a nigger streak?"

For answer she said: "Supposing it was you, John, with a quadroon girl or octoroon, could you still love her?"

"Me! I'd sooner love a toad!"

Her heart stopped dead.

They ordered an orange drink in a little white shop, but she merely played with the straws. She had no desire to go to any place of amusement. He could not tease any spirit into her nor draw out any conversation. Presently she said she had a headache and would like to go home.

"It's the worry you had in getting away. An evening begun badly always ends up badly," he said, just to say something.

He went out to call a taxicab and brought back from the drug store some aspirins which she would not take.

"They're no good," she said. "I must sleep it off."

She lounged heavily back in the taxicab.

"Gee, Angie!" he cried. "You ought to let me see your people and brave this thing out. You've got to be game. And when it's over everything will be setting pretty."

"All right," she agreed. "I think it's about time I told them."

"Good, Angie! I knew you'd act like a brave girl at the right time."

He kissed her demonstratively, but she was unresponsive.

"John, if you don't mind, I'd like to drive straight home—alone."

"All right, dear, and when shall we meet next?"

"I'll telephone ... perhaps to show you to the folk at last." She smiled faintly.

He gave her a long grateful kiss. He was so happy that he did not feel how cold and nerveless her mouth was.

As she descended from the taxicab the phonograph mocked her with a wretched wail of sentimentality: Butterfly! Butterfly!

In her room the canary, glowing like a little ball of sulphur in the gloom of the window, seemed a spiteful little thing. She dropped the broken stick of herself in the easy-chair.

She thought of that delicious night, they two together, how his eyes had glowed over her flesh and his lips had praised, and she shuddered, remembering the sweet caress of his hand ... their bodies warm together ...

A toad! A toad! O god! a toad!

46

"The Pink Hat"

Caroline Bond Day

Caroline Bond Day (1889–1948) was a fiction writer, educator, and anthropologist whose academic work focused on interracial families. Day, who was born in Alabama, received an A.B. from Atlanta University in 1912 and continued her education as an English major at Radcliffe College in 1916, earning a second A.B. there in 1919. Day worked as a college teacher and dean in Texas and Atlanta and returned to Radcliffe as a graduate student of anthropology, gathering data on racially mixed families. She also began to publish essays and short stories. She earned her M.A. in 1930; the cumulative report of her work, *A Study of Some Negro-White Families in the United States*, appeared in 1932. The short story included here, "The Pink Hat," was published in *Opportunity* in 1926.

This hat has become to me a symbol. It represents the respective advantages and disadvantages of my life here. It is at once my magic-carpet, my enchanted cloak, my Aladdin's lamp. Yet it is a plain, rough, straw hat, "pour le sport," as was the recently famous green one.

Before its purchase, life was wont to become periodically flat for me. Teaching is an exhausting profession unless there are wells to draw from, and the soil of my world seems hard and dry. One needs adventure and touch with the main current of human life, and contact with many of one's kind to keep from "going stale on the job." I had not had these things and heretofore had passed back and forth from the town a more or less drab figure eliciting no attention.

Then suddenly one day with the self-confidence bred of a becoming hat, careful grooming, and satisfactory clothes I stepped on to a street car, and lo! the world was reversed. A portly gentleman of obvious rank arose and offered me a seat. Shortly afterwards as I alighted a comely young lad jumped to rescue my gloves. Walking on into the store where I always shopped, I was startled to hear the sales-girl sweetly drawl, "Miss or Mrs.?" as I gave the customary initials. I heard myself answering reassuringly "Mrs." Was this myself? I, who was frequently addressed as "Sarah." For you see this is south of the Mason and Dixon line, and I am a Negro woman of mixed blood unaccustomed to these respectable prefixes.

I had been mistaken for other than a Negro, yet I look like hundreds of other colored women—yellow-skinned and slightly heavy featured, with frizzy brown hair. My maternal grand-parents were Scotch-Irish and English quadroons; paternal grand-parents Cherokee Indian and full blooded Negro; but the ruddy pigment of the Scotch-Irish ancestry is my inheritance, and it is this which shows through my yellow skin, and in the reflection of my pink hat glows pink. Loosely speaking, I should be called a mulatto—anthropologically speaking, I am a dominant of the white type of the F^3 generation of secondary crossings. There is a tendency known to the initiated persons of mixed Negro blood in this climate to "breed white" as we say, propagandists to the contrary notwithstanding. In this sense the Proud Race is, as it were, really dominant. The cause? I'll save that for another time.

Coming back to the hat—when I realized what had made me the recipient of those unlooked for, yet common courtesies, I decided to experiment further.

So I wore it to town again one day when visiting an art store looking for prints for my school room. Here, where formerly I had met with indifference and poor service, I encountered a new girl today who was the essence of courtesy. She pulled out drawer after drawer of prints as we talked and compared from Giotto to Sargent. Yet she agreed that Giorgione had a sweet, worldly taste, that he was not sufficiently appreciated, that Titian did over-shadow him. We went back to Velasquez as the master technician and had about decided on "The Forge of Vulcan" as appropriate for my needs when suddenly she asked, "but where do you teach?" I answered, and she recognized the name of a Negro university. Well—I felt sorry for her. She had blundered. She had been chatting familiarly, almost intimately with a Negro woman. I spared her by leaving quickly, and murmured that I would send for the package.

My mood forced me to walk—and I walked on and on until I stood at the "curbmarket." I do love markets, and at this one they sell flowers as well as vegetables. A feeble old man came up beside me. I noticed that he was near-sighted. "Lady," he began, "would you tell me—is them dahlias or peernies up there?" Then, "market smells so good—don't it?"

I recognized a kindred spirit. He sniffed about among the flowers, and was about to say more—a nice old man—I should have liked to stop and talk with him after the leisurely southern fashion, but he was a white old man—and I moved on hastily.

I walked home the long way and in doing so passed the city library. I thought of my far away Boston—no Abbey nor Puvis de Chauvannes here, no marble stairs, no spirit of studiousness of which I might become a part. Then I saw a notice of a lecture by Drinkwater at the women's club—I was starved for something good—and starvation of body or soul sometimes breeds criminals.

So then I deliberately set out to deceive. Now, I decided, I would enjoy all that had previously been impossible. When necessary I would add a bit of rouge and the frizzy hair (thanks to the marcel) could be crimped into smoothness. I supposed also that a well-modulated voice and assurance of manner would be assets.

So thus disguised, for a brief space of time, I enjoyed everything from the attentions of an expert Chiropodist, to grand opera, avoiding only the restaurants—I could not have borne the questioning eyes of colored waiters.

I would press on my Aladdin's lamp and presto, I could be comforted with a hot drink at the same soda-fountain where ordinarily I should have been hissed at. I could pull my hat down a bit and buy a ticket to see my favorite movie star while the play was still new.

I could wrap my enchanted cloak about me and have the decent comfort of ladies' rest-rooms. I could have my shoes fitted in the best shops, and be shown the best values in all of the stores—not the common styles "which all the darkies buy, you know." At one of these times a policeman helped me across the street. A sales-girl in the most human way once said, "I wouldn't get that, Sweetie, you and me is the same style and I know." How warming to be like the rest of the world, albeit a slangy and gum-chewing world!

But it was best of all of an afternoon when it was impossible to correct any more papers or to look longer at my own Lares and Penates, to sit upon my magic-carpet and be transported into the midst of a local art exhibit, to enjoy the freshness of George Inness and the vague charm of Brangwyn, and to see white-folk enjoying Tanner—really nice, likable, folk too, when they don't know one. Again it was good to be transported into the midst of a great expectant throng, awaiting the pealing of the Christmas carols at the Municipal Pageant. One could not enjoy this without compunction, however, for there was not a dark face to be seen among all of those thousands of people, and my two hundred bright-eyed youngsters should have been there.

Finally—and the last time that I dared upon my carpet, was to answer the call of a Greek play to be given on the lawn of a State University. I drank it all in. Marvellous beauty! Perfection of speech and gesture on a velvet greensward, music, color, life!

Then a crash came. I suppose I was nervous—one does have "horrible imaginings and present fears" down here, sub-conscious pictures of hooded figures and burning crosses. Anyway in hurrying out to avoid the crowd, I fell and broke an anklebone.

Someone took me home. My doctor talked plaster-casts. "No," I said, "I'll try osteopathy," but there was no chance for magic now. I was home in bed with my family—a colored family—and in a colored section of the town. A friend interceded with the doctor whom I had named. "No," he said, "it is against the rules of the osteopathic association to serve Negroes."

I waited a day—perhaps my foot would be better—then they talked bone-surgery. I am afraid of doctors. Three operations have been enough for me. Then a friend said, "try Christian Science." Perhaps I had been taking matters too much in my own hands, I thought. Yes, that would be the thing. Would she find a practitioner for me?

Dear, loyal daughter of New England—as loyal to the Freedmen's children as she had been to them. She tried to spare me. "They will give you absent treatments and when you are better we will go down." I regret now having said, "Where, to the back door?" What was the need of wounding my friend?

Besides, I have recovered somehow—I am only a wee bit lame now. And mirabile dictu! My spirit has knit together as well as my bones. My hat has grown useless. I am so glad to be well again, and back at my desk. My brown boys and girls have become reservoirs of interest. One is attending Radcliffe this year. My neighborly friend needs me now to while away the hours for her. We've gone back to Chaucer and dug out forgotten romances to be read aloud. The little boy next door has a new family of Belgian hares with which we play wonderful games. And the man and I have ordered seed catalogues for spring.

Health, a job, young minds and souls to touch, a friend, some books, a child, a garden, Spring! Who'd want a hat?

47

"Ballad of Pearl May Lee"

Gwendolyn Brooks

The poet Gwendolyn Brooks (1917–2000) practiced a lifelong creative and social commitment to the Afro-American community. Brooks, who was born in Kansas and raised in Chicago, began reading and writing poetry at an early age; she published her first poem, "Eventide," in *American Childhood Magazine* in 1930. After her graduation from Wilson Junior College in 1936, she became a regular poetry contributor to the *Chicago Defender*. Brooks achieved national recognition as a poet in 1943, when she won the Midwestern Writers' Conference Poetry Award. Her first two poetry collections, *A Street in Bronzeville* (1945) and *Annie Allen* (1949), combine racial concern with an awareness of gender inequality and examine the intersections between the two. Brooks experimented in a variety of poetic forms, and she also published prose fiction, most notably *Maud Martha* (1953). In 1950 Brooks became the first Afro-American to win a Pulitzer Prize. She was also the first black woman to be elected to the National Institute of Arts and Letters and to be appointed Illinois poet laureate. In 1967 Brooks committed herself to the Black Arts movement, spotlighting racial oppression in her poetry and shifting from the white mainstream press to publish her own works. She formed Brooks Press (later the David Company) in 1980. From 1993 until her death, she was Distinguished Professor of English at Chicago State University. The poem reprinted here, "Ballad of Pearl May Lee," is from *A Street in Bronzeville*.

Then off they took you, off to the jail,
A hundred hooting after.
And you should have heard me at my house.
I cut my lungs with my laughter,
    Laughter,
    Laughter.
I cut my lungs with my laughter.

They dragged you into a dusty cell.
And a rat was in the corner.
And what was I doing? Laughing still.
Though never was a poor gal lorner,
    Lorner,

Lorner.
Though never was a poor gal lorner.

The sheriff, he peeped in through the bars,
And (the red old thing) he told you,
"You son of a bitch, you're going to hell!"
'Cause you wanted white arms to enfold you,
    Enfold you,
    Enfold you.
'Cause you wanted white arms to enfold you.

But you paid for your white arms, Sammy boy,
And you didn't pay with money.
You paid with your hide and my heart, Sammy boy,
For your taste of pink and white honey,
    Honey,
    Honey.
For your taste of pink and white honey.

Oh, dig me out of my don't-despair.
Pull me out of my poor-me.
Get me a garment of red to wear.
You had it coming surely,
    Surely,
    Surely,
You had it coming surely.

At school, your girls were the bright little girls.
You couldn't abide dark meat.
Yellow was for to look at,
Black for the famished to eat.
Yellow was for to look at,
Black for the famished to eat.

You grew up with bright skins on the brain,
And me in your black folks bed.
Often and often you cut me cold,
And often I wished you dead.
Often and often you cut me cold.
Often I wished you dead.

Then a white girl passed you by one day,
And, the vixen, she gave you the wink.
And your stomach got sick and your legs liquefied.
And you thought till you couldn't think.

You thought,
    You thought,
You thought till you couldn't think.

I fancy you out on the fringe of town,
The moon an owl's eye minding;
The sweet and thick of the cricket-belled dark,
The fire within you winding ....
    Winding,
    Winding ....
The fire within you winding.

Say, she was white like milk, though, wasn't she?
And her breasts were cups of cream.
In the back of her Buick you drank your fill.
Then she roused you out of your dream.
In the back of her Buick you drank your fill.
Then she roused you out of your dream.

"You raped me, nigger," she softly said.
(The shame was threading through.)
"You raped me, nigger," and what the hell
Do you think I'm going to do?
    What the hell,
    What the hell
Do you think I'm going to do?

"I'll tell every white man in this town.
I'll tell them all of my sorrow.
You got my body tonight, nigger boy.
I'll get your body tomorrow.
    Tomorrow.
    Tomorrow.
I'll get your body tomorrow."

And my glory but Sammy she did! She did!
And they stole you out of the jail.
They wrapped you around a cottonwood tree.
And they laughed when they heard you wail.
    Laughed,
    Laughed.
They laughed when they heard you wail.

And I was laughing, down at my house.
Laughing fit to kill.

You got what you wanted for dinner,
But brother you paid the bill.
    Brother,
    Brother,
Brother you paid the bill.

You paid for your dinner, Sammy boy,
And you didn't pay with money.
You paid with your hide and my heart, Sammy boy,
For your taste of pink and white honey,
    Honey,
    Honey.
For your taste of pink and white honey.

Oh, dig me out of my don't-despair.
Oh, pull me out of my poor-me.
Oh, get me a garment of red to wear.
You had it coming surely.
    Surely.
    Surely.
You had it coming surely.

From the 1960s to the Present

The years since the 1960s have brought a renewed interest in the representation of interracial relations and their historical prohibition. The writers of the present actively engage with many facets of the earlier literature, from Adrienne Kennedy's experimental creation of a multiply divided dramatic character to Charles Johnson's ironic use of a historicizing first-person singular, from Rita Dove's modern Oedipus drama and Francesca J. Petrosino's ritual play to Itabari Njeri's playful engagement with the symbolic significance of the most iconic American tap dancer. One senses in the most recent works an ironic employment of what were once racializing clichés or hopeful sentimental inventions in a new spirit made possible by the full arrival of an interracial consciousness that occasionally bridges (yet is also careful not to forget the historical depth of) the rift between black and white in Western culture.

48

The Owl Answers

Adrienne Kennedy

The playwright Adrienne Kennedy (b. 1931) has received numerous awards, including fellowships from the Guggenheim Foundation and the National Endowment for the Arts. Kennedy was born in Pittsburgh and grew up in Cleveland; she received a B.A. from Ohio State University and moved to New York to study playwriting. Her first published work, a short story entitled "Because of the King of France," appeared in *Black Orpheus* in 1963. Her major work in drama followed, informed by forms ranging from Greek tragedy to the theatre of the absurd. The experimental one-act play *Funnyhouse of a Negro* (1964), coproduced by Edward Albee, won Kennedy her first Obie award. It presents a central self's suicidal refusal to accept part of a divided heritage—or to recognize herself in that part. In *A Rat's Mass* (1966), the siblings who are the main characters are surrealistically represented as half animal and half human. In *The Owl Answers* (1963), which is reprinted here, Clara Passmore's changing identities are examined, as she is white man's "blood" daughter, black cook's daughter, black reverend's foster daughter, Virgin Mary, and owl, and the set is a collage of Old and New World places, all of which strangely coexist. The play is representative of Kennedy's complex style. Among her other plays are *A Lesson in Dead Language* (1966), *An Evening with Dead Essex* (1972), *A Movie Star Has to Star in Black and White* (1976), and a drama cycle, *The Alexander Plays* (1992)—including *She Talks to Beethoven*, *The Ohio State Murders*, *The Film Club*, and *The Dramatic Circle*. Kennedy's *Electra and Orestes* (1980) is an adaptation of Euripides. She also published the autobiography *People Who Led to My Plays* (1987) and drew on it for her play *June and Jean in Concert* (1995).

Characters

SHE who is CLARA PASSMORE who is the VIRGIN MARY who is the BASTARD who is the OWL.

BASTARD'S BLACK MOTHER who is the REVEREND'S WIFE who is ANNE BOLEYN.

GODDAM FATHER who is the RICHEST WHITE MAN IN THE TOWN who is the DEAD WHITE FATHER who is REVEREND PASSMORE.

THE WHITE BIRD who is REVEREND PASSMORE'S CANARY who is GOD'S DOVE.

THE NEGRO MAN.

SHAKESPEARE, CHAUCER, WILLIAM THE CONQUEROR.

The characters change slowly back and forth into and out of themselves, leaving some garment from their previous selves upon them always to remind us of the nature of

She who is Clara Passmore who is the Virgin Mary who is the Bastard who is the Owl's world.

SCENE: *The scene is a New York subway is the Tower of London is a Harlem hotel room is St. Peter's. The scene is shaped like a subway car. The sounds are subway sounds and the main props of a subway are visible—poles. Two seats on the scene are like seats on the subway, the seat in which* SHE WHO IS *sits and* NEGRO MAN's *seat.*

Seated is a plain, pallid NEGRO WOMAN, *wearing a cotton summer dress that is too long, a pair of white wedged sandals. She sits staring into space. She is* CLARA PASSMORE *who is the* VIRGIN MARY *who is the* BASTARD *who is the* OWL. SHE WHO IS *speaks in a soft voice as a Negro schoolteacher from Savannah would.* SHE WHO IS *carries white handkerchiefs,* SHE WHO IS *carries notebooks that throughout the play like the handkerchiefs fall. She will pick them up, glance frenziedly at a page from a notebook, be distracted, place the notebooks in a disorderly pile, drop them again, etc. The scene should lurch, lights flash, gates slam. When* THEY *come in and exit they move in the manner of people on a train, too there is the noise of the train, the sound of moving steel on the track. The* WHITE BIRD's *wings should flutter loudly. The gates, the High Altar, the ceiling and the Dome are like St. Peter's, the walls are like the Tower of London.*

The music which SHE WHO IS *hears at the most violent times of her experience should be Haydn's "Concerto for Horn in D" (Third Movement).*

Objects on the stage (beards, wigs, faces) should be used in the manner that people use everyday objects such as spoons or newspapers. The Tower Gate should be black, yet slam like a subway door. The GATES SLAM. Four people enter from different directions. They are SHAKESPEARE, WILLIAM THE CONQUEROR, CHAUCER *and* ANNE BOLEYN. *They are dressed in costumes of Shakespeare, William the Conqueror, Chaucer and Anne Boleyn but too they are strangers entering a subway on a summer night, too they are the guards in the Tower of London. Their lines throughout the play are not spoken specifically by one person but by all or part of them.*

THEY. Bastard. (*They start at a distance, eventually crowding her. Their lines are spoken coldly.* SHE WHO IS *is only a prisoner to them.*)
You are not his ancestor.
Keep her locked there, guard.
Bastard.
SHE. You must let me go down to the chapel to see him. He is my father.
THEY. Your father? (*Jeering.*)
SHE. He is my father.
THEY. Keep her locked there, guard.
(SHAKESPEARE *crosses to gate and raises hands. There is a SLAM as if great door is being closed.*)
SHE. We came this morning. We were visiting the place of our ancestors, my father and I. We had a lovely morning, we rose in darkness, took a taxi past Hyde Park

through the Marble Arch to Buckingham Palace, we had our morning tea at Lyons then came out to the Tower. We were wandering about the gardens, my father leaning on my arm, speaking of you, William the Conqueror. My father loved you, William....

THEY. *(Interrupting.)* If you are his ancestor why are you a Negro?

Yes, why is it you are a Negro if you are his ancestor?

Keep her locked there.

SHE. You must let me go down to the Chapel to see him.

(SUBWAY STOPS. Doors open. CHAUCER exits. ANNE BOLEYN and WILLIAM THE CONQUEROR remain staring at HER. CHAUCER and SHAKESPEARE return carrying a stiff dead man in a black suit. The most noticeable thing about him is his hair, long, silky, white hair that hangs as they bring him through the gate and place him at her feet.)

THEY. Here is your father.

(They then all exit through various gate entrances. SHE picks up the dead man, drags him to a dark, carved high-backed chair on the Right. At the same time a dark NEGRO MAN, with a dark suit and black glasses on, enters from the Right gate and sits on the other subway seat. Flashing, movement, slamming the gate. The scene revolves one and one-quarter turns as next action takes place. The NEGRO MAN sits up very straight and proceeds to watch SHE WHO IS. Until he speaks to her he watches her constantly with a wild, cold stare. The DEAD FATHER appears dead. He is dead. Yet as SHE watches, he moves and comes to life. The DEAD FATHER removes his hair, takes off his white face, from the chair he takes a white church robe and puts it on. Beneath his white hair is dark Negro hair. He is now REVEREND PASSMORE. After he dresses he looks about as if something is missing. SUBWAY STOPS, doors open. FATHER exits and returns with a gold bird cage that hangs near the chair and a white battered Bible. Very matter-of-factly he sits down in the chair, stares for a moment at the cage, then opens the Bible, starting to read. SHE watches, highly distracted, until he falls asleep. Scene revolves one turn as ANNE BOLEYN throws red rice at SHE WHO IS and the DEAD FATHER who is now REVEREND PASSMORE. They see her. SHE exits and returns with a great black gate and places the gate where the pole is. SHE WHO IS runs to ANNE BOLEYN.)

SHE. Anne, Anne Boleyn. *(Throws rice upon SHE WHO IS CLARA PASSMORE who is the VIRGIN MARY who is the BASTARD who is the OWL.)* Anne, you know so much of love, won't you help me? They took my father away and will not let me see him. They locked me in this tower and I can see them taking his body across to the Chapel to be buried and see his white hair hanging down. Let me into the Chapel. He is my blood father. I am almost white, am I not? Let me into St. Paul's Chapel. Let me please go down to St. Paul's Chapel. I am his daughter. *(ANNE appears to listen quite attentively but her reply is to turn into the BASTARD's BLACK MOTHER. She takes off part of her own long dress and puts on a rose-colored, cheap lace dress. While she does this there is a terrific SCREECH. SHE WHO IS's reaction is to run back to her subway seat. She drops her notebooks. The BASTARD's BLACK MOTHER opens her arms to SHE WHO IS. SHE returns to the gate.)* Anne. *(As if trying to bring back ANNE BOLEYN.)*

BBM (BASTARD's BLACK MOTHER). *(Laughs and throws a white bridal bouquet at her.)* Clara, I am not Anne. I am the Bastard's Black Mother, who cooked for somebody. (*Still holding out her arms, she kneels by the gate, her kinky hair awry. Eyes closed, she stares upward, praying. Suddenly she stops praying and pulls at* SHE WHO IS *through the gate.*)

(*The* WHITE BIRD, *with very loud fluttering wings, flies down from St. Peter's Dome and goes into the cage.* REVEREND PASSMORE *gets up and closes the cage door.*)

SHE. Anne, it is I.

BBM. Clara, you were conceived by your Goddam Father who was The Richest White Man in the Town and somebody that cooked for him. That's why you're an owl. (*Laughs.*) That's why when I see you, Mary, I cry. I cry when I see Marys, cry for their deaths.

(WHITE BIRD *flies.* REVEREND *reads. The* BASTARD'S BLACK MOTHER *stands at the gate, watches, then takes off rose lace dress and black face [beneath her black face is a more pallid Negro face], pulls down her hair, longer dark hair, and puts on a white dress. From a fold in the dress she takes out a picture of Christ, then kneels and stares upward. She is the* REVEREND'S WIFE. *While she does this the scene revolves one turn.*)

REVEREND'S WIFE. (*Kneeling.* REVEREND *stands and watches her.* REVEREND'S WIFE *takes a vial from her gown and holds it up.*) These are the fruits of my maidenhead, owl blood Clara who is the Bastard Clara Passmore to whom we gave our name, see the Owl blood, that is why I cry when I see Marys, cry for their deaths, Owl Mary Passmore.

(SHE *gets up, exits from a side gate. SUBWAY STOPS, gates open, they come in, gates close. SUBWAY STARTS.* SHE WHO IS *goes to the* REVEREND *as if to implore him. He then changes into the* DEAD FATHER, *resuming his dirty white hair.* THEY *stand about.*)

SHE. Dear Father, My Goddam Father who was the Richest White Man in the Town, who is Dead Father—you know that England is the home of dear Chaucer, Dickens and dearest Shakespeare. Winters we spent here at the Tower, our chambers were in the Queen's House, summers we spent at Stratford with dearest Shakespeare. It was all so lovely. I spoke to Anne Boleyn, Dead Father. She knows so much of love and suffering and I believe she is going to try to help me. (*Takes a sheaf of papers from her notebooks; they fall to the floor.*) Communications, all communications to get you the proper burial, the one you deserve in St. Paul's Chapel, they are letting you rot, my Goddam Father who was the Richest White Man in the Town—they are letting you rot in that town in Georgia. I haven't been able to see the king. I'll speak again to Anne Boleyn. She knows so much of love. (*Shows the papers to the* DEAD FATHER *who sits with his hair hanging down, dead, at which point scene revolves clock-wise one-half turn. There are SCREECHES, and bird flaps wings. The* REVEREND'S WIFE *enters and prays at gate.*)

DEAD FATHER. If you are my ancestor why are you a Negro, Bastard? What is a Negro doing at the Tower of London, staying at the Queen's House? Clara, I am your Goddam Father who was the Richest White Man in the Town and you are a schoolteacher in Savannah who spends her summers in Teachers College. You are not my ancestor. You are my bastard. Keep her locked there, William.

SHE. (*They stare at her like passengers on a subway, standing, holding the hand straps.*) We were wandering about the garden, you leaning on my arm, speaking of William the Conqueror. We sat on the stone bench to rest, when we stood up you stumbled and fell onto the walk—dead. Dead. I called the guard. Then I called the Warder and told him my father had just died, that we had been visiting London together, the place of our ancestors and all the lovely English, and my father just died. (*She reaches out to touch him.*)

DEAD FATHER. You are not my ancestor.

SHE. They jeered. They brought me to this tower and locked me up. I can see they're afraid of me. From the tower I saw them drag you across the court ... your hair hanging down. They have taken off your shoes and you are stiff. You are stiff. (*Touches him.*) My dear father. (*MUSIC: Haydn.*)

DEAD FATHER. Daughter of somebody that cooked for me. (*Smiles. He then ignores* SHE WHO IS, *changes into the* REVEREND, *takes the Bible and starts to read. The* WHITE BIRD *flies into the cage. Wings flutter. The* REVEREND'S WIFE *prays, lights a candle. The* REVEREND *watches the* BIRD. REVEREND'S WIFE *then puts on her black face, rose dress. Some of the red rice has fallen near her, she says, "Oww," and starts to peck at it like a bird.* SHE WHO IS *wanders about, then comes to speak to the* BASTARD'S BLACK MOTHER *who remains seated like an owl. END MUSIC.*)

SHE. It was you, the Bastard's Black Mother, who told me. I asked you where did Mr. William Mattheson's family come from and you, my Black Mother, said: I believe his father came from England. England, I said. England is the Brontës' home. Did you know, Black Bastard's Mother, who cooked for somebody, in the Reverend's parlor—there in a glass bookcase are books and England is the home of Chaucer, Dickens and Shakespeare. Black Mother who cooked for somebody, Mr. William Mattheson died today. I was at the College. The Reverend's Wife called me, Clara who is the Bastard who is the Virgin Mary who is the Owl. Clara, who is the Bastard who is the Virgin Mary who is the Owl, Clara, she said, the Reverend told me to call you and tell you Mr. William Mattheson died today or it was yesterday he died yesterday. It was yesterday. The Reverend told me to tell you it was yesterday he died and it is today they're burying him. Clara who is the Bastard, you mustn't come. Don't do anything foolish like come to the funeral, Mary. You've always been such a fool about that white man, Clara. But I am coming, the Black Bastard's Mother. I am coming, my Goddam Father who was the Richest White Man in Jacksonville, Georgia. When I arrive in London, I'll go out to Buckingham Palace, see the Thames at dusk and Big Ben. I'll go for lovely walks through Hyde Park, and to innumerable little tearooms with great bay windows and white tablecloths on little white tables and order tea. I will go all over and it will be June. Then I'll go out to the Tower to see you, my father.

(*SUBWAY STOPS. Doors open.* THEY *enter.*)

THEY. If you are his ancestor, what are you doing on the subway at night looking for men?

What are you doing looking for men to take to a hotel room in Harlem?

Negro men?

Negro men, Clara Passmore?

(*GATES CLOSE, SUBWAY STARTS,* BIRD'S *wings flap.*)

SHE. (*Runs to the* BIRD.) My dead father's bird: God's Dove. My father died today.

BIRD. (*Mocking.*) My father died today, God's Dove.

SHE. He was the Richest White Man in our Town. I was conceived by him and somebody that cooked for him.

BIRD. What are you doing in the Tower of London then?

(*The* REVEREND *becomes the* DEAD FATHER *who comes forward, pantomimes catching
the* BIRD, *puts him in the cage, shuts the door.*)

SHE. My father. (*He turns, stares at her and comes toward her and dies. There is a
CLANG.*) What were you saying to William, my father, you loved William so? (*She
holds him in her arms. He opens his eyes.*)

DEAD FATHER. (*Waking.*) Mary, at last you are coming to me. (*MUSIC: Haydn.*)

SHE. I am not Mary, I am Clara, your daughter, Reverend Passmore—I mean Dead
Father. (BIRD *flies in the cage.*)

DEAD FATHER. Yes, my Mary, you are coming into my world. You are filled with
dreams of my world. I sense it all.

(*Scene revolves counterclockwise one and one-quarter turns. LIGHTS FLASH.* SHE
WHO IS, *trying to escape, runs into* NEGRO MAN.)

NEGRO MAN. At last you are coming to me. (*Smiles.*)

DEAD FATHER. Mary, come in here for eternity. Are you confused? Yes, I can see you
are confused. (THEY *come on.*)

THEY. Are you confused? (*One of them,* CHAUCER, *is now dressed as the* REVEREND.
*He comes, falls down onto the empty high-backed chair and sits staring into the
Bible.*)

DEAD FATHER. So at last you are coming to me, Bastard.

(BASTARD'S BLACK MOTHER *exits from gate, returns, part owl with owl feathers upon
her, dragging a great dark bed through the gate.*)

BBM. Why be confused? The Owl was your beginning, Mary. (*There is a GREAT
CLANG. Begins to build with the bed and feathers the High Altar. Feathers fly.*)

SHE. He came to me in the outhouse, he came to me under the porch, in the garden,
in the fig tree. He told me you are an owl, ow, oww, I am your beginning, ow. You
belong here with us owls in the fig tree, not to somebody that cooks for your Goddam Father, oww, and I ran to the outhouse in the night crying oww. Bastard they
say, the people in the town all say Bastard, but I—I belong to God and the owls,
ow, and I sat in the fig tree. My Goddam Father is the Richest White Man in the
Town, but I belong to the owls, till Reverend Passmore adopted me they all said
Bastard ... then my father was a reverend. He preached in the Holy Baptist Church
on the top of the hill, on the top of the Holy Hill and everybody in the town knew
then my name was Mary. My father was the Baptist preacher and I was Mary.
(*SUBWAY STOPS, GATES OPEN.* THEY *enter. GATES CLOSE. SUBWAY
STARTS.* SHE *sits next to* NEGRO MAN.) I who am the ancestor of Shakespeare,
Chaucer and William the Conqueror, I went to London—the Queen Elizabeth.
London. They all said who ever heard of anybody going to London but I went. I
stayed in my cabin the whole crossing, solitary. I was the only Negro there. I read
books on subjects like the History of London, the Life of Anne Boleyn, Mary
Queen of Scots and Sonnets. When I wasn't in the cabin I wrapped myself in a
great sweater and sat over the dark desks in the writing room and wrote my father.
I wrote him every day of my journey. I met my father once when my mother took

me to visit him and we had to go into the back door of his house. I was married once briefly. On my wedding day the Reverend's Wife came to me and said when I see Marys I cry for their deaths, when I see brides, Clara, I cry for their deaths. But the past years I've spent teaching alone in Savannah. And alone I'm almost thirty-four, I who am the ancestor of somebody that cooked for somebody and William the Conqueror. (DEAD FATHER *rises, goes to her, then dies again. GREAT CLANG.* BLACK MOTHER *shakes a rattle at* SHE. SHE *screams at the* DEAD FATHER *and the* MOTHER.) You must know how it is to be filled with yearning.

(THEY *laugh.* MOTHER *bangs at the bed.*)

NEGRO MAN. (*Touches her.*) And what exactly do you yearn for?

SHE. You know.

NEGRO MAN. No, what is it?

SHE. I want what I think everyone wants.

NEGRO MAN. And what is that?

SHE. I don't know. Love or something, I guess.

NEGRO MAN. Out there Owl?

DEAD FATHER. In St. Paul's Chapel Owl?

THEY. Keep her locked there, guard. (*GREAT CLANG.*)

BBM. Is this love to come from out there?

SHE. I don't know what you mean.

DEAD FATHER. I know you don't.

THEY. We know you don't.

SHE. Call me Mary.

NEGRO MAN. Mary?

THEY. Keep her locked there.

DEAD FATHER. If you are Mary what are you doing in the Tower of London?

NEGRO MAN. Mary?

(*The* REVEREND *gets up, goes to chair, puts on robe, sits. The* BASTARD'S BLACK MOTHER *reappears on the other side of the gate, owl feathers about her, bearing a vial, still wearing the long black hair of the* REVEREND'S WIFE.)

BBM. When I see sweet Marys I cry for their deaths, Clara. The Reverend took my maidenhead and I am not a Virgin anymore and that is why you must be Mary, always be Mary, Clara.

SHE. Mama. (BLACK MOTHER *rises. Steps in costume of* ANNE BOLEYN.) Mama. (*Watches her change to* ANNE BOLEYN. *They watch.*)

BBM. What are you doing on the subway if you are his ancestor?

(ANNE *makes circular cross around stage until* SHE *is back in same position* SHE *started at.*)

SHE. I am Clara Passmore. I am not His ancestor. I ride, look for men to take to a Harlem hotel room, to love, dress them as my father, beg to take me.

THEY. Take you?

SHE. Yes, take me, Clara Passmore.

THEY. Take you, Bastard?

SHE. There is a bed there.

(*The* WHITE BIRD *laughs like the mother.*)

WILL. And do they take you?

SHE. No, William.

WILL. No?

SHE. Something happens.

WILL. Happens?

CHAUCER. Happens?

SHE. Something strange always happens, Chaucer.

CHAUCER. Where?

SHE. In the hotel room. It's how I've passed my summer in New York, nights I come to the subway, look for men. It's how I've passed my summer. If they would only take me! But something strange happens.

ANNE. Take you, Mary. Why, Mary? (ANNE *has now reached gate.*)

(BLACK MOTHER *steps out of costume, crosses to bed.* SHE *talks to* ANNE *as if she were there.*)

SHE. Anne, you must help me. They, my Black Mother and my Goddam Father and the Reverend and his wife, they and the teachers at the school where I teach, and Professor Johnson, the principal to whom I'm engaged, they all say, "London, who in the hell ever heard of anybody going to London?" Of course I shouldn't go. They said I had lost my mind, read so much, buried myself in my books. They said I should stay and teach summer school to the kids up from Oglethorpe. But I went. All the way from Piccadilly Circus out there in the black taxi, my cold hands were colder than ever. Then it happened. No sooner than I left the taxi and passed down a grey walk through a dark gate and into a garden where there were black ravens on the grass when I broke down. I broke down and started to cry, oh the Tower, winters in Queen's House, right in front of everybody. People came and stared. I was the only Negro there. The Guard came and stared, the ravens flew and finally a man with a black hat on helped me out through the gate into the street. I am never going back, Anne. Anne, I am never going back. I will not go.

(*SUBWAY STOPS, GATES OPEN.*)

THEY. Keep her locked there, guard.

(*LIGHT comes through gates as if opened.* SHE *makes crown of paper, and places on* NEGRO MAN's *head.*)

SHE. God, do you see it? Do you see? They are opening the cell door to let me go.

NEGRO MAN. See it, Mary?

SHE. They are opening the cell door to let me go down to St. Paul's Chapel where I am yearning to go. Do you see it?

NEGRO MAN. Love? Love Mary?

SHE. Love?

NEGRO MAN. Love in St. Paul's Chapel? (*He tries to grab at her.*)

SHE. No, no, the love that exists between you and me. Do you see it?

NEGRO MAN. Love Mary? (*He takes her hand, with his other hand, he tries to undress her.*)

SHE. Love God.

NEGRO MAN. Love Mary?

SHE. Love God.

THEY. (*Simultaneously.*) Bastard, you are not His ancestor, you are not God's ancestor. (*There is a SCREECH as* THEY *bring the* DEAD FATHER *and leave him at her feet.*)

NEGRO MAN. Love Mary?

SHE. Love God. Yes.

BBM. (*Calls.*) Clara. Clara. (*The* REVEREND *watching.*)

THEY. Open the door. Let her go, let her go, guards. Open the cell door. (THEY *exit, leaving the gates open.*)

(NEGRO MAN *will not release* SHE WHO IS *Clara who is the Bastard who is the Virgin Mary who is the Owl.*)

SHE. Go away. Go away. (*The* NEGRO MAN *will not release her.*)

(*The* REVEREND'S WIFE *goes on building the High Altar with owl feathers, prays, builds, prays, stops, holds out her hand to* SHE WHO IS, *puts up candles, puts up owl feathers, laughs, puts more candles on the High Altar.*)

REVEREND'S WIFE. (*Calls.*) Owl, come sit by me. (*The* REVEREND'S WIFE *does not look at* SHE WHO IS, *but rather stares feverishly upward, her gestures possessing the fervent quality of Biblical images. Sitting on the High Altar, she holds one of her hands over her shoulder as though she drew near the fingers of a deity. Suddenly her hand reaches inside her gown and she pulls up a butcher knife.*) Clara. (*Staring upward, holding the knife.*)

SHE. Yes, the Reverend's Wife who came to me on my wedding day and said I cry for the death of brides. Yes?

REVEREND'S WIFE. I told the Reverend if he ever came near me again ... (*She turns the butcher knife around.*) Does he not know I am Mary, Christ's bride? What does he think? Does he think I am like your black mother who was the biggest whore in town? He must know I'm Mary. Only Mary would marry the Reverend Passmore of the church on the top of the Holy Hill. (*Turns the knife around, staring at it.* SHE *is leaving with* NEGRO MAN. REVEREND'S WIFE *is pulling her.*) We adopted you, took you from your bastard birth, Owl.

(SHE *and* NEGRO MAN *exit. GATES CLOSE. SUBWAY STARTS.* REVEREND'S WIFE *drags bed onto Center Stage. She enters with* NEGRO MAN *Down Center.*)

SHE. Home, God, we're home. Did you know we came from England, God? It's the Brontës' home too. Winters we spent here at the Tower. Our chambers were in the Queen's House. Summers we spent at Stratford. It was so lovely. God, do you remember the loveliness?

(*LIGHTS FLASH. Scene revolves clockwise one and one-quarter turns.* BIRD *flaps wings. LIGHT comes up on him.*)

BIRD. If you are the Virgin, what are you doing with this Negro in a Harlem hotel room? Mary?

SHE. My name is Clara Passmore.

BIRD. Mary. (WHITE BIRD *laughs like the* MOTHER. *The* REVEREND'S WIFE *lights candles.*)

NEGRO MAN. (*Going to her.*) What is it?

SHE. Call me Mary, God.

NEGRO MAN. Mary?

SHE. God, do you remember the loveliness?

REVEREND'S WIFE. (*Lights more candles and moves closer with the butcher knife, calling:*) Clara. (*The* BIRD *flies wildly, the* REVEREND *sits in the chair reading the white tattered Bible.*)

NEGRO MAN. What is it? What is it? What is wrong? (*He tries to undress her. Underneath her body is black. He throws off the crown she has placed on him. She is wildly trying to get away from him.*) What is it? (*The* WHITE BIRD *flies toward them and about the green room.*) Are you sick?

SHE. (*Smiles.*) No, God. (*She is in a trance.*) No, I am not sick. I only have a dream of love. A dream. Open the cell door and let me go down to St. Paul's Chapel. (*The blue crepe shawl is half about her. She shows the* NEGRO MAN *her notebooks, from which a mass of papers fall. She crazily tries to gather them up. During this* SHE *walks around bed. He follows her.*) Communications, God, communications, letters to my father. I am making it into my thesis. I write my father every day of the year.

God, I who am the Bastard who is the Virgin Mary who is the Owl, I came here this morning with my father. We were visiting England, the place of our ancestors, my father and I who am the Bastard who is the Virgin Mary who is the Owl. We had a lovely morning. We rose in darkness, took a taxi past Hyde Park, through the Marble Arch to Buckingham Palace. We had our morning tea at Lyons and then we came out to the Tower.

And I started to cry and a man with a black hat on helped me out of the gate to the street. I was the only Negro here.

They took him away and would not let me see him. They who are my Black Mother and my Goddam Father locked me in the fig tree and took his body away and his white hair hung down.

Now they, my Black Mother and my Goddam Father who pretend to be Chaucer, Shakespeare and Eliot and all my beloved English, come to my cell and stare and I can see they despise me and I despise them.

They are dragging his body across the green his white hair hanging down. They are taking off his shoes and he is stiff. I must get into the chapel to see him. I must. He is my blood father. God, let me into his burial. (*He grabs her Down Center.* SHE, *kneeling.*) I call God and the Owl answers. (*Softer.*) It haunts my Tower calling, its feathers are blowing against the cell wall, speckled in the garden on the fig tree, it comes, feathered, great hollow-eyed with yellow skin and yellow eyes, the flying bastard. From my Tower I keep calling and the only answer is the Owl, God. (*Pause. Stands.*) I am only yearning for our kingdom, God.

(*The* WHITE BIRD *flies back into the cage,* REVEREND *reads smiling, the* DEAD FATHER *lies on cell floor. The* MOTHER, *now part the black mother and part the* REVEREND'S WIFE *in a white dress, wild kinky hair, part feathered, comes closer to* CLARA.)

MOTHER. Owl in the fig tree, owl under the house, owl in outhouse. (*Calling cheerfully the way one would call a child, kissing* SHE WHO IS.) There is a way from owldom. (*Kissing her again.*) Clara who is the Bastard who is the Virgin who is the Owl.

SHE. (*Goes to* MOTHER.) My Black Mother who cooked for somebody who is the Reverend's Wife. Where is Anne Boleyn?

MOTHER. Owl in the fig tree, do you know it? Do you? Do you know the way to St. Paul's Chapel, Clara? (*Takes her hand.*) I do. Kneel, Mary, by the gate and pray with me who is your black mother who is Christ's Bride. (*She holds up the butcher knife.*) Kneel by the High Altar and pray with me. (*They kneel; she smiles.*) Do you know it, Clara, do you, Clara Bastard? (*Kisses her.*) Clara, I know the way to St. Paul's Chapel. I know the way to St. Paul's Chapel, Clara.

(MOTHER *lifts knife. She stabs herself. At this moment,* BIRD *flaps wings, scene moves counterclockwise one turn. There is a SCREECH of a SUBWAY. Then the Haydn plays. When revolve stops,* NEGRO MAN *tries to kiss* HER *and pin* HER *down on bed.* SHE *is fighting him off. The* WHITE BIRD *descends steps.*)

SHE. God, say, "You know I love you, Mary, yes, I love you. That love is the oldest, purest testament in my heart." Say, "Mary, it was a testament imprinted on my soul long before the world began. I pray to you, Mary." God, say, "Mary, I pray to you. Darling, come to my kingdom. Mary, leave owldom—come to my kingdom. I am awaiting you." (*The* NEGRO MAN *tries again to kiss* HER. *The* WHITE BIRD *picks up the* DEAD MOTHER *and takes her to the top of St. Peter's Dome. They remain there, watching down. The* REVEREND *reads the Bible, smiling.*)

NEGRO MAN. What is wrong?

SHE. Wrong, God?

NEGRO MAN. God?

SHE. Wrong, God?

NEGRO MAN. God? (*They are upon the burning High Altar. He tries to force her down, yet at the same time he is frightened by her. The* DEAD FATHER *who has been holding the candles, smiles.*)

SHE. Negro! (*MUSIC ENDS.*) Keep her locked there, guard. (*They struggle.*) I cry for the death of Marys. (*They struggle.* SHE *screeches.*) Negro! (*She tries to get out of the room, but he will not let her go.*) Let me go to St. Paul's Chapel. Let me go down to see my Goddam Father who was the Richest White Man in the Town. (*They struggle, he is frightened now.*) God, God, call me, Mary. (SHE *screeches louder.*) God!! (*Suddenly she breaks away, withdraws the butcher knife, still with blood and feathers upon it, and very quickly tries to attack him, holds the knife up, aiming it at him, but then dropping it just as suddenly in a gesture of wild weariness. He backs farther. She falls down onto the side of the burning bed. The* NEGRO MAN *backs farther out through the gate.* SHE, *fallen at the side of the Altar burning, her head bowed, both hands conceal her face, feathers fly, green lights are strong, Altar burning,* WHITE BIRD *laughs from the Dome.* SHE WHO IS *Clara who is the Bastard who is the Virgin Mary suddenly looks like an owl, and lifts her bowed head, stares into space and speaks:*) Ow ... oww. (FATHER *rises and slowly blows out candles on bed.*)

CURTAIN

49

From *Oxherding Tale*

Charles Johnson

Charles Johnson (b. 1948) trained at Southern Illinois University and SUNY Stony Brook, majoring in philosophy. After some work as a published cartoonist, he turned to writing fiction and became attracted to the tradition of the philosophical novel. His first novel was *Faith and the Good Thing* (1974), and his short story collection *The Sorcerer's Apprentice* (1986) was nominated for the PEN/Faulkner Award. He received the National Book Award for his third novel, *Middle Passage* (1990). His novel *Dreamer* (1998) creates the figure of a *doppelgänger* of Martin Luther King. Johnson has also written screenplays for the Public Broadcasting Service. He received fellowships from the National Endowment for the Humanities and the Guggenheim Foundation and is a professor of English at the University of Washington in Seattle. Johnson achieved his aesthetic breakthrough with his second novel, *Oxherding Tale* (1982), the first chapter of which is reprinted here. The book is in the form of a mock-autobiography inspired both by the eighteenth-century novel and the slave narrative tradition. It takes its title from the "Oxherding pictures" of a 12th-century Zen artist, as Johnson draws on Buddhist sources as well as on philosophers from Plato to Hegel.

My Origins

Précis of My Education
My Life at Cripplegate
The Agreement

Long ago my father and I were servants at Cripplegate, a cotton plantation in South Carolina. That distant place, the world of my childhood, is ruin now, mere parable, but what history I have begins there in an unrecorded accident before the Civil War, late one evening when my father, George Hawkins, still worked in the Big House, watched over his owner's interests, and often drank with his Master—this was Jonathan Polkinghorne—on the front porch after a heavy meal. It was a warm night. An autumn night of fine-spun moonlight blurred first by Madeira, then home-brewed beer as they played Rummy, their feet propped on the knife-whittled porch rail, the dark two-story house behind them, creaking sometimes in the wind. My father had finished his chores early, for he was (he says) the best butler in the country, and took great pride in his position, but he wasn't eager to go home. He stayed clear of his cabin when my stepmother played host for the Ladies Prayer Circle. They were strange, George thought. Those women were harmless enough by themselves, when sewing or cleaning, but together their collective prayers had a mysterious power that filled his whitewashed cabin with presences—Shades, he called them, because they moved furniture in the cabin, destroyed the laws of physics, which George swore by, and drove him outside to sleep in the shed. (Not that my father knew a whole lot about physics, being a slave, but George knew sorcery when he saw it, and kept his distance.) He was, as all Hodges knew, a practical, God-fearing man who liked to keep things simple so he could enjoy them. He was overly cautious and unnerved by little things. So he avoided his cabin and talked about commonsense things like politics and the price of potatoes on his Master's porch long after the last pine-knot candles winked out in the quarters. Whiskey burned, then exploded like gas in his belly. He felt his face expand. His eyes slid slowly out of focus. Hard old leaves on magnolias overhanging the porch clacked, like shells, in a September wind sprinkled with rain.

Twelve o'clock. A typical Saturday night.

"George," said Jonathan, his voice harsh after consuming forty-eight ounces of Madeira in what my father figured to be half an hour, "if I go up to bed at this advanced hour, smelling of spirits, my Anna will brain me with a milkstool." Low and deep, George laughed, then hiccoughed. He rubbed his legs to start blood circulating again. "And your wife, Mattie," Jonathan added, passing his bottle to my father, "she'll chew your fat good, won't she, George?"

Because he had not thought of this, my father stopped laughing, then breathing for a second. My stepmother frowned on drinking—she frowned, in fact, on most things about George. She was no famous beauty, fat as she was, with brown freckles, a rich spangled voice, and more chins (lately) than a Chinese social register, but my stepmother had—or so George believed when Jonathan arranged their wedding—beautiful ways. Her previous owners, friends of the Polkinghornes, were an old New England family that landed with the Pilgrims at Cape Cod Bay. Mattie, their servant, was sure some days that she had married below herself. She was spiritual, high-strung, respected books, and above all else was dedicated to developing George into a real gentleman, even if it killed him—she selected his clothes for him, corrected his speech, and watched him narrowly for the slightest lapse into Negroness, as she called it. Added to which, and most of all, George liked his women big and smart (you could have cut two good-sized maids out of Mattie and still had leftovers). As he uncorked a bottle of gin, poured a glass for Jonathan, then toasted his Master's health, he could not bear the thought of disappointing her by stumbling into their cabin reeking of liquor—it would destroy her faith that he was not, after all, a common nigger with no appreciation for the finer things; she would be waiting, he knew, turning the tissue-thin pages of her Bible, holding her finger on some flight of poetry in Psalms, which she planned to read to George for his "general improvement." She made him bend his knees beside her each night, their heads tipped and thighs brushing, praying that neither jealousy nor evil temper, boredom nor temptation, poverty nor padderolls, would destroy their devotion to each other. "You have me, I have you," Mattie whispered, "and we both have Jesus." It made George shudder. Why were black women so mystical? Religion was fine, but if you carried on too much about it, people were liable to think something was wrong with you. "No," he said, shaking his head, glancing left at Jonathan, "I'd best not go home tonight."

"Nor I." Jonathan sat back heavily on his cane-seat chair, crossing his knees, and lit a cigar. "But there must be *some* alternative."

My father raised his shoulders in a shrug.

They drank on in the darkness, grinning more and more now under the influence of gin-and-water. The porch fogged with smoke. At length, Jonathan lifted his head and touched my father's knee.

"George, I have it."

"Yessir?"

"*I* can't go upstairs to face my Anna. And *you* can't return to the quarters." Thoughtful, he picked at his lip. "Are these premises correct so far?"

"Yessir," George rocked his head. "I think so."

"But there's no harm in switching places for one night, is there, with me sleeping in the quarters, and you upstairs?"

George gave him a look. He was sure it was the gin, not Jonathan, talking.

"George, when*ever* I advance an idea you have a most annoying way of looking at me as if I'd just suggested that we strangle a child and sell its body to science. No good will come of this. Goodnight," Jonathan said, steadying himself with one hand on the porch rail as he stood. He rocked off for George's cabin. "I'll see you at breakfast."

How long George waited on the front porch, sweating from the soles of his feet upward, is impossible to tell—my father seldom speaks of this night, but the great Swiss clock in Jonathan's parlor chimed twice and, in perfect submission to his Master's will, he turned inside and walked like a man waistdeep in weeds down a hallway where every surface, every shape was warped by frail lamplight from Jonathan's study. His Master's house was solid and rich; it was established, quiet, and so different from the squalid quarters, with vases, a vast library, and great rooms of imported furniture that had cost the Polkinghornes dearly—a house of such heavily upholstered luxuriance and antiques that George now took small, mincing steps for fear of breaking something. In the kitchen, he uncovered a pot of beef on the table, prepared a plate for Mattie (he always brought my stepmother something when he worked in the house), wrapped it in paper, drained his bottle of gin, then lit a candle. Now he was ready.

My father negotiated the wide, straight staircase to Anna's bedchamber, but stopped in the doorway. In candlelight like this, on her high bed with its pewterized nickel headboard, Anna Polkinghorne was a whole landscape of flesh, white as the moon, with rolling hills, mounds, and bottomless gorges. He sat down on a chair by her bed. He stood up. He sat down again—George had never seen the old woman so beautiful. Blurred by the violence of his feelings, or the gin, his eyes clamped shut and he swallowed. Wouldn't a man rise new-made and cured of all his troubles after a night in this immense bed? And the Prayer Circle? Didn't his wife say whatever happened was, in the end, the Lord's will? George put his plate on the chair. He stared—and stared—as Anna turned in her sleep. He yanked off his shirt—wooden buttons flew everywhere, then his coarse Lowell breeches and, like a man listening to the voice of a mesmerist, slipped himself under the bedsheets. What happened next, he had not expected. Sleepily, Anna turned and soldered herself to George. She crushed him in a clinch so strong his spine cracked. Now he had fallen too far to stop. She talked to George, a wild stream of gibberish, which scared him plenty, but he was not a man to leave his chores half-finished, and plowed on. Springs in the mattress snapped, and Anna, gripping the headboard, groaned, "Oh *gawd*, Jonathan!"

"No, ma'am. It ain't Jonathan."

"Ge*o-o-o*-orge?" Her voice pulled at the vowel like taffy. She yanked her sheet to her chin. "Is this *George?*"

"Yo husband's in the quarters." George was on his feet. "He's, uh, with my wife." None of it made sense now. How in God's name had he gotten himself into this? He went down on all fours, holding the plate for Mattie over his head, groping around the furniture for his trousers. "Mrs. Polkinghorne, I kin explain, I think. You know how a li'l corn kin confuse yo thinkin'? Well, we was downstairs on the porch, you know, drinkin', Master Polkinghorne and me...."

Anna let fly a scream.

She was still howling, so he says, when George, hauling hips outside, fell, splattering himself from head to foot with mud deltaed in the yard, whooping too when he arrived flushed, naked, and fighting for breath at his own place, the plate of beef still miraculously covered. He heard from inside yet another scream, higher, and then Jonathan came flying like a chicken fleeing a hawk through the cabin door, carrying his boots, his shirt, his suspenders. For an instant, both men paused as they churned past each other in the night and shouted (stretto):

"George, whose fat idea was this?"

"Suh, it was *you* who told *me*...."

This, I have been told, was my origin.

It is, at least, my father's version of the story; I would tell you Anna Polkinghorne's, but I was never privileged to hear it. While Jonathan survived this incident, his reputation unblemished, George Hawkins was to be changed forever. Anna, of course, was never quite herself again. All this may seem comic to some, but from it we may date the end of tranquility at Cripplegate. Predictably, my birth played hob with George's marriage (it didn't help Master Polkinghorne's much either) and, just as predictably, for twenty years whenever George or Jonathan entered the same room as Mattie, my stepmother found something to do elsewhere. She never forgave George, who never forgave Jonathan, who blamed Anna for letting things go too far, and *she* demanded a divorce but settled, finally, on living in a separate wing of the house. George, who looked astonished for the rest of his life, even when sleeping, was sent to work in the fields. This Fall, he decided, was the wage of false pride—he had long hours to ponder such things as Providence and Destiny now that he was a shepherd of oxen and sheep. It was God's will, for hitherto he and Mattie—especially Mattie—had been sadditty and felt superior to the fieldhands who, George decided, had a world-historical mission. He had been a traitor. A tool. He refused Jonathan's apologies and joked bleakly of shooting him or, late at night when he had me clean his eyes with cloth after a day of sacking wool, even more bleakly of spiritual and physical bondage, arguing his beliefs loudly, if ineffectively, on the ridiculously tangled subject Race. My father had a talent for ridiculing slaveholders in general and the Polkinghornes in particular—who knew them better than their butler?—that ultimately went over big in Cripplegate's quarters. When I look back on my life, it seems that I belonged by error or accident— call it what you will—to both house and field, but I was popular in neither, because the war between these two families focused, as it were, on me, and I found myself caught from my fifth year forward in their crossfire.

It started in 1843 when Jonathan realized he would have no children, what with Anna holed up with his flintlock and twenty-five rounds of ammunition in one half of the house. What had been a comfortable, cushiony marriage with only minor flare-ups, easily fixed by flowers or Anna's favorite chocolates, was now a truce with his wife denying him access to the common room, top floors, and dining area (he slept in his study); what was once a beautiful woman whose voice sang as lovely as any in this world when she sat at the black, boatlike piano in the parlor, one foot gently vibrating on the sostenuto pedal, was now an irascible old woman who haunted the place like a dead man demanding justice, who left terrible notes on the kitchen table, under Jonathan's cup, who, locked in her bedchamber like a prisoner, finished the plates the housemaid left outside her door, but would not throw the latch: a rotten business, in Jonathan's opinion. He came half-asleep to her door night after night, night after night, night after night, and asked helplessly, "Can we talk about it?"

She sat up and shouted, "No!"

"We *all* make mistakes, Anna. For God's sake, George and I meant no harm...." He paused. The inevitable question still nagged him. "Anna, you *wanted* George, not me, to be there, didn't you?"

Silence. After a second: "Is that boy still here?"

"In the quarters," he said. "He's living with George, and he's beautiful, Anna. He has your hair, your—"

"You send him away!"

The old man gulped. "He's your son as much as George's, isn't he?" He rubbed the floor with the toe of his slipper. "We should do for him, you know, like he was ours...."

"I know no such thing!" Her voice became flat and tired. "Go away."

"This is *my* house!" he barked, trembling with fury. "I live here, too!"

"Go *away!*"

Exactly five years to the day George sprang from Anna's bedsheets, Jonathan sat in his study until dawn, writing advertisements for a tutor, which he sent to the best schools. So September, October, and November passed; and on a cold morning in December a gloomy but gifted teacher—a graduate of William and Mary—arrived unannounced on foot from Hodges. By a riverboat, by a stagecoach, by a wagon, by a horse, by a rail—by traveling for five weeks he came with a stupendous headcold to Cripplegate, bearing letters of reference from Amos Bronson Alcott, Caleb Sprague Henry, and Noah Porter, who wrote, "This candidate knows as much about metaphysics as any man alive, and has traveled in India, but you must never leave him alone for long in a room with a little girl."

Porter wrote:

"He is, let us say, born to Transcendentalism by virtue of a peculiar quirk of cognition that, like the Tibetan mystic, lets him perceive the interior of objects, why no one knows; whatever his faults, he is perhaps the only man in North America who truly understands the *Mahàbhárata*, and has a splendid future as an Orientalist ordained for him, provided he isn't hanged, say, for high treason, or heresy. He is well suited for the tutorial position you advertise if, and only if, you do not set him off. Never," wrote Porter, "mention his mother."

That winter, the worst in South Carolina's history, five men froze to their horses. Up in the hills, they weren't found until March thaw, their bodies white pap and bloated fingers inside the horses' bellies for the bloodwarmth. In this bitter season, snow sat on the rooftops, where its weight cracked wooden beams like kindling; snow brought a silence like sleep to the quarters, where it frosted the great family house and, like a glacial spell, sealed off the hills, the forests, and the fields in blue ice. This drowse of winter released a figure who evolved in pieces from the snowdrifts, first a patch of bloodless fingers and a prayerbook, then a black coat, a hatbrim dusted with ice crystals. Snow lay like a cloak on his shoulders and like spats on the tops of his boots. He sloshed, coughing, up a path made by the wagons to the paddocks—it was eight-thirty—and there he stamped his feet. Jonathan bounded outside in his house-coat, he picked up the stranger's portmanteau, then pushed a tumbler of claret at him. My tutor brushed it aside. "I never drink before noon."

"Nor I," chuckled Jonathan. "But it must be noon *some*where." He threw down the tumbler, then took the stranger's arm:

"How are you called?"

Dropping his gloves into his hat, he pulled back, did a heelclick in the hallway, and bowed. "My Christian name is Ezekiel William Sykes-Withers."

"Of course," Jonathan said, blinking—he couldn't stand people with two last names. "I wouldn't have it any other way."

They sat, these two, on straw chairs by the windows in the study. As Jonathan served hot cups of milk tea with honey, dickered over Ezekiel's wages, and spelled out his chores, Anna must have whiffed trouble, because the slumbrous feel of the morning was broken by a crash from her bedchamber upstairs, then a groan; the plank-ribbed ceiling buckled, Jonathan spilled boiling tea on his lap, and yelped, "Pay no attention—we're having some work done upstairs." In the doorway, I listened; the interview did not seem to be edited for my benefit.

"You're welcome to the guestroom," said Jonathan. "It's right below my wife's bedroom, so you can look in when she rings her bell."

"By your leave," sniffed Ezekiel—he blew his nose into his handkerchief, looked inside to see what he'd got, and said, "I will sleep closer to the boy."

"My thought exactly." Jonathan finished his tea, then placed his cup and saucer on a candlestand. Unconsciously, he swung his left foot. What he thought we shall never know, but this was clear: my tutor, he learned, was, as Porter hinted, an Anarchist and member of George Ripley's Transcendental Club—a brilliant man, a mystic whose pockets bulged with letters, scraps of paper, news clippings, notes scribbled on his handkerchiefs, his shirtcuffs, and stuffed inside his hat. He looked in the study's weak light like engravings I'd seen of Thomas Paine, or a Medieval scholar peering up from his scrolls, and at other times reminded me of a storybook preacher (Calvinist), and was, we learned, one of the two or three authorities on the Rhineland sermons of Meister Eckhart. He was thin as a line in Zeno, with a craglike face, wild goatish eyes, and blood pressure so staggeringly high that twice during the interview he ran outside to rub his wrists with snow. His tight, pale lips were the whole Jeffersonian idea of Insurrection. Whenever he pronounced the words "perceiver" and "perceived," which he referred to often that morning, he smothered them in his long nose into "per-r-rceiver" and "per-r-rceived" with a kind of solemn quiver as he rolled them out. He smelled of laudanum. He smoked while he was eating, disdained comfort, and died, ten years later, under circumstances that left the exact cause of death a mystery. "You don't drink heavily, do you, Ezekiel?" asked Jonathan. "No," he said. "Or take opium?" "No." "And you have no wife, no relations?" Ezekiel's brow wrinkled and he shook his head violently. "I've stayed to myself since the death of my parents, Mr. Polkinghorne."

"I'm sorry." Jonathan tapped the end of his broad, bell-shaped nose. "I lost my father not long ago, too—I know how you must feel."

"*My* father," said Ezekiel, "deeply loved the things of this world, he held his family and work in the highest esteem. He was piously religious to his Creator, loyal to his country, faithful to his wife, a kind relation, a lasting friend, and charitable to the poor." He sat stiffly on his chair, fists clenched tight. "He shot my mother and sister, and would have blown me to Kingdom Come, too, I assure you, had I not been away that evening. When I arrived home, they were all dead, over their *apéritif*, at the dinner table. Have you," Ezekiel asked, "ever considered suicide?"

"Why no!" Jonathan rubbed his nose. "Never!"

Ezekiel said, "You should."

"And what is *that* supposed to mean?"

"I only mean," said Ezekiel, "that we do not think of death until we are well within her jaws." What he meant by this, he did not say. From his pocket he withdrew a tobacco pouch and a big Nuremberg pipe, thumbed down a pinch of Latakia, and said, "This boy, you say, is a mulatto?"

Jonathan nodded yes.

"In his horoscope Mars confronts Mercury at three angles, and this is promising," said Ezekiel. "It signifies the birth of a philosopher. Is he yours?"

Witheringly, Jonathan glanced toward the door, wagged his head, and said, "No." The reply and gesture nihilated each other. "What I mean to say is that Andrew is my property and that his value will increase with proper training." He looked away, quickly, from the door, then sighed. And what was I thinking? What did I feel? Try as I might, I could not have told you what my body rested on, or what was under my feet—the hallway had the feel of pasteboard and papier-mâché. A new train of thoughts were made to live in my mind. Jonathan hung his head a little. He said to Ezekiel, without looking up from the floor, "Five dollars monthly, and board, are all I can offer. Are you still interested?"

Ezekiel's face wrinkled into an infernal, Faustian leer. "He *isn't* your son?"

"Are you," Jonathan asked, crossly, "interested?"

"I will teach the boy, yes, using a program modeled on that of James Mill for his son John Stuart, but I am never to be disturbed on Sundays, or during the evening. I never eat meat. Or eggs. I would like one wall of my room covered with mirrors. Don't ask why—I live a bit to one side of things. Do you," he asked, stretching out a hand soft and white as raw dough toward Jonathan, "agree to these conditions?"

"Yes." My Master blinked and pushed back his chair. "Agreed."

By the age of eight I began, with Ezekiel, learning Greek; by the time I was twelve I had read Xenophon and Plato. Next came Voice, Elocution, and Piano lessons. He gave George and Mattie orders that I was not to touch silver, gold, or paper currency; nor was I allowed to listen to the Mixed Lydian and Hyperlydian Modes in music, lest these melancholy strains foul Ezekiel's plans for what was—in his view—a perfect moral education. By the age of fifteen I began to fare badly. I could ask to use the silver chamber pot in George's cabin, where I slept curled up on a pallet, in Latin more perfect than my native tongue; I received lectures on monadology, classical philology, and Oriental thought—the better to fathom Schopenhauer, a favorite of Ezekiel, who often spent days in his cabin, reading Hegel and Thoreau, with whom he'd corresponded earlier, and Marx, who paid him a visit at Cripplegate in 1850. (Of Karl Marx's social call more will be said later.) He taught me the 165 Considerations, Four Noble Truths, the Eight-Fold Path, the 3,000 Good Manners, and 80,000 Graceful Conducts; but I must confess that reading Chinese thought was a little like eating Chinese food: the more one read Lao tzu and Chaung tzu, or ate subgum chop suey, the emptier one's head and stomach felt hours later. Too, I could never remember if it was ▽ before ⊥ except after 솖, or 阕 before 맍 except after 쌈, and always got the meanings confused. And there is also this to say:

Soon all life left my studies—why I couldn't say, but I had, at least, this theory: these vain studies of things moral, things transcendental, things metaphysical were, all in all, rich food for the soul, but in Cripplegate's quarters all that was considered as making life worth living was utterly wanting. And so I became restless and unquiet. So restless, in fact, that on the eve of my twentieth birthday, a rainy Sunday evening, I rose from my pallet in George's dreary, two-room cabin, and carried all my confusions to Master Polkinghorne.

May 6 of the year of grace 1858.

My clothes were soaking, my frock bunched up like a woman's bustle in the back as I scaled a hillslope between the quarters and house. The yard, as wide as a playing field, was wet and slippery to my feet. Farther on, around the lee side and behind long chintz draperies, a chandelier glowed faintly with fumes of golden light like luminous gas in one ground-floor window. For an instant, I paused beside the broad bay window, watching an old woman, all wrinkled, nothing but pleats and folds, almost bedridden now, burnt down to eighty pounds, dying faster than Dr. Horace Crimshaw in Hodges could feed her pills for migraines, pills for stomach cramps, and potions (Veronal and chloral hydrate) for rest. Jonathan loved his old woman, I knew, and me as well, but could not live with us both. He would slip away some evenings, yes, riding his one-horse chaise off on the remains of old plank roads to tumble, it was rumored, the wives of farmers gone to market in Greenwood. He became, in fact, a hunter of women—a broken-down old man, perfumed, who wore powdered wigs and ribbons in his hair like a Creole dandy. The sort of man who told women, "My wife and I live like brother and sister," or, "Older men make, of course, the best lovers." So it was for years with my Master before sickness brought his wife back downstairs. His chest shrank, his stomach filled, and duty replaced his desire for Anna. But he never thought—he was too loyal to think—of abandoning her, although now she could only stare back at him through burnt-out eyes, coughing blood into her brass thunderpot, crepitations like the dry induviae of brittle leaves in the folds of her nightgown: a fragile mass of living jelly, and no more wife to Jonathan now than a stump of firewood.

A thousand drubbing fingers of rain flew against my face as I leaned forward from my hips and climbed the six wooden steps of the dry-rotted porch. The nerves of my teeth reacted to the cold. Shivering, I lifted, then let fall once—twice—the long brass knocker on the door, waited, then stepped back quickly. For now the latch was thrown, and the huge door opened with a splinter of milkblue candlelight and a dragging sound. It opened, old hinges grating for want of oil. And in the doorway stood my Master, his back hooped like a horseshoe, breathing as if he'd been running for hours. His eyelids were puffy. He scuffed in his stiff, sliding walk onto the porch, lifted his candle higher, oblivious to hot wax trickling down his forearm into his sleeve, and winced when he saw me. A tic twitched in one of his eyes. He saddled his nose with wide spectacles, and asked, full of affection (for the old quop did, indeed, love me like a son), "Is this Andrew?"

"It is, Master Polkinghorne." He pressed his cold lips in a moist kiss against my forehead, and I, in return, affectionately squeezed his arm. "May I come in, sir?"

"You can't stay," he said. "My wife is up and about, you see."

"This won't take long." I coughed into my right hand to clear my throat. "You'll not be troubled by me again."

"You're not in any trouble, are you? You haven't murdered someone, have you?" Jonathan signed. "If so, I hope it wasn't anybody white, Andrew."

"No, sir. Nothing like that." At that moment I decided to tell him nothing, and confide only in you of my brief but unsettling encounter earlier that afternoon. Near the southern hills, close to the backroad, just where the plantation approaches a dark stretch of woods, I had been herding my father's Brown Swiss calves, his Leicester sheep, when the girl—this was Minty—appeared in an osnaburg skirt and white blouse, beneath an old Leghorn hat, with a blue satin ribbon, toting a washtub of clothes. I had known her since childhood—whenever she saw me, her lips made a kissing-sound and she called me away. To Master Polkinghorne's big twelve-stanchion barn. There, beside bins of old oats going bad, in a loft of straw and musty hay, I think I saw her—*really* saw her for the first time. Not, I say, as the wild daughter of Jonathan's maid, who teased me when I traipsed off for my sessions with Ezekiel, hid my books, and mocked my speech, but as all the highbreasted women in calico and taffeta, in lace-trimmed gingham poke bonnets and black net hose, that I had ever wanted and secretly, hopelessly loved. What seemed physical shortcomings, defects in her childhood—eyes too heavy for a child's small head, a shower of sienna hair always entangling itself in farm machinery—seemed (to me) that afternoon to be purified features in a Whole, where no particular facet was striking because all fused together to offer a flawed, haunting beauty the likes of which you have never seen. Do not laugh, sir: I was stung sorely, riveted to the spot, relieved, Lord knows, of my reason. How much of her beauty lay in Minty, and how much in my head, was a mystery to me. Was beauty truly *in* things? Was touch in me or in the things I touched? These things so ensorceled me and baffled my wits that I prayed mightily, *Give me Minty*. And, God's own truth, I promised in that evanescent instant that she and I, George and Mattie—all the bondsmen in Cripplegate's quarters and abroad—would grow old in the skins of free man. (Perhaps I was not too clear in the head at that moment.) But how long would this take? Forty years? Fifty years? My heart knocked violently for manumission. Especially when, as we straightened our garments, I saw her eyes—eyes green as icy mountain meltwater, with a hint of blue shadow and a drowse of sensuality that made her seem voluptuously sleepy, distant, as though she had been lifted long ago from a melancholy African landscape overrich with the colors and warm smells of autumn—a sad, out-of-season beauty suddenly precious to me because it was imperfect and perhaps illusory like moonlight on pond water, sensuously alive, but delivering itself over, as if in sacrifice, to inevitable slow death in the fields. Her name, now that I think on it, might have been Zeudi—Ethiopian, ancient, as remote and strange, now that something in me had awoken, as Inca ruins or shards of pottery from the long-buried cities of Mu. But this is not what I said to Master Polkinghorne. I said:

"She has never liked me, has she?"

"Perhaps you will find forgiveness in your heart for her, Andrew." Now we entered his study. "Our relations are somewhat on the stiff side." There was a bureau with swinging brass handles, a diamond-paned bookcase, and a soft calf-bound set of Hawthorne. On an elbow-chair near the fireplace my Master lowered his weight, then looked up. "Would you rub me along the shoulders, Andrew—the pain is there again." As I did so, Jonathan talked on, as if to himself. "My Anna is mad, gloriously mad, and it's all my doing." He forced a laugh, full of gloom. "And I'll tell you true, I hate her sometimes. Many a night I stand by her door, listening to Anna breathe—it's horrible. Just *horrible!*" His voice began to shake. "I pray that her lungs will fail, and when they *do* stop, faltering sometimes in a hideous rattle, I pray just as desperately for her to breathe again, and when this happens … ah, Andrew, I'm sorry once again." He rubbed his face with both hands as I crossed to the fireplace and stood with my back to the flames, facing him, opening my palms to catch the heat, closing them. The next time he looked up there were tears in his eyes. "What business brings you here tonight?"

"With your permission," I said, "I have come to tell you that Minty, your seamstress, and I plan to be married. That, however, is not all, sir."

"Oh?" He squinted suspiciously.

"Meaning no disrespect to you, sir, I want you to draw up my deed of manumission."

My Master was silent so long I could hear rain patter, lightly, against the windowpanes. Make no mistake. That night I trembled. A pulse began to throb in my temple. Beneath the sausage-tight skin of slavery I could be, depending on the roll of the dice, the swerve of the indifferent atom, forever poised between two worlds, or—with a little luck—a wealthy man who had made his way in the world and married the woman he loved. All right—be realistic, I thought. Consider the facts: Like a man who had fallen or been rudely flung into the world, I owned nothing. My knowledge, my clothes, my language, even, were shamefully second-hand, made by, and perhaps for, other men. I was a living lie, that was the heart of it. My argument was: Whatever my origin, I would be wholly responsible for the shape I gave myself in the future, for shirting myself handsomely with a new life that called me like a siren to possibilities that were real but forever out of reach. My Master sat, blinking into the fire, then up at me, the corners of his mouth tucked in, his expression exactly that of a man who has come suddenly across cat fur in a bowl of soup. I walked to the study window. Air outside still smelled of rain. Breezes flew over the grass like shadows or grandfather spirits—so I imagined—in search of their graves. Clearly, I remember the night sky as applegreen, the chirring of grasshoppers in a crazy sort of chorus. Abruptly, Jonathan Polkinghorne brought out:

"You haven't been smoking rabbit tobacco again, have you, Andrew?"

"No, sir."

His eyebrows drew inward.

"Touch your thumb to your nose."

I did so.

"Now say, 'The rain in Spain falls mainly on the plain.'"

I assured him I was sober.

"Then, Andrew," he said, "you will understand that you are too young for these freedom papers. All our bondsmen will be released after Anna and I close our eyes. This is in our will. You haven't long, I suppose, to wait." His face was pale and strained and vague—Jonathan rather hated all discussions of death, especially his own. Moving toward the door, his shoe knocked a chair, and he swore irritably. Massaging his toe, he turned to ask, "Is there anything else?"

"Sir," I said, struggling, the reflections of the balls of my eyes so utterly without depth in the window that even I could not tell what I was thinking. "Long ago, you would not have me, and you turned me out to the quarters, then over to a teacher...."

"Ezekiel Sykes-Withers." He drew his mouth down. "That was a mistake. The man was crazy as a mouse in a milkcan. Should've been a monk. He was hired to teach you useful *skills*, Andrew—things like book-keeping, and market research, and furniture repair, and what have we to show for his time here?"

"He taught me to read," I said.

"Well, that's some consolation."

"He taught me to control my heart and, when I walk, leave no footprints."

"Are these what they call *metaphors*, Andrew?" As always when facing figurative language, my Master was a little flummoxed. "I think I'm a pretty clear-witted man," he said, "but this outdoes me, Andrew." It's only about once in a lifetime that you stumble upon a first-rate philosophical metaphor, and when you do, people are bound to say, "Huh?" and take all the starch out of it. "You got out of bed to tell me all this?" He scratched his head. "Manumission and marriage?"

"Yes, sir."

"And what shall you do if I sign these papers?"

"Work for myself," I said, too loudly. "Within a year I'll be back to buy Minty, then George and Mattie from you." Our eyes met—mine squinted, small as sewing needles, like a murderer's; my Master's cold and critical, the eyes of an eagle, infinitely wise.

Softly, the clock in the corner chimed twice.

"I see."

He did not, I knew, see it at all.

"Then I tell you what, you *will* have an opportunity to work for yourself—or at least work this foolishness out of your system." He went to his bureau, taking out paper, ink, and a quill, but his jaw was set—that meant something. "However, as I say, I will sign no freedom papers until you return, as promised, with the money for the others."

"You will have it," I said. "Every penny."

Glasses clamped on his nose, he wrote quietly while I paced, and in a cramped, arthritic script that made his letter resemble a cross between cuneiform, Arabic, and Morse code. When he finished this tortured message, he folded the paper, and pressed it into my hand.

"This letter will see that you get work with one of my old acquaintances in Abbeville. We have not corresponded in years, but I believe she will put you to work." He said this woman—Flo Hatfield—would see to all my needs (he didn't say what needs), and would keep me busy (he didn't say how). Standing, he rumpled my hair, which I hated, and said, "Now go and tell George and Mattie where you're off to."

I started to hug him, then thought better of it, and ran down the hallway, though I had no reason, and leaped from the porch. The beauty of the night made me shout a cry that set sleeping dogs to barking and hummed for minutes afterwards in my ears. A fine rain fell. I sang out, now to trees that nodded respectfully in return, now to invisible blackbirds that called back from the bushes. Then I hurried on through foamy mud to the quarters, the letter tucked inside my shirt, sank slowly to sleep, and, dreaming, saw myself counting coins at the end of the week.

But first I had to work for Flo Hatfield.

50

From *The Darker Face of the Earth*

Rita Dove

Rita Dove (b. 1952) has achieved early and lasting critical acclaim for her poetry. She was born in Ohio and earned a B.A. from Miami University (Ohio) and an M.F.A. from the University of Iowa Writers' Workshop. Her first poetry collection, *The Yellow House on the Corner* (1980), was followed by several smaller poetry compilations, which were all well received. Throughout the late 1970s and 1980s she won many awards, including fellowships from the Guggenheim Foundation, the National Endowment for the Arts, and the National Endowment for the Humanities. Her 1986 collection, *Thomas and Beulah*, a poetic retelling of her family history, earned Dove the Pulitzer Prize in poetry; she was only the second African American (after Gwendolyn Brooks) to receive the honor. In 1993 Dove became the first African American to be named poet laureate of the United States. Though she is primarily known as a poet, Dove has also produced work in other genres, such as her 1992 novel *Through the Ivory Gate* and her play *The Darker Face of the Earth*, excerpted here from the 2000 revised edition. Originally published in 1994, the play was first performed at the Oregon Shakespeare Festival in 1996. Dove's poetry collection *On the Bus with Rosa Parks* was published in 1999.

CAST

Female slaves:

PHEBE

PSYCHE, in her mid-teens

SCYLLA, pronounced "Skilla"

TICEY, a house slave

DIANA, a young girl about 12 years old

SLAVE WOMAN/NARRATOR

Male slaves:

HECTOR, an African

ALEXANDER

SCIPIO, pronounced "Sippio"

AUGUSTUS NEWCASTLE, a mulatto

The whites:

AMALIA JENNINGS LAFARGE

LOUIS LAFARGE, Amalia's husband

DOCTOR, in his fifties
JONES, the overseer, in his thirties

The black conspirators:
LEADER
BENJAMIN SKEENE
HENRY BLAKE

Other slaves and conspirators

TIME
Prologue: about 1820.
Acts I and II: Twenty years later.

PLACE
The action takes place in antebellum South Carolina,
on the Jennings Plantation and in its environs.

The characters of Psyche and Diana, as well as the Doctor and Jones, can be played by the same actors, as long as it is made clear to the audience that they are different people.

On occasion, the slaves comment upon the play somewhat in the manner of a Greek chorus. Individual characters are bound by time and circumstance; the chorus of slaves is more detached and omnipresent. By moving and speaking in a ritualized manner, they provide vocal and percussive counterpoint to the action. The slave woman who occasionally steps forward as the narrator, is quietly present in all slave scenes.

ACT ONE
Scene 5

The cotton fields. The light brightens: high noon. JONES *enters, looks at the sun and cracks his whip as he calls out.*

JONES. Noon!
     (*He exits, wiping his brow with a huge handkerchief. The* SLAVES *groan and*
        sigh as they settle down with their provisions—cornpone and salt pork
        and gourds of water.)
ALEXANDER. (*Making sure that* JONES *is out of earshot.*)
     I swear on all my years
     there's nothing I hate so much as cotton.
     Picking, toting, weighing, tramping:
     the work keeps coming.
SCIPIO. No end in sight, and that's the truth!
     (*Leans back, hands under head.*)
     Now what I'd fancy is a life at sea.
     Sun and sky and blue water,

> with just a sip of rum
> every once in a while.
> You been to sea, Augustus.
> What's it like?

AUGUSTUS. It ain't the easy life.

  SCIPIO. But what's it like, man?
> The closest I been to the sea
> was when the cotton gin came in
> to Charleston port. All those fine
> flapping sails and tall masts,
> cotton bales stacked to heaven …
> Did you visit lots of strange places?

AUGUSTUS. We sailed the West Indies route.
> Stocked up rum, tobacco, beads—

  SCYLLA. (*Scathingly.*)
> —and traded them for slaves.
> Did you have to ride cargo?

AUGUSTUS. (*With a sharp look, sarcastically.*)
> Cap'n Newcastle was a generous master.
> (*Resuming his story.*)
> But those ports! Sand so white,
> from far off it looked like
> spilled cream. Palm trees taller
> than our masts, loaded with coconuts.

  DIANA. What's a coconut?

AUGUSTUS. It's a big brown gourd
> with hair on it like a dog,
> and when you break it open
> sweet milk pours out.

  DIANA. What does it taste like?

AUGUSTUS. It tastes like …
> just coconut. There's nothing like it.

  SCYLLA. Your stories stir up trouble,
> young man.
> (PHEBE *moves as if to stop him; he motions her back.*)

AUGUSTUS. Seems you're the only one
> who's riled up, Scylla.

  SCYLLA. You're what we call an uppity nigger.
> And uppity niggers always trip themselves up.

AUGUSTUS. Are you going to put a curse on me, too,
> Scylla? Cross your eyes
> and wave a few roots in the air
> until I fall on my knees?

  SCYLLA. No need to curse you;
> you have been cursed already.

AUGUSTUS. You feed on ignorance
  and call it magic. What kind of prophet
  works against her own people?
  (*The* SLAVES *murmur.* SCYLLA *stands up.*)
SCYLLA. Oh, you may dance now,
  but you will fall.
  The evil inside you
  will cut you down to your knees,
  and you will crawl—crawl in front of us all!
  (*Lights dim, then grow mottled and swamp-green as all exit.*)

Scene 6

The swamp. Lights remain mottled and swamp-green. Night sounds filter in as HECTOR *enters.*

HECTOR. Easy, easy: don't tell the cook
  the meat's gone bad.
  (*Slashes at the underbrush.*)
  We got to cut it out.
  Ya! Ya!
  (*Hacks in rhythm for a moment.*)
  I can smell it. Pah!
  (*Sniffs, then peers.*)
  But there's a rose in the gravy, oh yes—
  a rose shining through the mists, a red smell.
  Red and mean.
  But how sweet she smelled!
  Cottons and flowers.
  And lemons that bite back
  when you touch them to the tongue.
  Shh! Don't tell the cook.
  Black folks fiddle, the white folks stare.
  (*There is a bird call;* HECTOR *conceals himself.* AUGUSTUS *enters; he ap-
    pears to be following the sound. He gives out a matching call, then
    bursts into a clearing in the swamp where a group of black men sit in a
    circle around a small fire, chanting softly. The* LEADER *of the group
    rises.*)
LEADER. There you are!
  We've called two nights.
AUGUSTUS. Who are you?
LEADER. Patience, Augustus Newcastle.
  Oh yes, we know all about you.
AUGUSTUS. What do you want?
LEADER. Your courage has been a beacon—

CONSPIRATORS. Amen! Selah!

> (*The* CONSPIRATORS *surround the* LEADER; *they react to his words in a call-and-response fashion; their movements are vaguely ritualistic and creepy, as if they were under a spell; this effect can be enhanced with dance and pantomime.* AUGUSTUS *stands still as the* CONSPIRATORS *swarm around him, occasionally trying to pull him among them.*)

LEADER.   —and we need men willing to fight
> for freedom! Tell me, Augustus Newcastle:
> are you prepared to sign your name
> with the revolutionary forces?

AUGUSTUS.   First tell me who you are.

LEADER.   So cautious? We expected a bit more daring
> from someone of your reputation.

AUGUSTUS.   I am many things, but I'm not a fool.

LEADER.   (*Laughs.*)
> Shall we show him, brothers?

CONSPIRATORS.   Selah!

LEADER.   Each of us has been called forth
> as a warrior of righteousness.
> Each wandered in darkness
> until he found the light of brotherhood!
> Take young Benjamin Skeene:
> (BENJAMIN *squares his shoulders as he steps forward; he is a trim young man who, judging from his clothes, must be either a house slave or a freeman.*)
> As a skilled carpenter, he enjoys
> a fair amount of freedom.

BENJAMIN.   The boss man's glad
> I can make his deliveries.

LEADER.   So we've arranged a few
> deposits of our own.
> Benjamin, can you find a way
> to fasten this blade to a pole?

BENJAMIN.   Easy.

LEADER.   Every man who can wield a stick
> shall have a bayonet!

CONSPIRATORS.   Selah!

LEADER.   A few were more reluctant …
> or shall I say cautious?
> Henry Blake, for instance:
> (HENRY, *a dark, middle-aged man, steps forward hesitantly.*)
> Fear had made him grateful
> for every crumb his master dropped him.
> (*The two act out the following exchange.*)

HENRY.   I don't want no part of this!

LEADER. You followed the sign;
    you have been called!

HENRY. Any fool knows a mockingbird
    when he hears one—and that
    weren't no mockingbird!

LEADER. (*Threatening.*)
    Are you prepared to slay
    our oppressors, male and female,
    when it is deemed time, according
    to the plans of insurrection drawn up
    and approved by members present?

HENRY. I'm against the white man
    much as all of you—but murder?
    "Thou shalt not kill," saith the
    Commandments.

LEADER. Who made your master?

HENRY. God.

LEADER. And who made you?

HENRY. God.

LEADER. Then aren't you as good as your master
    if God made you both?

HENRY. I'm not a vengeful man.

LEADER. But our Lord is a vengeful God.
    "Whoever steals a man," He says,
    "whether he sells him or
    is found in possession of him,
    shall be put to death."
    Who is not with us
    is against us.
    You answered the call.
    If you turn back now …
    (HENRY *slowly lifts his head, squares his shoulders, and remains frozen in*
        the spotlight while the LEADER *speaks to* AUGUSTUS.)

LEADER. He was brought to reason.

CONSPIRATORS. Selah.

LEADER. So the one becomes many
    and the many, one.
    Hence our password:
    "May Fate be with you—

CONSPIRATORS. And with us all!"

AUGUSTUS. Now I see who you are.

LEADER. Augustus Newcastle: are you prepared
    to slay our oppressors,
    male and female,
    when it is deemed time, according

to the plans of insurrection
drawn up and approved by members present?

AUGUSTUS. I am.

LEADER. Enter your name in the Book of Redemption!
(AUGUSTUS *signs the book.*)

CONSPIRATORS. Selah! Selah!

AUGUSTUS. Tell me what to do.

LEADER. You'll need a second-in-command.
Report your choice to us;
we will send out the sign.
(*Turning to the group.*)
My brothers, it is time to be free!
Maps are being prepared
of the city and its surroundings
along with the chief points of attack.
Bullets wait in kegs under the dock.
Destiny calls!

CONSPIRATORS. Amen!

LEADER. There are barrels of gun powder
stacked in a cave outside Dawson's Plantation.
Our Toby has been busy—
(CONSPIRATORS *nod and laugh in consent.*)
but he cannot risk further expeditions.
Henry Blake!
(HENRY *steps forward.*)
Your owner praised you in the marketplace
as the most trustworthy nigger
he ever had the fortune of owning.
Now it is up to you
to put your master's trust to the test.
(HENRY *bows his head in assent, steps back into the group.*)
Destiny calls us! The reckoning is nigh!
But remember: trust no-one.
All those who are not with us
are against us, blacks as well
as whites. Oh, do not falter!
Bolster your heart with the memory
of the atrocities committed upon your mothers.
Gird your loins with vengeance,
strap on the shining sword of freedom!

CONSPIRATORS. Selah!

LEADER. Brothers, are you with me?

CONSPIRATORS. Right behind you!

LEADER. Then nothing can stop us now!

AUGUSTUS. (*Blurting out.*)
> My orders! What are my orders?

LEADER. (*A little taken aback, but decides on the role of the amused patriarch.*)
> Patience, my son! Patience and cunning.
> Sow discontent among your brethren,
> inspire them to fury.

AUGUSTUS. I can do more. Read maps, write passes—

LEADER. That is all for now.
> Is that clear?
> (*Strained silence; the* LEADER *speaks reassuringly.*)
> You will recognize the signal.
> (*The* CONSPIRATORS *begin humming "Steal Away".*)

LEADER. Go to your people and test their minds;
> so when the fires of redemption
> lick the skies of Charleston,
> they will rise up, up—
> a mighty army
> marching into battle!

CONSPIRATORS. Steal away, steal away,
> Steal away to Jesus!
> Steal away, steal away home,
> I ain't got long to stay here.
> (*The* CONSPIRATORS *continue singing as they exchange farewells and slip off.* HECTOR *appears at the edge of the undergrowth, a dead snake in his outstretched arms.*)

> *Blackout.*

Scene 7
The cotton fields.

NARRATOR. A sniff of freedom's all it takes
> to feel history's sting;
> there's danger by-and-by
> when the slaves won't sing.
> (JONES *supervises the picking, which transpires without singing; the silence is eerie.* JONES' *appearance is slovenly, as if he's already been drinking.*)

JONES. Move it, nigger! Faster!
> What you glaring at? Faster!
> (*The* SLAVES *continue picking at the same rate.* JONES *looks at the sun, then cracks his whip.*)
> Aw, the hell with ya! Noon!
> (*He stumbles offstage. The* SLAVES *divide into two groups: some hum spirituals while the others gather around* AUGUSTUS.)

SCIPIO. Come on, Augustus, what else?
AUGUSTUS. Did you know there are slaves
    who have set themselves free?
SCIPIO. (*Almost afraid to ask.*)
    How'd they do that?
AUGUSTUS. Santo Domingo, San Domingue, Hispaniola—
    three names for an island
    rising like a fortress
    from the waters of the Caribbean.
    An island of sun and forest,
    wild fruit and mosquitoes—
    and slaves, many slaves—half a million.
    Slaves to chop sugar, slaves
    to pick coffee beans, slaves to do
    their French masters' every bidding.

    Then one summer, news came
    from the old country: Revolution!
    Plantation owners broke into a sweat;
    their slaves served cool drinks
    while the masters rocked on their verandas,
    discussing each outrage:
    people marching against the king,
    crowds pouring into the streets,
    shouting three words:
    Liberté!
SLAVES. We shall be free!
AUGUSTUS. *Égalité*!
SLAVES. Master and slave.
AUGUSTUS. *Fraternité*!
SLAVES. Brothers and sisters!
AUGUSTUS. *Liberté, Égalité, Fraternité*—three words
    were all the island masters talked about
    that summer, while their slaves
    served carefully and listened.
SLAVES. *Liberté, Égalité, Fraternité*!
    (*During the following speech, a smouldering growl among the* SLAVES *grows
      louder and louder, until it explodes in a shout.*)
AUGUSTUS. Black men meeting in the forest:
    Eight days, they whispered,
    and we'll be free. For eight days
    bonfires flashed in the hills:
    Equality. For eight days
    tom-toms spoke in the mountains:
    Liberty. For eight days

the tom-toms sang: Brothers and sisters.
And on the eighth day, swift as lightning,
the slaves attacked.

SLAVES. Yah!

(AMALIA *enters, unseen, and stands listening.*)

AUGUSTUS. They came down the mountains
to the sound of tambourines and conch shells.
With torches they swept onto the plantations,
with the long harvest knives
they chopped white men down
like sugar cane. For three weeks
the flames raged; then the sun
broke through the smoke and shone
upon a new nation, a black nation—
Haiti!

SLAVES. Haiti!

AUGUSTUS. (*Looking intently at the faces around him.*)
Now do you see
why they've kept this from us,
brothers and sisters?

AMALIA. A lovely speech.

(*The* SLAVES *are horrified.* AUGUSTUS *stands impassive.*)

I see you're a poet
as well as a rebel.

(JONES *rushes in.*)

JONES. Anything wrong, Miss Jennings?

AMALIA. Not a thing, Jones. Just passing
the time of day with my happy flock—
which is more than I see you doing.

JONES. But it's noon, Miss Jennings!
They need nourishment
if we're going to get this crop in.

AMALIA. It appears they've been getting
a different sort of sustenance.

JONES. (*Uncomprehending.*)
Beg pardon, Ma'am?

AMALIA. (*Impatient with* JONES.)
See that they work an extra hour tonight.
I don't care if they have to pick by moonlight!

(*To* AUGUSTUS.)

As for you: I'll see you
up at the house. Come at sunset—
the view over the fields
is most enchanting then.

(*She strides off. Blackout.*)

Scene 8

The big house, Louis' *study and the parlor.*

Twilight filters through the curtains; the frogs have started up in the swamp.

Louis *paces back and forth in his room, holding a chart; he stops to stare at it for a moment, then waves it in disgust and paces once more.*

Louis. Something's out there: I can feel it!
What a discovery it would be.
But no—
(*Grabs his brandy.*)
No new coin shines
for Louis LaFarge
among the stars!
(*He stops at the window and stares out.*)
(Amalia *sits in the parlor reading, a decanter of sherry and a tea service on
the table next to the sofa. The evening song of the* Slaves *floats in from
the fields—a plaintive air with a compelling affirmation of life, a
strange melody with no distinct beat or tune.* Ticey, *the old house slave,
enters.*)
Ticey. Miss Amalia?
Amalia. (*Without turning.*)
Yes?
Ticey. That new slave, Ma'am—
he's standing at the front porch!
Amalia. (*Amused.*)
The front porch? Well, show him in, Ticey!
(Ticey *exits;* Amalia *rises and goes to the window. She is looking out to-
ward the fields when* Augustus *appears in the doorway. Although she
knows he is there, she does not turn around.*)
Amalia. What are they singing?
Augustus. No words you'd understand.
No tune you'd recognise.
Amalia. And how is it they all sing together?
Augustus. It's the sorrow songs.
They don't need a psalm book.
Amalia. (*Resumes her imperious manner.*)
"Personal servant to Captain Newcastle
of the schooner *Victoria*. Ports of call:
St Thomas, Tobago, St Croix,
Martinique"—in other words,
a slave ship.
Augustus. Yes.

AMALIA. And what did you learn
    under your captain's tutelage?

AUGUSTUS. Reading. Writing. Figures.

AMALIA. What did you read?

AUGUSTUS. Milton. The Bible.
    And the Tales of the Greeks.

AMALIA. (*Thrusting the book she's been reading at him.*)
    See the blue ribbon sticking out?
    You may start there.
    (AUGUSTUS *turns the book over to read the title, then looks at her for a mo-*
        ment before returning it. She snatches the book.)

AMALIA. Too difficult? No doubt you'd do better
    with the Greek original—
    (*Slyly.*)
    but we are not that cultured a household.
    (*Circling him.*)
    I wondered could there be a nigger alive
    smart as this one's claimed to be?
    Of course, if there were, he might
    be smart enough to pretend
    he wasn't smart at all.

AUGUSTUS. No pretense. I've read that one already.
    In my opinion, the Greeks
    were a bit too predictable.

AMALIA. A slave has no opinion!
    (*Regaining her composure.*)
    I could have you flogged to your bones
    for what you did today.

AUGUSTUS. Why didn't you?
    (*The* SLAVES *stop singing.*)

AMALIA. Daddy said a master knows his slaves
    better than they know themselves.
    And he never flogged a slave—
    he said it was a poor businessman
    who damaged his own merchandise.

AUGUSTUS. (*Sarcastically.*)
    An enlightened man, your father.

AMALIA. He let me run wild until
    it was time to put on crinolines.
    My playmates were sent to the fields,
    and I was sent to the parlor with needlework—
    a scented, dutiful daughter.

AUGUSTUS. Most men find intelligence troubling
    in a woman—even fathers.

AMALIA. Then, off I went to finishing school: Miss Peeters'

Academy for Elocution and Deportment!
"The art of conversation," she used to say—
please, sit down!—"is to make
the passing of time agreeable."
(*Arranging her dress as she sits on the sofa.*)
"suitable subjects are—"
Sit down, I said!
(*Softer, but with an edge.*)
One does not conduct conversation
while standing.
(*She indicates a chair, upholstered in champagne-colored tufted damask.*
 AUGUSTUS *moves toward it but swiftly and gracefully drops cross-*
 legged to the floor, daringly close to AMALIA*'s slippered feet. She starts*
 to pull away—then slowly extends her feet again.)
"Suitable subjects for
genteel conversation are:"
(*Ticking them off on her fingers.*)
"Nature. Travel. History.
And above all, culture—
painting, music, and books."
We'll, we're done with books!
Tell me, Mr Newcastle—
was the weather in the Indies
very different from here?

AUGUSTUS. Warmer.

AMALIA. Is that all?

AUGUSTUS. There was always a breeze.

AMALIA. And an abundance of exotic
foods, I'm sure.

AUGUSTUS. We had our share of papaya.
(*The* SLAVES *start up a new song, more African in rhythm and harmonies.*)

AMALIA. Imagine that. Subject number two:
Travel. So many ports!
(*Shaking her head charmingly.*)
Did Captain Newcastle
allow you to go ashore
at St Thomas, Tobago, Martinique?

AUGUSTUS. (*On guard.*)
No.

AMALIA. Charleston has welcomed a fair share
of immigrants to her shores.
(*Laughs delicately.*)
There was that Haiti business around the time
I was born. Over five hundred French plantation owners
fled here. The whole city was in panic.

Why, my dear husband—hear him pacing
up there, wearing out the floorboards?—
little Louis showed up in Charleston harbor
that year, with his blue blood *maman* and *papa*.
Liberté, Égalité, Fraternité!
(*Looking directly at* AUGUSTUS.)
It was a brilliant revolution.
I've often wondered why our niggers
don't revolt. I've said to myself:
"Amalia, if you had been a slave,
you most certainly would have plotted
an insurrection by now."
(*Turns away from* AUGUSTUS.)
But we say all sorts of things
to ourselves, don't we?
There's no telling what we'd do
if the moment were there for the taking.
(*Lights up on* LOUIS, *still staring out the window.*)

LOUIS. You can't hide forever.
There's a hole in the heavens,
and you're throbbing right behind it.
(*Whispers.*)
I can feel you.

AMALIA. Have you ever heard of the *Amistad*?

AUGUSTUS. Why?

AMALIA. The *Amistad*: a slave ship.
Three days off the port of Principe
the Africans freed themselves
and attacked with machetes and harpoons.
Cinque, their leader, spared two sailors
to steer them back to Africa.
But Cinque was unfamiliar with the stars
in our hemisphere. Each morning
he set course east by the sun;
each night the sailors turned the ship
and steered west—until they managed
to land on our coast and deliver
Cinque and his followers to execution.

AUGUSTUS. A bit of a storybook ending, isn't it?

AMALIA. What's that supposed to mean?

AUGUSTUS. It's just so perfect a lesson.

AMALIA. You don't believe me?
It was in the newspapers.
(*Significantly.*)
You followed your precious captain

> everywhere; you were there when
> he loaded slave cargo into the hold
> or plotted a new course.
> What an admirable science, navigation!
> It must be terribly complicated,
> even for you.

AUGUSTUS. (*Getting up from the floor.*)
> Now I have a story for you.
> Once there was a preacher slave
> went by the name of Isaac.
> When God called him
> he was a boy, out hunting rice birds.
> Killing rice birds is easy—
> just pinch off their heads.
> (*Indicating the sherry.*)
> May I?
> (AMALIA *flinches, nods. He pours the sherry expertly.*)
> But one day, halfway up the tree
> where a nest of babies chirped,
> a voice called out: "Don't do it, Isaac."
> It was an angel, shining
> in the crook of a branch.
> Massa let him preach.
> What harm could it do?
> (*Sitting down in the damask chair.*)
> Then a slave uprising in Virginia
> had all the white folks
> watching their own niggers
> for signs of treachery.
> No more prayer meetings, Isaac!
> But God would not wait,
> so Isaac kept on preaching
> at night, in the woods.
> Of course he was caught.
> Three of his congregation
> were shot on the spot, three others branded
> and their feet pierced.
> But what to do about Isaac,
> gentle Isaac who had turned traitor?

AMALIA. Is there a point to this?

AUGUSTUS. I'm just passing the time of evening
> with … conversation.
> (*Upstairs,* LOUIS *positions his telescope at the window and searches the heavens.*)

LOUIS. There it is … no, wait!

Gone.
(*Shakes his head in despair.*)
Sometimes I catch
a glimmer, a hot blue flash—
then it disappears.
Show yourself, demon!
(*In the parlor,* AUGUSTUS *takes a sip of sherry and continues.*)

AUGUSTUS. First they flogged him. Then
   they pickled the wounds with salt water,
   and when they were nearly healed,
   he was flogged again, and the wounds
   pickled again, and on and on for weeks
   while Massa sold off Isaac's children
   one by one. They took him to see
   his wife on the auction block,
   baby at her breast.
   A week later it was his turn.
   His back had finally healed;
   but as his new owner led him
   from the auction block,
   Isaac dropped down dead.
   (*Pause; more to himself than to* AMALIA.)
   They couldn't break his spirit,
   so they broke his heart.
   (*They stare at each other for a moment; then* AMALIA *rises and walks to the*
     window. It has gotten dark outside.)

AMALIA. They're still singing.
   How can they have songs left?

AUGUSTUS. (*Joining her at the window.*)
   As many songs as sorrows.

AMALIA. And you, Augustus? Were you ever happy?

AUGUSTUS. Happy? No.

AMALIA. Never? Not even on the ship
   with the whole sea around you?

AUGUSTUS. I was a boy. I felt lucky, not happy.

AMALIA. I was happy once.
   I traded it for luck.

AUGUSTUS. Luck's a dangerous master.

AMALIA. Half my life I spent dreaming,
   the other half burying dreams.
   (*Bitter laugh, turns to* AUGUSTUS.)
   Funny, isn't it?

AUGUSTUS. (*Turns away from her with difficulty, stares out the window.*)
   One soft spring night
   when the pear blossoms

cast their pale faces
on the darker face of the earth,
Massa stood up from the porch swing
and said to himself, "I think
I'll make me another bright-eyed pickaninny."
Then he stretched and headed
for my mother's cabin. And now—
that pickaninny, who started out
no more than the twinkle in a white man's eye
and the shame between his mama's legs—
now he stands in the parlor of
another massa, entertaining the pretty mistress
with stories of whippings and heartbreak.

AMALIA. (*Half to herself.*)
Pretty? Am I pretty?

AUGUSTUS. (*Answers in spite of himself.*)
You can put a rose in a vase
with a bunch of other flowers;
but when you walk into the room
the rose is the only thing you see.
(AMALIA *touches his wrist, then traces the vein up his arm, as if remembering.*)

AMALIA. Imagine! A life without even
a smidgen of happiness …

AUGUSTUS. (*Wrestling with desire.*)
I'm not one of your dreams.

AMALIA. No? Perhaps not. What a pity.
(*She touches his cheek; he holds her hand there. They lean towards each other slowly, as the* SLAVES' *sorrow song surges—but before their lips touch, there is a blackout.*)

ACT TWO

Scene 1

Dream sequence.

*Dimly lit, the light rather blue. Each group is in its appointed "place" on stage—*AMALIA *in her parlour with* TICEY *standing impassively in the background;* LOUIS *above, in his study; most* SLAVES *going about their chores;* SCYLLA *isolated, with her herbs and potions. In the swamp,* HECTOR *searches for snakes; the* CONSPIRATORS *huddle, occasionally lifting a fist into the circle.* AUGUSTUS *stands front and centre, back to the audience, gazing at* AMALIA. *Mostly silhouettes are seen, except when a single voice rises out of the chanting, which will grow to cacophony at the end of the sequence.*

SLAVES. They have bowed our heads,
   they have bent our backs.
   Mercy, mercy,
   Lord above, mercy.
AMALIA. I slept, but my heart was awake.
   How beautiful he is!
SLAVES. Lord have mercy.
   They have bowed our heads …
SCYLLA. There's a curse on the land.
   The net draws closer.
HECTOR. Under rocks, 'twixt reeds and roots …
SLAVES. They have bent our backs,
   they have snatched our songs …
AUGUSTUS. (*Singing.*)
   Sometimes I feel like a motherless child …
SLAVES. (*Joining in.*)
   A motherless child, a motherless child,
   sometimes I feel like a motherless child—
   (*Continue humming through most of the scene.*)
LOUIS. (*In a scientific voice, detached, as if reciting.*)
   Every night at the same hour, each star appears
   slightly to the west of its previous position.
   Scientists calculate that the 12 houses of the zodiac
   have shifted so radically since ancient times,
   their relation to each other
   may now signify completely different portents.
HECTOR. So many, so many.
SLAVES. (*Singing.*)
   A long way from home.
AUGUSTUS. One soft night, Massa stood up—
CONSPIRATORS. Selah.
AUGUSTUS. —and laughed to himself.
CONSPIRATORS. It is time.
SCYLLA. The net draws tighter.
CONSPIRATORS. Selah!
AUGUSTUS. One darkening evening, I stood up—
   (SLAVES *humming,* CONSPIRATORS *chanting "Selah" in a barely audible*
    whisper.)
   —and she was mine,
   mine all night, until
   the day breathed fire
   and the shadows fled.
AMALIA. Look, how beautiful he is!
CONSPIRATORS. Rise up!
SLAVES. (*Simultaneously.*)

                   Mercy, mercy.
AMALIA. His eyes, his brow, his cheeks—
CONSPIRATORS. Rise up!
AMALIA. —his lips …
AUGUSTUS. … until the day breathed fire …
HECTOR. Eshu Elewa … ogo … gbogbo.
SLAVES. They have bowed our heads,
              they have bent our backs.
SCYLLA. Closer …
              (PHEBE *dashes to center-stage, hands out-stretched as if to hold back a*
                  flood.)
PHEBE. Stop it! Stop!!!
              (*Everyone freezes.*) …

                            Scene 8

The big house: AMALIA*'s bedroom,* LOUIS*' study and the hallway.*

Evening: LOUIS *stands at the open window of his study, looking through the telescope, alternately at the night sky and down over the plantation grounds.*

AMALIA *sits on the window seat in her bedroom.* PHEBE *enters.*

PHEBE. You wanted me, Ma'am?
AMALIA. Good evening, Phebe!
              I was sitting at the window,
              catching the last rays of sunlight,
              when I happened to see you
              darting from group to group,
              talking to this slave and that,
              and I said to myself: "Perhaps
              Phebe would like to talk to me, too."
PHEBE. (*On her guard.*)
              I'm pleased to talk conversation
              whenever you like, Miss Amalia.
AMALIA. (*Slightly sarcastic.*)
              It seems you're mighty pleased
              with other people's conversations
              these days.
PHEBE. I don't follow your meaning, Ma'am.
AMALIA. Oh, really? I notice
              you and Augustus have no problem
              following each other's meaning.
PHEBE. Augustus ain't nothing
              but a friend, Ma'am.

I don't recollect talking to him
any more than anyone else.
(*Laughs nervously.*)
Me and my big mouth always be
yakking at somebody or another.

AMALIA. Don't talk yourself
into trouble, Phebe.

PHEBE. Beg pardon, Ma'am.
I didn't mean nothing by it.

AMALIA. Everyone can see
you're making a fool of yourself
over him! Have you spoken
to Augustus today?

PHEBE. I can't rightly say, Ma'am.
(*At a warning look from* AMALIA.)
That is—I talked to a lot of people
and he was amongst them, but
we didn't say more than a how-de-do.

AMALIA. Tell Augustus I want to see him.

PHEBE. (*Thrown into panic.*)
I don't know—I mean—

AMALIA. What's the matter, Phebe?

PHEBE. Nothing, Ma'am.
It might take a while, is all.

AMALIA. (*Sarcastic.*)
And why is that?

PHEBE. It's just—well, Augustus been keeping
to himself lately. I seen him
going off in the direction of the swamp;
he's got some crazy idea
about fixing up Hector's shack.

AMALIA. (*Haunted.*)
Oh.
When he returns, send him up.

PHEBE. Yes, Ma'am.
(PHEBE *exits. In the hallway she runs into* AUGUSTUS. *He is very agitated.*)

PHEBE. (*Whispering.*)
You! Here?

AUGUSTUS. Yes. They sent me back.

PHEBE. I thought for sure they was going to do
something awful to you.

AUGUSTUS. The sun travels its appointed track,
a knot of fire, day in day out—
what could be more awful?

PHEBE. Augustus, what is it?

Can I help?

AUGUSTUS. This job I do alone.

   PHEBE. But surely you can take a minute
            to go in there and smooth
            that she-hawk's feathers down
            so's the rest of us can—
            (AMALIA *steps out and peers into the dim hall.* AUGUSTUS *shrinks into the*
               shadows.)

AMALIA. Is that you, Phebe?

   PHEBE. Yes'm. I was just on my way downstairs.

AMALIA. I heard voices.

   PHEBE. That was me, Ma'am.
            I twisted my foot in the dark—
            guess I was talking to it.
            (*Laughs nervously.*)
            My mama used to say it helps
            to talk the hurt out.

AMALIA. Well, do your talking
            elsewhere. Go on!
            (PHEBE *hesitates, then exits.* AMALIA *stands looking into the darkness for a*
               moment, then goes back into her room. AUGUSTUS *steps out of hiding,*
               holding a knife. The CONSPIRATORS *can be heard in the background.*)

LEADER. Prove you haven't betrayed the cause!

BENJAMIN. Kill them both—

   HENRY. —your mistress
            and her foolish husband.

AUGUSTUS. That's fate for you, Amalia.
            (*Looks at the knife.*)
            That white throat, bared for kisses ...
            one quick pass, and it will flow
            redder than a thousand roses.
            Everything was so simple before!
            Hate and be hated.
            But this—love or freedom—
            is the devil's choice.
            (*Steeling himself, he heads for* LOUIS' *room. Lights up on* LOUIS, *who is sit-*
               ting with his right hand tucked nervously in the lap of his dressing
               gown. His back is to AUGUSTUS, *who enters stealthily.*)

   LOUIS. (*Startling* AUGUSTUS, *who stops in his tracks.*)
            No-one has come through that door
            for years. You're the new one, aren't you?
            (*Unseen by* AUGUSTUS, *he pulls a pistol out of his lap.*)
            A wild nigger, I hear. Amalia's latest indulgence.

AUGUSTUS. So this is the great white master,
            trembling in his dressing gown!

LOUIS. Beware of the Moon in the house of Mars!
> (*Stands up and turns, hiding the pistol as he and* AUGUSTUS *face off.*)
> The stars can tell you everything—
> war and pestilence, love and betrayal.

AUGUSTUS. War? Yes, this is war. Say your prayers,
> Massa—you have a hard ride ahead of you.

LOUIS. A hard ride, me? I don't think so.
> (*Aims his pistol at* AUGUSTUS.)
> A man should be able to kill
> when he has to, don't you agree?
> (*Startled by this unexpected turn of events,* AUGUSTUS *freezes.* LOUIS
>   *reaches for the bottle on the table with his other hand.*)
> Perhaps you'd care for a bit of bourbon
> to warm your way?

AUGUSTUS. (*Trying to compose himself.*)
> You can't stop what's coming
> over the hill.

LOUIS. (*Shakes his pistol at* AUGUSTUS, *shouting.*)
> This time I won't leave things up to chance!
> (*Muttering.*)
> What a fool I was!
> I should have smothered the bastard
> right there in the basket.
> That's the man's way.

AUGUSTUS. Basket? What basket?

LOUIS. Amalia's of course. Amalia's basket.
> It was—
> (*Slight pause; distracted.*)
> The doctor refused to kill it.
> What else was there to do?
> (AUGUSTUS *lunges, knocking the gun from* LOUIS' *hand and overpowering*
>   *him.*)

AUGUSTUS. There goes your last chance, fool!
> (*Drags* LOUIS *by the collar toward center-stage.*)
> This basket—what did it look like?

LOUIS. What do you care?

AUGUSTUS. (*Holds the knife to* LOUIS' *throat.*)
> Enough to slit your throat.

LOUIS. (*Whimpering.*)
> Oh, it was beautiful! White wicker,
> lined in blue satin, tiny red rosettes
> marching along the rim …

AUGUSTUS. (*Slowly lets go of* LOUIS' *collar.*)
> And your spurs slipped right inside.

LOUIS. Amalia's Christmas present.

Oh, was the good doctor relieved!
"It's a miracle," he said,
"but the child's still alive!"

AUGUSTUS. And still lives to this day.
Spurs bite into a horse's belly—
think what they can do
to a newborn child!
(*Rips open his shirt.*)

LOUIS. You?

AUGUSTUS. All my life I tried to imagine
what you would look like.
Would you be tall or stooped over?
Blue eyes, or brown?
Would you dress in white linen
or dash around in a dusty greatcoat?
to think that your blood flows
through my veins—
(*Advances on* LOUIS, *who staggers back into the chair.*)

LOUIS. My blood?

AUGUSTUS. When I think of you forcing
your wretched seed into my mother,
I want to rip you—

LOUIS. Me, your father?
You think I'm your father?

AUGUSTUS. I heard it from your own lips.

LOUIS. (*Bursts into laughter.*)
Of course! Of course!
The stars said it all:
who is born into violence
shall live to fulfill it.
Who shuns violence
will die by the sword.

AUGUSTUS. (*Pulls* LOUIS *from the chair, knife at his throat.*)
What happened to my mother?
What did you do to her?

LOUIS. (*In a crafty voice.*)
I haven't touched her since.
Ask Amalia—
she runs this plantation.
She knows your mother better than anyone!

AUGUSTUS. Amalia? Of course!
Missy wanted the bastard child dead.
Now I understand: It's an old story.

LOUIS. You understand nothing.
(*A sudden shout outside; the revolt has begun. Both men freeze, listening.*)

AUGUSTUS. It's time!
> (*Stabs* LOUIS *as the sounds of the revolt grow.*)

LOUIS. You were there … all along …

AUGUSTUS. (*Letting* LOUIS' *body drop.*)
> So, Amalia—and to think
> I tried to bargain for your life!

SLAVES. Freedom! Freedom! Selah! Selah!
> (AUGUSTUS *heads for* AMALIA's *room; lights come up on* AMALIA, *who*
> *has stepped into the hall.*)

AMALIA. Augustus, there you are! What's happening?
> I called Ticey, but she won't come!

AUGUSTUS. (*Backing her into the room.*)
> I thought you didn't care
> what happened out there.

AMALIA. Why are they shouting?
> Why doesn't Jones make them stop?

AUGUSTUS. I reckon the dead don't make good overseers.
> Your slaves are rebelling, Missy.
> *Liberté, Égalité, Fraternité!*

AMALIA. (*Stares at him uncomprehendingly, then runs to the window.*)
> Rebelling? My slaves?
> Augustus, make them stop!
> They'll listen to you!

AUGUSTUS. Like I listened to you?
> You led me into your parlour
> like a dog on a leash. Sit, dog!
> Heel! Care for a sherry? A fairy tale?

AMALIA. No, you were different!
> You were—

AUGUSTUS. (*Grabs her.*)
> No more conversation!
> Where is my mother?

AMALIA. Your mother? How would I know a thing like that?

AUGUSTUS. Your husband confessed.

AMALIA. (*Aware of danger on all sides, seeking escape.*)
> What could Louis have to confess?

AUGUSTUS. A shrewd piece of planning,
> to destroy him with his own son
> after you had failed to destroy
> the son himself!
> But you had to be patient.
> Twenty years you had to wait
> before you could buy me back.

AMALIA. Louis, your father? You must be joking!

AUGUSTUS. Shall I help you remember?

You supplied the basket yourself—

AMALIA. Basket?

AUGUSTUS. —lined in blue satin, trimmed with rosettes—

AMALIA. *Red* rosettes?

AUGUSTUS. Monsieur LaFarge agreed
        to sell his own baby—but that wasn't enough,
        was it? You wanted the child dead.
        So you slipped a pair of riding spurs
        into the sewing basket.
        And you know the kind of scars
        spurs leave, Missy. Like crowns …
        or exploding suns.

AMALIA. My God.

AUGUSTUS. The woman who patched me up
        kept that basket as a reminder.

AMALIA. No …

AUGUSTUS. (*Shakes her.*)
        What did you do with my mother?
        Who is she?
        (*Slaps her.*)
        Tell me!

AMALIA. (*Wrenches free to face him; her voice trembling.*)
        So you want to know who your mother is?
        You think, if I tell you,
        the sad tale of your life
        will find its storybook ending?
        Well then, this will be my last story—
        and when I have finished,
        you will wish you had never
        stroked my hair or kissed my mouth.
        You will wish you had no eyes to see
        or ears to hear. You will wish
        you had never been born.

AUGUSTUS. I've heard grown men scream,
        watched as the branding iron
        sank into their flesh. I've seen
        pregnant women slit open like melon,
        runaways staked to the ground
        and whipped until
        they floated in their own blood and piss.
        Don't think you can frighten me, Missy:
        Nothing your lips can tell
        can be worse than what
        these eyes have seen.

AMALIA. Bravo! What a speech!

But you've seen nothing.
(*Backs up to appraise him, smiling, slightly delirious.*)
That same expression! How could I forget?
My lover then stood as tall as you now.

AUGUSTUS. Your lover?
(PHEBE *bursts in.*)

PHEBE. They're coming, Augustus!
They're coming to see if you did
what you were told! Oh, Augustus—
you were supposed to kill her!

AUGUSTUS. (*Shaking himself into action, threatening* AMALIA.)
My mother, who is my mother?
Out with it!

AMALIA. Phebe, you tell him.
You were there.
Everyone was there—
under my window,
waiting for news …

PHEBE. That … was the night
we all came to wait out the birth.

AUGUSTUS. What birth?

AMALIA. Hector on the porch.

AUGUSTUS. What about Hector?
(*More shouts outside; compelled by the urgency of the growing revolution,*
PHEBE *tries to distract* AUGUSTUS.)

PHEBE. There's no time!

AUGUSTUS. (*Grabs* AMALIA *as if to slit her throat.*)
What about Hector?

AMALIA. Chick in a basket, going to market!
They said you died, poor thing.
That's why Hector went to the swamp.
(AUGUSTUS *stares desperately at her.* PHEBE *turns, thunderstruck.*)

AUGUSTUS. Hector?

AMALIA. But you didn't die. You're here …
(*Reaches for him; he draws back.*)

PHEBE. (*Looks from* AMALIA *to* AUGUSTUS, *horror growing, recites tonelessly.*)
Stepped on a pin, the pin bent,
and that's the way the story went.

AMALIA. (*Sadly, in a small voice.*)
Silk for my prince, and a canopy of roses!
You were so tiny—so sweet and tiny.
I didn't know about the spurs.

PHEBE. You sold your own child.
Hector's child.

AUGUSTUS. Hector …

(*The knife slips from his fingers.*)

AMALIA. I was trying to save you!

AUGUSTUS. Save me?

AMALIA. (*Extremely agitated.*)
I felt like they had hacked out my heart.
But I wouldn't let them see me cry.

AUGUSTUS. (*Wrestling with the horror.*)
You? My mother?

AMALIA. (*Clutching herself.*)
It was like missing an arm or a leg
that pains and throbs, even though
you can look right where it was
and see there's nothing left.
(*She stops abruptly.*)

AUGUSTUS. My own mother gave me away.
But I found my way back ...
a worm crawling into its hole.

AMALIA. For weeks afterwards
my breasts ached with milk.

AUGUSTUS. (*Sinking to his knees.*)
Better I had bled to death in that basket.
(*A great shout goes up as the insurrectionists gain entry to the main house.* AMALIA *takes advantage of the ensuing distraction to pick up the knife.*)

PHEBE. Augustus!

AUGUSTUS. (*Passive.*)
The Day of Redemption is here.

PHEBE. They'll kill you, Augustus!

AUGUSTUS. Time to be free.

AMALIA. Poor baby! I thought
I could keep you from harm—
and here you are,
right in harm's way.
(PHEBE *gasps;* AMALIA *stabs herself as* AUGUSTUS, *alerted by* PHEBE'S *gasp, jumps up, too late to stop her. The room turns red as the out-buildings go up in flames.*)

AUGUSTUS. Amalia!
(*Catching her as she falls.*)
No ...
(*Calling out in anguish.*)
Eshu Elewa ogo gbogbo!
(*The chanting of the rebelling* SLAVES *grows louder.*)

PHEBE. Oh, Augustus ...

AUGUSTUS. (*Lays* AMALIA'S *body down, gently.*)
I had the sun and the moon

once. And the stars
with their cool gaze.
Now it's dark.

PHEBE. It's alright. You'll be alright now.

AUGUSTUS. (*Staring as if trying to make out something in the distance.*)
Who's there? How she stares,
like a cat at midnight!

PHEBE. Nobody's there, Augustus.

AUGUSTUS. Don't you see her?
(PHEBE *shakes her head, terrified.*)
Look, she's hidden behind a tree.

PHEBE. Oh, Augus—

AUGUSTUS. Shh! You'll frighten her. There's another one—
he's been flogged and pickled in brine.
That skinny boy ate dirt; that's why he staggers.
So many of them, limping, with brands
on their cheeks! Oh, I can't bear it!

PHEBE. Come along, now.

AUGUSTUS. (*Calling out to the "ghosts".*)
I came to save you!
(*The* SLAVES *burst in, brandishing bayonets and torches.*)

BENJAMIN. He did it.

SLAVES. Selah! We're free!
(*The* SLAVES *lift* AUGUSTUS *onto their shoulders. The* SLAVE
WOMAN/NARRATOR *stands at the door, holding a torch, taking in the
scene.*)

SLAVES. Freedom, freedom, freedom …
(*The "Freedom!" chant grows louder and more persistent as the* SLAVES *parade out of the room,* AUGUSTUS *on their shoulders;* PHEBE *follows
them, sobbing.* SCYLLA *takes the torch from the* SLAVE WOMAN/NAR-
RATOR *and sets fire to the window's billowing curtains as she slowly
straightens up to her full height.*)

Blackout.

The End.

51

From *Buck*

Francesca J. Petrosino

The earliest works of the playwright Francesca J. Petrosino (b. 1981) were produced while she was earning her undergraduate degree in Afro-American studies at Harvard. Petrosino, the daughter of public school teachers, was born in Baltimore and spent much of her childhood in Shrewsbury, Pennsylvania, a small, predominantly white town where her biracial heritage was a painful issue. She began to explore playwriting in 1998, the year she entered Harvard. In 2000 Petrosino produced and directed her first play, *Snatch*, which employed the wordplay and themes of racial crossover that are featured in much of her work. Subsequent plays included *Second Coming*, a sexual farce, and *Rosehips*, a series of monologues and dialogues on women and body image. *Buck*, which is excerpted here, was first produced in 2002.

CHARACTERS

Lincoln Washington, 25, a black farmhand
Jane McNeill, 22, a girl
WHITE MAN
WHITE WOMAN

SETTING: rural Mississippi

TIME: late 1930s

ACT I

Scene 1

The stage is assembled as such: taking up about a third of the stage at stage right is an open cotton field where Lincoln works. At the far right is a large shade tree with a patch of grass beneath it overlooking the fields. Painted background flats give the illusion of endless white-capped fields, simultaneously beautiful and painful.

At stage left, lifted on stage flats, is a bedroom setting with a bed, a night table, and a window with long white drapes. The bed linens are also white. The bedroom, the site of the principal action, takes up two-thirds of the stage.

As the story begins, however, we are greeted by LINCOLN *downstage. Lights are down over both the fields and the bedroom.*

As lights come up, we see LINCOLN *seated, knees drawn to his chest. He would appear small and frightened were it not for the belligerence with which he stares at his audience. Regardless of their actual composition,* LINCOLN *speaks and behaves as though his listeners are all white.*

LINCOLN *is naked. A stack of clothing and a pair of worn-out shoes are next to him as he speaks.*

LINCOLN. Sunflower County, Mississippi, ladies and gentlemen, is where it all began. It is where *I* began, if that even matters. But, being born, raised, and killed in Sunflower County, Mississippi, I know that it doesn't matter at all.

(squints at audience) You've all come here to see me, haven't you? What do you want to see? I assume you've already seen my fingers and toes, as the good people at Crenshaw's Market were good enough to display them in the window for you. *And* offer a two-for-one deal on round steaks this week, too. Good folks. What you'd call the salt of the earth. I'm guessing you've already seen me doing my dance from the end of a tree branch.

I know exactly what you came to see. *(stands up to reveal his nakedness; he stands quietly a moment, and in the silence, there is a sense of the power in that body, of the past it has endured, of what it could have been) (like an Uncle Tom)* Anything else I can do for ya? Massa? Missus? *(pretends to think with exaggeration)* I plumb fergot! I's here ta welcome ya'll to Sunflower County, Mi'ssippi. *(makes wide, cartoonish hand and facial gestures)* Greetin's and sal-u-tations from the Chamber of Commerce and the Ku Klux Klan. We sho do hope ya'll enjoy ya'lls stay and come back again real soon!

(approaches the end of the stage) Who, me? *(looks around; wide-eyed and incredulous)* Ya want *me* to show you around Sunflower County? That's mighty nice of ya to think of me, mighty nice, Massa. I been here all my life, and I know all they is to know 'bout this part of Mi'ssippi. I's got stories to tell ya, plenty stories, but … *(self-deprecating; shakes his head)* naw, I wouldn't want to take ya'lls time with my talkin'. Ya'll probably got plenty mo' impo'tant things to do than listen to this here nigger talk 'bout hisself. *(pauses; eyes widen again)* But if ya got a minute … well, maybe jes the one story. But don't you tell my Massa I'm out here a-talkin' away. I s'posed to be out in da fields.

De mos' impo'tant thing 'bout these parts of Mi'ssippi is de lan'. *(waves his arms toward the cotton field; lights come up to reveal it)* This is cotton plantin' country, and you come by just at pickin' time. I's one of the niggers 'roun here what does a lot of the pickin'. *(picks up clothing and dresses as he speaks; his clothes are ragged at the edges, faded, dirty).* We bags as much cotton as we can, then we empty our sacks and go back an' get more. Massa Brett say I must be the best picker in the county. *(smiles)* That makes me real proud to hear. You know you got the bes' cotton picker in Sunflower County talkin' to ya right now?

(finished dressing, Lincoln faces the audience, smile quickly fleeing; in a grave voice) Welcome to the twentieth century in Mississippi.

Scene 2

LINCOLN *walks toward the field and stands next to the tree.*

LINCOLN. This tree is the first and last thing I remember about Sunflower County. Look at it. *(looks up, thoughtfully regarding the tree)* Have you ever seen a tree better formed, tall and strong in the trunk, wide limbs and leaves, perfect for shade on a summer day? I spent a lot of time under this tree. At midday, we would leave the fields, my father and brothers and I, and look for shady spots for our lunch.

(sits down beneath the tree; sighs) There we go. Still the same old spot I came to every single day from the time I was eight until I was twenty-five. *(leans back and places his arms behind his head)* I used to daydream a lot. Look out over those fields and just dream away …

(WHITE MAN *enters. He is in the persona of William Brett, a wealthy planter. He is wearing slacks, a dress shirt with the sleeves rolled up, suspenders, and a tie. He is sweating a little and speaks harshly in a deep Southern accent.)*

BRETT. Ain't you supposed to be workin', nigger?

LINCOLN. *(to audience)* This is William Brett. He owns every last acre of this cotton plantation. Someone in his family has had it since about 18-something. A long time ago. There used to be about a hundred slaves working this plantation. *(ironically)* But now, thanks to the Emancipation Proclamation, Reconstruction, and the Thirteenth, Fourteenth, and Fifteenth Amendments, there are about a hundred sharecroppers working this plantation. And William Brett has never been anything but a very wealthy man.

BRETT. *(harshly; slapping the back of* LINCOLN's *head)* Nigger, didn't you hear me? I said why ain't you out workin' like I'm payin' you for? I ain't about to accommodate no lazy niggers 'round here.

LINCOLN. *(immediately penitent)* I's sorry, Mr. Brett. I's just takin' my midday break to set here 'til the hot sun go 'way.

BRETT. *(disgusted)* You are one stupid nigger. I never seen anybody lazy as you. Don't you know we already behind on this year's harvest? I ain't got no time to be worryin' over you and your break time. That sun ain't all that hot, and you ain't no old lady. You better get your lazy ass out there!

LINCOLN. *(rising quickly)* I's sorry, Mr. Brett! So sorry!

BRETT. *(suspiciously)* What you call me?

LINCOLN. *(cautiously)* I said—

BRETT. You called me "Mr. Brett," didn't you, nigger?

LINCOLN. Well, I—I s'pose—

BRETT. *(slaps* LINCOLN, *who falls and holds his face)* What did I tell you to call me at all times? What?

LINCOLN. *(weakly)* Massa … Massa Brett.

BRETT. *(satisfied)* That's right. Because I *am* the master around here. *(kicks* LINCOLN *savagely)* You won't forget that again, will you?

LINCOLN. Naw … Nawsuh.

BRETT. Good. Now get on. You had enough time to rest.

(BRETT *watches as* LINCOLN *struggles to stand. He gets frustrated and yanks* LINCOLN *by the arm.*)

BRETT. Come on, nigger, you ain't hurt that bad.

LINCOLN. *(holds his side and winces)* Nawsuh, I ain't hurt that bad.

BRETT. That's right. You my best picker, right here.

LINCOLN. Yassuh.

BRETT. My best.

(*Lights go down.*)

Scene 3

Lights go up over downstage. LINCOLN *appears.*

LINCOLN. Didn't matter how much I wanted to kick him back. Just had to content myself with being the best cotton-picker in Sunflower County.

Now, William Brett may have forced us to call him "Massa," and we may well have done it, but we knew, and so did he, that he had to pay us for our work. One of the things I dreamed about under that big shade tree was how I'd save up to move to New York City. I heard there were all kinds of Negroes in New York, Negroes with jobs, Negroes who'd gone to college. That's where I wanted to have a family. Raise children. My children would be Northerners, not some nappy-headed, no-tooth-havin', no-book-readin' pickaninnies that Mississippi clawed at like fleas on a dog.

One day, I got to my spot under the tree only to discover that someone else had heard about it.

(*Lights go back up over field.* JANE *enters in a simple dress with a cotton sack. She sets down the sack with a sigh and removes the straw hat she's wearing. She wipes her brow with her hand and stands with a hand on her hip, looking out over the fields. She is only twenty-two, but she's been at this for a long time. There is something strong and ultimately subversive in the way she gazes at the fields. It is almost as though she owns them.*)

(LINCOLN *walks toward the tree. He eyes* JANE *suspiciously.*)

LINCOLN. Girl, what you doin' here?

(JANE *turns. She is not at all startled.*)

JANE. It's midday. I was just lookin' for a place to sit.

LINCOLN. *(sitting down)* All the seats here is taken.

JANE. Who are you, nigger? You talkin' like you some white man on the bus.

LINCOLN. Since when is you takin' the bus? You got time to ride on some buses?

JANE. *(defensively)* Maybe. These here fields ain't my whole life.

LINCOLN. Well, now, that's cuz Massa Brett ain't takin' a shine to ya like he done me.

JANE. *(skeptically)* Really.

LINCOLN. Sho 'nuff. He say I'm his best picker, maybe the best picker in the whole county. *(looks in* JANE's *sack)* That all you picked this mornin'? You got some catchin' up ta do—

JANE. Nigger, that's my fourth one of the day already.

LINCOLN. *(subdued)* Oh.

JANE. *Now* can I sit down?

LINCOLN. Naw, you can't. Massa Brett say we ain't supposed to be takin' no breaks when we so behind on the harvest.

JANE. Massa Brett? You still callin' him Massa like we on some old-time plantation?

LINCOLN. He say he want us to call him that.

JANE. So? It ain't slavery time no more. We got to do everything he wants?

LINCOLN. When he's the one givin' me my money.

JANE. Uh-huh. When was the last time you saw some money?

LINCOLN. (scratches his head) Well … now … I don't know. I was gonna get some last Christmas, but then Massa Brett had to pay for some new tools and clothes and stuff, and—

JANE. And you didn't get nothin', did ya?

LINCOLN. Maybe this Christmas?

JANE. (shaking her head) Christmas a long way off, nigger. What's your name? I got to teach you some things 'bout dealin' with these white folks.

LINCOLN. My name's Lincoln Washington.

JANE. Rolly's boy, huh? I'd a thought he'd taught you better than to believe everything the white man say.

LINCOLN. My daddy taught me to pick my cotton and keep my words to myself if I wanted to live.

JANE. You ain't got to hold your tongue around me, Lincoln. Ain't no white folk around ta hear ya.

LINCOLN. Sho there is. White folk is everywhere. Sometimes they black up an' go out in the fields with us just to hear what we thinkin'.

JANE. (laughs) I tell ya, I been knowin' a lot of white folk in my lifetime, an' I ain't never met one that ever wanted to black up and go out into the field. Not for nobody!

LINCOLN. You from around here?

JANE. Naw, I come from Coahoma County. My name's Jane McNeill.

LINCOLN. Now where did a nigger like you get a Irish name like that?

JANE. (shrugs) Somebody's master a long time ago.

LINCOLN. Well, come on and sit down if you gonna. (moves over to make room)

(JANE sits down with her knees drawn up; her skirt comes above her knees a little.)

LINCOLN. That ain't no way for a lady to sit.

JANE. What way?

LINCOLN. That way. With your knees all out and your skirt hiked up. Like some two-bit floozy. You got to have some manners if you a lady.

JANE. I'm out there pickin' cotton every day like you, ain't I?

LINCOLN. Yeah.

JANE. Then I guess I ain't much of a lady.

LINCOLN. You could be even if you is a nigger. You got to have some dignity.

JANE. Yeah? So do you.

LINCOLN. I got plenty dignity. I work, I make my own money, I'm good at my job.

JANE. You know what I mean. (slips out of black vernacular English) So when you're with me, you can talk like a human being, not somebody's buck-dancing darky.

LINCOLN. (in standard English) But only when I'm with you.

JANE. Right. Because when Brett's around, you're still—
LINCOLN. The bes' picker they is!
(*Lights go down.*) …

ACT II
Scene 1

LINCOLN *is seated under the shade tree as lights go up. He is barefoot and is daydreaming.* BRETT *approaches.*

BRETT. What ya up to, nigger?
LINCOLN. (*rising*) Nothin', Massa Brett. Sho is nice ta see you this mornin'.
BRETT. You enjoyin' the day off?
LINCOLN. Oh, sho 'nuff, Massa Brett. I jes love settin' here under this tree an' watchin' the day go by. I declare, if'n you hadn't been good enough to give me a job, I'd be settin' under this tree my whole life long.
BRETT. I do my part for the niggers.
LINCOLN. Yes, you sho do, Massa Brett. We is lucky to have white folk like you around.
BRETT. (*thoughtfully*) What's your name, nigger?
LINCOLN. Lincoln Washington, Massa. I's Rolly's boy.
BRETT. Lincoln *and* Washington, eh? Named after two presidents—one of 'em great, the other one not so great.
LINCOLN. Yassuh.
BRETT. What's that mean, nigger? You wanna be president someday? Cuz you got the names for it?
LINCOLN. (*shaking his head*) Oh, nawsuh. I jes wants to stay here on this plantation an' keep workin' cuz that's what I do best. We niggers ain't good for nothin' but workin' in the field. (*to audience*) It wasn't hard to tell William Brett what he wanted to hear.
BRETT. (*happily*) Well, I wish all our niggers around here thought like you, Lincoln. Too many of 'em runnin' around tryin' to vote and own businesses and go to school with white folk. It ain't proper.
LINCOLN. Nawsuh, it ain't.
BRETT. We are different colors for a reason, you know.
LINCOLN. Yassuh.
BRETT. The Lord wants us to be separate. Do you believe in the Lord, Lincoln?
LINCOLN. Yassuh. I loves the Lord with all my heart.
BRETT. Good. You're a good worker, Lincoln, and a good Christian.
LINCOLN. Thank you, Massa Brett.
BRETT. I tell ya, Lincoln—naw, never mind.
LINCOLN. Somethin' on your mind, Massa Brett?
BRETT. Well … yes, but … aw, you wouldn't understand. It's white men's trouble.
LINCOLN. I may not understan' all of it, Massa, but I sho can listen if they's somethin' ya need to get off ya chest.

Brett. Well, Lincoln … hell, you seem like a good nigger. I know you won't go tellin' the world what I'm about ta say.

Lincoln. Oh, nawsuh.

Brett. It's my wife.

Lincoln. Missus Brett?

Brett. Uh-huh. Seems as though she just … lost interest in … her wifely duties, if you catch my meanin'.

Lincoln. Yassuh, I does. I hear this happens all the time with the womenfolk.

Brett. Yes. Well, I tell you, I don't know what to do. Seems as though I'm just not good enough for her anymore.

Lincoln. Now, Massa Brett, I know that ain't true. You the envy of jes about every woman in Sunflower County.

Brett. Oh, you'd be surprised, Lincoln. I may be wealthy and successful, but in the bedroom, my wife just couldn't be bothered with me.

Lincoln. Aw, now that's a shame, Massa. *(to audience)* He certainly was taking a long time to get to what he really wanted.

Brett. I'm beginnin' to think … that I'm not the right, uh, fit for her anymore.

Lincoln. What do ya mean?

Brett. I mean, I think she is no longer … satisfied by what I … have to offer. I think she needs somethin' what I can't give her. *(slowly, looking at Lincoln)* But … I know someone who can …

Lincoln. Massa Brett?

Brett. You got a girl, nigger?

Lincoln. Nawsuh, I's too busy workin' to be foolin' with no gal.

Brett. Aw, I don't believe that for a second. There ain't no little nigger gal waitin' up at night for you?

Lincoln. Nawsuh.

Brett. I know you must be lyin' ta me. *(looking Lincoln up and down)* You one of them big, black niggers. I'm surprised you ain't got no gal. *(pauses)* You are one big son of a bitch. You big all over?

Lincoln. Suh? I don' understand.

Brett. Big, nigger. *(suggestively)* Are you big?

Lincoln. I—I s'pose so, suh—

Brett. Good. *(thoughtful)* I think you'll do us just fine.

Lincoln. *(wondering)* Do ya jes fine …? *(after a pause in which he is presumably figuring out just what Brett means)* Massa Brett! You ain't sayin' what I think you sayin'!

Brett. What do you think I'm sayin'?

Lincoln. Well, I … Massa Brett, you know I can't say it out loud! It ain't nothin' for proper folk to talk about!

Brett. Proper folk? Well, Lincoln, look at me! I'm talkin' 'bout it, and it don't get no properer than William Brett. You've said so yourself a dozen times.

Lincoln. You is sho 'nuff right, suh. B-but 'round these parts, I could get killed just for jes thinkin' 'bout what you're thinkin' 'bout!

BRETT. Aw, now, Lincoln, I won't tell anybody. You can trust me. Ain't I made sure you and your daddy and your brother had good jobs the past twenty years now?

LINCOLN. Yassuh.

BRETT. Then who you gonna trust if you ain't gonna trust the man who gives you your pay?

LINCOLN. You right, Massa Brett.

BRETT. Then what do you think I'm getting at?

LINCOLN. You think ... you think Missus Brett might ... might—

BRETT. Spit it out, boy!

LINCOLN. *(trembling)* Might want a ... a bigger, uh, bigger—

BRETT. *(coaxing)* That's right, a bigger one. And who's got a bigger one to give her?

LINCOLN. I don't know, suh.

BRETT. Sure you do.

LINCOLN. Nawsuh.

BRETT. *(getting angry)* I've had enough of these games, nigger. You tell me what I want you to tell me!

LINCOLN. Nawsuh! Nawsuh, I can't say it!

BRETT. Say it! *(slaps him)* You say it right now or you'll be sorry! I'll make you one sorry nigger!

LINCOLN. *(begging)* Please, Massa Brett! I's a good Christian! Dis ain't right wit de Lawd!

BRETT. *(enraged)* You gon' try to tell me about the Lord, you ignorant black bastard! You want me to send you to him?

(BRETT *punches* LINCOLN, *wrestles him to the ground, and stands over him with his foot on his chest.*)

BRETT. Say it! You say it, you goddamned no-good nigger trash!

LINCOLN. It's me! You want me to do it to her!

BRETT. *(fiercely)* That's right. And you gonna do it right, ain't ya?

LINCOLN. Yassuh ... yassuh.

BRETT. And you ain't gonna tell anyone.

LINCOLN. Nawsuh.

BRETT. Good. *(moves away from Lincoln, who doesn't get up)* You come to the house tonight at nine o'clock, you hear? It won't be too long. You just getting her warmed up for me.

(*Lights go down.*)

Scene 2

Lights go up over bedroom. MRS. BRETT *is on the bed in a nightgown.* BRETT *is standing in front of her, arms crossed. He has just finished telling her what he told Lincoln—in less violent terms.*

MRS. BRETT. Have you plumb lost your mind, William?

BRETT. Aw, come on, Adele.

Mrs. Brett. I don't know why you thought I would go in for all of this. Imagine! Some big sweaty nigger going at it on top of me! Why, I think I would just die from the stench.

Brett. Aw, I doubt it.

Mrs. Brett. You could have consulted me, William. You didn't have to go to these lengths—

Brett. *(frustrated)* Didn't I? You been makin' it clear the last few months how little you want me in our bed. You've grown so cold to me, Adele. An' I don't know why.

Mrs. Brett. And you think this is the way to fix things?

Brett. I don't know! It's somethin'! I don't see you doin' anything to warm up your side of the bed.

Mrs. Brett. But a nigger? Some common field nigger with cotton between his toes?

Brett. He's a common nigger, yes, but niggers, they got … you know … things that white men just don't have.

Mrs. Brett. Like what?

Brett. Don't make me say it, Adele. You know what I mean.

Mrs. Brett. I'm sure I don't. I'm not in the habit of sleeping with niggers.

Brett. It's just the one time, darlin'. And he's just gonna warm ya up for me, then I'll make him go away.

Mrs. Brett. William, you're my husband and I love you, but I don't see how I can go along with this. It's just plain wrong!

(There is a knock.)

Brett. That must be him now. *(calling)* Come in, Lincoln!

Mrs. Brett. Come in? William, are you listenin' to me? There is no way I am givin' myself to this nigger!

Brett. *(angry)* You'll do as I tell you! You're the wife here, and I'm the husband. I say what you do and don't do. And if I want you to have relations with this nigger, you will!

Mrs. Brett. But William—

Brett. *(slapping his wife)* You shut your goddamned mouth!

(Mrs. Brett holds her cheek and falls silent. Brett comes closer.)

Brett. *(nuzzling Mrs. Brett)* Now, then, Mrs. Brett, why you wanna get ugly? I'm just doin' this for you and me.

Mrs. Brett. But I don't want this nigger, William!

Brett. *(low, seductive)* Aw, come on now, you mean to tell me you ain't never thought just once about havin' a nigger? Havin' his big strong thing inside a you? Never once?

Mrs. Brett. *(clears her throat and swallows nervously)* I-I thought that was just a myth, all that talk about what they have down there.

Brett. It ain't no myth, honey, believe you me. I seen 'em, an' what they got makes what I got look like a lil' ol' string bean.

Mrs. Brett. *(shocked but excited in spite of herself)* William!

Brett. I'm tellin' the truth. You heard it a million times before, I bet. Bet you thought about it just as many times. *(strokes Mrs. Brett's shoulders and breasts; he is murmuring in her ear)* You never dreamed just once that some big black buck would come bustin' through your door, push you down on the bed, and take you like some nigger bitch?

(MRS. BRETT *looks increasingly hot and bothered.*)

BRETT. And you never thought about riding on top of some black bronco who fills you up all the way to your belly? *(rubs Mrs. Brett's thighs; she moans softly)*

MRS. BRETT. *(whispers)* Maybe once or twice …

(LINCOLN *enters and stands in the doorway uncomfortably.* BRETT *pulls away from his wife abruptly.*)

BRETT. Come on in here, Lincoln. I want you to meet my wife.

(LINCOLN *comes into the room and stands at the foot of the bed.*)

BRETT. Lincoln, this is Missus Brett. You've seen her before.

LINCOLN. *(quietly)* Yassuh.

BRETT. Honey, say hello to Lincoln.

MRS. BRETT. *(quietly)* Hello, Lincoln.

BRETT. Now, Lincoln. You remember what we talked about.

LINCOLN. Yassuh.

BRETT. All right. You remember then, you just get her warmed up for me. Nothing more.

LINCOLN. *(pauses; looks at* MRS. BRETT*)* What, uh, what should I do, Massa Brett?

BRETT. Don't tell me you've never done this before?

LINCOLN. Aww, of course I have, Massa Brett.

BRETT. Then just come up here on the bed and do like you normally do.

LINCOLN. Missus?

MRS. BRETT. It's all right, Lincoln.

(LINCOLN *awkwardly kneels on the bed.*)

BRETT. Don't you wanna touch her?

LINCOLN. Huh?

BRETT. Ain't you gonna do nothin'? You just sittin' there.

LINCOLN. I's sorry, Massa Brett. I's a little nervous.

BRETT. Look, Lincoln, I'm givin' you your biggest wish, ain't I? Here she is, a pure white woman, just waitin' for ya. Ain't that what you always wanted?

LINCOLN. *(to* BRETT*)* Yassuh.

BRETT. Then take her. *(pushes* MRS. BRETT *toward* LINCOLN*)* Take her.

(LINCOLN *hesitantly moves closer to* MRS. BRETT. *He kisses her slowly while* BRETT *watches.*)

BRETT. Good! Good, that's good. Now, Lincoln, you just push her down on that bed—

(LINCOLN, *still kissing* MRS. BRETT, *pushes her on the bed.*)

BRETT. And you just take off them pants and go at it.

(LINCOLN, *not looking at* BRETT, *still kissing* MRS. BRETT, *undoes his pants and gets on top of* MRS. BRETT. *He pulls the sheets over the two of them and begins to charge in and out of her rhythmically.* MRS. BRETT *begins to moan.*)

BRETT. *(watching)* You like that, honey? That good?

MRS. BRETT. Ooh … yes … yes.

(LINCOLN *begins to move faster;* MRS. BRETT*'s moans grow louder.*)

BRETT. How you doin', honey? You about ready for me?

MRS. BRETT. Uhh ... yeah ... yeah.

(BRETT *undoes his pants and puts a hand on* LINCOLN'*s shoulder.*)

BRETT. All right, boy. You're done.

LINCOLN. *(still moving on top of* MRS. BRETT*)* What?

BRETT. I said you're done, boy. You warmed her up, and now you're done.

LINCOLN. Oh. *(stops moving)* Right.

(LINCOLN *dismounts and gets out of bed.* BRETT *moves past him and begins kissing* MRS. BRETT. *He mounts her and begins moving on top of her while* LINCOLN *is still in the room. He can't help but stare.*)

BRETT. *(panting; to* LINCOLN*)* Boy ... get out of here, boy ...

LINCOLN. I's sorry.

BRETT. *(close to climax; so is* MRS. BRETT*)* Now, boy! Get ... out ... now!

(LINCOLN *exits. Lights go down over bedroom, but we can still hear the bed moving.* LINCOLN *moves downstage, and lights go up downstage. He is fixing his pants.*)

Scene 3

LINCOLN: So, my friends. I'm sorry if that disturbed you. You had to see it. Would you have believed me otherwise?

(BRETT *and* MRS. BRETT *both announce very loud orgasms. When they finish, the bed stops creaking and* LINCOLN *is silent a moment, letting the quiet sink in.*)

My job there was complete.

Brett said something rather interesting just now—did you catch it? He assumed that what just happened was for me better than Christmas—the chance not only to touch but to enter a "pure white woman" in the open, without fear, without punishment, without blood ... wasn't that what I always wanted? Wasn't that some sort of slave's dream come true?

(looks at audience scornfully) Let me be honest. Mrs. Brett was hardly the first white woman I'd ever had. In fact, one of my first was white—not my very first, mind you. Not the second or third either. She was far enough down the line that I can't recall exactly what number she was or get emotional about her, but important enough that I can remember the incident, which is more than I can say for some other encounters. Her name was Amanda, and her family ran Crenshaw's Market in the center of town. When I was about fifteen, I took on some extra work after I finished in the fields delivering groceries for Mr. Crenshaw. And when I was finished running a dozen eggs to Mrs. Sanders or a quart of milk to Mrs. Hamilton, I'd run back to the market one last time to see if Mr. Crenshaw could keep me on just a while longer. I'd help stock things. Lift more boxes and bags.

Mr. and Mrs. Crenshaw lived above the store. It was a nice place; I was the only nigger in town who got to see it. They were good white folk who didn't allow colored in their house. Didn't want to dirty their nice white napkins, I guess. Mrs. Crenshaw was a tiny little sliver of humanity. Her hair was very light brown and very thin, and she wore long dresses and a sweater even in August because she was always cold. I think she secretly thought that blackness just flaked off us niggers like old paint. If she were to let one in her pristine house, she'd have to run behind him with her broom.

But sometimes in the evenings, Mr. Crenshaw needed some help carrying boxes from the store all the way up the long staircase. One night, I got back from making deliveries just as Mr. Crenshaw was struggling to pick up a huge watermelon. He saw me coming, and his relief was palpable. For some reason, my being a nigger qualified me to carry this watermelon with the minimum of physical strain. "Here, Lincoln," he said, standing back and pointing to the melon with a crooked finger. "Why don't you take that upstairs for me? My wife will cut it up and send you home with a piece."

Crenshaw paid me for my work. It just wasn't always in money. My being a nigger meant that watermelon was as valid form of tender as dollar bills.

I heaved the watermelon over my shoulder. Crenshaw always went ahead of me on the steps so he could warn his wife that the Negro was on his way up, but just for a minute, then he'd be on his way. But tonight, Crenshaw waved at me to start up without him. "I forgot another box out in the shed. I'll be back, you go on up." I wondered at this unexpected development but shrugged and went on. Evidently, I had attained the status of "good nigger." So good and obedient and asexual that I could be trusted to enter the white man's home unchaperoned.

The door swung open just as I reached the threshold. Standing on the other side of it, arms akimbo, brows furrowed, was Crenshaw's sixteen-year-old daughter Amanda. Much as her parents liked to ignore it, Amanda had such a loose reputation on the white side of town that even us niggers knew about it. Word was that she had slept with the entire football team over at the white high school. We Negroes snickered to ourselves and wondered if Amanda was the reason why the Negro schools didn't have football teams.

A good bit of Amanda's tarnish stemmed from her total lack of fear. Even now, she glowered at the colored man at her doorstep when her mother would have gone under the couch to find refuge with the dustbunnies. "What are you doin' here?" she asked belligerently.

I put the watermelon on the step and explained that her father was on his way.

She picked up the melon—a true feat, for it had even been a challenge for me—and told me rather crossly that I was not to be in their home without her father to escort me. But then she cocked her head at me. She could smell a rule just waiting to be broken.

"But since you're already here," she said, "you wanna see my bedroom?"

Her mama wasn't home. Amanda smiled and turned, and I followed her. Her words stuck in my head. She had said "bedroom." She wanted me to see her "bedroom." Not the living room or the dining room where the normal, observable functions of life occurred, where it was all right even for a Negro to peek in from time to time. She wanted me to see the room where she kept her bed, where she slept. She wanted me to see the white sheets she lay down on every night and the thin cotton nightgowns she wore strewn so carelessly but so tantalizingly across the floor. She intrigued me, this girl. I had seen Negro girls all my life, had seen what their skin looked and felt like, the places where it tended to wrinkle, the places where it would assume lighter or darker tone. But this girl, this white girl, was a new country to me. I stepped into her room, and the smell of her was everywhere, that very particular white girl smell that exists only in white girls' bedrooms. There was a wooden hairbrush on the bureau near the door, and I looked at it and saw long, straight strands of blondish-brown hair. I was fascinated at the thought of straight, light hair. It was as though everything about Amanda was softer, lighter, more beautiful, more refined than anything any Negro girl had ever owned. Even the bed was softer than any I'd ever sat on.

I remember feeling like it was all too good for me as she started to undress me. I was suddenly embarrassed because I knew there would be corns on my feet when her little white hands took off my shoes. I knew there would be rings of dirt around my socks and the cuffs of my pants. But Amanda didn't seem at all bothered by any of it. When she kissed me … I felt lost. I couldn't feel her lips, I wasn't used to lips so thin. I was worried that I would bruise her with my big nigger lips, and I was ashamed of how black I looked next to her white skin and her white sheets.

But Amanda took me inside her, and she did not stop, not even when Mr. Crenshaw's footsteps creaked up the stairway and into earshot. She waited for me to finish, and then she helped me out the window.

(thoughtfully) It's funny how neither of us ever spoke during the whole thing. And after that, whenever I saw her, she was as cold to me as she was to every other Negro. She and I both knew better than to breathe a word of what had happened. Although on one occasion, when we were both helping out at the market, she caught my eye, and I saw her smile at me.

So where does all of this get us? There were women before and after Amanda, all of them Negro. And I noticed that what it felt like inside Amanda … that was exactly how it felt inside the rest of them. No better, no worse. The finish was no better and no worse. So, no, Mrs. Brett was most certainly not the realization of some long-suppressed fantasy. I wanted a white woman no more or less than I wanted any other woman. There you have it. My great case for the equality of the races.

But William Brett had no way of knowing any of this. In fact, he would congratulate himself for his great idea for a long time to come. My input, as it were, seemed to do the trick for him and Mrs. Brett.

As for me, well, I wasn't ready for sleep when I left the Bretts that evening …

Scene 4

Lights go up over fields. JANE *is under the tree; it is nighttime.* LINCOLN *approaches.*
JANE. *(rising)* Lincoln!
LINCOLN. I thought I'd find you here.
JANE. What are you doing—
(JANE *is interrupted when* LINCOLN *pulls her to him and kisses her. The two drop down to the earth together, still kissing, as lights fade over the fields. The stage is completely dark.)* …

ACT III

Scene 5

Lights go up over field. LINCOLN *is under the tree, cotton sack by his side. He doesn't seem concerned about* BRETT's *no-breaks rule. His knees are drawn up, and he rests his right calf on his left knee.*

WHITE MAN *approaches as* ROBERT ANNISTON. *He is a schoolteacher and is wearing a suit and glasses and carries a handful of books. He stops when he sees* LINCOLN. LINCOLN *rises and bows, smiling wide.* ANNISTON *smiles as well, and the two pantomime a conversation. The theater is silent as this occurs.*

ANNISTON's *smile disappears as he explains something rather serious to* LINCOLN. LINCOLN *frowns and nods, then mouths a response.* ANNISTON *doesn't care for this response and argues with him.* LINCOLN *shakes his head and picks up his cotton sack, preparing to go. As* LINCOLN *turns to go,* ANNISTON *makes one last attempt:*
ANNISTON. I'll pay you!
(*Lincoln stops and turns around. A smile spreads slowly across his face as lights go down.*)

Scene 6

LINCOLN *appears as lights come up. There is a thoughtful smile on his face.*

LINCOLN. Robert Anniston wasn't from around here, as the folk say. He wasn't from the North, but he was from Virginia, which was about as far north as any of us—white and colored alike—had ever been. Crozet, I think, was the town where he grew up. His people used to be small planters there in slavery time—little corn, little tobacco. Only had about five or six slaves of their own. On a plantation like that, well, white and colored folk tend to get a little close. Almost like family, if you can call it that. So when Emancipation came, most of the Anniston slaves stayed put, helped old Massa Anniston rebuild the farm and keep it running right on into the next century. When Robert came along, he wasn't too interested in taking over the farm from his daddy. He left that to his brother John and instead went to the University of Virginia and studied history. When he left, there wasn't much else to do but teach school. He started teaching up in Virginia, but got into some trouble when he started courting Miss Sarah Bellow, whom he did not know was actually the wife of a Major Harold Bellow. When the war ended, Major Bellow came home, and Robert Anniston's hopes of a June wedding were summarily dashed. He took off as fast as his feet would take him and ended up in Sunflower County, Mississippi.
Anniston started teaching in the white high school in town. He kind of stuck out around here—in a town full of farmers in overalls, he wore three-piece suits, carried around big stacks of books, and went to the library. People stared at him. Especially Walter Street, whom you met earlier. If you couldn't tell, Walter's the jealous sort, and he didn't much like having this know-it-all in town who knew things Walter couldn't even dream of. I do believe Walter Street hated Robert Anniston even more than he hated William Brett.

The women in town decided that the best thing for Robert Anniston would be to marry up right quick with one of their choicest young ladies. Nothing like a little legitimacy to get people like Walter Street off your back. So, round about three years ago, Mr. Anniston wed a right proper young lady right out in the town square. His lady had somewhat of a spotty past, but standing there in her white dress with the daisies curling through her hair, she was as lovely and pure a woman as any white man could want. She brushed her hair a hundred strokes every night with a wooden hairbrush she's had since she was a girl.

And now it seemed as though things had cooled in the happy marriage bed, and Robert Anniston had overheard a conversation between Walter Street and the barber, Ralph Hymes. Seems there was a nigger in town—a real well-hung nigger—who William Brett was hiring out to warm up their wives' beds all over town. And Walter Street, who was seen smiling from ear to ear on a daily basis nowadays, could attest to just how well this nigger did his appointed task. Didn't cost him a dime, either. And Robert Anniston thought back to his own marriage and to the long-snuffed fire inside himself and inside his wife, and he left school early one day to find that nigger out in William Brett's cotton fields.

When that nigger started to resist—as Walter Street said he might—Anniston knew a little money would sweeten the deal. The coloreds were always poor and looking for money. Stupid nigger would probably blow it all on Cokes on the way home. But it was money, and the nigger took it with a smile. Anniston breathed relief, but not before he made sure the nigger would be discreet about the whole thing. His wife was from a prominent family in town, and it wouldn't do for the entire town to know that some black buck nigger had fucked the life out of Amanda Crenshaw Anniston....

ACT V

Scene 3

Lights go up over bedroom. JANE *enters with a basket of laundry. She sets it on the bed and begins taking clothes out of it.* WHITE MAN, *as* BRETT, *enters and sees* JANE *bent over with her back to him. He runs his eyes along her body and smiles salaciously.* JANE *is not aware of his presence.*

BRETT. *(low)* Hey, Honey.
JANE. *(startled)* Massa Brett! I didn't see ya there.
BRETT. That's cuz I meant ta sneak up on ya.
JANE. You been watchin' me?
BRETT. You know I been watchin' ya every day since you started workin' in the house.
JANE. Well, I's might glad ya brought me in here ta work, Massa. I like it a whole heap better than pickin' out in the fields.
BRETT. I thought you might. *(sits on bed)* Why don't ya come over here and let's get better acquainted?
JANE. *(bashful)* Now, Massa Brett, I s'posed ta be workin'.

BRETT. It's all right, Honey. Come here. *(pats the bed)*

(JANE *sits next to* BRETT. *He immediately begins pawing her.*)

BRETT. *(breathing deeply)* You smell so good, Honey. I been waitin' so long just to get you alone.

JANE. I been waitin', too, Massa.

BRETT. *(pleased)* I knew it! I knew you were just bein' a tease last time. You must know I been watchin' ya, that's why you come around here lookin' and smellin' so good. You know I don't miss nothin' when it comes to you.

JANE. I know. But Massa, I's scared that I won't be as good as the other gals you been with.

BRETT. Oh, you will. *(looks her up and down in the visual equivalent of licking his chops)* I can tell just by lookin' at ya.

JANE. Would you tell me a little bit more about that gal Harriet you mentioned before? It sounded like she was real good to you.

BRETT. She was. *(touches* JANE*'s neck)* Her mother was the housekeeper here, and they lived in the house up the back staircase. I would go on up there sometimes and see her.

JANE. An' did she like you?

BRETT. I don't know. I reckon I didn't much care.

JANE. But you know I like you, don't you?

BRETT. *(smiles)* I reckon I don't much care 'bout that, neither, so long as you sit here by me a while.

JANE. What happened ta her?

BRETT. Who?

JANE. Harriet.

BRETT. Oh, her. I dunno. She moved away when I was a young man. I hear she was in some kind a trouble.

JANE. Trouble? What kind?

BRETT. What other trouble is there for a nigger gal ta get into? With child, I'm guessin'. I think she had a nigger beau who worked in the fields. Maybe her beau already had a gal, I dunno. *(voice becomes more seductive)* Let's forget about her, Honey. This is just you and me right now. *(tries to kiss her)*

JANE. But, Massa, wait, they's somethin' I gotta tell ya—

(BRETT *kisses* JANE.)

JANE. *(jumps up and slaps* BRETT*)* I'm your daughter, for God's sake! I'm your own daughter! *(she spits)*

(BRETT *blinks.*)

BRETT. What you say, girl?

JANE. Me! I'm your own blood, the child you made with Harriet!

BRETT. *(indignant)* Couldn't be! I never had a child with no nigger bitch!

JANE. Yes you did! My mother told me all about you. She told me how she used to work for a man named Brett in Sunflower County and how he just had to have some of her *(mocking)* honey. Then when she got in trouble, she had to pick up and leave because she knew you'd never help her.

BRETT. I take care of all my niggers! Always have.

JANE. *(disgusted)* You didn't care about her. You used her up until you'd had your fill, and that was it. And you tried to do the same to me. You're so sick that you almost slept with your own blood!

BRETT. Girl, you better keep that voice down!

JANE. I'm not afraid of you!

BRETT. *(furious)* You oughta be, you no-good whore! You better get the hell outta this town. I got friends here, and they'll make sure you don't have enough breath left in you ta spread your lies.

JANE. It would be worth it! To die if I could tell everyone who you really are.

BRETT. You might just get your wish if you keep talkin' like that! Now get outta here and don't let me see you again!

JANE. *(laughs harshly)* You think you can make this go away? Come on, *William*! I've been waiting twenty-two years for this! Don't act like you didn't see it coming!

BRETT. I most certainly did not! How was I supposed to know about all this? Harriet moved away when I was very young, before I even got married.

JANE. You didn't think it was odd that this light-skinned girl just showed up here one day, came all the way from Coahoma County just to pick cotton on your farm?

BRETT. I dunno! You niggers are always pickin' up and movin' from place to place for no apparent reason.

JANE. Well. I had a reason, didn't I? And it's only a matter of time before the whole town finds out why this particular nigger ended up here.

BRETT. *(furious)* You will not! You will not say a word!

JANE. *(laughs)* This usually works for you, doesn't it? Say the word and it's done.

BRETT. *(insulted and enraged)* Don't you know who I am? You know you're dealin' with William Brett! I own this goddamn county! William Brett, that means somethin' to a lotta people around here.

JANE. *(sarcastic)* It's always meant so much to me *(smiles wickedly)* Father—

BRETT. *(enraged)* Don't you ever—!

(BRETT *grabs* JANE *by the throat and forces her on the bed.* JANE *struggles and makes choking sounds, but* BRETT *does not relent. Suddenly,* JANE *is quiet.* BRETT *slowly releases her throat and steps away from the bed.*)

(*Lights go down.*)

Scene 4

Lights go up over bedroom. LINCOLN *and* WHITE WOMAN, *as* AMANDA, *sitting together on the bed, kissing.*

LINCOLN. *(pulling away)* You all right, Missus?

AMANDA. Yes, Lincoln. But I think you may call me Amanda from now on.

LINCOLN. Yes'm—I mean, Amanda.

(AMANDA *kisses* LINCOLN *again.*)

AMANDA. You know I don't love you, Lincoln.

LINCOLN. I know.

(AMANDA *pulls* LINCOLN *to her and helps him out of his shirt. They get beneath the sheets, where* LINCOLN'S *pants are next to go. He is naked, but below the waist he is concealed by the sheet.* LINCOLN *mounts* AMANDA *and begins moving on top of her.*)

LINCOLN. You like that?

AMANDA. *(panting)* Yes ... yes ...

(LINCOLN *continues. After a few moments,* AMANDA *grips his back and lets out a loud moan.*)

LINCOLN. *(stops)* I better go get Mr. Anniston—

AMANDA. No! No, you stay.

LINCOLN. I'm only s'posed ta get things started—

AMANDA. Stay *(kisses* LINCOLN*)* stay *(kisses him again)* I want you to ... I want ... *(kisses him)*

(LINCOLN *responds to* AMANDA'S *kiss and continues his lovemaking.* AMANDA'S *moans grow louder and are joined by* LINCOLN'S. *Just as both reach climax, the door swings open.* WHITE MAN, *as* ANNISTON, *storms in.*)

ANNISTON. Good Lord!

(ANNISTON *pulls* LINCOLN *off* AMANDA. *Both are breathless.*)

AMANDA. Robert, stop!

ANNISTON. *(slaps* LINCOLN*)* You stupid nigger! Didn't I tell you you were only to start her? I finish her, not you!

LINCOLN. *(genuinely afraid)* Yassuh, yassuh. I's so sorry, suh! I didn't mean to!

ANNISTON. You expect me to believe this was all an accident?

AMANDA. *(rising; entreating)* Please don't be angry, Robert, I asked him to stay. He was going to go get you, but I told him to stay—

(AMANDA *is silenced by the back of* ANNISTON'S *hand.*)

ANNISTON. I don't believe it. This nigger probably got you to lie for him. *(to Lincoln)* Didn't you? *Didn't you?*

LINCOLN. Nawsuh! It was jes like she said it was!

ANNISTON. *(furious)* You're a liar! This *(pointing to* AMANDA*)* is a good white woman. She doesn't want anything to do with your filth. She tried to push you off, didn't she? And you wouldn't go. You had to finish your dirty work, and you finished inside of her even as she was struggling to get away, didn't you?

LINCOLN. Nawsuh!

ANNISTON. Get out of my bed!

(ANNISTON *tears the sheets off the bed and reveals a naked* LINCOLN. LINCOLN *jumps up and tries to gather his clothes.*)

ANNISTON. Get out of here! You better run, and you better run fast, nigger! Because there'll be a lynch mob out for you tonight! I'll make sure everybody in this town knows that you raped a white woman tonight.

LINCOLN. It wasn't rape!

AMANDA. Robert, no!

ANNISTON. The rule was that you didn't finish. You didn't! You got up and left the best part of it to the husbands. *(screaming now)* But you got greedy, didn't you, you dirty bastard!

AMANDA. Lincoln, run!

(LINCOLN, *still naked, exits. Lights go down in the bedroom and follow him downstage. He runs offstage in search of a place to hide.*) ...

Scene 6

Lights slowly come up over the fields. As they rise, we hear a mournful woman's voice singing "Strange Fruit." JANE *is the singer; she wanders out and looks up at the tree. Lights reveal a noose hanging from a branch. As* JANE *finishes singing, she sits with her back against the tree, looking at the noose, as lights go down.*

52

From *The Secret Life of Fred Astaire*

Itabari Njeri

The award-winning author Itabari Njeri (b. 1952) was at first interested in a career in music. Njeri (originally named Jill Moreland) was born in Brooklyn, studied vocal music at New York's High School for Music and Art, and entered Boston University as an opera student. As the 1970s progressed, her interests veered from classical music to jazz, and she became increasingly active in the Black Arts movement championed by Amiri Baraka. After earning an undergraduate degree in public communication from Boston University and a master's degree in journalism from Columbia, Njeri worked as a reporter and features writer for the *Greenville News* (South Carolina), the *Miami Herald*, and the *Los Angeles Times*. She won an Associated Press award in 1981, a fellowship from the National Endowment for the Humanities, and an American Book Award for her first book, *Every Good-Bye Ain't Gone* (1990). She was also a finalist for the Pulitzer Prize in 1992. From 1994 to 2000, Njeri was a writer-in-residence and lecturer in Afro-American studies at Washington University in St. Louis, and she is currently a doctoral student in the history of American civilization at Harvard. Her second book, *The Last Plantation*, appeared in 1997; *The Secret Life of Fred Astaire*, excerpted here, is a novel in progress.

Chapter 1

Fred Astaire rose before dawn each day of the week. He ate one boiled egg with a cup of bouillon for breakfast. He took long walks and choreographed dance routines in his head as the sun tried to catch him. He had soup for lunch, preferably homemade. He drank two Manhattans and ate five peanuts at the cocktail hour. He disliked wines except for Dom Perignon and drank as much of that as he wanted, when he wanted. But he never ate dessert or women. Rhea Verney was determined to change the latter; change it tonight.

"I want to be your china bowl." Her honey-dipped alto was soft but resonant. It possessed the assured refinement of a pearl-draped, Junior League matron auctioning a magnificent porcelain *objet* for a charity fundraiser: ... *and who wouldn't desire this exquisitely rendered piece from the Ming dynasty?* Her tenure at elite finishing schools, foreign and domestic, left their mark—though she bolted before any one of them finished with her. Still, she owned an elegance that, in one so young, must have come from the marrow. The hint of lasciviousness was in her bold, penetrating gaze.

Fred stared into his champagne glass then halfway up at her without moving his bony head. He allowed his mouth to ease into a tired smile. It was the half indulgent response of a familiar to a loved one's often heard but unfulfilled plea. He watched her eyes gleam brighter the longer he remained silent. The locomotive force of Ella Fitzgerald swinging "St. Louis Woman" whipped through the void.... *yeah he may be your man, but he comes up to see me sometime....* Fred started drumming time on the table. "I love the way she does this, those hard driving four-four rhythms then cha-cha and back again," he said, turning musicologist and friendly stranger at the neighborhood bar. Rhea's fork froze midway between her plate and mouth. He felt like a man dropping ice cubes in hell. Her almond-shaped eyes eased shut in response, then she languidly placed a piece of lamb in her mouth. He watched her savor the silken morsel of fat attached to the meat. To someone who didn't know her, it might seem an act of delayed gratification. He knew it was an act of resolve. She was determined to run out the clock; to wear him down. The tip of her tongue lingered on a glistening spot at the corner of her mouth.

"I really enjoyed that," he told her. Half a chop with all its fat remained on his plate. He reached for her dish.

"No, relax. I'll do that. You look a little weak tonight." Drought, he thought, that's what she sounded like; a long, long drought.

Shoeless, legs bare, Rhea floated past him in a white halter dress patterned with exotic birds. The voluminous skirt of her dress gently billowed and swirled around her muscular, dancer's calves. Any second she might fly away, airborne by her ballooning skirt of fantastic birds painted fresh-blood red and solar yellow, taking with her the complications of his life. He wanted an uncomplicated life. She must want the same thing. Doesn't everybody? Half his divided self always told him so. The other half put him here.

The French doors between the cottage dining room and patio were open, framing a ridiculous full moon; a balloon on the horizon fit for a cartoon.... *yeah he may be your man, but he comes up to see me sometime ... wouldn't give a crippled crab a crutch, ain't gonna give ya* nothin' *cause ya ain't so such a much....* A needle riding vinyl kept Ella's voice sailing through the unusually warm, mist-filled spring breeze blowing from Long Island Sound. The secluded, Tudor-style cottage was once a guest house on a North Shore estate. After World War II, the land was subdivided. A friend lent the place to Fred whenever he came to New York and wanted the kind of privacy a hotel couldn't afford. About now, he felt a bomb shelter would be better.

There was a short shelf life to this sort of thing. Fred convinced himself that each meeting with Rhea would be their last. Yet, he further complicated his life by buying this house and the surrounding five acres. He planned to put the deed in Rhea's name. Next month would be the third anniversary of their meeting in Paris, and the land not only was a gift but something to secure her financial future. If that wasn't love, he didn't know what was. He *was* tight with a dollar, but Rhea was in diapers during the Depression. He saw what could happen to the richest people back then. Even with his decades of success and careful investments, what could be shakier than a performer's life? She should be damn glad. Still, it would have been better if he told her about the house and land right off. Now it would seem like leaving money on the dresser—a very nice chunk of money. He caught himself in a body rocking nod, arms across his chest, underscoring the thought. This already was valuable land. Who knew what it would be worth ten, fifteen years from now? Who knew what she would do with it? She was so young. He was a year older than the century, as one recent magazine story annoyingly reminded him, but he didn't feel his age. He knew he hadn't been his usual performing self in the bedroom a few times in the past year, but that had more to do with Rhea.

"My face is not a deck," he snapped one night, when her tongue started swabbing it. He hated sloppy kissing, and she knew it. Then she started pouting, about the same thing. He wouldn't eat her. There were things, though, that he desired that she wouldn't do. As far as he was concerned, that evened the carnal score. What she did do, he loved; and more than unadorned lust that tied him to her. It was the nature of their early lovemaking, the timing of it in the broken rhythm of his life, that made him feel emotionally indebted to her.

He met Rhea the year his wife died, a year that crawled like an abandoned, thirsty man crawls through the desert groping through sand for water. He went into the Beverly Hills night and painted his neighbors' mailboxes yellow. Then he cried. Then he drank. Then he looked for Luna Pharr.

"She's dead," her sister said, then he heard the receiver bludgeon the cradle of the phone. He didn't believe it, though no one had seen Luna Pharr for more than twenty years.

He had loved Luna with an unsettling passion that threatened more than his career. It threatened his existence. He could stay a *kind* of white man; one abandoned by his family, one abandoned by his country, one living at the edge of even bohemian worlds. During the twenties, far from the States, he and Luna existed in a sealed sphere guarded by a group of Europeans and expatriate Americans. He knew they had to breathe the air of the real world eventually. He convinced himself that no time, no place could sustain the eddying tangle of desires that snaked his ravenous tongue toward her womb, an altar on which any part of him that could ecstatically dwelled in the nurturing dark of creation, and joyfully died to be resurrected, longing to travel again that tight night of flesh that could explode with the sea of birth.

At first, it was the stirring blackness of Luna that drew him. She was dark, darker than the sweet-faced, brown girl his bellhop friends from Harlem introduced him to, and dared him to kiss. He was thirteen and so was she. When the boys pushed them in the closet, and they did kiss, she put her tongue in his mouth and took him around the world. Slow, fast, her tongue traveled everywhere and never left his mouth for the dizzying trip, except to lick his lips. No one had ever done that to him before, and he liked it. When he told the boys and they teased the girl, she cried in Fred's face, "You a lie, you a big lie." Then she told them all to get out of her house before her Mama came home. Luna was darker than that little girl, darker than any of the brown girls he had known his many years on the road. Luna was so dark he wanted to rub up against her blackness as soon as he saw her. There was so much of it, surely she could afford to let him keep a smidgen of the black gold that covered her; surely she could afford to let him borrow some, at least. For years, it perplexed him that her very blackness so allured him; that he attached such beauty to it, even power. In the end, he felt that finding meaning was a burden. In the end, all he could taste, think, feel was an enduring sweetness. Between her legs lay home; one he never found again.

He had loved his wife and found with her a deep, calm pleasure that kept his divided self in check. Protecting his career policed him, too. Widowed, he became a walking wound; its scab pulled and dangling at the serrated edge of loneliness. Rhea assuaged his lonely heart. Together they danced at the edge of the abyss, where the free fall is an invitation to death, death defied by the shock to the heart from molten kisses that meld souls; where passion is a floating cloud of tender nerves aroused in the stillest atmosphere, tender nerves charged, engorged by the infinitesimal vibrations of a distant dove's wings; where shadowed desires invade flesh and erupt as the cry-scream of sweet force and surrender; where survival lies only in each other's arms because there is no one and nothing else to cling to when the mind, consumed by such passion, remembers to think of the dangers at all. But he refused to leap to that place with Rhea, as he had with Luna; especially now, as he felt a similar whirlpool of desire.

Fred leaned back, expelled a sigh, then instructed his well-trained muscles to relax. He was determined to keep the evening temperate, defy the unseasonable April heat, disobey his desires; all of them.

Rhea was not going to dance with him on television. End of story. She badgered him about dancing together almost as much as eating her. If he wouldn't, at least, make her his professional partner after their years together, they were done. He looked toward the kitchen. He heard a lot of dish rattling back there, an annoying accompaniment to the word bouncing inside his head: Coward. He knew that's what she would call him, too much of one to risk anything even at this point in his life. But his career wasn't over. He wanted some serious acting roles. Maybe he'd direct, too. His dancing days were ending though, and he wanted this television special to *be* special; nothing nostalgic, something fresh, imaginative, provocative. Rhea would be too provocative. The audience would fix on her; a pale, suspiciously slant-eyed girl with a spray of freckles on her nose, deep waves of mink-colored hair, and tantalizing lips that verged on a dangerously revealing Negro pout. Who would pay attention to the great choreography he planned? To him? And the press would want to know everything about her. She was Fred Astaire's new partner. He knew he couldn't find a better one, either.

He never saw a woman who danced exactly like her. She possessed her own assured style. Modern, ballet—she was accomplished at both. The vertical lift of her torso, the elegant undulations of her arms, inspired the image of Pavlova. Her sleek sensuality and precision reminded him of Cyd Charisse. The classical training and the modern technique were at her disposal; but Rhea was a hoofer. She could lay down iron like a man. Her taps were clean, clear—her feet sang. And she worked the ground—all of her—torso toward the earth, knee bone bent. "Got to," she teased him as they traded steps one day. "In Congo Square they used to say, 'don't want you be taken for a corpse, so gimme the knee bone bent.'" Her versatility gave her an inventive edge— she was always creating new combinations, and executing them with a power and lyricism that made her singular. Yet, when the dance demanded, she became a seamless extension of him, a yielding stream of energy in his arms. Luna's body was like a weapon on the dance floor, yielding nothing to him there, only in their bed.

Rhea was one reason he insisted that negotiations between his agent, the television network, and the sponsors of the TV special be confidential. He hoped to manage the damage from the fallout. The embarrassment of failure concerned him more, though; and things did look shaky for a while. The sponsors didn't believe an audience would watch him for a full hour. After all, "he *is* a year older than the century," Leo Sull jabbed in his "Whose Talking?" column. The caption under Fred's picture would have read, "In the Era of Elvis, Can Mr. Top Hat and Tails Conquer TV Too?" That's exactly the kind of publicity he wanted to avoid. His agent traded in a favor and had the item pulled. Even though the sponsors were behind him now, "keep a lid on it," Fred insisted. If he could have controlled gravity he would have—did his best to dancing on the ceiling once.

Rhea went through six cabinets before she found what she wanted; a small plate the color of a delphinium, edged in gold. She stood in the kitchen with a paring knife in one hand and a peach in the other. She wanted one riper, just ready to give up its juice but still firm to the blade. She fingered two other peaches and found one right to the touch. One moment she was drying the washed fruit in a tea towel then, after time she could not calculate, she discovered herself leaning against the sink, staring at the phone, peach flesh and juice seeping through the towel's pores. She loosened her grip and found a wounded peach where her fingers had been. She would call her aunts later.

Until this afternoon, she didn't think anything momentous would happen during this visit. Fred's cable simply said he missed her and could meet her in New York—not that he would or could say much in a cable.

Her cabaret act toured Europe for three months; and the cold, last stop was London. It was great to find New York so warm in April and Fred smiling broadly when he embraced her inside his waiting car at the airport. She arrived early and they made slow love all morning; they filled the bright hours with teasing, languid explorations that fueled anticipation; they made love interspersed with his dry kisses.

It was maddening that his mouth refused her. Fred was like a prostitute who allowed a John every invasion but the intimacy of her mouth. He held his tongue in captivity. Rhea might feel a warm moistness from his thin lips as they brushed her body, but they never fully parted to take her. Still, he so masterfully, elegantly—he demanded everything be done with an elegance he defined—manipulated her body with smooth, deft hands that she momentarily gave up the quest for his mouth.

By afternoon, though, he was quiet, preoccupied. The only things that held his interest were Ella and a collection of new books on modern art. Except for *Variety* and the daily paper, art books were the only thing he read. All evening, he seemed to be juggling some unsettling emotions. He looked his age tonight, Rhea thought, despite the recent nip and tuck.

She realized that Fred had the vanity and apprehensions of most aging men facing their mortality and harboring fears of diminished virility—a chink in his armor that increased her resolve. Oral sex, which she was always happy to give, never failed to please her; and it gave every man—particularly a flagging one—a potent sense of accomplishment with less wear and tear on him. That *Look* cover story proclaiming him "a year older than the century" ran a year ago, but he was still bitching about it.

"Why don't they just put me in a diaper, give me a long white beard and call me Father Time?" he griped. But the facts were cold. Despite his robust health and athletic dancer's life, actuarial tables presumed he could fall down dead any minute—but not before he ate her.

The uncertainty she saw tugging at his face all night was good. Fred was a deliberate man, or tried to be. If they were going to play the night without a script, she had the advantage. Improvisation was not his thing; not in his life, not in his art. Since she was a little girl, all the Verney women—dancing queens and the last word on everything, especially Fred—beat her eardrums with that.

The last word on everything, she repeated to herself. A row with her aunts now, or later? A row now *and* later? Rhea picked up the phone.

Fred heard her angry voice. It jarred him, broke his sense of vulnerability. He had to tell her. He turned off the record player. On the patio, stretched on a chaise, he studied the gargantuan moon.

The light in the dining room behind him dimmed. He felt Rhea's hands on his shoulders. "Who were you talking to?" he asked.

"I wanted to make sure my aunts got the wire I sent from London. I changed my travel schedule after your cable. They expected to see me earlier in the week."

"That's all? I could hear you out here. Do they know where you are?"

"I really don't want to talk about it." She eased herself onto his lap then cupped his face in her hands.

Fred opened his mouth to speak, shut it, then grunted. "It's too hot for all this togetherness," he finally said, then gripped her waist and lifted her as he stood. He felt the tug of her hands on his arms and allowed her to feel his weight on her back, his neck against hers. "I need to shave."

She pressed her cheek harder against his. "No you don't. Someone used to tell me life is like licking honey off a thorn."

"Life is like—" He pulled away. "That may be the corniest thing I ever heard come out of your mouth. Diabetes and a shredded tongue, not my idea of the good life." He turned on all the dining room lights Rhea had turned off, then sat at the piano.

He began an energetic version of "Liza" that was at odds with his somber eyes. She leaned on the piano and studied his long fingers. He played good stride. Even her aunts would allow that. Maybe not.

There always seemed to be a cuss word or two and cackling sounds when Rhea heard her aunts talking about Fred. Dessadra sucked her teeth and her head jerked back as if something stunk. "Fred's no hoofer."

"He's good with things." Out of Aquanetta's mouth, the *s* in "things" was a hissing missile.

"Yeah," Dessadra responded, "props."

Only Luna defended him. "He's no pure hoofer," she said, "but he's probably the greatest all around dancer we'll ever see." When she said that one time too many,

Aquanetta uncoiled her slow tongue and, building momentum with each word, declared, "Why *any ... dusty ...* Negro ... I picked off a back country Georgia road could dance better than Fred Astaire. So shut up." Aquanetta's contempt was so stinging, so final, that the sisters burst out laughing and fell on the floor. When the women looked up, Rhea—all four feet of her—towered over them and smiled curiously. That was the last time she saw all the sisters together and happy. It also was the day she left her aunts to live with Luna Pharr.

When Rhea came to her grandmother's isolated farm, she was certain that she was six and that Queen Isabelle would come for her soon. Her aunts had told her so. Queen Isabelle got sick. Queen Isabelle didn't come. What came was uncertainty. Rhea lost track of time and her place in it. Luna allowed no clocks in her house, no radio, no newspapers. Just books, a library of books, and even more records.

What time is it? What day is it? Luna laughed incredulously when Rhea asked. "We are dancers, tap dancers. We *are* time. If you're any grandchild of mine, you should feel the rhythm of time." Time, she told her, was ancient, in the memory of muscle, the beat of the heart. If her concern was as basic as the rhythm of months passing, look to the night sky. "Watch the phases of the moon. Watch me in the heavens. I am the ultimate projection of time. Watch me and I will tell you when to bleed, little girl; just wait and see."

Rhea came to like moonless nights best; and started marking time by the movies of the man whose name she so often heard whispered: Fred Astaire. It was years before she saw him in a movie in a regular theater. Her first movie house was her grandmother's converted barn. It housed a dance studio on one side and a small theater with a projection room on the other. Rhea squinted to read the year in roman numerals at the end of each film. It proved confusing. *Swingtime* was made in 1936, but she didn't see it until 1942; something it took her years to realize.

On Luna's farm, even her birthday became an obscurity, one that melded into singular moments: Warring squirrels that charged each other over a nut as they traversed the naked limbs of trees in a cold, gray light; sitting on the Aubusson rug next to her grandmother's chair and stroking the stray kitten she was permitted to keep one vague season of her birth. Rhea liked to watch the squirrels fight; but in that frigid season, the pale sun vanished in the bat of a drowsy child's eye. In the quickening dark, battling sleep, Luna would take her to the theater in the barn and make her watch a silent, grainy, black and white film in which Fred and Luna danced. Each season, Luna repeated, "A villa in Venice. The Countess. There's Cole Porter." Then she wished Rhea "a very happy birthday."

In time, Rhea realized there was more than a dance between her grandmother and Fred. The cold silences his name sparked were eventually filled by physical and psychological noise. Explosions expressed in the rapid-fire clack of metal taps across the dance studio's maple floor; days spent in bed when Luna Pharr refused to dress or eat; then her nighttime reemergence, during which she waltzed alone in the cavernous barn, the vacant right sleeve of her dress flapping as she spun in the dark to the music of her mind.

In the dark, by stealth, in the light, led willingly by her grandmother, Rhea studied Luna's every step. Then, in the half-light of a late afternoon, a curvaceous body, led by an enormous bosom, arrived. Against that bosom Rhea cried out the loneliness of kissless seasons in the lingering cold. The warm, generous body had a head crowned by a tower of curly white hair. Her face resembled Luna's, only kinder, more beautiful. Queen Isabelle found Luna in bed, glassy-eyed and morose. "I'd smack you shitless if I thought it'd do any good," the Queen told her. Luna's right brow jumped when her mother spoke, but she said nothing.

Beneath a sliver of moon, Queen Isabelle took Rhea away in her Packard Super 8, 180 Touring limousine. Dust and gravel bombarded them as the driver plowed along the rough, farm road; then north, to Montreal.

Rhea loved New Orleans after the cold of Canada. She loved being with her great-grandmother and wanted to live with her every day; but the Queen wouldn't allow it. Rhea stayed with her grown-up cousins, each a pale-skinned variation of the other. She liked her cousins, but escaped once a day to the Queen's house for breakfast, lunch, or dinner. If it was dinner, she claimed she was too tired to move; or she claimed that dinner had given her a tummy ache so bad she might die if she wasn't put in her bed right away. "Why can't I stay with you?" she moaned one night, holding on to a bloated belly she had filled with cookies, milk and Coke before eating the chicken *étouffée*.

The Queen gently held her by the shoulders. "In this family, you can be a traitor or a spy. When you're older, you make the choice. For now, you're staying with the spies."

With the spies, Rhea went to her first real movie theater. They sat downstairs with all the other white-looking people. The people who looked like the Queen sat in the balcony. Rhea could hardly watch the picture show for twisting to stare at the people near the ceiling, the place she wanted to be.

Year after year, Rhea went to that theater and grew more comfortable with her place in it, grew more eager to enter the celluloid world she saw in the dark. The first time she saw Fred on the giant screen, she wondered what Luna saw in such a skinny man with big ears. As she got older, he seemed different to her; enchanting. She felt a sense of delight watching him and forgot what he looked like, though he didn't look bad. The girls in her ballet class thought so, too. Even some of the colored hoofers who streamed through Queen Isabelle's house said, "*Oh yeah*, he's got style. His feet know something."

Just before Sunday at the Queen's house, Rhea lay on her bed in a knot whimpering. "What's your problem?" the Queen demanded. Rhea sat up. "She did it. She did it to me."

"Who did what?"

Rhea smelled chicken frying and biscuits baking, but the house smelled of garlic too. She knew dinner was almost ready and the Queen impatient. Isabelle Andriani Des Verney served hot food to her guests. Rhea couldn't help herself. She flopped back on the bed with her palms pressed together and clamped between her thighs. Her eyes met a spot of spaghetti sauce on the Queen's white apron. "Rhea, stop looking like Ned in the first reader. Stop looking simple. What is the matter with you?"

"I'm bleeding," she blurted. "Luna said she'd make me bleed."

Queen Isabelle sat on the bed and put Rhea's head on her warm lap. "Not hardly. Luna hasn't done a darn thing to you, and she is never going to."

Within a year, Queen Isabelle watched Rhea get out of the bathtub and shook her head. "You look like a grown, horseback woman." One boys wanted to ride. But Rhea held herself aloof. She liked older men; men with finesse.

In the cool dark of a movie theater, Rhea studied Fred and thought the simple bend of his wrist was a study in grace. Several nights in one week, she and two friends escaped their French boarding school to see *Easter Parade*—just to watch the way Fred's wrist curled when he spun Ann Miller to the reprise of "It Only Happens When I Dance with You."

In time, Rhea discovered that Fred's cinematic grace was studied, as much as natural. In almost everything, most certainly the dance, he never made an unrehearsed move. When they first met in Paris, she invited him to a recording session with some jazz musicians and hoofers. He refused to jam. His behavior was counter to everything she learned in the hoofer's orbit; and it gave her the clearest measure of him as a dancer and a man. He was not just a perfectionist. He feared spontaneity. He feared his deepest impulses. He had to control everything. If he would not improvise, he was no hoofer, and she understood why her aunts had viewed him with a true hoofer's derision.

Still, she thought him brilliant. The Nicholas Brothers had greater technique and equal versatility. John Bubbles—the man whose every move, according to her aunts, Fred copied—was both elegant and the greatest rhythm tapper of Fred's generation. Yet Fred, beyond personifying elegance as mere refinement, elevated it to the level of the sublime. He choreographed his material and was a more inventive dancer than the rest. And he defined dance for the film. If she had not been around great dancers all of her life, if she had not known that there *were* dozens of Negroes on dusty roads who might have outdone him given the chance, she would be more awestruck than she was. Fred had the chance. Fred set the benchmark. When Rhea sorted her feelings for Fred and the shadowed feats of the colored dancers who formed her, she decided this: Being great stars in vaudeville was one thing. Bubbles, Bojangles, the Whitman Sisters, and her aunts could easily claim that and more. To choreograph and define dance for film, though, the most important art form of the century, put Fred in another category. It seemed to Rhea that whatever he borrowed—stole, stole, stole, Luna eventually charged—passed through the artistic filter of a great instrument, his body, and ultimately transformed, even transcended, the source of his inspiration.

When Rhea returned to the farm as a grown, horseback-woman for real, she said all these things about Fred to Luna. She had been his partner, and danced with him, too. She said she was greater than Luna had been and still imagined herself to be. For these crimes, Luna Pharr disowned her son's child.

"Disown me?" Rhea said coolly. "You are an evil, withered-pussy bitch who never gave a damn about me." Rhea flinched when she saw Luna raise the hand she had left. Luna merely cupped her chin then walked away.

Rhea packed the few things she brought with her and got in her car. It was late summer and bright, but the wind that blew from Canada already hinted at the coming arctic blast. Rhea drove down the gravel driveway and out of the corner of her eye saw something red spiraling toward the sky and whipped by the wind. Luna stood on the porch wearing a long crimson scarf around her neck and nothing but taut, muscular flesh.

Rhea ceased to see anything but a curtain of white, feel anything but dizzying heat, when she thought about that taunting spiral of red above Luna's rocket breasts; when she thought about Fred and Luna together. She wondered if she would feel that way about any other woman and Fred. She did know that no one should ever give her a gun.

Rhea's fingers raked her hair now as she watched Fred. Her hand became a fist she pressed against the spot that used to rest on Luna's empty sleeve.

"I feel way off schedule," Fred told her. "I'm a little tired but don't really feel sleepy."

"I'm ready for bed," she told him.

He picked out the last few notes of "Liza" with one finger. "There's something I wanted to talk to you about."

"What is it?"

He did not avoid her eyes. "What's your next job?" He'd ease into it.

She looked at the ceiling. "What do the gods have in store for this gypsy? What is this, career-counseling night?"

"I'm just interested," he said vaguely.

"If we danced together, you'd know what I'd be doing."

"Rhea, I've just made my last musical."

"You've said that before. Besides, movies aren't the only option." He stiffened. "You could do a limited theater engagement."

"I am out of vaudeville," he said.

She rolled her eyes. "Vaudeville? Hardly."

"I want to do some serious acting, or try to. Especially after this last picture. I am not pleased, not pleased at all," he told her.

"You're never satisfied. What's the problem?"

"I look tired, I, I wanted to do this rock 'n roll number and I realize now it was a mistake. I look like some kind of parody of me. An antique in top hat and tails trying to be Elvis—The Pelvis."

"There's never been much pelvis in your dancing," she jabbed. She placed a finger on the top of her head and began to pivot, gyrating her hips like an arthritic. "*I left my hat in Haiti*," she sang, "*in some forgotten shack in Haiti.*"

"I always meant to ask you, why did they put that no dancin', no rhythm, munchkin in fuzzy, blue house slippers for that number? Too bad you didn't get Garland, at least we could have enjoyed the singing."

He didn't say a word.

This was not the battle she wanted to fight tonight and backed off. "To answer your original question, I have several auditions lined up. I have to talk to my agent about the details next week."

He told her, "That sounds good. I wish you every success."

"Well, I thank you for your kind encouragement, Mr. Freeze."

"You should probably go to bed," he said.

"Don't patronize me."

"Look," he snapped, "I'm tired."

"Now you're tired?"

"Yes. Tired, wound up, can't sleep. You just need to leave me alone right now." He could be curt and cold, but seldom with her—except when she pressed him for the one thing she wanted and had yet to get tonight. Midnight was several hours away, but it had been a long day. She let him alone.

He lay on the couch in silence. He felt ill knowing he would lose her. He felt fear at the thought of giving up so much if they did not part. He felt shame because he was a coward.

He was still wallowing in self pity—wide awake, eyes closed—when Rhea returned. He felt her before he saw her. She moved toward him in a virginal white negligée. He saw the glint of the small knife she held in one hand before noticing the plate in the other. She seemed to float toward him through water, pushing against the tide of his resistance, pulled by the undertow of his pulsing desire. It was spring, it was night, it was eighty-one degrees Fahrenheit. He felt a slender thread of sweat roll from his armpit. She was the undulating motion of heat waves caught in the moon beams and candle light that stole darkness from the room. She cut a thin slice of peach delicate enough to rest between tender folds of flesh. She let the fruit brush his lips, "Don't do that," he said, and wiped the wetness with the back of his hand. He spoke more harshly than intended and saw the fierceness he knew leave her eyes. His face softened, saddened, and the two lovers silently appraised each other in the moments it took a cloud to traverse the face of the moon.

The next morning, Rhea rose to a sunless spring sky and a familiar pain. As usual, Fred had left their bed early. She tried to sit up but fell to her side of the mattress. She took a deep breath, swung her legs over the side of the bed and made it to the bathroom to fill the tub. The steaming, velvet-textured water leeched some of the pain between her legs. She would stay in this spot all day if she could.

She reached the bedroom phone, then called Wilson Scott, the groundsman and chauffeur.

He was a trim, balding, efficient Negro who seemed to see everything and say little but good morning, good evening and thank you, while managing to be congenial. He wasn't much more than forty, but Rhea spoke to him with a deference usually accorded much older men. To her, he was always Mr. Scott. Rhea asked him to bring the car around in twenty minutes. She wondered where Fred was. It was late morning.

Rhea gripped the banister and inched her way to the first floor. She left a note for Fred on the dining room table, the spot of her triumph. She had made him a pearl diver last night and came harder sitting on his face than she had in all their time together. Right now, she hurt too much to savor the victory. The only orifice he did not invade was her ears. Now, she moved so gingerly toward her only goal, the front door, that she nearly missed Fred's note.

Rhea,
Something's come up. I must get back to L.A. We'll get our schedules together soon.
                                                              Love,

F

Like a captive in an airless room, she felt the panic of a slow but certain death. She didn't know how many times she read *We'll get our schedules together* before the doorbell mobilized her. "Are you all right, Miss Verney," Wilson Scott asked without expression.

"It's just my leg," she told him.

From the Long Island Expressway, they headed to downtown Brooklyn, passed the Academy of Music in Ft. Green, and finally reached Auburn Hill. He stopped the '57 Lincoln in front of a double, four-story brownstone on Fablio Lane.

The chauffeur took Rhea's suitcase and led her by the elbow to the stoop. "No, please, let's go through the ground floor."

A petite woman with high cheekbones and copper-brown skin opened the wrought iron gate. She started to speak but closed her mouth when she saw the unknown man. Frowning, the woman said, "Come in," and "please," as an afterthought.

Mr. Scott held back and looked unblinkingly at the colored woman.

"Please, would you like anything?" Rhea asked him.

"No thank you," he answered smoothly. "I'm fine. I need to get back. But is there anything else you'd like me to do?"

"No. You've been a big help. Thanks."

Wilson Scott got into the car and lit up a Winston. He studied the long Brooklyn block in his rearview mirror. Most adults were still at work, but kids were out for spring break. Halfway down the block, a group of girls jumped rope. Ahead of him, a kid in pink overalls was skating down the street, her long dark pony tail in the wind. There was a store at the next corner. A knot of mostly balding men sat on boxes and metal chairs talking, playing chess, a cloud of cigar smoke circling their heads. In a public playground in the next block, he saw older kids, mostly boys, playing stick ball. Everywhere he looked, he saw colored faces. He chuckled to himself and slowly pulled out of his parking space. The girl in pink overalls raced against the light. Easing toward the intersection, Wilson Scott tapped the horn and waited until she was safely on the curb, then drove back to Long Island.

Helen Van Ah winced like an artist struggling to gain perspective on a canvas. Deflated by the left hook of astonishment, her voice was flat and singsong. "I don't want to touch this." She backed away from Rhea.

Dessadra Verney pulled a stale Lucky Strike from the aging pack she kept in the dresser drawer. "You couldn't," she said pacing, "keep your legs closed a few more days? Mrs. Rawls, right across the street, her son is in Memphis this minute representing dozens of colored students beaten and jailed for demonstrating. And for what?" The retired dancer spun hard on the wood floor, grabbed a lighter, and lit her cigarette so fast that when she faced her grandniece again it was hard to tell what force ignited the flame. "Not, as you are always pooh-poohing, for a goddamn hamburger at the Woolworth, but to get people registered—to vote. This show is raising money for a legal defense fund. This is serious business."

"Aunt D, please," Rhea moaned, writhing on the bed. "Let me rest. Just put some ice packs on it," she told Helen. "I'll be fine."

"No you won't." Helen was a nurse and family friend who rented the top floor of Dessadra Verney's Brooklyn brownstone. "I've never seen anything like it."

Dessadra tossed her hands in the air. "Well, if you're goin' to hell, might as well go in a chariot."

Rhea's whole body throbbed in empathy with her eaten lips. "Aunt Dess, I know Negroes are getting hosed, beaten, lynched. This is fucking America. If I don't dance, I'll write a goddamn check."

Rhea caught the heat from their incinerating eyes. It felt worse than the stabbing pain between her legs. She turned on her side and pushed the ice pack against her crotch.

Dessadra lowered her voice but it quivered. "I guess it's too much to think he might have taken you, or arranged for you, to go to a hospital on the island."

"He didn't even know when I left."

"Well," Helen said, "before you go to hell in a chariot, I suggest we get one to the hospital."

Dessadra opened the bedroom door and yelled, "Jasper."

Three doctors examined Rhea. Word spread. Nurses came to investigate. A duo in starched white peeked under the sheet and concurred. A football—the left side of her vagina was as big as a football. It was an infected Bartholin's gland all right, but no one had ever seen a vagina as distended as hers.

"I'm going to lance it," the doctor said.

"No, I don't wanna be cut."

"It'll be a picnic compared to what you're feeling now. Do you feel this?"

"No."

"Do you feel this?"

"No."

"Do you feel—"

She felt it. The shriek rattled the whole corridor.

"Get outta here." Helen had heard the rumors about Rhea and Fred. Anything and everything happened on Fablio Court. But she wasn't into gossip.

"That girl is crazy," said Dessadra. "She let that man maim her. Reminds me of the time Aquanetta and I were on the road with Lump Leonard's band and Sheila Sh-bop Wilson was the singer. He had to fire her for missing three gigs in one week."

"Why?" Helen asked.

"She was screwing the heavyweight champ, and his equipment is legendary. I remember going to the hospital. Her stuff was almost as jacked up as Rhea's. But as soon as she got out the place—I mean get me in a taxi honey—she was humping the champ again. Rhea's addicted, too."

"Who'd a thunk," Helen said. "The man looks like an asexual, boiled chicken. But something too big was definitely rubbing something too hard."

"You can take it to the bank," Dessadra told her. "That ofay's packin' some mutant equipment between those skinny thighs."

Sources

Cleobulus, "Riddle," in *The Greek Anthology V*, trans. W. R. Paton (London: Heinemann/Loeb Classical Library, 1918), 76–77.

Wolfram von Eschenbach, *Parzival: A Knightly Epic*, trans. Jessie L. Weston (London: D. Nutt, 1894).

The Book of the Thousand Nights and One Night, trans. John Payne, 9 vols. (London, 1901).

Masuccio Salernitano, *The Novellino*, trans. W. G. Waters (London, [ca. 1900]).

Giambattista Giraldi Cinzio, *Hecatommithi* (1565), English translation by John Edward Taylor (1855), in *Othello*, a new variorum edition of Shakespeare, ed. Horace Howard Furness, vol. 6 (Philadelphia: J. B. Lippincott, [1886]).

Giambattista Marino, "The Beautiful Slave-Girl" (1614), English translation by Norman R. Shapiro published here for the first time. Italian original of "Bella schiava" in *Amori*, ed. Alessandro Martini (Milan: Bibliotecca Universale Rizzoli, 1982).

George Herbert, "A Negress Courts Cestus, a Man of a Different Colour," in *The Complete Works in Verse and Prose of George Herbert*, ed. Alexander B. Grosart (London: Robson and Sons, 1874).

John Cleveland, "A Faire Nimph Scorning a Black Boy Courting Her," in *The Poems of John Cleveland*, ed. Brian Morris and Eleanor Withington (Oxford: Clarendon Press, 1967), 22–23.

Eldred Revett, "The Inversion," "One Enamour'd on a *Black-moor*," "A Black Nymph Scorning a Fair Boy Courting Her," in *Selected Poems: Humane and Divine*, ed. Donald M. Friedman (Liverpool: Liverpool University Press, 1966), 21–24, 36–40.

Edward Herbert of Cherbury, "To Mrs. Diana Cecyll," "The Brown Beauty," "Sonnet of Black Beauty," "Another Sonnet to Black It Self," in *The Poems of Herbert of Cherbury*, ed. G. C. Moore Smith (Oxford: Clarendon Press, 1923), 38, 39, 60.

James De la Cour, "In Laudem Æthiopissæ," in *Poems* (Cork: Thomas White, 1778).

Henry Neville, *The Isle of Pines* (London: Allen Banks, 1668).

Thomas Southerne, *Oroonoko: A Tragedy in Five Acts* (London: Longman, [ca. 1806]).

John Whaley, "On a Young Lady's Weeping at *Oroonooko*," "To a Gentleman in Love with a Negro Woman," in *A Collection of Poems* (London: J. Willis and J. Boddington, 1732).

Story of Inkle and Yarico, *Spectator*, no. 11 (1715), reprinted in *The Spectator*, ed. David F. Bond (Oxford: Clarendon Press, 1965).

"The Story of Inkle and Yarico," *London Magazine*, May 1734.

Thomas Day and John Bicknell, *The Dying Negro* (London: W. Flexney, 1773).

Gustavus Vassa [Olaudah Equiano], "Letter to J. T. Esq., author of the book called *Cursory Remarks* and *Rejoinder*," *Public Advertiser* (London), January 28, 1788, reprinted in *The Interesting Narrative of the Life of Olaudah Equiano, or Gustavus Vassa, the African, Written by Himself*, ed. Werner Sollors (New York: W. W. Norton, 2001).

Heinrich von Kleist, *The Engagement in Santo Domingo* (1811), trans. Martin Greenberg, in *The Marquise of O—— and Other Stories* (New York: Criterion Books, 1954).

Claire de Duras, *Ourika*, trans. George Wallis Haven (Boston: Carter and Hendee, 1829).

Alexander Pushkin, "The Blackamoor of Peter the Great" (1827–1828), trans. Paul Debreczeny, in *Complete Prose Fiction* (Stanford: Stanford University Press, 1983). © 1983 by the Board of Trustees of the Leland Stanford Junior University. Reprinted by permission of the Stanford University Press.

L. Maria Child, "The Quadroons," in *Fact and Fiction* (New York: C. S. Francis, 1846).

Alexandre Dumas, *Georges* (1843), in *The Works of Alexandre Dumas, in Thirty Volumes* (New York: P. F. Collier, n.d. [ca. 1900]).

Theodor Storm, *From Beyond the Seas* (1863–1864). English translation by Judith Ryan published here for the first time.

Henry Wadsworth Longfellow, "The Quadroon Girl" (1842), in *The Poetical Works* (London: Henry Froude, 1912).

Elizabeth Barrett Browning, "The Runaway Slave at Pilgrim's Point" (1848), in *The Complete Works of Elizabeth Barrett Browning*, ed. with introductions and notes by Charlotte Porter and Helen A. Clarke (New York, Crowell, 1900).

William Dean Howells, "The Pilot's Story," *Atlantic Monthly* 6, no. 35 (September 1860).

Hans Christian Andersen, *Mulatto: An Original Romantic Drama in Five Acts* (1840), trans. Werner Sollors, with the help of Jesper Sørensen and Christoph Lohmann, published here for the first time.

Dion Boucicault, *The Octoroon; or, Life in Louisiana: A Play in Five Acts* (1859; photo reprint Upper Saddle River, N.J.: Literature House, 1970) and *Plays by Dion Boucicault*, ed. Peter Thomson (Cambridge: Cambridge University Press, 1984).

Wilkie Collins and Charles Fechter, *Black and White: A Drama in Three Acts* (New York: R. M. De Witt, [1869]).

David Goodman Croly and George Wakeman, *Miscegenation: The Theory of the Blending of the Races, Applied to the American White Man and Negro* (New York, 1863).

George Washington Cable, *Madame Delphine* (1881), repr. in *Old Creole Days* (Boston: Charles Scribner, 1893).

James Edwin Campbell, "The Pariah," in *Echoes from the Cabin and Elsewhere* (Chicago, 1895).

Guy de Maupassant, "Boitelle" (1889), in *The Works of Maupassant: Short Stories* (New York, [ca. 1900]).

Kate Chopin, "The Father of Désirée's Baby," *Vogue* (January 14, 1893), 70–71, 74.

Charles W. Chesnutt, "Uncle Wellington's Wives," in *The Wife of His Youth and Other Stories of the Color Line* (Boston: Houghton Mifflin, 1899).

Joseph Seamon Cotter, Jr., "The Mulatto to His Critics," in *Negro Poets and Their Poems*, ed. Robert T. Kerlin (Washington, D.C.: Associated Publishers, 1923). Reprinted by permission of the Association for the Study of African-American Life and History, Inc.

Georgia Douglas Johnson, "The Octoroon," "Cosmopolite," in *Bronze: A Book of Verse*, introd. W. E. B. Du Bois (Boston: B. J. Brimmer, 1922); "The Riddle," in *The New Negro*, ed. Alain Locke (New York: Boni, 1925). © 1923, 1925. Reprinted by permission of Gale Publishing.

William Pickens, *The Vengeance of the Gods and Other Stories of Real American Color Line Life* (Philadelphia: A.M.E. Book Concern, 1922).

Waldo Frank, "Hope," *Secession* 3 (August 1922). © 1922 by Waldo Frank. Reprinted by permission of Jonathan Frank.

Jean Toomer, "Withered Skin of Berries" (1923), in *The Wayward and the Seeking: A Collection of Writings by Jean Toomer*, ed. Darwin T. Turner (Washington, D.C.: Howard University Press, 1980). © 1980 by Darwin T. Turner and Marjorie Content Toomer. By permission of Margot Latimer and of The Permissions Company, P.O. Box 243, High Bridge, N.J., U.S.A. on behalf of Howard University Press. All rights reserved.

Margery Latimer, "Confession" (1929), in *The New American Caravan*, ed. Alfred Kreymborg, Lewis Mumford, and Paul Rosenfeld (New York: Macaulay, 1929). © 1929 by Margery Latimer. Reprinted by permission of Margot Latimer.

Eugene O'Neill, *All God's Chillun Got Wings, American Mercury* 1, no. 2 (February 1924). © 1924 by Eugene O'Neill. Reprinted by permission of Yale University. United States and non-United States copyright Yale University.

Countée Cullen, "Near White," "Two Who Crossed a Line," in *Color* (New York: Harper and Brothers, 1925). © 1925 by Harper and Brothers; copyright renewed by Ida M. Cullen. Reprinted by permission of GRM Associates, Inc., Agents for the Estate of Ida M. Cullen.

Langston Hughes, "Cross" (1925), "Mulatto" (1927), in *The Selected Poems of Langston Hughes* (New York: Knopf, 1994). © 1994 by the Estate of Langston Hughes. Reprinted by permission of Alfred A. Knopf, a division of Random House.

Langston Hughes, *Mulatto: A Tragedy of the Deep South* (1931), in *Five Plays by Langston Hughes*, ed. Webster Smalley (Bloomington: Indiana University Press, 1963), 1–35. © 1931 by Langston Hughes. Reprinted by permission of Harold Ober Associates Incorporated.

Claude McKay, "The Mulatto," *Bookman* (1925), © 1925; "Near-White," in *Gingertown* (New York: Harper, 1932), © 1932. Courtesy of the Literary Representative for the works of Claude McKay, Schomburg Center for Research in Black Culture, the New York Public Library, Astor, Lenox and Tilden Foundations.

Caroline Bond Day, "The Pink Hat" (1926), in *Blacks at Harvard: A Documentary History of African-American Experience at Harvard and Radcliffe* (New York: New York University Press, 1993). © 1926 by Caroline Bond Day. Reprinted by permission of New York University Press.

Gwendolyn Brooks, "Ballad of Pearl May Lee" (1945), in *Blacks* (Chicago: David, 1987). © 1945 by Gwendolyn Brooks. Reprinted by permission of the Estate of Gwendolyn Brooks.

Adrienne Kennedy, *The Owl Answers* (1963), in *The Adrienne Kennedy Reader* (Minneapolis: University of Minnesota Press, 2001). © 1963 by Adrienne Kennedy. Reprinted by permission of the author and the University of Minnesota Press.

Index

Note: Names of authors are given in **boldface**, titles of works in *italics*, and first lines of poems in roman font.

Aethiopissa ambit Cestum diversi coloris Virum, 99
All God's Chillun Got Wings, 504–29
"Ambiguous of race they stand," 530
Andersen, Hans Christian, 292–99
Another Sonnet to Black It Self, 109
Arabian Nights **see** *Thousand Nights and One Night, The Book of the*
"Ashamed of my race?," 461
"At Fate's approach whilst Oroonooko Groans," 143

Ballad of Pearl May Lee, 577–80
Beautiful Slave-Girl, The, 98
"Because I am the white man's son—his own," 559
Bella schiava, 97
Bicknell, John, 152–60
Blackamoor of Peter the Great, The, 208–31
Black and White: A Drama in Three Acts, 337–49
"Black beauty, which above that common light," 109
Black Nymph Scorning a Fair Boy Courting Her, A, 106
"Black you are, one of Nature's monsters, yes," 98
"Blest with thy last sad gift—the power to dye," 153
Boitelle, 424–30
Boucicault, Dion, 300–336
Brooks, Gwendolyn, 577–80
Brown Beauty, The, 108–9
Browning, Elizabeth Barrett, 280–87
Buck, 634–52

Cable, George Washington, 383–420
Campbell, James Edwin, 421–23
Chesnutt, Charles W., 436–58
Child, Lydia Maria, 232–39
Chopin, Kate, 431–35
Cinzio see **Giraldi Cinzio**
Cleobulus, 7
Cleveland, John, 101–2
Collins, Wilkie, 337–49
Confession, 498–503
Cosmopolite, 463
Cotter, Jr., Joseph Seamon, 461
Cour, James de la see **de la Cour, James**
Croly, David Goodman, 350–80
Cross, 532
Cullen, Countée, 530–31

Darker Face of the Earth, The, 606–33
Day, Caroline Bond, 573–76
Day, Thomas, 152–60
de la Cour, James, 110–11
Désirée's Baby see *Father of Désirée's Baby, The*
"*Diana Cecyll*, that rare beauty thou dost show," 107
"Don't Blush, dear Sir, your Flame to own," 143–44
Dove, Rita, 606–33
Dumas, Alexandre, 240–52
Duras, Claire de, 189–207
Dying Negro, The, 152–60

Engagement in Santo Domingo, The, 167–88
Equiano, Olaudah, 161–63
"Est mihi (siqua mihi est)," 110

Faire Nimph Scorning a Black Boy Courting Her, A, 101–2
Father of Désirée's Baby, The, 431–35
Fechter, Charles, 337–49
Feirefis, 31–53
"Fond Boy, thy vain pursuit give o're," 106
Frank, Waldo, 473–75
From Beyond the Seas, 253–77
"From where she stood the air she craved," 530

Gamuret, 8–31
Georges, 240–52
Giraldi Cinzio, Giambattista, 85–93

Hecatommithi, Gli, 85–93
He Crosses, 531
"He rode across like a cavalier," 531
Herbert, George, 99–100
Herbert of Cherbury, Edward, 107–9
Hope, 473–75
Howells, William Dean, 288–91
Hughes, Langston, 532–58

"I am your son, white man!" 533
"If unfaith in the heart find dwelling," 9
Inkle and Yarico, 145–51
In Laudem Æthiopissæ, 110
In Praise of a Negress, 110–11
Inversion, The, 103–4

Isle of Pines, The, 115–31
"I stand on the mark beside the shore," 280
"It was a story the pilot told, with his back to his hearers," 288

Johnson, Charles, 594–605
Johnson, Georgia Douglas, 462–63

Kennedy, Adrienne, 583–93
Kleist, Heinrich von, 167–88

Lady of Trapani Becomes Enamoured of a Moor, A, 69–76
Latimer, Margery, 498–503
Letter to James Tobin, 161–63
Longfellow, Henry Wadsworth, 278–79

Madame Delphine, 383–420
Marino, Giambattista, 97–98
Masuccio Salernitano, 69–84
Maupassant, Guy de, 424–30
McKay, Claude, 559–72
Miscegenation: The Theory of the Blending of the Races, Applied to the American White Man and Negro, 350–80
Moorish Captain Takes to Wife a Venetian Dame, A, 85–93
Mulatto (poem), 533–34
Mulatto: An Original Romantic Drama in Five Acts, 292–99
Mulatto: A Tragedy of the Deep South, 534–58
Mulatto, The (poem), 559
Mulatto to His Critics, The, 461
"My old man's a white old man," 532

Near White (poem), 530
Near-White (short story), 560–72
"Negra sì, ma se' bella," 97
Negress Courts Cestus, a Man of a Different Colour, A, 99–100
Neville, Henry, 115–31
Njeri, Itabari, 653–65
"Not wholly this or that," 463
Novellino, Il, 69–84

Octoroon, The (play), 300–336
Octoroon, The (poem), 462
On a Young Lady's Weeping at Oroonooko, 143
One Enamour'd on a Black-moor, 104–6
"One drop of midnight in the dawn of life's pulsating stream," 462
One Enamour'd on a Black-moor, 104–6
O'Neill, Eugene, 504–29
Oroonoko: A Tragedy in Five Acts, 132–42
Ourika, 189–207
Owl Answers, The, 583–93
"Own'd her father all the fact'ries," 421
Oxherding Tale, 594–605

Pariah, The, 421–23
Parzival, 8–53
Petrosino, Francesca J., 634–52
Pickens, William, 464–72
Pilot's Story, The, 288–91
Pink Hat, The, 573–76
Pushkin, Alexander, 208–31

Quadroon Girl, The, 278–79
Quadroons, The, 232–39
"Quid mihi si facies nigra est?," 99

Revett, Eldred, 103–6
Riddle, 7
Riddle, The (poem), 463
Runaway Slave at Pilgrim's Point, The, 280–87

Secret Life of Fred Astaire, The, 653–65
She Crosses, 530
Sonnet of Black Beauty, 109
Southerne, Thomas, 132–42
"Stand off, and let me take the aire," 101
"Stand off fair Boy, thou wilt affright," 103
Storm, Theodor, 253–77
Story of King Shehriyar and His Brother, 57–62
Story of the Enchanted Youth, 62–68

"Then off they took you, off to the jail," 577
"The Slaver in the broad lagoon," 278
"Thou Black, wherein all colours are compos'd," 109
Thousand Nights and One Night, The Book of the, 57–68
To a Gentleman in Love with a Negro Woman, 143–44
To Mrs. Diana Cecyll, 107–8
Toomer, Jean, 476–97
Two Who Crossed a Line, 530–31

Uncle Wellington's Wives, 436–58

Vassa, Gustavus see Equiano, Olaudah
Vengeance of the Gods, The, 464–72

Wakeman, George, 350–80
Whaley, John, 143–44
"What a strange love doth me invade," 104
"What if my face be black?," 99
"What shape I have, that form is all my own," 110
"While the two contraries of Black and White," 108
"White men's children spread over the earth," 463
Withered Skin of Berries, 476–97
Wolfram von Eschenbach, 8–53

"Ye virgin train, an artless *dame* inspire," 148
Young Girl Is Beloved by Many Suitors, A, 80–84
Young Man Loves a Certain Lady Who Does Not Love Him in Return, A, 76–80

About the Editor

Werner Sollors teaches Afro-American studies and English at Harvard University and is the author, editor, and coeditor of several books, including *The Multilingual Anthology of American Literature; Blacks at Harvard: A Documentary History of African-American Experience at Harvard and Radcliffe; Multilingual America: Transnationalism, Ethnicity, and the Languages of American Literature;* and *Theories of Ethnicity: A Classical Reader,* all available from New York University Press.